Preisreduziertes
Mängelexemplar

Philosophie in synthetischer Absicht

Synthesis in Mind

Herausgegeben von
Marcelo Stamm

Klett-Cotta

Inhalt

Vorwort 9

Hann Trier: In synthetischer Absicht – Gouache 13
Dieter Henrich: Welt-Bilder 15

I.
Subjektivität, Naturalismus, Ich-Gedanken
Mind, Nature, Stances of the Self

Jürgen Mittelstraß: Das philosophische Kreuz mit dem
   Bewußtsein 21
Arthur C. Danto: History and Representation 37
Roderick M. Chisholm: On the Simplicitiy of the Soul ... 53
Colin McGinn: Solving the Philosophical Mind-Body Problem 63
John Perry: Myself and I 83
Wolfgang Carl: Ich und Spontaneität 105
Donald Davidson: The Irreducibility of the Concept
   of the Self 123

II.
Wissensbegründung und Skepsis
Skepticism and the Question of Knowledge

Hans Sluga: Von der Uneinheitlichkeit des Wissens 133
Charles Parsons: Intuition and the Abstract 155
Dagfinn Føllesdal: Husserl's Idealism 189
Ernest Sosa: Epistemic Circularity: Sextus, Descartes,
   and Epistemology Today 203
Hilary Putnam: Skepticism 239

III.
Themen und Wege der Metaphysik
Metaphysics: Topics and Methods

Paul Guyer: Self-Understanding and Philosophy:
  The Strategy of Kant's *Groundwork* 271
Helmut Fahrenbach: Meinen, Wissen, Glauben 299
Vincenzo Vitiello: Epistemische Zeit und historische Zeit . . . 347
Michael Dummett: The Metaphysics of Time 361
Michael Theunissen: Rekonstruktion der Realität 375

IV.
Konzeptionen der Ethik, Orientierung des Lebens
Ethical Reasoning, Leading a Life

Gianni Vattimo: The Demand for Ethics and Philosophy's
  Responsibility 419
Bernard Williams: Naturalismus und Genealogie 431
Wolfgang Schluchter: Max Weber am Ausgang eines
  Denkweges 451
Harry Frankfurt: On Caring, and a Certain Parallel 465
Richard Wollheim: Emotion, the Malformation of Emotion,
  and J.-P. Sartre 477
Ernst Tugendhat: Gedanken über den Tod 487

V.
Perspektiven in Religion und Kultur
Prospects of Civilization

Wolfhart Pannenberg: Moral und Religion 515
Robert Spaemann: Gottesbeweise nach Nietzsche 527
Henry E. Allison: Beauty as Mediator between Nature
  and Freedom 539

Inhalt

Stanley Cavell: Benjamin and Wittgenstein: Signals
and Affinities 565
Ernst H. Gombrich: Zeit, Zahl und Zeichen 583
Hans-Georg Gadamer: Wissen zwischen gestern und morgen . 599

Autorenverzeichnis 613

Bildlegenden 625

Vorwort

Die Programmformel *Philosophie in synthetischer Absicht*, unter der die hier versammelten Beiträge ausgeschrieben waren, erwies sich allen davon abgeleiteten Titelentwürfen überlegen und avancierte darum auch zum Titelthema des Buches. So ist diese Formel, in der ein Kant-Echo hörbar ist, keine nachträgliche Erfindung und kein Kunstgriff, um disparate Abhandlungen in vordergründiger Weise zusammenzuhalten.

Mit der Rede von „Absicht" ist einerseits ein Gedanke der möglichen oder zugestandenen Unabgeschlossenheit dessen verbunden, was gemäß der Absicht geschieht, andererseits auch ein Orientierungsmotiv. Die Absicht ist hier, wie sich sagen läßt, leitend. Ihre Wirksamkeit bemißt sich im Vollzug des jeweiligen Gedankenganges. Leitend ist eine solche synthetische Absicht insofern nicht vor der Zieldimension eines synthetischen Resultats. Sie geht also nicht primär auf eine Synthese im Thema bzw. Gegenstand. Das bedeutet auch, daß Auslegungssinne der Formel „in synthetischer Absicht", die von der Sache und vom Ergebnis her geschehen, offen lassen, ob im Gang selbst eine entsprechende Absicht manifest wird. Gleiches gilt vom Orientierungsgedanken: Versteht man ihn von der Sache her, nimmt der Orientierungsgrad in dem Maße zu, in dem sich Zusammenhänge und Perspektiven herstellen und bewähren lassen. Gegen den professionellen Partikularismus in der Philosophie, der sich zumeist in detailgenauen Spezialuntersuchungen artikuliert, steht insofern die Forderung, das Erbrachte historisch und systematisch zu kontextualisieren, überhaupt erst in eine Perspektive einzusetzen oder das Ergebnis in einem Debattengang oder theoretischen Problemraum zu verorten. In den vorliegenden Beiträgen geschieht dies auch. Aber es ist nicht ihr primäres Ziel. Versteht man „Orientierung" nicht vom Resultat, sondern von der Arbeit bzw. Anstrengung des Sich-Orientierens her, kann auch dort Philosophie in synthetischer Absicht ins Werk gesetzt sein, wo ihr *Ergebnis* negativ oder partikularistisch erscheint. Insofern die Absicht im Bewegungsvollzug manifest wird, ist sie auch nicht schlechterdings in einen spezifischen

Methodenbegriff übersetzbar. Daß unterschiedliche Wege offenstehen, dem entspricht die je eigene Weise, in der sich die einzelnen Autoren des Bandes auf sein Programm eingelassen haben. Jedes konkrete Sich-Orientieren geschieht relativ zu einer „Umgebung" der Verhältnisse, Zwecke und Ziele. Schon aus diesem Grund haben unbedingte Richtungsvorgaben eine kurze Zerfallszeit. Wenn Wegweisungen darum auch nicht übertragbar sind, bleibt der Vorgang, sich zu orientieren, hingegen als solcher unabweisbar. Der Gedanke, daß die Philosophie eine Kultur der Orientierung tradieren kann, steht dann auch einem späten Motiv Wittgensteins gegenüber, demzufolge die eigentliche Einsicht in die Natur einer Reihe, deren Konstruktionsprinzipien man gewahr geworden ist, darin besteht, die Reihe abzubrechen. Die Fähigkeit, die einem dies erlauben würde, ist eben zugleich das Vermögen, die Reihe auch wieder zu eröffnen und die Orientierung im Philosophieren immer neu ins Werk zu setzen. Wo dies gelingt, können die Autoren mit ihren Beiträgen eine weitere Absicht verbinden: Dieter Henrich und sein Werk zu ehren. Ihm sind die Beiträge dieses Bandes gewidmet.

Kein Beitrag geht primär – und vordergründig genug – darauf aus, sich von einer Themen- oder Argumentationstradition abzusetzen, die als Gegenstellung zu einer synthetischen Absicht aufzufassen oder auszulegen wäre. So, wie das Programm konträre Methodenbegriffe einschließen kann und die beteiligten Autoren ganz unterschiedlichen philosophischen Traditionen angehören, wird auch deutlich, daß ein – zumal zur Stilbezeichnung oder zur Bekundung eines Anspruchs auf intellektuelle Lauterkeit geläuterter – Traditionsbegriff der „analytischen Philosophie", gegen den eine Philosophie in *synthetischer* Absicht intoniert sein könnte, hier als Oppositionsbegriff obsolet ist.

Die Weise, in der eine Aufnahme und Umsetzung des Programms in *synthetischer Absicht* erfolgt, ist zumeist kein eigener Gegenstand der Beiträge. Darin liegt kein Mangel. Wer die Wege der Autoren begehen will, muß dies im Selbstvollzug tun. Dies gilt auch für die vorliegende Bandgliederung. Die Beiträge erscheinen nach Themengebieten geordnet. Daß der Band weitgehend zweisprachig angelegt ist, folgt der Überzeugung, die Beiträge, wo immer möglich, im originalen Profil erscheinen zu lassen. Buch- und Abteilungstitel finden so auch keine Übersetzung, sondern ein Pendant. Die sachliche Ordnung der Beiträge läßt es offen bzw. fordert dazu heraus, zu einer Ordnung im eigenen Gang und im Lichte der in ihr enagierten synthetischen Absicht zu gelangen.

Für die vorliegende Sammlung von Abhandlungen hat Hann Trier zwei Bilder zur Verfügung gestellt: eine Tuschpinselzeichnung als Vorlage für den Umschlag und eine Gouache, die den Band eröffnet und dessen Titelthema aufnimmt. An entlegener Stelle sind Gedanken Dieter Henrichs zu Hann Triers Bildern erschienen, die die Arbeiten des Malerfreundes begleiten. Wir suchen, so Dieter Henrich in seinem Raisonnement zu Triers Malerei, in der Welt, was sie selbst ist, und gehen, von ihr befangen, einzelne Wege der Betrachtung in ihr. Der Gedanke der Offenheit und des Befangenseins im Weltverhältnis gilt für Triers Bilder und die Bewegungen im Denken gleichermaßen. Hier wie dort zeigen sich Verlaufswege in einer Bewegungskonstellation. Wo die Beiträge dieses Bandes und die Bewegungen der Farben in Triers Malerei einzelne Wege des In-, Zu- und Gegeneinander ausmachen, sind sie dennoch, wenn sie Dichte und Fülle haben und „welthaft" sind, für das „Ganze der Konstellation" offen, in der sie stehen.

Hann Trier gebührt besonderer Dank dafür, daß er sich auf die Konzeption des Bandes in so großzügiger Weise eingelassen hat, sowie allen Autoren für ihre Beiträge und ihre weit darüber hinausgehende Zusammenarbeit. Der Beitrag, den Chr. Klotz zu dem Projekt in seiner ersten Phase erbracht hat, verdient, besonders hervorgehoben zu werden. Gedankt sei auch K. Ameriks, G. Bücherl, G. Dry, O. Eller, J. Malpas, F. Michelini, R. Pippin, J. Roberts, T. Rosefeldt, E. Stark, J. Weyenschops und A. Zweig für wertvolle Hilfe und Rat sowie den Verantwortlichen und Mitarbeitern im Verlag Klett-Cotta für die ausgezeichnete Betreuung des Projekts.

Hann Trier – In synthetischer Absicht

Dieter Henrich

Welt-Bilder

Eine Betrachtung
zu Hann Triers Malerei*

Früher sprach man vom Buch, das die Natur oder die Welt ist. Und man wollte damit sagen, daß der Sinn, den sie in sich trägt, nur dem erschlossen wird, der sich darauf versteht, in ihr zu lesen. Es zu lernen und zu tun, war das Geschäft der Philosophen.

Die so sprachen, dachten an Geschriebenes noch im Singular, – an ein Buch, das wir niemals beiseite legen, von dem wir uns nur gelegentlich abwenden, über dem uns eher die Augen zufallen.

Tafelbilder, so meint Hann Trier oft, sind wie Bücher, die man nicht zuschlagen kann. Sind sie nicht Bildrollen aus dem Osten und nicht in ein Magazin gesammelt, so müssen sie sich immerzu offen zeigen. Sie umgeben uns zwar nicht, und wir sind nicht in ihnen und Teil von ihnen so, wie wir Weltwesen sind. Wenn sie aber anders sind als edlere Gebrauchsdinge, die uns erinnern oder in Erregung oder Ruhe halten, so begegnen sie uns wie die Welt selbst.

Die Welt setzt dem nichts entgegen, daß wir uns betrachtend in ihr ergehen. Doch sie informiert uns auch über nichts, gibt keine Halt- oder Handlungssignale, die uns stracks über sie hinweg zu irgendeiner Sache bringen. Wir suchen in ihr nur, was sie selbst ist. Damit ist auch gesagt, daß wir, wenn wir sie betrachten, so wenig etwas irgendwo in ihr finden wollen, wie wir durch sie etwas anderes zu finden hoffen. So können wir, wie in älterem Deutsch schön zu sagen war, von ihr „befangen" sein, weder timide abgewandt noch irgendwie veranlaßt oder auch nur fähig, uns über sie hinwegzuheben.

Was offen für uns ist, so daß es uns befängt, kann nicht fadenscheinig sein, – wie ein Gewebe, dem Stoff und Glanz vergingen und dessen Machart nun zum Vorschein kommt. Dauerhafte Dichte oder

Fülle muß es haben, – aber nicht die, welche auch eine Lade oder eine Tasche hat, in die manches gestopft ist. Denn das gerade ist Anfüllung ohne Offenheit.

Weder verbirgt die Welt sich uns, noch legt sie es nahe, uns einen Reim auf sie zu machen. Wir gehen Wege der Betrachtung, die sich uns auftun, – lesen in ihr, können aber schwerlich sagen, daß wir sie ausgelesen und dann weggelegt haben, weil wir schon gar nichts von ihr ablesen.

Es ist ein verläßliches Axiom für das Philosophieren, daß die Welt nicht einfacher sein kann als der komplexeste Gedanke, dessen wir hinsichtlich ihrer fähig sind. Auf nur einem Wege allein kann sich solch' ein Gedanke nicht ergeben. Er entspricht jedem von ihnen – also im Prinzip allen Wegen zugleich, – und dazu der Umgebung, in der sie sich ausfalten.

So ist, wenn es welthaft ist, auch ein Bild. Welt und Bild sind deshalb aber nicht so etwas wie ein Geheimnis. Wären sie dies, so ginge es wieder – wie beim versiegelten Buch – um den verborgenen Sinn, – ob er nun ewig verschlossen bleibt oder am Ende sich aufschließt. Welt und Bild sind aber aufgeschlagen. Sie sind auch nicht wie ein Vexierspiel, das einmal dies, dann ganz anderes, und zwar offenkundig, zu zeigen scheint, – für eine Weile den Hasen und dann plötzlich die Ente, erst nur den Baum und dann endlich den bösen Mann. Offen zu sein meint auch, daß der Einheitssinn ganz außer Frage steht. Wir entdecken kein neues Bild, nur Neues in ihm und auf neuen Wegen.

Hann Trier malt solche Bilder.

Da er aus dem Gestus malt und den Gestus auch zeigen will, meint man, dies sei das einzig Wesentliche in seinem Werk, daß seine Grapheme kraftvoll und geistreich zugleich ausgespannt sind. Was Hann Trier malt, sind aber Kraft*felder*. Bewegungsverläufe und Bewegungspotentiale bilden eine Bewegungskonstellation – je eine Welt von Bewegtheit. Man kann, in anderer Sprache, auch sagen, daß die Bewegungsverläufe seiner Bilder polyphon sind. Im Bild gehen viele Verläufe, in-, zu- und gegeneinander: großflächige und kleingespitzte Pinselschwünge, schnelle und träge, dunkel-geschlossene und farbig-durchleuchtete Kaskaden und Protuberanzen, weit ausholende und

Welt-Bilder

im Engen in sich zurückgetriebene Spurenwirbel. Die meisten dieser Bewegungswege sind so angelegt, daß man jedem einzelnen für sich nachgehen und von ihm her die Konstellation als solche auffassen kann, was verlangt, daß sie formstark in sich sind. Man kann sich sogar an einen solchen Weg und an die Aussichten, die er eröffnet, gewöhnen. Aber dann sind doch andere Wege zu finden. Geht man auf ihnen, so wird man frühere Wege erinnern, schließlich vielleicht mehrere zugleich durcheilen lernen. So wird man bemerken, daß noch manche andere Bewegungswege immer schon dahin wirkten, der ganzen Bewegungs-Konstellation ihre Form zu geben. Dabei überfüllt sich das Bild aber nicht etwa und verwirrt sich nicht. Sein Einheitssinn tritt nur klarer hervor.

Wegen dieser Wandlungsfähigkeit ohne Einheitsverlust sind Hann Triers Bilder luzide. Denn es gibt keine befreiende Klarheit, die aus dem Verdrängen der Vielfalt der Einsätze zu in sich folgerichtigen Lebensbewegungen kommt. Klarheit geht hervor, wenn wir im Standhalten nicht in gepreßte Sinnesart geraten. Nur wirkliche Kunst ist deshalb wirklich klar, während die Produkte des Bildermachens bestenfalls durchsichtig sind.

Aus solcher Klarheit kann Hann Trier Deckenbilder malen, die wie keine anderen Bilder für Räume sind. Sie lassen die Tageszeiten gewähren, deren Lichtwechsel diese oder jene Wege in ihnen zu auffälligem Vorschein bringt, – aber ohne das Bild nur in bedeutsame Vagheit zu ziehen und Sinn auf Kosten der Sichtbarkeit zu evozieren.

Eben darum sind Hann Triers Bilder auch Bilder zum Meditieren. Wie dem Wandel des Lichts, so geben sie auch der freien Bewegung des betrachtenden Gedankens einen anderen Raum.

Es gibt viele Weisen der Meditation, zunächst die über ein Thema. Aber Hann Triers Bilder bringen kein solches Thema auf, das in ein bedeutsames Sinnen versetzt, das seinerseits vom Bild selbst weggleitet, wobei dies Bild noch das Gestimmtsein verbreitet, das Sinnen aufkommen läßt und wachhält.

Dann gibt es die Meditation hinein in die Stille einer reinen Gegenwart. Aber Hann Triers Bilder sind Bewegungswelten, – das eigentliche Gegenteil von Einladungen zur Reinheit des Lichts oder der großen Leere. Auch sind sie nicht, wie ein Koan, Sinnrätsel, deren Lösung sich dem beharrlich Meditierenden am Ende aus ihnen selbst heraus auftut.

Die diesen Bildern gemäße Meditation hat kein Ziel. Nicht das „Meditieren über ..." und auch nicht das „Meditieren zu ..." wird von ihnen eingeladen. Sie sind selbstgenügsame Plafonds und Medien eines anderen Meditierens, das als ein „Meditieren in ..." zu verstehen ist.

Diese Bilder sind nicht die Welt selbst; ihnen fehlt schon die Widerständigkeit der Dinge, die aus sich selbst heraus sich zu erhalten scheinen. Aber sie sind *wie* die Welt, insofern die Welt als Ganze in Gedanken gefaßt werden soll. Auch die Welt ist dem Denken nicht, was die Sphinx dem Ödipus oder das Kreuz der heiligen Theresa war. Nur wer sie immer aufs neue ausschreitet, auf vielen und neuen Wegen, und wer die Entfernungen und Bewegungen auf diesen Wegen versteht, kann zu sagen versuchen, was Wegsinn und Bewandtnis in ihr ausmacht, und dann vielleicht auch, was als ihre eigene Bewandtnis mit ihr aufscheint. Er sagt es, indem er über die Wege und die Wegenetze spricht, die sich in der Welt auftun.

Hann Triers Bilder sind nicht ausgedacht. Sie sind auch nicht Bilder, die in irgendeinem thematischen Sinn nachdenklich machen wollen. Gerade so können sie dem Denken als solchem vertraut sein.

Anmerkung

* Der vorliegende Text wurde aus Anlaß der Ausstellung von Werken Hann Triers des Kölnischen Kunstvereins (vom 7. September bis 7. Oktober 1979) geschrieben und erschien in dem Begleitband *Hann Trier* zu dieser Ausstellung, S. 67–70. Er wurde wiederabgedruckt in einer Dokumentation zur Ausstellung der Galerie Hennemann, Bonn (im November 1980) mit dem Titel *Hann Trier*, ed. Manfred de la Motte, Bonn 1980, S. 54 f. Der Text erscheint hier mit wenigen kleinen Veränderungen.

I.

Subjektivität, Naturalismus, Ich-Gedanken

Mind, Nature, Stances of the Self

Jürgen Mittelstraß

Das philosophische Kreuz mit dem Bewußtsein

Bewußtsein ist in mannigfacher Weise ein Schlüsselbegriff der Selbstwerdung des Denkens und eine Erfindung der Philosophie. Vielleicht hätten wir die Probleme, die sich mit diesem Begriff in unterschiedlichen Kontexten, von den klassischen Zeugnissen der Metaphysik bis zur modernen Neurophysiologie, verbinden, gar nicht oder in gänzlich anderer Weise, wenn die philosophische Sprache, vor allem die des durch Kant begründeten Idealismus, ärmer ausgefallen wäre. Doch eine derartige Vermutung ist müßig angesichts der Wirkung dieser philosophischen Begriffsbildung sowie angesichts des Umstandes, daß der wissenschaftliche Geist, der sich als empirischer Geist versteht, seit langem damit beschäftigt ist, Bewußtsein auch in seinen Kategorien zu denken, zu analysieren und abzuarbeiten. Wenn die Welt (nach Wittgenstein) alles ist, was der Fall ist, dann gehört zu dieser Welt auch das Bewußtsein – sei es als ein empirisches Faktum oder als eine philosophische Erfindung mit wissenschaftlicher Zukunft.

Seine Karriere beginnt mit der dualistischen Konzeption Descartes', in der sich die ursprüngliche Aristotelische Konzeption einer Einheit von Leib und Seele, in der scholastischen Philosophie im Rahmen der sogenannten *forma-substantialis*-Theorie weitergeführt, zugunsten getrennter Welten des Körperlichen und des Denkens auflöst:

> „Es gibt gewisse Eigenschaften, die wir ‚körperliche' nennen, wie Größe, Gestalt, Bewegung [...], und die Substanz, der sie zukommen, nennen wir ‚Körper'. [...] Es gibt aber auch noch andere Eigenschaften, die wir ‚bewußte' nennen, wie Einsehen, Wollen, Sich-etwas-Einbilden, Empfinden; sie fallen alle unter den gemeinsamen Begriff der bewußten Handlung oder der Wahrnehmung oder des Bewußtseins. Und die Substanz, der sie zukommen, nennen wir ‚bewußtes Seiendes' oder ‚Geist'."[1]

Diese Konzeption wird zur Grundlage aller späteren Theorien des Bewußtseins, auch derjenigen Kants und des Deutschen Idealismus. Allerdings ist auch hier die Spannweite der Begriffsbildung groß. So versteht Kant unter dem Begriff des Bewußtseins in erster Linie die synthetischen Leistungen des Denkens bzw. der Subjektivität, erst in zweiter Linie eine Eigenschaft des wissensbildenden Subjekts. Dabei wird die Begriffsbildung zugleich um die Unterscheidung zwischen einem empirischen und einem transzendentalen Bewußtsein („Bewußtsein überhaupt") erweitert:

> „Alle Vorstellungen haben eine notwendige Beziehung auf ein *mögliches* empirisches Bewußtsein: denn hätten sie dieses nicht, und wäre es gänzlich unmöglich, sich ihrer bewußt zu werden: so würde das so viel sagen, sie existierten gar nicht. Alles empirische Bewußtsein hat aber eine notwendige Beziehung auf ein transzendentales (vor aller besondern Erfahrung hervorgehendes) Bewußtsein, nämlich das Bewußtsein meiner selbst, als die ursprüngliche Apperzeption. [...] Der synthetische Satz: daß alles verschiedene *empirische Bewußtsein* in einem einigen Selbstbewußtsein verbunden sein müsse, ist der schlechthin erste und synthetische Grundsatz unseres Denkens überhaupt. Es ist aber nicht aus der Acht zu lassen, daß die bloße Vorstellung *Ich* in Beziehung auf alle andere [...] das transzendentale Bewußtsein sei."[2]

Diese Vorstellung wird insbesondere von Fichte ausgearbeitet, zugleich aber auch wieder (etwa bei Hölderlin) problematisiert. Es geht nunmehr um die

> „Trennung zwischen der Begründungsweise Fichtes, welche die Dynamik ausarbeitet, die im Für-sich-Sein des Subjektes, das er ‚das Ich' nannte, und in dessen ausgezeichneter Einheit angelegt ist, und einer anderen Begründungsart, die nicht anerkennt, daß eine solche Subjekteinheit dem Philosophieren eine letzte Begründung zu geben vermag"[3].

In beiden Formen wird das Bewußtsein endgültig zu derjenigen Instanz, von der alles (philosophische) Wissen seinen Ausgang nimmt und auf die alles (philosophische) Wissen zurückführt.

Doch nicht von diesem Umstand und seiner Geschichte soll hier die Rede sein, sondern von der Karriere des Bewußtseins in wissenschaftlichen Forschungsprogrammen. Tatsächlich ist Bewußtsein auch zu einem wissenschaftlichen Problem geworden, und zwar – entgegen mancher wissenschaftlicher Selbstwahrnehmung – zu einem solchen, in dem immer noch mehr Philosophie steckt, als die Wissenschaft in der Regel zu bemerken scheint. Das gilt heute vor allem im Rahmen des sogenannten, von Philosophie und Wissenschaft wieder intensiv diskutierten Leib-Seele-Problems.[4]

I
Zwischen Monismus und Dualismus

In der Philosophie wird das Leib-Seele-Problem häufig ein Cartesisches ‚Restproblem' genannt, weil es aus der Zwei-Substanzen-Metaphysik Descartes' entstanden ist, die Probleme der Wechselwirkung zwischen (in klassischer Terminologie) Leib und Seele, damit auch zwischen Materie und Bewußtsein, zu einem Geheimnis werden läßt. Die ersten philosophischen ‚Lösungen' dieses Problems, schon bei Descartes angesichts zeitgenössischer Kritik, sind *dualistischer* Art, d. h., sie empfehlen die Annahme einer gegeneinander isolierbaren Selbständigkeit, eben einer Dualität von Leib und Seele, Materie und Bewußtsein.[5] Descartes selbst ist dabei reichlich unschlüssig. So vertritt er einerseits eine *interaktionistische* Annahme, die eine organische Vermittlung beider Substanzen über die Zirbeldrüse (Epiphyse) vorsieht[6], begnügt sich aber (im Blick auf die systematische Inkonsequenz einer solchen Annahme) auch mit dem schlichten Hinweis auf alltägliche Erfahrungsbestände.[7]

Im Cartesianismus lebt diese Unbestimmtheit in Form zweier alternativer ‚Lösungen' weiter, dem sogenannten *Influxionismus*, der eine tatsächliche physische Verbindung beider Substanzen annimmt, und dem sogenannten *Okkasionalismus*, der das Paradox einer physischen Verbindung und kausalen Wechselwirkung zwischen Physischem und Nicht-Physischem durch ‚gelegentliche' göttliche Eingriffe bzw. (zur Entlastung Gottes) durch eine von Gott bewirkte andauernde Korrespondenz beider Substanzen zu erklären sucht. Letzterem verwandt sind Leibnizens Annahme einer *prästabilierten Harmonie* zwischen Leib und Seele (die zugleich die Seele der Philosophie vor allzu niveaulosen Einfällen rettet) und Spinozas Deutung beider als Attribute einer göttlichen Substanz. Zugleich begründen derartige Versuche die Konzeption eines *psychophysischen Parallelismus*, die später auch zur Lösung des Problems der empirischen Korrespondenz zwischen objektiv-physischen Reizen und subjektiv-psychischen Sinnesempfindungen vertreten wird (z. B. von Fechner, Wundt und Mach).

Kein Wunder, daß derartige ‚Lösungen' ihrerseits *monistische* Konzeptionen auf den Plan rufen. Zu diesen Konzeptionen gehören sowohl *idealistische Reduktionen*, etwa in Form des von Berkeley vertretenen *Immaterialismus*, als auch *physikalistische* bzw. *materialistische Reduktionen* älterer und neuerer Art. Beispiele für physikalistische bzw. materialistische Reduktionen sind der *Behaviorismus* und die *Identitäts*theorie. Jeder Versuch, eine Steuerung mentaler Vorgänge ‚von außen', d. h. nicht an Gehirnsubstanz gebunden, anzunehmen, wird hier als Rückfall in philosophische Naivitäten gedeutet. Hierhin gehört im übrigen auch (mit gewissen Einschränkungen) der sogenannte *Epiphänomenalismus*, sofern dieser psychische Zustände und Prozesse als ‚Begleiterscheinungen' physischer bzw. physiologischer Zustände und Prozesse deutet, die ihrerseits ein in sich geschlossenes, von psychischen Einwirkungen freies System bilden.

Ergänzt werden derartige monistische Alternativen zur dualistischen Erklärung durch neuere *informationstheoretische* Ansätze, in deren Rahmen psychische und geistige Prozesse als komplexe Datentransformationen sowie Leib und Seele, Materie und Bewußtsein als unterschiedliche Strukturen von Informationszuständen aufgefaßt werden. Auch diese Ansätze sind ihrer Struktur nach monistisch und physikalisch-materialistisch. Das Gehirn erscheint als eine ‚Rechenmaschine'. Dabei wird auch hier wie in den erwähnten monistischen Erklärungskonzeptionen deutlich, in welch intensiver Weise sich ursprünglich rein philosophische Ansätze mit Forschungen der Neurophysiologie und Neuropsychologie über empirische Zusammenhänge und wechselseitige Abhängigkeiten zwischen physischen und psychischen Zuständen und Prozessen verbinden. Die Zukunft der Philosophie scheint auch in Sachen Leib-Seele-Problem in der Wissenschaft, d. h. in der wissenschaftlichen Bearbeitung ihrer Intuitionen zu liegen. Nicht unwidersprochen, wie moderne *dualistische* Versionen deutlich machen.

II
Das Ich und sein Gehirn

Reduktionsprogramme aller Art leiden darunter, das Kind – hier: einen abgewogenen, spekulationsfreien Zugang zum Begriff des Bewußtseins – mit dem Bade – hier: mit dualistischen Widersprüchen – auszuschütten. Ein moderner Versuch, diesem Unglück zu wehren, ist der reduktionskritische, interaktionistische Dualismus von Popper und Eccles[8], dessen zentrale Bestandteile eine Antireduktionismusthese und eine Realitätsthese sind.[9]

Die *Antireduktionismusthese*, d. h. die Behauptung, daß sich unterschiedliche Wirklichkeitsbereiche wie Physik, Chemie, Biologie und Soziologie nicht aufeinander reduzieren lassen, wird durch ein wissenschaftshistorisches Analogieargument – es gibt, historisch, keine erfolgreichen Reduktionen; was als Reduktion erscheint, ist im wesentlichen Korrektur – und durch ein evolutionäres ‚Kreativitätsargument' – höhere Ebenen der Organisation führen zu Erscheinungen, die sich aus Prozessen der niederen Ebenen nicht ableiten lassen – zu begründen versucht. Diese Begründung hält jedoch, näher betrachtet, einer kritischen Analyse nicht stand. Das gleiche gilt für die *Realitätsthese*, d. h. für die Behauptung, daß es drei Welten gibt – die ‚erste' Welt der physischen Körper, die ‚zweite' Welt der geistig-seelischen Zustände und die ‚dritte' Welt der ‚objektiven Gedankeninhalte' (die schon bei Frege[10] auftritt) – und daß diese drei Welten jede für sich wirklich sind. Die Charakterisierung als *wirklich* schließt hier die Behauptung ein, daß diese Welten in gleicher Weise auch *kausal* aufeinander wirken können. Dies müßte dann insbesondere für das Verhältnis von Welt 3, der Welt der Theorien, zu Welt 2, der Welt unseres Denkens, gelten, da ja eine ‚Reduktion' der Theorien auf das Denken dieser Konzeption nach nicht möglich ist.

Dieser (philosophisch problematische) Umstand führt Popper und Eccles nicht nur dazu, gegen monistische Erklärungskonzeptionen die ‚dualistische' Selbständigkeit von psychischen und physischen Zuständen bzw. Prozessen zu behaupten, sondern darüber hinaus die Selbständigkeit und Identität des Ich (oder Ichbewußtseins) gegenüber seinen auch physischen Repräsentationen – pointiert in der Wendung „das Ich und sein Gehirn" ausgedrückt. Dabei gehört nach dieser Vorstellung das Gehirn dem Ich, nicht umgekehrt das Ich dem Gehirn. Das Ich ist der Programmierer des Computers ‚Gehirn', der Steuermann, nicht der Gesteuerte. Eccles, für den das selbstbewußte Ich, der selbstbewußte Geist, in der Welt 2 verankert ist, übersetzt diese Vorstellung in eine neurobiologische Sprache. Danach kontrolliert und interpretiert das Ich die Neuronenprozesse, es sucht aktiv nach Hirnereignissen, die in seinem Interessenbereich liegen, und integriert sie zu einer vereinheitlichten und bewußten Erfahrung. Es tastet ständig kollektive Interaktionen unzähliger Neuronen ab, die gegenüber einer Wechselwirkung mit der Welt 2 offen sind (‚Liaison-Hirn'). Die Einheit der bewußten Erfahrung, so Eccles' zentrale These, wird „durch den selbstbewußten Geist vermittelt [...] und nicht durch die neurale Maschinerie der Liaison-Zentren der Großhirnhemisphäre"[11].

Wie das im einzelnen zu verstehen ist, d. h., wie der behauptete Interaktionismus von selbstbewußtem Ich oder selbstbewußtem Geist und Gehirn tatsächlich vonstatten geht, bleibt allerdings offen – wie schon bei Descartes. Auch als Forschungsprogramm aufgefaßt reicht daher dieser Dualismus über die klassischen dualistischen Positionen – trotz der neurobiologischen Sprache, die er spricht – wenig hinaus. Als ein solches Programm mag er vielleicht sympathischer sein als seine reduktionistischen Kontrahenten; zu zeigen, daß er diesen auf ihrem eigenen Felde, der Erklärung neurobiologischer Zustände und Prozesse, überlegen ist, bleibt er (jedenfalls bisher) schuldig.

III
Identität und pragmatischer Dualismus

Gegen dualistische Vorstellungen, etwa nach Art der Konzeption von Popper und Eccles, steht die monistische Vorstellung, daß neurophysiologische und psychische Zustände und Prozesse *identisch* sind. Doch auch diese Vorstellung ist unbefriedigend; sie läßt sich durch irgendwelche physikalische Gesetze nicht stützen. Für eine monistische Reduktion ist auch nicht hinreichend, daß sich zwischen psychischen Zuständen und Prozessen auf der einen Seite und bestimmten neurophysiologischen Zuständen und Prozessen auf der anderen Seite eine umkehrbar eindeutige *Korrelation* herstellen läßt. Nur auf derartige Korrelationen aber stützen sich in der Regel monistische Vorstellungen wie im Falle der Identitätstheorie, d. h. der These, daß sich psychische Zustände und Prozesse letztendlich als physische Zustände und Prozesse erweisen. Hier wird festgestellt, daß der psychische Zustand oder Prozeß a genau dann auftritt, wenn auch der neurophysiologische Zustand oder Prozeß a^1 nachweisbar ist. So korrelieren z. B. gewisse Empfindungen mit einer (durch Kernspintomographie feststellbaren) veränderten Stoffwechselaktivität in bestimmten Hirnbereichen. Für eine Identität beider aber gibt es keine Argumente. Die Situation ist vielmehr die gleiche wie im Falle von guten Meßgeräten. Auch hier korreliert ein Zustand des Meßgerätes mit einem bestimmten Zustand außerhalb desselben. So *verweist* das Signal bei einer Kernspintomographie auf Protonenpräsenz, ist aber mit dieser nicht identisch. Desgleichen *zeigt* die Bahn in einer Nebelkammer den Durchgang eines Teilchens an, ist aber mit diesem nicht identisch. Nur unzureichendes Wissen mag hier dazu führen, beides (fälschlich) miteinander zu identifizieren. Außerdem reicht die Bedingung einer Übersetzbarkeit von Begriffen einer Theorie in eine andere Theorie nicht aus, um Identität zu gewährleisten; es muß vielmehr auch eine Übersetzbarkeit von einschlägigen Gesetzen gegeben sein. Damit ist aber die Vorstellung, daß psychische Zustände und Prozesse auf neurophysiologische Zustände und Prozesse ontologisch reduziert wären, eine bisher nicht eingelöste Behauptung.

Nun könnte dem auch der Anhänger eines identitätstheoretischen Monismus zustimmen und dennoch Monist bleiben, nämlich im Sinne der behaupteten Durchführbarkeit eines Reduktions*programmes* – das gegenüber dem dualistischen Programm dann auch noch den (aus Sicht der Wissenschaft) Vorteil hätte, ohne Philosophie auskommen zu können. Doch erstens muß dieses nicht unbedingt ein Vorteil sein, und zweitens lassen sich auch hier keine strengen Kriterien für ein erfolgversprechendes Reduktionsprogramm angeben. Auch Verweise auf reduktive Leistungen in anderen Wissenschaftsbereichen helfen da nicht weiter. Es ist wie in der Philosophie: „Eine Hauptursache philosophischer Krankheiten – einseitige Diät: man nährt sein Denken mit nur einer Art von Beispielen"[12], d. h., man verweist in diesem Falle auf die erfolgreichen Reduktionen in der Physik und übersieht die gescheiterten in der Psychologie. Das Schicksal des *behavioristischen* Reduktionsprogrammes sollte an dieser Stelle zu denken geben. Schließlich ist kein Grund erkennbar, warum das analoge neurophysiologische Reduktionsprogramm erfolgreicher sein sollte.

An dieser Stelle hilft möglicherweise die Interpretation kognitiver Begriffe, mit denen wir nicht-reduktionistisch über menschliches Verhalten sprechen, als *theoretischer Begriffe* weiter. Theoretische Begriffe sind solche, die nicht in Begriffe einer theorieunabhängigen Beobachtungssprache übersetzt werden können, d. h. deren Bedeutung auf eine Theorie insgesamt und auf die Bedingungen ihrer empirischen Bewährung bezogen bleibt. Das bedeutet nicht, daß man in besonderen Fällen keine geeigneten Indikatoren hat. So auch im Falle der Psychologie, in der über die Anwendbarkeit von theoretischen Begriffen in einer gegebenen Situation anhand von Verhaltensindikatoren zu entscheiden wäre, wobei jedoch deren Bedeutung durch die Summe der Verhaltensindikatoren nicht erschöpft wird. Die Einführung theoretischer Begriffe in unserem Problemzusammenhang schließt in dieser Form die Einsicht ein, daß es eine Eigenschaft gerade fruchtbarer wissenschaftlicher Begriffe ist, eine ‚überschüssige Bedeutung' zu besitzen, d. h. eine Bedeutung über ihren operationalen Gehalt hinaus, und daß es offene Begriffe sind, deren zugeordnete Beobachtungsindikatoren sich im Gang des Wissenschaftsprozesses ändern mögen. Es sieht so aus, als setzte ein monistisches Reduktionsprogramm im Sinne der Identitätstheorie dagegen auf eine starre Fixierung psychologischer Konzepte an ihre neurophysiologischen Indikatoren. Das aber ist wissenschaftstheoretisch gesehen der Stand der Theoriediskussion der 20er Jahre dieses Jahrhunderts. Warum also sollte die Philosophie der Biologie die Fehler der Wissenschaftstheorie der Physik wiederholen?

Dies ist natürlich eine *wissenschaftstheoretische*, keine biologische bzw. neurophysiologische Argumentation. Die ontologische Frage nach der Identität von Bewußtsein (oder Geist) und neurophysiologischen Zuständen und Prozessen wurde übersetzt in die wissenschaftstheoretische Frage, ob eigenständige psychologische Begriffe prinzipiell fruchtbar sein können oder prinzipiell zu vermeiden sind. Argumentiert wurde zugunsten ihrer prinzipiellen Fruchtbarkeit und damit für einen *pragmatischen Dualismus*. Hier werden, mit anderen Worten, keine Gründe für einen tatsächlichen Unterschied zwischen physischen und psychischen Zuständen und Prozessen angeführt, sondern allein Gründe dafür, daß es besser ist, einen derartigen Unterschied nicht von vornherein auszuschließen. Positiv gewendet: Eigenständige psychologische (kognitive) Begriffe lassen sich als *Erklärungskonstruktionen* rechtfertigen. Die Frage, ob diese Konstruktionen irgendeine ontologische Referenz haben, ist die allgemeine wissenschaftstheoretische Frage nach der Existenz von Referenten theoretischer Begriffe, und diese Frage ist derzeit ungeklärt. Das heißt aber auch, daß sie sich nicht vorab in neurophysiologischen Zusammenhängen klären läßt.

So gesehen kommt daher auch die reduktionistische Kritik am Dualismus, wonach der Geist die zweifelhafte Rolle eines ‚deus ex machina' spiele[13], methodisch zu früh; vor allem dann, wenn gleichzeitig auch von reduktionistischer bzw. monistischer Seite erklärt wird, daß unser Bild der Welt stets eine *Konstruktion* sei.[14] Was von diesem Bild gilt, muß auch von unserem biologischen Wissen von Bewußtseinsprozessen gelten. Anders ausgedrückt: Wenn alles, was wir landläufig über die Welt wissen, zumindest partiell eine Konstruktion des Gehirns ist, dann kann auch das, was die Biologie über das Gehirn weiß, nicht seinerseits von Konstruktionen unabhängig sein.

Das wird auch von Teilen der neurophysiologischen Forschung so gesehen, z. B. von Creutzfeld, wenn dieser von der Fähigkeit des menschlichen Gehirns zur *symbolischen Repräsentation* spricht und dabei betont, daß die Symbole selbst weder eine Leistung des Nervensystems, noch das Nervensystem, noch die Welt selbst sind.[15] Creutzfeld zieht daraus selbst eine dualistische Konsequenz, pointiert von ihm in der Weise ausgedrückt, „daß Dualismus – d. h. das Sich-selbst-gegenübergestellt-sein – die Natur von Bewußtsein ist"[16]. Es ist klar, daß dies kein Satz der Neurophysiologie, sondern ein *philosophischer* Satz ist. Er muß deshalb nach dem über einen pragmatischen Dualismus Gesagten kein sinnloser Satz sein. Das gilt, wenn auch mit gewissen Einschränkungen, auch von den folgenden Bemerkungen: Die Symbole „bilden unabhängig eine eigene Welt, auf die sich unser Gehirn wiederum ständig bezieht: die Welt des Geistes"[17]. Und:

„Alle reduktionistischen Theorien werden diesem Wesen des Bewußtseins nicht gerecht. Sie erfassen nur die eine Seite, nämlich die Hirnmechanismen, aber nicht die andere, nämlich die Welt der Symbole, mit denen diese Mechanismen, also das Gehirn, sich selbst konfrontiert und die so real ist, wie die natürliche Welt."[18]

„Die Welt des Geistes" und „die Welt der Symbole" – diese Formeln atmen den Geist der klassischen Philosophie, nicht den der vergleichsweise nüchternen modernen Wissenschaftstheorie. Dennoch sind auch sie, was die Betonung des konstruktiven Charakters aller Orientierungen, auch der wissenschaftlichen Orientierungen, und die Kritik der reduktionistischen These einer Identität von Hirnmechanismen und Bewußtsein betrifft, mit dem hier vertretenen pragmatischen Dualismus verträglich. Das Entscheidende ist, daß über der Praxis der Biologie nicht wieder der reine Geist aufzieht, sondern diese Praxis in ihren theoretischen Forschungsprogrammen unter Perspektiven einer wissenschaftstheoretischen Aufklärung gesehen wird. Ob dazu auch die Realität der Welt der Symbole oder die von Creutzfeld im gleichen Zusammenhang betonte Einheit des Bewußtseins gehören müssen, ist demgegenüber eine nachgeordnete Frage.

IV
Bewußtsein und Selbstverständnis

Die bisherige Darstellung könnte den Eindruck erwecken, daß in Sachen Bewußtsein die Aufgabe der Philosophie mit ihren wissenschaftstheoretischen Aufklärungsbemühungen beendet ist und daß die weitergehenden Behauptungen von Popper/Eccles und Creutzfeld eigentlich unzulässige Erweiterungen dieser Bemühungen sind. Im Falle des von Popper/Eccles vertretenen interaktionistischen Dualismus wird man letzterem zustimmen können, doch ist damit noch nicht über die Begrenzung philosophischer Kompetenzen auf wissenschaftstheoretische Kompetenzen entschieden. Bewußtsein ist philosophisch gesehen nicht nur ein wissenschaftstheoretischer Begriff (und dies, historisch gesehen, sogar nur in äußerst seltenen Fällen). Das bedeutet nicht, daß die Philosophie am Ende eben dasjenige Bewußtsein erklären soll, das die Wissenschaft zu erklären versucht. Auch wird, mit den Worten Creutzfelds, niemand

„bestreiten, daß unsere Erfahrungen und Reaktionen auf der Fähigkeit des Nervensystems beruhen, bestimmte physikalische Reize aufzunehmen, als Aktionspotentialsequenzen zu kodieren und diese Information in entsprechende Sequenzen der motorischen Systeme umzuwandeln, was dem Reduktionismus hinreichende Erklärung gibt"[19].

Nur, darum geht es beim Begriff des Bewußtseins, philosophisch gesehen, auch gar nicht.

Die Philosophie soll keine Probleme lösen wollen, die die Wissenschaft besser lösen kann – und die daher auch als wissenschaftliche, nicht als philosophische Probleme definiert werden. Ihre Aufgabe ist die Herstellung von Klarheit in allen Bereichen unserer Selbst- und Situationsverständnisse, auch der wissenschaftlichen Verständnisse. Letzterem dient sie als Wissenschaftstheorie. Das Besondere dabei ist, daß sie sich dieser Aufgabe *denkend*, nicht *forschend* unterzieht. Das wiederum bedeutet nicht, daß die Forschung nicht denkt, sondern daß das philosophische Denken nicht Forschung in derselben Weise ist, in der die Wissenschaft – im Lichte von Theorien und mit empirischen Methoden – forscht. ‚Bewußtsein', ‚Selbstbewußtsein', ‚Selbstverständnis' sind Titel dieser besonderen philosophischen Art, sich im Denken und durch das Denken zu orientieren. Und diese Orientierung ist weder ein kultureller Luxus, den sich eine rationale Gesellschaft neben ihrem Arbeits- und wissenschaftlichen Wissensbildungsalltag leistet, noch kann sie durch Wissenschaft selbst geleistet werden. Pointiert formuliert: Sokrates' Frage nach dem richtigen Selbst- und Situationsverständnis des Menschen wird nicht dadurch beantwortet oder auch nur leichter beantwortbar, daß sich der Mensch wissenschaftliche Kenntnisse über sein Gehirn verschafft. Dies würde wieder nur bedeuten, daß wir glaubten, alles begriffen zu haben, wenn wir uns nur neurophysiologisch richtig begriffen hätten. In diesem Sinne aber ist der hier vertretene pragmatische Dualismus nicht nur ein *theoretischer*, sondern auch ein *praktischer* Dualismus.

Natürlich soll das nicht als Aufforderung an die Philosophen aufgefaßt werden, mit der Rede von Bewußtsein etc. frohgemut so fortzufahren, als sei die Neurophysiologie noch nicht erfunden. Wissenschaftliche Kenntnisse vermeiden auch hier gewisse Naivitäten, mit denen sich philosophische Ansichten allzu gerne an die Stelle von wissenschaftlichen Forschungen zu setzen suchen. Auch ist es wichtig, sich hier an sprachanalytische Untersuchungen über das Leib-Seele-Problem innerhalb der Philosophie zu erinnern, etwa an Wittgensteins Kritik philosophischer Verwechslungen von Aussagen in mentaler Rede mit Aussagen über die Realität einer psychischen Welt oder an Ryles Kritik psychologistischer und physikalistischer Orientierungen innerhalb einer ‚Philosophie des Geistes'.[20]

Allerdings ist es mit der in diesem philosophischen Rahmen (bei Wittgenstein und Ryle) erfolgten Deklaration des Leib-Seele-Problems zum *Scheinproblem* noch nicht getan. Wäre dies der Fall, bliebe am Ende ja doch nur wieder der Weg, entweder zwischen unverbindlichen Ansichten und Meinungen oder wissenschaftlichen Orientierungen zu wählen. Diese aber beschreiben eine Lebenswelt, in der sich das Subjekt kaum wiederzuerkennen vermag:

„Die Welt stellt sich dem Gehirn über die Sinnesorgane dar. Bereits hier wird ihre Einheit in eine Vielfalt von Erscheinungsformen zerlegt, indem jedes Sinnesorgan nur für einen begrenzten Bereich der Energieübertragung empfindlich ist: das Auge für den engen Wellenlängenbereich des ‚sichtbaren' Lichts, das Ohr für einen engen Bereich mechanischer Schwingungen, die Hautsinne für langwellige Wärmestrahlungen und für niederfrequente mechanische Schwingungen und die Geruchs- und Geschmackssinne schließlich für einen engbegrenzten Bereich von Konzentrationen bestimmter Moleküle. Die Welt, wie sie sich uns darstellt, ist somit auf einen engen Bereich physikalischer und chemischer Phänomene beschränkt. Dies aber ist unsere Lebenswelt."[21]

Ist sie dies wirklich? Dagegen steht schon das im Sinne eines pragmatischen Dualismus über Konstruktionen der Wirklichkeit Gesagte. Und mehr noch: Wir sind Lebewesen, die nicht nur die Welt, in der sie leben – ihre Welt – konstruieren, sondern die sich auch selbst konstruieren, indem sie in ihren und mit ihren Selbstverständnissen leben. Es ist eben etwas anderes: sich ein *wissenschaftliches Wissen über sich selbst* und sich ein *Selbstverständnis von sich selbst* zu bilden. Auch dafür aber steht, unter anderem, der Begriff des Bewußtseins. Insofern ist dann sogar Popper zuzustimmen mit der Bemerkung:

„Wie erlangen wir ein Wissen von uns selbst? Nicht durch Selbstbeobachtung [...], sondern dadurch, daß man ein Ich wird, und daß man Theorien über sich selbst entwickelt."[22]

Selbst der Satz, daß nicht das Ich dem Gehirn, sondern das Gehirn dem Ich gehört, gewinnt, wenn man ihn unter einer lebensweltlichen praktischen, nicht einer wissenschaftlichen theoretischen Optik betrachtet, einen guten Sinn. Man denke nur daran, daß sich jemand nicht gerade heiter an seinen Schreibtisch begibt und sich selbst auffordert, nunmehr, und wenn es auch schwerfallen sollte, zu denken (z. B. weil eine Arbeit über den Begriff des Bewußtseins fertig werden muß). Ändern da wissenschaftliche Kenntnisse irgend etwas an dieser Situation? Sicher nicht. Auch verstehen wir uns in der Regel recht gut, wenn wir uns als Herren (und Herrinnen) im eigenen Haus, zu dem auch unser Gehirn gehört, verstehen. ‚Wissenschaftlicher' Erklärungen, wie sie der Dualismus und der Monismus suchen, bedarf es dazu nicht.

Auch das aber soll nicht dazu führen, die philosophische und die wissenschaftliche Kultur auf allzu fern voneinander liegenden Inseln anzusiedeln, vor allem, wenn es um Fragen geht, auf die beide eine

Antwort wissen – um dann meist festzustellen, daß sie doch verschiedene Fragen beantwortet haben. Creutzfeld, der hier wiederholt zu Worte kam, beendet seine Überlegungen, auf das Problem der Einheit des Bewußtseins zu sprechen kommend, mit der Bemerkung: „Die Antwort des Neurophysiologen ist der Beginn des Fragens der Philosophen."[23] Das ist wohl, zumindest in diesem Falle, wahr (vielen Philosophen allerdings wissenschaftliche Kenntnisse unterstellend, die sie nicht haben). Richtig ist aber auch, daß die Antwort auf die Frage des Philosophen in diesem Falle auch eine wissenschaftlich beratene sein sollte. Andernfalls geschähe das, was man leider mit manchem Recht der Philosophie gelegentlich vorzuwerfen pflegt: daß sie der Wirklichkeit durch Spekulation zu entkommen sucht, statt sie durch das Denken zu begreifen.

Anmerkungen

1 *Meditationes*, Obj. III 2, Resp. *(Oeuvres*, I–XII, ed. C. Adam et P. Tannery, Paris 1897–1910; Neue Ausg., I–XI, 1964–1974, VII, S. 176).
2 *Kritik der reinen Vernunft* A 117 f.
3 D. Henrich, *Der Grund im Bewußtsein. Untersuchungen zu Hölderlins Denken (1794–1795)*, Stuttgart 1992, S. 21.
4 Die folgende Darstellung gibt die Kernthesen einer früheren, einführenden Darstellung wieder: J. Mittelstraß, „Vorbereitende Bemerkungen zu einer pragmatischen Philosophie des Bewußtseins", in: *Zeitschrift für Wissenschaftsforschung* 4, Nr. 2 (1988), S. 139–151. Die hier vertretene Konzeption ist mittlerweile zu einer Theorie des pragmatischen Dualismus ausgearbeitet in: M. Carrier u. J. Mittelstraß, *Geist, Gehirn, Verhalten. Das Leib-Seele-Problem und die Philosophie der Psychologie*, Berlin, New York 1989 (engl., überarbeitet und ergänzt, unter dem Titel *Mind, Brain, Behavior. The Mind-Body Problem and the Philosophy of Psychology*, Berlin, New York 1991). Cf. ferner H. Schleichert, *Der Begriff des Bewußtseins. Eine Bedeutungsanalyse*, Frankfurt a. M. 1992.
5 Systematisch korrekt müßte eigentlich, bezogen auf den historischen Kontext des Problems, zwischen einem Leib-Seele-Problem, einem Leib-

Geist-Problem oder Leib-Bewußtsein-Problem und einem Materie-Leben-Problem unterschieden werden.
6 Cf. *Oeuvres* XI (cf. Anm. 1), S. 180.
7 Zu den Cartesischen Bemühungen um eine Lösung des Leib-Seele-Problems und der Fortsetzung dieser Bemühungen im Cartesianismus, ferner bei Leibniz und Kant, cf. M. Carrier u. J. Mittelstraß, op. cit. (cf. Anm. 4), S. 17–29 („Descartes und die Folgen"); in der englischen Fassung S. 16–27 („Descartes and the Aftermath").
8 Cf. K. R. Popper u. J. C. Eccles, *The Self and Its Brain. An Argument for Interactionism*, Berlin u. a. 1977 (dt. *Das Ich und sein Gehirn*, München u. a. 1977).
9 Zu systematischen Details cf. wiederum M. Carrier u. J. Mittelstraß, op. cit. (cf. Anm. 4), S. 121–132 („Das Ich als Steuermann"); in der englischen Fassung S. 114–125 („The Self as Pilot").
10 Cf. G. Frege, „Der Gedanke. Eine logische Untersuchung" (1918/1919), in: ders., *Logische Untersuchungen*, ed. G. Patzig, Göttingen 1966, S. 30–53. Cf. dazu auch Chr. Thiel, „Frege", in: *Enzyklopädie Philosophie und Wissenschaftstheorie* I, ed. J. Mittelstraß, Mannheim u. a. 1980, Stuttgart u. a. 1995, S. 671–674.
11 Loc. cit. (cf. Anm. 8) (dt. Ausgabe), S. 436.
12 L. Wittgenstein, *Philosophische Untersuchungen* § 593.
13 Cf. E. Pöppel, *Grenzen des Bewußtseins. Über Wirklichkeit und Welterfahrung*, Stuttgart 1985, S. 145 f.
14 Cf. loc. cit., S. 66 f.
15 Cf. O. Creutzfeld, „Bewußtsein und Selbstbewußtsein als neurophysiologisches Problem der Philosophie", in: *Reproduktion des Menschen. Beiträge zu einer interdisziplinären Anthropologie*, Frankfurt a. M. u. a. 1981 (Schriften der Carl Friedrich von Siemens Stiftung 5), S. 43.
16 Loc. cit., 42.
17 Ibid.
18 Loc. cit., S. 43.
19 Loc. cit., S. 33.
20 Cf. G. Ryle, *The Concept of Mind*, London, New York 1949, London 1988 (dt. *Der Begriff des Geistes*, Stuttgart 1969, 1982).
21 O. Creutzfeld, loc. cit. (cf. Anm. 15), S. 34.
22 Loc. cit. (cf. Anm. 8), S. 45.
23 Loc. cit. (cf. Anm. 15), S. 43.

Arthur C. Danto

History and Representation*

> But this very entity, Dasein, is in itself "historical," so that its ownmost ontological elucidation necessarily becomes an "historiological" Interpretation.
> Martin Heidegger, *Being and Time*, Int. II, § 8

> Joyce suddenly asked some such question as, "How could the idealist Hume write a history?" Beckett replied, "A history of representations."
> Richard Ellmann, *James Joyce*

Here is Konrad Lorenz, endeavoring to describe an animal rather considerably lower in the scale of evolution than the dogs and geese, his fine observations of whom enlightened us all, and earned him a Nobel prize. I draw attention to the fact that he describes these beings – paramecia, as it happens – in a language he or we might use to characterize the conduct of dogs and geese or, for the matter, the conduct of one another.

> "Even the primitive way in which the paramecium takes avoiding action when it collides with an obstacle, by first reversing and then swimming forward in another direction determined by accident, suggests that it 'knows' something about the external world which may literally be described as 'objective fact'. *Obiecere* means 'to throw against': the 'object' is something that is thrown in our advance, the impenetrable something with which we collide. All the paramecium 'knows' about the 'object' is that it impedes continuation of its movement in a particular direction, and this 'knowledge' stands up to the criticism which we are able to exercise from the point of view of our richer and more detailed picture of the world. True, we might advise the creature to move in more favorable directions than the one it took at random, but what it 'knows' is still quite correct: 'The way straight ahead is barred.'"[1]

This passage bristles with cautionary punctuation. There are inverted commas around such words as "knows", "knowledge", "object" – though, oddly enough, not around "quite correct", as if the little phrase in the Language of Thought for paramecia, as gnomic as if a fragment from some Pre-socratic philosopher – "The way straight ahead is barred" – were *true*. All this hedging circumspection vanishes from a gloss on the passage by the distinguished art historian, Sir Ernst Gombrich, who otherwise cites Lorenz's text with great approval, subject only to a Popperian emendation, in his own book on ornamentation, *The Sense of Order*. I find the following a pure example of heavy professorial pedantry seeking to lighten itself with jocularity, but inadvertently comical because it is hysterically wrong while taking itself to be obviously and unarguably right.

> "Strictly speaking [I find myself wanting to write this in a heavy Teutonic accent!], as Popper would remind us and as Lorenz knows [no single quotes here!] the creature's reactions are not based on knowledge [and here the Materialists among us want to break into applause, stifled, alas, as Gombrich goes on to say] but on a hypothesis [groan]; they rest on the implicit assumption that the object which gives it a jolt would continue to remain at that point, for otherwise a change of course might bring the animal into collision with the same obstacle. It need hardly be added [it is this "It need hardly be added" which I find so indescribably funny, emblemizing as it does all the complacent professors of my student years] that the term 'hypothesis' is here used in a less specialized sense than in scientific research."[2]

Our little Popperian cell, accordingly, is vested with a certain competence in scientific method, less specialized than that employed by those who study the behavior of paramecia, but not so dauntingly different that in studying paramecia one is doing anything remarkably different from studying, as scientists, one another. It seems innately to be equipped with an on the whole satisfactory metaphysics through which it confidently ascribes sameness and stability to the objects it encounters. It holds a view of the external world regarding which it entertains true – and false – hypotheses. A chap, on balance, much like you and me. Students of Heidegger might even find parallels in the way in which things present themselves *as obstacles* to the paramecium when an obstacle "loses its ready-to-hand in a certain way. [...] It does not vanish simply, but takes its farewell, as it were, in the conspicuousness of the unusable."³ In standing in the way, something becomes an object for the paramecium, who discovers the configurations of its world the way we discover the configurations of our own.

So much, for the moment at least, for the cognitive endowment of the paramecium, and for its *Dasein*. And, since *Dasein* calls up the thought of *design*, I turn my attention to the fairly simple body of *paramecium aurelia*, that slipper-shaped animalcule which consists of but a single cell. Unicellular though it is, paramecium aurelia is rather more than a single nucleus surrounded by cytoplasm, and I shall briefly describe the relevant anatomy, much of it brought to light with the advent of the electron microscope, and so unknown when cytologists had only the light microscope to work with. There is, to begin and, for our purposes to end with, an excitable membrane or *pellicle*, and then a certain number of ciliae, which are the organelles of this animal's locomotion. Ciliary beating propels the animal along a left-handedly helical course – until it encounters the obstacle, chemical or physical as the case may be, at which point the ciliae reverse directions, like propellers on a boat, which in turn reverses the paramecium's path. At a certain point, the ciliae resume their habitual direction, the animalcule embarks on a new forward course and either reencounters the obstacle (hypothesis false, according to Lorenz-Popper-Gombrich), or, having evaded it, swims free through the medium in which it lives out its *Geworfenheit* (hypothesis true so far, according to the same authorities). Looking down through our electron microscopes, like Zeus from on Mount Ida, we can see whether or not the paramecium is headed in the right direction. But unlike Zeus we lack a system of signs through which we can communicate our superior knowledge to the struggling creature below, who must find the unbarred path without aid from on high.

Against this picture of the pathfinding protozoon, so like in fact or in metaphor to dogs, geese, and to ourselves, it is irresistible to ascribe to it a life of reason: a system of internal representations, the power of practical inference, and a structure through which representations become executed as actions guided in effect by maxims of prudence. That may seem like a great deal to ascribe to a unicellular being, but I only communicated a fragment of what we know of its physiology, replete with mitochondria, the Golgi complex, chloroplasts, ribosomes, and, as we say in advertising, much, much more. But alas, as Homer would say, it was not to be. I think we now know enough to say that this entire way of representing paramecial behavior is merely picturesque. The behavior the paramecium exhibits turns out not even to be teleological. For the matter, it is probably already too much to describe it as behavior.

Here then is the true story. The direction and rate of ciliary beat now seem demonstrably to be a function of differences in electrical potential distributed across the membrane's surface. In the normal state of resting potential, rearward ciliary beat occurs without excitation, this being the way the paramecium is built – its default state, to use the convenient computer term. Ciliary reversal correlates with the depolarization of the membrane, due to an influx of cations, this due to electrochemical reactions to the environment. As the environment changes, the membrane reverts to resting potential, the default position of normal ciliary beat takes over, and mere contingencies of the electro-chemical *Umwelt* account for such changes in direction as are read, by fantasists such as Lorenz, as calculated efforts on the part of paramecium to get round the obstacles that bar its path. What happens is smoothly narrated in terms of electrical changes translated into physical motion on the part of an animal constructed in a certain way.

"In a certain way": in fact something over three hundred strains of paramecium aurelia have been identified, each of which reacts somewhat differently in relation to a norm that I conjecture must be regarded as merely statistical. The obstacles I shall discuss are chemical, viz. a trace of a sodium chloride. Some paramecia over-react violently, recoiling to distances vastly in excess of the norm. Some are phlegmatic, back up so short a distance as to suggest indifference. Some change directions without benefit of sodium chloride, as if exercising free will. Or, since we are being psychological, as if paranoid, suspecting salinity at every turn. And then there are those that appear truly indifferent, sailing through concentrations of salinity that define the normal, and whose conduct would have to be classed as superogatory in the language of morals. There is indeed enough variation to license a psychology of humors, or a psychopathology of the kind we use to classify deviant or perverse behavior, ranging from unreasonable to irrational, in case avoidance of sodium chloride in some degree is actually adaptive rather than, let us say, aesthetic. But none of this survives the understanding that comes with electrochemical explanation. The strains are marked by differences in membranal curvature, and the distribution of charges, which determine completely the rate and direction of ciliary reversal. The account I have sketched is compact, leaving no room for the intervention of will, the efficacy of practical syllogisms, the weighting of hypothetical alternatives, the language of thought, a Popperian methodology. I would venture even a claim that we know enough already to recognize that the so-called "Intentional Stance" proposed by Daniel Dennett is appropriate only as a jocular *façon de parler*. Paramecium aurelia, in all its versions, does not reverse beat and hence direction *in order* to cope with obstacles strewn in its path. Rather, it forms with its environment a single electrochemical system. The design of the system suffices all our explanatory ends. It is the product of evolution and not of design.

Lorenz's punctuationally hedged account was finally false. Everything is fully explained in a way which requires no reference to cognition, to "objects" in the intensional sense assigned that term by Lorenz, viz. the way something is an object of thought or consciousness, or that which answers to the *da* – to the indexical "there" – in *Da-sein*. There is no World of the Paramecium. Or, to bring it closer to contemporary analytical distinctions, there is nothing it is like to be a paramecium, any more than there is something it is like to be a lump of cobalt. There is enough of a resemblance to the way a far more evolved animal than it deals with obstacles – to the way we deal with obstacles, say – to say that based on what that resemblance consists in, a Turing Test would fail to discriminate paramecium aurelia from such animals, or from us. It would, by Turing criteria, be insupportable to ascribe rationality to creatures like ourselves and withhold it from paramecium aurelia. It is by tacit appeal to Turing-like considerations that Lorenz and Gombrich use the idiom of hypothesis, knowledge, obstacle, and the like. So much the worse for the Turing Test then. The Turing Test recommends that parity of behavior requires parity of explanation. If we were Zeus, watching the behavior, say, of Odysseus from a cloud, we might say: Odysseus has encountered an obstacle on his way back to Ithaca. He realizes that the way home is barred. He reflects, changes course, and is on his way. If Zeus liked him more he would have communicated some useful facts. Lorenz cannot help the protozoon, who has, like Odysseus, to work things out for itself. It works out its own practical syllogisms, and finds its own way through the wine-dark Petri dish. But as we saw, nothing like this happens at all. Parity notwithstanding, we are not required to explain paramecium aurelia's conduct as we do that of Odysseus. Or, we could use the Turing Test in a reverse way. Since it proved not to be required to use the explanatory apparatus of practical reason in the case of paramecium aurelia, whose "behavior" (let me help myself to some fudging punctuation) so resembles ours that it seems altogether natural to describe it as we would our own, how can we be that sure that such descriptions are finally fitting in our own case? So that if it is illegitimate in the case of paramecium aurelia, what makes it legitimate in our *own* case?

Philosophical turnabout is metaphysical fair play. Are we finally in any deep or serious way all that different from paramecium aurelia? As the simplest of animals, paramecium aurelia is still an animal, and must with its one cell perform all the functions essential to animal life performed by us with our system of organs and network of often specialized cells – must find food and flee danger, register something like awareness of its environment, respire, eliminate, and reproduce. The transmission of nervous impulse through interchange of sodium and potassium ions is not so amazingly different from the depolarization of the pellicle through the movement of positively and negatively charged ions. Now we have seen how, with the advantage of the electron microscope, we have been able to learn enough simply to discard, as altogether irrelevant to the description and explanation of paramecial behavior, the language of cognitive function. We do not know enough to be able to do this with human beings, at least not as yet. But from the perspective of an extrapolated neurochemistry, have we any reason to believe that the descriptions found so irrelevant, so picturesque, so merely *façon de parler* in the case of paramecium aurelia, will not be similarly found so in our own case? Scientists like Lorenz, finding no difference in kind but only in quantity between ourselves and paramecia, found it irresistible to describe the latter in terms altogether natural in describing us. I am taking the other direction: having found that description finally empty in the case of paramecia, what is to prevent us from going, as the French say, *jusqu'au bout* with the Eliminativists in the philosophy of mind, who claim preemptively that the language of everyday psychology must give way in time to the descriptions to be made available through an advanced neurochemistry? The Turing Test runs in two directions, down the slippery slope when there is nothing to arrest it, and up the slippery slope when there is nothing to arrest it. Turing was anxious to ascribe thought to what he called "computing machinery" when its behavior was indiscriminable from ours. The Eliminativist, reversely, is anxious to deny thought when our behavior is indiscriminable from that of an animal in the explanation of whose behavior thought has no place. How can we possibly fault him?

Let us at this point turn our attention from paramecium aurelia, who has served us well or dubiously, depending upon your vision of the universe, to us.

Whatever one may think of the ingenious thought experiment designed a few years back by John Searle[4], it does something rather rarely done in these discussions: he has undertaken to insert himself into the argument, when he asked, against the evidence of consciousness, whether it could be true of him, whatever his outward behavior, that he understands something when, introspectively, he finds that he does not. Remember, the outward behavior in Searle's imagined case was indistinguishable from that of a native sinolect: he printed out – let's imagine him equipped with a keyboard – in chinese characters, the very array of marks a literate sinolect would print out in answer to a question, itself in chinese characters, and did this over a sustained period, so that there was no discernible difference between his "output" and that of a native sinolect. That is the way things are set up by Turing in his classical statement of the "guessing game": the thought was that if there is no discernible difference between the output of a machine and of a human being, one could not invoke reason in explanation of the one while withholding it in the case of the other. And Searle has thrust himself into the pilot's seat, producing in response to questions answers indiscernible from those of a Chinese speaker, making it, on Turing grounds, unacceptable that competence in Chinese should be ascribed to the latter and withheld from Searle himself. In the famous Peer Review system of the *Journal of Behavioral and Brain Science*, in which Searle's Chinese Room argument first appeared[5], many of the commentators bit the bullet and insisted that whatever he said, Searle really had to understand Chinese. (Some said that while he may not have understood Chinese, the system in which he was a component understood it.) Now we do, sometimes, assure people who are not confident in their English that they understand the language they are so apologetic about, and we may observe that we are the better judges of the matter: if *we* say they understand it they do, however uncertain they feel. But Searle insists that he is not just uncertain in this way. Rather, he is altogether certain that he knows not a word of Chinese – he just has mattered some rules for combining symbols. Milton's daughters used to read Latin, Greek, even Hebrew to the blind poet, without knowing what they were reading – they just had mastered the rules of pronunciation. The printed words were input, the uttered words the output, but while their output might have been indiscernible from someone who read these learned languages aloud knowing what he read, they really did not know these languages at all. And this is what Searle is insisting upon in his own case.

    I do not want to be distracted by the example, however: I am only drawing attention to Searle's sense that he belonged somewhere in the picture he was painting, a matter of almost standard amnesia, where scientists and philosophers leave themselves outside the situation they try to depict for us. As though science and philosophy were ontologically weightless, always logically external to the world as they address it from across a Cartesian distance, never asking, as it were, where would science or philosophy be if what science or philosophy said were true. Where would the Eliminativist be, for example, if what he or she said were true? How would we deal with Eliminativism as an activity if all we had were the language of neurochemistry to do it with? Or will Eliminativism too disappear with the psychology it assures us must disappear when neurochemistry prevails? And if Eliminativism is swept away by neurochemistry, what will happen to neurochemistry itself, considered as a scientific practice? Will neurochemistry's content be rich enough to represent itself? A science, neurochemistry itself included, is a system of representations. It is a system arrived at by exercising that sort of cognitive endowment we giggled a bit in seeing thinkers like Gombrich and Lorenz seriously ascribe to paramecia: projecting hypotheses, testing and revising them in the light of falsifying observations, arriving at hypotheses which carry us securely from experience to experience in such a way that we are prepared to call them true. Can this activity be described in the idiom of neurochemistry? Well, no. At least not in the case of paramecia. The moment we got the electrochemical story right, the story of hypothesis, testing, observation, revision, falsity and truth disappeared. But what would the science of neurochemistry be from which all this disappeared? It could not be the story of a scientific practice! The moment we try to bring scientific practice into its own picture, the picture becomes subject to grave pressures indeed: there seems to be no room for it. It was science which gave us the correct picture of what takes place in paramecium aurelia. And it will be science, surely, which will give us a true picture of ourselves. But will science itself have to disappear from that true picture? If so, how is science, as a practice, to be accounted for? It is surely among the things human beings do, and indeed do best. How strange that there should be no room for it in the final picture of the world science is to draw up! How can we even talk about it if Eliminativism is right?

In the late years of the Nineteenth Century, philosophers struggled to formulate a distinction between two kinds of science, and enlisted a sufficient number of bad metaphysical arguments in support of a sharp difference between the sciences of nature and the sciences of man – between the so-called *Naturwissenschaften* and the so-called *Geisteswissenschaften* – that it failed to make a lasting impression on the Anglo-American philosophical world, leery in any case of dualisms. Here the overall attitude was polemically expressed in the title of that series in which so many of the great monographs of high Positivism were published – *The Encyclopedia of Unified Science*. Actually the notion of unified science was a way of speaking of a unified world, and the strategies of definition and reduction within the sciences was the linguistic strategy for speaking of a world in which there were no final divisions between orders and kinds of things. My sense is that the controversy today, between certain strong versions of Eliminativist Materialism and certain realist versions of The Language of Thought, reflects this controversy. If we can succeed in representing ourselves in such terms as those with which we have succeeded in representing paramecia, then there is a single continuous line connecting the simplest of animals and the most complex, at just that juncture where, if they resembled us, they would be unicellular scientists aswim in their salty worlds, or, if we resembled them, we would be storms of ions and nothing more. But my thought is that if we bring ourselves into the picture, and ask, as scientists, how in electro- or neurochemical terms we are to represent what we as scientists do – represent the features of scientific activity – the formation of hypotheses, the inferring to observations, the performance of tasks, and that after all human all too human concern that truth prevail, we are suddenly faced with the possibility that the *Naturwissenschaften*, being after all something humans do, are finally part of the *Geisteswissenschaften*, which represent, interpret, and seek to understand what humans, scientists included, do. Can we give a natural science account of natural scientific practice, or must we in fact remain satisfied with a human-science account, using the language one of the natural sciences – neurochemistry – was to have eliminated?

Each of the animal functions we share with paramecium aurelia marks an entry point for culture in our case, though not in the case of protozoa, and hence is subject to a historical evolution of a kind even animals greatly advanced over paramecium aurelia know nothing of. But none of these cultural and historical differences penetrate the human genome, so that if there were some catastrophic erasure, in which everything achieved by history were obliterated, the human being would find itself coping very much the way its first ancestors did, however many hundreds of thousands of years ago. With paramecium aurelia, there is nothing to obliterate. It lives as it has always lived, since it first emerged. Genomic change takes place only through mutation. So history washes over the genetic endowment like waves against the hardest rock, making no difference to it whatever. The DNA of Homer is not especially different from the DNA that specifies you and me. In the last centuries, scholars judging by the sparse color vocabulary of the epics, supposed the Greeks lived in a chromatically reduced universe. Since the work of Berlin and Kaye, we know that Greek color vocabulary is what one might expect at that stage of a culture. Their ability to differentiate colors were of apiece with ours. Color perception is not indexed to culture in that way at all. A cartoon in *Science* has one bystander explaining to another the project of a colleague as: trying to identify the gene that accounts for our making our living by studying genes. It is (mildly) comical because we would not expect genetics, as a science, to be coded for in the genes. It is not a genetic product. It is a product of science, and science itself may be the result of culture modifying what could be coded, namely the disposition to form beliefs and the like, which scientists share with everyone else, and which cannot today be at all different from what we see in Odysseus when he computes the best strategy for slipping free of Cyclops. The *content* of the beliefs of course will differ, but that is where history and culture have their genetically intransmissible effects. The history of science is the history of representational change, and if there are representations coded for genetically, they would not change except under mutation.

The data I reported on regarding the anatomy of paramecium aurelia were, as I mentioned, made possible by a great deal of laboratory technology, including the electron microscope. They were published in 1976.[6] But the history of beliefs about protozoa begins almost exactly three centuries earlier, when they were first described by

Leeuwenhoek, in a letter of 1676. There he characterizes a free, living animalcule, which he discovered in standing rainwater by means of a simple microscope. Beliefs may very well be – very likely are – modifications of nervous tissue. Electrochemically, human nervous tissue is as it has been since the appearance of the genome. But before 1676, there was no human tissue so modified as to be a belief about protozoa. There were none before the invention of the microscope. The concept of protozoa is surely nowhere to be found in the genetic endowment of microscopists, even if their nervous tissue is in the course of education modified in the form of beliefs about them.

Here is the thrilling passage from Leeuwenhoek's letter to the Royal Society in October, 1676:

> "In the year 1675, about half-way through September [...] I discovered new living creatures in rain, which had stood but a few days in a new tub, that was painted blue within. This observation provoked me to investigate this water more narrowly; and especially because these little animals were, to my eye, more than ten thousand times smaller than animalculae which Swamerdam has portrayed and called by the name of Water-flea or Water-louse, and which you can see alive and moving in water with the bare eye."[7]

Leeuwenhoek calls these "living atoms", his observation of which the Royal Society sought to confirm in 1677, at first with no success, leading to a certain skepticism, or efforts to explain away what the Dutchman actually saw. But on November 15, things were seen which "by all who saw them were verily believed to be animals; and that there could be no fallacy in the appearance".

Leeuwenhoek discovered ciliae in 1677, and in fact formed a good account of their function. But in general the early microscopists lacked the concepts they needed to understand what they saw through the lenses of their marvelously ornamental instruments. F. J. Cole, in his *History of Protozoology*, writes this way:

> "When we first read the writing of the old naturalists we experience a feeling of disappointment if not of contempt. Their statements appear to be indefinite and incoherent, as if they had no real conception of the phenomena with which they were grappling."[8]

But it is instructive to reflect on how nearly impossible it would be to express in language Leeuwenhoek could have grasped the discoveries published in 1976 about the animalcule he was the very first to know about. The first clear description of paramecia appeared in 1703, in which transverse fission was observed for the first time. But its meaning did not become clearly manifest until the work of Trembley in 1745, which became in a sense *the* scientific excitement of the 18th century, largely because of the philosophical views, widely held, with which it collided. Trembley's polyp, if chopped up, will bud into as many polyps as there are pieces, roughly speaking, and the question was whether this meant that the soul was divisible as well as the body. The theory of the cell comes into place only in 1837. The hot question for the classical microscopists was whether these animals were spontaneously generated, it being greatly to Leeuwenhoek's credit that he was doubtful, probably by analogical reasoning from what he found out about the flea, which until then was widely supposed to come from sand. Leeuwenhoek discovered spermatozoa in insects, but had no model for how things could work with paramecia, and spontaneous generation remained a question into the time of Pasteur. The important fact is that different scientists at either end of this history had vastly different beliefs, and in a sense to explain to a naturalist of 1676 what protozoologists of 1976 found out, would have to be instructed in chemistry, the theory of electrolysis, cytology, to mention only the most obvious things. And to understand the beliefs of 1676 would require taking on the ignorances of the men of that period, their wild beliefs, their extravagant reservations as to whether God ever meant for us to see such things in the first place, having made the eye as He had.

But Leeuwenhoek was made much as we are made, a product of the same genetic material, with eyes that worked the way our eyes work, and whose nervous anatomy cannot have differed any more from ours than the anatomy of the first sighted paramecium differed in membrane and organelles from its descendents of today. But Leeuwenhoek's system of representations cannot have been the same, and that difference cannot be explained through genetics or through the organization of nervous tissue, or through the anatomy of the brain. It can only be explained through history. The advent of his beliefs calls upon explanatory considerations very different from the advent of ours, made three centuries after his powerful discoveries – which themselves enter into the explanation of our beliefs. But nothing with which Leeuwenhoek physically interacted has anything to do with us today. It is these matters that I am seeking to make central by bringing science into the world, asking what must be in place for scientists to represent the world as they do, and what must be true of representations that they can form histories of the sort that the history of protozoology exemplifies when the human body circa 1676 and 1976 has no historical development to speak of, and is the same at either end of that remarkable history.

Eliminativism, in eliminating psychology or what it dismissively speaks of as Folk Psychology, eliminates history, and so treats the human animal as it would the unicellular animalcule as behaving in the same way under principles of electrochemistry from century to century. But it could not conceivably explain its own behavior that way, and certainly not the behavior of the sciences whose future findings it supposes will enable a full description and explanation of human behavior without any of the terms we require in order to describe and explain science as a practice. It is ironic that the Eliminativist appeals to history – for what after all is being spoken of if not the future of an historical development – and at the same time projects a picture of language which has no room for history in it. Without history, it cannot so much as state its position. So what are we to say when its position has no place for history?

Let me conclude with a perhaps tenuous analogy. Consider the photochemical side of photography. Typically it is a process that depends upon the sensitivity to light of silver compounds: silver bromide is emulsified in a gelatine, which coats a support – a plate, a piece of film – and after exposure, the exposed bromide is reduced to metallic silver, which forms an image corresponding to the light intensity to which the emulsified silver was initially exposed. This is the basic process. The relationship between image and metallic silver is perhaps philosophically not so different from the relationship between mental representations and nervous tissue. The latter is unquestionably more complex. Little really is known about what the "emulsion" is or how it gets "fixed" – and here I avail myself of the same hedging punctuation with which Konrad Lorenz insinuated a certain psychological story into his description of the paramecium – or about anything at that level where body and mind interface. But in some way the apparatus of material and formal cause applies, as much so as it does in photography. You can say, in a materialist tone, that the photograph is nothing but metallic silver, caused to be arrayed as it is by varying intensities of light on emulsified silver compound and the subsequent dissolving of the unexposed compound by hyposulphate. And in a sense you would be right. Chemically speaking, what else is there? But in a sense obvious to us all, something is left out which has no place in the language of chemistry. There is a technical history to photography, from Niepce's first success with an unfixed positive in silver chloride, through the work of Daguerre, the collodion emulsion, and on through Land's polaroid process. The curator of photography at the Museum of Modern Art in New York, Peter Galassi, described the histories of photography that existed when he took up the subject. They were histories without images. But in a sense obvious to us all the history of photography is image-driven. And to talk about images, what they meant and why they were made, and how they changed, is to bring in factors for which no account can be given with the resources of photochemistry alone.

And this is the kind of thing I want to say is true of us. Just getting to the point where we understand the physiology of representations, which corresponds to the forming and fixing of images on the photographic support, is at the present moment far away. Needless to say, some physiological account will have to be given of how beliefs about protozoa are inscribed in the nervous tissue of Leeuwenhoek and everyone else. But then we have to give an historical explanation of how that tissue was exposed. There is, for us, a history of representations for which *jusqu'au boutisme* allows us no conceptual room. And since that extreme position characterizes something philosophers of a certain persuasion find attractive, it might be prudent to pause and ask ourselves how, if it were true, we could account for our discussion of it in the only terms it is prepared to allow?

Arthur C. Danto

Notes

*   An earlier version of this essay was presented, at Dieter Henrich's invitation, before the Institut für Philosophie at the Ludwig-Maximilians-Universität München in 1995. On that occasion I benefited immensely from Professor Henrich's observations and criticisms, most particularly on the analogies between the paper's chief argument, and transcendental argumentation in Kant. I hope I have been able to incorporate the insights he communicated into this version. I never sought to publish the paper, as I had thought I would base a book on it someday. Perhaps I shall, perhaps not. All the greater reason for contributing it to this volume in honor of my esteemed colleague and friend.
1   K. Lorenz, *Die Rückseite des Spiegels. Versuch einer Naturgeschichte menschlichen Erkennens* (München: Piper, 1973); passage translated and cited by E. Gombrich, *The Sense of Order* (London: Phaidon, 1979), p. 2.
2   Ibid.
3   M. Heidegger, *Being and Time* (San Francisco: Harper, 1962), p. 74.
4   J. R. Searle, "Minds, Brains, and Programs", in: *Journal of Behavioral and Brain Sciences* 3 (1980), pp. 417–424.
5   Cf. also: J. R. Searle, "The Chinese Room Revisited: Response to Further Commentaries on 'Minds, Brains, and Programs'", in: *Journal of Behavioral and Brain Sciences* 5 (1982), pp. 345–348.
6   Cf. R. Eckert, "Bioelectric Control of Ciliary Activity: Locomotion in Ciliated Protozoa", in: *Science* 176 (May 5, 1972), pp. 473–481.
7   Letter from 9th October, 1676 (modernized translation); cf. Antoni van Leeuwenhoek, *The Collected Letters of Antoni van Leeuwenhoek*, issued and annotated under the auspices of the Leeuwenhoek-Commission of the Royal Netherlands Acad. of Sciences and Letters (Lisse: Swets & Zeitlinger, Vol. 2 (1676–1679), 1941), letter No. 26 (pp. 60–161), here p. 65; cf. as well loc. cit., letter No. 28 from 11th November, 1676 (pp. 168–189), esp. p. 171.
8   Fr. J. Cole, *History of Protozoology* (London: London University Press, 1926), p. 5.

Roderick M. Chisholm

On the Simplicity of the Soul
Some Logical Considerations

Introduction

There is something that is metaphysically unique about persons, such entities as you and me. We have a nature wholly unlike anything that is known to be true of things that are known to be compound physical things.

I will defend this thesis in what follows and will show how it coheres with the traditional doctrine of "the simplicity of the soul". And I will argue that the doctrine of the simplicity of the soul is, in William James' terms, very much of a live option.

I
The soul as incorporeal

I am using the word "soul" in the way in which St. Augustine, Descartes, Bolzano and many others have used it: to mean the same thing as "person". In this use of the word, you and I and everyone else can be said to be souls. And if we are said to *be* souls, then it would be a little misleading also to say that we *have* souls.

The thesis of "the simplicity of the soul" says that we are *substances* but *not* compounds of substances. We are not like pieces of furniture, for such things are composed of other substances – as this chair is composed of back, seat and legs. Why, then, say that you and I are simple substances? The hypothesis may seem somewhat shocking.

I will use the first person and begin with the familiar question: "What is the relation between *me* and my body?"

There are three possibilities. The first is that I am identical with my body. The second is that I am identical with a proper part of my body. And the third is that I am not identical with *any* body. (Whatever else I may be, surely I am not identical with any bodily thing having parts that are not shared by *this* body.) Isn't the hypothesis that I am identical with some proper part of this body more plausible than the hypothesis that I am identical with the whole of this gross body that you see before you? This hand, say, is not an essential part of me. I could have lost it, after all, just as I have lost other parts, without thereby ceasing to be.

A simple substance, or monad, is a substance that has no substance as a proper part. Therefore a simple substance is *incorporeal*, in the sense in which St. Augustine and Descartes understood the word "incorporeal": it is not an extended physical body.

The thesis that we are *incorporeal* things is not the same as the thesis that we are things *composed of incorporeal stuff*. If we are composed of incorporeal stuff, then, of course, we are incorporeal. But we can be incorporeal without being composed of any stuff at all, as would be the case if we were simple substances, or monads.

A *simple* substance, therefore, does not require a kind of stuff that is foreign to the world of physics. Indeed, there is very good reason to believe that the existence of extended physical substances presupposes the existence of non-extended and therefore simple substances.

I will try to show, then, that persons or souls – such entities as you and I – have a kind of property that no compound thing, no extended physical thing, is known to have.

II

A Cartesian approach

I propose that we treat these difficult questions from a Cartesian point of view. This means two things.

It means, first, that we should begin by considering the nature of our *mental* properties. We should begin here for the very good reason that our mental properties provide us with the most assured information that we have about *any* individual thing or substance. On the basis of what we know about our own thinking, we may derive certain conclusions about the nature of ourselves.

A Cartesian approach has a second feature. In investigating these questions, we presuppose that we are *rational* beings. This means, in part, that we are able to "conceive things that are purely intelligible", such *entia rationis* as numbers and properties or attributes.[1] And in conceiving these things, we are able to distinguish one from another and to see just what it is that they logically require in order to be exemplified. For example, the property of *being a body*, if it is to be exemplified, logically requires an individual thing that has other individual things as proper parts; but the property of *thinking* does not logically require that its bearer have any proper parts at all.

If we take a Cartesian approach, and I suggest that we do, then we will consider the nature of mental properties and ask ourselves what kind of entity *could* have such properties.

III
A structural mark of the thinking subject

To defend the thesis that there is something metaphysically unique about persons, I will describe a certain "structural feature" of thinking. Our mental life, as many philosophers have said, has the property of being *qualitative*. To say what the relevant sense of "qualitative" is, I will list certain formal or structural marks of the property of thinking.

1. If thinking is going on, then there is a *substance*, or *individual thing*, that is doing the thinking.

Consider any familiar mental property – say, judging, wondering, wishing, hoping, enjoying oneself, being sad, being depressed, having a sensation or dreaming. What kinds of things can *have* such a property? In grasping the nature of such properties, we can see that they are properties that can be exemplified only by *substances*, or *individual things*. Judging, wondering, wishing, hoping cannot possibly be properties of *states* of things, or of *processes*. And they cannot be properties of *abstract objects* such as properties, numbers, and relations. *You* can hope for rain, but no state or number or property or relation can hope for rain.

In other words, the fact that a certain mental property is exemplified – the fact, say, that the property of hoping for rain is exemplified – logically implies that there is a *substance* that has that property. This is a fact about the property itself: the property of hoping for rain is necessarily such that the only things that can have it are substances. And analogously for the other mental properties.

What more does a mental property require in order to be exemplified? The answer is: very little – indeed astonishingly little. This brings us to a feature of thinking that points in the direction of the simplicity of the soul.

2. So far as *logical* requirements are concerned, mental properties are such that they may be had by simple substances. Those of our activities that are not mental do not have this feature. The property of rowing a boat, for example, is not like that. The property of rowing a boat logically requires the existence of ever so many substances *in addition to* the person who is rowing the boat. But the property of *thinking about rowing a boat* doesn't logically require a single substance other than the person who is thinking. And this means that it doesn't *logically* require that the substance have any proper parts. You could *think about* rowing a boat even if you were a monad or simple substance.

What I have just said is true of the relatively simple thought that you have when you think about rowing a boat. But the thought may be as complex as you like and yet not require to be exemplified in a more complex substance. Suppose, for example, you are very methodical and have this thought: "I will row my boat on the fourth of July, unless I go to the ball game, in which case I will row it the following day provided that it is not raining in Wisconsin, where I think I will probably be." This thought, too, does not logically require any complexity on the part of the substance that thinks it. You could think in such a way even if you were only a simple substance.

But there are possible misunderstandings.

The Simplicity of the Soul

Presumably nothing can think unless it has a brain. The property of thinking, therefore, may causally require the existence of a brain. But this fact is quite consistent with what I have just said. When we say that thinking causally requires a brain, we mean that it is *physically* necessary – or *causally* necessary – that whatever thinks has a brain. But when we say that the property of thinking does not logically require that the things that have it have proper parts, we are saying only that it is *logically possible* that the thinker is an unextended thing. Clearly no *logical* contradiction is involved in saying that the thinker is unextended.

There is an elementary point here that is sometimes missed. I need a brain in order to think just as I need eyes in order to see and ears in order to hear. But I see *with*, or *by means of* my eyes and I hear *with*, or *by means of* my ears. Those physical organs do not do my seeing and hearing for me. As Bishop Butler said, I see with my eyes in the same sense in which I see with my glasses.[2] And analogously for my brain. *I* may want to take a walk tomorrow and *I* may wonder whether you are interested in this particular point. But *my brain* doesn't want to take a walk tomorrow. And *it* does not wonder whether you are interested in anything that I am saying; unlike me it will not be in the least disappointed if you are not.

Let us now generalize upon this second feature of mental properties. Mental properties, in order to be had, need no substances other than a single simple substance. And yet such properties are *open* to any number of substances. For any number you like, there are mental properties that may be exemplified by just *that* number of things.

3. Mental properties are *repeatable*: anything that can have such a property is possibly such that it does not have but did have and will have that property. (I have recommended that we take a Cartesian approach to these questions. But so far as repeatability is concerned, I think Descartes went wrong. He had held somewhat implausibly, that the property of *thinking* – the property of *being conscious* – is *not* repeatable. Once you lose it, according to him, you cease to be. This point is quite essential to what is called Cartesian philosophy, but I see no reason why we should accept it.)

The next two structural features of the mental have to do with parts of substances – where the term "part" is so understood that we may say that a *part* of a substance is itself a substance. Following St. Augustine and Descartes, I have said that "a compound substance" is a substance that has *other* substances as its parts.

4. There is one thing that is known to characterize certain properties of compound things and that is also known *not* to hold of any mental property. This is the feature of being "compositive". Consider such properties as being magnetized, being warm, being heavy. If a physical thing is composed of two parts, each of which is magnetized or warm or heavy, then that physical thing itself is magnetized or warm or heavy. A compositive property is a property of this nature: anything that is composed of things that have it is itself a thing that has it.[3]

Of course, not *all* physical properties are compositive. If a thing is composed of two parts each of which weighs exactly 10 pounds, then it would be a mistake to suppose that that physical thing itself weighs exactly 10 pounds. But although some physical properties are compositive and some are not, *no* mental property is compositive.

Any whole composed of parts that are extended is itself extended; and analogously for being green, being in motion and for being either a positive or a negative electric charge. But from the fact that an aggregate is composed of two persons each of whom is thinking, it does not follow that the aggregate is thinking. You could want the weather to be colder and I could want it to be warmer; but that heap or aggregate which is the pair of us (that thing that weighs 300 pounds if you and I each weigh 150 pounds) does not want anything at all.

5. A closely related feature of mental properties is that of being what we may call *"divisive".* If a property is divisive, then whatever has it has a proper part that has it. Mental properties are not divisive. The fact that I am hoping for rain does not imply that I have a proper part that is hoping for rain. That is to say, the fact that I am a substance that hopes for rain does not imply that there is *another* substance that is a proper part of me and that *that* substance *also* hopes for rain.

The Simplicity of the Soul

I come now to the sixth and final feature of the mental. After saying what *it* is, we may stir all these ingredients together, so to speak, and then exhibit a structural feature that is unique to the properties of thinking things or persons.

6. Mental properties are among those properties that have traditionally been called *internal*, or *nonrelational* properties. If an individual has properties that consist in *relating* that individual to *other* individuals, then that individual also has internal properties, properties that do *not* consist in relating it to other individuals.

Roughly speaking, we may say that my internal properties are those of my properties that would not tell you anything about any substance other than myself. If you know that I have the property of being married, then you are in a position to know that there is a person who has a property that I don't have – namely, that of having married me. But if I tell you that I feel well or that I do not feel well, then what I tell you does not logically imply anything about anyone else but me. We may put this point a little more precisely by saying that an *internal* property of a substance tells you something about the substance itself but doesn't tell you anything about the properties of any other substance. It includes every property of substances that it implies.

These six features give us a special philosophical concept – that of being *qualitative*. They provide us with a sense of "qualitative property" which is such that, so far as we know, only substances that are capable of thinking may be said to have qualitative properties. Certain technical niceties aside, we may say that a qualitative property is a property that has the features just singled out. It may be exemplified only by substances; it may be exemplified by simple substances; it may be exemplified by any number of substances; it is repeatable and internal; and it is neither compositive nor divisive.[4]

Anything that has a qualitative property, then, is a substance that is capable of thinking.

IV
A philosophical argument

Where are we, then?

I have been speaking about the simplicity of the soul. We can hardly be said to have a *proof* of the simplicity of the soul. But we can formulate a philosophical argument that does have a significant conclusion.

The argument has three premises. The first is an empirical proposition stating certain things about our psychological properties. The second and third premises are Cartesian: they tell us what rational beings can know about the nature of the psychological properties that they have.

I will state the argument using the first person plural.

(1) We have qualitative properties.
(2) Every qualitative property that we are acquainted with is known to be such that it may be exemplified by simple substances.
(3) No qualitative property is known to be such that it may be exemplified by compound substances.

Hence:

(4) Some of our properties are known to be such that simple substances can have them and are not known to be such that compound substances can have them.

Therefore:

(5) We have a nature which is wholly unlike the nature that anything known to be a compound physical thing is known to have.

V
Souls and complete human beings

I have said that we *are* souls and that souls are simple substances. But it is also said, even by those who have held that the soul is simple, that *persons* are compound things having souls as parts. Can we have it both ways?

If the soul is simple and the person is a compound of soul and body, which would I be – the simple substance which is the soul or the compound substance which has the soul as one of its parts?

If we say, as Descartes seems to have said, (1) that I am a thinking being and (2) that a thinking being and a soul are one and the same thing, then we should also say (3) that *I am* a soul; and therefore (if we take "have" in its ordinary sense) we should say (4) that I do not *have* a soul.

The correct view, I think, was set forth by St. Thomas Aquinas in Article II of his treatise entitled *On Spiritual Creatures*. The view is not that of St. Thomas himself, but he puts it as clearly as anyone could wish. He tells us it is a view that Gregory of Nyssa attributed to Plato. The passage is this:

> "Gregory of Nyssa tells us Plato asserted that the intellectual substance which is called the soul is united to the body by a kind of spiritual contact; and this is understood in the sense in which a thing that moves or acts touches the thing that is moved or is passive. And hence Plato used to say, as the aforesaid Gregory relates, that man is not something that is composed of soul and body, but is a soul using a body, so that he is understood to be in a body in somewhat the same way as a sailor is in a ship."[5]

Notes

1 Cf. R. Descartes, *The Principles of Philosophy* (Dordrecht: Reidel, 1983) Part I, Section 32.
2 Cf. J. Butler, *The Analogy of Religion*, Part I, Chapter 1 ("Of a Future Life"); in: *The Whole Works of Joseph Butler*, LL. D. (London: Thomas Tegg, 1839), p. 7. Cf. B. Bolzano, *Athanasia oder Gründe für die Unsterblichkeit der Seele* (Sulzbach: J. G. v. Seidelsche Buchhandlung, 1838), p. 60. Bolzano's discussion of these questions (esp. pp. 21–68) is the best that is known to me. Unfortunately his work has not been translated into English.

3 The term "compositive" is suggested by the following sense of "being composed of". A compound object A may be said to be *composed of* two compound objects B and C, provided only that (i) B and C are parts of A, (ii) B and C have no parts in common and (iii) every part of A has a part in common either with B or with C. This definition was proposed, in somewhat different terms, by A. N. Whitehead, in *The Organization of Thought* (London: Williams and Norgate, 1917), pp. 159–60.
4 These niceties are spelled out in a paper having the same title as this one which appeared in the "Philosophy of Religion" issue of *Philosophical Perspectives*, Vol. V: *Philosophy of Religion*, ed. J. E. Tomberlin (Atascadero: Ridgeview, 1991).
5 The citation is from pages 35 f. of the translation by M. C. Fitzpatrick and J. C. Wellmuth of *On Spiritual Creatures* (Milwaukee: Marquette University Press, 1949). The translators note that another version of the text reads: Plato "does not mean that man is made up of body and soul, but that he is a soul using a body and, as it were, clothed with a body" (p. 35 note).

Colin McGinn

Solving the Philosophical Mind-Body Problem

I

I began my 1989 paper, "Can We Solve the Mind-Body Problem?", with this quotation from Thomas Huxley, writing in 1886: "How it is that anything so remarkable as a state of consciousness comes about as a result of irritating nervous tissue, is just as unaccountable as the appearance of the djinn when Aladdin rubbed his lamp in the story."[1] That succinctly states the essence of the philosophical problem about mind and body, about consciousness and the brain: something "remarkable" seems to result from something unremarkable, and in a way that is unprecedented in nature. The problem can be put this way: if you rub most physical objects, even lamps, you do not usually get a djinn to appear; yet Aladdin's lamp has the power to do just that – and it seems not to differ in any fundamental way from the objects that fail to harbour djinns. So how does it happen that *this* physical object manages so unique a feat? Analogously, if you "irritate" most physical objects, even organs of the body, no conscious state appears; yet the brain has the power to generate conscious states – and it seems not to differ in any fundamental way from objects that fail to harbour consciousness. So how does it happen that *this* physical object manages so unique a feat? What underlying difference explains this difference of generative power between brains and other physical objects? Indeed, what explains the difference between states of the brain that do yield conscious states and states that do not? All brain states look much the same, physically speaking, yet some are "associated with" consciousness and some are not: how is this marked difference consistent with the evident similarity manifest at the neural level? It seems no more intelligible that neurons should produce conscious states than that kidney cells should, or sawdust for that matter. We seem to be confronted with a kind of spontaneous generation in which a deep ontological gulf is miraculously bridged. The question then is whether this impression of miracle can be removed – whether, that is, the djinn of consciousness can find a naturalistic place in the lamp of the brain. And the problem is hard because it is so atrociously difficult to see how the fit is supposed to work. Brain states cause conscious states – that is what observation suggests: but the question is how such a thing is so much as *possible*.

Consider, as a thought experiment, the following imaginary scenario. The brain is actually not the real basis of consciousness but acts merely as an interface between the real basis and bodily behaviour. The real basis lies elsewhere, perhaps up in the sky, perhaps underground, and the whole system works by transmitting signals from the basis to the brain and hence controlling behaviour. Thus conscious states are really located roughly where the real basis is located, since the location of the mind is parasitic on the location of its physical basis. (Don't ask how such an odd set-up could have resulted from evolution – this is meant to be an imaginary thought experiment designed to make a certain conceptual point, not a genuine empirical possibility.) Now the crucial point is that the real basis is actually totally different in structure and composition from the brain; in fact, it is like nothing else we have ever encountered in nature, running by means of principles unique to it. Moreover, we can suppose that were we to discover this basis its relation to conscious states would strike us as transparently intelligible – unlike the organ that actually sits in our heads. Nevertheless, there are systematic correlations between brain states and conscious states, as one would expect given that the brain acts as a kind of transmitter of signals from the real basis. States of the basis cause conscious states, which are in turn correlated with brain states, as the body is remotely controlled from the basis. So there is a kind of illusion an investigator would be subject to, in that it would be natural (though false) to conclude that the brain is the basis of consciousness, despite the fact that (by hypothesis) it is quite incapable of acting as the origin of consciousness. An investigator would naturally take the brain to be the basis of consciousness, not knowing about the strange way things are really arranged, and would therefore frame questions along these lines: how is it possible for the brain to be the cause of consciousness when it looks incapable of being so, in view of its similarity to other physical systems that have not a hint of consciousness in them? And the point is that this question is misconceived in view of the true situation, since the brain is unable to act as the basis of consciousness. No doubt some thinkers in this imaginary world would assert manfully that conscious states just are brain states, though in our stipulated set-up they are not; while others might opt for Cartesian dualism or eliminativism or behaviourism or whatever. But we know better, having stipulated the case, correctly locating consciousness in another physical object of a radically different, and more suitable, design.

The lesson I want to draw from this thought experiment is that our epistemic situation with respect to mind and brain is significantly analogous to this strange story. It is as if the brain *appears* to us be a mere mediator of conscious states and not their ultimate origin, given our knowledge of its operations. In fact, if we simply shift the real basis in our imaginary case from outside the brain to *inside* it we get a precise analogue to our current epistemic predicament. Suppose then that the real basis is hidden somewhere inside the observable brain, perhaps too microscopic to be accessible to us; it actually sits at the precise midpoint of the reticular formation, say (again, remember this is an imaginary thought-experiment). Then again we would be quite wrong in assigning to the gross brain the role of causal basis of conscious states – the brain simply transmits messages from the real miniature basis whose properties are radically different from those of the observable brain. And now we can take one more step towards the probably actual situation and suppose that the real basis of consciousness lies not in the properties of nerve cells as currently conceived but rather in some new properties that serve to distinguish cells that yield conscious states from cells that do not. The mind-body problem then is the problem of finding out what these special distinguishing properties are. In the thought-experiment we set it up so that the properties in question were not regular neural properties, but this only serves to highlight the epistemic situation in which we stand in the actual world; and it acts as a warning against those who opt for more conservative responses to the problem stated so trenchantly by Huxley – since such responses would be false by hypothesis in the imaginary case. The challenge posed by the thought-experiment is simply this: if the standard responses are wrong in that case, why are we so sure that they are sensible in the actual case, in which much the same problem is presented by the observed phenomena? In any case, the philosophical problem can be formulated as the problem of identifying the real basis of consciousness, given that the ordinary neural properties of the brain are inadequate to do the job. What, that is, is the nature of the *epistemically* remote basis of consciousness? What is inside the brain lamp such that it can produce a consciousness djinn when you rub it?

In my 1989 paper I answered the question that forms its title ("Can we solve the mind-body problem?") with the words "No and Yes". No, in that we cannot identify the real basis of consciousness, so we cannot explain what it is about the brain that yields conscious states; but Yes, in that we can nevertheless solve the philosophical problem generated by the mind-brain nexus. Critics and expositors have focused on the negative part of my position, wondering whether my pessimism is warranted; but there has been very little discussion of the positive aspect of my position – the philosophical good news, as it were. This is unfortunate because I took the negative part to be a piece of an overall position with a positive message: it was not intended as pessimism for its own sake, but rather as a stepping-stone to ridding ourselves of intractable philosophical perplexity. So in this paper I will accentuate the positive and set out my reasons for supposing that my position actually *solves* the philosophical mind-body problem. I will not attempt to defend my cognitive closure thesis here but instead dwell upon its role in dissolving philosophical perplexity. Part of my point here is that the label "mysterian" as applied to my position can be misleading, since there is also a strongly anti-mysterian component to the view; indeed the mysterian element is invoked to advance an anti-mysterian agenda.[2] I am really just another kind of naturalist (though this label too can be misleading), not a purveyor of thrilling quasi-mystical doctrines. This paper could have been subtitled "Why I am not a Mysterian" and not be wildly wide of the mark.

Clearly, if my answer to the question whether we can solve the mind-body problem is "No and Yes" I must be supposing that there are two distinct questions here, on pain of self-contradiction; and one of these questions cannot be answered while the other can. We cannot answer the question of what the basis of consciousness is, but we can answer the question of how to respond to the philosophical perplexities raised by this difficulty. Using some earlier terminology, I want to distinguish between a "constructive" and a "nonconstructive" solution to the mind-body problem: to give a constructive solution would be to *produce* the property or theory that explains how the brain causes consciousness; but a nonconstructive solution requires only that we find reason to suppose that such a property or theory *exists*, whether we can produce it or not. If we had reason to believe such a property to exist, and reason to believe that we could not identify it, then we would have an explanation of why we find the problem so hard and why we tend to go in for unsatisfying constructive solutions for it. Put simply, the aim is to remove the suspicion that the world is behaving very strangely – almost paradoxically – when conscious states are generated by the brain, without having to produce the theory that explains how things are actually working. We want to save common sense without having to come up with a theory of how the brain operates to yield consciousness. Let me now sketch the way this nonconstructive solution is intended to dissolve our perplexities – what intellectual work it does for us.

II

It is of prime importance to recognize that what makes the mind-body problem philosophical is not simply that we have not yet identified the basis of consciousness – that we have an unsolved problem on our hands. For this does not distinguish a philosophical problem from a merely scientific one: our problem is more fundamental, more conceptual. Compare the problem of what caused the dinosaurs to go extinct. Here we have an array of possible explanations, each of which has the right form to explain the extinction of a species, yet we cannot settle by empirical means which of these is the true explanation. There were dinosaurs, they did go extinct – but was it the result of a meteor impact or changing climate or increased competition from other species or alien intervention? Each of these *would* explain the extinction, but the evidence for selecting one theory over another is lacking. But this is precisely what is not the case with respect to the question of what causes the existence of consciousness: we do not have a plethora of theoretically adequate options from among which we cannot empirically choose; rather, nothing that we can think of has a chance of explaining what needs to be explained. We don't know what a possible explanation of consciousness would even *look like* – hence the feeling of deep conceptual intractability. Instead, we have a range of characteristically philosophical "positions" *(attitudes)* that are offered in response to the manifest lack of understanding. These positions display a typical form, and it is this form that signals the existence of a philosophical problem: I call this form the DIME shape. So the idea is that the philosophical mind-body problem leads to the DIME shape, which constitutes a set of variously unsatisfactory responses to the explanatory problem we face.[3]

The DIME shape comprises the following options: "D" stands for deflationary reductionism; "I" stands for outright irreducibility; "M" stands for eerily magical; "E" stands for ontological elimination. I will not discuss this taxonomy of philosophical responses in any depth here, having done so elsewhere; but I think it is clear enough that this is precisely the set of responses that cluster around the mind-body problem. Thus we have reductive materialism or behaviourism or functionalism; we have claims of *sui generis* irreducibility; we have supernatural dualisms of various forms; and we have the suggestion that there is no such thing as consciousness after all. Now my point is that it is the presence of the DIME shape that makes the mind-body problem specifically philosophical; and it does so because none of these options can command any consensus – the topic is permanently controversial. We have nothing like this with respect to the problem of dinosaur extinction: we don't find some theorists holding that dinosaurs are really some other species in disguise, where that species does have a known explanation for its extinction (as it might be, Dodos); other theorists who claim that the extinction has no explanation but is just a brute fact about nature; others who maintain that it was some supernatural event that caused the extinction (God got tired of dinosaurs one day and zapped them with a divine ray); and yet others who sincerely assert that there were not any dinosaurs after all, which is why we are having so much trouble explaining how they went out of existence. All such positions would seem ludicrously extreme in respect of the dinosaur problem, but they are exactly the positions that insinuate themselves when we ask what causes consciousness. The essence of the philosophical problem, then – what makes the mind-brain relation so conceptually perplexing – is that we seem impaled on the DIME shape. In other words, none of the available options is intrinsically appealing; all seem more or less desperate responses to a deep explanatory conundrum. In particular, we feel under pressure either to accept ontological peculiarities in the world or to deny the very existence of consciousness. What I am calling the philosophical mind-body problem is the problem of getting out from under this pressure, so that we can acknowledge that consciousness is both real and nonmiraculous. The task is to show how consciousness is *possible*, despite the appearances. So when I say that the philosophical problem can be solved, I mean to be speaking of *that* problem – escaping the clutches of the DIME shape, not succumbing to the pressures it creates. And my suggestion is that we can do that without constructively solving the problem, i. e. without actually identifying the objective basis of consciousness.

III

Is consciousness mysterious? The core of my position is that this question is seriously ambiguous: does it ask whether consciousness has an occult nonnatural *nature*, or does it ask simply whether we do or can *understand* the nature of consciousness? The first reading is ontological or metaphysical, the second is purely epistemological. My thesis is that consciousness is not mysterious in the first sense but it is in the second sense. I am an ontological anti-mysterian and an epistemological mysterian. The key point is that I think the sense of deep mystery we have, which naturally expresses itself in ontological rhetoric, is really entirely epistemic; the mystery is *relative* to the human intellect as it attempts to come to terms with the problem. This is, if you like, a deflationary view of the issue, since it locates the apparent oddity of consciousness entirely in the eye of the beholder. The world itself is as smoothly natural and seamless as one could wish; it is just that we lack the conceptual resources with which to discover its objective lineaments. And this perspective gives us a way both to escape the DIME shape and to explain its seeming compulsoriness. Consciousness indubitably exists, yet it is not magical, nor irreducible, nor reducible to the usual kinds of physical basis. It only *seems* magical because we have no grasp of what explains it; it only *seems* irreducible because we cannot find the right explanation; it only *seems* as if physicalism is the only possible naturalistic theory because that is what we are conceptually limited to; and it only *seems* to invite elimination because we can find no explanation for it from within our conceptual scheme. We solve the philosophical problem by diagnosing how it arises and asserting that consciousness is not nonnatural despite all appearances to the contrary. It is because we cannot in principle discover the constructive solution that we find ourselves under so much philosophical pressure; but we can relieve this pressure by accepting our theoretical limitations. That is what I mean by solving the philosophical mind-body problem. The negative "mysterian" part of my position thus serves to underpin the positive "naturalist" part. Wittgenstein spoke of the "unbridgeable gulf" that seems to separate conscious states from the brain[4], and he correctly diagnosed this as the source of the philosophical problem; my answer to the problem consists in rendering the gulf ontologically innocuous, by locating it entirely in our cognitive biases and limitations. Objectively, there *is* no such gulf – the gulf is a kind of illusion resulting from cognitive closure.

Solving the Mind-Body Problem

Let me present an analogy to illustrate how this solution is meant to work. We all have the notion of an unperceived object, i. e. an object that exists while not being an object of sensory observation. This is a basic element in our general picture of the world; it is part of what we mean by the objectivity of physical objects. How do we form this conception? The answer is obvious enough: we have a conception of space in which objects and our own bodies are located, and we conceive of independent objects in terms of their being located at a point in space at which our sense-organs are not directed, and which therefore do not exert causal influence on our sensory state. Thus our notion of independently existing objects – of objects that persist while not being observed – involves conceiving of them in spatial and causal terms. If we are asked how unperceived existence is possible, then we reply with the spatial story just adumbrated. But now consider a race of beings who perceive physical objects but who lack the conceptual framework of space and its causally active occupants: they don't have the conceptual resources with which to conceive of the objects of their experience in terms of their relative locations in space, including their own located bodies, along with the causal concepts that enable us to explain the possibility of unperceived objects. They are cognitively closed with respect to this spatial-cum-causal theory. When they have a visual experience of a red sphere, say, the object is presented to them as phenomenally "outer", but they do not have the concepts and theoretical capacity that would make this appearance intelligible. They thus do not know how unperceived existence is possible, though we may suppose them to have raised the question to themselves. They ask themselves whether objects could exist without being perceived, but they lack the concepts that are necessary to answering that question. Perhaps they are convinced that reality consists of such unperceived objects, but they are at a loss to understand the nature of that reality. They accordingly find themselves in deep philosophical perplexity over the question.

I conjecture that the philosophers among these cognitively limited beings will find themselves in thrall to an array of unsatisfactory DIME options. The deflationary position might be that objects are really nothing but potentialities for sensation, so that to say that an object exists unperceived is just to say that certain counterfactuals are true about the course of their experience; or perhaps so-called unperceived objects are really nothing but ideas in the mind of God. The irreducibility position will be that the notion of unperceived existence admits of no explanation, being just a brute fact with no further conceptual articulation. The magical position, prompted no doubt by the weaknesses of the first two positions, might be that the object somehow springs out of the sense-impression by a sort of miracle (rather like the djinn springing out of the lamp) – that it is a kind of ghost of the sense-impression that persists when the impression ceases. Maybe God performs this miracle every time they close their eyes. This may make them take an attitude of unusual reverence towards unperceived objects, even arguing to the existence of God on the strength of what needs to be assumed in order to explain such a remarkable thing (compare the attitude of some human beings towards consciousness). Finally, sterner souls may seek to sidestep the entire controversy, with all its handwaving and denunciations and intellectual sleights-of-hand, and declare roundly that objects do not exist unperceived at all – that there is really nothing in the world save sense-impressions and the minds that house them. Loftier commentators may wonder how they could have found themselves locked into these unsatisfactory options and hunger for some new perspective to relieve their intellectual cramps. In any case, *we* can see, no doubt with some wry condescension, that each of these DIME options is mistaken, arising as they do from a limited and distorted view of the nature of the objects of perception. It is apparent to us that their perplexities arise from a cognitive deficit on their part – not understanding how objects are located in space and so on. We can also see that they are not condemned to enslavement to the DIME, since it is open to them to hold that their perplexities spring from a conceptual blindspot. Their mistake in cleaving to the DIME options is basically that of overestimating their cognitive powers, trying to force unperceived objects into the conceptual categories they have available. If they could only acknowledge that the nature of objects exceeds their conceptual resources, then they could hold that objects do exist unperceived without benefit of miracle and in a fully robust sense, but in virtue of having properties they are prohibited from conceiving. Thus they could solve their philosophical problem, by relieving the pressure to accept what is not rationally acceptable. It only *seems* to them that objects call for these bizarre and revisionary theories because they lack a proper conception of their underlying nature as spatial entities.

I say it is like this with us and the mind-body problem. Consciousness and the brain do have a nature that renders their union perspicuous and natural, but we are blocked from grasping this nature, so we are apt to pin ourselves to the DIME shape. If this is correct, then we have the resources with which to dissolve the philosophical problem – construed as the problem of avoiding those perennially unappealing options. Consciousness exists, it is not nonnatural, it is not something else in disguise, and it has an explanation: it is just that its nature is deeply hidden to us. This diagnosis explains the appeal of the DIME options and also provides an alternative to them. We can thus relax in the face of the explanatory vacuum and not feel forced to interpret it in terms we cannot really live with. The basic expression of this relief is the recognition that consciousness is nothing extraordinary after all – that it is not a glitch in the natural order. As I like to put it, consciousness is no more remarkable to God's mind than digestion is to ours – though that truth is something we will never be able properly to absorb, given the way the psychophysical nexus strikes us.

Let me give one more analogy, this time of a more scientific sort. Consider the correlation between the temperature of a gas and its pressure, and compare this to the correlation between brain states and conscious states. In the gas case, there seems no a priori reason for such a correlation to exist – it is scarcely a conceptual truth about "pressure" and "temperature". Rather, it is an empirically established law that such a correlation exists. This correlation naturally prompts the question *why* it obtains – what is it about gases that makes their temperature and pressure correlate in this way? What unites these apparently distinct magnitudes? The answer, we now know, lies in the molecular conception of gases: the rapid movement of molecules gives rise *both* to the pressure of the gas and to its temperature, since pressure is the result of the molecules striking the interior of the container and temperature is just the mean kinetic energy of molecules. In this way we explain the correlation and render it "unmiraculous". But if you had a mind that was prevented from forming the idea of constituent molecules and their movements, this explanation would be closed to you, and you would find yourself faced with a brute correlation. My claim is that this is essentially our predicament with respect to psychophysical correlations: we lack the unifying underlying theory, so we are deeply puzzled about the observed correlations. But this is not in itself a reason to beat our heads against the DIME shape; we need simply to accept our deep ignorance. Then we will see that what strikes us as unintelligible might have an objectively straightforward explanation.

IV

I regard this as a demystifying answer to the mind-body problem; for it takes the mystery out of the mystery, so to speak. The impression that consciousness arises from the brain in the miraculous way the djinn emerges from the lamp is given a deflationary account: it is an artifact of our cognitive gaps, not a veridical indication of ontological oddity. I also intend the view to stem from a naturalistic conception of human cognitive powers: the human mind is an evolved collection of biologically driven mechanisms and strategies, responsive to the usual evolutionary pressures. No doubt human reason is a remarkable product of evolution, permitting all sorts of adaptation-transcendent feats of thought; but that is not to exempt it from all biological constraint and bias. As Chomsky points out, the human language faculty is also a remarkable cognitive achievement, conferring all sorts of powers on our minds, but it is a biologically structured natural faculty with intrinsic biases and limitations nonetheless.[5] Our minds have certain epistemic strengths and weaknesses, most apparent in perception and memory, but also present in the so-called higher cognitive functions. So my thesis of cognitive inac-

Solving the Mind-Body Problem

cessibility with respect to the mind-brain link is intended as just one more limitation on human cognitive capacity, not fundamentally different in kind from our inability to remember more than eight digit sequences. We should always remember that intelligence is just one form of biological adaptation, recently evolved, and no doubt set to evolve further, so that it is subject to the same kinds of architectural and functional limitations as any other evolved trait; it is not something that somehow elevates us to the level of epistemic gods. So if I am a mysterian about the mind-brain link, it is because I am a naturalist about the human mind; indeed, since consciousness appears essential to scientific and philosophical understanding, I am a mysterian about consciousness precisely because I am a naturalist about it. Our conscious thinking has its natural limits and that is why it is a mystery to us. Nagel sees correctly into the spirit of my position when he remarks that it is too demystifying for him: he finds it hard to believe that the sense of profundity we feel about problems of mind could be simply a result of naturally-based cognitive lacks.[6] And anyone who feels that the world is a more intrinsically mysterious place than I am willing to recognize will brand me unacceptably anti-mysterian. This response seems to me far more apposite than the usual one, namely that I am a peddler of revamped religious mysteries; indeed, part of my point is to block the way to all such religious metaphysical outlooks. Certainly, I myself find the startling aspect of my view to be the suggestion that the profundity of the mind-body problem is a kind of projective illusion; this is the aspect I have to repeat to myself over and over again with shocked incredulity, and I am not at bit surprised if people find it hard to accept. In comparison the thesis of terminal cognitive closure seems like a mild and banal claim, and I find myself puzzled at the vehemence with which it is often rejected. It is the hard-core naturalism that should take one's breath away, not the soft-core mysterianism.

It might be helpful to compare my view with Wittgenstein's general metaphilosophical outlook. He recognizes that it is a mark of a philosophically interesting concept that intimations of the "queer" and "occult" and "sublime" should surround our thinking about that concept. Thus meaning and reference are apt to strike us in this way

– we naturally suppose that something extraordinary is involved in these things.[7] He also appreciates the dialectic that is apt to spring up around such intimations – misplaced reductionism, eliminativism, radical dualism. His view, of course, is that all this flows from certain identifiable sources of philosophical error – particularly, misunderstandings of our ordinary language for speaking about meaning and reference. Now my position clearly does not agree with Wittgenstein's diagnostically, but there is agreement over the role of those intimations of supernaturalism and over the conceptual deformations they are likely to produce. Where Wittgenstein thinks we can dispel the philosophical clouds by reminding ourselves of our actual language-games, I think we should do so by acknowledging our cognitive limitations. Where he thinks nothing is hidden, I think hiddenness is exactly the problem. Nevertheless, at a certain abstract level, I am agreeing with Wittgenstein's conception of the form of a philosophical problem, and I am likewise proposing a deflationary response to the perplexities generated. We both think that *ontologically* there is nothing "funny" going on; nothing is "queer" *de re*. Consciousness, I say, is really just a particular biological phenomenon, and quite a primitive one at that, found quite far down the phylogenetic scale (remember that by "consciousness" we simply mean "conscious states", and these include such humble items as simple perceptual experiences of the environment). It is a great mistake to suppose just because consciousness is especially problematic that it must therefore belong to what we deem the highest of human faculties; on the contrary, quite lowly species – bats, reptiles, birds – have consciousness in an equally problematic way, since they are conscious of their environment, feel pain, and so on. There would be a deep philosophical problem of consciousness even if evolution had never progressed the dinosaurs. To my mind, this strongly suggests that our inability to solve the mind-body problem is the result of a quite specific *bias* in our faculties of comprehension: we are cognitively targeted away from understanding consciousness and towards some quite different kind of entity, namely physical objects in space. But the point I am making now is that the refractoriness of the problem of consciousness is no sure guide to its ranking in terms of objective complexity or biological sophistication, since that reflects our cognitive slant as much as the nature of reality.

The general upshot is that the negative part of my position should not be seen as pessimism for its own sake but rather as a component of an overall position that is intended to ease our philosophical perplexities about consciousness. When we have the right explanation for our failure to solve the problem we see why it is that the DIME options are not forced upon us, and thus we are relieved of the philosophical pressure they seem to exert.

V

I said just now that our minds are biased away from arriving at an understanding of the mind-brain link. What kind of bias might this be – where might it stem from? We can only be speculative about this question, but I think that the role of physical space in our thinking must be at least part of the story. As I have argued elsewhere, conscious experiences are not aptly conceived in ordinary spatial terms, as extended occupants of space with the standard spatial properties.[8] Yet the neural processes with which experiences are correlated are *bona fide* spatial entities. This puts an obstacle in the way of theories that attempt to assimilate conscious states to brain states of the standard type, since this would require doing violence to the very essence of consciousness; so materialist reduction looks misguided granted the nonspatiality of the mind. Because of this we cannot conceive of conscious states as combinatorial products of brain constituents, since that would be to try to derive the nonspatial from the spatial by mere combination or aggregation. The underlying problem here is that our spatial methods of understanding the world fail to yield the right relation between consciousness and the brain: higher-level phenomena are standardly conceived as complex combinatorial emergents, but this mode of understanding is inadequate to explain how conscious states emerge from brain states – since conscious states are not themselves spatial entities. So our cognitive bias towards spatial modes of understanding lets us down in the present case. The combinatorial paradigm cannot subsume the mind-brain relation. But this is no reason to suppose that anything nonnatural is afoot: that *we* think in combinatorial spatial terms is not a reason to think that nature itself must always operate in those terms. There must be noncombinatorial principles that link conscious states to brain states, since that is how nature appears to be working here; it is just that our bias towards the spatial prevents us from gaining insight into these principles.[9]

These remarks are just a summary of my diagnosis of the source of cognitive closure with respect to the mind-body problem; they are intended to illustrate the *kind* of explanation that might exist for the negative part of my position, and to show how it feeds into the positive part. The DIME shape tempts us because of our deepseated spatial combinatorialism about the natural world, but we can break its hold on our thinking by recognizing that nature may not always work by means of forms of spatial aggregation. In the case of the mind there is really no reason to suppose that the mode of thought that works so well for the nonmental world should carry over to the mental world. Here, bias leads inevitably to distortion. The way out is to recognize the bias and draw the appropriate epistemic conclusion.

It is instructive to compare the problem here with an opposite problem faced by some forms of idealism. Suppose we hold that only minds are real and that minds are nonspatial substances in the style of Descartes. Then a question arises about the nature of ordinary objects like tables and chairs: they seem to have spatial qualities, but how is this possible if nothing is spatial? Perception presents these objects to us as spatial, but the assumed metaphysics has no room for the spatial. The question here is the converse of the question posed by mental states for a materialist metaphysics: since everything is spatial according to that metaphysics, what are we to make of the apparent nonspatiality of the mind? The idealist, for her part, is faced with some unpalatable choices when it comes to ordinary objects: she can either say there are no tables and chairs after all, since they would have to be spatial and nothing is spatial, or she could try to maintain that there are tables and chairs but they are not spatial, thus convicting perceptual experience of a radical form of error. Better, perhaps, to question the revisionary idealist metaphysics. In the same way, a materialist might try to maintain that experiences only seem nonspatial but are really spatial, thus convicting introspection of a form of radical error. Just as the idealist has trouble finding room for ordinary objects in her nonspatial world of pure minds, so the materialist has trouble finding a place for conscious states in his purely spatial world. Seeing this analogy can help to encourage appreciation for the problem posed for materialism by the apparent nonspatiality of conscious states. Against an idealist background of universal nonspatiality, ordinary objects are an anomaly that prompts revisionary manoeuvres; against a materialist background of universal spatiality, conscious states are an anomaly that prompts comparable revisionary manoeuvres. We are much more accustomed in this century to the latter kind of manoeuvering, but it is worth remembering that in periods of thought of idealist cast the converse would have seemed far more reasonable. The right response, in both cases, is extreme chariness about the kinds of tendentious revisionism enforced by the metaphysical outlooks in question.

VI

I began this paper by recalling Huxley's formulation of the mind-body problem; I can now summarize my response to the problem thus posed. If we did come across a lamp that produced a djinn when rubbed, we would be justified in concluding that it had properties going far beyond any that are apparent to us – it could not be simply a *lamp*. Not knowing these properties, we might be tempted to reduce the djinn to a mere puff of innocuous smoke (go reductionist about djinns), or to declare that we are up against a primitive inexplicable natural law linking (some) lamps and djinns (opt for radical irreducibility), or to concede that there are miracles out there after all (accept the magical and supernatural), or simply to deny that anything comes out of the lamp at all (embrace eliminativism). None of these responses would be reasonable, I maintain; the right response is that there is more to some lamps (and their djinns) than meets the eye. If there were not, then indeed we would have a problem, since there would then be no escaping the DIME options with all their discomfort – we would *have* to accept a deflationary reduction of djinns on pain of miracles or elimination. But once we have accepted that reality exceeds our grasp here we can carry on rubbing lamps and getting djinns out of them without fearing that we will be engulfed in philosophical perplexity. Djinns exist, as we can see, and they have a natural explanation; it is just that the lamps that produce them have properties that lie outside of our ken.[10] We thus solve the philosophical djinn-lamp problem – while accepting that we cannot explain the djinn-lamp link. Nature has solved the djinn-lamp problem, though we cannot see how; and that is all we really need to know.

Notes

1 The paper originally appeared in *Mind* 98, no. 891 (July 1989), and is reprinted in my *The Problem of Consciousness* (Oxford: Basil Blackwell, 1991). In that paper I misattributed the quotation from Thomas Huxley to Julian Huxley, for uninteresting reasons, as Nicholas Humphrey first pointed out to me.
2 The label "mysterian" was first introduced by O. Flanagan in *The Science of Mind* (Cambridge, Mass.: MIT Press, 1984) to describe the views of Thomas Nagel, myself and others. Actually, Nagel has never advanced the strong unknowability thesis I defend and is quite sceptical about it. The label is strictly speaking quite accurate in describing my position, since I do regard the mind-body problem as an insoluble (epistemic) mystery, but the connotations of anti-naturalism are misleading, so I do not use it self-referentially.
3 For an extended discussion of the DIME shape, cf. my *Problems in Philosophy: the Limits of Enquiry* (Oxford: Basil Blackwell, 1993). My general thesis in that book is that there are a range of other philosophical problems that display the same form as the problem of consciousness.
4 Wittgenstein writes: "The feeling of an unbridgeable gulf between con-

sciousness and brain-process: how does it come about that this idea does not come into the considerations of our ordinary life? This idea of a difference in kind is accompanied by slight giddiness, – which occurs when we are performing a piece of logical sleight-of-hand. (The same giddiness attacks us when we think of certain theorems in set theory.)" *Philosophical Investigations* (Oxford: Basil Blackwell, 1953), § 412.

5 Cf., for example, N. Chomsky, *Reflections on Language* (New York: Pantheon, 1975). Language, like reason, confers creativity, but only because it has its own fixed structure. The mistake is to think that creativity requires the myth of the *tabula rasa*, the inherently featureless cognitive receptacle.

6 Cf. Th. Nagel, *The Last Word* (New York: Oxford University Press, 1997), p. 131, note 9.

7 Cf., for example, § 38 of *Philosophical Investigations*. It should be obvious that Wittgenstein's use of "occult" and similar terms is not intended to be equivalent to "non-physical" (whatever that may mean); he is clearly not advancing a materialist programme in invoking these notions. My own use of "non-natural" is similarly not confined to that which flouts "physicalist" scruples.

8 Cf. my "Consciousness and Space", in: *Conscious Experience*, ed. Th. Metzinger (Paderborn: Schöningh/Imprint Academic, 1995).

9 For discussion of the combinatorial paradigm, cf. my *Problems in Philosophy*, cited in note 3. In that book, I call this the CALM format – combinatorial atomism with lawlike mappings.

10 Just for the record, I do not of course believe in djinns! I am speaking metaphorically.

John Perry

Myself and I

Introduction

In this essay I distinguish three kinds of *self-knowledge*. I call these three kinds *agent-relative knowledge, self-attached knowledge* and *knowledge of the person one happens to be.* These aspects of self-knowledge differ in how the knower or agent is represented. Most of what I say will be applicable to beliefs as well as knowledge, and to other kinds of attitudes and thoughts, such as desire, as well.[1]

Agent-relative knowledge is knowledge from the perspective of a particular agent. To have this sort of knowledge, the agent need not have an idea of self, or a notion of himself or herself. This sort of knowledge can be expressed by a simple sentence containing a demonstrative for a place or object, and without any term referring to the speaker. For example, "There is an apple" or "that is a toaster".

(Ideas of specific objects I call *notions*. Ideas of properties and relations I just call *ideas*. A judgement involves an idea being associated with a notion. A notion together with all of the ideas associated with it is a *file*.)

In self-attached knowledge, the agent has an idea of self, which is associated with a notion, which I call a *self-notion*. This is the kind of knowledge that is expressed with the word "I" – what Shoemaker calls "first-person knowledge".[2] For example, "I am a philosopher", or "I see a toaster" or "I have a headache". In the last section of this paper, I try to explain why that is an apt name – why it is that the word "I" is so intimately connected with the expression of this sort of "self-thought".

In knowledge of the person one happens to be, the agent is represented to herself in just the same way that other people are represented to her. The agent has just the same kind of idea of herself as she has of other people. This kind of knowledge can be expressed with a name for third person demonstrative. For example, "John Perry is a philosopher" or, pointing to myself in a mirror, "That man is a shabby pedagogue".

I
Agent-relative knowledge

1. Two facts about the human condition

Everything we learn about other objects we learn by employing methods that are appropriate because those objects stand in certain relations to us. And however remote from us the object we are ultimately learning about may be, our inquiry will involve detecting the properties of things in our immediate vicinity.

I may learn that Bill Clinton visited the Bay Area by reading the paper, or seeing pictures on television, or hearing the radio. I learn about Clinton by reading what is written on the paper, seeing what is portrayed on the television screen, or hearing the sounds coming from the radio. Being the radio I am listening to, or the television I am watching, or the newpaper I am reading, are all what I call *agent-relative roles*: roles that other individuals play in the lives of agents. These are agent-relative roles, because an object plays or doesn't play such a role relative to a given agent, at a given time. For example, my computer is playing the role of *object in front* right now, relative to me, but not relative to you.

When I read about him, or watched him on TV, or listened to a report of what he was doing on the radio, Clinton was also playing an agent-relative role in my life, one that was derived from the role these other objects were playing, and his relation to them. For example, Clinton was the object read about, because the newspaper was the object read, and Clinton was the object the newspaper story was about.

This is the first of two very general facts I want to emphasize: any object we learn about plays some agent-relative role, basic or derived, in our life. We learn about the object by using an epistemic method connected to the role, a way of finding out about the object or person playing that role. The way to find out about the object in front of you is to look at it, or perhaps to walk up to it and touch it. The way to find out about the object that the document in front of you is about is to read the document. Finding out about the objects around us is a way of finding out about other objects, given general facts about the way things work and specific facts about how things are related. If Clinton is the source of the image on my television, then I can find out things about him by finding out things about that image.

The second fact is that however complex our lives are, everything we do comes down to performing operations on the objects around us – objects in front of us, behind us, above us; objects we are holding; objects we can see. By doing these things, we do things to objects in less basic relations to us. By speaking into the phone I hold, I speak to the person I called, the person to whom the signals that pass through the phone I hold are ultimately directed. I know how to move my body so as to effect objects around me, and I know how effecting those objects will effect other objects related to them in certain ways.

There are then two kinds of methods connected with agent-relative roles, epistemic methods and pragmatic methods. These two kinds of methods are the key to all human intelligence and purposive activity. We know how to find out what kinds of objects occupy these roles, and we know how to perform various operations on them. Technology extends the methods, so that we can find out about things in more and more complex relations to us, and do things that will change them in predictable ways.

Our practical knowledge then, the knowledge that enables us to do things, forms a structure at whose base is information about the objects that play relatively basic agent-relative roles in our lives.

2. Knowledge concerning the self

Consider a simple successful transaction involving such a basic agent-relative role, and epistemic and pragmatic methods associated with it. I am hungry. I see an apple before me. I pick it up and eat it. The complex movement of arm, hand, fingers, neck and jaw was successful in getting the apple into my mouth, because of the distance and direction the apple was from *me*. What I learned from perception, then, must have been the distance and direction of the apple from *me*. Or consider a transaction with a fax machine. To press certain buttons on it, I have to move my fingers a certain distance and direction from *me*. It isn't enough to know where the buttons were relative to one another, or where the fax machine was in the building or the room. I had to know where these things were relative to *me*.

It seems then, that these basic methods already require me to have some notion of myself. For it seems I need to know who it is, for example, from whom the apple is a certain distance and direction. If it is that distance and direction from you, or President Clinton, then moving the way I did would not be a way of eating it.

However, I think this is misleading. A natural way for me to report what I saw would be to simply say:

"That's an apple."

or:

"There is an apple there."

There is nothing in this remark that refers to me. And after all, why should there be? I didn't see myself, I saw an apple. But, one might reply, we saw above that I got the information that the apple was a certain distance and direction from me. Otherwise, how did I know that I could reach it?

When we perceive, we learn how things are around us. But that remark is a bit ambiguous. Suppose I say that when you look at an accurate clock, you learn what time it is in the time zone you are in. That's true. But is it true if said of a child, who doesn't know what time zones are? It's still true in a way. The child learns what time it is in the time zone she is in, as opposed to learning what time it is in some other time zone. But there is nothing in her thinking that reflects that she is this time zone rather than that one, so it is misleading.

Is there something defective in the child's approach to time? That depends. Given the child's life, does she need to keep track of timezones? Does it matter to her that there are other time-zones? Perhaps it does; perhaps she talks to her grandmother in Denver, and finds the whole thing very confusing. But perhaps it doesn't. Perhaps she never talks to anyone outside her time zone, and never travels. In that case, there is no point in her thinking, as she sees the clock, "It is 3 p. m., Pacific Time".

The general point is this. Sometimes all of the facts we deal with involving a certain n-ary relation involve the same object occupying one of the argument roles. In that case, we don't need to worry about that argument role; we don't need to keep track of its occupant, because it never changes. We can, so to speak, pack it into the relation. For centuries people in Europe assumed that *being a summer month* was a property of months. July was a summer month, December was not. Once they started to visit the Southern Hemisphere, they had to take account of the relativity to places. July was a summer month in the Northern Hemisphere, but not in the Southern Hemisphere. A child who is unconcerned about and even unaware of the weather anywhere but where he is, can treat the issue of whether it is raining or not as a property of a time, rather than a relation between times and places. He says, "It is raining now" rather than "It is raining here now". (In this case the argument role is not always occupied by the same place, but always occupied by a place with a fixed relation to the agent, the place he is at.) The child we thought of above says "It is *now* 7 o'clock p. m.", treating *being 7 o'clock p. m.* as a property of the present time, rather than a relation between that time and a place or time zone. Before Einstein, we could treat simultaneity as a 2-ary relation between events, rather than as a 3-ary relation between a pair of events and an inertial frame, because in our daily life we never need to worry about alternative inertial frames.

In all of these cases, I say that the judgement *concerns* the fixed, unarticulated object, even though it is not explicitly about it.[3] The judgement concerns the object because its truth-value depends on the object, even when it is not explicitly represented in thought. The child is right when he thinks "It is 7 o'clock" because it is 7 o'clock Pacific Coast Time; he is right when he judges "It is raining now", if it is raining where he is.

Let us then return to the remark that I said was ambiguous, that when we perceive we learn how things are around us. When we perceive how the world is around us and act upon it, we need to judge what distance and direction things stand relative to ourselves. But we do not need to keep track of who it is that we are judging things to be in front of or to the left of, at least as long as we are basing our actions on simple perceptual knowledge. In this case, our knowledge concerns ourselves but need not involve an explicit representation of ourselves.

Of course, humans use a wide variety of knowledge, not only the input from immediate perception. They combine this input with all sorts of facts and general principles that they know from previous experience and communication of various sorts. All of this requires a notion of themselves, and once we have one, there is an easy transition from "There is an apple" or "Apple in front" to "There is an apple in front of me". But if our cognizing were confined to discovering facts about the objects around us and acting upon them, we would only need selfless thoughts. There are systems that perceive, and use the information about their circumstances they get through perception, that do not know that it is *their* circumstances they are learning about. During our formative stages and in certain moods later on, we may be such systems.

This then is the first aspect of self-knowledge, agent-relative knowledge of things that play various roles in our lives. This kind of knowledge is self-knowledge, in that it embodies knowledge of the relations things stand in to the agent; the thoughts are true because of facts about the agent. But it does not require that the agent have an idea of self or a notion of itself.

II
The detach and recognize information game

The concept of agent-relative knowledge fits into what I call the "detach and recognize information game"[4]. We live in a world where we encounter the same objects on different occasions. On each of these occasions we are in a position to learn some facts about the object. If we can accumulate this knowledge, then in later encounters we will be able to deal with the object in light of this whole file of information, rather than simply what we can pick up on that occasion.

Suppose I am talking to you at a conference. You are occupying a number of agent-relative roles in my life: the person in front of me, the person I am talking to, the person talking to me, the person I see, and so forth. I am taking in a lot of information about you and deciding what to say to you and in general how to treat you. I accumulate information – the way I am thinking about it, this means I associate ideas to the notion I have formed of you. During this whole period, this notion is *attached* to the perceptions I have of you, to roles you are playing in my life and hence to the epistemic and pragmatic methods connected with those roles. It is what I call a *buffer*.

The conference is over; you go one way, I go another. I still have a notion of you. But now it is *detached*. The notion is no longer a buffer, but what I call an *enduring notion*. It is not connected to any agent-relative roles and epistemic and pragmatic methods. I may want to ask you a question, or tell you something, or hit you or shake your hand. The ideas in my file may give me good reasons to do all of those things. And I do know how to ask questions, tell people things, hit them and shake their hands. But only when they are playing certain roles in my life. To do these things, I need to get my notion of you attached to the appropriate roles.

Suppose then we meet again. At first I don't recognize you. I see you, form a notion, a buffer, and begin to collect information. After a while I recognize you as the person I saw before. This time the buffer doesn't endure; the information is transferred to my old notion of you, which is now attached to the stream of perceptual information.

Now I am in a position to ask you a question or shake your hand. That's what recognition is: getting one's file on a person or thing attached to the roles that the person is playing in one's life, so one can bring one's information about the object to bear on one's decisions about what to say and do. Misrecognition is attaching one's file to roles that some other object is playing; failure to recognize is not attaching one's file of an object to a role the object is playing.

In our lives, of course, we are not dependent on perception of objects to form notions of them and learn a lot about them. We can learn of people, and learn a lot about them, by talking to third parties about them, and by reading things that they have written and that have been written about them. Suppose you think W. V. O. Quine is a great philosopher; you have read many of his works and many articles about him. You understand he is going to be at a philosophy department reception; you go. You have all sorts of things you want to say to him. You have a notion of Quine, formed when you first read about him or heard your philosophy professor talk about him. You have all sorts of ideas associated with your Quine notion – that he wrote *Word and Object*, that he is sort of a modern Pythagorean, arguing that all we need to believe in is set theory; that he has a pleasant, friendly face, looking a little like David Hume might have had he gone on a successful diet and taken up vigorous walking. You have a rich mental file on Quine.

This same notion is also involved in certain desires you have. You'd like to shake Quine's hand, and tell him how much you enjoy his works, and ask him if he is serious about his Pythagoreanism.

You read that Quine will be at a reception given by the Philosophy Department. You go to the reception. You are standing in front of Quine. Let's say for a while that you don't recognize him – he looks a little older than the picture of him on your book. There are a couple of other people that you think might be Quine. But eventually, partly on the basis of your memory of how he looks, and partly on the basis of how one of the candidates seems to talk and act like a modest but great philosopher might, things sort of click and you take one of them to be Quine.

Let's focus on this period when you have seen Quine, and are noticing things about him, but haven't quite recognized him. During this period, you have two notions of the same person. One of them is the one we talked about earlier. You acquired it when you first heard of Quine. Since that time information has been accumulating around it, and desires have been forming on the basis of this information. One thing associated with that notion is the desire to shake his hand. But of course there is no simple *method* for shaking Quine's hand. You have to know where he is relative to you to do this. This sort of information, where Quine is relative to you, isn't part of your notion. Or rather nothing very specific is – you think that he is at the same reception as you are, but that's not specific enough to support handshaking.

You have a second notion of Quine, a buffer, that you formed when you entered the room, and noticed him as one of the Quine candidates. Now this notion is associated with his position relative to you. As he moves or you move you "track him", keeping his position relative to you associated with the notion, so if you conclude that it is Quine you can strike.

Now you are standing next to Quine. The next-to relation is connected with epistemic and pragmatic methods. That is, there are certain ways of finding out more information about the person next to you, and there are certain ways of effecting the person next to you. You can find out more about him by looking. You can make him move by shoving. And you can shake his hand by turning towards him, extending yours, and smiling.

At this point you want to shake Quine's hand, and Quine is the person standing next to you, and you know how to shake the hand of the person next to you. So why don't you do it? Not because you don't see him there; you are looking at him very intently, almost staring. Because you don't quite recognize him; you're not sure. The desire to shake Quine's hand is associated with one notion of him, your enduring notion of him, the method for shaking hands is connected with another, your perceptual buffer of him as the person next to you. Only when you bring these together do you turn, smile, and extend your hand.

Suppose that F is an idea. That is, F is a cognitive particular in the mind of some person that combines with notions in that person's mind to produce judgements about the objects the notions are of. We might think of notions as names and ideas as predicates in a language of thought. Or we might think of notions and ideas as different sorts of nodes in a network that can be associated by edges of some sort. All I require of an idea is that it provide a way that notions can be modified.

What makes it the case that F was an idea of some agent-relative role R? It is by being associated to the epistemic and pragmatic methods that are associated with R. I'll call these "normally R-informative ways of knowing" and "normally R-effecting ways of acting".

A notion that is associated with F, an F-notion, will serve as the *repository* of information that is normally acquired by methods for finding out about the object that plays the F role, and the *motivator* of actions that are directed at (whose success depends upon) the nature of things that play the role.

A notion, whether buffer or enduring notion, that is associated with the idea of a role R, I call an "R-notion", for as long as the association continues. Of course, this is not an enduring trait of notions, since typically the same object will not play a given agent-relative role in our lives for very long. The apple is in front of me now, but won't be a moment from now. My apple notion is an *In-front* notion now, but won't be a moment from now. There are exceptions, of course. The role of being the planet I live on the surface of, for example, is one that has been occupied by Earth since I was born, and presumably will continue in that role until I die.

III
Mach and the shabby pedagogue

In 1885 Ernst Mach wrote:

> "Not long ago, after a trying railway journey by night, when I was very tired, I got into an omnibus, just as another man appeared at the other end. 'What a shabby pedagogue that is, that has just entered', thought I."[5]

In this case, Mach had agent-relative knowledge of a certain person, which he describes as "that man". He knows how to find out whether or not a man he sees at the other end of a bus is a shabby pedagogue. He is thinking of the man he sees as a man in front of him at some distance away, for to find out more about that man he uses the methods appropriate for someone playing that role. Now in this particular case Mach wasn't motivated to do much of anything. We can suppose that he saw a bunch of lint on the man's vest. There are methods for getting the lint removed from the vest of a man a few yards in front of one, if one cares a lot about it. One can shout, "Brush that lint off your vest, you shabby pedagogue", or one can walk forward and stretch out one's hand and brush it off for him. Mach no doubt would have used those methods, had he cared that much about the lint he saw, and not gone on to make an important discovery:

> "It was myself: opposite me hung a large mirror. The physiognomy of my class, accordingly, was better known to me than my own."[6]

During the period when he didn't know who he was looking at, Mach could be said to have known something about himself in the following sense. He knew something about a certain person, the man he was looking at, the man he referred to as "that man". And this man, that he knew something about, was in fact Ernst Mach. Let's assume Mach's belief was true. What made it true was that Mach himself was a shabby pedagogue. It was a case of Mach knowing something about Mach, and in that sense, self-knowledge.

But it wasn't what we would ordinarily call self-knowledge. Mach only had that after he recognized himself, and was ready to say, "I am a shabby pedagogue". What Mach had, before he recognized himself, was knowledge of the person he happened to be. He knew about someone whom he thought of as "that man", and that person happened to be him.

This was a failure of *perceptual* recognition; Mach failed to recognize himself as the person he was perceiving. Another kind of case of recognition and failure of recognition is what I'll call *documentary*. One fails to recognize someone that one knows as the person one is reading about (or seeing a video about or a portrait of).

Suppose that Mach, when he gets off the bus, hits his head and as a result has amnesia. "He doesn't know who he is", we would say. When he wakes up in the hospital he sees a story in the paper, "Famous Scientist is Missing". It goes on to say that Ernst Mach never returned home, and his family and colleagues at the university are upset. We can imagine Mach reading this and not recognizing himself as Mach, not knowing that he is the missing person, not remembering his name and his profession. This is a failure of documentary self-recognition. This is another case of Mach having knowledge of the person he happens to be, but not what we would ordinarily call self-knowledge.

IV
Self-attached knowledge

Ordinarily all ones knowledge about oneself is integrated around a special sort of idea or notion of oneself that we express with "I". While my perception that the beer is in front of me may not require a representation of myself, the information I acquire is immediately integrated into self-attached knowledge, that I might express with "I see a beer" or "there is a beer in front of me". And when I read a piece of e-mail, that says that John Perry's paper is overdue, I integrate this information into self-attached knowledge, "My paper is overdue", and I realize that it is me that has to get to work. I would think, "There is a beer in front of *me*, but *I* have a paper to do". So

Myself and I

I want to turn to the question of this kind of knowledge. What did Mach lack, when he "didn't recognize himself"?

The view I advocate is simply that identity is a basic relation, and that our idea of self ("being me") is the idea of the agent-relative role *is identical*. This is the role we each play in our own lives. That is, identity, like being in front or behind or above, is a basic relation relative to which we have epistemic and pragmatic methods. There are certain methods for picking up information about the person identical with us, and certain methods for having an effect on that person. The notion that is the repository of information gained via those methods, and the motivator of actions associated with that relation, is our self-notion. The person this notion is of, is the person we take ourselves to be.

An uncharitable summary of the view I am putting forward would be that my idea of *me* is just the idea of *the person identical with me*, which seems clearly circular, since the defining idea seems to contain the idea of *me*, the very idea being defined. It is agent-relative knowledge that keeps the account from circularity. It is not the idea, *person identical with me* that I need, but only the role-idea, *person identical*. My idea of *me* is not a part of this idea.

But why should we think that "being identical" is one of these epistemic-pragmatic relations?

Suppose I am at a party. I bend over to pick something up, and I hear a ripping sound that is characteristic of trousers splitting. I suspect that the trousers that have just ripped are my own. But they might not be. You can hear other people's trousers splitting. Then I feel a hot flush in my face. So I am aware that someone is blushing. But who? It's a silly question. Of course it is me. It is my own blushing of which I am aware. I can be aware of the blushing of others. But I can't be aware of it in the same way that I can be aware of my own blushing. I feel myself blush, and anytime I am aware of blushing by feeling it, I know that it is I who am blushing.

This is an example of what I shall call a *reflexive method* of knowing. This is a method for finding out whether someone has some property or does not, that we can each use to find out about ourselves, but can't use to find out about others. What one finds out may be accessible to others, using different methods. But the particular method in question can only be used by the person in question to find out about himself or herself. Feeling hunger is normally a way of detecting that one's own stomach is short of food. Feeling thirst is a way of knowing that one's throat is parched or that one's body is short of water. There is a certain feeling, that children are trained to recognize, that signals that one's bladder is full. In each case, someone else can determine the same thing, using a different technique. This alternative technique may even be superior. Perhaps you can tell that I am blushing, by looking, when I am not sure. Perhaps you can be sure that my stomach is full, having noticed what I have put into it, when I am still in that charming interval between being full and feeling full. Parents are often better judges of the states of their children's bladder than the children themselves are. So the point isn't that our reflexive methods of knowing about ourselves are always infallible or superior to any other methods. It is that only we can use them.

In these examples, the fact that these methods of discovering a person's states are for the exclusive use of the person in question, is a matter of quite reliable but not quite necessary facts. We could imagine, for example, cases involving spinal columns that are connected across bodies which had the result that one person knew about the state of another person's stomach in the way that we normally know only of the states of our own stomach.

We also have reflexive methods of knowing our own mental states, and in these cases it seems quite plausible to suppose that this is a matter of necessity. There are ways that I have of knowing whether I have a headache, or a throbbing tooth, or believe that Berkeley is west of Santa Cruz, that I employ to find out about my own mental states, and others employ to find out about theirs. It is very difficult to imagine even a science fiction case in which one uses these methods to find out about someone else's mental states.

On Locke's theory of personal identity, at least according to one way of interpreting and developing it, this special way of knowing one's own mental states guarantees identity by bestowing identity. An instance of being aware of an experience, and the experience of which one is aware is known, necessarily belong to the same person, because it is in terms of this relation, that "same person" is defined.

Locke says that this method of knowing experiences and actions may be extended back in time. It seems that what he has in mind is what we might call first-person memory. Compare:

(1) I remember Mach wrote *The Analysis of Sensation.*
(2) I remember Mach writing *The Analysis of Sensation.*
(3) I remember writing *The Analysis of Sensation.*

(1) might be said truly by any of us who remember that Mach wrote the book; (2) might be said by any of his family and colleagues who remember him laboring on it, but (3) could be truly said only by Mach. It seems to be getting at a way of remembering, "remembering from the inside", in Shoemaker's phrase, that we each have of remembering our own past experiences, and with which we can remember no others.[7]

But in the case of memory from the inside, it is not so clear that the link is a necessary one. In his influential paper "Persons and Their Pasts", Shoemaker develops some examples in which it seems we can remember[8] in this way experiences we did not have.

There are also reflexive ways of acting. These are ways of bringing it about that someone has a property, that each person can use to bring it about that he or she has a property, but cannot use to bring it about that others have it. Towards the end of the movie "Spellbound" Leo. G. Carroll points his gun at Ingrid Bergman as she walks out the door of his office, having just disclosed that she knows that he framed Gregory Peck. We see this from Leo. G. Carroll's perspective. Then we see the hand holding the gun turn slowly, until the barrel of the gun is all that is visible on the screen. Then it fires. We know what Carroll has done, and to whom. He has killed someone, and the someone is him. The way Carroll held and fired the gun was a reflexive way of killing.

V
What is special about self-notions

So far I have emphasized the analogy between self-notions, notions that are associated with the role-idea of *being identical*, and notions that are associated with ideas of other agent-relative roles. But there is one important disanalogy. As we saw above, the other cases (or most of them), the attachment between notion and role cannot be permanent, because different objects occupy the same roles relative to us at different times. We noted one exception, the role of being the planet lived on. And of course there are indefinitely many others based on the same general idea: being star that warms, being the part of the universe relied on most, etc. Clearly, the person with whom I am identical falls into this category of non-shifting roles, but in this case the reliability is not a contingent matter. It is logically possible that I will move to Mars, or even to a planet in the solar system of another sun. But it is not possible that I will ever be identical with anyone other than me. If I have picked out the right notion to be my self-notion once, it will continue to be the right one.

This is not to say people cannot be wrong, nor that they might not change their self-notion. My parents might have, as sort of a practical joke, raised me believing I was really Al Smith, former Governor of New York and Democratic Presidential candidate. They tell me that in an extreme use of the witness protection program, I was shrunken and made child-like. My memory was obliterated and then I was passed off as John Perry, the real John Perry having died in 1944 as an infant. They recommend that I go along with the story, and pretend to believe that I am really John Perry. At some point I do a bit of research, uncover the prank, and realize that Al Smith really did die in 1944, and I am John Perry, just as everyone but me and, as I thought, my parents, had always believed. At that point my Al Smith notion would cease to be my self-notion, and my John Perry notion take over that job. And I might become convinced, at some point in the future when I sink into madness or senility, that I am really Napoleon and not John Perry. One can be mistaken about who one is.

But for most of us most of the time, possessed of sober parents and a sound mind, there will never be any reason to detach our self-notion from our enduring notion of the person we are, and we and everyone who knows us takes us to be.

VI
Back to Mach

Now let us see if this analysis provides us with a plausible candidate for what Mach lacked in the two cases we considered.

When he looks to the far end of the bus, Mach gets information about himself in a way that is not normally self-informative, but normally "person-in-front-and-looked-at"-informative. So this information doesn't pass into his self-notion; it is not combined with information got in reflexive ways. And it doesn't motivate normally reflexive actions.

Suppose Mach looks down at his own vest and sees a big piece of lint. (Mach himself provides us with a picture of the way one's front characteristically looks to oneself.) He would have associated the idea of having a large piece of lint on one's vest with his self-notion. That's what I mean by saying that the self-notion is the repository of normally self-informative perception. Now if Mach had desired not to have large pieces of lint on himself, he would have reached out and removed in a way that works when the piece of lint is on one's own vest. If he has this desire, and the idea of having lint on one's vest is associated with his self-notion, we would expect him to take such a normally self-directed action. That's what I mean by saying that the self-notion is the motivator of normally self-directed actions.

But when Mach sees a piece of lint on the vest of the person in the mirror he does not act in this way. The information is not gotten in the normally self-informative way.[9] So it is not combined with the other information in the self-notion, and doesn't lead to the action that works to remove lint from oneself. At the beginning of the episode, Mach formed a notion for the person he saw, whom he took to be getting on the other end of the bus. This was a notion of himself, but not a self-notion. We assume Mach knew who he was, and so that he had a notion of Ernst Mach as having all of the well-known properties of Ernst Mach that was also a self-notion. Mach's beliefs change, during the episode, in that he transfers the information associated with the new notion formed when he got on the bus to his old self-notion. If, after he has made the transfer, he notices that the person in the mirror has a piece of lint on his vest, he will pick the lint of his own vest in the normally self-dependent and self-effecting way of picking lint off one's vest.

Now let us turn to the case of Mach the amnesiac, reading about himself in the paper. He plays the role in his own life of "person being read about". He forms a notion of this person; he knows he is called "Mach", is a scientist, and is missing. Even in the middle of a bout of amnesia Mach would have had at least a self-buffer, a notion tied to normally self-informative action and perception. He realizes that the table he sees in front is in front of him, the same person who is reading the paper and can't remember who he is. He does not associate the ideas he picks up from reading the paper, of being named "Mach", being a scientist, and being missing, with his self-notion; that is, that role remains unattached to the self-notion.

VII
Self-notions and "I"

The word "I" refers to the speaker or writer. Thus the meaning of the first person associates it with a role in the situation of discourse. One reason for having such a word is that it puts a modest cognitive load on the hearer in a variety of common speech situations. One is a face to face speech situation, in which some of the information a speaker is providing will be likely to motivate actions towards the speaker. So, for example, you and I are sitting at a table and I say: "I'd like some salt." I want you to hand the salt to me. You, being an agreeable sort, will hand the salt to anyone who wants it. In order for my request to work, I simply have to depend on you knowing

English, and being able to tell that the person speaking to you is the person playing a certain perceptual role. You don't have to know anything more about me.

If, on the other hand, I were to say, "John Perry would like some salt", there is no telling what you might do. Perhaps you would say, "Good for him". My request puts a larger cognitive load on you; you need to know more in order to be expected to accede to it. You need to have recognized the person before you as a person named "John Perry". Even if I'm pretty certain that you do know who I am – perhaps we are old friends – it will still sound odd and sort of pompous to say "John Perry wants salt". The only fact relevant to your passing the salt would usually be that I am a human being who wants the salt.

On the other hand, use of the first person is inappropriate in other situations. If I call you on the phone, and you clearly don't recognize my voice, I need to tell you my name, and it's impolite to do otherwise.

The first person also puts a relatively light cognitive load on the speaker. When Mach had amnesia, he still referred to himself with "I" – or "ich" at any rate. To know that he was doing so he needed to know i) the meaning of "I" and ii) that he was the utterer of the words he was speaking. That is, he needed to realize that the words he was going to speak, the one's he was planning to say, would be spoken by him. There is in fact a certain way of knowing whom words are spoken by, when the words are the result of one's own planning and articulating; they will be spoken by the planner and articulator, and hence, if the word is "I", will refer to that person. Thus, a person who has forgotten who they are, and so no longer has an enduring notion associated with the self-role, may nevertheless successfully and confidently refer to himself or herself.

Most of us don't get amnesia, so having a referring device that enables us to refer to ourselves without knowing very much about ourselves isn't all that important. But in philosophy, having such a device is often of great value. The point isn't that we don't know much about ourselves, but that we don't want to assume much about ourselves. Why should Descartes say "I think" rather than "Descartes thinks?"[10] When he says "I think" he does not assume that there is a person with a past like Descartes has and a name "Descartes". He can use the method of doubt to bracket all of that knowledge he has of himself.

Now what Descartes can't quite do is to refer to himself without assuming anything except what he is entitled to at the beginning of the Second Meditation. For to refer to himself with "I" (or "je") he needs to assume that there is a language with a word in it that refers to the person who uses it. But, to be fair, to write his *Meditations*, as opposed to merely meditating them, Descartes does need to assume that, or at least play along with his inclination to believe that, there is a language.

The first person, then, does not give philosophers as secure a way of talking about themselves as their self-notions give them of thinking about themselves. I can think about myself so long as I exist and have a self-notion, even if there is no language at all, although in the case I cannot refer to myself. But first person pronouns, like "I", "ich" and "je", give philosophers a pretty secure way of referring to themselves, one that should satisfy all but the most dedicated solipsists. The most dedicated solipsists don't write very much anyway.

Notes

1 The first sections of this paper are intended to present basically the same account that was developed in J. Perry, "Self-Notions", in: *Logos* (1990), pp. 17–31, from which it borrows some examples and prose. I believe this essay is clearer about the structure of agent-relative knowledge and the relations between the three kinds of knowledge, and connects with the ideas developed in "Rip Van Winkle and Other Characters" (cf. note 4).
2 Cf. S. Shoemaker, *Identity, Cause, and Mind* (Cambridge: Cambridge University Press, 1984) and *The First-Person Perspective and Other Essays* (Cambridge: Cambridge University Press, 1996); (cf. also note 7)

3   Cf. J. Perry, "Thought Without Representation", in: *Supplementary Proceedings of the Aristotelian Society* 60 (1986), pp. 263–83. Reprinted in J. Perry, *The Problem of the Essential Indexical* (New York: Oxford University Press, 1993).
4   J. Perry, "Rip Van Winkle and Other Characters", in: *European Review of Philosophy* 2 (1997), pp. 13–40.
5   Ernst Mach, *The Analysis of Sensations*, translated by C. M. Williams and S. Waterlow (Chicago, London: Open Court, 1914), p. 4n.
6   Ibid.
7   S. Shoemaker, "Persons and Their Pasts", in: *American Philosophical Quarterly* 7 (1970), pp. 269–285.
8   Or at least "quasi-remember"; one quasi-remembers an experience if one fulfills all of the conditions other than being the original experiencer (cf. also note 2).
9   In many situations, looking into a mirror is a normally self-informative way of getting information. In Mach's case the mirror was far away and not set up for self-viewing, and he didn't seem to realize at first that he was looking into a mirror.
10 Cf. E. G. M. Anscombe, "The First Person", in: *Demonstratives*, ed. P. Yourgrau (Oxford: Oxford University Press, 1990), p. 136. Originally published in: *Mind and Language*, ed. S. Guttenplan (Oxford: Clarendon Press, 1975), pp. 45–64.

de
Wolfgang Carl

Ich und Spontaneität

Es ist eine Besonderheit des Wortes „ich", daß seine philosophische Betrachtung sowohl Beziehungen zwischen verschiedenen philosophischen Disziplinen als auch Verbindungen gegenwärtiger Philosophien mit den Überlegungen der Philosophen der Vergangenheit herauszustellen erlaubt. Semantische Theorien zur indexikalischen Referenz, epistemologische Betrachtungen zum Verhältnis unseres Wissens von unserem Denken und Wollen zu unserem Wissen von einer von uns unabhängigen Welt und Erörterungen des Begriffs des Bewußtseins und des Mentalen überhaupt überschneiden sich bei einer Analyse von Phänomenen, die wir sprachlich nur durch die Verwendung des Wortes „ich" zum Ausdruck bringen können. Die Beschäftigung mit solchen Phänomenen zieht sich wie ein roter Faden durch die philosophische Entwicklung Wittgensteins, von den frühen „Tagebüchern" bis zu den späten Aufzeichnungen der „Philosophischen Psychologie". Aber es handelt sich hier nicht um eine fixe Idee der Philosophen dieses Jahrhunderts, sondern Philosophen wie Descartes und Kant haben Behauptungen wie „cogito sum" oder „Das *Ich denke* muß alle meine Vorstellungen begleiten können" eine zentrale Rolle für die Erklärung der Möglichkeit von Erkenntnis zugesprochen. Es ist zu vermuten, daß sie diese Rolle nicht haben können, ohne daß das Wort „ich" gebraucht wird. Seine philosophische Betrachtung lädt dazu ein, systematische Überlegungen mit philosophisch-historischen Untersuchungen, die gegenwärtige Philosophie mit ihrer Geschichte zu verbinden. Der Komplexität dieses Themas werden die folgenden Gedanken nur in sehr bescheidener Weise, wenn überhaupt, gerecht. Sie sind nicht mehr als eine Skizze, die im Anschluß an Kants Konzeption der Apperzeption entwickelt wird.

Das Interesse, das gegenwärtige Philosophen an dieser Konzeption nehmen, ist im wesentlichen von den Argumentationsstrategien her bestimmt, in denen diese Konzeption eine Rolle spielt, – von der Destruktion eines cartesianischen Ich-Begriffs im „Paralogismus"-Kapitel einerseits und von dem Nachweis der objektiven Gültigkeit der Kategorien im Deduktions-Kapitel andererseits. Im Kontext der analytischen Philosophie hat dies dazu geführt, daß der Begriff der Apperzeption nur im Hinblick darauf betrachtet wird, was er zu einer Widerlegung des cartesianischen Dualismus und des Skeptizismus beiträgt.[1] Was jedoch bei dieser restringierten Rezeption nicht in den Blick kommt, sind die Konzeption selbst und die sie konstituierenden Begriffe. Es ist daher kein Zufall, daß Kants Überlegungen zur Spontaneität und zum Ich-Begriff kaum zur Kenntnis genommen werden. Dies hat aber zur Folge, daß seine Beiträge zur Diskussion eines der zentralen Probleme der gegenwärtigen Philosophie übersehen werden. Ich meine die Rolle, die der sogenannte „Standpunkt der ersten Person" für das Verstehen von uns selbst und anderen und für die Möglichkeit von Wissen überhaupt hat. Dieser „blinde Fleck" auf der nicht undifferenzierten Landkarte gegenwärtiger Kant-Rezeption ist um so bedauerlicher, als er einer der ersten, wenn nicht der erste gewesen ist, der diese Rolle erkannt hat.

Das Besondere seiner Position wird deutlich, wenn man das bemerkenswerte, aber – soweit ich sehe – bislang nicht bemerkte Faktum betrachtet, daß Wittgenstein im „Blue Book" eine Unterscheidung trifft, die nicht nur aus terminologischen Gründen zu einem Vergleich mit einer entsprechenden kantischen Unterscheidung einlädt.[2] Es handelt sich um die Unterscheidung zwischen der Verwendung des Ausdrucks „ich" als „Subjekt" und als „Objekt". Wittgenstein hat diese Terminologie später nicht mehr verwendet, aber es ist nicht schwierig, das Thema selbst in seinen späteren, artikulierteren Überlegungen wiederzuerkennen. Die Unterscheidung im *Blue Book* ist zugleich der Ausgangspunkt für eine Reihe von wichtigen Beiträgen zum Ich-Begriff gewesen.[3] Auch Kant unterscheidet zwischen einem „Ich als Subjekt" und einem „Ich als Objekt"[4] und verbindet mit dieser Unterscheidung eine transzendentalphilosophische Erklärung des Ich-Begriffs, die von einer Betrachtung dieses Begriffs im Rahmen der empirischen Psychologie abgegrenzt wird. Um Kants Projekt deutlich zu machen, ist es sinnvoll, das Verhältnis der von beiden Philosophen getroffenen Unterscheidung genauer zu betrachten.

Wittgenstein erörtert zwei Verwendungen des Ausdrucks „ich", die sich aufgrund der Prädikate, die ich mir selber zuschreibe, voneinander unterscheiden. Der Ausdruck wird als Objekt verwendet, wenn ich etwa sage, daß ich drei Zentimeter gewachsen bin oder mir den Arm gebrochen habe; er wird dagegen als Subjekt verwendet, wenn ich sage, daß ich Schmerzen habe oder glaube, daß es regnen wird. Worin besteht der Unterschied? Im ersten Fall geht es darum, eine bestimmte Person zu identifizieren, und dabei kann die Möglichkeit eines Irrtums nicht ausgeschlossen werden: „The possibility of an error has been provided for."[5] Im zweiten Fall dagegen kann eine solche Möglichkeit nicht auftreten: Ich kann nicht wissen, daß jemand Schmerzen hat, aber mir im unklaren darüber sein, ob ich es bin, der sie hat. Die Gefahr, daß ich mich mit einem anderen verwechsle, besteht nicht. Wittgenstein zieht daraus den Schluß, daß die Äußerung des Satzes „ich habe Schmerzen" überhaupt gar keine Behauptung über eine bestimmte Person ist.[6]

Die Unterscheidung, die Wittgenstein macht, muß im Lichte dieser Schlußfolgerung gesehen werden. Es geht ihm darum, zwei Arten von Selbstzuschreibungen so voneinander zu unterscheiden, daß im einen Fall von einer genuinen Referenz, die der Möglichkeit des Irrtums und der Verwechslung ausgesetzt ist, geredet werden kann, während im anderen Fall eine solche Möglichkeit nicht gegeben ist und daher die Annahme einer referentiellen Bezugnahme auf mich selbst bezweifelt werden muß. Gegeben die zusätzliche, m. E. irrige Annahme, daß die Verwendung des Ausdrucks „ich" als Subjekt nur bei der Selbstzuschreibung mentaler Prädikate auftritt, so ist zumindest verständlich, wie Wittgenstein in seinen gleichzeitigen *Notes for Lectures on Private Experience and Sense Data* zu der Auffassung gelangt, daß „the idea of the ego inhabiting a body [has] to be abolished"[7], und wie er dann zu einer nicht-deskriptiven und daher auch nicht-kognitiven Interpretation mentaler Selbstzuschreibung in der ersten Person kommt. Betrachtet man die Unterscheidung des Ichs als „Subjekt" vom Ich als „Objekt" in diesem größeren Zusammenhang, so wird deutlich, daß es Wittgenstein eigentlich nicht darum geht, eine Unterscheidung zu treffen, sondern vielmehr darum, die sinnvolle Verwendung des „ich" als „Subjekt" und die Möglichkeit eines Wissens mentaler Selbstzuschreibungen in der ersten Person in Zweifel zu ziehen.

Kants Unterscheidung zwischen dem „Ich als Subjekt" und dem „Ich als Objekt" differiert nicht nur in der Sache von derjenigen Wittgensteins, sondern auch in der Absicht, mit der sie getroffen wird. Kant geht es nicht darum, die verschiedenen Rollen voneinander abzugrenzen, die ein erkennendes Wesen innerhalb der ihm möglichen Erkenntnisse zu übernehmen hat. Ein solches Wesen besitzt „das Vermögen, zu sich selbst ich zu sagen"[8], und muß als ein erkennendes Wesen ein Bewußtsein davon haben, daß es sowohl eine Spontaneität des Verstandes als auch eine Rezeptivität der Sinnlichkeit besitzt. Auf der Grundlage dieser beiden konstitutiven Merkmale von Erkenntnis ergibt sich die Bestimmung des Ichs als Subjekt des Denkens einerseits und die Bestimmung des Ichs als Objekt sinnlicher Wahrnehmung andererseits. Es handelt sich nicht um ein doppeltes Ich, „welches widersprechend wäre"[9], sondern darum, daß „Ich, als denkendes Wesen, […] mit Mir, als Sinnenwesen, ein und dasselbe Subject bin"[10]. Das Wissen, das ein solches Subjekt von seiner Erkenntnismöglichkeit besitzt, artikuliert sich in einem Bewußtsein des „Ich der Reflexion"[11], auch „*reine* Apperzeption" genannt, und in einem Bewußtsein des Ich der „Apprehension" oder empirischen Apperzeption.[12]

Schon diese grobe Skizze zeigt deutlich, daß Kants Unterscheidung nicht in der Tradition einer letztlich Descartes verpflichteten Differenzierung der Selbstzuschreibungen von Prädikaten steht, sondern in den Kontext einer Analyse der uns möglichen Erkenntnis gehört. Da Spontaneität und Rezeptivität Bedingungen einer solchen Erkenntnis abgeben, können das „Ich als Subjekt" und das „Ich als Objekt" auch keine Arten von Wissen und keine Inhalte der Erkenntnis voneinander abgrenzen. Nicht Elimination, sondern Integration des „Ichs als Subjekt" in eine Theorie der formalen Bedingungen von Erkenntnis ist das Ziel von Kants Überlegungen. Gerade an seiner Analyse dieses Ichs wird der fundamentale Unterschied zwischen ihm und Wittgenstein und auch der Tradition, in der dieser immer noch steht, faßbar.

Um diesen Unterschied ins rechte Licht zu setzen, ist es nötig, einen Blick auf Kants Konzeption der synthetischen Einheit der Apperzeption zu werfen. Sie kann als eine Analyse der Bedingungen verstanden werden, unter denen die Rede von „meinen Vorstellungen" steht. In moderner Terminologie formuliert, geht es um Selbstzuschreibungen von Meinungen vom Standpunkt der ersten Person aus. Über solche Vorstellungen zu verfügen, ist eine notwendige Bedingung für die Möglichkeit, Erkenntnisse zu haben und zu erwerben, sofern man von der Voraussetzung ausgeht, daß diese Möglichkeit mit Hilfe des Begriffs der Vorstellung zu erklären ist. Kants Konzeption der Apperzeption enthält drei Gesichtspunkte, die bei einer solchen Erklärung zu berücksichtigen sind. Das „Denken, das meine Vorstellungen muß begleiten können", ist nichts anderes, als daß ich von jeder meiner Vorstellungen wissen und urteilen kann, daß es meine Vorstellung ist. Meine Vorstellungen sind Vorstellungen von diesem und jenem, aber daß es meine Vorstellungen sind, weiß ich oder kann ich wissen ganz unabhängig davon, ob sie korrekt oder adäquat sind. Das Denken, das sie muß begleiten können, besteht darin, daß ich urteile, solche Vorstellungen zu haben; und dasjenige, was gedacht wird oder Inhalt des Urteils ist, ist der Umstand, daß ich sie habe. Selbstzuschreibung von Mentalem, so kann man auch sagen, impliziert die Fähigkeit, Urteile vom Standpunkt der ersten Person aus zu fällen. Der Ausdruck „ich denke" steht für diese Form des Urteils. Trägt man nun dem Umstand Rechnung, daß meine sinnlichen Vorstellungen oder Anschauungen stets eine Mannigfaltigkeit bilden, dann besagt dies, daß die Verwendung des Ausdrucks „ich denke" mit der Annahme verbunden werden muß, daß es ein und dasselbe Subjekt ist, das verschiedene Vorstellungen hat. Die Spontaneität des Urteilens steht unter der Bedingung der Identität desjenigen, der im Hinblick auf seine gegebenen Vorstellungen und auf ihrer Grundlage Urteile fällt.

Der zweite Gesichtspunkt knüpft an die besondere Art des Wissens an, das mit der Selbstzuschreibung des eigenen Mentalen zu verbinden ist und das in der philosophischen Tradition als Bewußtsein bestimmt wurde. Es ist ein Wissen, für das es keine Kriterien gibt und für welches das Subjekt der Selbstzuschreibung eine besondere Autorität besitzt.[13] Kant führt hier den Begriff der Apperzeption[14] ein, wobei er sich im Rahmen seiner transzendentalen Betrachtung auf den Fall der „reinen Apperzeption" beschränkt, die als eine formale Bedingung von Erkenntnis sowohl von der empirischen Apperzeption als auch von der empirischen Selbsterkenntnis zu unterscheiden ist.

Der dritte Gesichtspunkt verbindet die Spontaneität der Verwendung von „ich denke" für eine Mannigfaltigkeit meiner gegebenen Vorstellungen mit dem Bewußtsein der Identität des Subjekts dieser Vorstellung, um die Einheit des Selbstbewußtseins herauszustellen. Es handelt sich um eine Einheit, die ihren Ausdruck in der Gemeinsamkeit findet, die meine Vorstellungen aufweisen, sofern sie unter den beiden zuerst genannten Gesichtspunkten betrachtet werden. Die Einheit des Selbstbewußtseins besteht darin, daß meine Vorstellungen Vorstellungen sind, die der Spontaneität meiner Verwendung von „ich denke" zugänglich sind und unter der Bedingung der Möglichkeit von Identitätsbewußtsein stehen. Daß diese Einheit als eine transzendentale Einheit angesehen wird, verweist auf die argumentative Rolle, die dem Begriff der Einheit der Apperzeption für die folgenden Überlegungen zukommt: Die Bedingung, die Vorstellungen erfüllen müssen, sofern sie als meine Vorstellungen anzusehen sind, soll als eine Bedingung ausgewiesen werden, die im Rahmen einer transzendentalen Erklärung von Erkenntnis eine Rolle spielt. Diese Bedingung besteht in der synthetischen Einheit der Apperzeption und besagt, daß eine Mannigfaltigkeit meiner Vorstellungen nur dann die Bedingungen der Selbstzuschreibung erfüllt, wenn meine Vorstellungen synthetisch verbunden sind und somit eine synthetische Einheit aufweisen. Ob Kant diese These bewiesen hat und, wenn ja, wie, braucht uns hier nicht zu interessieren.

Was uns beschäftigt, ist vielmehr die Frage, weshalb Kant den ersten Gesichtspunkt seiner Konzeption der synthetischen Einheit der Apperzeption, also den Akt der Spontaneität der Beurteilung meiner gegebenen Vorstellungen, mit der Verwendung des Ausdrucks „ich" verbindet. Es ist ein bemerkenswertes Faktum, daß er die Rolle, welche die reine Apperzeption als eine formale Bedingung von Denken oder Erkennen spielen soll, stets mit Hilfe der Verwendung des Ausdrucks „ich" beschreibt. Es ist ja ein „Ich denke", das alle meine Vorstellungen muß begleiten können; das „Subjekt der Apperzeption" wird als ein Ich, als ein „logisches Ich"[15] gedacht, und es ist das „Ich als Subjekt des Denkens", von dem Kant erklärt, daß es „die reine Apperzeption bedeutet"[16]. Wie erklärt sich der Zusammenhang zwischen dem Begriff der Apperzeption und der Rede vom „ich"?

Eine mögliche Antwort ergibt sich, wenn man Kants Konzeption der Apperzeption von Descartes aus versteht und, wie etwa Henrich, annimmt, daß das Selbstbewußtsein „in cartesianischer Gewißheit erschlossen ist".[17] Meint man mit dieser Gewißheit das unmittelbare, d. h. „kriterienlose" Wissen, das Descartes einem denkenden Wesen als ein Wissen von seinen mentalen Zuständen zusprach, so kann eine solche Gewißheit zwar erklären, weshalb es sich um ein Wissen handelt, das nur vom Standpunkt der ersten Person aus zugänglich und daher auch nur durch die Verwendung des Ausdrucks „ich" formulierbar ist. Aber diese Interpretation verkennt den formalen Charakter der Apperzeption und macht aus einer Bedingung, die die Form des Denkens betrifft, eine inhaltliche Erkenntnis des epistemischen Subjekts, die Kant ausdrücklich als eine empirische Erkenntnis bezeichnet hat.[18]

Eine andere Erklärung des Zusammenhangs von Apperzeption und der Verwendung des Ausdrucks „ich" könnte darin bestehen, diesen Ausdruck als eine Art Variable zu verstehen, die unter einer gegebenen Interpretation durch eine geeignete Individuenkonstante zu ersetzen ist. Wer immer denkt oder Vorstellungen hat, muß auch imstande sein können, zu urteilen, daß er denkt oder Vorstellungen hat. Der Gebrauch von „ich" ergibt sich durch die von Kant gemeinte Allgemeinheit einer formalen Bedingung von Denken und Vorstellen und kann in jedem Einzelfall durch die Verwendung von Namen und Kennzeichnungen ersetzt werden.

Gegen diese Auffassung spricht jedoch, daß Kant immer wieder auf die fundamentale Bedeutung des Standpunkts der ersten Person für das menschliche Denken und Handeln hingewiesen hat[19] und es daher geboten ist, dieser Überzeugung bei der Interpretation der Apperzeption Rechnung zu tragen. Wesen, die in ihrer „Vorstellung das Ich haben" können, sind Personen,[20] und Personen sind Wesen, die ein Bewußtsein ihrer numerischen Identität haben.[21] Kant hat sich bereits in den siebziger Jahren ausführlich mit dem Zusammenhang von Ich und Person beschäftigt, und diese Überlegungen, die sich in „Reflexionen" zu Metaphysik- und Anthropologie-Vorlesungen, aber auch in den Nachschriften zu diesen Vorlesungen selbst erhalten haben, dienen der Klärung des Apperzeptions-Begriffs.

Daß „der Mensch in seiner Vorstellung das Ich haben kann", unterscheidet ihn von allen anderen Lebewesen.[22] Der Unterschied beruht darauf, daß andere Lebewesen zwar Vorstellungen äußerer Sinne, nicht aber Vorstellungen, die auf dem inneren Sinn beruhen, besitzen.[23] Diese Vorstellungen stehen unter der „allgemeinen Bedingung des inneren Sinnes; Bewußtseyn"[24]. Da Kant wohl kaum bestreiten will, daß Tiere in der Lage sind, Schmerzen zu empfinden, muß der Begriff der inneren Vorstellung von dieser Bedingung her verstanden werden; und dieses Bewußtsein, das für innere Vorstellungen charakteristisch ist, kann nicht als ein Empfinden oder Gewahrwerden, sondern muß als ein „Bewußtseyn seiner Selbst" gedacht werden.[25] Innere Vorstellungen sind daher nicht bloß thematisch als Vorstellungen von Nicht-Körperlichem, von Mentalem zu charakterisieren; es sind vielmehr die Ich-Zentriertheit des Mentalen, die Selbstzuschreibung und die Möglichkeit, eben dieses vom Standpunkt der ersten Person aus zu wissen, weitere Gesichtspunkte, die für ein adäquates Verständnis des Begriffs der inneren Vorstellung zu berücksichtigen sind. Die von Kant vorgenommene Abgrenzung der Menschen von den Tieren beruht also auf der spezifischen „Subjektivität des Mentalen"[26] und auf der Behauptung, daß nur derjenige den Ausdruck „ich" sinnvoll verwenden kann, der sich selbst Mentales zuschreiben kann. Dies bedeutet nicht, daß jemand, der den Ausdruck verwenden kann, sich nicht auch als Person im Sinne Strawsons, d. h. als Träger körperlicher *und* mentaler Eigenschaften verstehen muß: „Das Ich kann in zweifachem Verstande genommen werden: Ich als Mensch, und Ich als Intelligenz. Ich, als ein Mensch, bin ein Gegenstand des inneren und äußeren Sinnes. Ich als Intelligenz bin ein Gegenstand des inneren Sinnes nur."[27] Aber, wie sich noch zeigen wird, soll dies nicht besagen, daß es sich um verschiedene Gegenstände handelt; keine „doppelte Persönlichkeit"[28], sondern eine „vermischte"[29] ist gemeint; es geht um verschiedene Zugangsweisen zu demselben, das auf nicht reduzierbare Weise komplex zu charakterisieren ist. Kant unterscheidet daher auch zwischen einem engen und einem weiten Sinn, d. h. der „Gegenstand des innern Sinnes, dieses Subject, [ist] das Bewußtsein", wobei wir von dem „Object des inneren Sinnes alles Aeußere abstrahiren"[30].

Für den Zusammenhang von Apperzeption und Ich ist jedoch nicht dieses Ich in *sensu stricto*, das man auch die „psychologische" Person nennen könnte,[31] sondern ein bestimmter Fall solcher Selbstzuschreibungen wichtig. Es geht um ein „Ich [...] welches der *singularis* der Handlungen des Denkens ist"[32] um ein Ich, das als „Subjekt" einer Handlung, d. h. als ihr Träger und Ursprung fungiert.[33] Die Handlung ist der Akt des Denkens oder Urteilens, und die Erklärung seiner Möglichkeit wird in direktem Zusammenhang mit der Begründung freien Handelns gesehen: „Die Frage, ob die Freyheit möglich sey, ist vielleicht mit der einerley, ob der Mensch eine wahre Person sey oder ob das Ich in einem Wesen von äußeren Bestimmungen möglich sey".[34] Die Frage nach diesem Ich ist die Frage nach der Referenz solcher mentalen Selbstzuschreibungen, die *nicht* durch äußere Bestimmungen, durch Affektionen unserer Sinne oder unseres Begehrungsvermögens determiniert sind. Positiv formuliert: Es geht um ein Ich, das von sich aus denkt und will. Ein solches Ich ist „selbsttätig: Spontaneität, sofern ich aus mir selbst denke und will"[35]. Kant bezeichnet dieses Ich auch als „logische Persönlichkeit"[36], als logisches Ich.[37]

Kants Unterscheidung von verschiedenen Ichs ist keine Unterscheidung verschiedener Dinge, sondern verschiedener Betrachtungsweisen der Referenz mentaler Selbstzuschreibungen. Diese Zuschreibungen werden vom Standpunkt der ersten Person aus vorgenommen: Sie beruhen auf dem, was ich von mir wissen kann, sofern „ich mir meiner bewußt bin"[38]. Kant ist der Überzeugung, daß auf dieser Grundlage zwei Klassen mentaler Selbstzuschreibungen voneinander abzugrenzen sind: diejenigen, die „das Ich als leidend" darstellen, und diejenigen, die „das Ich als selbsttätig" hinstellen.[39] Nach seiner Meinung ist diese Einteilung vollständig und exklusiv.

Im Rahmen der theoretischen Philosophie läßt sich diese Unterscheidung mit der von Sinnlichkeit und Verstand korrelieren, die als Vermögen gedacht werden können, dasjenige zu haben oder zu erwerben, was ich mir als mentale Zustände zuschreibe. Diese können eingeteilt werden in mir gegebene Vorstellungen einerseits und in Vorstellungen meiner Spontaneität andererseits. In den *Prolegomena* heißt es: „Wenn uns Erscheinung gegeben ist, so sind wir noch ganz frei, wie wir die Sache daraus beurtheilen wollen. Jene, nämlich Erscheinung, beruhte auf den Sinnen, diese Beurtheilung aber auf dem Verstande."[40] Es ist nun das logische Ich, das als Träger und Ursprung der Beurteilung dessen, was immer mir gegeben sein mag, fungiert. Dieses Ich ist keine konkrete Person; es ist auch keine mentale Entität, die durch Introspektion erfaßt werden kann, sondern dient nur dazu, die mentalen Selbstzuschreibungen, die sich auf die Beurteilung durch den Verstand beziehen, von denen abzugrenzen, die auf das verweisen, was mir gegeben und daher durch von mir unabhängige Umstände bedingt ist. Da diese Selbstzuschreibungen vom Standpunkt der ersten Person aus erfolgen, liefern sie eine bestimmte Betrachtung von mir als einem logischen Ich, d. h. als einem Referenten dieser Beschreibungen, der als „frey und eine reine Selbstthätigkeit, die durch nichts anderes als sich selbst bestimmt ist", vorgestellt wird.[41] Das logische Ich ist nichts anderes als dasjenige, was als Referent der mentalen Selbstzuschreibungen fungiert, die sich auf die Beurteilung beziehen, d. h. auf den Akt des Urteils auf der Grundlage von gegebenen Vorstellungen und im Hinblick auf diese. Aber dieser Referent ist kein besonderer Gegenstand, sondern eine besondere Betrachtungsweise von Gegenständen, in diesem Falle von Personen oder Menschen, sofern sie als dasjenige fungieren, worauf mentale Selbstzuschreibungen einer besonderen Klasse von Prädikaten referieren. Kurz formuliert: Das logische Ich steht nicht für einen bestimmten Gegenstand, sondern für eine bestimmte Klasse von Prädikaten, genauer: für die Eigentümlichkeit, die ihre Selbstzuschreibung vom Standpunkt der ersten Person aus aufweist.

Zum Abschluß will ich Kants Konzeption des logischen Ichs auf dem Hintergrund von Wittgensteins Überlegungen zum „Ich als Subjekt" betrachten. Wittgenstein ging es um mentale Selbstzuschreibungen vom Standpunkt der ersten Person, und sein Ziel war es, den besonderen Status des Wissens um solche Zuschreibungen und den Träger dieses Wissens in Zweifel zu ziehen. Als Grundlage dieser auf Descartes zielenden Kritik diente ihm die Beobachtung, daß bei solchen Selbstzuschreibungen die Verwendung von „ich" immun gegenüber Irrtümern der Identifikation ist.[42] Die sich daran anschließende Diskussion hat gezeigt, daß diese Immunität nicht nur für mentale Selbstzuschreibungen gilt[43] und daß wir auch dann sinnvoll von Selbstreferenz reden können, wenn keine Identifikation vorgenommen wird.[44] Damit geraten die Grundlagen für Wittgensteins nichtdeskriptive und daher nicht-kognitive Deutung mentaler Selbstzuschreibungen ins Wanken. Seine grundsätzliche Kritik an Descartes' Annahme einer Autonomie des Wissens um das eigene Mentale wird durch diese Kritik jedoch nicht betroffen: Die Selbstzuschreibung mentaler Prädikate vom Standpunkt der ersten Person aus verlangt erstens die Selbstzuschreibung nicht-mentaler Prädikate von diesem Standpunkt aus und zweitens die Zuschreibung von mentalen Prädikaten an andere. Eine Kritik an der Autonomie des Wissens um das eigene Mentale findet sich denn auch bei Kant in seiner Widerlegung des Skeptizismus, aber sie hat nichts mit seinen Überlegungen zum logischen Ich zu tun.

Es ist wichtig, darauf hinzuweisen, daß diese Überlegungen Kants weder von Wittgensteins grundsätzlicher Kritik an Descartes noch von seinen irrigen Betrachtungen zum Gebrauch von „ich" bei mentalen Selbstzuschreibungen betroffen sind. Denn das logische Ich fungiert nicht ganz allgemein als Referent mentaler Selbstzuschreibungen vom Standpunkt der ersten Person aus. Kant geht es darum, eine bestimmte Betrachtung einer Person auszuzeichnen, die mit einer besonderen Klasse von Prädikaten verbunden wird, die sie vom Standpunkt der ersten Person aus sich selbst zuschreibt. Diese Prädikate bringen eine Beurteilung, eine assertorische Stellungnahme zu gegebenen Vorstellungen zum Ausdruck; und ein solches Prädikat vom Standpunkt der ersten Person sich selbst zuzuschreiben besagt, daß man als Träger und Grund einer solchen Beurteilung fungiert, daß man einen Akt der Spontaneität vollzieht. Kant interessiert sich dabei nicht für die Bedingungen mentaler Selbstzuschreibungen, noch will er die Kriterien für die Identität desjenigen formulieren, der sich selbst etwas zuschreibt. Daher lassen sich seine Überlegungen nicht in die von Wittgenstein geprägte Diskussion über mentale Selbstzuschreibungen integrieren. Das bedeutet aber nicht, daß das logische Ich als Träger und Grund einer spontanen Handlung für ein angemessenes Verständnis der Verwendung des Ausdrucks „ich" unerheblich ist.

Es ist bekanntlich Austin gewesen, der uns auf „explizite Performativa" aufmerksam gemacht hat, bei denen, wie er sich ausdrückt, "the 'I' who is doing the action does [...] come essentially into the picture".[45] Der Gebrauch des Wortes „ich" in performativen Äußerungen wird selten genauer betrachtet, wenn Philosophen sich mit diesem Wort beschäftigen. Denn das Besondere dieser Verwendung kommt nicht in den Blick, solange man sich an die beiden Standardfragen hält, die in der gegenwärtigen Philosophie diskutiert werden: Welche Rolle spielen Beschreibungen vom Standpunkt der ersten Person für unser Denken und Handeln,[46] und wie läßt sich die Rolle von „ich" als "essential indexical" gegenüber anderen singulären Termini abgrenzen?[47] Mit Kants Konzeption des logischen Ichs verhält es sich anders.

Performative Äußerungen haben zwar eine grammatische Ähnlichkeit mit Sätzen, die eine deskriptive Selbstzuschreibung vom Standpunkt der ersten Person geben, aber ein wichtiger Unterschied fällt sofort auf. Solche Sätze beschreiben meine Erfahrungen und Zustände von einem subjektiven Standpunkt aus, während performative Äußerungen Handlungen darstellen. Um ich-zentrierte Beschreibungen verstehen zu können, muß ich auch verstehen können, daß andere mir so etwas zuschreiben können. Diese wechselseitige Abhängigkeit der Standpunkte der ersten und dritten Person gilt sicherlich auch für performative Äußerungen, aber sie impliziert in diesem Falle nicht eine Differenz zwischen zwei Beschreibungen desselben, sondern zwischen dem Vollzug einer Handlung und dem Konstatieren dieses Vollzugs. Die Möglichkeit, dies zu Recht zu konstatieren, setzt voraus, daß eine solche Handlung durch eine performative Äußerung vollzogen wird, aber nicht umgekehrt. Die wechselseitige Abhängigkeit unter dem

Gesichtspunkt der Verständlichkeit schließt eine einseitige reale Abhängigkeit nicht aus. Das „ich", das in solchen Äußerungen verwendet wird, steht für den Grund und den Träger der Handlung und zeigt ein Wesen, das eines „Aktus der Spontaneität" fähig ist, aber beschreibt und identifiziert es nicht. Daher sagt Kant zu Recht, daß das „ich denke", verstanden als „ich urteile", ein Aktus der Spontaneität ist.

Das „ich", das in performativen Äußerungen verwendet wird, ist ohne Zweifel ein "essential indexical", denn seine Ersetzung durch eine Kennzeichnung oder auch einen Namen zerstört in der Regel den performativen Charakter der Äußerung. Die Diskussion über indexikalische Ausdrücke hat zwar gezeigt, daß die Semantik von „ich" nicht nach dem Vorbild von Namen oder Kennzeichnungen modelliert werden kann, aber sie hat dem performativen Charakter von Äußerungen, in denen „ich" als "essential indexical" vorkommt, nicht Rechnung getragen. Kant hat sich nicht für die Besonderheiten indexikalischer Referenz interessiert; es geht ihm um das Ich, das, wie es in einer Reflexion zur Metaphysik heißt, „der *singularis* der Handlungen des Denkens ist"[48]. Solche Verwendungen des Ausdrucks „ich" bringen eine Stellungnahme und Bewertung gegebener Vorstellungen oder Meinungen zum Ausdruck, die ihrer Form nach mit Intentionen zweiter Stufe vergleichbar sind.

Frankfurt hat auf solche Intentionen aufmerksam gemacht, um den Begriff der Person zu erläutern. Intentionen zweiter Stufe sind Intentionen, die sich auf Intentionen erster Stufe beziehen. Es ist leicht zu sehen, daß dieser allgemeine Begriff nicht ausreicht, um die von Frankfurt und Dennett vertretene These zu charakterisieren, daß die Fähigkeit einer „reflective self-evaluation that is manifested in the formation of second-order desires" eine wesentliche Eigenschaft von Personen ist.[49] Denn eine solche Stellungnahme ist nur dann eine Stellungnahme zu den eigenen Intentionen, kann daher nur dann den Charakter reflexiver Selbstbewertung haben, wenn sich die Intention zweiter Stufe in der Form der Selbstzuschreibung auf eine Intention erster Stufe bezieht, die wiederum auf diese Weise zugeschrieben wird. Dies ist aber nur dann möglich, wenn wir das Schema „x intendiert, daß y intendiert" so interpretieren, daß nicht nur gilt, daß x identisch mit y ist, sondern daß weiterhin gilt, daß die

Variablen durch den Ausdruck „ich" ersetzt werden. Selbstzuschreibungen verlangen die Verwendung dieses Worts, und die Möglichkeit von Stellungnahmen, die den Charakter „reflexiver Selbstbewertung" haben, ist auf die nicht-eliminierbare Verwendung des Wortes „ich" angewiesen. Der Gebrauch von koextensiven Namen oder Kennzeichnungen kann hier nicht genügen.

Es ist ein Irrtum zu glauben, daß solche reflexiven Selbstbewertungen nur im Bereich des Handelns von Bedeutung sind – ein Irrtum, wie er z. B. Tugendhats Abgrenzung des epistemischen Selbstbewußtseins vom praktischen Selbstverhältnis zugrunde liegt. Für ihn „fallen diese nicht unter eine einheitliche Gattung"[50], und „dasjenige Wissen von uns selbst, das wir ohnehin haben, kann nicht praktisch relevant sein"[51]. Während die letzte Behauptung ebenso dogmatisch wie unplausibel wirkt, ist die erstere Behauptung leicht zu widerlegen. Nicht nur ist für beide Bereiche der Standpunkt der ersten Person von entscheidender Bedeutung,[52] sondern wir sind auch in beiden Fällen mit dem Phänomen reflexiver Selbstbewertung konfrontiert. Wie schon Frege deutlich gesehen hat, ist das Verständnis der Möglichkeit des Irrtums für unseren Begriff der Meinung, des „Fürwahrhaltens", konstitutiv.[53] Diese Möglichkeit setzt nicht nur die Unterscheidung zwischen wahren und falschen Meinungen voraus, sondern auch, daß man sich eine Meinung über seine eigene Meinung bildet, also eine Meinung zweiter Stufe, die den Charakter reflexiver Selbstbewertung hat. Die Fähigkeit, unsere Meinungen zu korrigieren, ist Teil einer allgemeinen Kompetenz der Beurteilung der Verläßlichkeit und Kohärenz unserer Überzeugungen. Diese Kompetenz ist an die Fähigkeit der Verwendung des Ausdrucks „ich" gebunden und gehört zu dem, was es heißt, den Standpunkt der ersten Person einzunehmen. Sie ist für unser Selbstverständnis als epistemische Subjekte nicht weniger wichtig als die Fähigkeit, Intentionen zweiter Stufe zu haben, für das Selbstverständnis als Personen. Es gibt eine philosophische Tradition, die jene Kompetenz der Beurteilung unserer Meinungen auf die cartesianische Gewißheit unserer Meinungen und somit auf einen besonderen Fall von Meinungen zweiter Stufe reduziert, also auf das, was Tugendhat „epistemisches Selbstbewußtsein" nennt. Diese Tradition gibt nicht nur im

Rahmen der theoretischen Philosophie ein unvollständiges und unbefriedigendes Bild des Standpunkts der ersten Person; sie verkennt auch, wie das Beispiel von Tugendhat zeigt, den Zusammenhang, der zwischen unserem Selbstverständnis als denkende Wesen und unserem Selbstverständnis als handelnde Personen besteht. Man kann daher sagen, daß Kants Konzeption des logischen Ichs nicht nur Wittgensteins eliminativer Analyse des „Ichs als Subjekt" überlegen ist, sondern auch gerade die Besonderheiten der Verwendung des Wortes „ich" ins Zentrum stellt, die in der heutigen Diskussion nicht berücksichtigt werden, aber, was das Beispiel der expliziten Performativa zeigt, für ein adäquates Verständnis seiner Verwendung unverzichtbar sind. Eine solche Betrachtung kann uns dazu bringen, diejenigen, die das Wort „ich" kompetent gebrauchen, als Wesen zu verstehen, die einer „reflexiven Selbstbewertung" ihres Denkens, Tuns und Wollens fähig sind. Nicht die cartesianischen Gewißheiten solcher Wesen, sondern die Spontaneität ihres Verstandesgebrauchs ist der eigentliche Ausgangspunkt für eine philosophische Analyse der Bedingungen der Möglichkeit von Denken und Erkennen, wie sie in der „Deduktion der Kategorien" versucht wird.

Anmerkungen

1   Cf. P. F. Strawson, *The Bounds of Sense*, London 1966, S. 97 ff., 162 ff.; J. McDowell, *Mind and World*, London 1994, S. 99 ff.
2   L. Wittgenstein, *The Blue and Brown Books*, Oxford 1958, S. 66 f.
3   Cf. G. E. M. Anscombe, „The First Person", in: *Self-Knowledge*, ed. Q. Cassam, Oxford 1994, S. 140 ff.; S. Shoemaker, „Self-Reference and Self-Awareness", in: *Journal of Philosophy* 65 (1968), S. 555 ff.; G. Evans, *The Varieties of Reference*, Oxford 1982, S. 215 ff.
4   Im folgenden wird Kant nach *Kant's gesammelten Schriften*, herausgegeben von der Königlich Preußischen Akademie der Wissenschaften und ihren Nachfolgern, Berlin 1900 ff. (= Akademie-Ausgabe [in der Folge: AA]) unter Angabe des Bandes in römischen und der Seitenangabe in arabischen Ziffern zitiert. Wo dies angezeigt erscheint, folgen zusätzlich

mit entsprechender Titelangabe bzw. nach Erstnennung mit Kurztitel die Seitenangaben der Originalausgabe(n) (A bzw. B); hier: AA VII 134 Anm., *Anthropologie in pragmatischer Hinsicht* [in der Folge: *Anthropologie*] BA 14 ff. Anm.; cf. auch AA XX 270, *Welches sind die wirklichen Fortschritte, die die Metaphysik seit Leibnitzens und Wolf's Zeiten in Deutschland gemacht hat?* [in der Folge: *Preisschrift: Fortschritte der Metaphysik*] A 35.
5 *The Blue and Brown Books* (cf. Anm. 2), S. 67.
6 Ibid.
7 „Notes for Lectures on 'Private Experience' and 'Sense Data'", in: *Philosophical Review* 77 (1968), S. 282; cf. auch *Wittgenstein und der Wiener Kreis von Friedrich Waismann*, ed. B. F. McGuinness, Frankfurt 1967, S. 49.
8 AA XX 270, *Preisschrift: Fortschritte der Metaphysik* A 35.
9 AA VII 134 Anm., *Anthropologie* BA 15 Anm.
10 AA VII 142, *Anthropologie* BA 27.
11 AA VII 141, *Anthropologie* BA 27.
12 AA VII, S. 134 Anm., *Anthropologie* BA 15 Anm.
13 Cf. D. Davidson, „Knowing One's Own Mind", in: Q. Cassam, loc. cit. (cf. Anm. 3), S. 43 ff., G. Evans, loc. cit. (cf. Anm. 3), S. 205 ff.
14 Cf. W. Carl, *Die Transzendentale Deduktion der Kategorien*, Frankfurt 1992, S. 60 ff.
15 AA XX 270, *Preisschrift: Fortschritte der Metaphysik* A 36.
16 AA VII 134 Anm., *Anthropologie* BA 15 Anm.
17 Cf. D. Henrich, *Identität und Objektivität*, Heidelberg 1976, S. 44.
18 AA III 275, *Kritik der reinen Vernunft* B 422 Anm.
19 Cf. AA VII 127, *Anthropologie* BA 3 f. (§ 1); sowie AA XX 270, *Preisschrift: Fortschritte der Metaphysik* A 36.
20 AA VII 127, *Anthropologie* BA 3.
21 Cf. AA III 268, *Kritik der reinen Vernunft* 408.
22 AA VII 127, *Anthropologie* BA 3; cf. auch XX 270, *Preisschrift: Fortschritte der Metaphysik* A 35; sowie AA XXVIII 275 f., *Vorlesungen über Metaphysik* L_1 (Psychologie nach Pölitz).
23 AA XXVIII 276, *Vorlesungen* (Bd. V), *Vorlesungen über Metaphysik* L_1 (Psychologie nach Pölitz).
24 AA XVII 468, *Kant's handschriftlicher Nachlaß* (Bd. IV), *Reflexionen zur Metaphysik* Refl. 4230.
25 AA XXVIII 276, *Vorlesungen* (Bd. V), *Vorlesungen über Metaphysik* L_1 (Psychologie nach Pölitz); cf. auch AA XVIII 72, *Kant's handschriftlicher Nachlaß* (Bd. V), *Reflexionen zur Metaphysik* Refl. 5049.
26 Cf. Th. Nagel, *The View from Nowhere*, Oxford 1986, S. 28 ff.

27 AA XXVIII 224, *Vorlesungen* (Bd. V), *Vorlesungen über Metaphysik L*$_1$ (Psychologie nach Pölitz).
28 AA XX 270, *Preisschrift: Fortschritte der Metaphysik* A 36.
29 AA XV 663, *Kant's handschriftlicher Nachlaß* (Bd. II), *Reflexionen zur Anthropologie* Refl. 1482.
30 AA XXVIII 265, *Vorlesungen* (Bd. V), *Vorlesungen über Metaphysik L*$_1$ (Psychologie nach Pölitz).
31 Cf. AA VII 134 Anm., *Anthropologie* BA 15 Anm.
32 AA XVII 470, *Kant's handschriftlicher Nachlaß* (Bd. IV), *Reflexionen zur Metaphysik* Refl. 4234.
33 Cf. AA XVII 573, *Kant's handschriftlicher Nachlaß* (Bd. IV), *Reflexionen zur Metaphysik* Refl. 4495.
34 AA XVII 464 f., *Kant's handschriftlicher Nachlaß* (Bd. IV), *Reflexionen zur Metaphysik* Refl. 4225.
35 AA XV 80, *Kant's handschriftlicher Nachlaß* (Bd. II), *Reflexionen zur Anthropologie* Refl. 208.
36 AA XVIII 72, *Kant's handschriftlicher Nachlaß* (Bd. V), *Reflexionen zur Metaphysik* Refl. 5049.
37 Cf. AA XX 270, *Preisschrift: Fortschritte der Metaphysik* A 36; sowie AA VII 134 Anm., *Anthropologie* BA 15 Anm.
38 AA XV 80, *Kant's handschriftlicher Nachlaß* (Bd. II), *Reflexionen zur Anthropologie* Refl. 208; cf. auch AA XX 270, *Preisschrift: Fortschritte der Metaphysik* A 36.
39 AA XV 80, *Kant's handschriftlicher Nachlaß* (Bd. II), *Reflexionen zur Anthropologie* Refl. 208.
40 AA IV 290, *Prolegomena* A 65.
41 AA XVIII 182, *Kant's handschriftlicher Nachlaß* (Bd. V), *Reflexionen zur Metaphysik* Refl. 5441.
42 L. Wittgenstein, *Philosophische Untersuchungen* § 404.
43 Cf. G. Evans, loc. cit. (cf. Anm. 3), S. 215/24; B. Garrett, „Wittgenstein and the First Person", in: *Australasian Journal of Philosophy* 73 (1955), S. 347 ff.
44 Cf. S. Shoemaker, loc. cit. (cf. Anm. 3), S. 560 ff.
45 J. L. Austin, *How to Do Things with Words*, Oxford 1962, S. 61.
46 Cf. Th. Nagel, loc. cit. (cf. Anm. 26), S. 3 ff.
47 Cf. J. Perry, „The Problem of the Essential Indexical", in: *Nous* 13 (1979), sowie D. Kaplan, „Thoughts on Demonstratives", in: *Demonstratives*, ed. P. Yourgrau, Oxford 1990, S. 34 ff.
48 AA XVII 470, *Kant's handschriftlicher Nachlaß* (Bd. IV), *Reflexionen zur Metaphysik* Refl. 4234.

49 Cf. H. Frankfurt, „Freedom of the Will and the Concept of a Person", in: *The Importance of What We Care About*, Cambridge 1988, S. 12; sowie D. Dennett, „Conditions of Personhood", in: *Brainstorms*, Brighton 1981, S. 283 f.
50 E. Tugendhat, *Selbstbewußtsein und Selbstbestimmung*, Frankfurt 1979, S. 32.
51 Loc. cit., S. 47.
52 Loc. cit., S. 33.
53 G. Frege, *Nachgelassene Schriften und wissenschaftlicher Briefwechsel*, ed. H. Hermes, F. Kambartel, F. Kaulbach, Hamburg 1969, Bd. 1, S. 2.

Donald Davidson

The Irreducibility of the Concept of the Self*

In his gentle, probing way, Dieter Henrich often asked me whether I thought the idea of the self was an irreducible or primitive concept. I replied that I did think so, but so far as I remember, I never said why. I remain in doubt what an adequate response calls for, but here I shall try to list some of the considerations that may be relevant to a fuller answer.

Of course, a concept is irreducible only relative to some specified resources. When it comes to the large, grand concepts that concern philosophers, like good, truth, belief, knowledge, physical object, cause, and event, I think of a concept as irreducible if it cannot be defined in terms that are as general, at least as clear, and do not lead in a circle. With respect to the concepts I have listed, I think the search for such a definition or analysis is doomed. The question is, is the concept of the self another of the essential, and therefore irreplaceable, conceptual building blocks of our thought and languages?

I better confess at once that I see no way to address this question directly, since the phrase "the self" doesn't play any clear role in ordinary speech. Philosophers introduce it when they want to discuss such topics as self-consciousness, or the question what unites the various experiences of a person. So my approach will of necessity be oblique.

Thomas Nagel asks us[1] to imagine a description of the universe that tells when and where everything happens relative to some objectively given space-time framework; the description names each person with his or her mental states along with the positions and properties of all other objects. The description includes a complete history of Nagel himself, all from a third person point of view. The one thing it doesn't contain, Nagel says, is the information that *he* is a particular one of the people described. Of course, since he may not know his name is Nagel. The only way he can with certainty locate himself in that world is by using the word "I". Thus the personal pronoun allows him to express knowledge that cannot be expressed in any other way. Clearly, there is something irreducible, irreplaceable, embodied in the use of the first person pronouns – all the first person pronouns. In fact, all sentences containing indexicals depend, for their interpretation and their truth value, on who utters them. But if I utter them, I know without observation that it is I who uttered them. In this way, I relate myself to places, objects, times and others by my use of "there" ("here", "behind me"), "that" ("this"), "now" ("tomorrow", all tensed verbs), "you". There is no substitute for this way of placing myself in the public world.

A less obvious, but equally important, function of indexicals is to provide an early and essential step into the domain of thought and language. For what we learn first is to associate what in the end turn out to be one word sentences ("Mama", "No", "Dog", "Blue") with situations, events, objects, and their features. Soon, or perhaps at once, the child learns the magical power of making sounds adults find appropriate and hence reward. These are only preliminaries to fully fledged talk and thought, for in the beginning the child lacks awareness of the distinction between what is believed and what is the case, what is asked or demanded and what is answered or done. But though only preliminaries, these primitive relations between two people in the presence of stimuli from a shared world contain the kernel of ostensive learning, and it is only in the context of such interactions that we come to grasp the propositional contents of beliefs, desires, intentions, and speech.

I am not, of course, trying to establish the truth of these claims here; I have argued for them elsewhere.[2] But if I am right, this view of the origin and nature of rational thought points to another sense in which the outlook on the world of each person differs irreducibly from that of any other person. The full force and meaning of this statement will emerge presently. But this much should be clear: the basic triangle of two people and a common world is one of which we must be aware if we have any thoughts at all. If I can think, I know that there are others with minds like my own, and that we inhabit a public time and space filled with objects and events many of which are (through the ostensions which made such thoughts available to us) known to others. In particular, I, like every other rational creature, have three kinds of knowledge: knowledge of the objective world (without numerous successful ostensions, I would have no thoughts); knowledge of the minds of others; and knowledge of the contents of my own mind. None of these three sorts of knowledge is reducible to either of the other two, or to the other two in combination. It does indeed *follow* from the fact that I have any one of these sorts of knowledge that I have the other two since the basic triangle is a condition of thought, but none is conceptually or temporally prior to the others.

If I had only knowledge of the contents of minds, perhaps of my own and that of others, there is no way I could construct my knowledge of the world we live in, for that requires the causal connections with that world provided by perception. Of course, if I had knowledge of the contents either of my own mind or of another mind, I would have knowledge of the public world, and would know that I did. But this does not mean I could *construct* such knowledge from my knowledge of the contents of minds.

My knowledge of another mind is not reducible to my knowledge of the contents of my own mind and of the natural world, though my knowledge of the minds of others is dependent on my perceptual knowledge of the movements of their bodies. But to suppose that mental states can be *defined* in terms drawn exclusively from the natural sciences (as some behaviorists once held) is to suppose that the intentional is reducible to the extensional, and such reduction is surely not in the cards.

That knowledge of the contents of my own mind is special, and basic to all my knowledge is, of course, part of the Cartesian and empiricist dreams. And this much is correct: such knowledge is basic in the sense that without it I would know nothing (though self-knowledge is not sufficient for the rest), and special in that it is irreducibly different from other sorts of knowledge.

What unites the three varieties of knowledge, and makes their interdependence the grounding of all thought, is best illustrated by describing the process of ostension. Consider the case of two people both of whom have developed languages. One asks, pointing, "What's that?" "A cormorant", the other answers. More questions and pointings may be needed before the learner gets it right, but astonishingly often, shared habits of generalization do the work at one try. Here we have the three mature forms of knowledge at work. The learner and teacher each know what is in the other's mind, and a vital element in this understanding depends on the shared perceptual stimulus. More important, however, is the way this triangular set of relations reveals the basis of the objectivity of thought, its ability to latch on to something in the public world. In our imagined scenario, both participants already have the concept of objective content and of truth; they know what a physical object is, and what it is for a belief to be true or false. Nevertheless, at the start of the ostension, the learner has nothing but a wordless, conceptless, stimulus to which to attach a concept and a word. Of course she has, we are supposing, plenty of concepts available; but which is the right one? Only the teacher can determine this. It takes two to triangulate the location of the distal stimulus, two to provide an objective test of correctness and failure. If this is so, it must be so from the start, before the learner has the idea of objectivity, and is learning, by way of ostensions which are, to begin with, no more than ways of establishing associations, what it is to *judge* what it is for a response to be right or wrong. The possibility of thought comes with company. Thus the gearing of verbal (and other) responses to situations, events, and objects through the prompting and perception of others plays a key role both in the acquisition of a first language, or the learning of a second language in the absence of an interpreter or bilingual dictionary.

Learning a first and learning a second language are, of course, very different enterprises. The former is a matter of entering the domain of thought for the first time, the latter is a matter of someone already at home in the realm of thought entering into the thought of someone else. However, both depend on similar mechanisms and similar cues. Furthermore, the contrast is weakened by the realization that in case of the child initiate, the two forms of learning mesh, for in absorbing the idea of an objective world, the child is simultaneously learning to communicate with others, which requires insight into the thoughts and intentions of those others.

Making sense of the verbal and non-verbal behavior of others is not an enterprise limited to the special cases of learning first or further languages or adding new words to one's own. Or we might say, treating the notion of a language more strictly than it is treated in ordinary talk, that all these are matters of learning a new language, since any addition to or alteration in our verbal resources makes ours a different, a new, language. Since if we look at the fine detail, no two idiolects are identical, nor is any person's language apt to remain unaltered for long, we are as interpreters constantly working out what others mean by what they say. We are also, both because of the interdependence of thought and speech and for obvious further reasons, constantly deciding what others think, intend, and want. Much of the time we assume we have things right enough for the purposes at hand, and most of the time what small adjustments are needed come so easily that we are aware of no mental effort. It is only now and then that we realize we are coping with old words used in ways new to us, or that some piece of grammar cannot be treated as familiar. In such cases we become conscious that our interpretive skills are being tested. It is here that the unique contribution of the first person point of view – the self – becomes most apparent.

The conceptually developed thinker has two basic interpretive resources at his or her disposal in coming to understand the utterances and actions of others: the assumption of sufficient rationality to make these actions intelligible, and knowledge of how perception yields the contents of belief. In the case of speech, this is easy to illustrate, and the lesson carries over to the propositional attitudes. Sentences, or rather the attitudes they express, owe their content, that is their meaning, to two things: their relations to other sentences or attitudes, and their relations, direct or indirect, to the world through perception. It is therefore impossible for an interpreter wholly to disregard the logical relations among a speaker's sentences or attitudes, or to suppose that they can utter sentences they understand without attending to how the contents of those sentences are related. This is not a matter of an effort on the part of agents to be consistent; it is a matter of their speech and behavior having the meaning they do because of how they hang together. Without sufficient coherence, there is no assigning propositional contents to their speech, beliefs, desires, or intentions. The interpreter's assumption of a degree of rationality on the part of those she wishes to understand is thus no more than a condition of understanding them at all.

The fundamental role of ostension in learning and interpreting speech guarantees that an interpreter cannot go wrong in generally supposing that a speaker's utterances reliably touched off by evident features of the observable world are true and about those features. Mistakes on the part of speaker or interpreter are to be expected, but these cannot be the rule, since errors take their content from a background of veridical thought and honest assertion. The crucial difference between the predominant, mostly banal, run-of-the-mill but on-target beliefs and assumptions and the occasional deviation is this: errors, confusions, irrationalities have particular explanations; getting things right, aside from hard cases, is to be expected.

I have said little about knowledge of the contents of our own minds. Like all knowledge, it cannot exist in isolation from its social beginnings; the concept of oneself as an independent entity depends on the realization of the existence of others, a realization that comes into its own with communication. But the vocabulary of the attitudes applies equally to oneself and to others, and the contents of the attitudes so attributed is likewise expressed in concepts that are in the public domain. My thought that Shakespeare was a woman is mine, but anyone can think as I do. What, then, is so special about my knowledge of my own mind?

I know not only what I think. I also know an infinity of things that I can express and which I know someone might believe or doubt or wonder about; the list is in a sense as large as the list of things expressible in my language, in concepts I command. These are the propositional contents to which I advert when I attribute attitudes to myself or to others. This rich reservoir of conceptual resources is what I must use in interpreting the utterances or actions of those around me. When I speak of "using" these resources, I do not mean it generally takes reflection or effort. It is done without notice, automatically. Even your slips of tongue, omissions, fragmented grammar, accidental substitutions of one name for another I silently, and often unconsciously, correct. Most of the time, your words strike my ear and I understand without an intermediate mental process. But my understanding proves that a process, however inarticulate or far from introspective investigation, has taken place, a process that deserves to be called, if not interpretation, then something much like it. It is interpretation in which conscious reasoning and explicit recourse to evidence and induction have been reduced to zero.

Interpretation in this etiolated sense can be described in terms, not of the observed process, but of the transition from input to outcome, for this transition is after all the same as the transition accomplished by conscious interpretation. Here the elements are as before: the search for coherence based on the assumption of rationality, and the perception of external cues which are within the ken of the speaker or actor. My interest here is not in the details of the process, but in a fact so obvious it may escape notice: that the standards of rationality and reality on which I depend in understanding others are my own, and there can be no appeal beyond them. This is not to deny that what standards I have would not exist if it were not for a history of communication and experience. Nor is it to suppose I cannot reflect on my own reasoning and consult with others for greater clarity, wisdom, and information. But in so far as I seek information directly by experiment and observation, I again can do no better or more than employ my own resources. And if I wonder whether the norms of rationality I employ in trying to comprehend others are correct, I can, of course, ask Sebastian whether I am as objective or reasonable as I should be in my account of Basil's thoughts and actions. But my understanding of Sebastian's reply will be one more exercise of my own standards and methods. There is another obvious indication of the irreducible singularity of my direct acquaintance with the contents of my own mind, and this is that such knowledge is unique in that it is, aside from unusual cases, unsupported by observation, evidence or reasons. This is due, at least in part, to the fact that here interpretation has no application. Drawing on my store of potential thoughts will yield nothing but tautologies when applied to those same thoughts. Self-consciousness of this kind can direct attention inward and promote self-criticism, but it can lead from insight to action only indirectly.

I do not think that because the ultimate court of appeal is personal that therefore my judgments are arbitrary or subjective, for they were formed in a social nexus which assures the objectivity if not the correctness of my beliefs. The intersubjective is the root of objectivity, not because what people agree on is necessarily true, but because intersubjectivity depends on interaction with the world. Though we could not have been at the point of comparing notes without prior interaction, it is private notes that in the end get compared. It is here that each person, each mind or self, reveals itself as part of a community of free selves. There would be no thought if individuals did not play the indispensable, and ultimately unavoidably creative, role of final arbiter.

Notes

* I have been greatly aided in writing this by Marcia Cavell, who joins me in her admiration for the work of Dieter Henrich, and in her gratitude for his friendship.
1 Cf. Th. Nagel's "The Objective Self", in: *Knowledge and Mind. Philosophical Essays*, ed. C. Ginet and S. Shoemaker (New York: Oxford University Press, 1983), pp. 211–232, which has been translated into German as "Das objektive Selbst", in: *Identität der Person. Aufsätze aus der nordamerikanischen Gegenwartsphilosophie*, ed. L. Siep (Basel und Stuttgart: Schwabe, 1983).
2 Cf. my "The Structure and Content of Truth", in: *The Journal of Philosophy* 87 (1990), pp. 279–328.

II.

Wissensbegründung und Skepsis

Skepticism and the Question of Knowledge

Hans Sluga

Von der Uneinheitlichkeit des Wissens

„Dies ist nun eben, worüber ich zweifelhaft bin und was ich durch mich selbst nicht hinreichend ergründen kann, die Erkenntnis, was die wohl sein mag."[1] So leitet Sokrates im Platonischen *Theätet* sein Gespräch mit dem Mathematiker Theätet ein. Der ist zugleich in diesem Dialog der Gegenspieler von Sokrates und auch sein Doppelgänger, diesem in Erscheinung wie in Charakter verwandt. Sokrates spricht anfänglich wie immer spielerisch kokettierend. Wie immer sucht er seinen Gesprächspartner in ein Paradox zu verfangen, um ihn so zum philosophischen Weiterdenken zu zwingen. Theätet, der sich so gut in der höheren Mathematik auskennt – so sucht er zu zeigen – vermag nicht zu sagen, was das Wissen selbst ist. Wie immer geht es auch hier um eine Ein- und Verführung zum philosophischen Denken.

In den mehr als zweitausend Jahren, die seitdem verstrichen sind, haben wir uns allerdings so sehr an die sokratische Frage nach dem Wesen menschlicher Erkenntnis gewöhnt, daß sie uns kaum mehr bemerkenswert erscheint. Wir sprechen heute von der Erkenntnistheorie als der Disziplin, die sich mit solchen Fragen befaßt. Diese erscheint in der Tat als ganz normales, ernstes Geschäft und hat als solches wenig Verführerisches an sich. Und dennoch liegt etwas höchst Seltsames in der Frage, was Wissen ist, sowie in den Bemühungen, sie zu beantworten. Was erwarten wir eigentlich von einer Antwort auf diese Frage? Warum soll es sich lohnen, sie zu finden, wenn es, wie sich herausstellt, so mühselig ist, diese Antwort zu finden. Die Frage, was das Wissen ist, ist ja keineswegs selbstverständlich. Niemand vor Platon hat sich jemals mit ihr befaßt. Der historische Sokrates jedenfalls hat, soweit uns bekannt ist, ganz andere Probleme gehabt. Ihm ging es anscheinend um eine neue Ethik und gar nicht um die Natur des Wissens. Vor Sokrates hat auch kein griechischer Philosoph je gefragt, was das Wissen selbst ist. Parmenides zum Beispiel hatte vom Unterschied zwischen Wissen und Meinen gesprochen, stellte sich jedoch niemals die Frage nach der Natur des Wissens selbst. Diese stammt also wahrscheinlich erst von Platon als dem Autor des *Theätet.* Er ist somit im eigentlichen Sinne der Urheber dieser merkwürdigen Disziplin, der Erkenntnistheorie, deren Name allerdings viel neueren Datums ist.

Hier gilt es anzumerken, daß gar nicht offensichtlich ist, welche Frage Platon eigentlich gestellt hat. Wir übersetzen seine Worte heute gewöhnlich mit „Was ist Wissen?" oder „Was ist Erkenntnis?"; aber haben wir damit richtig getroffen, was er meinte, wenn er „τί ἔστιν ἐπιστήμη?" fragte? Wir sollten wohl erst einmal ganz einfach linguistisch fragen: Was heißt in diesem Zusammenhang ἐπιστήμη? Dieses Hauptwort, so die Auskunft des Wörterbuchs, kommt von dem Verbum ἐπίσταμαι, dessen Wurzel σταν mit unserem deutschen „Stehen" verwandt ist. *Epistamai* bedeutet demnach soviel wie: auf etwas gestanden sein. Wir sagen vielleicht besser „sich auf etwas verstehen", und ἐπιστήμη heißt dementsprechend: das „Sich-auf-etwas-Verstehen". Es lohnt sich, dies anzumerken, weil es die platonische Frage in ein noch merkwürdigeres Licht setzt.

Warum nämlich soll es überhaupt eine Antwort auf die Frage geben, was das Sich-auf-etwas-Verstehen selbst und an sich sei? Ist nicht ein solches Sich-auf-etwas-Verstehen der Natur nach ebenso vielfältig wie alle die Dinge, auf die man sich solchermaßen versteht? Warum soll es, wenn ich etwa zu laufen, zu tanzen, zu kochen, zu schreiben oder zu philosophieren verstehe, überhaupt ein bestimmtes „Sich-auf-diese-Dinge-Verstehen" geben, das es philosophisch zu definieren und festzunageln gilt?

Der Einwand liegt so nahe, daß Platon ihn selbst gleich zu Beginn seines Dialogs vorbringt. Er läßt Theätet nämlich erst einmal auf die Frage „τί ἔστιν ἐπιστήμη?" mit einer Aufzählung verschiedener Wissensgebiete reagieren. Darauf antwortet ihm der platonische Sokrates allerdings: „Das Gefragte aber war nicht dieses, wovon es Erkenntnis gäbe, noch auch, wievielerlei sie wäre. Denn wir fragen nicht in der Absicht, sie aufzuzählen, sondern um die [ἐπιστήμη] Erkenntnis selbst zu begreifen, was sie wohl sein mag."[2] Platon sagt hier, daß Wissen, Erkennen, Verstehen (wie immer wir es nennen wollen) eine

Die Uneinheitlichkeit des Wissens

ganz bestimmte Beziehung zwischen einem Wissenden und einem Wissensgegenstand ist und daß diese Beziehung ein und dieselbe für alle Wissenden und alle Wissensgegenstände sein muß. Das heißt, mit anderen Worten, daß Wissen ein bestimmtes Ausgerichtetsein, eine bestimmte Sorte von Intentionalität ist, die zwischen einem Subjekt und einem Objekt bestehen kann; dieses Ausgerichtetsein muß von beiden, dem Subjekt wie dem Objekt der Beziehung, getrennt werden, ebenso wie wir bei der Jagd zwischen dem Jäger, dem Jagdwild und dem Zielen des Jägers auf sein Wild unterscheiden müssen.

Platon war sich allerdings bewußt, wie schwer die Frage „τί ἔστιν ἐπιστήμη?" zu beantworten ist. Zunächst erwog er den Gedanken, daß Wissen vielleicht dasselbe wie Wahrnehmen (αἴσθησις) sei. Das ist nicht unplausibel, wenn wir das Wort im griechischen Sinne verstehen, wo es auch Erkenntnis und Erfahrung bedeuten kann. Die Formel, daß Wissen Erfahrung ist, wird heute noch von gewissen Empirikern für wahr gehalten. Platon aber läßt sich nicht auf diese Gleichung ein. Denn zum einen kann Erfahrung täuschen, zum anderen ist ungewiß, wie abstrakte Begriffe und Wahrheiten durch Erfahrung gekannt werden können, zum dritten muß Wissen etwas Stabiles und Dauerhaftes sein. Wahrnehmungen sind aber, wie Platon sagt, immer relativ und veränderlich; sie resultieren aus der Wechselwirkung zwischen einem sich stetig ändernden Subjekt und einem gleichfalls sich stetig ändernden Gegenstand. Wissen ist nun auch, zweitens, kein bloßes Glauben oder Für-wahr-Halten, denn das kann trotz aller Gewißheit grundsätzlich falsch sein. Es genügt hier nicht hinzuzufügen, daß ein solcher Glaube wahr sein muß, denn dieser Glaube kann noch immer aus ganz falschen Gründen für wahr gehalten werden. Wenn mich die Fernsehwerbung überredet zu glauben, daß OMO weißer wäscht als andere Mittel, dann habe ich noch kein wirkliches Wissen, selbst wenn OMO in der Tat effektiver wäscht. Das ist jedenfalls Platons Gedanke. Aber er betrachtet es, drittens, auch nicht als zureichend, Wissen als einen begründeten, gerechtfertigten, bewiesenen wahren Glauben zu definieren. Denn alles Begründen, Rechtfertigen und Beweisen muß doch irgendwo einen Anfang haben, und wenn das, was begründet, gerechtfertigt oder bewiesen wird, Wissen sein soll, dann muß doch auch der Anfang dieses Begründens, Rechtfertigens und Beweisens ein Wissen darstellen. Denn von nichts kann doch nichts kommen, von Nichtwissen kann doch kein Wissen abgeleitet werden. Im *Theätet* erwägt Platon genau diese drei Charakterisierungen des Wissens, ist aber von keiner von ihnen befriedigt. Sein Dialog endet so in der Ratlosigkeit – in der Aporie, wie es heißt. Der platonische Sokrates sieht sich am Ende gezwungen, im Hinblick auf die verschiedenen Erklärungsversuche zuzugeben: „Unsere Geburtshelferkunst hat von diesen allen gesagt, es wären nur Windeier und nicht wert, daß man sie aufziehe."[3] Und er rät Theätet, den Mißerfolg zum Anlaß zu nehmen, „besonnenerweise nicht [zu] glauben zu wissen, was du nicht weißt".[4]

Das platonische Gespräch scheint es allerdings zunächst offenzulassen, ob sich nicht vielleicht bei einem neuerlichen Versuch zuletzt doch eine zureichende Definition des Wissens finden lassen würde oder ob eine solche Suche von Anfang an vergebens ist. Platon hatte vermutlich das zweite im Sinne und wollte uns mit dem aporetischen Schluß des Dialogs wohl davon überzeugen, daß wir wissen können, was Wissen ist, ohne eine Definition des Wissens zu haben oder zu benötigen. Denn alles Definieren ist ein Analysieren, wie der Dialog sagt, und dieser Prozeß muß irgendwo ein Ende haben. Die Elemente unserer Analysen, die Endpunkte unserer Definitionen, müssen wir aber ohne weitere Analysen und Definitionen kennen können. Der Begriff des Wissens – so dürfen wir vielleicht den Gedankengang von anderen platonischen Texten her ergänzen – ist nun eine dieser einfachen Ideen, die sich nur direkt, niemals aber durch eine Definition erfassen lassen. Unser Wissen vom Wissen ist also zuletzt – nunmehr jedoch in einem radikal neuen Sinne – grundlegend Erfahrung, nicht jedoch empirische Erfahrung eines sich fortwährend ändernden Gegenstandes durch ein sich fortwährend änderndes Subjekt, sondern die Erfahrung eines Bleibenden – der Ideen selbst – durch ein anderes Bleibendes, nämlich die Seele, die den Ideen ähnlich ist. Dies alles wird aber im *Theätet* nur angedeutet; als explizit formulierter Schluß bleibt hingegen die negative Folgerung, daß die versuchten Definitionen des Wissens unbrauchbar sind und daß Wissen insofern möglicherweise nicht definierbar ist.

Die spätere erkenntnistheoretische Debatte ist Platon in dieser Hinsicht nicht gefolgt. Denn die moderne Erkenntnistheorie – und hier denke ich insbesondere an die analytische Erkenntnistheorie, an die Diskussion der bekannten Gettier-Paradoxien, und die Beiträge Fred Dretskes, Robert Nozicks und Saul Kripkes zu dieser Diskussion – die moderne Erkenntnistheorie ist noch immer auf der Suche nach der richtigen Definition des Wissens, meist in der Hoffnung, daß sich die dritte platonische Definition oder eine Modifikation und Verbesserung von ihr doch noch als zureichend herausstellen möge. Was Platon und die Erkenntnistheoretiker dabei trotz aller Differenzen allerdings gemeinsam haben, ist eine wichtige Annahme: der Glaube, daß es überhaupt so etwas wie *das* Wissen gibt, mithin, daß „τί ἔστιν ἐπιστήμη?" eine Frage mit einer definiten Antwort ist.

Aber sind wir überhaupt berechtigt anzunehmen, daß in verschiedenem Wissen die Wissensinhalte zwar verschieden sein mögen, die Art ihres Gewußtwerdens aber stets ein und dieselbe ist? Zweifel erheben sich hier erst einmal wegen des offensichtlichen Unterschiedes zwischen theoretischem und praktischem Wissen, wie Platon selbst schon erkannte. Wird z. B. in den Sätzen:

(1) Einstein wußte, daß Gleichzeitigkeit ein relativer Begriff ist.

und

(2) Goethe wußte sein Leben zu führen.

etwa im selben Sinne von Wissen gesprochen? Ist das Gewußtwerden, von dem hier die Rede ist, in beiden Fällen dasselbe? Soviel scheint zunächst einmal gewiß: In diesen zwei Fällen manifestiert sich das Wissen jeweils in ganz verschiedener Weise. Das eine Wissen zeigt sich darin, daß Einstein bestimmte Überlegungen anstellte und bestimmte Gedanken bejahte, daß der Inhalt seines Wissens in einem Satz ausgedrückt werden kann, und auch, daß er selbst sagen konnte:

(3) Gleichzeitigkeit ist ein relativer Begriff;

oder genauer:

(4) Ich weiß, daß Gleichzeitigkeit ein relativer Begriff ist.

Im Unterschied dazu zeigte sich Goethes Lebensweisheit in seinem täglichen Handeln darin, wie er mit Menschen umzugehen verstand, und in dem, was er aus sich machte. Der Inhalt seines Lebensverständnisses braucht sich gar nicht in Satzform fassen zu lassen. (Wie sähe ein solcher Satz denn auch aus? Müßte er nicht Goethes ganzes Leben beschreiben?) Und es ist sicherlich auch nicht wesentlich für die Wahrheit des Satzes (2), daß Goethe von sich selbst sagen konnte:

(5) Ich weiß mein Leben zu führen.

Nun ließe sich aber doch argumentieren, daß diese zwei Arten von Wissen trotz bestimmter Unterschiede wesentlich gleich sind. Platon war jedenfalls davon überzeugt. Er argumentierte, daß der Handwerker, der seine Werkzeuge zu gebrauchen versteht, eigentlich gar kein Wissen hat, solange er es nicht als Idee besitzt, und das heißt hier auch: solange er es nicht in Worten ausdrücken kann. Für Platon gilt daher, daß der Satz:

(6) Der Tischler weiß seine Hobel zu führen.

so lange nicht wahr ist, als der Tischler nicht sagen kann:

(7) Man muß die Hobel in dieser und jener Weise führen, um das Brett zu glätten;

oder genauer:

(8) Ich weiß, daß man die Hobel in dieser Weise und jener Weise führen muß, um das Brett zu glätten.

Platon glaubte, mit anderen Worten, daß praktisches Wissen eigentlich nur eine Form des propositionalen oder theoretischen Wissens ist. Wir können diesen Standpunkt mit einem modernen Wort Kognitivismus nennen. Dieser Kognitivismus ist aber nun auch der Grund für Platons Überzeugung, daß der Begriff des Wissens, obwohl er ein eindeutiger, definiter Begriff ist, zugleich doch nicht definierbar ist. Denn aus seinen Bedenken gegenüber den verschiedenen Definitionen des Wissens, die er im *Theätet* erörtert, geht nicht hervor, daß keinerlei Definition nachweislich richtig sein kann. Um letzteres zu zeigen, bedarf es anderer und stärkerer Argumente. Die

Die Uneinheitlichkeit des Wissens

liegen nun genau in Platons Kognitivismus. Denn alles Wissen schließt diesem Kognitivismus zufolge immer schon den Begriff des Wissens selbst in sich ein. Um diese Einsicht plausibel auszudrücken, müssen wir uns daran erinnern, daß ἐπιστήμη nicht nur Wissen, sondern auch Erkennen und Verstehen bedeutet. Und so lautet Platons Gedanke dann: Den Begriff des Wissens mit Hilfe einer Definition zu erkennen bedeutet, ihn mit Hilfe von den Begriffen zu erkennen, die im Definiens dieser Definition vorkommen. Das aber bedeutet auch, daß wir diese definierenden Begriffe selbst bereits kennen müssen. Wiederum einen Begriff zu kennen heißt jedoch der kognitivistischen Annahme zufolge immer, daß wir *wissen*, daß dieser Begriff so und so beschaffen ist. Und um das zu verstehen, müssen wir den Begriff des Wissens selbst bereits besitzen. Alle möglichen Definitionen des Wissens sind demnach notwendigerweise zirkulär. Wissen muß ein undefinierbarer Grundbegriff sein.

Mir geht es hier natürlich nicht darum, dieses platonische Argument zu rechtfertigen. Vielmehr wollte ich nur zeigen, daß Platons Wendung gegen die Definierbarkeit des Wissens eine Folge seines Kognitivismus ist. Dieser Kognitivismus hat nun allerdings viele Gründe gegen sich. Insbesondere ergibt sich aus ihm, daß alle Wesen, die begrifflichen Denkens nicht fähig sind, auch kein Wissen haben können. Das heißt dann, daß der Vogel oder die Biene oder mein Hund nichts wissen, wenn sie zu wissen scheinen, wo ihr Nest, wie weit die Blüte entfernt bzw. wer sein Herr ist.

Nun läßt sich aber Platons Anhänglichkeit an den Kognitivismus daraus verständlich machen, daß er glaubte, der Begriff des Wissens sei eindeutig und definit. Wenn wir diesen Kognitivismus fallenlassen, erscheint der Begriff des Wissens in wenigstens einer wichtigen Hinsicht als zweideutig, weil dann ein unüberbrückbarer Unterschied zwischen praktischem und theoretischem Wissen besteht. Man könnte nun einfach die Unüberbrückbarkeit zwischen Theorie und Praxis zugeben und zugleich insistieren, daß zumindest der Begriff des theoretischen, propositionalen Wissens eindeutig und definierbar sei. Oder man könnte umgekehrt auch darauf bestehen, daß die Natur des Wissens in Theorie und Praxis dieselbe sei, jedoch die Einheit des Wissens nicht durch den platonischen Kognitivismus, sondern durch jene Tatsache richtig erklärt werde, daß alles Wissen letztendlich praktischer Art sei, weil sich theoretisches Wissen letztlich in Überlegen, Denken und Reden und damit in Handlungen manifestiere. Wollte man dagegen geltend machen, daß ein Handeln mit Begriffen doch etwas anderes ist als ein nicht-begriffliches und nicht-sprachliches Handeln, so ließe sich darauf antworten, daß unser begriffliches und sprachliches Handeln am Ende nur dadurch seine Bedeutung erhält, daß es mit nicht-begrifflichen und nicht-sprachlichen Handlungen verbunden ist. Überlegungen dieser Art sind uns aus der philosophischen Literatur unseres Jahrhunderts vertraut. Sie lassen sich vereinfacht mit dem Wort Pragmatismus bezeichnen. Der Pragmatismus, so scheint es, gibt uns genügenden Grund, an der scharfen Trennung von Theorie und Praxis zu zweifeln.

Dieser Pragmatismus zeigt allerdings nur, daß es keinen absoluten Trennungsstrich zwischen theoretischem und praktischem Wissen gibt; er beweist nicht, daß das Gewußtwerden in verschiedenem Wissen immer genau ein und dasselbe ist. Im Gegenteil macht er uns darauf aufmerksam, nicht nur wie sehr sich theoretisches und praktisches Wissen unterscheiden können, sondern auch wie verschieden ein theoretisches Wissen von einem anderen theoretischen Wissen und ein praktisches Wissen von einem anderen praktischen Wissen sein kann.

Und dies führt uns nun zu einem anderen, und – so scheint es – zwingenderen Argument dafür, warum Wissen überhaupt kein eindeutiger, definiter Begriff sein kann. Sehen wir uns die verschiedenen Wissenssituationen noch einmal genauer an. Einstein wußte, daß Gleichzeitigkeit ein relativer Begriff ist; er wußte dies aufgrund von Spekulationen über Raum und Zeit, die auf wissenschaftlichen Beobachtungen und mathematischen Berechnungen beruhen. Alle Kriterien, die uns aus der Physik bekannt sind, bestätigen uns, daß Einstein ein bestimmtes Wissen hatte. Aber wie ist es nun, wenn

(8) Sabine weiß, daß morgen mein Geburtstag ist?

Hier bedarf es doch nicht der Kriterien der Physik. Hier geht es nicht um wissenschaftliche Beobachtungen und mathematische Kalkulationen. Ich bin mir sicher, daß Sabine das Datum meines Geburtstags weiß, weil ich es ihr gesagt habe, weil sie mich selbst daran erinnert hat und weil sie schon jetzt dabei ist, einen Kuchen zu backen. Und wenn wir uns nun das Wissen des Mathematikers und Logikers ansehen, so stellen wir fest, daß es, im Unterschied zu Einsteins und zu Sabines Wissen, ausschließlich auf Selbstevidenz und deduktiven Beweisen beruht. Das Wissen des Literaturwissenschaftlers wiederum beruht auf Einfühlung, auf Plausibilitätsüberlegungen, auf der Einfallskraft seiner Interpretationen. Das heißt nicht, daß theoretisches Wissen je nach dem Fach, zu dem es gehört, jeweils ein anderes ist. Denn algebraisches Wissen ist noch einmal von anderer Art und wird nach anderen Kriterien gemessen als geometrische Erkenntnis, das Wissen des Erforschers des Nibelungenliedes nach anderen Kriterien als das des Goethe-Interpreten. Ich meine damit nicht, daß in jedem Fall das Gewußte ein anderes ist, sondern daß die *Kriterien*, nach denen wir jeweils beurteilen, ob jemand Wissen hat, immer wieder verschieden sind. Und das heißt doch auch wohl, daß in diesem Falle das Gewußtwerden selbst ebenso jeweils ein anderes ist. Was hier für das theoretische Wissen gesagt worden ist, läßt sich natürlich auch für das praktische Wissen wiederholen. Denn die Kriterien, die wir gebrauchen, um zu entscheiden, ob einer sein Leben zu führen, den Hobel zu führen, eine Sprache zu sprechen oder Schach zu spielen weiß, sind wiederum gänzlich voneinander verschieden. Und so haben wir es auch in all diesen Fällen immer wieder mit verschiedenen Arten von Wissen zu tun.

Wir können das bisher Gesagte noch einmal im Rückgriff auf die letzte der drei von Platon erwogenen und verworfenen Definitionen des Wissens verschärfen. Diese dritte Definition besagte, daß Wissen ein gerechtfertigtes Glauben an etwas Wahres sei. Die erkenntnistheoretische Diskussion hat sich immer wieder an diese Definition als die plausibelste geklammert, nicht zuletzt um zu beweisen, daß sie mit einem definiten Gegenstand, nämlich dem Wissen selbst, befaßt ist. Wir können nun aber kritisch anmerken, daß diese Definition in jedem Fall nur eine Leerformel und systematisch mehrdeutig ist. Denn der Begriff der Rechtfertigung ist selbst mehrdeutig und kann so den des Wissens nicht vereindeutigen.

Nun könnte man aber zugeben, daß in verschiedenen Fällen des

Wissens die Kriterien des Wissens (die Natur des Glaubens, der Rechtfertigung und der Wahrheit selbst) jeweils andere sind; zugleich ließe sich dann allerdings fragen, ob dadurch die Art des Gewußtwerdens jeweils eine andere sein muß. Verhält es sich hier nicht wie im Falle von Meßurteilen? Wir sagen, daß der Tisch zwei Meter lang, daß der Mond so-und-so-viele Kilometer von der Erde entfernt ist und daß ein Sauerstoffatom diesen oder jenen Durchmesser hat. Insofern sich die Meßmethoden für die verschiedenen Abstände unterscheiden, sind die Kriterien, die unseren Aussagen zugrunde liegen, jeweils andere, und doch sprechen wir in jedem Fall von demselben System von Maßeinheiten. Können wir nicht im gleichen Sinne sagen, daß die Kriterien des Gewußtseins in der Mathematik, der Physik, der Germanistik und im alltäglichen Leben jeweils andere sein mögen, daß es aber dennoch einen gemeinsamen Nenner für die Gesamtheit der theoretischen Wissenszustände gibt – nämlich das Wissen selbst, die ἐπιστήμη, die Platon als erster philosophisch identifiziert hat? Und besteht dieses Gemeinsame nicht zuletzt darin, daß in jedem einzelnen Fall das Wissen eine besondere Art des Gerichtetseins eines Bewußtseins auf einen Wissensinhalt ist?

Was aber nötigt uns eigentlich dazu anzunehmen, daß es einen intentionalen Zustand des Wissens überhaupt gibt? Rührt die Veranlassung dazu letztlich nicht daher, daß in all den Sätzen, in denen wir über verschiedene Arten des Wissens reden, immer wieder das eine Zeitwort „wissen" vorkommt? Aber was ergibt sich denn aus dem syntaktischen Faktum, daß alle diese Sätze die Struktur „S weiß x" haben? Haben wir das Recht, daraus zu schließen, daß alle diese Sätze in ein und demselben Sinne von Wissen handeln müssen? Wilhelm Jerusalem hat einmal erklärt, daß Husserl zwar berechtigt gewesen sei, die Unterscheidung zwischen einem intentionalen Prädikat und seinem Gegenstand zu machen, daß aber die Unterscheidung keineswegs die Existenz eines wirklichen Unterschiedes garantiere und damit die Existenz von intentionalen Gegenständen. Wir können sein Argument hier variieren, indem wir sagen, daß die Syntax unserer Sprache uns erlaubt, in bestimmten Sätzen ein intentionales Prädikat des Wissens zu unterscheiden, daß dies aber in keiner Weise die Existenz einer intentionalen Beziehung des Wissens garantieren kann. Denn es besteht die Möglichkeit, daß das Wort „weiß" in Sätzen der Form „S weiß x" nur ein synkategorematischer Ausdruck ist und dieser daher ebenso wie die logischen Partikel „und" und „oder" für sich allein genommen gar keine definite Bedeutung hat, sondern nur, wenn die gekennzeichneten Leerstellen mit geeigneten Ausdrücken gefüllt sind.

Die Mindestbedingung für den Schluß, daß das Wort „weiß" in Sätzen der genannten Form eine eigene Bedeutung hat – und zwar dieselbe in allen Sätzen dieser Form – ist doch wohl, daß wir die vermeintliche Bedeutung dieses Bestandteils von den Bedeutungen der anderen Satzbestandteile zu trennen vermögen. Gelingt dies nicht, hat der Satz als ganzer vielleicht eine Bedeutung, aber wir sind kaum berechtigt zu sagen, daß das intentionale Prädikat für sich genommen eine Bedeutung hat. Um dem Prädikat eine solche Bedeutung beizulegen, müssen wir mit anderen Worten sowohl einen Begriff des Subjekts des Wissens als auch den eines Gegenstands des Wissens haben. Die platonische Frage, was Wissen sei, ist also mit den Fragen nach der Natur des Wissens-Subjekts und der Natur des Wissens-Inhalts unabdingbar verknüpft.

Platon selbst hat dies verstanden, und so ist sein Gespräch über das Wissen zugleich auch eine Abhandlung über die menschliche Seele als dem, was ihm zufolge Wissen hat. Dies wird aus der Wendung sichtbar, die das Gespräch nimmt, nachdem Sokrates erklärt hat, daß Wissen nicht mit Sinneswahrnehmung identisch sein könne, weil nämlich zumindest einiges Wissen auf Schlüssen beruhe. An diesem Punkt angelangt stellt Sokrates dem Theätet die Frage, ob dieser vielleicht annehmen wolle, daß beides, Sinneswahrnehmung und schließendes Denken, Formen von Wissen sein können: „Willst du nun jenes und dieses dasselbe nennen, da beides so große Verschiedenheiten zeigt?"[5] lautet seine Frage. Diese zu bejahen würde bedeuten, daß Wissen zumindest zwei ganz verschiedene Formen haben könnte: Es könnte einerseits ein Wahrnehmungswissen und andererseits ein begriffliches Wissen sein. Von der Einheit des theoretischen Wissens wäre dann keine Rede mehr. Platon läßt den Theätet aber noch einmal die Einheit des Wissens bekräftigen. Wissen kann nicht sowohl Wahrnehmen wie begriffliches Wissen sein; und wenn es manchmal begriffliches Wissen ist, dann muß es nach dieser Logik immer begriffliches Wissen sein. So kann Sokrates resümieren, daß wir in der Frage nach der Erkenntnis „nun wenigstens so weit vorgeschritten [sind], daß wir sie ganz und gar nicht unter der Wahrnehmung suchen wollen". Statt dessen suchen wir sie „unter demjenigen Namen, den die Seele führt, wenn sie sich für sich selbst mit dem, was ist, beschäftigt".[6] Und mit dieser Bemerkung ist eine Brücke zwischen der Frage „τί ἔστιν ἐπιστήμη?" und der Frage nach der Natur der Seele als dem Subjekt des Wissens geschlagen.

Aus dem, was Platon hier sagt, ergeben sich in der Tat zwei wichtige Folgerungen, nämlich erstens, daß Wissen ein definiter und einzigartiger Zustand ist, und zweitens, daß Wissen der Zustand einer Seele oder eines Geistes ist. Hieraus läßt sich zugleich auch ersehen, wie wenig aporetisch das Gespräch zwischen Sokrates und Theätet in Wirklichkeit ist. Natürlich beantwortet der Dialog nicht die Hauptfrage, die er sich stellt (die Frage „τί ἔστιν ἐπιστήμη?"), aber Platon, dem es nie allein um ein isoliertes Thema geht, kommt doch zu positiven Antworten bezüglich einiger anderer Fragen. Denn zum ersten argumentiert das Gespräch für eine scharfe Unterscheidung von Sinnes- und Seelentätigkeit und so für die generelle Unterscheidung von Körper und Seele. Zum zweiten legt sich der Text darauf fest, daß Wissen und Denken intentionale Beziehungen sind, und zum dritten deutet er an, daß Wissen auf einer Affinität zwischen dem wissenden Subjekt und den Wissensinhalten beruhen muß. So gesehen dürfte Platon eigentlich mit den positiven Ergebnissen des *Theätet* zufrieden sein. Zwar hat er nicht das Wissen definiert, aber er hat doch die Weichen für die gesamte künftige erkenntnistheoretische Diskussion gestellt.

Der Satz, daß Wissen notwendigerweise ein geistiger Zustand ist, ergibt sich für Platon, wie wir soeben gesehen haben, aus der Annahme, daß Wissen etwas Einheitliches ist, denn wenn es etwas Einheitliches ist (so sagt er), kann es nur ein Seelenzustand sein. Aber was sollte uns dazu bringen, das Wissen als einen solchen Seelenzustand zu bestimmen, wenn wir nicht schon von Anfang an glauben, daß Wissen ein einheitlicher Zustand ist? Für Platon war Wissen der Zustand eines wissenden Subjekts. Dieses Subjekt sollte zugleich

Die Uneinheitlichkeit des Wissens

aber nichtkörperlich sein: ein Ich oder eine Seele. Dieser Standpunkt ist in neuerer Zeit von Descartes noch einmal bekräftigt worden, der ohnehin viel dazu beigetragen hat, die platonischen Ansätze in die moderne Erkenntnistheorie zu injizieren. Descartes erklärt nämlich sowohl, daß es ein nichtkörperliches Ich gibt, das verschiedener Modi und Akte fähig ist, die wir zusammengenommen Denken nennen, als auch, daß Wissen ein solcher definiter Modus des Denkens ist.

Was aber ist denn diese Seele, dieser Geist, deren Zustand das Wissen sein soll? Ist das Ich überhaupt ein definites Objekt? Von Kritikern ist immer wieder gesagt worden, daß es ein solches wissendes Subjekt gar nicht gebe, daß das Ich gar kein Gegenstand sein könne und daß sich dies darin offenbare, daß das Wort „ich" kein Name ist und nicht als Name gebraucht wird. Solche Kritik will das Ich als Produkt einer grammatischen Täuschung und als Ergebnis einer mißverstandenen Analogie entlarven. Und so heißt es dann, daß wir eigentlich „es denkt", „es erkennt", „es weiß" sagen sollten (wie wir auch „es regnet" sagen) und nicht „ich denke", „ich erkenne" und „ich weiß". Nun fragt sich aber doch, warum eine solche Sprachreform sich in der Praxis als undurchführbar erweist. Und hierzu muß hinzugefügt werden, daß die Tatsache, daß das Wort „ich" nicht als Name gebraucht wird, nicht beweist, daß es keine Seele oder keinen Geist gibt. Das Wort „hier" zum Beispiel ist ebensowenig ein Name und wird auch nicht als Name eines Ortes gebraucht; dennoch gibt es den Ort, von dem wir mit seiner Hilfe reden. Warum sollte es nicht ebenso im Falle des Wortes „ich" sein?

Allgemeiner gesprochen: Es ist unklar, wieso die Existenz des Ich aufgrund von logischen und grammatischen Überlegungen entscheidbar sein sollte. Was es gibt oder nicht gibt, läßt sich nicht unbedingt von den Formen unserer Sprache ablesen, denn diese Sprache kann ja defektiv oder unvollständig sein. Natürlich stimmt es auch, daß wir dem eigenen Ich nicht wie einem Gegenstand gegenüberstehen. Dazu ließe sich allerdings erstens anmerken, daß wir auch dem eigenen Leib nicht wie einem gewöhnlichen Gegenstand gegenüberstehen (und ebensowenig Personen oder Gegenständen, die uns bekannt und von Bedeutung sind). Und zweitens ist zu bedenken, daß uns das eigene Ich durchaus manchmal als fremd erscheint, daß wir ihm gelegentlich als einem ganz anderen gegenüberstehen (so zum Beispiel, wenn uns unser eigenes Verhalten im nachhinein unverständlich ist). Natürlich ist auch die Beobachtung richtig, daß die Selbstreflexion uns mit Bewußtseinszuständen bekannt macht; allerdings nicht mit einem Ich, das von diesen Zuständen getrennt werden kann. Das gleiche gilt ebenso von jedem beliebigen Gegenstand (und insbesondere von unserem eigenen Leib), denn diesen können wir uns auch nicht von seinen Eigenschaften getrennt vorstellen.

In seiner Faktizität erscheint das Ich jedenfalls als etwas, über das ich keineswegs vollständig verfüge. Ich habe zum Beispiel einen Charakter, der sich mir als Faktum präsentiert. Wenn ich mich frage, wer ich bin, dann antworte ich damit, daß ich mich auf meine Herkunft berufe, auf mein Leben, auf meine Erinnerungen und meine Erwartungen. Das sind Fakten, die meine Identität bestimmen, ob ich es mag oder nicht. Ich bin mir auch bewußt, daß ich meinen Charakter keineswegs aufs Geratewohl ändern kann. Ich weiß, daß ich oft meine Gefühle unterdrücke bis zu dem Punkt, an dem sie plötzlich unkontrollierbar hervorbrechen. Das ist ein Charakterfehler, den ich bedauern mag, an dem ich aber wenig ändern kann. Ich erkläre mir: So bin ich eben. Was ich „Charakter" in mir nenne, ist wohl zum Teil das Ergebnis gelebter Umstände und Erfahrungen, manches daran ist aber auch ererbte Veranlagung. Ich erkenne in mir, zum eigenen Erstaunen, die Charakterzüge meiner Eltern und Großeltern. Auch hier kann ich nicht voll über mich selbst verfügen. Das Ich ist sicher kein Gegenstand für mich wie irgendein anderer, und doch ist etwas Gegebenes an ihm.

Die philosophische Diskussion stellt uns hier immer vor zwei Möglichkeiten. Sie sagt: Entweder nehmen wir an, daß das Ich eine Illusion ist – das Resultat einer grammatischen oder logischen Täuschung – oder wir sind verpflichtet zu schließen, daß es das Ich als Substanz gibt. Dazwischen liegt aber in Wirklichkeit noch ein Drittes: Das Ich ist etwas Konstituiertes und Konstruiertes und als solches (und nur als solches) real. Es gibt etwas, auf das wir mit dem Ich-Wort verweisen, das aber weder eine platonische Psyche noch eine cartesische

Die Uneinheitlichkeit des Wissens

Geistsubstanz ist. Das Ich ist vielmehr eine Bewußtseinsstruktur, deren Formierung, wie Freud und Piaget gezeigt haben, sich genetisch beschreiben und analysieren läßt. Und dieses formierte Ich ist nun, wie eine solche Analyse erweist, aus Bewußtseinszuständen, Erfahrungen, Erinnerungen, Gedanken, aus Überzeugungen und Wissenszuständen konstituiert. Dieses Ich ist das Prinzip, das all diese Zustände in einer – zugegeben: unsicheren, prekären, instabilen – Ordnung vereinigt. Ein solches Verständnis des Ich scheint in der Tat die Probleme zu umgehen, welche den zwei überkommenen philosophischen Positionen anhängen. Sie macht uns einerseits verständlich, warum wir nicht ohne die Annahme eines Ich auskommen und andererseits auch, warum dieses Ich nur in seinen Zuständen vor uns tritt.

Hierzu ließe sich sicher noch vieles anmerken. Für uns ist die Sache gegenwärtig nur insofern von Bedeutung, als sie die Frage betrifft, wie das menschliche Wissen zu verstehen ist. Wir waren dahin gelangt zu fragen, ob sich das Wissen als Zustand der Seele, des Geistes, oder des Ich beschreiben ließe. Es stellt sich nunmehr heraus, daß das Ich selbst nur aus seinen Zuständen begriffen werden kann; daß insbesondere das, was ich bin, davon abhängt, was ich weiß und wie und warum ich es weiß. Der Versuch, das Wissen selbst als etwas Einheitliches, als einen spezifischen und definiten Absichtszustand der Seele zu verstehen, schlägt also fehl. Wenn Platon erklärt, Wissen sei der Zustand der Seele, in dem sie „sich für sich selbst mit dem, was ist, beschäftigt"[7], zeigt er damit keineswegs, daß der Begriff des Wissens eindeutig und definit ist. Denn erstens ist, so wie wir es jetzt sehen, die Seele oder das Ich selbst keine Einheit, sondern als Vielfalt seelischer Zustände konstituiert, und zum zweiten ist Platons Beschreibung zirkulär, weil die Beschreibung der Seele schon voraussetzt, daß wir wissen, was die Wissenszustände dieser Seele sind.

Es gibt nun vielleicht noch eine letzte Möglichkeit, die Eindeutigkeit des Wissens aufrechtzuerhalten. Sie besteht darin anzunehmen, daß es ein Reich der Wissensinhalte oder Wissensobjekte gibt, und daß Wissen selbst ein spezifisches Ausgerichtetsein auf diese Inhalte oder Objekte ist. Platon hat schließlich auch diese Möglichkeit erwogen. Die platonischen Ideen sind nämlich nichts anderes als solche ausgezeichneten Objekte des Wissens. Sie eröffnen sich allein dem, der echtes Wissen besitzt. Wissen ist solchermaßen Zugang zu den Ideen. In neuerer Zeit hat Hermann Lotze von Wahrheiten an sich gesprochen, die an und für sich gültig sind unabhängig davon, ob sie von uns erfahren werden, oder nicht. Wissen ist diesem Begriff zufolge Ausgerichtetsein auf Wahrheiten an sich.

Die Annahme eines objektiven Reiches von Wissensinhalten ist allerdings selbst wieder problematisch. Denn zum einen ist der metaphysische Status dieses Feldes ungeklärt. Nun haben Philosophen von Platon bis zu Popper immer wieder gesagt, daß wir nicht um die Annahme objektiver Wissensinhalte herumkommen, ohne die Möglichkeit objektiven Wissens überhaupt in Frage zu stellen: Wie kann es Wissenschaft geben, wenn es keine objektiven Inhalte gibt, deren Wahrheit nicht von uns abhängt und über die wir gemeinsam nachdenken können? Aber hier ließe sich zurückfragen: Wie kann der Appell an ein Reich objektiver Inhalte uns helfen, wenn wir nicht einmal richtig verstehen, wo dieses Reich existieren soll, welcher Art seine Wirklichkeit ist, und in welcher Beziehung es zu unserer gewöhnlichen, zeitlichen Welt steht? Das Dunkel läßt sich schließlich nicht mit der Finsternis erhellen.

Die Finsternis, die in der Annahme eines Reichs objektiver Wissensinhalte liegt, wird offenbar, wenn wir im nächsten Schritt fragen, wieso Wesen wie wir, die aus Fleisch und Blut gemacht sind und im Zeitlichen leben, überhaupt von einer solchen anderen Wirklichkeit wissen können. Natürlich wird Platon uns antworten, daß die Seele selbst dem Wesen nach gar nicht zeitlich, sondern ewig, gleichbleibend und den Ideen, d. h. also den Wissensinhalten ähnlich ist. Aber wir haben bereits gesagt, daß wir keinerlei Grund zu der Auffassung haben, daß die Seele, das Ich, eine Substanz sei, sondern vielmehr: eine Konstruktion aus vielfältigen, zeitlichen Erfahrungen. Und es hilft auch nicht weiter zu sagen, daß uns das Reich der objektiven Wissens- und Denkinhalte als Korrelat unserer intentionalen Akte des Wissens und Denkens gegeben ist. Denn es steht ja gerade zur Diskussion, ob es überhaupt eine intentionale Beziehung des Wissens gibt. Wir hatten zuerst versucht, den intentionalen Begriff des Wissens direkt zu erklären. Als uns dies nicht gelang, versuchten wir,

Die Uneinheitlichkeit des Wissens

eine Erklärung über den Begriff des wissenden Subjekts zu gewinnen. Auch dies mißlang, und so vermuteten wir schließlich, daß wir das Wissen vielleicht im Rückgriff auf die Wissensinhalte charakterisieren könnten. Jetzt sieht es aber so aus, als seien die vermeintlichen Wissensinhalte selbst wieder nur mit Bezug auf den Wissensbegriff spezifizierbar. Wir bewegen uns, so scheint es, im Kreise.

Was aber sind diese Wissensinhalte oder -objekte, von denen wir bislang immer sprechen? Sind es Gedanken, Theorien, Wahrheiten, die nur geistig wahrgenommen werden können? Wissen, so lohnt es sich hier zu erinnern, existiert gar nicht immer nur im menschlichen Denken. Es existiert genausogut in Büchern, Tabellen, Bildern, Karten oder Computern, in der Struktur unserer Bauwerke, Brücken, Werkzeuge, Maschinen und Kunstwerke. Es existiert insbesondere in Form von Sätzen, Formeln, Gleichungen und Diagrammen. Wissen wird manchmal im stillen Denken produziert, aber oft auch beim Sprechen und Schreiben. Es lohnt sich hier z. B. zu fragen, wie Wissen sich beim Schreiben manifestiert und was sich daraus über die Natur des Wissens selbst ergibt.

Vergegenwärtigen wir uns, wie wir beim philosophischen Denken und Schreiben ein verstehendes Wissen hervorzubringen versuchen. Zunächst einmal läßt dieser Prozeß erkennen, daß ein solches Denken kein Sehen oder Erfassen, sondern ein Machen und Konstruieren ist. Dieses Konstruieren beginnt als Sammeln und Suchen, geht von dem aus, was sich findet und was einem einfällt. Da sind Worte, Ideen, einzelne Formulierungen, plötzlich erinnerte Sätze und Zitate, isolierte Denkbewegungen, die sich aufdrängen. Aber philosophisches Schreiben ist nicht nur ein Anhäufen einzelner Bausteine, sondern auch ein Ordnen und Organisieren nach Plan und Schema, denn unsere Sätze sollen zusammenhängen, sie sollen eine „logische" Folge ergeben. Im Unterschied zum Hausbau sind das Zusammentragen der Steine und das Planen des ganzen Gebäudes allerdings merkwürdig verschränkt: Bei einem solchen Schreiben werden die Einzelideen und Einzelsätze immer wieder gegen das Schema und das Schema immer wieder gegen die Einzelideen abgewogen. Alles Bauen ist hier bereits stets zugleich ein Umbauen und Umplanen, alles Schreiben ein Umschreiben.

Philosophisches Schreiben wird so zu einem Reflexionsprozeß. Der einmal produzierte Text wird in stetig wiederholten Operationen überholt. In immer neuen Lesungen wird der bereits vorhandene Text neuen Deutungen unterworfen. Entstandene Fassungen werden ständig durch neue Zusätze, Streichungen und Umordnungen stets von neuem modifiziert. Im Zuge dieser Arbeit werden die Bestandteile des Textes zunehmend integriert, wird ein immer dichteres und komplexeres Netz von Beziehungen zwischen den Textteilen geschaffen. Aber das Ziel der vollendeten Einheit ist zugleich eine Chimäre, die sich uns in dem Maße entrückt, in dem wir ihr nahekommen wollen. Denn der Prozeß des Bauens und Umbauens verhängt über uns zugleich beständig neue Diskrepanzen. Die Netzstrukturen des Textes erweisen sich immer von neuem als unvollständig und brüchig. Denkstrukturen bleiben verzettelt und undurchsichtig verknotet. Abschlüsse sind jeweils vorläufig oder von außen erzwungen, nie aber von der Logik des Textes selbst gefordert.

Wissensinhalte haben so, wenn wir von der Erfahrung eines solchen Schreibens ausgehen, keineswegs die Eigenschaften, die ihnen die platonische Auffassung wiederholt zugeschrieben hat. Sie sind Produktionen, Werke des Menschen und wie alles Menschliche provisorisch, jedoch keinesfalls „an sich", zeitlos oder objektiv. Sie sind unstabil, unvollkommen, unvollständig, uneinheitlich, miteinander unvereinbar, widersprüchlich. Sie befinden sich in einem stetigen Konstitutionsprozeß, stets im Aufbau und Umbau, den keine interne Logik zur Ruhe bringt. Das Gebiet unseres Wissens ist in der Tat kein homogenes Feld, sondern eine Zerstreuungsstruktur, in der Wissensinhalte manchmal eng beieinander und manchmal weit auseinander liegen, in der die Übergänge vom einen zum anderen Häufungspunkt nie gleichförmig sind und in der im Fortgang der Zeit vielleicht gar nicht die Integration, sondern vielmehr die Zerstreuung zunimmt.

Wir hatten mit dem Versuch eingesetzt, das Wissen selbst zu charakterisieren. Weil uns das nicht gelang, versuchten wir, es im Bezug auf das wissende Subjekt zu erklären. Dieses Subjekt erwies sich aber nicht als stabiler Bezugspunkt. Die Einheit des Wissens ließ sich nicht aus der Einheit des Subjekts erklären. Dies führte uns zu dem Ver-

Die Uneinheitlichkeit des Wissens

such, das Wissen in seiner Relation zu den Wissensinhalten zu charakterisieren. Aber auch diese sind instabil und keineswegs einheitlich. Das Wissen als Beziehung eines Subjektes zu einem Gegenstand ist offensichtlich in dem selben Fluktuationsprozeß begriffen, der die bezogenen Elemente, das Ich und die Wissensinhalte, einbegreift. Und damit ergibt sich, daß wir auch keinen Begriff des Wissens selbst haben können, der ein für allemal fixiert werden könnte.

Platon stellte im *Theätet* die Frage, was Wissen sei, fand jedoch keine Antwort, die ihn befriedigte. Unser Gedankengang, so stellen wir fest, bestätigt die platonische Aporie erneut. Wir wissen jedenfalls nicht, wie Wissen zu definieren ist. Unsere Schlußfolgerung scheint allerdings in noch stärkerem Maße aporetisch zu sein als diejenige Platons. Sein Dialog sagt uns nicht, was Wissen ist, deutet jedoch an, daß wir das Wissen selbst, wenn nicht in einer Formel, so doch im sehenden Denken als einen eindeutigen, definiten Begriff erfassen können. Wissen soll ein Zustand sein, durch den ein Subjekt auf einen Wissensinhalt ausgerichtet ist. Platon hat damit der Erkenntnistheorie einen bestimmten und fragwürdigen Begriff der Intentionalität mit auf den Weg gegeben. Wir haben dagegen eingesehen, daß Wissen gar nicht *ein* Ding ist, daß es keinen definiten intentionalen Zustand des Wissens gibt und daß sich der Begriff des Wissens aus diesem Grunde der einheitlichen Erfassung entzieht.

Ich weiß von keinem Philosophen, der dies so scharf erkannt hat wie Michel Foucault in seinen archäologischen und genealogischen Untersuchungen. Denn Foucault hat erkannt, daß es nicht ein Wissen, eine ἐπιστήμη gibt, sondern viele Formen des Wissens, viele *Epistemen*, wie er es selbst verschiedentlich ausdrückt. In diesem Wechsel von der Einzahl zur Mehrzahl liegt, wie ich es sehe, implizit eine grundlegende Kritik von Platon und der gesamten erkenntnistheoretischen Tradition, die auf dem platonischen Boden erwachsen ist. Wenn Foucault von *Epistemen* spricht, dann will er, so wie ich ihn jetzt lese, nicht nur sagen, daß es verschieden gestaltete Totalitäten von Wissensinhalten gibt (das entspräche etwa der Ansicht von Thomas Kuhn), sondern daß Wissen selbst jeweils verschiedene Formen annehmen kann. Zu Platon nimmt er so die genaue Gegenstellung in bezug auf die Frage „τί ἔστιν ἐπιστήμη?" ein. Denn für Foucault ist eine *Episteme* jeweils sowohl durch ein wissendes Subjekt wie einen Wissensinhalt konstituiert und ist damit notwendigerweise jeweils zugleich eine neue Art von Beziehung zwischen den beiden.

Foucaults Gegenposition zum platonischen Projekt und all dem, was aus ihm folgt, ist also radikal. Folgen wir ihr, dürfen wir nicht länger von der Einheit des Wissens und auch nicht von der Einheit des Ich oder von einem einheitlichen Wissensinhalt reden. Wissen, so müssen wir jetzt sagen, ist ein vielfältiges, systematisch mehrdeutiges Phänomen, das Ich eine mannigfaltige Struktur, die Wissensinhalte sind divers in Form und Inhalt. Erkenntnistheorie ist bis jetzt stets der Versuch gewesen, diese Mannigfaltigkeit auf einen Nenner zu bringen. Wir müssen dagegen die Vielfalt als Faktum (an)erkennen und fragen, wie zu verschiedenen Zeiten und unter verschiedenen Umständen, in verschiedenen Diskursen und Disziplinen das wissende Subjekt und sein Wissensfeld und so das Wissen selbst jeweils neu konstituiert sind.

Wir begannen mit der platonischen Frage „τί ἔστιν ἐπιστήμη?" und fragten uns zunächst, worin ihre Bedeutung bestehe. Erst jetzt kommen wir zu diesem Thema zurück. Denn Foucaults Werk läßt einen gewahr werden, daß mit der platonischen Frage nicht nur die Einheit des Wissens auf dem Spiel steht, sondern auch das, was wir bisher Erkenntnistheorie genannt haben, und schließlich auch die Philosophie als ganze, wie sie bis jetzt immer verstanden worden ist. Alles Philosophieren bis in die Gegenwart ist noch immer platonisch gewesen, indem es immer wieder die Einheit hinter der Vielheit der Dinge gesucht hat. Foucaults Werk (ähnlich wie das des späten Wittgenstein) bricht endlich mit dieser Annahme und erweist sich so als philosophisch nur in radikal unphilosophischer Weise. Die Bedeutung der platonischen Frage bestand dann, so sehen wir jetzt im Rückblick, hierin: Sie lud zu einer bestimmten Art von Denken ein, in der Wissen selbst, das wissende Ich und sein Wissensfeld unter dem Begriff der Einheit gedacht werden sollten. Sie war in diesem Sinne eine Ein- und Verführung in solche Philosophie, wie sie sich seit Platon entwickelt hat. Sie war, so können wir jetzt auch sagen, das Unternehmen, eine bestimmte *Episteme* zu konstituieren, nämlich die *Episteme* des philosophischen Feldes. Für uns, die wir die platonischen Annahmen nicht länger teilen können, wird sie aber zugleich zur Einführung in ein anderes Fragen: ein Fragen, in dem die Vielfalt der *Epistemen* Sache der Untersuchung wird und damit auch die *Episteme* des philosophischen Denkens.

Anmerkungen

1 Platon, *Theätet*, 146 a, zitiert nach der Übersetzung von Fr. Schleiermacher.
2 Loc. cit. 146 d.
3 Loc. cit. 210 b.
4 Loc. cit. 210 c.
5 Loc. cit. 186 d.
6 Loc. cit. 187 a.
7 Ibid.

Charles Parsons

Intuition and the Abstract*

I
The concept of intuition

The concept of intuition occupies an uneasy place among the different notions deployed by philosophers and others in order to describe knowledge and belief. Some such notions, such as that of knowledge itself, have been thought to be definite enough in pre-philosophical usage and of sufficient importance so that considerable philosophical effort has been devoted to their "analysis", in the hope of giving in clearer terms necessary and sufficient conditions for knowledge, or, failing that, stating interesting general principles. Others have been from the beginning technical terms, so that no one has hoped to get from them a better understanding than can be derived from philosophers' explanations. Kant's terms "analytic" and "synthetic" would be examples.

The word "intuition" undoubtedly has a pre-philosophical use from which its use in philosophy in some way derives. But there does not seem to be conviction on the part of philosophers that there is a fundamental notion behind that use, which philosophical analysis might make clear. On the other hand, at least in comparatively recent discussion there is also not a technical usage to which writers discussing intuition have been ready to defer, except in rather restricted contexts such as the interpretation of Kant. To be sure, the use of the term in linguistics, when the "intuitions" of native speakers of a language are discussed, may be an exception to this state of affairs. But probably this generalizes at best by analogy. Thus in his useful encyclopedia article on intuition, Richard Rorty goes so far as to say that "nothing can be said about intuition in general".[1]

My own work on the concept of intuition has been in application to mathematics. There the general difficulty I mentioned is very much in evidence, and it is not at all clear that those who defend the idea of mathematical intuition, and those who attack it, have the same concept in mind. In our time there has not been a developed positive conception of mathematical intuition that is sufficiently salient either as a model to be developed and defended or as a target to be attacked. One might contrast this state of affairs with what prevailed in the late nineteenth and early twentieth centuries, where Kant offered a kind of paradigm of a philosophical conception of intuition applied to mathematics (whether or not he was interpreted correctly or even consistently). That is no longer the case.

One can, however, make some elementary distinctions about intuition that apply generally. In the philosophical tradition, intuition is spoken of both in relation to objects and in relation to propositions, that is to say as a propositional attitude.[2] I have used the terms "intuition *of*" and "intuition *that*" to mark this distinction. The philosophy of Kant gives the basic place to intuition of, but it certainly allows for intuitive knowledge or evidence that would be a species of intuition that. I think it is quite clear that Kant has such a conception, but he doesn't designate it by the term *Anschauung* or even use such a phrase as *anschauliche Erkenntnis*. It is not so clear that this priority of intuition of is always preserved in the rather loosely Kantian talk about intuition in late nineteenth and early twentieth century writing about the foundations of mathematics, but it is in the most important developments of broadly Kantian conceptions of intuition in this period, in the work of Brouwer and Hilbert.

An important dimension on which uses of "intuition" as a propositional attitude differ is in how much they are epistemically loaded. The most loaded use would have it that intuition is by definition or by its nature knowledge. That would make it natural to talk of intuition of truths as what is to be contrasted with intuition of objects. Such a use does have precedents in the tradition. What Descartes in the *Rules for the Direction of the Mind* calls *intuitio* is in our terms intuition that and is not genuine unless it is knowledge.[3] Rorty distinguishes four meanings of the term. The first two are instances of intuition that; the last two of intuition of. But all but the first are by definition knowledge. His sense (2), which he justifiably regards as philosophically most important, is worth quoting:

> "Intuition as immediate knowledge of the truth of a proposition, where 'immediate' means 'not preceded by inference'."[4]

This is a good first approximation to a characterization covering the important uses of intuition that. But today at least, "intuition" is not so commonly used so as to connote knowledge. In particular, it is not necessarily factive. If one has the intuition that p, it by no means always follows that p. When a philosopher talks of his or others' intuitions, that usually means what the person concerned is inclined to believe at the outset of an inquiry, or as a matter of common sense; intuitions in this sense not only need not be true but can be very fallible guides to the truth. To take another example, the intuitions of a native speaker about when a sentence is grammatical are again not necessarily correct, although in this case they are, in contemporary grammatical theory, taken as very important guides to truth. In fact, it is not so easy to find factive uses of the term in contemporary philosophy. Use of "intuition" with the connotation of knowledge, and therefore of truth, is likely to cause misunderstanding in the circumstances of today; it may even lead a reader to think one has in mind something like intuitions in a less strict sense with the extra property of being infallible. When one wants to make clear one is speaking of knowledge, it is probably best to use a term like "intuitive knowledge" rather than simply "intuition". Obviously, however, what would count as intuitive knowledge would depend on the underlying conception of intuition, as is shown by the fact that in the philosophy of mathematics "intuitive knowledge" has had a more special sense, connected with Hilbert's version of a roughly Kantian notion of intuition.[5]

Even if one agrees to use "intuition" so that it is not *ipso facto* knowledge and one's having the intuition that p doesn't imply the truth of p, differences are still possible as to how epistemically loaded the notion is, or how much is or ought to be claimed for intuition as a source of knowledge or as a guide to the truth. What philosophers call their intuitions are not generally claimed to be an autonomous source of knowledge, and their reliability will vary greatly. But, as we noted, the intuitions of native speakers of a language do create a presumption of truth. Moreover it could be that in some domain intuition, if carefully enough cultivated, is a source of knowledge and a quite reliable guide to the truth, without actually constituting knowledge in the sense (again) that an agent's having the intuition that p implies p. It can, I believe, be shown quite convincingly that that is the way Kurt Gödel, the twentieth-century philosopher who claims the most for mathematical intuition, intends to use the term.[6] It should be clear that the issue between this usage and that of Descartes is first of all terminological: suppose one has what is to all appearances a convincing intuition that p, but after a time something comes to light that causes one to withdraw assent to p. (Perhaps p, together with other equally convincing assumptions, leads to a contradiction.) On Descartes' usage, one will then say that one did not really have intuition that p; on the usage I am attributing to Gödel, it can be that one had intuition that turned out to be deceptive. Someone who believes that under the right circumstances and by exercising sufficient care one can get into a state which *guarantees* the truth of what one is claiming is more likely to adopt the Cartesian usage, but such a belief is not a necessary condition for it. Note that the locution "see that" is factive, but no one would think that a sufficient reason for holding that infallible perceptual judgment is possible.

These observations suggest what would be the opposite of the Cartesian usage on the dimension of epistemic loading: intuition as simply belief or inclination to believe, presumably not on the basis of inference or ordinary perception, where the attribution of intuition does not regard it as more than a very minimal guide to the truth.[7]

Descartes contrasted intuition with deduction; on his usage the conclusion of an inference would not be an intuition. In describing possible sources of knowledge, not only would intuition be distinguishable from the results of arguments involving inferences, but such results could not be intuitions, although possibly the same proposition could be, or could have been, known by intuition. Descartes' usage agrees with the most common present-day usage; what is most distinctive about what are called intuitions is that they are *not* the conclusions of arguments. More properly, the status of a proposition as an intuition cannot result from its being the conclusion of an argument, although in philosophy and other fields, even to some extent in mathematics, an argument may be defended on the ground that its conclusions agree with intuition.

In this usage, what is most characteristic of intuition is that it is belief, or inclination toward belief, independent of any articulation of its grounds, possibly coupled with expression of doubt as to whether it *could* be reinforced by grounds of another kind, that is by argument (taking this word in its most general sense, which would incorporate deductive arguments, including mathematical proof, empirical or "inductive" arguments, and arguments of a less rigorous structure such as are characteristic of philosophy).

Evidently Rorty, in the definition of his sense (2) cited above, takes this as what the "immediacy" of intuition that consists in. That is no doubt true for many uses of the term. But it cannot be the whole story for the uses that most interest us. For if it were, the simplest and most evident *logical* truths would be intuitively known, and the immediacy of the simplest logical inferences would also be of the same type as what we would call intuitive. It is not usual to view them in that way. The reason is, I think, that the intuitive is contrasted not just with what is inferred but also with the conceptual. This is the usage of Kant, which has been followed by philosophers who are not particularly Kantian in other respects. For example the "knowledge without observation" that we have of our own intentional bodily movements is not usually described as intuition or intuitive knowledge, although it satisfies Rorty's definition. On this point the philosophical tradition divides. In insisting that only sensibility gives rise to intuitions, Kant is breaking both terminologically and substantively from the earlier rationalistic tradition, for which "intuitive knowledge" can represent a high development of what we would call conceptual. This earlier tradition has not lost its influence, and moreover there are uses of "intuition" that are neutral on the issues it would raise. The development of the concept in my own writings on the subject is in the Kantian tradition, and conceptions that agree in this respect with Kant's will be our main concern in what follows.[8] But one should keep the other tradition in view.

Another ambiguity is also worth mentioning: The distinction between intuition of and intuition that does not quite coincide with that between intuition with non-propositional and intuition with propositional objects. For if one takes propositions seriously as objects, in principle one might grant that one could intuit a proposition, in such a way that one could conclude its existence and perhaps something about its structure, while emphasizing that such intuition of the proposition as an object is not apprehension of its *truth*. In other words, intuition *of* the proposition that p as object is not the same as intuition *that p*.

II
Intuition and perception

At this point we need to turn to intuition of. Though Kant, at least in his official explanations, did think of intuition as knowledge[9], it is knowledge *of objects* and not in the first instance propositional knowledge.[10] His *Anschauung* is a case of intuition of. This is forced by what we might anachronistically call its "logical form": an intuition is a singular representation, contrasted with concepts, which are general.[11] Intuitions are also said to be "immediate"; the meaning of this has been a matter of controversy.[12] One aspect that is not controversial is that empirical intuition arises from perception. A situation in which a subject has an empirical intuition of an object, however it is described further, is one in which he perceives the object; in particular, he is affected by the object. Kant's notion of intuition in this sense generalizes the concept of a representation arising from perception. One element of the controversy about Kant's notion of intuition is how much of the presence to the mind of the object in perception carries over to other cases of intuition.

It is hard to see what could make a cognitive relation to objects count as intuition if not some analogy with perception. And indeed we find such an analogy claimed or appealed to by writers advancing very different conceptions. Thus in our own time Gödel famously claimed that "we do have something like a perception of the objects of set theory".[13] In the paper "Is mathematics syntax of language?" that he worked on in the 1950's but never published, he also stresses this analogy, going so far as to speak of an analogy between reason and an "additional sense".[14] But Gödel is not alone in discerning such an analogy.

The Latin *intuitio* is derived from *intueri*, meaning "to look at, to gaze at". Descartes' explanation of *intuitio* in the *Rules* relies on the analogy with perception only in this choice of terminology, on which no doubt nothing in particular turns. It is clearly intuition that; the examples that he gives in Rule Three are all propositional. The analogy with perception is, however, used in Descartes' later definition of clear and distinct perception:

> "I call a perception "clear" when it is present and accessible to the attentive mind – just as we say that we see something clearly when it is present to the eye's gaze and stimulates it with a sufficient degree of strength and accessibility. I call a perception "distinct" if, as well as being clear, it is so sharply separated from all other perceptions that it contains within itself only what is clear."[15]

On the other hand Leibniz does not use such analogies in his explanations of clear and distinct knowledge in "Meditationes de cognitione, veritate, et ideis" (1684). There he makes a contrast between intuitive and "blind or symbolic" knowledge; knowledge of a notion is intuitive when we can "consider all of its component notions at the same time".[16]

Edmund Husserl is a philosopher for whom the notion of intuition takes on a very general significance. He makes a sustained attempt to develop a theory both of knowledge of abstract objects and of rational evidence based on an analogy with perception. Basic to his theory of meaning is a distinction between meaning intentions and their fulfillment. The acts or intentional experiences that constitute our consciousness have intentionality, relation to an object. Such a relation is realized or fulfilled if the object is present in intuition (or at least represented in imagination)[17]; in the case of actual intuition, where there is a certain kind of unity of the intended sense and the sense of the act fulfilling it, one has knowledge of the object. Intuitions are in one place described as "the acts that in knowledge are called to the fulfillment of other intentions".[18] The examples by which Husserl explains these ideas tend to be perceptual. Acts of outer perception have the characteristic that they contain both fulfilled and unfulfilled intentions; for example a perception of a cup sitting on a table will represent it as having a bottom, but since the bottom is not visible that intention is not fulfilled.

In the context of the *Logische Untersuchungen*, the introduction of intuition where the object may be abstract is explicitly represented as an extension of the concept and that of perception. The intention/fulfillment schema invites generalizing the notion of intuition in a way that parallels the generalization of the notion of object:

„So werden, und in allgemein gebräuchlicher Rede, Inbegriffe, unbestimmte Vielheiten, Allheiten, Anzahlen, Disjunktiva, Prädikate *(das Gerecht-sein)*, Sachverhalte zu ‚Gegenständen', die Akte, durch die sie als gegeben erscheinen, zu ‚Wahrnehmungen'."[19]

Something common to Kant, Husserl, and Gödel is a close connection between what I am calling intuition that and intuition of. According to Kant, intuition (which as I have remarked is intuition of) in mathematics confers evidence that is immediate. He says that axioms are "immediately certain" and remarks:

„Die Mathematik dagegen ist der Axiomen fähig, weil sie vermittelst der Konstruktion der Begriffe in der Anschauung des Gegenstandes die Prädikate desselben a priori und unmittelbar verknüpfen kann, z. B. daß drei Punkte jederzeit in einer Ebene liegen."[20]

Evidently the immediacy of the *judgment* derives from a construction "in the intuition of the *object*".[21]

Husserl seems to regard intuition that as a species of intuition of: evidence of a judgment is a situation in which the state of affairs that obtains if it is true is "itself given". Since, typically, a proposition involves reference to objects, evidence will involve intuition of those objects, but they play the role of constituents of a state of affairs that is also intuitively present, at least in the ideal case.[22]

For Gödel, that we have "something like a perception of the objects of set theory" is supposed to be "seen from the fact that the axioms force themselves upon us as being true". The latter appears to be a matter of intuition that; it is clearly a matter of the evident character of certain *statements*. Even if we grant this, why should it follow that there is *intuition* of "the objects of set theory"? Gödel's particular reason for thinking this was very probably that in talking of the objects of set theory, he had in mind not only sets but also concepts, and for him rational evidence of a proposition involved "perception" of the concepts occurring in it.[23] What Gödel calls perception would in our terminology be intuition, since it is clearly perception only in an extended sense.[24]

That intuition that should in some way rest on, or at least be intimately connected with, intuition of is what one would expect if intuition that is analogous to perception, since one of the central elements of perception is the presence of the object perceived; one knows by perception *that* my bicycle is blue by seeing my bicycle. Someone who has never seen my bicycle might know this, but he would not know it by perception in the most straightforward sense.

It is this that makes Gödel's inference natural, even apart from the particular context of his views about concepts and perception of concepts. In what follows I will use the term "intuition" so that a mode of evidence does not count as intuition unless it is analogous to perception in a definite way. In the case of some proposed kind of intuition that, one way in which the analogy can be made out is that it involves intuition of certain objects. Unlike Gödel, I do not maintain that all rational evidence of principles that are not the conclusions of deductive or empirical arguments is a case of intuition, or even that intuition extends very far into the conceptual domain. The following inquiry will be in the tradition of Kant, for whom intuition and reason are of a different nature, rather than in the tradition of Spinoza and Leibniz, for whom intuitive knowledge is possible at high levels of abstraction and rational integration. Taking the analogy with perception as what distinguishes intuition that from other forms of "intrinsic plausibility" that statements might have does not force one to be in Kant's rather than the other camp on this matter (as the example of Gödel shows), but the adherent of the other tradition is required to stretch the analogy much further, as one can see by comparing Gödel's remarks in "Is Mathematics Syntax of Language?" with the conception of intuition presented in my own writings on mathematical intuition.[25]

In these writings I have argued that a form of intuition of in which the objects can be described as mathematical exists, and I have used an associated conception of intuitive knowledge. But the very idea of such an intuition seems at first sight outrageous, and the defense of intuition in the tradition of Kant may seem to deny the accomplishments in the foundations of mathematics since the late nineteenth century, so much of which was directed against either Kant's own views or views deriving from Kant. Both the objections one needs to consider and the defenses against them are more general, concerning the applicability of the concept of intuition where the object is abstract.

III
Objections to the very idea of mathematical intuition

Many critics of theories of mathematical intuition such as Gödel's accuse these theories of postulating a special faculty of intuition. Even if this criticism can be answered in the particular case where it is advanced, behind it lies a point that has to be taken seriously. By its very nature, intuition is not the sort of thing that should be "postulated". If mathematical or other abstract objects are given to us in a way similar to that in which physical objects are given to our senses, should it not be *obvious* that this is so? But the history of philosophical discussion about mathematics seems to show that it is not. Whatever mysteries and philosophical puzzles there may be about perception, it works to a large extent as a straightforward empirical concept. We can make a lot of assured judgments about when we perceive something, and confidence about this description of our experience can often survive doubt about what it is an experience of. Thus the proposition that I now *see* before me a computer with text on its screen is one that I expect that no other philosopher, were he now in the room where I am writing, would dispute except on the basis of skeptical arguments, and many of these would not touch weaker statements such as that it *looks* to me as if I see these things. There is a phenomenological datum here that is as close to being undisputed as anything is in philosophy.

It is hard to maintain that the case is the same for mathematical objects. Is it *obvious* that there is an experience of intuiting the number 7, or a triangle, or at least of its "looking" as if I were intuiting 7 or a triangle? But if it isn't obvious, how could it be true, or how could our intuiting these objects have a relevance to mathematical knowledge comparable to that my seeing my computer screen has to my knowledge that, for example, some sentence I have just typed contains a typographical error? One can put the question in another way by asking whether there are any experiences we can appeal to in the mathematical cases that are anywhere nearly as undisputed as my present experience of seeing the computer screen. If we don't know what to point to, that appears to be already a serious disanalogy between sense-perception and whatever consciousness we have of mathematical objects.

This embarrassment is connected with an obvious disanalogy. In normal cases of perception, there is a physical action of the object perceived on our sense-organs. Our perception is in some way founded on this action, and there are serious reasons for holding that such a causal relation is a necessary condition for perceiving an object. But it would be implausible to hold that in *mathematical* intuition there is a causal action of a mathematical object on the mind. And this point is more general, since it is natural to take not standing in causal relations as a defining mark of abstract objects. In fact that there is such action is no part of the view of the upholders of mathematical intuition that I have mentioned, though it is sometimes included in popular conceptions of platonism or attributed to philosophers like Gödel by their critics.[26] But though in the case of

Gödel it is not justified by the texts, it is not an unnatural error, since one might expect that if mathematical intuition is like perception it should share with it this central feature.

In the first instance these difficulties apply to intuition of mathematical objects, to which both Husserl and Gödel have to be interpreted as being committed. Kant does not say this straightforwardly, and indeed mathematical objects do not play an explicit role in his philosophy of mathematics. There have been differences of opinion about the question to what extent Kant has or can have a conception of mathematical objects.

Still, Kant expresses a puzzlement about how intuition can be a priori that is related to the difficulty about causality. In *Prolegomena*, after introducing the notion of pure intuition, he writes:

> „Anschauung ist eine Vorstellung, so wie sie unmittelbar von der Gegenwart des Gegenstandes abhängen würde. Daher scheint es unmöglich, a priori *ursprünglich* anzuschauen, weil die Anschauung alsdann ohne einen weder vorher noch jetzt gegenwärtigen Gegenstand, worauf sie sich bezöge, stattfinden müßte und also nicht Anschauung sein könnte. […] Allein wie kann *Anschauung* des Gegenstandes vor dem Gegenstande selbst vorhergehen?"[27]

It is clear from the context that by "object" Kant means here *real* object, in practice physical object. The problem does not directly concern intuition of mathematical objects, except insofar as such intuition is to yield mathematics that is applicable to the real world. The question is how it is possible for a priori intuition to be "of" objects that are not given a priori.

Kant's own solution to the puzzle, given in § 9 of the *Prolegomena*, appeals to the idea that a priori intuition contains only the form of our sensibility. This evidently removes the causal dependence of intuition on the object. It is a nice question what is left of the characterization of intuition that gives rise to the puzzle.[28] Kant's solution seems to allow the *phenomenological* presence of an object to be preserved, but it is a further question whether what one has is a representation of a physical object, not individually identified and not really present, or a representation of a mathematical object. The former is not ruled out by the a priori character of pure intuition, since the "presence" might be that characteristic of *imagination* rather than sense. In fact, a number of passages in Kant indicate that just that is his position.

Kant's puzzle may have force for us, but we are not likely to accept the view that pure intuition contains only the form of our sensibility, a central part of Kant's transcendental idealism, at least not as Kant understood it. I have not claimed that mathematical intuition is a priori, but this concession does not remove the force of the puzzle. For suppose that intuition of certain objects underlies our knowledge of a mathematical truth, say $7+5 = 12$. We have this intuition at a certain place and time, and yet the proposition is general in its implications; it is applicable to the "first three minutes" after the Big Bang and also to the world long after we are dead. Moreover, we generally understand such statements to be necessary. Someone who defends mathematical intuition owes us a solution to Kant's puzzle.

Another difficulty for the idea of intuition of mathematical objects is posed by the structuralist view of such objects. According to it, the properties and relations of mathematical objects that matter for mathematics are those determined by the basic relations of some system or structure to which all the objects involved belong, or perhaps several such structures and mappings between them. For applications, what I would call external relations also matter, for example the correspondences between initial segments of the natural numbers and sets of objects numbered. But these are independent of a choice of realization for a given type of structure.

On the structuralist view, mathematical objects are in a way not individually identifiable at all. But then how is it possible that they should be objects of intuition? For example, unless one is presupposing a structure including numbers and sets, it seems indeterminate whether the number 2 is identical to the one-element set $\{\{\emptyset\}\}$, the two-element set $\{\emptyset, \{\emptyset\}\}$ or neither. How can this be if numbers and sets are objects of mathematical intuition? Can such intuition be a significant source of mathematical knowledge if it does not determine the answers to such simple questions?

It is for pure mathematical objects such as the elements of the various number systems and pure sets that the structuralist view is most persuasive. These are pure abstract objects, in that they are characterized by conditions of a highly abstract character involving objects in general. In particular, they do not have anything that could be called an intrinsic concrete instantiation or representation. The other setting besides mathematics in which pure abstract objects arise is metaphysics, particularly in ontological investigations. I do not propose to pursue the idea of a general conception of intuition that would also take in pure abstract objects. I have argued elsewhere that already natural numbers are not objects of intuition on the particular conception I have developed.[29] But the objection just made does have some force for objects of the kind that are the most favorable cases for a Kantian conception of intuition. These are quasi-concrete objects, which do have an intrinsic concrete or perhaps perceptual representation. Examples relevant to mathematics are expression-types and geometrical figures. The difficulty is that they are still incomplete in Leibniz's sense. That they have intrinsic concrete instantiations is not enough to endow them with the range of properties and relations a concrete object would have. The trivial example of numbers and sets given above might be taken as a case of indeterminacy of identity. That such indeterminacy will not arise in quasi-concrete cases is not evident. This is shown by the fact that in the development of mathematics nothing that the mathematician normally attends to is lost by thinking of them in a structural way, so that expressions, for example, are simply built up from arbitrary objects called "symbols" by a relation called "concatenation" that is specified in a purely structural way. On that way of looking at them, their relation to their tokens is an external relation.

To summarize, one might object to the idea of intuition of mathematical objects, and abstract objects generally, that its existence does not have the obviousness that intuition ought to have, that it could not be analogous to perception given that its objects do not stand in causal relations, that it would convey knowledge that, if not fully a priori, is at least general enough so that it is puzzling how it could anticipate our encounters with the objects to which it applies, and that it is incompatible with the incompleteness that even quasi-concrete mathematical objects suffer from.

The objections put forth in this section have all been to the idea of intuition of mathematical objects. Intuition as a propositional attitude is not at the outset as questionable an idea. First of all, there is no doubt that principles in mathematics and other domains have what one might call intrinsic plausibility, and in mathematics at least, reductionist programs that would remove any necessity to rely on this plausibility have not fared very well. But then, as I have structured the question, whether we should talk of intuition depends on whether we can make out a significant analogy with perceptual knowledge. If, as I have suggested is likely, part of this analogy will be dependence on intuition of, the above objections become relevant. The "obviousness" objection does have some independent force. One might put it this way: if on reflection we do not find a certain principle (such as an axiom of set theory) obvious without appealing to a proof, then it is doubtful that we can regard it as a deliverance of intuition. However, it would be a greater task than I can undertake here to separate issues concerning intuition, where a significant analogy with perception is demanded, from issues concerning rational evidence in general. For that reason, my focus here will be primarily on intuition of.

IV
Perception and the abstract

The best reply to these objections would be to motivate and develop a defensible concept of intuition and to show that the objections are not decisive against it. I have undertaken to do this elsewhere[30]; what I shall try to do here is to deal with the objections in a more general setting, without particularly focusing on mathematics.

The observation from which I will start is that consciousness of objects that in the usual classification count as abstract is pervasive and commonplace and closely intertwined with perception. In my view it is closely enough intertwined so that in many cases it is appropriate to call the consciousness itself perception or intuition. An appropriate example with which to begin is what in the empiricist tradition are called sense-qualities. We all perceive colors, and a natural way of describing such experiences is as seeing this or that color, say red or blue. To see red is not the same as to see that some object is red, although of course they are related. Looking to the left of my computer, I see bright blue. It is also true that I see a folder that *is* bright blue, but I could see bright blue without seeing that the folder is blue, either because I fail to identify it, or because there is something in the setting that misleads me about the color of the folder and in fact it isn't bright blue although it looks so. It is the latter possibility that is of greatest importance in the philosophical discussion of color, but I would like to dwell for a moment on the former. If in fact there is a bright blue folder before me, and looking in that direction I see bright blue, then in the absence of some grossly abnormal conditions I do see a bright blue folder. But seeing the color is different from seeing that the folder has that color, or even from seeing, of some demonstratively identified object, that it has that color. One thing that marks the difference is individuation. If, in similar lighting, I look at another folder just like this one, I will see the same color but not the same folder. In semi-darkness, I may be able to see the same folder but not see its color at all. This difference is also enough to distinguish seeing bright blue from seeing a bright blue object, even though under normal conditions they go together (at least if one counts something like a flash of light as an object).

There are two kinds of conditions in which they appear not to go together. The first is where lighting or other conditions might cause an object to look some color other than its real color. Then it seems that I might look at a green object and see bright blue, because the object looks bright blue to me. That seems to me to be the natural way to describe this sort of case, particularly since if my color vision is normal the blue that I see is a real physical phenomenon. The second type of case is an after-image or hallucination, where I might "see" a color but there is no object out there that I am seeing at all. Someone might deny in this sort of case that I really see the color, because the experience is not a perception of a real color phenomenon in my immediate environment. For the purpose of the present discussion it is not of great moment whether such cases are or are not accepted as genuine cases of seeing colors.

It appears that the color we see is a universal, in the sense that it can be instantiated at a great variety of places and times. Although I see bright blue in a certain location, that is not to say that the color itself is located. What is located is not the color but its manifestations, typically objects that have that color or at least look that color to an observer.[31] It may be that what we see is still something more particular than a color as identified by a color-word. For example, a blue computer disk on my table is not quite the same color as the folder. In each case I can properly be described as seeing blue, but one might say that this is only by virtue of my seeing a color that is a variety of blue, so that my seeing blue while looking at the disk and my seeing blue while looking at the folder are not cases of seeing the same color. This does not alter the fact that what is seen is individuated differently from the individuation of spatio-temporal objects.

Color and color perception have many special complications, and so I will not pursue the subject further. One other example, closer to mathematics, should reinforce the claim that perception of objects that are abstract is a commonplace experience and acknowledged as such in our perceptual vocabulary. That is language.

The vocabulary of seeing and hearing is often used with objects that are linguistic and not particular events or physical objects. Thus one often talks of seeing letters, words, and sentences, and of hearing words and sentences.[32] Often when what is heard or seen is a particular event, it is still naturally described in terms referring to linguistic objects, for example as someone's uttering certain words. The word "hear" is also used with what would be called propositional objects; that is, one hears what someone said and could naturally report this using a that-clause. That-clauses also occur in descriptions where the object of hearing is legitimately construed as an event; one can say that one heard someone say that p.[33] One would take in the same information visually by reading it, but we usually talk of reading what someone says or writes rather than seeing it.

The cases of reports by that-clauses obviously introduce a serious complication, as is indicated by the continuing disagreement as to what, if any, the objects of indirect discourse and propositional attitudes are. I want to leave that at one side, since there is no doubt that we do talk of seeing and hearing words and sentences, and at least seeing letters, and there is not the same disagreement as to what these objects are. Here, however, it may be objected that in talk of syntactic objects such as words and sentences, the objects might be types or tokens. If we understand written tokens as physical inscriptions, and spoken tokens as particular events,[34] then perception of tokens is no counterexample to the view that the objects of perception are always concrete. But it seems to me evident that the vocabulary of perception is used where the natural reading is to take the objects as being types, as for example when I report what I heard someone say by giving the exact words. The question whether another hearer heard the same will be answered in the affirmative if he reports the same words, and where that is at issue (i. e. where an indirect-discourse report that would involve paraphrase or translation is not what is called for) not otherwise. And I may also report that I heard a certain word or sentence in a situation where I could not identify the speaker or the location from which the sound came. In such a case in a sense I identify what I heard, namely this or that linguistic expression, but I do not identify a particular object or event. This kind of case is less significant for my claim, however, because in cases where abstract objects are not at issue one's identification of what one perceives can be very partial, and this kind of case can be described in that way. I also think one can talk of perception of linguistic expressions in situations where the perception of an actual object or event is illusory or mistaken, and there was not actually a speaker in the neighborhood who uttered those words, but even if that is agreed its significance can be read in different ways, and I will not insist on it.

Just what is involved in the perception of words and sentences will be as complex as other questions about perception, perhaps more so just because the objects are linguistic, and specifically linguistic abilities are exercised. None of the above is evidently incompatible with the possibility of describing cases of perception of linguistic types in ways that remove the commitment to types.[35] All I have tried to do in this discussion is to make the case that talk of perception of types is something normal and everyday. A convinced nominalist might still respond to this by saying that there must be a reduction in which such talk is shown not really to be committed to types.

V
Replies

The first of the objections raised in III was that if there is intuition of abstract objects, it should be obvious that this is so, and it is not. In IV I pointed to a number of phenomena that surely are obvious and are naturally glossed as something like perception where the object is abstract according to the criterion I have used. Once the kind of intuition of strings of symbols that Hilbert relied on in his explanations of finitism has been explained, it can be seen to rest on something equally obvious. Geometric intuition, where the objects are figures, is in a broad way similar but poses difficulties that Hilbertian intuition does not, because of the fact that although one can defend the idea of perception of shapes on the same grounds as those on which I defended the idea of perception of colors, the relation of experience to mathematical exactness is especially problematic in the case of geometric figures.

It must be admitted that it is less obvious that the description of these phenomena as perception of something abstract is correct. To that extent I do not in the end agree with the premise of the objection. The closeness between our awareness of shapes, colors, and linguistic expressions and undisputed cases of perception is something that has to be pointed out and about which there is room for argument. One might compare my thesis with the thesis that there is perception of *physical objects*. In principle one might deny that even this thesis meets the obviousness condition, since although that appears to be the way we ordinarily talk (and also talk in reporting scientific experiments), a lot of room is still left for argument as to how to take this, in view of the old representationalist view that the only objects of our "direct" perceptual consciousness are ideas or sense-impressions and of the possible project of a phenomenalist reduction of talk about bodies.[36] An analogue of the latter in the case of types has been alluded to, namely a possible nominalist reduction. There is no analogue of the former that is so direct, but the idea that types have to be thought of as equivalence classes or properties of tokens might be developed so as to have the analogous feature, that types are a theoretical construction based on a prior concept of token.

Some arguments about these matters take the form of disputes about how close a cognitive phenomenon is to perception. That brings us to the disanalogy already mentioned between ordinary perception and any intuition of objects where the objects are abstract: We can't say in the latter case that the object itself causes either the intuition or something underlying it (as physiological processes underlie perception), since that would violate the acausality of abstract objects. Although this is a genuine disanalogy, I wish to say that it is not so great as might appear at first sight. One has to recall two things. One is that in many cases, in particular the specifically mathematical ones, intuition of an abstract object requires a certain conceptualization brought to the situation by the subject. The other is that although it is in our usage a criterion for being abstract that an object not stand in causal relations, this is in a way a grammatical point. Abstract objects can be referred to in descriptions of events that do stand in causal relations, and these descriptions can figure in causal explanations. Intuition of a string of symbols from some alphabet is typically founded on perception of one of its tokens. That a token *of that type* acted on the sense-organs of the perceiver could perfectly well be part of a causal explanation of the perceiver's perceiving a token of that type and thus of his having intuition of the type. But we do not gloss this in such a way that causal efficacy is attributed to the type. The underlying reason is no doubt that it is only instantiations of forms at particular places and times, and not the forms themselves, that are said to emit light or otherwise transmit energy to us.

Some locutions might seem to attribute causal efficacy to linguistic expressions or shapes or colors. Suppose for example someone were to say to me, "You have no right to call yourself a philosopher". I might comment on this by saying, "His words made me furious". But if we are thinking of the words as types, surely what made me furious was his uttering them. It was that that made them *his*, and his uttering them in that context made them addressed to me. So that once again we have a situation where the cause is an event that we describe in a way involving reference to an abstract object (the sentence type) that is instantiated in it.[37]

Consider now a case involving a simple artificial "language", such as is discussed in writings of Hilbert and Bernays and some of my own[38]. We need only the simplest case, where there is only a single symbol '|', and the expressions of the language are strings of occurrences of this symbol. For future reference I will call this language *L*. Suppose now that someone A sees a token of '|||' but does not have the concept of strings of this language and so does not think of it as a string of our language, still less intuit such a string, with the case where another person B intuits '|||', perhaps on the basis of a perception of the same token very similar in its other outward aspects such as orientation and lighting. The fact that the token is of the type it is will very likely enter into the explanation of why B's experience is as it is, but it is not clear that its role will be causal, since the difference between B's situation and A's is that B is exercising a conceptual apparatus that includes the capacity to recognize tokens as being of a certain type. Moreover, if a token of a certain type is present to a perceiver, then it follows *necessarily* that the type is instantiated there. Thus one can't distinguish the two cases by saying that in the outer world the type is present in B's case but not in A's. It is hard to say that the *type* is responsible for the difference. But it would not be reasonable to expect that, since the case is precisely one of a difference in the subject's conceptual resources.

The reply we have given to the objection concerning causality is along the lines of a response made some years ago by Mark Steiner to Paul Benacerraf's problem of reconciling reference to mathematical objects with a causal theory of knowledge.[39] Steiner's reply was that although mathematical objects do not stand in causal relations, they do play a role in causal explanations. I am not claiming that by appealing to the distinction between causal relations and causal explanation one can rescue a causal theory of knowledge about abstract objects, only that one can make clearer the relation of such objects, and especially mathematical objects, to the causal order and dissipate the impression that they constitute a "realm apart".

It might be desirable, however, to have our response on this point not depend on the distinction between causal relations and causal explanation. If we reject it, however, then there is another line of response that has already been developed by Jaegwon Kim.[40] The background of Kim's discussion is his well-known rejection of the idea of events as particulars and his view that it is properties, relations, and states of affairs that stand in causal relations. If one takes that view, then one will reject the criterion of abstractness with which I have been working, according to which abstract objects do not stand in causal relations. And that is what Kim does.[41] We might ask whether Kim's view allows a causal relation between objects of the sort of intuition that concerns us and our own cognitive states. Since Kim's focus is different, on simple numerical facts and the objects that might be said to be constituents of them, such as small sets of concrete objects, one cannot read off an answer from his text. But if I am right the fact that an object is a token of a certain type might figure in a causal explanation of someone's knowledge concerning that type, it appears that on Kim's view types might be at least constituents of the states of affairs that stand in causal relations to cognitive states. Although my own tendency is to accept a view of events closer to Davidson's, Kim's discussion makes clear that the contrary view does not put us in a worse position with regard to the relation of abstract objects to the causal order and to perception.

The disanalogy between intuition and perception is reduced by these considerations but does not disappear altogether. A further disanalogy arises from the fact that intuition may be founded on imagination rather than on actual perception; in that case the causal role of objects in the outer world is much more indirect. Furthermore, there is no phenomenon in perception corresponding to that of imagining an arbitrary instance of an intuitive concept, which plays a central role in instances of intuitive knowledge.[42]

Let us now turn to Kant's puzzle. Are we, in order to accept the view that single intuitions can have general implications, forced to accept the conclusion Kant drew from this, particularly in the radical form that the spatio-temporal form of our experience is contributed by our own minds? A problem we face, already in interpreting Kant, is to see what it is specifically about intuition that should drive us to this conclusion. We know that if the earth still exists 2000 years from now, and the earth is a satellite of the sun, then at least one satellite of the sun will exist 2000 years from now. This is a truth of logic and presumably not in any way a deliverance of intuition. Yet it talks of the world 2000 years from now, and obtains its evidence without the use of whatever procedures might be used in physics or astronomy to extrapolate so far and come to a reasonable hypothesis as to whether the earth will exist 2000 years from now. We don't, however, think of its truth as contributed by our own minds in a way that other truths, such as that the earth existed 1000 years ago, are not.[43]

With respect to Kant, a difficulty in understanding the Aesthetic, and the parallel parts of the *Prolegomena*, is why it should be exactly a priori *intuition* that requires that its content should be due to our own cognitive faculties and not to how things are in themselves. Kant's statements on the matter are often dogmatic[44], and he does not seem to me to make a convincing case. Once we take account of the fact that the object of the intuition that concerns us is abstract (as the formulation of the puzzle in the *Prolegomena* does not), then the difference of intuition and concepts is much less evident. On the Hilbertian interpretation of arithmetic as a theory of strings concatenated from a single symbol '¡', it may be held that it is intuitively evident that $7 + 5 = 12$.[45] That statement will be equally true, whatever tokens of the relevant strings are produced 2000 years from now. But on the interpretation at issue it concerns strings as types. Is the relation of type to token so different from that of concept to instance that in the first case our knowledge of a truth concerning types should have the consequence that it is only possible if the ground of the truth is a factor in knowledge contributed entirely by ourselves, while this need not be true in a case of the latter kind?[46] In a case of recalcitrant future data in the intuitive case, it will be open to us to say that the tokens encountered are not of the relevant types, just as in the other cases it will be open to us to say that the instances encountered are not instances of the relevant concepts.

Moreover, there is a difficulty of principle that Kant's position suffers from: Given our inability to know things as they are in themselves, how can it be possible to identify a particular part of our knowledge that is due *entirely* to ourselves or to separate our own contribution to our knowledge from that of the external world? Generally, our knowledge results from our own cognitive faculties and from the world. What Kant's position requires is that one be able to identify some knowledge in which the role of the "world" factor is zero, even though there is no knowledge in which the role of the other factor is zero. We have to be able to identify this knowledge without being able to get at the other factor ("things in themselves"). But if we can't do that, how can we be sure that the other factor plays no role? I do not wish to claim that this difficulty arises on any possible interpretation of Kant's distinction of appearances and things in themselves. I do question, however, how any interpretation can leave intact the claim that the spatio-temporal form of what is intuited is entirely due to ourselves, at least if that is something we know on the basis of an argument like those to be found in the Aesthetic.

The last objection put forth in III derived from the structuralist view of mathematical objects. Although the usual formulations of that view do not hold for quasi-concrete objects, the fact that they have intrinsic concrete instantiations may not be enough to endow them with the range of properties that a concrete object would have; moreover, it is not clear that they do not suffer from the indeterminacy of identity. We cannot rule out the possibility that they are incomplete in the sense that not every predicate is determinately true or false of them.

Let us first consider sentences of a natural language with respect to this issue. Ordinary thought seems to me to treat even quasi-concrete abstract objects as of a different category from physical bodies or other ordinary concrete objects, so if we ask whether a sentence has a property that such objects might have, such as being red or round, the answer will be no straight away; a slightly more sophisticated version of the answer will be that it makes no sense to say of a sentence that it is red or round. Linguistic expressions may be limited in their properties and relations to linguistic ones (broadly construed) and certain relations having to do with their instantiations, such as being uttered on certain occasions. If that is so, then certainly the general tendency of ordinary thought about them would be to hold other predicates false or nonsense in application to them. Some ordinary properties such as being located at a particular place and time are applied to them but not in quite the same way as to bodies. To say that an expression is at a certain place means that a token of it is there, and that of course does not exclude its being elsewhere at the same time. These facts about expressions don't present any particular obstacle to intuition or perception of them beyond those that arise from their being abstract and have already been discussed.

What is said above about expressions of natural language is surely also the case for the strings of an artificial symbolism; that is, initially they have only the properties and relations that either come with their being instantiated in the way they are or are mathematical properties and relations internal to the system of strings. Strings will be, in effect, a logical type. There is a difference with expressions of natural language, however, although it is conceivable that the difference could disappear or be mitigated when the latter are considered in theoretical linguistics. That is that in the further development of a mathematics in which reference to strings plays a role, we may abandon the position in which strings of this language are a logical type. One way this could happen is by generalization of the notion of string-type, so that some tokens are admitted as being of the same type as string tokens that were not previously. But a more relevant one is that strings might come to be talked about in a first-order theory that also talks about mathematical objects of other kinds. It appears that stipulations have to be made about the identity of the strings and the other objects; the initial position according to which no string is identical to anything described in another way (except in the development of the theory of strings, where for example terms introduced by recursions might arise) is not legislative. Hilbert and Bernays, in their practice of finitist arithmetic, identified natural numbers with strings. To consider another more contrived case, if one began to talk of a language in which 'l' was just one of the symbols of the alphabet, it would be extremely natural (indeed, almost forced by that description of the situation), to identify the expressions of our language L introduced above with the strings of the new language that contained only 'l'.

One might see a difficulty in this for intuition of strings. To simplify things, let L' be the language with three symbols, 'l', '\', and '/'. Consider now a person A to whom L has been explained and who thus acquires the ability to intuit strings of L. It seems perfectly conceivable that he might not have the ability to intuit strings of L' containing the additional symbols. But if our own conception makes L a part of L', then according to it A is intuiting strings of L', even though he may not be able to distinguish them and might even, for example, take '\' to be just a badly written version of 'll'.

What this example seems to me to show is that the requirement that one have the concept of a string in order to intuit a string implies that 'intuit' generates an intensional context. Thus it is not quite accurate to say that A is intuiting strings of L', the more accurate description is that A is intuiting strings that are in fact strings of L'. How the behavior of 'intuit' resembles and differs from other referential attitudes is a question that may be worth some investigation.

However, I don't think that topic is especially relevant to what has concerned us here. Our main goal has been to make clear that something that can legitimately be called *intuition* where the object is *abstract* belongs to our cognitive apparatus and is not especially esoteric or mysterious or even confined to the mathematical realm.

Intuition and the Abstract

Notes

* This paper incorporates some material written while the author was a Fellow of the Center for Advanced Study in the Behavioral Sciences, with support from the Andrew W. Mellon Foundation. Thanks are due to both institutions. I also wish to thank Richard Tieszen for his comments on some of what I wrote then and for discussions of intuition over a longer period. The connection with Dieter Henrich's work is not very close, but since Kant is in the background throughout, I should state how much I owe in general to his writings about Kant and to some more specific suggestions he made relevant to work of mine on Kant. I have also benefited from other writings of his and from his efforts to make the German philosophical tradition better known and understood.

1 "Intuition", in: *The Encyclopedia of Philosophy*, ed. P. Edwards (New York: Macmillan, 1967), Vol. 3, p. 204. Rorty does, however, proceed to distinguish four principal meanings of the term; see below.
2 I try to use the term "proposition" as neutrally as possible.
3 I take this to be implied by his characterization in Rule Three of intuition as "the conception of a clear and attentive mind, which is so easy and distinct that there can be no room for doubt about what we are understanding" (Descartes, *Œuvres* (second edition, Vols I–XI), ed. C. Adam et P. Tannery, Vol. X (Paris: Vrin, 1974), p. 368; translation from *The Philosophical Writings of Descartes*, trans. J. Cottingham, R. Stoothoff, and D. Murdoch (Cambridge: Cambridge University Press, 1985), Vol. I, p. 114). Concerning Descartes' mature notion of clear and distinct perception, however, the possibility that one has clearly and distinctly perceived that p and yet p is false is a live one until his argument for the truth of clear and distinct perception, appealing to the veracity of God, has been carried out.
4 Loc. cit. (cf. note 1), p. 204.
5 Consider, for example, the use of the terms „anschauliche Evidenz" and „anschauliche Erkenntnis" in K. Gödel, „Über eine bisher noch nicht benützte Erweiterung des finiten Standpunktes" (1958), in: *Collected Works*, Vol. II: *Publications 1938–1974*, ed. S. Feferman et al. (New York and Oxford: Oxford University Press, 1990), pp. 240 and 242. Gödel is referring to conceptions from the Hilbert school. For evidence that Hilbert and particularly Bernays did rely on such a conception, see § 2 of

my "Finitism and Intuitive Knowledge", in: *The Philosophy of Mathematics Today*, ed. M. Schirn (Oxford: Clarendon Press, 1998).

6 See §§ 4–5 of my "Platonism and Mathematical Intuition in Kurt Gödel's Thought", in: *The Bulletin of Symbolic Logic* 1 (1995), pp. 44–74.

7 Cf. Rorty's first meaning: "unjustified true belief not preceded by inference; in this (the commonest) sense 'an intuition' means 'a hunch'", loc. cit. (cf. note 1), p. 204. The qualification "true" seems to me out of place; Rorty may have inserted it because he was thinking of *claims* of intuition, that is first-person attributions.

8 In this respect I am probably swimming against the tide at least in choice of terminology. It is interesting to compare Rorty's article (cf. note 1) with the one with the same title by George Bealer in *The Encylopedia of Philosophy Supplement*, ed. D. M. Borchert (New York: Macmillan Reference USA, 1996), pp. 268–269. Rorty is roughly neutral between the Kantian and the earlier rationalistic usage; Bealer regards the Kantian usage as "out of fashion" and concentrates on a usage derived from the rationalistic one. I believe he is approximately correct in his perception of how the term is most widely used today. He is also a strong defender of a rationalistic conception of intuition; cf. also his "On the Possibility of Philosophical Knowledge", in: *Philosophical Perspectives* 10: *Metaphysics*, ed. J. E. Tomberlin (Atascadero: Ridgeview, 1996), pp. 1–34.

9 Cf. e. g. *Kritik der reinen Vernunft* A 320/B 376 f.

10 Of course it does not follow that there is essentially non-propositional knowledge according to Kant. His view that intuitions without concepts are blind, and that the use the understanding makes of concepts is to judge by means of them (cf. *Kritik der reinen Vernunft* A 68/B 93), implies that knowledge of objects is manifested by propositional knowledge about them.

One should be cautious in attributing to Kant's *Erkenntnis* everything that for us goes with the word "knowledge"; some writers in English on Kant have preferred the translation "cognition" (in part because *Erkenntnis* in Kant's usage is a count noun, while "knowledge" is not). In particular, it is not evident that where an *Erkenntnis* is propositional (that is a judgment) it must be true.

11 Apart from the *Kritik der reinen Vernunft* A 320/B 376 f., see also Kant's *Logik* § 1, in: *Kant's gesammelte Schriften*, ed. Deutsche (formerly Königlich Preußische) Akademie der Wissenschaften, Vol. IX, (Berlin: Walter de Gruyter, 1923), p. 91.

12 Cf. my *Mathematics in Philosophy* (Ithaca: Cornell University Press, 1983),

pp. 111–115, 142–145, and the writings of Hintikka, Howell, and Thompson cited there, also section I of my "The Transcendental Aesthetic", in: *The Cambridge Companion to Kant*, ed. P. Guyer (Cambridge: Cambridge University Press, 1992).

13 "What is Cantor's Continuum Problem?" (1964 version), in: K. Gödel, *Collected Works*, Vol. II: *Publications 1938–1974*, ed. S. Feferman et. al. (New York and Oxford: Oxford University Press, 1990), p. 268.

14 For example in version III, published in: K. Gödel, *Collected Works*, Vol. III: *Unpublished Essays and Lectures*, ed. S. Feferman et al. (New York and Oxford: Oxford University Press, 1995), pp. 353 n. 43 and 354.

15 *Principia philosophiae*, Pars prima: XLV, in: *Œuvres* (cf. note 3), Vol. VIII,1; trans.: *Principles of Philosophy*, in: loc. cit. (cf. note 3), pp. 207 f.

16 In: *Die philosophischen Schriften von G. W. Leibniz*, ed. C. I. Gerhardt, Vol. IV (Berlin: Weidmann, 1880), p. 423; translation from *Philosophical Essays*, trans. and ed. R. Ariew and D. Garber (Indianapolis: Hackett, 1989), p. 25. I would conjecture that this essay had an influence on Gödel, but Gödel could hardly have derived from it the idea of thinking of reason as an "additional sense". It is also unlikely that Husserl was a major influence; the various versions of "Is mathematics syntax of language?" were in all probability written before Gödel began his serious study of Husserl (in 1959).

17 Cf. *Logische Untersuchungen* I, § 9 and § 14, in: E. Husserl: *Husserliana*, ed. U. Panzer, Vols. XIX.1 and XIX.2 (Den Haag: Nijhoff, 1984). The distinction between intention and fulfillment and the relations between them are explored more thoroughly in Investigation VI.

18 *Logische Untersuchungen* VI, § 10, A 511/B_2 39 (cf. note 17).

19 *Logische Untersuchungen* VI, § 45, A 615/B_2 143 (cf. note 17): "Thus, also in generally customary speech, aggregates, indeterminate multitudes, totalities, numbers, disjunctives, predicates *(being just)*, and states of affairs become 'objects'; the acts, through which they appear as given, become 'perceptions'." [my translation].

20 *Critique of Pure Reason* A 732/B 760.

21 Kant does not explicitly claim immediate certainty for all mathematical propositions; the question naturally arises whether it is limited to axioms. In the Hilbert school and later, the idea of intuitive evidence has been applied also to the results of proof, with, however, strong restrictions on the admissible methods. It is doubtful that Kant would make such an extension; for example he glosses "propositions that are synthetic and immediately certain" as "*indemonstrabilia*" (cf. *Critique of Pure Reason*

A 164/B 204). Here, where he is talking about arithmetic, he clearly has in mind numerical formulae such as $7 + 5 = 12$, which he does not call axioms because they are singular. Clearly in these cases, however, one needs to carry out the operations (which Kant certainly thought of as constructions). Although apparently a construction is sufficient to make such propositions evident, the construction can be quite complex, and in the case of large numbers evidently will be. For this reason one should not read "immediately certain" as "self-evident", as Frege did (cf. G. Frege: *Grundlagen der Arithmetik. Eine logisch mathematische Untersuchung über den Begriff der Zahl* (Breslau: Koebner, 1884), § 5).

22 In his discussion of truth, Husserl talks of the "ideal of final fulfillment" *(Logische Untersuchungen* VI, §§ 37–39 (cf. note 17)). But that final fulfillment is even ideally possible in Husserl's sense conflicts with his view that it is essential to objects of external perception that they can be perceived only inadequately. The complexities of Husserl's views on truth and evidence in *Logische Untersuchungen* (cf. note 17) and *Ideen zu einer reinen Phänomenologie und phänomenologischen Philosophie,* Buch 1 (in: *Husserliana,* ed. W. Biemel, Vol. III (Den Haag: Nijhoff, 1950)) are instructively discussed in Gail Soffer, *Husserl and the Question of Relativism* (Dordrecht: Kluwer, 1991), ch. 3.

23 This claim is documented in "Platonism and Mathematical Intuition in Kurt Gödel's Thought" (cf. note 6).

24 When Gödel uses the term "intuition", he usually means intuition that, but this is not always the case, in particular not when he is talking about a Kantian notion of intuition.

25 "Mathematical Intuition", in: *Proceedings of the Aristotelian Society* 80 (1979–80), pp. 145–168; modified and amplified in "Intuition in Constructive Mathematics", in: *Language, Mind, and Logic,* ed. J. Butterfield, (Cambridge: Cambridge University Press, 1986), pp. 211–229, and "On Some Difficulties Concerning Intuition and Intuitive Knowledge", in: *Mind* 102 (1993), pp. 233–245.

26 Thus Paul Benacerraf writes: "He [Gödel] sees, I think, that something must be said to bridge the chasm created by his realistic and platonistic interpretation of mathematical propositions, between the entities that form the subject matter of mathematics and the human knower. Instead of tinkering with the logical form of mathematical propositions or with the nature of the objects known, he postulates a special faculty through which we "interact" with these objects." ("Mathematical Truth", in: *The Journal of Philosophy* 70 (1973), pp. 661–679, p. 675.) The quotes around

"interact" indicate that Benacerraf thinks that even for Gödel such talk is not to be taken literally, but it is not clear to me what he thinks Gödel wishes to substitute for literal action of mathematical objects on this "special faculty".

My own reading of Gödel's conception of mathematical intuition does not give place to anything like interaction of ourselves with mathematical objects or the "concepts" that are more prominent in Gödel's discussion of these matters; cf. "Platonism and Mathematical Intuition in Kurt Gödel's Thought" (cf. note 6), §§ 4–5. I agree with the earlier criticism of Benacerraf's remark by Tait, "Truth and Proof", *Synthese* 69 (1986), pp. 341–370, footnote 3, although I do not entirely agree with the interpretation Tait proposes to put in its place; cf. loc cit. (cf. note 6), pp. 66–67, and n. 44.

27 *Prolegomena* A 50 f. (§ 8).
28 In fact, the characterization does not comport fully with Kant's conception of intuition as explained and deployed elsewhere.
29 "Intuition and Number", in: *Mathematics and Mind*, ed. A. George (New York and Oxford: Oxford University Press, 1994), pp. 141–157.
30 Cf. note 25.
31 Whether that should count as a "manifestation" of the color is a question that would have to be addressed in a fuller account of color. Some philosophers have maintained that there are "abstract particulars", in our example what one might call the particular blue of my folder. On such a view that might properly be called the manifestation of the color. This would allow one to hold that seeing bright blue is a case of seeing that something is bright blue; namely one sees the color-particular, and sees that it is bright blue. Husserl, for example, would distinguish between the color-moment of the folder, which is just such an abstract particular, and the color blue, which is a universal. The former is quite properly located. The question arises for this view whether even the folder's looking bright blue now (even if, perhaps, it isn't really) has a particular moment of the folder corresponding to it.
32 Hearing letters probably does occur, but only when a particular letter sound is salient.
33 If I hear someone say that p, then I might sensibly say that I have heard that p. If I see someone write that p, something further is needed for me to see that p.
34 According to the criterion I have relied on, events are concrete rather than abstract, since they are located in space and time and stand in causal relations.

35 S. Bromberger and M. Halle, "The Ontology of Phonology", in: S. Bromberger, *On What We Know We Don't Know* (Chicago: University of Chicago Press, and Stanford: Center for the Study of Language and Information, 1992), pp. 209–228, argue that expression-types are not fundamental objects in phonology, that phonology need not be committed to them, that they are merely a *façon de parler* (p. 226). I am not entirely convinced by their case. Their claims do not contradict mine directly, however: I am claiming that the straightforward reading of certain ordinary locutions about perception of language will be in terms of perception of types. Whether reference to types can be eliminated in a certain linguistic theory, phonology, is another matter.

36 Although the possibility of such a reduction is not taken very seriously today, it was not so long ago, at least up through the 1950's.

37 Although that isn't exactly what the imagined comment intends, it might be more accurate to say that what caused my anger was his saying *that* I had no right to call myself a philosopher. Then the event is described using indirect discourse. Most accounts of indirect discourse have it involving reference to a sentence or proposition, thus again to something abstract. The influential account of Davidson appears to introduce only reference to utterances, but carrying it through may require modifying it to introduce reference to sentences and their structure; cf. J. Higginbotham, "Linguistic Theory and Davidson's Program in Semantics", in: *Truth and Interpretation*, ed. E. Lepore (Oxford: Blackwell, 1986).

38 Cf. note 25.

39 See Steiner, *Mathematical Knowledge* (Ithaca: Cornell University Press, 1975), ch. 4. Benacerraf's problem was posed in "Mathematical Truth" (cf. note 26). As noted in "Mathematical Intuition", n. 12 (cf. note 25), Kant's puzzle in the *Prolegomena* is a related problem.

40 "The Role of Perception in A Priori Knowledge: Some Remarks", in: *Philosophical Studies* 40 (1981), pp. 339–354.

41 Cf. op. cit. (cf. note 40), p. 347.

42 See in particular "Mathematical Intuition" (cf. note 25), section V.

43 The reader, thinking of conventionalist views of logical truth, will naturally ask: Yes, but we do consider the view that, though all truth depends both on the world (outside us) and language (a human creation), some truths, and in particular logical truths, are such that the contribution of the former is zero. But if they thus depend only on language, then they are contributed only by us. Kant's view should probably be seen in a similar light. I am not concerned to show that no *general* view of this

kind can be right. They have the feature that there is some factor contributed by "us" that *all* knowledge depends on. That seems to me to be the primary point, not whether there is some knowledge that depends only on this factor. As indicated below in the text with reference to Kant, I do have difficulty with the latter conclusion (for Quinean reasons). But my main concern is to argue that the kind of intuition I am concerned with does not force the particularly Kantian version of this dependence.

44 See e. g. *Kritik der reinen Vernunft* B 41.
45 This would be an implication of the introduction of the concepts of finitist arithmetic in Hilbert and Bernays, *Grundlagen der Mathematik I* (Berlin: Springer, 1934); cf. my "Finitism and Intuitive Knowledge" (cf. note 5), § 5.
46 In the end Kant holds that it is true also in the conceptual case whenever the proposition involved is a priori and expresses genuine knowledge of objects. In view of the role of the forms of intuition in the deduction of the categories, it is very doubtful that he intends an argument for this conclusion that would be independent of the claims concerning intuition, although the transcendental unity of apperception is given in some passages a legislative role that parallels the "forming" role of the forms of intuition.

Dagfinn Føllesdal

Husserl's Idealism

Husserl's turn to transcendental idealism in 1905–08 was regretted by many of his students and is also criticized by many present-day phenomenologists. Roman Ingarden (1893–1970) wrote a small book and a number of articles against it.[1] Husserl protested that he was misunderstood, and contended that his idealism was different from traditional idealisms.[2] Husserl insisted again and again that his idealism was at the core of his phenomenology. The following often quoted passage from the *Cartesian Meditations*[3] is typical:

> "Only those who misunderstand the most profound sense of the intentional method or the transcendental reduction or even of both, may want to separate phenomenology from transcendental idealism."[4]

Husserl's transcendental idealism is so intimately intertwined with the rest of his philosophy that in order to get it right we have to have an accurate understanding of the totality of which it is a part. Unfortunately, good and careful Husserl scholars have misconstrued central points in his philosophy. This has led them to a wrong conception of Husserl's idealism, which in turn has made it an easy prey for their criticism. In what follows, I will first give a brief presentation of the main points in Husserl's idealism as an integral part of Husserl's phenomenology. The finer points are then brought out in a critical examination of one of the most careful and well-documented discussions of Husserl's idealism from recent years, that of Herman Philipse in his article "Transcendental Idealism" in *The Cambridge Companion to Husserl*.[5] My aim is not so much to criticize Philipse, whom I regard as a competent and careful Husserl scholar, but to use his presentation and discussion of Husserl's idealism as an occasion to bring out certain crucial features of Husserl's idealism that are often misunderstood, not only by Philipse, but also by many others.

Dagfinn Føllesdal

I
Intentionality

Husserl's notion of intentionality is the key notion of his phenomenology and, as he points out in the quotation above from the *Cartesian Meditations* and in several other places, it is crucial for a proper understanding of his idealism. There are particularly *six* features of Husserl's notion of intentionality that are pivotal:

1. Objects of acts

First, Husserl retains the following basic idea of Brentano's:

> "We understand by intentionality the peculiarity of experiences to be 'consciousness *of* something'." [6]

Husserl's quotation marks are, I think, put in to indicate that there are cases where an object is missing, but that nevertheless consciousness has the property of always being *as-if-of* an object. There is abundant and explicit evidence in several of Husserl's works that this is his view. This interpretation of Husserl has been criticized, it has been claimed that according to Husserl every act has an object.[7] I have rebutted this objection elsewhere and shall not discuss it here.

What interests the phenomenologists is not whether or not there is an object, but what the features are of consciousness that makes it always be *as if of* an object. These three words, 'as if of' are the key to Husserl's notion of intentionality. To account for the directedness of consciousness by saying only that consciousness is directed towards an object, and letting it remain with that, leaves us in the dark with regard to what that directedness is. Husserl wanted to throw light on just this issue: what does the directedness of consciousness consist in?

2. What is directedness?

Husserl uses the label 'noema' for those features of consciousness that manifest its directedness. I shall not discuss the notion of *noema*

Husserl's Idealism

now.⁸ Let us merely note that for Husserl intentionality does not simply consist in consciousness directing itself towards objects that are already there. Intentionality for Husserl means that consciousness in a certain way "brings about" that there are objects. Consciousness "constitutes" objects, Husserl said, borrowing a word from the German idealists, but using it in a different sense. I put the phrase 'bringing about' in quotation marks to indicate that Husserl does not mean that we create or cause the world and its objects. 'Intentionality' and 'constitution' mean merely that the various components of our consciousness are interconnected in such a way that we have an experience as of one object. To quote Husserl:

> "[T]he object is 'constituted' – 'whether or not it is actual' – in certain concatenations of consciousness which in themselves bear a discernible unity in so far as they, by virtue of their essence, carry with themselves the consciousness of an identical X."⁹

3. Transcendent objects

Objects are experienced as having a great number of properties, normally, as in the case of a material object, many more than can ever be exhausted in our experience of it. This might be thought to go against idealism. However, it manifests a characteristic feature of Husserl's version of idealism. Most of the objects we experience are experienced as being independent of our experience of them. They have a richness of features that will largely remain unexperienced by anybody. Many of these objects were there before we were born and will continue to be around after we are gone. They are transcendent, Husserl said. He did not mean by this that they are not experiencable, merely that there will always be more to them than we can ever get around to experience. The transcendent objects are just what we experience in acts. They should not be thought of as something like Kant's *Ding an sich*, a notion that Husserl rejected.

Husserl also talks about transcend*al* objects. This is a quite different notion. Transcendental objects are objects that are crucial to our experience, but are not normally noticed by us, such as the *noema*, the *noesis* and the *hyle*. They become objects of our acts only in a special act of reflection upon our own consciousness, what Husserl called the *transcendental reduction*.

4. The *hyle*

I shall here not talk about the *noesis*. However, the *hyle* is important for understanding Husserl's idealism. According to Husserl, *hyle* are experiences which we typically have when our sense organs are affected, as in perception, but also in some other cases, such as when we are affected by drugs, fever and the like.

In acts of perception the *hyle* play a constraining role. While in acts of imagination our acts can have a wide variety of *noemata* and corresponding objects, independently of what goes on at our sense organs, acts of perception are constrained to having *noemata* that are compatible with the *hyle*. This notion of compatibility is rather intricate, the *hyle* are experiences, they do not have properties that correspond to the properties of the object nor to properties of the *noema* of the object. The *hyle* have no colors and no shapes. They do have a temporal duration, but this duration does not correspond to the duration of the object, which usually outlasts our experience of it. Also, *hyle* cannot be reidentified from one act to another, different act, as has been claimed by Gurwitsch.[10] The *hyle* of each act depend on the structural connections within which they appear, that is, the *noema* of the act.

5. Intersubjectivity

Although the *hyle*, that are so crucial in perception, are private experiences, not shared by others, Husserl emphasizes, early and late, that the world we intend and thereby constitute, is not our own private world, but an intersubjective world, common to and accessible to all of us. Thus in the *Ideas* he writes:

> "I continually find at hand as something confronting me a spatiotemporal reality [*Wirklichkeit*] to which I belong like all other human beings who are to be found in it and who are related to it as I am."[11]

Husserl stresses the shared, intersubjective nature of the world particularly in § 29 of the *Ideas*, which he entitles "The 'Other' Ego-subjects and the Intersubjective Natural Surrounding World". He there says:

> "I take their surrounding world and mine objectively as one and the same world of which we are conscious, only in different ways [*Weise*] [...] For all that, we come to an understanding with our fellow human beings and together with them posit an objective spatiotemporal reality".[12]

In the later works one finds similar ideas, particularly in the many texts that have been collected by Iso Kern in the three volumes of the *Husserliana* devoted to intersubjectivity[13], but also in many other works, for example in the *Crisis*:

> "Thus in general the world exists not only for isolated men but for the community of men; and this is due to the fact that even what is straightforwardly perceptual is communal."[14]

Husserl discusses in great detail empathy and the many other varieties of intersubjective adaptation that enable us to intend a common, intersubjective world. For these discussions I refer to the three volumes on intersubjectivity that I just mentioned.

This, then, is a further feature of Husserl's idealism. It is not a solipsism. The constituted world in which we find ourselves, is a shared world, experienced by each of us only from a perspective. This communal nature of the world and of the objects we perceive is another characteristic of their transcendence. In addition to the innumerable aspects of transcendent objects that we ourselves have not yet explored, they also have lots of aspects that are there for others to explore. Some of these other aspects might not even be accessible to us. If, for example, I am colorblind, I will not see the colors of the world. Still, in virtue of my life together with others, I constitute the world as having colors. Also, to use an example used by Hilary Putnam in another context: although I am not myself able to tell elms from beeches, I live in a world where there is such a distinction to be drawn.

6. The thetic character of acts

Our acts and their *noemata* have a further feature, which is crucial for a correct understanding of Husserl's idealism. They are not merely object-directed, they are also directed towards their object in different ways. While in one act we perceive the object, in another we remember it, etc. This different „thetic" character of the act is studied in phenomenology, along with the complex structure which makes it as if of an object. Husserl correspondingly distinguished two main components in the *noema* of an act: the *thetic* component, which differentiates acts of perception from acts of remembering, imagining, etc., and the *noematic sense* [Sinn], which gives the act its object-directedness. Two acts can have the same thetic character, e. g., be acts of perception, and yet have different objects. And two acts may have different thetic characters, e. g., be acts of perceiving and of remembering, and yet have the same object.

The thetic character of acts is highly important in Husserl's idealism. The study of the thetic character gives us insight into what it means for the world and its objects to be:

> "Phenomenological idealism does not deny the factual [*wirklich*] existence of the real [*real*] world (and in the first instance nature) as if it deemed it an illusion [...]. Its only task and accomplishment is to clarify the sense [*Sinn*] of this world, just that sense in which we all regard it as really existing and as really valid. That the world exists [...] is quite indubitable. Another matter is to understand this indubitability which is the basis for life and science and clarify the basis for its claim."[15]

In fact, just the difference between our notions of illusion and reality is one of the contrasts that phenomenology seeks to clarify.

II
Reality

Phenomenology is a study of these structures of our consciousness, those that relate to the noematic sense as well as those that pertain to the thetic character. An important task for phenomenology is to throw light on the sense in which we regard the world as real, as existing. Husserl claims as we have noted that the world is experienced as transcendent, intersubjective and constantly at hand. He was particularly concerned with what gives reality-character to the world. Like William James, whom he read already when he made the transition to phenomenology in the mid nineties, he stressed the importance of the body, and the inflictions upon our body, for our sense of reality. As James put it: „Sensible vividness or pungency is then the vital factor in reality."[16] Husserl goes much more into depth and detail than James concerning the role of the body.

The existence of the world is, according to Husserl, indubitable. In a manuscript from 1917 Husserl introduced the word 'lifeworld' for this world in which we find ourselves living and which is experienced by us as real. In the *Crisis* (1936), where he first uses this word in print, he writes:

> "[T]he lifeworld, for us who wakingly live in it, is always there, existing in advance for us, the 'ground' of all praxis, whether theoretical or extratheoretical. The world is pregiven to us, the waking, always somehow practically interested subjects, not occasionally but always and necessarily as the universal field of all actual and possible praxis, as horizon. To live is always to live-in-certainty-of-the-world."[17]

Husserl's idealism does hence not consist in rejecting the reality of the world, or regarding it as an illusion. On the contrary, the very notion of an illusion presupposes the reality-character of the world. To say that the world is an illusion would verge on a contradiction. It would be to undercut the very sense of what is claimed. There are certain parallels to this in the earlier German idealists, notably Fichte. However, Husserl's position seems to me to be better thought through, and it differs in important respects from the positions that are commonly labeled 'idealism'. Husserl was notorious for his lack of skill in understanding other philosophers and for his ineptitude in using their terms. Thus, for example, terms like 'ontology' and 'metaphysics' are used in a very idiosyncratic way by Husserl. My own view is that the traditional idealism/realism distinction is ill suited to capture Husserl's position, and that here, as in the rest of his philosophy, he might have been better off avoiding traditional philosophic terminology. This is confirmed by a letter he wrote in 1934 to Abbé Baudin: "No ordinary 'realist' has ever been as realistic and concrete as I, the phenomenological 'idealist' (a word which by the way I no longer use)."[18]

III
Philipse's interpretation and criticism of Husserl's idealism

As already mentioned, Herman Philipse has recently written a long and thorough article on Husserl's idealism which, I will argue, is based upon a misinterpretation of Husserl, but gives me an occasion to stress, elaborate and defend some of the points concerning Husserl's idealism that have been stated above.

Philipse argues that "Husserl's transcendental idealism is closer to traditional idealist positions such as Berkeley's or Kant's than is commonly thought".[19] His strategy is to present a new view on Husserl's development from *Logical Investigations* (1900/1901) to *Ideas* (1913). In arguing for his position Philipse depends especially strongly on the *first* edition of the *Logical Investigations* and an article by Husserl from 1903, in his article series „Bericht über deutsche Schriften zur Logik in den Jahren 1895 – 99".[20]

Philipse shows that these early texts contain passages that lead to an interpretation of phenomenology that makes Husserl's idealism implausible and incoherent. Now, the pertinent passages in the *Logical Investigations* were changed by Husserl in the second edition of this work (1913). Philipse's view is that "Husserl deleted or modified most of these passages in the second edition. They had been rendered obsolete by transcendental idealism".[21] My own view is that these passages clash already with other parts of the first edition of the *Logical Investigations*, and that there is no need to go to his later, idealist, works in order to see that the passages need to be revised. The passages misrepresent Husserl's view, even the view he had in 1900/01, and he therefore revised them.

There will not be space here to go into all the points Philipse makes in his long paper, although it would have been useful to do so before he expands it into a planned monograph. I will concentrate here on just one point, which plays a central role in his argument. Philipse argues that

> "Husserl endorsed a theory of outer perception that was popular in the second half of the nineteenth century, the so-called *projective theory of perception*. According to the projective theory, the perceptual apperception is a projective mental function by which the impressions or sensations we have when we perceive an external object, sensations which, in fact, are nothing but subjective mental modifications, are 'projected' outside, that is, are localized at a place different from the one in which the perceiving subject localizes itself. This projective function would endow the sensations with the illusory appearance of independent existence. If this hypothesis is correct, Husserl's 'objective sense' is nothing but this illusory appearance of 'independent existence' of phenomenal objects, which we project or posit on the basis of our sensations, and his 'objectifying perceptual apperception' is nothing but projection. In other words, Husserl's key-term 'constitution' simply means projective interpretation, at least in the case of outer perception."[22]

The allegation that Husserl had a projective theory of perception comes back again and again in Philipse's article[23] and is an assumption required for several other of his arguments.

Philipse is well aware that his interpretation of Husserl's theory of perception is crucial for his argument. He writes: "I shall contend that Husserl's very problems concerning experience cannot be understood unless one reconstructs them on the basis of his theory of perception."[24] However, the interpretation of Husserl's theory of perception which Philipse presents in the long passage I have quoted above is quite different from the one I presented above, in my discussion of Husserl's notion of *hyle*. There are very many passages in Husserl's writings that support my interpretation, as I have documented in an article on Husserl's philosophy of perception in 1974.[25] Philipse's interpretation certainly conflicts with all these passages. What textual evidence is there then for Philipse's interpretation? Philipse focuses on two passages, one in the first edition of the *Logical Investigations*, which was changed in the second edition, and one in the 1903 article I mentioned earlier. Here is the first passage:

> "[T]he things of the **phenomenal** [the emphasis is Husserl's] world, that is to say all their characteristics, are constituted out of *the same stuff* [the italics are Philipse's], which, as sensations, we consider to belong to the content of consciousness."[26]

This is clearly at odds with my interpretation. Husserl, too, found it at odds with what he wanted to say. So he changed it. I count this in favor of my interpretation, and against Philipse's.

The second crucial passage is not quoted in full by Philipse. He only states:

> "This interpretative hypothesis is confirmed by another casual passage, this time in a review from 1903 to which Husserl often refers. For he there characterizes the objectifying apperception in outer perception as an *interpretative externalization* [*deutende Hinausverlegung*]. The hypothesis also explains why the phenomenal world is constituted out of the same stuff as sensations are."[27]

However, if we read the words italicized by Philipse in context, they do not support his interpretation. This is what Husserl writes (I quote the original German to avoid any inaccuracy):

> „Indessen, aus eben diesen vorkritischen Objektivierungen – mit ihren [...] deutenden Hinausverlegungen von physischen Dingen und Zuständen [...] entspringen die Schwierigkeiten des metaphysischen Problems der Möglichkeit der Erkenntnis."[28]

So, the phrase „deutende Hinausverlegung" is used by Husserl to characterize a position that he finds problematic and precritical. Of course, Husserl held, as we have seen earlier, that the physical objects we perceive are outside us, one aim of phenomenology is to throw light on this and in general on the transcendence of the physical object. But he certainly did not hold, as Philipse claims in his characterization of the projective theory of perception, that

> "the impressions or sensations we have when we perceive an external object, sensations which, in fact, are nothing but subjective mental

modifications, are 'projected' outside, that is, are localized at a place different from the one in which the perceiving subject localizes itself".[29]

Husserl, like most of us, did not always find the most felicitous expressions to state his view. Fortunately, he repeatedly went back over his texts and rectified them. A good interpretation should not attribute to Husserl a view from which he distanced himself. It should rather find confirmation in the fact that certain passages that clash with the interpretation were also found by Husserl himself to be unsatisfactory.

There is much more that can and should be said about Philipse's interpretation of Husserl, for example about his view that Husserl's notion of *noema* is an expansion of the notion of sense. I have put forth this view, in 1962, but I would certainly not subscribe to Philipse's most radical expansion, when he says:

> "It follows from Husserl's theory of perception that transcendent objects are 'senses', for they are the product of a projective interpretation of sensations."[30]

Numerous passages from Husserl can be cited against this view. And they count not only against Philipse's view that transcendent objects are senses, but also against his attribution to Husserl of a projective theory of perception and against his interpretation of Husserl's idealism. This is not the place for a full discussion of Philipse's article. In lectures and articles, since 1962 on, I have presented a fuller interpretation of Husserl's idealism within the context of his whole philosophy, with close attention to Husserl's arguments and the textual evidence. Eventually I hope to bring this out in its entirety. However, I hope that the above sketch will be of some use, especially since even these few elementary points are not regarded as obvious by all Husserl scholars.

Dagfinn Føllesdal

Notes

1 Cf. R. Ingarden, *On the Motives Which Led Husserl to Transcendental Idealism*, translation from the Polish by A. Hannibalsson (Den Haag: Nijhoff, 1975) (= Phaenomenologica 64). For a discussion of Ingarden see I. M. Wallner, "In Defense of Husserl's Transcendental Idealism: Roman Ingarden's Critique Re-Examined", in: *Husserl Studies* 4 (1987), pp. 3–44.
2 Cf. E. Husserl, *Briefe an Ingarden*, ed. R. Ingarden (Den Haag: Nijhoff, 1968), esp. p. 156.
3 All references to Husserl's writings are to *Husserliana: Gesammelte Werke* (= in the following: Husserliana), ed. H. L. van Breda et al. (Den Haag: Nijhoff et al., 1950–1996), providing the volume in Roman numerals, followed by the page number and the lines cited (in brackets). Thereafter follow an abbrevation for the work cited and references to sections or to the pagination of the first edition, indicated as "A". Where not stated otherwise, translations are mine.
4 Husserliana I 119 (8–11), *Cartesianische Meditationen* IV, § 41.
5 Cf. H. Philipse, "Transcendental Idealism", in: *The Cambridge Companion to Husserl*, ed. B. Smith and D. W. Smith (Cambridge: Cambridge University Press, 1995), pp. 239–322.
6 Husserliana III.1 188 (19–20), *Ideen* § 184, A 168. The emphasis is Husserl's.
7 Cf. D. Bell, "Reference, Experience, and Intentionality", in: *Mind, Meaning, and Mathematics: Essays on the Philosophical Views of Husserl and Frege*, ed. L. Haaparanta (Dordrecht: Kluwer, 1994) (= Synthese Library 237). My response is forthcoming in a Festschrift for Burton Dreben.
8 Cf. my "Husserl's Notion of Noema", in: *The Journal of Philosophy* 66 (1969), pp. 680–87.
9 Husserliana III.1 313 (16–20), *Ideen* § 135, A 281, translation by F. Kersten (The Hague, London: Nijhoff 1982) [= Kersten-trans. p. 325].
10 Cf. A. Gurwitsch, *Studies in Phenomenology and Psychology* (Evanston, Ill.: Northwestern University Press, 1966), p. 256. That *hyle* cannot be re-identified from act to act is stressed by Husserl at several places, for example in the manuscripts published in *Analysen zur passiven Synthesis. 1918–1926*, ed. M. Fleischer: cf., e. g., Husserliana XI 363, *Beilage VI: Sinn und Anschauung*.
11 Husserliana III.1 61 (15–18), *Ideen* § 30, A 52 [Kersten-trans. pp. 56f., slightly modified by me].

12 Husserliana III.1 60 (16–26), *Ideen* § 29, A 52 [Kersten-trans. pp. 55 f.].
13 Cf. Husserliana XIII–XV, *Zur Phänomenologie der Intersubjektivität*, 3 Tle. (1905–1935), ed. I. Kern (Den Haag: Nijhoff, 1973).
14 Husserliana VI 166 (19–22), *Krisis* § 47, translation by D. Carr (Evanston: Northwestern University Press, 1970) [= Carr-trans. p. 163].
15 Husserliana V, 152 f. (32 ff.), *Nachwort* (= Preface to the Gibson-translation of *Ideas* (London: Allen et Unwin, 1931)). The passage is cited here from the German *Nachwort*-version in Husserliana V [my translation].
16 W. James, *The Principles of Psychology*, Vol. 2 (New York: Dover 1950) Ch. XXI, p. 301.
17 Husserliana VI 145 (24–32), *Krisis* § 37 [Carr-trans. p.142].
18 Letter quoted in I. Kern, *Husserl und Kant. Eine Untersuchung über Husserls Verhältnis zu Kant und zum Neukantianismus* (Den Haag: Nijhoff, 1964) (= Phaenomenologica 16), p. 276n. Also other interpreters of Husserl find that 'idealism' is not a good label for Husserl's position, thus, e. g., Harrison Hall in "Was Husserl a Realist or an Idealist?", in: *Husserl, Intentionality, and Cognitive Science*, ed. H. L. Dreyfus and H. Hall (Cambridge, Mass.: MIT Press, 1982). Among the many others who find Husserl's use of 'idealism' misleading I will mention only two: Elisabeth Ströker, in *Husserls transzendentale Phänomenologie* (Frankfurt a. M.: Klostermann, 1987), and I. M. Wallner, in the article referred to in note 1.
19 Philipse, "Transcendental Idealism" (cf. note 5), p. 242.
20 Cf. the third article in the series, in *Archiv für systematische Philosophie* 9 (1903), pp. 393–408; reprinted in Husserliana XXII 201–215, *Aufsätze und Rezensionen 1890–1910*.
21 Philipse, "Transcendental Idealism" (cf. note 5), p. 262.
22 Loc. cit. (cf. note 5), p. 265 f., the italics are Philipse's.
23 Cf. loc. cit. (cf. note 5), pp. 269 f., 270, 278 f., 280, 283, 296, 298, 305.
24 Loc. cit. (cf. note 5), p. 249.
25 Cf. "Phenomenology", in: *Handbook of Perception*, Vol. I, ed. C. C. Carterette and M. P. Friedman (New York: Academic Press, 1974), ch. 19, pp. 377–386. Cf. also my article "Brentano and Husserl on intentional objects and perception", in: *Grazer philosophische Studien* 5 (1978), pp. 83–94.
26 Husserliana XIX.2 764, footnote 0, *Logische Untersuchungen* VI, *Beilage* A 706, cited with Philipse's italics (loc. cit. p. 265).
27 Loc. cit. (cf. note 5), p. 266, the italics are Philipse's.

28 Husserliana XXII 206 (13–23), *Bericht über deutsche Schriften zur Logik* (cf. note 20), A 398 f.
29 Cf. note 21.
30 Loc. cit. (cf. note 5), p. 283.

Ernest Sosa

Epistemic Circularity: Sextus, Descartes, and Epistemology Today*

A main epistemic problematic, found already in Aristotle's *Posterior Analytics*, presents a threefold choice on how a belief may be justified: either through infinitely regressive reasoning, or through circular reasoning, or through reasoning resting ultimately on some foundation. Aristotle himself takes the foundationalist option when he argues that rational intuition is a foundational source of scientific knowledge: one that yields starting points, not conclusions, of our reasoning. The five modes of Agrippa, which pertain to knowledge generally, again pose that same problematic, the "Pyrrhonian" problematic. And here Galen and the Stoics also opt for foundations.

Sections I and II below explore that foundationalist option. Section III draws some lessons. Section IV uses these to interpret Descartes. I argue that Descartes shows us the way beyond the Pyrrhonian problematic, although his way is not that traditionally attributed to him. On these basic issues of epistemology, Descartes is no Cartesian. Section V, finally, applies the lessons learned to the recrudescence of a famous controversy in earlier decades of the current century. I mean the problematic of the given which much exercised analytic philosophy from its earliest days.

I

According to Galen,

"nature has given us two things: the criteria themselves, and untaught trust in them. Now the criteria themselves are the sense-organs and the faculties which use these organs; and an untaught and natural trust in them is found not only in men but in the other animals too."[1]

For the Stoics, as Sextus reports,

> "nature has given us our perceptual faculty and the impressions which arise through it as, so to speak a light for the recognition of truth, and it would be absurd to reject such a faculty and to deprive ourselves of, as it were, the light."[2]

Epictetus adds that

> "it is the nature of the mind to assent to truths, to dissent from falsities, to suspend judgment with regard to what is unclear. 'What's the evidence for that?' Feel now, if you can, that it is night. 'Impossible.' Reject the feeling that it's day. 'Impossible.' Feel or reject the feeling that the stars are even in number. 'Impossible'."[3]

From these passages, Jonathan Barnes draws the following "theory of natural belief":

> "x has a natural belief that P just in case (i) it is the fact that P which causes it to seem to x that P, and (ii) it is the fact that it seems to x that P which causes x to believe that P."[4]

This Barnes holds to be "fundamentally correct as a description of the basis of Hellenistic Dogmatism".[5] As he explains,

> "the Stoics hold that x is justified in believing that P (where P is a basic belief) provided that (β^*) Because P is impressed on x by nature, x believes that P.
>
> They do *not* hold that, in addition, it must be true that:
>
> (α^*) Because x believes that P is impressed on x by nature, x believes that P."[6]

Earlier in that same work, Barnes had held it to be characteristic of an externalist epistemology that it maintains the likes of β^* rather than α^* as a condition necessary for x to be justified in believing that P. "Hence the Stoics, maintaining (β^*) rather than (α^*), are marked as externalists."[7]

Indeed the view attributed by Barnes to the Stoics, that "natural beliefs" (in his sense) are thereby epistemically justified and can thus amount to knowledge is akin to a contemporary causal theory, advocated by Alvin Goldman, according to which one knows something when one is caused to believe it by the very fact believed in that belief.[8] Knowing requires no meta-grasp that one's belief is so-caused, or that one knows, or the like. Simply being caused to believe in that distinctive way is enough: such causation can work its epistemic magic outside the ken of its beneficiary.

Other causal or dependence relations have been advanced in recent decades as sources of epistemic justification for beliefs that stand in them. For example, Robert Nozick proposes the following:

> "S knows that p IFF it is true that p, S believes that p, and both: if it were not true that p S would not believe it, and if it were true that p S would believe it."[9]

This requires, in a word, that S's belief "track" the truth. Otherwise put, S must "mirror" in his belief the truth or falsehood of the proposition that p, believing it if it were true, not believing it if it were not true. Here again one apparently needs no awareness that one's belief tracks the truth of the fact believed. One need only track, whether one knows it or not.

II

Such externalist epistemologies have prompted much controversy. Internalists have rejected them as unworthy of human epistemic dignity. Externalism has been denigrated as a "thermometer" model of knowledge inadequate to the full complexity of human cognition.[10] Despite recent decades of such controversy, we can still learn from our ancient predecessors, or so I will suggest. The Pyrrhonists oppose the externalism of Galen and the Stoics. Sextus, in particular, invokes similes that illuminate our issue, such as the following:

> "Let us imagine that some people are looking for gold in a dark room full of treasures. [...] [N]one of them will be persuaded that he has hit upon the gold even if he *has* in fact hit upon it. In the same way, the crowd of philosophers has come into the world, as into a vast house,

in search of truth. But it is reasonable that the man who grasps the truth should doubt whether he has been successful."[11]

Most would not disdain the good fortune of those who strike it rich in the dark, but it is no doubt a lesser state than that of finding gold guided by good eyesight in clear light. Enlightened discovery is more admirable than is any comparable luck that may reward groping in the dark. For one thing, enlightened discovery is success attributable to the agent; luck in the dark is not.[12]

Suppose that, concerning a certain subject matter, you ask yourself whether you know, and you have to answer either "Definitely not" or "Who knows?". In that case, is there not some straightforward and widely shared sense in which you do *not* really know?

Similarly, suppose that, concerning a certain choice or action of yours, you ask yourself whether it is right and you have to answer "Definitely not" or "Who knows?". Isn't there some sense in which your action or choice *automatically* falls short?

That all may amount to nothing more than this: It is better to believe and to act in ways that are *reflectively* right than in ways that happen to be right but unreflectively so.

III

Let us now focus on such *reflective* knowledge or justification, knowledge or justification that is, as suggested by Sextus's simile, "enlightened".[13] If one knows (reflectively), then one must believe one knows, at least *implicitly*, in that if one faced the question consciously, one would assent. But there is more: surely *this* belief, the belief that one knows, could hardly buttress one's being in the high-grade state of reflective knowledge if it were either (a) false, or (b) arbitrary or irrational, or (c) otherwise unjustified or of low epistemic quality. Surely this belief must itself be justified. We arrive thus at the following principle of epistemic ascent:

EA   If one knows that p, and one also grasps (understands) the proposition that one knows that p, then one must be justified in believing that one knows that p (in believing it at least implicitly, in that if one were to ask oneself whether one knows that p, one would assent).[14]

Consider, moreover, a principle of the "transfer of justification through justifiedly believed entailment":

TJJE One must be justified in believing whatever one justifiedly believes to be entailed by any given proposition that one is justified in believing. (Otherwise put: If one is justified in believing X and justified in believing that X necessarily entails Y, then one must also be justified in believing Y.)[15]

And consider also a "principle of exclusion":

PE One must be justified in believing to be false whatever one justifiedly believes to be necessarily excluded by one's knowing any given proposition. (Otherwise put: If one knows that P and justifiedly believes that one's knowing that P entails that Not-Q, then one must be justified in believing that Not-Q.)

Principles EA and TJJE enable an independent argument for PE:

1. One knows that P. *(By assumption.)*
2. One justifiedly believes that one's knowing that P necessarily excludes the possibility that Q. *(By assumption.)*
3. One grasps the proposition that one knows that P. *(From 2, since one can know that one's knowing that P excludes something only if one grasps the proposition that one knows that P.)*
4. One is justified in believing that one knows that P. *(From 1 and 3, by conjunction and EA.)*
5. One is justified in believing that Not-Q. *(From 4 and 2, by TJJE.)*
6. One must be justified in believing to be false whatever one justifiedly believes to be necessarily excluded by one's knowing any given proposition. (Otherwise put: If one knows that P and justi-

207

fiedly believes that one's knowing that P necessarily excludes the possibility that Q, then one must be justified in believing that Not-Q.) *(From 1, 2, and 5, by conditionalization.)*

This principle – PE – in turn yields a "principle of the criterion" PC. Here is how.

Note first the following:

> One's knowing that P necessarily excludes the possibility that the sources of one's belief that P be extremely unreliable. (Otherwise put: One's knowing that P necessarily entails that NOT-(the sources of one's belief that P are extremely UNreliable).[16]

Not only is this so. We justifiedly believe it to be so. Therefore, by combining this knowledge with our principle of exclusion, PE above, we may derive our "principle of the criterion":

> PC   One knows that p and grasps (understands) the proposition that one knows that p, only if one is justified in believing that the sources of one's belief that p are at least minimally reliable (i. e., not extremely unreliable).[17]

IV

Aware of the Pyrrhonian critique of knowledge, Descartes confronts the epistemic problematic found in the five modes of Agrippa.[18] But in so doing he finds himself in a circle that many have found vicious. Interpreting Descartes as a rationalist foundationalist, however, opens a plausible way to make sense of otherwise puzzling passages and enables a compelling account of the Circle.[19] One advantage claimed for the foundationalist interpretation concerns the notorious fourth paragraph of the Third Meditation, where Descartes seems to contradict himself, in suggesting *first* that he can be certain in taking two and three to make five, *and, second,* that one can doubt one's ability to do even the simplest sums correctly, absent knowledge of God's veracity. The same apparent inconsistency arises with regard to the *cogito* itself, since Descartes had already affirmed, in the second paragraph: "I am certain that I am a thing which thinks." How then can he now concede that even this is subject to doubt until we prove God's veracity?

The key to the foundationalist interpretation is a distinction between two propositions:

(A) For all P, if I clearly and distinctly perceive that P, then I am certain that P.

(B) I am certain that (for all P, if I clearly and distinctly perceive that P, then P).[20]

This distinction enables an interpretation meant to resolve puzzles that bedevil other accounts, and to open an escape from the Circle. According to this interpretation, here "are the things of which Descartes is certain, listed in the order in which he becomes certain of them:

(1) *I think*, the causal maxims, etc.
>Propositions known because they are clearly and distinctly perceived.

(2) *God exists, God is no deceiver.*
>Propositions known because they are clearly and distinctly perceived to follow from premises at level (1).

(3) *Whatever I perceive clearly and distinctly is certain.*
>Principle known because it is clearly and distinctly perceived to follow from propositions at level (2).

(4) *I perceive clearly and distinctly that I think*, etc.
>New premises, one corresponding to each premise at level (1).

(5) *I am certain that I think,* etc.

> Propositions known because they are clearly and distinctly perceived to follow from propositions at levels (3) and (4)."[21]

It's because of level 1 that, on this interpretation, Descartes is a foundationalist.[22]

My own view is that, while the interpretation proposed has important advantages, in the end it does not fit Descartes's writings satisfactorily. Therefore, even if outright foundationalists (rationalist foundationalists, among others) *could* escape charges of circularity brought against them, this does not satisfactorily enable us to escape the problem of circularity that arises *for Descartes* – since he cannot be interpreted satisfactorily as being just an outright foundationalist. Here is why.

Consider again the apparent self-contradictions early in the Third Meditation. The foundationalist account proposes to explain them by suggesting that those passages reveal only that by the fourth paragraph Descartes has reached a stage where A is true of him but B is not. Thus, when Descartes grants in that notorious paragraph that he might have been fooled even with regard to clear and distinct propositions, he is granting not the falsity of A but only the falsity of B. And this seems quite consistent.

However, that is insufficient to resolve the puzzle entirely. In the last sentence of that same paragraph, speaking of the "metaphysical" doubt that he has raised, Descartes has this to say: "[I]n order to be able altogether to remove it, I must inquire whether there is a God as soon as the occasion presents itself; and if I find that there is a God, I must also inquire whether he may be a deceiver; for without a knowledge of these two truths I do not see that I can ever be certain of anything." If this is so, then not even A can have been established by that stage so as to explain how it can be certain to him that $2 + 3 = 5$, or that he thinks.[23]

Consider indeed the form of that problematic proposition: *I cannot know anything unless I know that p.* How can all my knowledge depend on knowledge of a fact that I do *not* know by unaided intuition, if only deduction will give me knowledge of whatever I do not know by unaided intuition? Any case of deduction would seem to depend on intuition epistemically prior to *that* (and any?) deduction. The problem is that for Descartes as foundationalist: (1) the proposition that there is a veracious God is not known merely by unaided intuition, while yet (2) only deduction can give us knowledge of whatever we do not know by unaided intuition. How then could "p" above be replaced by "there is a veracious God"? It seems incoherent for Descartes to contend that he cannot know anything unless he knows that there is a veracious God.[24]

That puzzle of the Third Meditation remains standing, therefore, and is not entirely removed by our foundationalist account.

The second advantage adduced for the foundationalist interpretation is that it enables us to understand the epistemic advantage that Descartes claims over the atheist. The advantage is now said to favor Descartes when they both remember having earlier perceived clearly and distinctly that p. Unlike the atheist, Descartes can know that p on the basis of that later memory, once he has proved the veracity of God. For, unlike the atheist, Descartes can then rest assured that anything perceived clearly and distinctly must be true.

Consider, however, a key passage in which Descartes claims epistemic advantage over the atheist:

> "The fact that an atheist can be 'clearly aware that the three angles of a triangle are equal to two right angles' is something I do not dispute. But I maintain that this awareness of his [*cognitionem*] is not true knowledge [*scientia*], since no act of awareness that can be rendered doubtful seems fit to be called knowledge [*scientia*]. Now since we are supposing that this individual is an atheist, he cannot be certain that he is not being deceived on matters which seem to him to be very evident (as I fully explained). And although this doubt may not occur to him, it can still crop up if someone else raises the point or if he looks into the matter himself. So he will never be free of this doubt until he acknowledges that God exists."[25]

Here Descartes is not claiming only *ex post facto* advantage. Take the moment when both are clearly and distinctly perceiving the fact that the three angles are equal to two right ones. *Even at that very moment,* according to Descartes, the atheist is at an epistemic disadvantage.

That, moreover, is not the only passage where Descartes claims or implies the specified *in situ* sort of advantage over the atheist. Here is another, the last paragraph of Meditation V:

> "And so I very clearly recognize that the certainty and truth of all knowledge depends alone on the knowledge of the true God, in so much that, before I knew Him, I could not have a perfect knowledge of any other thing."

Recall the five levels that Descartes traverses, according to the foundationalist interpretation, on the way to his well-founded belief (and knowledge) that *he is certain* that he exists, that he thinks, etc. The foundationalism of that interpretation is unqualified because only one epistemic state of certain knowledge is recognized, and it is conferred on the propositions at level 1 for epistemic subjects *simply in virtue of their clear and distinct perception of those propositions.* It is this that runs counter to the Cartesian passages already indicated, including those in which Descartes claims an epistemic advantage over the atheist.

Evidently, Descartes is unwilling to settle for any straightforward foundationalist answer. The important, more specific, point is moreover this: *For Descartes the clearness and distinctness of a proposition to a subject at a time does not suffice to confer on that subject's acceptance (perception, belief, ...) of that proposition the most desirable epistemic status of certain knowledge: I mean the preferred, highest such status, to wit, scientia.*[26]

Already in the early passages of his *Meditations,* Descartes grapples with the problem posed by our "principle of the criterion" PC, or the like. Recall his desire to counteract the recurrent doubt that the source or faculty yielding one's belief is, in the circumstances, not reliable. Thus the doubts deriving from the fallibility of the senses, from the possibility that one be dreaming, that one fall victim to an evil demon, etc. In each case, the problem is posed by a possibility that the source of one's belief be in fact unreliable, i. e., would not with sufficient reliability yield beliefs bound to be true. And note well Descartes's reaction: in order to remove such doubts, he wishes to establish that the deep source of our beliefs is indeed a reliable source of truth. Of course, this might be attributed only to Descartes's aim to establish that our source is reliable, *without* implying that we attain true knowledge only once we achieve that aim. But that would misinterpret Descartes's intentions, as is shown for example by the passage about the atheist already cited.[27]

Recall our "Principle of the Criterion":

PC One knows that p and grasps (understands) the proposition that one knows that p, only if one is justified in believing that the sources of one's belief that p are reliable (i. e., not unreliable).

This principle sufficiently explains why Descartes will not be satisfied with unqualified foundationalism. After all, enlightened, reflective, *scientia* requires the satisfaction of this principle, and will not be attained through mere external foundations in the dark, nor even when the foundational source is "internal" and as reliable as rational intuition is said to be.

Descartes will not settle for mere cognitio, not even for *internalist, a priori*, reason-derived cognitio, as attained by the atheist mathematician. Descartes wants *reflective, enlightened* scientia. It is *this* that sets up the problem of the Cartesian Circle. Since Descartes wants not just reliable, truth-conducive cognitio, since he wants the enlightened attainment of reflective scientia, he needs a defense against skeptical doubts about his intellectual faculties, not only his faculties of perception, memory, and introspection, but even his faculty of intuitive reason, by which he might know that $3 + 2 = 5$, that if he thinks he exists, and the like. He believes he can defend against such doubts *only* by coherence-inducing theological reasoning that yields an epistemic perspective on himself and his world, in terms of which he can feel confident about the reliability of his faculties. And these faculties must include the very faculties employed in arriving, via *a priori* theological reasoning, at his perspective on himself and his world, the perspective that enables confidence in the reliability of such faculties.[28]

Our account explicates Descartes's project by placing it in the context of the Pyrrhonian problematic. It also helps explain why the circle is virtuous, and how certain stages of the Cartesian project, which might seem incoherent at first blush, may be seen as coherent in the end. (Example: the apparently incoherent claim about needing to first prove the veracity of God.)

Descartes seems enmeshed in a Cartesian Circle because he appears committed to each of the following propositions:

(1) I can know with certainty that (p) whatever I perceive clearly and distinctly is true only if I first know with certainty that (q) there is a veracious God.

(2) I can know with certainty that (q) there is a veracious God only if I first know with certainty that (p) whatever I perceive clearly and distinctly is true.

Yet, avoiding a vicious circle seems to require denying either (1) or (2).[29]

If "knowledge" and "certainty" are univocal terms in (1) and (2), then no adequate view can accept them both. One thing we might mean by "knowledge" is just "cognitio", for example, while "certainty" we reserved for "certain (or highest grade) cognitio". If we opt for these senses of the crucial epistemic terms, then Descartes *is* best read as a rationalist foundationalist: High grade, certain cognitio derives from intuition or deduction. Deductive cognitio is derivative from the already known. Intuitive cognitio is foundational. On this account, we deny (2).

As we have seen, however, that does not suffice to give a satisfactory account of Cartesian epistemology. Nor does it do justice to deeply intuitive sources of the Pyrrhonian problematic. The Pyrrhonist will not be satisfied by the appeal to "blind" intuition, and will demand "enlightened" intuition. It is Descartes's sensitivity to the appeal of such a (Pyrrhonian) stance that motivates important (and puzzling) structural features of his epistemology, or so I am suggesting.

Is there an account with the following features?

(a) It allows Descartes to be certain *both* that p *and* that q (with p and q as above).

(b) It rejects *neither* (1) *nor* (2) above.

It would seem not. How can (a) and (b) come together in a single coherent account? In fact they can, however, if we find ambiguity in (1) and (2) above. Using Descartes's own terms, we might reformulate them thus:[30]

(1′) I can have certain *scientia* that p only if I first have certain *cognitio* that q. (Where 'p' and 'q' represent again what they represent in (1) and (2).)

(2′) I can have certain *scientia* that q only if I first have certain *cognitio* that p.

These two propositions – (1′) and (2′) – are compatible, and it is these that Descartes wished to affirm. These, moreover, are sufficient to make sense of the Cartesian epistemological project. Descartes's aim of developing a coherent world-view within which he could validate his cognitive faculties is sufficiently supported by the desire for reflective knowledge (especially reflective knowledge that in other respects also reaches the level of *scientia*). And this desire is sufficiently justified by the evidently higher quality of such knowledge as compared with the mere *cognitio* of the atheist mathematician, or the mere animal (thermometer-like) "knowledge" of the unreflective. We must compare here apples with apples. The unreflective knowledge of the atheist mathematician does not bear comparison with the reflective knowledge that might accompany an old farmer's empirical lore. The proper comparison, according to Descartes, pairs the unreflective mathematical cognitio attainable by an atheist, on one side, with such reflective knowledge as one might attain aided by *both* mathematics and theology. Descartes was perhaps too san-

215

guine in his theological ambition, but that is quite different from being doomed to vicious regress or circle through the very logical structure of his inquiry.

In the barest sketch, here is how I see Descartes's epistemological project. First he meditates along, attaining the kind of epistemic justification and even "certainty" that might be found in an atheist mathematician's reasonings, one deprived of a world view within which the universe may be seen as epistemically propitious. Descartes's reasoning at that stage *can* be evaluated, of course, just as can an atheist mathematician's reasoning. After all, atheist mathematicians will differ in the worth of their mathematical reasonings. Absent an appropriate world view, however, no such reasoning can rise above the level of *cognitio*. If we persist in such reasoning, nevertheless, enough pieces may eventually come together into a view of ourselves and our place in the universe that is sufficiently comprehensive and coherent to raise us above the level of mere *cognitio* and into the realm of higher, reflective, enlightened knowledge, or *scientia*. There is in none of that any circle that vitiates the project.[31]

Admittedly I have done little more than to sketch my proposed interpretation of Descartes's epistemological project. A proper defense would require a full textual study. My own reading inspires optimism, but the full project must await another occasion.[32]

One important question I would like to mention before moving on, although I will not be able to do much more than that: What could possibly give to reflective knowledge a higher epistemic status than the corresponding unreflective cognitio(n)? And, more particularly, what could possibly do so within the epistemological framework favored by Descartes?

What favors reflective over unreflective knowledge? Recall that reflective acquisition of knowledge is like acquisition of gold in the light, whereas unreflective acquisition of knowledge is like acquisition of gold in the dark. In each case the former is distinguished from the latter in being a more admirable occurrence, and one that so far might be ascribed admiringly to the protagonist, as his doing. Allied to that is our ability to shape our cognitive practices, individually and collectively, so as to enhance their epistemic virtue, their effectiveness in putting us in touch with how matters stand. This does not require that our every belief be freely chosen and deliberate. A tennis champion reacts "instinctively" at the net, even though such reactions result from highly deliberate and autonomously chosen training carried out voluntarily over a period of years. Even when already in place, moreover, such "instinctive" reactions are still subject to fine tuning through further practice and training. The same is true of a bird watcher and his binocular-aided "instinctive" beliefs. And the same is true of us all and our most ordinary visual beliefs, aided by the tutelage of daily practice and, eventually, the hard lessons taught by diminishing acuity.[33]

A further advantage of reflective knowledge is the increment of comprehensive coherence that it entails. Interestingly, Descartes himself accepts comprehensive coherence as a source of epistemic worth, indeed as a source of certainty. In Principle CCV of his *Principles of Philosophy*, for example, he notes that if he can interpret a long stretch of otherwise undecipherable writing by supposing that it is written in "one-off language," where the alphabet has all been switched forward by one letter, etc., this provides good reason for that interpretation. There he also argues in favor of his scientific account of physical reality that "it would hardly have been possible for so many items to fall into a coherent pattern if the original principles had been false".

Since the propositions that form the coherent pattern are "deduced" from the "original" principles, therefore if the coherence of the implicands signifies the truth of the principles, it likewise, derivatively, signifies the truth of the implicands themselves forming the pattern. Descartes seems therefore here again, as elsewhere, to be adopting a kind of reliabilism in defending the epistemological power of coherence – its ability to impart certainty – by appeal to its reliability as a source of the truth of what renders it certain.[34]

Admittedly, in that same Principle (CCV) Descartes claims only *moral* certainty for his coherence-validated beliefs about the alphabet or about the natural world. However, in the very next principle (CCVI) he claims *more* than moral certainty for his scientific principles, and does so, again, at least in part through appeal to explanatory coherence (when he adduces that they "appear to be the only possible explanations of the phenomena they present").

But why is reflective *scientia* better than unreflective *cognitio*? First, because it is reason-molded, at least in the way of a champion's "instinctive" play. Second, because a knowledge that enjoys the support of a comprehensively coherent and explanatory world-view is better. But is it *epistemically* better? Is it better with a view to getting at the truth? That Descartes would respond affirmatively even here is made plausible by key passages in which he explicitly recognizes the epistemic power of explanatory coherence.

In sum, Descartes was a foundationalist, *and* a coherentist, *and* a reliabilist. Each of these doctrines may be seen to apply, in some illuminating respect, to a system whose architectural elegance survives the erosion of its individual stones.

Our baroque Cartesian structure enables a revealing perspective on that most foundationalist of issues, the problematic of the given. Descartes's contribution, though distorted by received views, in fact offers an unusual way beyond that problematic, as the next section attempts to show.

V

A moderate foundationalism was once proposed by Carl Hempel as follows: "When an experiential sentence is accepted 'on the basis of experiential evidence', it is indeed not accepted arbitrarily; but to describe the evidence in question would simply mean to repeat the experiential statement itself. Hence, in the context of cognitive justification, the sentence functions in the manner of a primitive sentence."[35]

If put in terms of beliefs rather than sentences, Hempel's point appears thus:

(H) Beliefs held on the basis of direct experiential evidence are not arbitrary. Yet to state the evidence for such a belief is just to voice the belief. Hence, in the context of cognitive justification, these beliefs function as primitive or basic.

Roderick Chisholm credits Hempel for this insight, and makes it central to his own epistemology. Chisholm defends a form of foundationalism that admits apprehensions of the given at the foundation of empirical knowledge. And he adopts a conception of that foundation in line with Hempel's insight H.[36]

Among the foundations defended by Chisholm, early and late, are sensory foundations or apprehensions of the given – as well as knowledge of one's own beliefs and other propositional attitudes, which are also said to satisfy Hempel's conditions for being primitive or basic.

A famous critique of such foundationalism is due to Wilfrid Sellars, another philosopher influenced by German philosophy, from Kant and Hegel through Carnap and logical positivism. Two main issues divided Sellars from Chisholm and fueled their long and widely followed controversy. Their disagreement involved, first, the relation of thought, or intentionality, to language, and, second, the relation of experience to empirical knowledge. On this second issue they thus continued the controversy of their predecessors from Central Europe: Neurath, Schlick, Carnap, and Hempel.

Sellars seems right in saying that Hempel's thesis points to inferences of the form.[37]

(α) It is a fact that a is F;
     So, it is reasonable (for me) to believe that a is F.

But his objection is now that any such argument as α will do its job only if the premise has authority, only if it is something which it is reasonable to believe. According to Sellars, this leads from α to the following alternative argument schema:

(β) It is reasonable to believe it to be a fact that a is F;
     So, it is reasonable to believe that a is F.

And this is of course, just as Sellars says, "obviously unilluminating".

That, again, is Sellars's critique. But the sort of problem he raises is not unique to his critique. A main theme of Richard Rorty's attack on foundationalism is the alleged "confusion of causation with justification" that he attributes to Locke and others. Donald Davidson also adds his voice:

> "As Rorty has put it, 'nothing counts as justification unless by reference to what we already accept, and there is no way to get outside our beliefs and our language so as to find some test other than coherence.' About this I am, as you see, in agreement with Rorty."[38]

Just how damaging is that line of objection against experiential foundations? Doesn't it beg the question against Hempel's insight H? The insight, recall, is that certain beliefs have authority simply in virtue of being true. It is their *truth* that makes them reasonable. The believer thus becomes reasonable (or at least nonarbitrary) in so believing, simply because of the truth of his specific belief (which is of course not to say that any true belief would be equally reasonable since true). Therefore the believer does not need to employ any such reasoning as α or β. The believer does not need to adduce reasons in order to be reasonable in *such* a belief. That is indeed what makes it a *foundationally* justified (or reasonable) belief, according to Hempel. Inferential backing is here not needed. Truth alone is sufficient (given the belief's content).

Hempel's insight hence appears to survive the sort of objection urged by Sellars, Rorty, and Davidson. But does it yield an acceptable foundationalism, as Chisholm believes? More specifically, does it adequately explain how it is that experience bears on knowledge? Shall we say that experientially given facts justify beliefs directly, merely through their truth? Shall we say, for example, that the mere fact that I have a headache suffices to justify my belief that I do?

What is the alternative to such foundationalism concerning how one is justified in believing that p? Circular or regressive reasoning will not adequately explain how that belief is justified. How could the belief that p derive its justification entirely from such reasoning? There is much to be said about this, but little time to say it here. So let me just gesture towards the problems involved by asking how, in either a pure regress or a pure circle, justification ever enters in the first place. Inferential reasoning serves to transfer justification but this presupposes that justification is already there in the premises of the reasoning, and that is precisely what neither the pure circle nor the pure regress is able to explain.[39] A full explanation of how one's belief that p gets to be justified must apparently take us back to ultimate premises that do not get all their justification from further premises yet. Must there not be ultimate premises that somehow get some of their justification by means other than reasoning from further premises? If not, it is hard to see how justification ever appropriately enters the line of reasoning (regressive or circular) that leads to one's being eventually justified in believing that p.

That sketches an argument in favor of the appeal to *foundations*. But note well the highly determinable character of these foundations. *All we have a right to suppose about our foundational beliefs, on the basis of our elimination of the circle and the regress, is that they are justified noninferentially.* Any more determinate and positive thesis would require further defense. In particular, we are in no position to conclude that the foundation must be constituted by direct apprehensions of the experiential given.

We have been considering how sensory experience bears on our empirical knowledge and justification. And we have found two opposing positions. On one side are Neurath, Sellars, Rorty, and Davidson, among others. According to this side, experience bears causally on our beliefs, but it is a serious mistake to confuse such causation with justification. Experience bears at most causally on our beliefs about external reality, even on our simplest perceptual beliefs. We do not *infer* such perceptual beliefs from beliefs about our sensory experience, nor is the justification for such beliefs a matter of their coherence with appropriate *beliefs* about our experience.

On the other side are Schlick, Hempel, C. I. Lewis, and Chisholm, among others. For these it is an "astounding error" to suppose that the mere coherence of a self-enclosed body of beliefs might suffice to confer justification on its members. And it is hard to see what, other than sensory experience, could serve to supplement coherence appropriately so as to explain empirical justification. Accordingly, they prefer rather to postulate beliefs about such experience, the takings or apprehensions of the given, through inference from which, or by coherence with which, one must attain one's empirical justification. But this side notoriously fails to find foundations contentful enough to found our rich knowledge of an external world.

As so often in philosophy, this controversy leaves middle ground untouched. Our coherentists and foundationalists share an assumption:

(A) Experience can bear epistemically on the justification of belief only by presenting itself to the believer in such a way that the believer directly and noninferentially believes it to be present, and can then use such belief as a premise from which to reach conclusions about the world beyond experience.

We can go beyond the traditional controversy by rejecting assumption A. Experience can bear epistemically on the justification of a perceptual belief *by* appropriately causing that belief.[40] Thus, while viewing a snowball in sunlight I may have visual experience as if I saw something white and round, which may prompt the corresponding perceptual belief. In that case it will be an important part of what makes my perceptual belief epistemically justified – and indeed of what makes it a perceptual belief – that it is caused by such experience.

But does that serve to provide *foundational* justification for perceptual beliefs? Take a perceptual belief prompted appropriately by a corresponding experience. Take a belief that this is white and round, one prompted by visual experience of a sunlit snowball in plain view. Is that perceptual belief *foundationally* justified simply in virtue of its causal aetiology? When Sellars inveighs against the myth of the given, he targets not only the radical version of the myth involving direct apprehensions of given experience. He objects also to the more moderate version that postulates foundational knowledge through perception. Indeed the key passage that encapsulates his opposition to a foundational epistemology targets not a foundation of introspective direct apprehension but a foundation of perception.

Here I avoid issues about the nature of thought and its relation to language and society. So I will take the liberty of transmuting

Sellars's argument into one pertaining directly to belief, justification, and knowledge, leaving aside whether to understand these in terms of moves in a language game governed by social rules. I am not *denying* that our main epistemic concepts are to be understood thus in terms of language and society. I am simply not joining Sellars in affirming it. Thus my preference for the transmuted argument that does not prejudge these issues. So transmuted, here then is the Sellarsian refutation of the epistemology of foundations:

> "We have seen that to constitute knowledge, an observational belief must not only *have* a certain epistemic status; this epistemic status must *in some sense* be recognized by the person whose belief it is. And this is a steep hurdle indeed. For if the positive epistemic status of the observational belief that this is green lies in the fact that the existence of green items appropriately related to the perceiver can be inferred from the occurrence of such observational beliefs, it follows that only a person who is able to draw this inference, and therefore has not only the concept *green*, but also the concept of an observational belief that this is green – indeed the concept of certain conditions of perception, those which would correctly be called 'standard conditions' – could be in a position to believe observationally that this is green in recognition of its epistemic status."[41]

In arguing thus, Sellars is of course rejecting externalist reliabilism. It is not enough that an observational belief manifest a tendency to believe that one faces a green object "if and only if a green object is being looked at in standard conditions". This may give the belief a certain minimal epistemic status. But if the belief is to constitute real knowledge then "this epistemic status must *in some sense* be recognized by the person whose belief it is". And this is the hurdle that Sellars regards as "steep indeed". It is this hurdle that in his eyes dooms foundationalism. If the hurdle is steep for the foundationalist, however, it seems no less steep for anyone else. How could anyone avoid the threatening circle or regress? How could one acquire the required knowledge about which conditions are standard, and the knowledge that those conditions are present, without *already* enjoying a lot of the observational knowledge the possibility of which is under explanation? Here now is Sellars's proposed solution (transmuted):

> "All the view I am defending requires is that no belief by S *now* that this is green is to count as observational knowledge unless it is also correct to say of S that he *now* knows the appropriate fact of the form *X is a reliable symptom of Y*, namely that the observational belief that this is green is a reliable indicator of the presence of green objects in standard conditions of perception. And while the correctness of this statement about Jones requires that Jones could *now* cite prior particular facts as evidence for the idea that such belief *is* a reliable indicator, it requires only that it is correct to say that Jones *now* knows, thus remembers, that these particular facts *did* obtain. It does not require that it be correct to say that at the time these facts did obtain he *then knew* them to obtain. And the regress disappears."[42]

By this stage Sellars had highlighted inadequacies not only of traditional givenist foundationalism, but also of a more recent externalist reliabilism – a neat trick since, at the time he wrote, such reliabilism had not yet appeared in print. Nevertheless, Sellars's positive proposal is problematic. In the first place, how realistic is it to suppose that at the later time one remembers that the particular facts in question *did* obtain? Think of any perceptual knowledge that you can attribute to yourself now. Think, perhaps, of your knowledge that you are perceiving a rectangular sheet of paper with a certain pattern of marks on it. Is it realistic to suppose that, in believing perceptually that before you there lies such a sheet, you are relying on recollected incidents in which you successfully perceived thus?

And there is a further problem. Our later access to earlier observational reactions is an exercise of memory. But memory itself seems to require, no less than perception, some meta-awareness of its reliability when exercised in circumstances of the sort in which it is now exercised.[43] And if there was a problem of regress attaching to the exercise of perception there would seem to be an equally disturbing problem of regress attaching to the exercise of memory. Perhaps the response would be that *just as* earlier proto-perceptions can become data supportive of generalizations about our perceptual reliability, generalizations that underlie later perceptual knowledge; *so, similarly,* earlier proto-memories can become data supportive of generalizations about our memorial reliability, generalizations that underlie later memorial knowledge. Perhaps, but this raises even more poignantly an objection akin to that raised earlier about perceptual knowledge: namely, that we cannot plausibly be said to remember particular earlier exercises of memory constitutive of a data bank which can later support our underwriting generalizations.

For a better solution we must go back, ironically, to a philosopher long miscast as the archetypal foundationalist and givenist. It is, I suggest, in Cartesian epistemology that we find a way beyond our regress or circle.

Ancient skepticism, as represented by Pyrrhonism, and modern skepticism, as presented by Descartes, have been regarded as radically different. How plausibly? Descartes does raise a certain skeptical problem that *is* limited by comparison with the radical skepticism of the ancients: namely, the problem of the external world. But this is by no means the only skepticism of interest to Descartes. It is obvious in the *Meditations* that his concerns are much broader, as when he wonders how he can know the truth even when he adds three and two or when he considers how many are the sides of a square. It is precisely the radical skepticism of the ancients that mainly concerns Descartes (and not only Hegel, who is emphatic on the point). Moreover, this skepticism is best seen in the light of the epistemic problematic found already in Aristotle's *Posterior Analytics*[44], where it is given a foundationalist resolution, and, more famously, in the five modes of Agrippa. To the latter incarnation of that problematic the Stoics, in kinship with Aristotle, offer a foundationalist response. Where Aristotle appeals to rational intuition as a way to found scientific knowledge, the Stoics appeal to natural, animal perception as a way to found ordinary and empirical knowledge.

The Pyrrhonists find such externalism unacceptable because it dignifies mere "groping in the dark" with the title of knowledge.[45] The Pyrrhonists highlight *enlightened* knowledge, which must be acquired and sustained in awareness of one's epistemic doings. Only this is "knowledge" worthy of the title. Sadly, they would prefer in their own practice to suspend judgment in specific case after specific case, with few if any exceptions, partly because they reject blind foundations. In their view, moreover, any attempt to move beyond foundations only misleads us into circles or regresses, viciously either way.

Descartes's response is balanced and sensitive to this Pyrrhonian dialectic. It grants the truth in foundationalism by allowing room for an inference-independent epistemic state of *cognitio*. Intuition gives us foundational cognitio, as suggested by Aristotle, and such unreflective knowledge is open even to the atheist mathematician. There is however a higher knowledge, reflective knowledge. Attaining such knowledge requires a view of ourselves – of our beliefs, our faculties, and our situation – in the light of which we can see the sources of our beliefs as reliable enough (and indeed as perfectly reliable if the *scientia* desired is absolute and perfect).

It is important to recognize, in assessing this Cartesian strategy, that while we do need to underwrite, at the later stage, the reliability of our faculties, what enables us to do so is the appropriate use of those very faculties in yielding a perspective from which reality may be seen as epistemically propitious. But we need not restrict ourselves to the use of rational intuition and deduction as the only faculties of any use in that endeavor. Descartes himself surely needed memory as well. And memory, by definition, operates over time. It is not a present-time-slice faculty. Nor, indeed, is deduction itself such a faculty, except where the whole proof can be seen in a flash. So memory, as a *cognitio*-level mechanism can join *cognitio*-level intuition and perception in yielding the pieces that, once present with sufficient comprehensiveness and coherence, can boost us to the level of reflective *scientia* with the ability to underwrite all such faculties. This means that we need not later exhume from memory any particular cases of reliable perception or reliable memory in order to support inductively the generalizations about the reliability of our faculties. It is enough that such generalizations be present because of the combined operation of past perception and memory (and, *perhaps*, a gradual "induction" over time, and/or appropriate innate principles). If through such *cognitio*-level cognitive processing enough of a coherent and comprehensive picture comes together, such a picture can still underwrite the continued use of those very faculties, now with reflective assurance, and now at the level of enlightened *scientia*.[46]

We have gone beyond the mythology of the given, first by rejecting the assumption that experience can bear on the epistemic justification of our beliefs only by providing premises yielding knowledge of a world external to experience. A better way to think of the epistemic efficacy of experience is perhaps this. Visual experience as if this is white and round may cause belief that this is white and round in the absence of any special reason for caution. That can yield perceptual knowledge that this is white and round, with no need to postulate any inference from one's experience to what lies beyond. *Maybe* there are such inferences, lightning inferences unconsciously or subconsciously yielding our perceptual beliefs as conclusions. But we need not enter that issue. It is enough that experience cause belief in some appropriate, standard way. Whether it does so via a lightning, unconscious inference we can leave open. Whether it does so or not, it may still endow the perceptual belief with appropriate epistemic status to constitute perceptual knowledge.

Nevertheless, a mere thermometer reaction to one's environment cannot constitute real knowledge, regardless of whether that reaction is causally mediated by experience. It is not enough that one respond to seeing white and round objects in good light with a "belief" or "proto-belief" that there is something white and round. Suppose one asks oneself "Do I know that this is white and round?" or "Am I justified in taking this to be white and round?" and has to answer "Definitely not" or even "Who knows? Maybe I do know, maybe I don't; maybe I'm justified, maybe I'm not". In that case one *automatically* falls short, one has attained only some lesser epistemic status, and not any "real, or enlightened, or reflective" knowledge. The latter requires some awareness of the status of one's belief, some ability to answer that one does know or that one is epistemically justified, and some ability to defend this through the reliability of one's relevant faculties when used in the relevant circumstances. But this leads to a threat of circle or regress, a main problematic, perhaps *the* main problematic of epistemology. Surprisingly, already in Descartes himself, in the founder of modern epistemology, we find a way beyond that problematic.[47]

Appendix

At the beginning of section III, we arrived at the following principle of epistemic ascent:

EA $\quad\quad K(P) \,\&\, GK(P) \Rightarrow J[K(P)]$

In other words, if one knows that p, and one also grasps (understands) the proposition that one knows that p, then one must be justified in believing that one knows that p (in believing it at least implicitly, in that if one were to ask oneself whether one knows that p, one would assent).

Consider, moreover, the following two principles:

TJJE $\quad\quad J(X) \,\&\, J(X - Y) \Rightarrow J(Y)$

This is a principle of the "transfer of justification through justifiedly believed entailment".

PE $\quad\quad \{K(P) \,\&\, J[K(P) \Rightarrow \sim Q]\} \Rightarrow J(\sim Q)$

This is a "principle of exclusion".

Principles EA and TJJE enable an independent argument for our "principle of exclusion" PE:

1. $K(P)$ — Assumption
2. $J[K(P) \Rightarrow \sim Q]$ — Assumption
3. $GK(P)$ — From 2, which requires that one grasp $K(P)$
4. $J[K(P)]$ — From 1 and 3, by conjunction and EA

5. J(~Q) From 4 and 2, by TJJE
6. {K(P) & J[K(P) ⇒ ~Q]} ⇒ J(~Q) Conditionalization

This principle – PE – in turn yields a further principle, the "principle of the criterion" PC. Here is how.

Note first that we justifiedly believe the following (at least implicitly, so long as the complexity of P does not put it beyond our grasp):

K(P) ⇒ (The sources of B(P) are at least minimally reliable)

or, otherwise put:

K(P) ⇒ ~(The sources of B(P) are extremely unreliable),

which, abbreviated, may be expressed thus:

K(P) ⇒ ~UB(P).

Again, this we believe justifiedly, if we grasp K(P); so we also have:

GK(P) ⇒ J[K(P) ⇒ ~UB(P)].

Plugging in 'UB(P)' for 'Q' in PE above, we obtain:

{K(P) & J[K(P) ⇒ ~UB(P)]} ⇒ J(~UB(P)).

But we had just seen that: GK(P) ⇒ J[K(P) ⇒ ~UB(P)]. So we may derive our "principle of the criterion":

PC [K(P) & GK(P)] ⇒ J(~UB(P)).

Or, spelled out:

PC One knows that p and grasps (understands) the proposition that one knows that p, only if one is justified in believing that the sources of one's belief that p are at least minimally reliable (i. e., not extremely unreliable).

Moreover, this is not just an accidental truth. We have seen it to follow necessarily from two facts each more than just an accidental truth, namely:

(a) {K(P) & J[K(P) ⇒ ~UB(P)]} ⇒ J(~UB(P))

and

(b) GK(P) ⇒ J[K(P) ⇒ ~UB(P)].

Since PC follows necessarily from (a) and (b), if each of (a) and (b) is in some sense necessary, necessary, too, is then PC itself, in that same sense. Now (a) is proposed as a principle that could not possibly be false. What about (b)? Suppose one were faced with the question whether [K(P) ⇒ ~UB(P)], while understanding that question fully. How could one possibly fail to assent? Would not failure to assent simply show that one had *not* understood the question fully? Compare [K(P) ⇒ T(P)] – the principle that if one knows that p then it must be true that p. Would not a failure to assent here again betray some failure to understand? If so, these propositions are both automatically believed (with justification, surely) by anyone who understands them – at least implicitly, so that one would always assent upon conscious consideration. These reflections make it plausible that neither (a) nor (b) could be false. If so, then, since PC follows necessarily from (a) and (b), it should seem equally plausible that PC could not be false.[48]

Epistemic Circularity

Notes

* I am delighted to participate in this volume honoring Dieter Henrich.
1 *The Doctrines of Hippocrates and Plato*, v 725, ed. C. G. Kuhn (Leipzig, 1821–33). Translations from the Greek by Jonathan Barnes, in *The Toils of Skepticism* (Cambridge, UK: Cambridge University Press, 1990).
2 *Against the Mathematicians*, orig. *Adversus Mathematicos*, in: *Sexti Empirici opera*, ed. H. Mutschmann (Bibliotheca scriptorum Graecorum et Romanorum Teubneriana VII), p. 259.
3 *Discourses* I xxviii 2–3.
4 Barnes, op. cit., p. 136.
5 Ibid.
6 Loc. cit., p. 137.
7 Ibid.
8 "A Causal Theory of Knowing", in: *The Journal of Philosophy* 64 (1967), pp. 357–72.
9 *Philosophical Explanations* (Cambridge, Mass.: Harvard University Press, 1981), Part 3.
10 Cf. W. Sellars's "Empiricism and the Philosophy of Mind", in: *Minnesota Volumes in the Philosophy of Science*, Vol. I (1956), section 36 of part VIII ("Does Empirical Knowledge Have a Foundation?").
11 *Against the Mathematicians* (cf. note 2), p 52.
12 In harmony with this Pyrrhonian sentiment, Confucius says in his *Analects*: "When you know, to know that you know. When you do not know, to know that you do not know. That is real knowledge."
13 For now we focus on such reflective knowledge, although a lower grade of "knowledge" will also be admitted in due course.
14 I would also defend the stronger principle that, more than being only justified in believing that one knows, one must also attain knowledge that one knows, or at least must attain knowledge of a sort – a sort that I will point to below when it comes into view.
15 At least so long as one has in mind, in one specious present, all three items: the belief X, the belief that X entails Y, and the question whether Y. Let us suppose this to be implicit whenever TJJE is invoked.
16 This is a first approximation. Since it is close enough for our purposes, we won't stop for a more exact statement, which would not be a trivial attainment. The following will indicate the sorts of problems we would face: "Sources" here means "total epistemically relevant sources". Percep-

tion may be in general a reliable source, but in a particular case the total epistemically relevant source may be not just perception but perception in certain (unpropitious) circumstances (object too far, or too small, or in poor light, etc.).

17 A symbolization in the Appendix may make the argument of this section more easily surveyable. There I also argue that PC is more than just a contingent truth.

18 He confronts that problematic, I say, a problematic that suffused the intellectual atmosphere of his age. Nevertheless, I do not say that he is responding to the modes specifically, as found in Sextus. Hegel, by contrast, was to focus *especially* on this problematic, and to the modes more specifically, as may be seen in *The Relation of Skepticism to Philosophy*, orig. *Verhältnis des Skeptizismus zur Philosophie*, in: *Jenaer Schriften 1801–1807*, Werke Bd. 2 (Frankfurt am Main: Suhrkamp, 1977), pp. 213 – 272. For a discussion of Hegel's view of ancient skepticism see M. Forster's *Hegel and Skepticism* (Cambridge, MA: Harvard University Press, 1989).

19 J. Van Cleve, "Foundationalism, Epistemic Principles, and the Cartesian Circle", in: *The Philosophical Review* 88 (1979), pp. 55 –91. Reprinted in *Knowledge and Justification*, ed. E. Sosa (Dartmouth Publishing Company Limited, 1994). While disagreeing with this account, I regard it as among the most enlightening. One other account in the vast literature on the Circle is an important antecedent to ours. I mean K. DeRose's "Descartes, Epistemic Principles, Epistemic Circularity, and *Scientia*", in: *Pacific Philosophical Quarterly* 73 (1992), pp. 220 –38. The main differences involve: (a) my emphasis on the Pyrrhonian background and the related notion of reflective (or enlightened) knowledge; (b) my defense of the Principle of the Criterion (PC) by appeal to that notion of reflective knowledge and its associated principles of Epistemic Ascent (EA) and of Exclusion (PE); and (c) my use of a notion of coherence in understanding Descartes's *scientia* and my reasons for taking Descartes to endorse such use. DeRose's paper is excellent, in any case, and our accounts and arguments are on the whole complementary.

20 Van Cleve, op. cit., p. 67. Compare Barnes's contrast between α^* and β^*, noted above.

21 Loc. cit., p. 72.

22 And, presumably, because of level 4 as well.

23 Van Cleve is well aware of this problem, and indeed forthrightly brings it up himself: "It must be said, however, that the final sentence of this

paragraph – 'Without a knowledge of these two truths [God exists and is not a deceiver] I do not see that I can ever be certain of anything' – is an embarrassment for almost any interpretation of Descartes." Loc. cit. (cf. note 19), p. 67.

24 This is hence a problem for any interpretation according to which Descartes is a rationalist foundationalist for whom intuition lays the foundation and deduction builds the superstructure.

25 This passage is from the Second Set of Replies as it appears in *The Philosophical Writings of Descartes*, ed J. Cottingham, R. Stoothoff, and D. Murdoch, op. cit., Vol. II, p. 101. However, I must add that where this translation says that an atheist can be "clearly aware," Descartes's Latin is "clare cognoscere".

26 Other passages may seem to cast doubt on this point. (See, for example, the reply to the third of the Objections II.) But they can be deflected through attention to the fact that *both cognitio* and *scientia* come in degrees of epistemic quality. One can attain the highest level of *cognitio* without the aid of *scientia*. But no matter how epistemically worthy may be a state of *cognitio* that p, the corresponding reflective *scientia* that p will be of higher quality. (By a state S of reflective *scientia* that p which "corresponds" to a state C of *cognitio* that p, I mean *scientia* that p which incorporates constitutively a state of *cognitio* of the same level of epistemic quality as C, and builds from there through a further reflective meta-state about that object state.) It is crucial, however, that merely by requiring ascent from the object level to the first metalevel, Descartes is not automatically committed to requiring ascent at *every* level up to the next higher level. Can't one improve one's epistemic state by ascent that keeps pace with understanding, even if our ascent cannot be limitless? Surely our epistemic state can improve through enhanced comprehensive coherence, and this can justify our preference for enlightened, reflective *scientia*, even if such improvement cannot be continued without limit up an infinite ladder of epistemic ascent.

27 This passage is important enough that I would like to have before us an alternative translation: "That an atheist can clearly know that the three angles of a triangle are equal to two right angles, I do not deny; I merely say that this knowledge of his *(cognitionem)* is not true science *(scientia)*, because no knowledge which can be rendered doubtful should, it seems, be called science. Since he is supposed to be an atheist, he cannot be certain that he is not deceived even in those things that seem most evident to him, as has been sufficiently shown; and although this doubt

may never occur to him, nevertheless it can occur to him, if he examines the question, or it may be suggested by someone else, and he will never be safe from it, unless he first acknowledges God." *The Philosophical Works of Descartes*, trans. Haldane & Ross (Cambridge, UK: Cambridge University Press, 1911), Vol. 2, p. 39. Cf. *Œuvres de Descartes*, ed. C. Adam and P. Tannery (Paris: Librairie Philosophique J. Vrin, 1964), Vol. IX, p. 111.

28 There is a telling analogy, not explicitly recognized by Descartes, between the role of dreams in his skepticism vis-a-vis perception, and a role assignable to paradoxes and aporias in a parallel skepticism vis-a-vis rational intuition.

29 Cf. Van Cleve, op. cit. (cf. note 19), pp. 55f.

30 But it is also important here to note that both *cognitio* and *scientia* might come in degrees of epistemic quality, up to the heights of the respectively appropriate "certainty".

31 Although we can thus offer a plausible account that bids fair to satisfy both (a) and (b), by interpreting 1 and 2 as 1' and 2' respectively, nevertheless it seems to me uncertain that Descartes really wished to make the claims of *priority* (temporal or epistemic) that are suggested by 1' and 2'. So I believe that more defensible attributions to Descartes would drop the word "first" from each of 1' and 2'. Moreover, among the pieces that need to come together in order to raise the belief-that-p above the level of cognitio, to the level of scientia, may well be found appropriate cognitio *that* one enjoys cognitio that p. And once the claims of priority *are* dropped, as I am proposing, then it might well be held not only that cognitio that p *and* cognitio that one enjoys cognitio that p, are both required for scientia that p. It might even be held that *scientia* that one has scientia that p is also required for scientia that p – so long as one grasps the proposition that one has scientia that p. So a form of the KK Principle seems accessible along this avenue.

32 Victor Caston poses an intriguing question: Did the Old Stoa already have the bi-level epistemology attributed here to Descartes? He reasons: "While they are usually arguing about 'secure impressions' *(kataleptike phantasia)*, which provide some kind of foundational basis, true knowledge *(episteme)* is the province of the wise man alone, who grasps truths in a systematic and integrated way that is "unshakable by reason," corresponding roughly to the distinction proposed between *cognitio* and *scientia*." See esp. Stobaeus, *Ecl.* 2. 73.16–74. 3 (= 41H in Long&Sedley, *The Hellenistic Philosophers*).

33 It must be granted, however, that Descartes's *cognitio*-level attainments are importantly different from the lucky grasp of gold by those in the dark room. The latter is more like a gambler's lucky guess. Undeniably, that distinction can and should be made. But it brings to the fore the fact that epistemic luck can be found at different levels and in different ways. Take a case where the gold-searcher enters a dark room that in fact happens to contain only gold objects, though he has no idea of this. Or take a case where there are several rooms before him, any of which he might enter, all dark and only one containing all gold objects. If he happens to choose that one while ignorant of the relevant facts, again it is no accident in one respect that he lays hold of some gold, while still that remains an accident in another respect. The Pyrrhonian gold-in-the-dark example can, I believe, be supplemented interestingly in the ways indicated, so as to support the intuition that one needs a reflective perspective rich and powerful enough to rule out more than just the weak possibility that one's belief be just as much a matter of blind luck as is a gambler's lucky guess.

34 This appeal is also found at the heart of Descartes's epistemology, when in the second paragraph of the third Meditation he writes: "Certainly in this first knowledge there is nothing that assures me of its truth, excepting the clear and distinct perception of that which I state, which would not indeed suffice to assure me that what I say is true, if it could ever happen that a thing which I conceived so clearly and distinctly could be false." Reliability is hence assumed to be at least necessary in an acceptable source of epistemic status. A belief is supposed to be certain if one is assured of it by its clearness and distinctness, which requires that clearness and distinctness be a (perfectly) reliable guarantor of truth. Note well: it is the clearness and distinctness of the perception that itself yields the certainty, at least in the first instance. What yields the certainty is *not* just an argument that *attributes* in a premise clearness and distinctness to one's perception of what one is led to accept as a conclusion of that argument. (As we have seen, such an argument may *boost* the epistemic status of one's belief in its conclusion, by making it a case of reflective *scientia*. But that belief already enjoys the highest level of certainty attainable as a state of *cognitio* simply through the perception of what it accepts with sufficient clearness and distinctness.)

35 "Some Theses on Empirical Certainty", in: *Review of Metaphysics* 5 (1952), pp. 621–29; p. 621. Carnap had spoken already in 1936 of the "confrontation of a statement with observation", and had proposed "acceptance

rules" for such confrontation: "If no foreign language or introduction of new terms is involved, the rules are trivial. For example: 'If one is hungry, the statement "I am hungry" may be accepted' ...." (From "Truth and Confirmation", in: *Readings in Philosophical Analysis*, ed. H. Feigl and W. S. Sellars (Appleton, 1949), p. 125. These claims appeared first in "Wahrheit und Bewährung", in: *Actes du congrès international de philosophie scientifique*, Vol. 4 (Paris, 1936), pp. 18–23.

36 In "The Theory of Knowledge", in: *Philosophy: The Princeton Studies: Humanistic Scholarship in America* (Garden City, NJ: Prentice-Hall, 1964). Chisholm cites Hempel's work, and also an earlier paper by C. J. Ducasse, "Propositions, Truth, and the Ultimate Criterion of Truth", in: *Philosophy and Phenomenological Research* 1 (1939), pp. 317–40.

37 See Sellars's "Epistemic Principles," in his lecture series, "The Structure of Knowledge", in: *Action, Knowledge, and Reality*, ed. H. N. Castañeda (Indianapolis: Bobbs Merrill, 1975), pp. 337 f.

38 "A Coherence Theory of Truth and Knowledge", in: *Kant oder Hegel?*, ed. D. Henrich (Stuttgart: Klett-Cotta, 1983), reprinted in E. LePore, *Truth and Interpretation* (Oxford: Blackwell, 1986), pp. 307–20; p. 310.

39 Again, I do not pretend that this is an adequate analysis of our issue (which I myself regard as quite complex); but here it will have to serve.

40 Actually this sort of approach is defended already by Thomas Reid.

41 "Empiricism and the Philosophy of Mind", in: *Minnesota Studies in the Philosophy of Science*, Vol. I, ed. H. Feigl and M. Scriven (Minneapolis: University of Minnesota Press, 1956), pp. 253–329. Reprinted in *Empirical Knowledge*, ed. R. M. Chisholm and R. J. Swartz (Englewood Cliffs: Prentice-Hall, 1973), pp. 471–541; p. 512.

42 Loc. cit., p. 513.

43 This requirement is defended in my *Knowledge in Perspective* (Cambridge University Press, 1991), pp. 280 ff.

44 Cf. A 3.

45 Cf. my reference to Sextus on page 205 f. above and note 11.

46 The combination of coherence and comprehensiveness comports with a concept of epistemic justification that is "internal". But it remains to be seen just where to draw the relevant boundaries: At the skin? At the boundaries of the "mind"? At the present-time-slice? At the boundaries of the subject's lifetime? Using some combination of the above? If so, which? And why? And why do we and should we care whether people are thus "internally" justified? My own answers would rest on a *subject-centered* conception of epistemic justification as intellectual virtue, and on

the importance to a social species of keeping track of the epistemic aptitude or ineptitude of oneself and one's fellows, especially where it is possible to exercise some measure of control, however indirect.

47 My *Knowledge in Perspective* (Cambridge, UK: Cambridge University Press, 1991) gives a central role to a distinction between animal knowledge and reflective knowledge analogous to Descartes's *cognitio/scientia* distinction, although my rationale is somewhat different and predates my awareness of Descartes's. Cf., e. g., pp. 240 and 282. I would now supplement that earlier rationale with our considerations here involving reflective knowledge, the Principle of the Criterion and its demonstration, and the Pyrrhonian Problematic. These considerations support use of the animal/reflective distinction in epistemology, no less than they support Descartes's use of the *cognitio/scientia* distinction. Of course, many since Descartes have groped for a similarly coherent way beyond the Pyrrhonian Problematic, and many have repudiated any such project. I discuss some of the most important recent work in "Philosophical Skepticism and Epistemic Circularity", in: *Proceedings of the Aristotelian Society* Supp. Vol. 68 (1994), pp. 268–90.

48 My warm thanks for comments on parts I – IV of this paper to Victor Caston, Matthew McGrath, and, especially, James Van Cleve.

Hilary Putnam

Skepticism*

What originally provoked these reflections is a certain movement away from Kant and back in the direction of Hume that is visible in Strawson's later philosophical writing. Like Hume, whom he explicitly cites as his model, Strawson argues that such beliefs as our belief in the uniformity of nature and the existence of the external world are not based on reasoning and can neither be undermined nor defended by it. This has led me to ask (a question Strawson has himself considered, in a more Kantian period) whether the *non*existence of the external world is really a coherent idea. In the first of the following sections of this essay I shall offer reasons for thinking that answer is "no, it isn't", or at least that we have not been so far enabled (by the skeptic or, for that matter, by his familiar opponent, the traditional epistemologist) to give it a coherent sense. In the second of the following sections I then consider what sort of failure to achieve intelligibility is involved here, and I argue that intelligibility is, in general, not a matter of words and syntax alone, but a matter of the circumstances under which a sentence is uttered, and that the failure of such a sentence as "We are immaterial beings undergoing the illusion of being in a material world" to achieve the kind of sense it would have to have to represent a challenge to our world-view is analogous to the failure of a sentence in a fairy tale to achieve the status of a claim whose truth-value could be seriously discussed. This emphasis on *context sensitivity* leads, in the third of the sections which follow, to a discussion of what I shall call the "occasion sensitivity" of the verb "know"; the fourth section thereby comments on the distinction between ordinary and "philosophical" doubt. The fifth section discusses the idea of the skeptic as "challenging our conceptual scheme as a whole", and the last section distinguishes my approach from an approach (due to Michael Williams) which also stresses the context sensitivity of claims to know, but does so in a way which, in my opinion, gives the skeptic far too much.

Because these reflections belong, in large part, to what is called "philosophy of language", they run the danger of giving the impression that (I hold the view that) skepticism has its powerful appeal simply because we make certain mistakes about the way language works. This would indeed be absurd. Rather, my view is that the appeal both of skepticism *and* a wrong way of viewing our language rest on much deeper facts about us – such as the fact that we humans oscillate between illusions of omnipotence and illusions of impotence with respect to so many of our powers (emotional, intentional, and cognitive alike). But to develop that thought must be a task for another occasion.[1]

I
The "external world"

Let us begin by considering that old chestnut, the "existence of the external world". Is it really clear that there is a coherent alternative?; clear, that is, that there is a coherently describable state of affairs which would properly be described as the existence of "external objects" being illusory?

Of course, for eighteenth century philosophers such a state of affairs seemed perfectly imaginable. Sense impressions were conceived of by rationalists and empiricists alike as immaterial; it was the coherence of the idea of *matter* that was thought (by certain empiricists) to be problematic. But today, not only do Berkeley's and Hume's difficulties with the conceivability of "unperceived matter" seem wrongheaded[2], but in addition the very idea of "sense data"[3] (Hume's "impressions and ideas"), thought of as immaterial particulars which alone we directly observe, has been repeatedly attacked by some of the best philosophical minds of the century. Without attempting to review a vast literature (and without attempting to deal with all of the confusions and unwarranted assumptions that hover around the notion of "experience" in the philosophical literature like a swarm of hornets) let me begin by making just three points here:

First of all, the very idea that experiencing something is being related to an immaterial particular or universal[4] ignores an obvious possibility (sometimes called the "adverbial" view of perception), namely the possibility that experiencing something is being in a certain state or condition, in short, *having a certain sort of predicate apply to one*, and not being in a mysterious relation R to a mysterious sort of entity[5]. The adverbial view has the advantage of being nicely neutral on a number of contested metaphysical issues.[6] Although, when I was young, one still found some philosophers who thought that the relational analysis of experience (i. e., the analysis that says that having a particular experience is being in a relation R – a relation of "directly experiencing" – to an immaterial something [a something which is not itself a state of the experiencer, although it may be dependent on his mind for its existence]) was *obviously* correct, indeed, thought that it was not an "analysis" at all, but just a report of the plain facts of (sufficiently sophisticated!) introspection, few if any philosophers think this today. Today, I believe, almost all philosophers of perception recognize that all of these "accounts" are compatible with the "subjective quality" of experience itself. Indeed, at one point in the *Investigations*[7], Wittgenstein seems to suggest that such accounts mistake what is just a new way of talking for the discovery of a novel feature of reality.

Secondly, the idea that the experiencing subject could herself be just a "collection of ideas and impressions" (this is Hume's account of the self) is enormously problematic. Not only did Hume himself, famously, see deep difficulties with his own account, but the fact is that we learn what perception is (as Strawson himself has more than once pointed out) in the course of talking about transactions between persons and a material world which they sometimes perceive rightly and sometimes wrongly. Indeed, in the *Metaphysical Foundation of Natural Science*, Kant suggests that even our idea of *color* involves notions of body, of surfaces of bodies, and of laws ["rules"] relating our perceptions to what goes on with the surfaces of bodies. The idea of taking away all the bodies (including the body of the experiencer) and leaving the experiences makes no more sense than the idea of taking away the Cheshire cat and leaving the grin.

Thirdly, our whole experience of persons, including ourselves, is as *embodied* beings. The Berkeleyan notion of a "spirit", is, as the etymology suggests[8], a survival of a time when the human mind was thought to consist of *wind*. Why should we grant that this is an intelligible notion?

If we take these points into account, then the natural upshot may well be a view of perception like the one that Strawson adopted in *Individuals*. The main elements of such a view are the following: (1) We understand persons as having special properties (Strawson's "P-predicates"), including experiential properties (as in the "adverbial view"), properties which figure in explanations of, in particular, the *reasons* for our attitudes and doings. (2) Because the analysis of conduct from the point of view of its intentional meaning and its justification or lack of justification in terms of reasons is a different enterprise from the enterprises of physics and chemistry, the explanations we give using "P-predicates" employ a different sense of "because" than do physical (or chemical, etc.) explanations of our bodily motions, and because the "becauses" are different, there is not, in principle, any *conflict* between the physical and the psychological perspectives on our behavior. (3) We need not be driven to a metaphysical dualism by the fact that P-predicates aren't reducible to physical (chemical, electro-chemical, etc.) predicates in any sense of "reducible" we presently possess. (4) Being a possessor of P-predicates is not the same thing as being an immaterial "spirit" or "soul" in a mysterious relation to a body.

But isn't it the case that from such a view claims that "nothing exists except spirits and their ideas [experiences]" (this was Berkeley's claim), and "nothing exists except ideas and impressions" (this was Hume's view, at least "in the study") rest on a misunderstanding of the necessary preconditions for ascribing predicates at all? If our conception of what an experience *is* indeed derives from our mastery of ordinary talk of *persons' experiencing particular objects, properties of objects, interactions between objects, etc.*, then *do* such ideas as the idea that persons might *be* experiences (or immaterial "spirits" plus experiences) really make sense? (In Hume, such talk was supposed to have the status of *scientific* talk – Hume famously compared his associationist psychology cum philosophy to Newtonian gravitational theory – Humean "ideas" and "impressions" being, as it were, the "particles" of the new theory of the mind, and association being the "gravitational force" that held them together.) The idea of an "immaterial spirit" has a kind of intelligibility in a ghost story (an intelligibility which becomes the more questionable the more seriously the ghost story is taken), but does it acquire a determinate sense *just* from Berkeley's philosophy?

II
But *are* the skeptical scenarios "rationally meaningful"?[9]

In *Skepticism and Naturalism: Some Varieties*, Strawson does briefly discuss the issue of the intelligibility of the skeptical challenge, or, rather, he briefly discusses *Stroud's* discussion of that issue[10]. The challenge to the intelligibility of the skeptical challenge that Strawson considers is Carnap's[11], and Stroud, in Strawson's summary, finds that "Carnap does not altogether miss the point [of the skeptical challenge], but seeks to smother or extinguish it by what Stroud finds an equally unacceptable verificationist dogmatism. It is all very well, Stroud says, to declare the philosophical question to be meaningless; but it does not *seem* to be meaningless. The skeptical challenge, the skeptical question, *seem* to be intelligible. We should at least need more argument to be convinced that they were not."[12] And Strawson adds *(loc. cit.)*: "Many philosophers would agree with Stroud, as against Carnap, on this point; and would indeed go further and contend [...] that the skeptical challenge is perfectly intelligible, rationally meaningful." In *Skepticism and Naturalism*, Strawson leaves unchallenged the view of "many philosophers" that "the skeptical challenge is perfectly intelligible, rationally meaningful", and instead takes a rather hard Humean line. Belief in the external world, or the uniformity of nature, is, he says, a matter of natural inclination, not received conviction, and we could not be brought to give such beliefs up by any reasons. Moreover, the skeptic's doubts and the various philosophical attempts to answer the skeptic are alike pointless; beliefs that are not based on reasoning can neither be undermined nor defended by it. (Contrast Strawson's own statement in *Individuals*, p. 35, that the skeptic's doubts "are unreal, not simply because they are logically irresoluble doubts, but because they amount to the rejection of the whole conceptual scheme within which alone such doubts make sense"!)

I am surprised at the fact that Strawson does not see his Humean tendencies and his Kantian tendencies as in conflict. In *Skepticism and Naturalism: Some Varieties*, he attempts to reconcile them in the following way: Kantian arguments show us how our concepts hang together, but do not speak to the skeptic's challenge to justify our conceptual scheme as a whole; Strawson's Humean contention that the question of justification cannot even be raised, because reasons are not and cannot be in question here, appears to speak to that challenge. But, the contention employs the wrong "cannot". Strawson's contention speaks to the issue of pointlessness given the way we are "hard-wired", not to the issue of intelligibility. Surely, the skeptic's challenge to justify "the uniformity of nature" and "the existence of the external world" presupposes that these can be *coherently* doubted. And that is just what the Kantian arguments call into question. How our concepts hang together has everything to do with whether there *is* an intelligible skeptical challenge.

Stroud (and, if he indeed agrees with him on this point, Strawson) is, of course, right that the way to meet the skeptical challenge *isn't* to resort to "verificationist dogmatism". But, as I have been explaining, there are grounds for doubting whether the traditional skeptical scenarios in connection with "the existence of the external world" really are meaningful, and none of the ones I have rehearsed turns upon a prior commitment to a philosophical theory (such as verificationism) that is supposed to yield a general method for assessing the meaningfulness of an arbitrary statement.

Let me now try to say in a more abstract way what the nature of such grounds is.

In chapter 10 of *Sense and Sensibilia*, Austin makes the remark that "It seems to be fairly generally realized that if you just take a bunch of sentences [...] impeccably formulated in some language or other, there can be no question of sorting them out into those that are true and those that are false; for (leaving out of account so called 'analytic' sentences) the question of truth and falsity does not turn only on what a sentence *is*, nor yet on what it *means*, but on, speaking very broadly, the circumstances in which it is uttered."[13] "Knowing the meaning" of the words in a sentence, in the sense of knowing how the words are used in a sufficient number of typical situations, isn't knowing a list of all the circumstances which might affect exactly what the sentence is used to say, and of the ways in which the words are to be used in those circumstances, nor does it require possession of an algorithm for calculating what the sentence is used to say in an arbitrary circumstance (that's something that has to be determined with the aid of what Kant called "good judgment"). In addition, this sort of occasion-sensitivity is not something that can or should be handled by postulating a host of different "meanings" for our words, one corresponding to each difference in the circumstances that affects the truth conditions. This is something that Austin argues at some length (in some special cases), in chapter 10 of *Sense and Sensibilia*.

I will give two examples that may help to indicate what I am talking about. (They are taken from articles by Charles Travis.[14]) I certainly know the meaning of the words, "there", "coffee", "a lot", "is", "on", "the" and "table". But that knowledge by itself does not determine the "truth value" of the sentence "There is a lot of coffee on the table"; in fact, the sentence, simply as a sentence, doesn't *have* a truth-value apart from particular circumstances. Moreover, the truth-conditions of the sentence "There is a lot of coffee on the table" are highly occasion-sensitive: depending upon the circumstances, the sentence can be used to say that there are many cups of coffee on a contextually definite table, or that there is a huge urn of coffee on the table in question, or that there are bags of coffee stacked on the table, or that coffee has been spilled on the table, etc.

A different sort of example: I have an ornamental tree in my garden with bronze-colored leaves. Suppose a prankster paints the leaves green. Depending upon who says it and to whom and why, the sentence "The tree has green leaves", said with my tree in mind, may be *true, false,* or *indeterminate*!

[Responding to the coffee example, a philosopher of language of my acquaintance – one wedded to Grice's distinction between the standard meaning of an utterance and its conversational implicatures[15] – suggested that the "standard meaning" of "there is a lot of coffee on the table" is that there are many (how many?) *molecules* of coffee on the table. But if that is right, the "standard" sense is a sense in which the words are never used!]

The idea of occasion-sensitivity that Austin referred to in the late 1950s is directly relevant to questions of skepticism, and the intelligibility of both skeptical challenges and various responses to those challenges. One can read Stanley Cavell's *The Claim of Reason* as an exercise in showing how Austinian and Wittgensteinian considerations of occasion-sensitivity can be brought to bear on philosophical skepticism. Cavell brings out how a skeptical claim to doubt a "best case" of knowledge and a counter-skeptical claim to "know", such as G. E. Moore's claim to know that "this is a hand", fail, in the end, to be intelligible as *claims*.[16]

Before applying the idea directly to the skeptical scenarios we have been discussing, let me mention one more example: we all "understand" the sentence "At the stroke of midnight, the coach turned into a pumpkin", in the sense of being able to enjoy *Cinderella*. But it does not follow that we should understand what was being said if – without providing any relevant context to indicate what he or she is doing – someone, obviously not engaged in telling a fairy tale, and with apparent seriousness, said "It has really happened that a coach turned into a pumpkin".[17] (And it would not be enough for the speaker to add: "I mean you to take this as a philosophical assertion".)

In the case of the tree on my property, someone who knows that my tree has (by nature) bronze-colored leaves might well be confused if I said, without explaining that a prankster had colored the leaves green, "The tree now has green leaves". But we would be much more confused if someone appeared to claim in all seriousness that a coach has turned into a pumpkin. Are the atoms of the coach supposed to have rearranged themselves? But the coach doesn't consist of the same *elements* as a pumpkin. And the mass of the coach is much greater than the mass of a pumpkin. There are, of course, possible occasions of use on which we could understand the claim. (E. g., the "coach" was a "prop", made to be used in puppet-shows, and it is part of its clever construction that it can "turn into a pumpkin" – that is, a pumpkin "prop".) But just saying "I mean it really happened", or "I am speaking in the context of philosophy" does nothing to make the alleged claim "rationally meaningful". (Recall the early modern dispute as to the meaningfulness of the doctrine of transubstantiation. The Christian claim that the communion wine "is" Jesus' blood is intelligible from the point of view of a committed Christian (and problematic from any other point of view[18]); but is the philosophical interpretation of that religious utterance, which holds that the communion wine has all the essential properties of blood but lacks the chemical composition of blood, supposed to be really intelligible, even from that point of view?) The point is not that we could not find an occasion of use for the expression "some coaches really do turn into pumpkins", but rather that here and now we cannot understand *what* those words are to be taken as asserting.

But if we cannot understand "Some coaches really do turn into pumpkins", how much less can we say we understand the claim that a person – indeed, oneself – might be a "disembodied spirit". At least we know what *pumpkins* are. But do we have any account at all of what disembodied spirits are? (Even the medieval schoolmen, or many of them, balked at the idea that the souls of the departed have literally *no* matter of any kind at all.[19]) Talk of disembodied spirits, ghosts, etc., does, obviously, have the kind of intelligibility appropriate to myth; but does that make such talk intelligible if intended as factual description?

One might, as a desperate last resort, try explaining the notion of one's being a disembodied spirit by a *via negativa*; "As a skeptical hypothesis, that you are a disembodied spirit need only mean that you have exactly the experiences you seem to yourself to have, but you don't actually have a body." But recall, the "possibility" that we don't actually have bodies was supposed to be *made intelligible* by pointing out that we "might be disembodied spirits"! Now we have come full circle. We would have to know just *how* we might actually not have bodies in order to know what it would be to be a "disembodied spirit", and we would have to know what a disembodied spirit was in order to understand the possibility that we might not really have bodies.[20]

As already mentioned, Hume, unlike Berkeley, thought he could explain how we might not really have material bodies *without* invoking the Berkeleyan notion of a "spirit". According to Hume, we are just collections of impressions and ideas. But, although Hume never faces it, this would seem to imply the scarcely intelligible possibility that there might be *experiences without any experiencer at all* (a problem that haunts the sense-datum tradition[21]); for if sense-data (ideas and impressions) are the atoms out of which "selves" are built, it would seem to be a purely contingent truth, if it is a truth, that all of these atoms belong to the sorts of bundles which constitute selves. Why should there not be stacks of them lying around which don't belong to any self? And if *that* is possible, why should there not be grins without grinners? To raise the question of the intelligibility of these skeptical hypotheses is by no means to commit oneself to verificationism, as Stroud (and, implicitly, Strawson) suggest. Very strange ways of using words like "idea" and "impression" (or, alternatively "experience") occur here; and the context of their use hardly clears up our difficulties. To say: "we do know the relevant context; it is the context of Hume's *Enquiry*", for example, is not to tell us *how* a person could be a bundle of experiences; the *Enquiry* simply takes that as already clear, for reasons which have to do with Hume's failure to see the weakness of some of his own key arguments. Denying, as I am, that Berkeley or Hume or any of their successors have provided us with a "rationally meaningful" scenario to discuss – denying that they have so much as made sense of the claim that we are nothing but "spirits and their ideas", or nothing but "ideas and impressions" – does indeed involve rejecting the idea that traditional philosophical claims are automatically to be allowed to be clear, to possess truth value, etc., without looking carefully at the different circumstances in which the key terms are non-philosophically used.[22] But rejecting that idea is putting the burden of proof back where it belongs, on the *prima facie* unintelligible claims, and that burden can be shifted without appealing to some controversial philosophical procedure for classifying all claims into those that are meaningful and those that are not.

III
The occasion-sensitivity of knowledge claims

I turn now to an exploration of some features of our ordinary use of "know". The phenomenon of the occasion-sensitivity of truth-claims in general that Austin remarked upon is especially important in connection with knowledge claims. The reason for this is that, as we actually use the word "know", a statement of the form "X knows that so-and-so" does not claim that either X or the speaker (who may be a third person) is in a position to defuse *every* conceivable "doubt" (or "possibility of error").

Here is a relevant example:

(1) I know (for example) that the color of my house is "off-white".
(2) I know the (obvious) implication: If some pranksters painted my house blue this morning, then the color of my house is now blue, and not off-white.
(3) But I do not *know* that some pranksters did not paint my house blue this morning (I have been at the office all day) – and, by the way, I also don't "not know" that some prankster did not paint my house blue this morning – in the absence of some legitimate reason for doubt, one can only say that the question does not arise.[23]

Moral: when we say "I know", what we mean is that we can rule out certain relevant "doubts", but *not* all possible "doubts". Which "doubts" depends on the circumstances; there is no rule that we can give once and for all that covers all the occasions on which we might use the word "know". We have to use good judgment, and assume that our conversational partners are attuned to us,[24] that they will share our implicit knowledge of what that comes to in the circumstances.

There is an intimate connection between this occasion-sensitivity of "I know" and Stanley Cavell's point that Moore's "I know that this is a hand" (said while holding up one of his hands) does not succeed in making a claim. Normally, we can tell which possibilities a speaker is claiming to be able to rule out and which he is not claiming to be able to rule out because we know the *point* of his assertion. If my hearers know that the point of my assertion is to tell them what color my house has, I do not have to guarantee (what is anyway beyond my power to guarantee) that there hasn't been a prank in the last few hours, unless, of course, there has been a rash of such pranks lately, and the questioner really is interested in the color of the house *this moment*. And this observation is not merely a piece of "pragmatics" as opposed to "semantics"; what determines *what* is being said, in such a case, is our understanding of *why* one would say it in such circumstances.

Contrast, now, this familiar use of "know" with G. E. Moore's. The point of Moore's utterance was what we call "philosophical" – that is to establish that he "really knows" that there are material objects, and not practical in the way in which my saying that I know I will be in Emerson Hall Wednesday week serves a practical purpose. But there is no standard of "really knowing" independent of an ordinary context for using the word(s) "know" (and "really"). One might understand the statement that one "really knows" that something is a hand if one were to encounter an ordinary context which gave sense to the question – a context which also gave sense to "not knowing" that it is a hand (for example, there could be doubt as to whether one could identify a hand, even one's own, if there were a real possibility that one had been brain damaged) – but to establish in such a context that one does really know that it is a hand would not answer the skeptic's doubt of the external world; it would only establish (on the basis of a fund of background knowledge) that one is not brain damaged (or whatever the problem might be), and this would lack the requisite generality to address the skeptical challenge. On the other hand, to use "know" with no specifiable point other than to establish that one "really knows" that there are material objects is to use it in such a way that it has come loose from the criteria that allow it to be recognizable as an application of our concept of knowledge.[25] And when "know" is used without a criterion we can just as well say (with the skeptic) that Moore *doesn't* know as that he does know. Moore wants to exploit the appropriateness of saying "I know" in a host of ordinary contexts without recognizing the *occasion sensitivity* which is part and parcel of the use of "know" in those ordinary contexts.

IV
Ordinary and "philosophical" doubt

I have said that the point of saying "I know" is to rule out certain "possibilities" that what one claims to know not be the case, and that *which* these are depends upon the *ordinary* context in which the knowledge claim is made.

"Ordinary context", here, is meant to contrast with "philosophical context"[26], not, for example, with technical, or scientific, or learned, context. I do not suppose that such a contrast is one that can be drawn once and for all, independently of what particular context is being characterized as "philosophical" and what the point of so characterizing it may be. Instead, let me illustrate the notion of a "philosophical context" by saying briefly how both the skeptical use of "know" and Moore's use of "know" go wrong, wrong in ways which are characteristic of philosophical discussions of knowledge.

These two ways of going wrong correspond to opposing ways of attempting to transcend the context-sensitivity of ordinary knowledge claims: both Moore and the skeptic attempt to use "know" in such a way that everything that ordinarily determines a human context – what our interests and objectives are, what our background knowledge is, what our loyalties, what our communal affiliations and disaffiliations, what our relations to the person(s) we are speaking to – become *irrelevant*. That attempt at an impossible transcendence is what I take to characterize a "philosophical context", for the purposes of this discussion.

Notoriously, skeptics will not allow one to ignore any "possibility" as too far fetched; they will also not allow one to appeal to background knowledge in one's reply (if one does, they will simply point to conceivable – or allegedly conceivable – "possibilities" of error with the background knowledge). But this makes the skeptics' use of "know" one in which it is virtually *tautological* that one does not "know" anything. The skeptic often conceals this (as does Descartes, for example, in his skeptical moment) by beginning as if all he were doing was insisting on "tightening up" our standards, and introducing some praiseworthy "methodological rigor" into our attributions of knowledge. But when the skeptic is done, what he says seems to have no methodological implications whatsoever. This fact is reflected in Stroud and others saying they are interested in a "special philosophical question". It is a live question whether this "philosophical" use of "know" hasn't just produced a homonym of our word if it doesn't feed back into any conclusions as to when we should attribute knowledge in the ordinary use.

The skeptic's use of "know" is one example of a "philosophical" use; but what of Moore's? Moore's claim, as we just said, trades on the use of "know" in ordinary contexts (his "I know that this is a hand" is a parody of such ordinary knowledge claims as "I know this is such and such a sort of object", "I know this is a tool for such and such a purpose", uttered in a context in which "what it is" is in genuine doubt); but precisely because it is not responsible to any ordinary context, what *licenses* Moore to make his claim is just as unclear as is the skeptical "possibility" that it is all a dream or a pervasive hallucination. We might say that the skeptic requires *absurd* criteria for knowledge, while Moore tries to make a knowledge claim *without* criteria.

But why are we tempted to suppose that such a use of "know" as the skeptic employs is part of the language game? Perhaps the deepest reason is the tendency to oscillate between illusions of omnipotence and illusions of impotence that I mentioned at the outset of this essay, or, to put it in a way that is only apparently different, the tendency to think that anything (any "knowledge") that isn't omnipotent is impotent.

A more superficial – but nonetheless very plausible – reason was once suggested by Max Black.[27] Black pointed out that we sometimes speak of using the word "know" in a "stricter" or "less strict" sense. And he suggested that this may give rise to the idea that the skeptic's "sense" is *the absolutely strict sense*. Perhaps that is why it seems that the skeptic's use of "know" is the proper one; why it seems that it is we who normally speak "loosely" – we who are being too "sloppy" to see the correct point the skeptic is making: that "strictly speaking" we do not know anything at all.

To help us resist this temptation, Black pointed out that at one time mathematicians thought that it made sense to speak of the "sum" of any infinite series at all – without reference to whether the series of partial sums converges or diverges. (A celebrated early nineteenth century mathematician suggested that the divergent series 1−1+1−1+1−... has the sum 1/2!) Just as it does not follow from the fact that the series 1−1+1−1+1−... can be calculated to any finite number of terms that there is such a thing as the "sum" of the whole infinite series, or such a thing as the "limit" of the partial sums, so from the fact that one can use "know" in increasingly strict senses (in certain contexts, anyway) it does not follow that there must be such a thing as "the absolutely strict sense". The limit of a series of stricter senses of "I know" may not be a sense of "I know" at all. And, indeed, the skeptic's "sense" of "I know" is one that cannot do the work that knowledge claims do.

In distinguishing in this way between ordinary and philosophical uses of "I know", I am in the ballpark of Peirce's celebrated distinction between "real" and "philosophical" doubt. Unfortunately, Peirce drew that distinction in psychological terms; and this has allowed some philosophers (including Michael Williams) to say that there is no difference, or only a verbal difference, between Peirce's rejection of skeptical doubt and Hume's observation that such doubt cannot be sustained outside the study. But Peirce's observation need not be understood in this way. The real point that Peirce – and after him James and Dewey – were making, I believe, is a genuinely logical point. The point is that *doubt requires justification as well as belief.* And pointing to remote possibilities of error, mere logical possibilities or even far fetched empirical possibilities, does not, in itself, justify doubt. That the language game is not played the way the skeptic plays it is a fact about the *structure* of our concepts. It is not a mere contingent fact about our psychology that we do not use "know" in such a way that the only knowledge-statement we can make is the one negative statement that we do not know anything; for such a use of "know" would defeat the purposes for which we have the concept, and *that* is as much a logical fact as is the fact that if we have one contradiction in a logical calculus (whose rules include the standard rules of two-valued logic) we can derive every statement as a theorem in the calculus, and then the calculus would be useless (if intended as a formalization of some branch of discourse).

V
Skepticism as a challenge
to the whole language game

A number of philosophers will find all this argumentation futile; indeed, they will find any attempt to show the incoherence of skeptical doubt futile. (My worry in this essay has been that Strawson seems to agree with these philosophers, at least in his Humean mood.) While their arguments against the enterprise vary, in the case of Barry Stroud's article cited by Strawson[28], a central reason seems to be that such an attempt necessarily proceeds from *within* our conceptual system itself. But the skeptic, they say, is offering a *challenge to our ordinary conceptual system as a whole.* The sort of criticism of the skeptic's argument we have been engaged in necessarily begs the whole question, they believe.

To this, there are two replies I would offer. First of all, it need not be – and it had better not be – our purpose to give a reply to the skeptic that *the skeptic must accept.* To think of the target as the skeptic, or even "the skeptic inside me" (this is a suggestion of Michael Williams) is to engage in a losing enterprise. The skeptic will go on asking "How do you know that", *ad infinitum*. The challenge of skepticism, insofar as it is an *intellectual* challenge at all (and, as Cavell has discussed at length in Part Four of *The Claim of Reason*, for the skeptic himself it is something much deeper) lies in the fact that the skeptic threatens our conceptual system from *inside*. The reason skepticism is of genuine intellectual interest – interest to the *nonskeptic* – is not unlike the reason that the logical paradoxes are of genuine intellectual interest: paradoxes force us to rethink and reformulate our commitments. But if the reason I undertake to show that the skeptical arguments need not be accepted is, at least in part, like the reason I undertake to avoid logical contradictions in pure mathematics (e. g., the Russell Paradox), or to find a way to talk about truth without such logical contradictions as the Liar Paradox; if my purpose is to put my own intellectual home in order, then what I need is a perspicuous representation of our talk of "knowing" that shows how it avoids the skeptical conclusion, and that my *nonskeptical* self can find satisfactory and convincing. (Just as a solution to the logical paradoxes does not have to convince the skeptic, or even convince all philosophers – there can be alternative ways to avoid the paradoxes – so a solution to what we may call "the skeptical paradoxes" does not have to convince the skeptic, or even convince all philosophers – perhaps here too there may be alternative solutions.) It is not a good objection to a resolution to an antinomy that the argument to the antinomy seems "perfectly intelligible", and, indeed, proceeds from what seem to be "intuitively correct" premises, while the resolution draws on ideas (the Theory of Types, in the case of the Russell Paradox; the theory of Levels of Language in the case of the Liar Paradox – and on much more complicated ideas than these as well, in the case of the follow-up discussions since Russell's and Tarski's) that are abstruse and to some extent controversial. That is the very nature of the resolution of antinomies. What I have tried to provide in this essay is an argument *that convinces me* that *the skeptic cannot provide a valid argument from premises I must accept to the conclusion that knowledge is impossible.* In the same way, Russell showed that (after we have carefully reconstructed out way of talking about sets) a skeptic – or whoever – cannot provide a valid argument from premises we must accept to the conclusion that mathematics is contradictory, and Tarski showed that (after we have carefully reconstructed our talk about truth) a skeptic – or whoever – cannot provide a valid argument from premises we must accept to the conclusion that talk about truth is contradictory.[29]

Secondly, the notion of challenging the conceptual system as a whole is (as I think it was the merit of the Kantian tradition to have seen) an incoherent one. To challenge the conceptual system "as a whole" would require standing outside of one's own concepts, and there is no place from which to do that. The idea that we have already criticized as incoherent, of a general problem of the existence of the external world, was a failed attempt to find just such a place. (Not surprisingly, it depended on the Humean cum Berkeleyan view of experiences – "ideas and impressions" – as free-standing objects.)

To be sure, the skeptic may, and often does, try to find a place "inside" our concepts from which he can formulate *something like* the traditional problems. The Brain in a Vat scenario that I discussed in *Reason, Truth and History* is just such an attempt. But incoherence is not the only problem to threaten the skeptic's attempt to criticize our conceptual scheme "as a whole". Let us think of what goes on in Brain in a Vat scenarios for a moment. Even if we bracket the question as to how, if we are indeed Brains in a Vat, we are supposed to be able to so much as refer to real vats, real objects, a real computer (which we have to do to so much as formulate the skeptical possibility), the fact is that such scenarios do not even attempt to describe a possible world in which there are no external objects at all. Not only are there external objects in a Brain in the Vat scenario (although the BIVs are supposed to be mistaken about which they are), but they are supposed to obey just the standard physical laws. So the Brain in a Vat scenario does not actually contradict either our "belief in an external world" *or* our "belief in the uniformity of nature". And it even concedes that we have the general character of the external world right and the general character of the physical laws right! It is the details we have wrong. But precisely because the scenario assumes just our standard picture of the physical world at the level of natural law, it is appropriate for us to point out to the skeptic that *the world picture which he needs to give content to his talk of computers, brains, electrical impulses, chemicals needed to keep the brains alive, etc.,* is simply stolen from *our* world picture, and our world picture does not imply that there is any serious likelihood of the existence of a computer large enough and powerful enough to simulate a "real world" so well as to fool billions of different human brains.[30] The skeptic can, indeed, say that the Brain in a Vat scenario is only meant as an *illustration* of the possibility that the external world is an illusion; but then he is back at the problem of giving *that* "possibility" content. Of course, we must concede that the possibility of constructing such scenarios from within our own world picture does show that what our claims rest on is not "deductive certainty". But, in the end, that is all the skeptic can get us to concede. And that is hardly news.

VI
The contextuality of knowledge claims

In the remaining sections of this essay, I shall further explore the occasion sensitivity of knowledge claims and the nature of skepticism by contrasting the view I have been defending with some views defended by Michael Williams in *Unnatural Doubts*.

Superficially, Michael Williams' views on skepticism resemble the ideas about the "occasion sensitivity" of knowledge claims that I have been defending. Insightfully, he sees the skeptic and his traditional opponent as sharing a view he calls "epistemic realism": in effect, the view that the knowledge relation is a natural kind, like the parent relation, or like the metric relation in General Relativity. For the epistemic realist, to say that one knows that *p* is always, no matter what the context, to say that one and the same relation R (the "natural kind" in question) obtains between the true proposition one claims to know and one's "evidence" (including memory and the "evidence of the senses"). This view implies that "knowing" cannot come to different things in different contexts; it implies that what reasons one has for claiming to "know", what doubts actually *arise* in the context, what is going to be *done* (and by whom) if one's knowledge claim is accepted, and the nature and seriousness of the possible consequences, are all irrelevant to whether one can say "I know".

In opposition to epistemic realism, Williams proposes the thesis that whether or not one knows depends very much on these contextual factors, and particularly on what doubts actually are at issue in the context. So far this resembles the claim I have attributed to various philosophers (J. L. Austin, Stanley Cavell and Charles Travis, in particular) that knowledge claims are, by their very nature, occasion sensitive. But clearly Michael Williams understands what he calls the "contextuality" of knowledge claims very differently than these authors. For he does *not* find skeptical arguments incoherent (although, significantly, he considers no skeptical arguments in detail, but only refers vaguely to the claim that external objects are an "illusion", and the like), and he finds Cavell's contention that Moore and the skeptic are alike trying to speak outside of our criteria too recherché to be a successful rejoinder to the skeptic's allegedly clear and convincing arguments.

According to Williams, what I have called "philosophical contexts" are conceptually in perfect order; it is just that in those contexts, contexts in which such possibilities as the possibility that the whole external world might be a "dream"[31] or an "illusion" are raised, *every doubt becomes relevant*, and hence, according to Williams, the skeptic is *right* (in those contexts) to say that we have no knowledge of external things. However, Williams adds, that does not mean that the skeptic is right *tout court*. In an *ordinary* context, one in which we don't think about either the skeptic's *arguments* or the traditional philosopher's responses – or, for that matter, Williams' own responses – to those arguments, one in which philosophical considerations do not even arise, it is *right* to say that we *do know* that, e. g., there are tables and chairs in the room. (In effect, Williams is offering a logical reconstruction of Hume's distinction between what we know in the "study" and what we know when we are not in the "study".[32])

One way in which one can see the difference between Williams' notion of contextuality and the notion of occasion sensitivity that I have defended is to examine the way Williams treats the dispute as to whether knowledge is "closed under known implication" (the very issue that first led me to think about the occasion sensitivity of knowledge claims). According to Williams, knowledge *is* closed under known implication. Thus, consistently with his position about the "contextual" truth of skepticism, Williams holds that in the sort of ordinary context just mentioned, in which I know, according to Williams, that there are tables and chairs, and that I see them, I also know (because it follows from the fact that I see real tables and chairs by an implication which is also known to me) that it is not the case that the external world as a whole is an illusion. *But I only know it when I don't think about it*; as soon as I think about the question whether the external world is an illusion, the skeptical doubts become relevant, and then my knowledge is destroyed. Williams explicitly "buys" the counter-intuitive consequence: there are true statements of the form "I know that *p*" that I can never know to be true at the time that they are true. I can *know* that the external world is not an illusion – indeed, most of the time I do know this – but I can never truly *claim* "I know that the external world is not an illusion".

I shall argue that there are at least three things wrong with this account:

(1) Williams is quite wrong about the concept of knowing.
(2) The particular way in which he is wrong makes him an "epistemic realist" *contre lui.*
(3) Williams misunderstands the nature of both skeptical and ordinary knowledge contexts.

I now take up each of these points in turn.

1. Misconceptions of the concept of knowing

Even though I cannot say "I know the external world is not an illusion" in an "ordinary" context, according to Williams (because to even think about the question would transform the context into a philosophical one), a third person – e. g., Williams himself – *can* say that I knew this in that context. In fact, according to his theory, Williams can say of himself that *when* he was in an ordinary context he knew (but did not know that he knew, and could not claim that he knew) that the external world was not an illusion. The theory thus implies that the following utterances are perfectly acceptable:

> 1) When I was counting the chairs to make sure there were enough for the party, I knew that the external world was not an illusion, but I do not know that now.
>
> 2) In some contexts I know that I will come to Emerson Hall next Wednesday, and in other contexts I do not know that I will come to Emerson Hall next Wednesday.
>
> 3) I would have known that I will come to Emerson Hall next Wednesday if you hadn't mentioned the fact that I might get killed in a traffic accident.

I submit that none of the above *is* a non-deviant English sentence. Our actual use of "know" has no place for such utterance-forms as "I would have known that p if you hadn't mentioned the fact that q" or "I know that p when I don't think about q" or "I know that p in that context but I don't know that p in this context". Williams is simply wrong about how the concept of knowledge functions. But how did it come about that, starting with promising observations about "epistemic realism" and "contextuality" as he did, he ended up with such mistaken (not to say bizarre) views about the concept of knowledge?

2. Has Williams really given up epistemic realism?

A central difficulty is that Williams has tried to handle the occasion sensitivity of knowledge claims by assimilating it to the kind of simple relativity we find with such predicates as "large". There is nothing wrong with saying that someone is "large for a man but small compared to an elephant", or that something is "large for a piece of fabric but small for a wall covering". That knowledge claims exhibit *some* relativity is something no one would deny; on *any* account, whether I know that p or not depends upon my *evidence*, my experiences, my memories, and my other beliefs. Thus it can be perfectly correct to say, "When I only had such and such evidence I did not know that *p*, but now that I have such and such additional evidence, I do know that *p*". Williams has tried to handle occasion sensitivity by simply adding such factors as *what doubts actually arise in the context* to the list of things (evidence, experiences, memories, other beliefs) on which knowledge depends. But *occasion sensitivity is quite a different phenomenon from dependence on evidence*. Indeed, the idea that *one* and the same knowledge relation is involved in all contexts (it is only that the *relata* are different in different contexts) is what Williams calls "epistemic realism", and, as we have just seen, Williams does not really give this idea up; instead, he simply expands the list of permissible relata. In this sense, Michael Williams is still an epistemic realist *contre lui*.

It is, of course, true that sometimes we have to take back or at least qualify a knowledge claim that we have made when new doubts become relevant. This can happen in two ways: the more drastic case arises when raising new doubts, doubts we had overlooked, actually cause us to stop believing that *p*, where *p* is whatever we claimed earlier to know. (So it isn't, in this case, just that we won't say "I know that *p*"; we won't even say "I think that *p*".) In such a case we certainly wouldn't say "Well, in the former context I knew that *p*"; rather we will say "I thought I knew, but I didn't, because I overlooked such and such a possibility". The less drastic case arises when we still believe that *p*, but the circumstances force us to qualify our claim to know. This could happen in a court of law, where one might admit the relevance of some possibility that in a less stringent context one would feel free to ignore, or, even outside of a law court, it might happen that the possible damage that will result if one turns out to be mistaken is greater than one thought, and so one hedges one's claim in various ways. In the latter kind of case one might say, "I still believe that *p*, but I was speaking loosely when I said I *knew* that *p*", but again one would not say "I *did* know that *p*, but I don't know in *this* context". The relevant features of the context determine whether one is licensed to make a knowledge claim at all; but they are not *relata*. (Indeed, strictly speaking even the evidence is not a *relatum*, for although I may say that "I did not know when I only had such and such evidence, but I do know now that I have further evidence", I will not say, even when I still believe the *p* in question to be true: "When I had only such and such evidence I did know that *p*, but now that I have additional evidence, I do not know that *p*"; for if the additional evidence causes me to retract my claim to know that *p* – perhaps by raising a "Gettier problem" with my earlier reasoning – then I will say "I *thought* I knew" about my earlier epistemic condition, not "I did know, relative to that evidence".)

These are not, needless to say, mere linguistic oddities. Rather, they reflect fundamental features of our cognitive situation: that we are *fallible* (knowledge claims are defeasible), and that *we have the right to claim to know, in certain situations, at certain times, and for certain purposes*. If these two features of our cognitive situation have come in for so much emphasis from pragmatist writers, it is because pragmatism has from the beginning been simultaneously *fallibilistic* and *antiskeptical*. While Williams also wishes to be fallibilistic (and to quarantine skepticism to philosophical contexts), the locutions he allows us: locutions like "I know it in this context, but I don't know it in that" cannot do the work of making knowledge claims, and without genuine knowledge claims, there is nothing to be fallibilistic about.

3. Misunderstanding the nature of both skeptical and ordinary knowledge contexts

This last remark about Williams' view may seem overly harsh. If I say, in a given context, "I know that *p*", I *have* made a genuine knowledge claim, Williams may reply; I haven't *merely* said "*relative to this context*, I know that *p*".

The problem, however, is that for Williams what fixes or changes a context is merely what doubts are *thought of*. And this makes knowledge contexts an essentially superficial matter. After all, the possibility of "illusion" may be mentioned in all sorts of contexts which are not technically philosophical! To revert to the law court example: a hostile attorney may say to the witness, "perhaps you only imagined it". If merely mentioning the possibility that what I claimed to see was only imagined, or only an illusion, or that I was dreaming, sufficed to change the context to a philosophical one (and if the skeptic is right, as soon as the context becomes a philosophical one, as Williams contends), then any attorney worth his salt could get anyone at all to admit that he doesn't know that *p*, no matter what the relevant *p*. Williams' account loses what I described as the pragmatist insight – that raising a doubt is something that requires a *justification*.

4. Is the skeptic making a straightforward conceptual blunder, misconstruing the grammar of our language?

For Michael Williams, the skeptic's argument is perfectly correct; however the skeptic has misconstrued the grammar of our language, and thus failed to see that from the fact that he (in his philosophical context) can truly say "We don't know there is an external world" it does not follow that in a different context one cannot perfectly well know (even if one cannot claim to know, because doing so would change the context!) that there is an external world. The skeptic is right (in the study), but, for conceptual reasons, it doesn't matter. But this account makes skepticism both less serious and more serious a matter than it is.

It makes skepticism less serious than it is, because it misses what one may call the *pathos* of skepticism. Even if we can show within our conceptual system, or within a plausible rational reconstruction thereof, that doubting whether we "know that the external world is not an illusion" is incoherent, this will not satisfy the skeptic – in fact, it would not satisfy the skeptic *even if it were intellectually invulnerable in every respect*. Even if skeptics were to concede that they cannot coherently state what worries them without doing violence to the concepts of "knowing" and "doubting" that we actually have, they would still not feel that their worries have been laid to rest by that discovery; they would only come to feel that their worries are unreal if they were able comfortably to *inhabit* our conceptual system, were able to make those concepts of knowledge and doubt *their own*, and the skeptics' problem, as Stanley Cavell has emphasized, is precisely their *alienation* from our concepts (an alienation which has, indeed, its positive aspect[33]), and not just a conceptual worry occasioned by an argument. For the skeptic, skepticism is not just or even primarily a conceptual problem. And Williams makes skepticism more serious than it is by conceding so easily, almost frivolously, that the skeptic's arguments are correct.

Notes

* One of the great learning experiences of my philosophical life was the opportunity to sit in on Dieter Henrich's lectures on the Transcendental Deduction at Harvard two decades or so ago. In the course of those lectures he more than once compared and contrasted his own interpretations with those of Peter Strawson, and that fact makes it not inappropriate to offer these reflections of my own on Strawson's work in a volume honoring Dieter Henrich. – I am deeply indebted to close readings and criticisms by Ruth Anna Putnam, James Conant, Paul Franks, Adam Leite and David Macarthur. (I am sure that none of them will feel that all of their criticisms have been adequately addressed however!)
1 A related diagnosis is developed brilliantly in Part IV of St. Cavell's seminal *The Claim of Reason* (Oxford: Oxford University Press, 1979).
2 Cf. the discussion of Berkeley's difficulties with the notion in "Language and Philosophy", reprinted in my *Philosophical Papers*, Vol. 2, *Mind, Language and Reality* (Cambridge: Cambridge University Press, 1975), particularly pp. 15–16.
3 Many terms have been used in the course of four hundred years of "modern" epistemology.
4 Russell thought sense data were immaterial universals.
5 In logical notation: "Helen experiences (or seems to herself to be experiencing) the presence of a blue sofa" trivially has the logical form P(Helen), but we do not have to agree with sense datum theorists that P has the "analysis": $P(x) = (Ey)(xRy \text{ \& } y \text{ is a blue sofa sense datum})$. Note that an adverbialist need not, as is often claimed by critics, analyze *all* the aspects of an experience as further properties $P', P'', \ldots$ of the subject: if I see a chair with certain features, the various qualifications of my experience can be analyzed as *properties of a property of me*, not as

simply further properties of me. I believe that, in fact, all the "formal" objections to the adverbial analysis are easy to meet.

6 These issues include the tenability of traditional mind-brain reductionism (Reichenbach thought that having a certain sort of experience is being in a particular brain-state, Sellars opposed this sort of reductionism on the ground that it was being in a kind of state which is *sui generis*); the question of functionalism (applied to experiences, this is the philosophical theory that having a certain sort of experience is being – or one's brain being – in a particular *computational state*; I proposed this view in a series of papers starting in 1960, but I reject it now, for reasons given in my *Representation and Reality* (Cambridge, Mass.: MIT Press, 1988)); and also the question whether we should think of the "qualitative identity" which (it is claimed) sometimes obtains between "veridical" and "nonveridical" perceptions as due to the presence of something which is "numerically identical".

7 *Philosophical Investigations*, § 400.

8 Not only in Indoeuropean languages: the Hebrew word for "spirit", *ruach*, originally means "wind"!

9 In what follows I have borrowed six or seven paragraphs from my "Strawson and Skepticism", forthcoming in *The Philosophy of Peter Strawson*, ed. L. Hahn (La Salle, Ill.: Open Court Publishing Co.).

10 The article Strawson discusses is B. Stroud's "The Significance of Skepticism," in: *Transcendental Arguments and Science*, ed. P. Bieri, R.-P. Horstmann, and L. Krüger (Dordrecht: Reidel, 1979), pp. 277–97.

11 R. Carnap, "Empiricism, Semantics and Ontology," in: *Revue Internationale de Philosophie* 11 (1950). Reprinted in: *Semantics and the Philosophy of Language*, ed. L. Linsky (Champaign: University of Illinois Press, 1952).

12 *Skepticism and Naturalism: Some Varieties* (New York: Columbia University Press, 1985), p. 7.

13 Austin, loc. cit. pp. 110 f. The "general realization" of which Austin speaks seems, in the meanwhile, to have been largely neutralized by the pretence – for that is what it is – that the dependence of the truth-conditions of a sentence (or better: of what is *said* when a sentence is used on a particular occasion) can be simply – indeed, mechanically – specified, by just giving the values of a few "indices", which, it is claimed, describe the relevant features of each of the circumstances in which one and the same sentence might be uttered. This claim is an instance of the prevalence of science fiction, often disguised under the name "cognitive science", in present day philosophy and linguistics; but it is not necessary

to go into that issue here. In his important book *The Uses of Sense* (Oxford: Oxford University Press, 1989) Charles Travis goes into it in detail.

14 Travis speaks of "occasion variability" and "S[peaking]-sensitivity" where I use "occasion sensitivity". I have changed his butter example to a coffee example.

15 Cf. Ch. Travis, "Anals of Analysis", in: *Mind* 100, no. 398 (April 1991), pp. 237–263 for a powerful criticism of Grice's procedures.

16 A radical – but I have come to believe correct – interpretation/application/extension of Cavell's and Travis's points due to Jim Conant holds that even when Moore says "This is a hand" (i. e., *before* he introduces the word "know") he has already failed to make a determinate statement. This seems extremely implausible at first, since we can think of many statements those words could be used to make (e. g., a teacher of English as a second language might use those words, and we would know exactly what she was saying – and she would have to be very cruel to say "this is a hand" if she was raising anything other than a hand!). But Moore was not making the statement that the English teacher was making, nor was he clearly making any other statement. What makes it hard to see this, I think, besides our adherence to the what Travis calls "classic semantics", is that we do think we know what Moore is saying – in fact, we naturally understanding him as saying that "this is a hand" is something he knows for certain (even before he introduces the word "know"). Whereas normally the intelligibility of "I know that p" presupposes the prior understanding of what p says in the context, in *this* context p itself is understood via the (illusion of) understanding "I know that p". But if "I know that p" has *no* determinate meaning, than neither does p, in Moore's case. One cannot give "This is a hand" a determinate use by just *staring* at one's hand.

17 An example of a relevant context for a related sentence (suggested by Paul Franks): in certain imaginable circumstances, someone very insightful might say to me "Your coach just turned into a pumpkin", and his remark might both be true and not adequately expressible in any other way.

18 Referring to a religious person speaking about the Judgement Day Wittgenstein says, "In one sense I understand all that he says – the English words 'God', 'separate', etc. I understand. I could say, 'I don't believe in this', and that would be true, meaning I haven't got these thoughts or anything that hangs together with them. But not that I could contradict

the thing." Ludwig Wittgenstein, *Lectures on Aesthetics, Psychology, and Religious Belief*, ed. Cyril Barrett (Berkeley: University of California Press, 1966), p. 55. A little later (p. 58) he says that he doesn't know "whether I understand him or not. I've read the same things as he's read. In a most important sense, I know what he means."

19 Cf. C. Walker Bynum, *The Resurrection of the Body in Western Christianity* (New York: Columbia University Press, 1995).

20 It is well to recall in this connection Austin's famous observation that "real" is a word whose sense in a context depends on what sort of "non-real" X is relevant in the context. "Is that a real duck?" – as opposed to a decoy? or as opposed to a goose? "Are our bodies real?" Well, they certainly aren't *fakes*.

21 As is amply evidenced in Moore's replies to his critics in the volume on him in *The philosophy of G. E. Moore* [The Library of Living Philosophers 4], ed. P. A. Schilpp (La Salle, Ill.: Open Court Publishing Co., 1968).

22 I believe that the resistance to acknowledging the pervasiveness (and the depth) of the phenomenon of occasion-sensitivity is related to the resistance that I have found people have to accepting that if we were "brains in a vat" we would not be able to *think* or *say* that we were. – And even more to the resistance to granting the next step in the argument I offered in *Reason, Truth, and History* (Cambridge: Cambridge University Press, 1981): if we couldn't think or say that we were brains in a vat if we were brains in a vat, then it follows that we *aren't* brains in a vat! We are, I think, deeply attracted to the idea (call it "semantic omnipotence") that we can refer to/think about *anything whatsoever*, independently of our environment and the nature of our embeddedness in the world.

23 At one time such examples convinced me that knowledge is not "closed under known implication". But, as Paul Franks has pointed out to me, that way of putting it already accepts the picture that there is some determinate set of things that I can be said to "know" *independent of what the context is in which the question is asked.*

24 The metaphor of attunement is Cavell's (cf. *The Claim of Reason*, cf. note 1).

25 Let me say that I follow Cavell (in *The Claim of Reason*, cf. note 1) in not taking "criteria" to be *necessary and sufficient conditions* for being an X, but rather for being the "grammatical" conditions which must be satisfied for it to be the case that what one is talking about/identifying/perhaps misidentifying is X's.

26 I am indebted to Cavell for suggesting that this is how Wittgenstein's notion of the ordinary is to be understood.

27 I have been unable to locate the place in which (I remember) Max Black makes this comparison.
28 "The Significance of Skepticism" (cf. note 10).
29 David Macarthur objects (in a private communication): "You don't offer a rational reconstruction but an attempt to explain the conditons of sense-making and how we are led to forget or overlook those conditions. This activity of 'trying to make sense' seems different from Tarski on truth, etc." It is true that I am more interested in describing our practice than in "reconstructing" it, but I have always believed that philosophically relevant descriptions of our practice always involve *some* element of "rational reconstruction".
30 Recall our Peircean principle, that doubt requires justification just as much as belief. If there is some version of the Brain in a Vat scenario that overcomes the semantical objections that I raised in *Reason, Truth, and History* (cf. note 22), I don't think a Peircean would say that "we know that we are not Brains in a Vat"; he would say "the question does not genuinely arise".
31 Of course, when this possibility is raised, the question of just how the dreamer (or his unconscious) is supposed to be able to dream a dream which is that complex and that coherent is never seriously discussed. In effect, the dreamer – or his brain – becomes the supercomputer in the Brain in a Vat scenario.
32 Unfortunately, Williams is quite wrong to think that Hume claimed that in the "study" we know the skeptic is right; as I have already pointed out, with respect to external (persisting) objects, the Hume of the "study" was an *idealist*, not a *skeptic*. The mistake about Hume is symptomatic of the larger error of supposing that so-called skeptical arguments are either simple or timeless, as if the Greek skeptics, Descartes, Hume, our contemporaries who imagine scenarios involving brains in a vat and computers all dealt with the same "skeptical arguments".
33 See my foreword to *Pursuits of Reason: Essays in Honor of Stanley Cavell*, ed. T. Cohen, P. Guyer, and H. Putnam (Lubbock, Texas: Texas Tech University Press, 1993).

III.

Themen und Wege der Metaphysik

Metaphysics: Topics and Methods

Paul Guyer

Self-Understanding and Philosophy: The Strategy of Kant's *Groundwork*

Above all, Dieter Henrich has been concerned to characterize philosophy's contribution to human self-understanding. Unlike Heidegger, as well as Schopenhauer before him and post-modernists of various stripe after him, Henrich has not considered our sense of selfhood an artifact of philosophy, an illusion constituted by bad philosophy and best absorbed into the oneness of Being or the web of words, but has instead recognized selfhood as the fundamental and ineliminable form of human life which though not created by philosophy needs to be understood by us with the help of philosophy. Kant's recognition that each of us is not merely part of a common world but also both a unique perspective on it and a free agent in it, and that this is both the most obvious fact about our form of life but at the same time the deepest mystery about it, the puzzle that philosophy must explicate if not entirely dissolve, is surely the basis of Henrich's lifelong fascination with Kant's philosophy. The twin poles of Kant's thought, the ideas that philosophy can show the form of our theoretical understanding of the world to be grounded in the form of our representation of our own selfhood, and that philosophy can save our practical self-understanding as free agents in the world from our own tendency to misunderstand ourselves as mere parts of the world, have also been the twin poles of Henrich's fascination with Kant. Here I want to bring Henrich's fundamental concerns to bear on the enduring puzzle of Kant's argumentative strategy in the *Groundwork of the Metaphysics of Morals* by examining the relationship between "common" and "philosophical" "rational cognition of morals" [*sittliche Vernunfterkenntnis*] that Kant has in mind in this much studied but still not well understood work.

One striking fact about the argument of the *Groundwork* is that philosophy appears in it in the guise of both "popular moral worldly wisdom" – here it may be best to translate *Weltweisheit* literally rather than as just an archaic word for "philosophy" – on the one hand and that of Kant's own "metaphysics of morals" and "critique of pure practical reason" on the other. More precisely, the *Groundwork* starts off by deriving its initial formulation of the categorical imperative from a "common rational cognition of morals" that every reasonable person is supposed to recognize as his or her own, and then relates both "popular worldly wisdom" and a genuine "metaphysics of morals" and "critique of pure practical reason" to this "common rational cognition of morals". What is the relation of these two forms of philosophy to each other and to the pre-philosophical self-understanding from which Kant's argument seems to begin?

One interpretation might be this: Kant thinks that every normal human being innately possesses or early acquires an understanding of the demands of moral duty and of its worth, which however can be corrupted by bad but popular philosophy or "worldly wisdom". Such philosophy, a kind of empiricism in the sense that it bases its prescription of how moral agents ought to behave on observation of how humans are actually observed to behave, could corrupt our innate sense of duty and its merit in two ways: it would confuse us about the principle of morality by presenting our own happiness rather than duty as the object of morally worthy action; and it would give us an excuse for lapsing from the stern demands of duty by appealing to determinism as an excuse for our own moral frailty or evil. Kant's strategy, then, would be to counteract the deleterious effects of this "popular worldly wisdom" by showing, in his "metaphysics of morals" (that is, Section II of the *Groundwork*) that happiness can never be the object prescribed by the categorical imperative that we are all in some way disposed to acknowledge, and by showing, in his "critique of pure practical reason" (that is, Section III of the *Groundwork*), that we really are always free to live up to the stern demands of morality no matter what our prior experience and history might seem to have determined us to do. In this way, a sound philosophy would save our innate self-understanding as moral agents from corruption by bad philosophy.

Such an interpretation of Kant's strategy in the *Groundwork* is almost right, but not quite. Henrich might seem to suggest such an interpretation when he writes:

> "Man subtly refines the moral law until it fits his inclination and his convenience, whether to free himself from it or to use the good for the justification of his own self-importance. Kant considers his entire philosophy an attempt to refute the sophistry of reason that is in the service of pleasure. In this way he also attempts to give firm insight into the good against dialectical artifices."[1]

But Henrich's references to the sophistry of reason, not to the sophistry of popular philosophy or "worldly wisdom", as well as to dialectical artifices, suggest a more subtle reading of Kant's argument. The risk to our moral self-understanding does not arise from without, from the wily artifices of corrupt philosophers who appear out of nowhere to darken our paths; the source of sophistry and corruption lies within us, in evil possibilities inherent to our own nature, which can in turn co-opt our own faculty of reason to produce a form of philosophy that would appear to justify our lapses from duty unless countered by a sounder philosophy that is itself another product of our own reason accessible to any of us by the reflective use of our own reason. Just as our theoretical reason is inherently liable to irresolvable dialectical disputes or antinomies until we fully understand the proper conditions for its use – dialectical disputes that find expression in speculative philosophy but are by no means mere artifices of speculative philosophers[2] – so our practical reason is inherently liable to undermine our common rational cognition of morals by a dialectic that is entirely natural to it, which is thus not caused by but merely expressed in popular moral philosophy or worldly wisdom, and which can only be resolved by a sounder philosophical reflection on the nature of our practical reason and the conditions of its use of which we are also capable. Kant's moral philosophy is not intended simply to rescue our moral self-understanding from bad philosophy contingently imposed upon us by bad philosophers. It is rather intended to give us the fuller self-understanding that we need in order to save our understanding of the moral law and its demands from our own self-misunderstanding and the bad philosophy that we create for ourselves.

This subtle strategy might not be entirely obvious from Kant's first statement of the need for his moral philosophy in the Preface to the *Groundwork*[3]:

> "A metaphysics of morals is therefore indispensably necessary, not merely because of a motive to speculation – for investigating the source of the practical basic principles that lie *a priori* in our reason – but also because morals themselves remain subject to all sorts of corruption as long as we are without that clue and supreme norm by which to appraise them correctly. For, in the case of what is to be morally good it is not enough that it conform with the moral law but it must also be done for the sake of the law; without this, that conformity is only very contingent and precarious, since a ground that is not moral will indeed now and then produce actions in conformity with the law, but it will also often produce actions contrary to the law. Now the moral law in its purity and genuineness (and in the practical this is what matters most) is to be sought nowhere else than in a pure philosophy."[4]

Initially, this passage simply leaves open the source of any tendencies to the corruption of morals. It then perhaps goes on to suggest that the problem is that while we may have a natural desire to conform to the requirements of morality, whatever they might be, without a clear recognition of the principle of morality and its requirements, particularly its requirement that we act for the sake of the moral law itself, we are open to all sorts of corruption. Thus we might suppose that Kant means to argue that our natural disposition to conform to the demands of morality has to be supplemented by a clearly formulated principle of morality, and that it is up to his moral philosophy to offer a sound one to compete with, and triumph over, the less sound ones offered by more popular worldly wisdom or philosophy.

The conclusion of Section I of the *Groundwork*, however, suggests the more subtle strategy I have ascribed to Kant. Here Kant writes:

> "Reason issues its precepts unremittingly, without thereby promising anything to the inclinations, and so, as it were, with disregard and contempt for those claims [...] But from this there arises a natural dialectic, that is, a propensity to rationalize against those strict laws of duty, and to cast doubt upon their validity, or at least upon their purity and strictness, and, where possible, to make them better suited to our

Self-Understanding and Philosophy

wishes and inclinations, that is, to corrupt them at their basis and to destroy all their dignity – something that even common practical reason cannot, in the end, call good.

In this way common human reason is impelled, not by some need of speculation (which never touches it as long as it is content to be mere sound reason), but on practical grounds themselves, to go out of its sphere and to take a step into the field of practical philosophy, in order to obtain there information and distinct instruction regarding the source of its principle and the correct determination of this principle in comparison with maxims based on need and inclination, so that it may escape from its predicament about claims from both sides and not run the risk of being deprived of all genuine moral principles through the ambiguity into which it easily falls. So there develops unnoticed in common practical reason as well, when it cultivates itself, a dialectic that constrains it to seek help in philosophy, just as happens in its theoretical use; and the former will, accordingly, find no more rest than the other except in a complete critique of our reason."[5]

The dialectic of practical philosophy is not academic but natural: that is, the corruption of "common human reason" is threatened not from without, but from within, and "popular worldly wisdom" is not an external threat to "common human reason" but is itself an expression of something natural to human beings that can be resolved only by the self-understanding afforded by a "complete critique of our reason". In particular, common human reason tends to confuse its natural recognition of the genuine principle of morality with "maxims based on need and inclination". Only a clear distinction between the fundamental principle of morality that we all intuitively recognize and any maxims based on need and inclination, but at the same time an equally clear understanding of the proper role of need and inclination in the conditions of human agency, will enable us to save ourselves from the dialectic of practical reason that is as natural to us as our recognition of the fundamental principle of morality itself.

This program of self-understanding is carried out in the *Groundwork*, I suggest, in the following steps.

(1) In Section I, Kant argues that a genuine even if less than entirely explicit understanding of the fundamental principle of morality is reflected in our common conceptions of good will and duty and in

the moral judgments that we make about particular cases of human action, especially when those cases are presented to us in ways that do not immediately involve our own interests. From our common conception of good will and duty and from such particular cases, a clear formulation of the genuine principle of morality can be extracted.[6] This clear recognition of our duty, however, is threatened by two factors that are as natural to our condition as is the recognition of our duty itself. First, it is entirely natural for us each to seek our own happiness, and thus the risk of substituting an imperative to seek our own happiness for the imperative to perform our duty is equally natural to us. We also try to dignify this tendency by adopting a philosophy that seems to entail hedonism. Second, as far as we can see, human beings frequently succumb to this confusion; thus insofar as we try to base our moral principles on actual examples of human conduct, and moreover even try to dignify this procedure by thinking of it as dictated by what appears to be a respectable empirical philosophy, we will tend to substitute the principle of happiness for the genuine principle of duty.

(2) In Section II of the *Groundwork*, Kant argues that this natural danger can be avoided only by making completely explicit the fundamental principle of morality that is merely implicit in our initial moral self-understanding. In the fuller development of his moral theory, however, he will also have to show how the interest in happiness, precisely since it is entirely natural to us and neither should not nor cannot be expected to be extirpated, is to be incorporated into the object of morality in the form of the highest good, the realization of happiness conditioned by the worthiness to be happy. If the principle of happiness were just a threat from bad moral philosophy, not an ineliminable feature of human nature, the theory of the highest good would not be a necessary part of Kant's moral philosophy.

(3) Section III of the *Groundwork* then takes up the second threat to our natural recognition of duty, a threat which is just as natural to us as the interest in happiness and just as much as that needs to find its proper place in a complete self-understanding of our moral agency. This is the threat of determinism, or as Kant himself calls it

"pre-determinism"[7], the doctrine that our actions at any given moment are thoroughly necessitated by events at prior moments, from which it seems to follow that it is not always in our power to live up to the stringent demands of duty, which must therefore be weakened. Such a doctrine of determinism is clearly, in Henrich's term, a sophistry of our own reason by which we can excuse our failure to act as we knew we should, and needs to be answered by a critique of pure practical reason that will show that we do indeed always have the power to act as duty requires no matter what our past might seem to predict. However, the doctrine of determinism is not just a rationalization of our moral weakness offered to us by popular philosophy (although of course historically it was a prominent doctrine of the empiricist philosophies of Locke and Hume), but is itself a genuine aspect of our self-understanding, indeed the indispensable foundation of our theoretical understanding of the world of nature and our place in it. Thus what is necessary is not a simple refutation of determinism, but rather a proper situation of it in the fuller self-understanding that we can reach through a sound philosophy – which must also lie ready in ourselves. This is of course what Kant attempts to provide through the transcendental idealism which he invokes in Section III of the *Groundwork* and then again in the *Critique of Practical Reason*.[8] Just as Kant's theory of the highest good is his recognition that we cannot simply dismiss the principle of happiness but must incorporate it into a proper position in our full understanding of the object of morality, so he also recognizes that we cannot simply dismiss determinism as a groundless threat to our sense of duty but must rather show its proper place in relation to the indisputable fact of our freedom in the transcendental idealism that gives fullest expression to our self-understanding as moral agents.

I will hardly have room here to explicate and argue for these three claims in the detail they require. I will just be able to present some of the key evidence for these claims and to comment on some of the issues that they raise.

I

From the outset of the *Groundwork*, Kant insists that everything essential in moral philosophy is readily accessible to the ordinary human being. The Preface maintains that "in moral matters human reason can easily be brought to a high degree of correctness and accomplishment, even in the most common understanding"[9]. The argument of Section I then takes the form of deriving the first formulation of the fundamental principle of morality from an analysis of the concept of a good will that is taken to be commonly acknowledged, where the common possession of this concept is itself confirmed by our common appraisal or judgment of hypothetical examples of the performance of duty, such as the case of the man who has been created without sympathetic inclinations or lost them through his own misfortunes who can nevertheless act virtuously out of his respect for duty.[10] We can consider this style of argument to be continued in Section II of the *Groundwork* when Kant appeals to commonly accepted examples of duty – now ranged in four classes – to confirm not the common concept of duty itself but rather the first and second formulations of the categorical imperative to which this concept of duty gives rise.[11] Throughout, Kant's strategy is to show that the moral principle that he proposes – which is hardly supposed to be a new invention, "as if, before him, the world had been ignorant of what duty is"[12] – is implied by the commonly shared conception of duty and expressed in commonly shared judgments about particular cases of dutiful action.

Kant does not make his assumption clear when he first introduces the analysis of the concept of a good will: here he just says, entirely without any methodological comment, that in order "to explicate the concept of a will that is to be esteemed in itself […] we shall set before ourselves the concept of *duty*".[13] Upon having derived his initial formulation of the only possible principle for the determination of the good will from this concept, however, he states that "Common human reason also agrees completely with this in its practical judgments and always has this principle before its eyes".[14] A page later, he reiterates that "we have arrived, within the moral cognition of common human reason, at its principle, which it admittedly does not think so abstractly in a universal form, but which it actually has before its eyes and uses as the norm for its judgments"[15]. The fundamental principle of morality is implicit in our common conception of duty and in our common judgments about duties, and if not already explicitly formulated by every normal human being will immediately be recognized and acknowledged when presented to any normal human being in its explicit form.

As I am here more concerned with the form of Kant's account than with its content, the details of his analysis and its confirmation can be recalled briefly. Kant analyses the concept of a good will by means of three propositions that are obviously supposed to be acknowledged by anyone with common moral cognition: (i) good will consists in acting from duty rather than from inclination[16]; (ii) "action from duty has its moral worth not in the purpose to be attained by it but in the maxim in accordance with which it is decided upon, and therefore does not depend upon the realization of the object of the action but merely upon the principle of volition"[17]; and (iii) "duty is the necessity of an action from respect for law"[18]. The first proposition of the analysis in particular is confirmed by an appeal to an example: we will all recognize that there is no manifestation of good will and thus no special moral worth in a grocer's maintaining a policy of honesty for the sake of his own long-term interest or in somebody preserving his life merely out of inclination[19], but we do recognize good will and thus moral worth when somebody "preserves his life without loving it" or continues to act benevolently even though his mind has been "overclouded by his own grief"[20]. Our judgments of moral worth in such cases can only be explained by our assumption that moral worth lies in the performance of actions out of the motive of duty rather than out of inclination or self-interest. The first phase of Kant's analysis of the concept of a good will in terms of the concept of duty is thus confirmed by commonly accepted moral judgments.

After completing his analysis of duty, Kant then derives the formula "I ought never to act except in such a way that I could also will that my maxim should become a universal law", which he will designate as the first formulation of the categorical imperative after he has introduced the concept of such an imperative in Section II, from the fact that since this analysis has "deprived the will of every impulse that could arise for it from obeying some law, nothing is left but the conformity of actions as such with universal law"[21]. The validity of this formula is then again confirmed by an example: if we consider whether we may make a promise without the intention of keeping it in order to get out of a current difficulty, we all realize that the relevant question is not whether it is possible or prudent to do so, but rather simply "would I indeed be content that my maxim (to get myself out of difficulties by a false promise) should hold as a universal law (for myself as well as for others)?"[22]. Kant's previously cited claims that his formulation of the principle of morality is reflected in the practical judgments of common human reason immediately precede and succeed the exposition of this example.[23] Kant's argument in *Groundwork* I thus has the following form: our common conception of good will as manifest in the performance of action from duty, which is supported by examples of virtuous action that we all recognize, combined with an analysis of the concept of duty that we all accept, gives rise to a formulation of the fundamental principle of morality, which, even if we do not explicitly recognize it in its most abstract form, is in fact the basis for the particular moral judgments that we make, as can again be confirmed by an appeal to any example of a duty that we all acknowledge.

Kant sums up this first stage of his work by saying that "there is no need of science and philosophy to know what one has to do in order to be honest and good, and even wise and virtuous"[24]. If this is so, why does the argument of the *Groundwork* have to continue into its Sections II and III? Kant's answer to this question is not that we need philosophy simply in order "to present the system of morals all the more completely and comprehensibly and to present its rules in a form more convenient for use", but rather that "innocence [...] is easily seduced", because the "human being feels within himself a powerful counterweight to all the commands of duty", namely, "the counterweight of his needs and inclinations, the entire satisfaction of which he sums up under the name happiness"[25]. The next stage of the argument of the *Groundwork*, which occupies Section II, must then be to distinguish clearly the principle of morality from the principle of happiness; in Kant's moral philosophy more broadly considered, however, the next stage of the argument must be not merely to distinguish the principle of morality from the natural pursuit of happiness but also to show how happiness, as the ineliminable natural end of human beings, does properly fit into the complete object of morality. Before turning to this next stage of Kant's argument, however, several comments on the character of its first stage are in order.

First, there is a question about what sort of moral principle could be derived by the appeal to common concepts and judgments that Kant presents in *Groundwork* I. Thus far, I have referred to both the fundamental principle of morality and the categorical imperative without distinction, but of course, these are not exactly the same: as Konrad Cramer has argued, the fundamental principle of morality can be considered a pure synthetic *a priori* principle, applicable to any and all rational beings, while the categorical imperative is an impure synthetic *a priori* principle, the form in which the fundamental principle of morality presents itself to beings like us, who empirically know ourselves to have inclinations and interests that may conflict with compliance with the fundamental principle of morality, and thus may experience the fundamental principle of morality as a constraining obligation – a categorical imperative – in a way that beings without such conflicting incentives would not.[26] Shouldn't a derivation of a moral principle that appeals to commonly shared concepts such as those of good will and duty and to commonly shared practical judgments or moral responses to particular examples of duties and dutiful sorts of persons yield at best an impure formulation of the fundamental principle of morality in the form of a categorical imperative applicable to beings like us only, rather than the fundamental principle of morality itself in its pure form? Indeed, shouldn't a derivation of a principle of morality in any form from common concepts and judgments yield only something empirical, not any sort of *a priori* principle at all, that is, a principle that is universally and necessarily valid for any species of rational agents, let alone all rational agents? To answer this question, we need to distinguish carefully between a derivation of the formulation of the principle of morality (in any form) and a derivation of its validity. It clearly cannot be Kant's position that we derive the validity of the moral law by any sort of empirical method from commonly accepted concepts and judgments. Rather, it is clearly his view that by reflection on our common concepts of good will and duty and on common moral judgments of particular examples of duties and dutiful persons we can see that we already acknowledge the validity of the moral law even in its purest form, its form as the fundamental principle of morality, as well as in its form as the categorical imperative, and even if we have not previously explicitly formulated the principle in any abstract terms at all. We immediately see that our recognition of the principle is what explains our acceptance of the concepts and judgments that we all do accept; we don't only come to accept the principle because of our response to particular cases. As Kant says, "Nor could one give worse advice to morality than by wanting to derive it from examples. For, every example of it represented to me must itself first be appraised in accordance with principles of morality, as to whether it is also worthy to serve as an original example."[27]

But at this point a second question about an argument involving appeal to examples arises. At the outset of Section II of the *Groundwork*, Kant inveighs against any attempt to derive the fundamental principle of morality in any form from actual examples of human conduct:

> "If we have so far drawn our concept of duty from the common use of our practical reason, it is by no means to be inferred from this that we have treated it as a concept of experience. On the contrary, if we attend to experience of people's conduct we meet frequent, and as we ourselves admit, just complaints that no certain example can be cited of the disposition to act from pure duty; that, though much may done in conformity with what duty commands, still it is always doubtful whether it is really done from duty and therefore has moral worth [...] In fact, it is absolutely impossible by means of experience to make out with complete certainty a single case in which the maxim of an action

otherwise in conformity with duty rested simply on moral grounds and on the representation of one's duty."[28]

Doesn't this blunt statement completely undermine any attempt to derive anything about the moral law from examples of any kind?

To answer this question, we need to draw a firm distinction between the use of actual and of hypothetical examples of moral conduct. Kant's initial argument in Section II is that we cannot be sure that any actual conduct, that of others or even our own, has been performed out of the pure motive of duty, and thus we would be hard-pressed to derive a fundamental principle of morality from actual human behavior in the face of uncertainty; indeed, we might even take him to go on to argue that we can be reasonably sure that almost all actual deeds, whether our own or others', have been motivated by inclination and self-interest, thus that if we attempt to formulate a fundamental principle of morality by induction from actual conduct we shall almost certainly come up with the wrong principle. In particular, we know that in actual cases of actions in any way affecting our own interests, our judgments are likely to be distorted by self-love.[29] But the examples in *Groundwork* I are not actual examples of human conduct, but hypothetical cases for moral judgment; and in the case of such examples what is at issue is only the question of how we judge that agents in such cases ought to be appraised, not whether we ourselves or anyone else ever actually lives up to such judgments. Kant's claim is precisely that in the appraisal of hypothetical cases and situations of human action, where the threat of self-love can be certain to be set aside, we all immediately recognize how human agents ought to be motivated and to behave, even if we are not sure that any of us has ever actually been motivated in that way. And the basis of such acknowledgments of the principle of morality, Kant insists, is not experience but pure practical reason. Examples need to be adduced for the confirmation of our common concepts of good will and duty because pure practical reason commonly expresses itself in the judgment of particulars rather than in abstractions, but not because these concepts rest on experience rather than pure reason.

II

Kant's argument in *Groundwork* II is that the true principle of morality can never be discovered by examples from ordinary experience; rather, it requires "pure rational concepts" and a "metaphysics of morals"[30], although once "the doctrine of morals" has been "first grounded on metaphysics" it can be "provided with access by means of popularity"[31]. By a "popular philosophy" (here he does use the word *Philosophie* instead of *Weltweisheit)* he means simply a method "that goes no farther than it can by groping with the help of examples"[32]. Thus, he does not explicitly identify "popular philosophy" with a specific school of academic moral philosophy, such as the moral-sense school as an applied form of academic empiricism. In fact, he clearly means to include the perfectionism of Wolff and his followers as well as the moral-sense philosophy of Hutcheson and Hume under this rubric – what we get if we attempt to discover the principle of "morality in that popular taste" is a hodgepodge of principles identifiable with those of all the popular schools of moral philosophy:

> "One will find now the special determination of human nature (but occasionally the idea of a rational nature as such along with it), now perfection, now happiness, here moral feeling, there fear of God, a bit of this and a bit of that in a marvelous mixture."[33]

But the overall argument of Section II is certainly a polemic against the idea that Kant assumes would be inevitably suggested by basing our conception of the fundamental principle of morality on observation of actual examples of human motivation and behavior, namely, the idea that what morality prescribes is the pursuit of happiness as such – as Hume puts it in his *Enquiry Concerning the Principles of Morals*, the cultivation of qualities useful and agreeable to ourselves and others.[34]

Kant carries on his polemic against any such principle in several stages. First, he derives the concept of a categorical imperative in general from what he clearly assumes to be the common understanding that the fundamental principle of morality must be an objectively necessitating principle, that is, a principle necessitating certain principles of action for all relevant agents[35], and then argues that a simple principle of pursuing happiness could never give rise to a categorical imperative but only a hypothetical one. Such a principle would be a hypothetical one not because it is entirely contingent whether anyone adopts happiness as an end – on the contrary, Kant recognizes it as a fact of nature, a "natural necessity"[36], that everyone does adopt happiness as an end – but rather because of the following sorts of considerations: it is contingent what particular ends it is the satisfaction of which would constitute anyone's happiness; it is contingent whether the various particular ends the satisfaction of which would constitute a single person's happiness are conjointly realizable[37]; and, as Kant adds in the *Critique of Practical Reason*, it is also contingent whether two or more different persons' conceptions of happiness are conjointly realizable.[38] For these sorts of reasons, then, although it is not exactly contingent that anyone has happiness as an end, it certainly would be contingent whether anyone has as his end a particular conception of happiness that could rationally be pursued in the actual circumstances of his life.

After his initial contrast between merely hypothetical imperatives and a categorical imperative, Kant argues that the very concept of a categorical imperative – again, presumably one that every normal human being has – gives rise to precisely the same formulation of the fundamental principle of morality that the previous analysis of the concepts of good will and duty yielded, the principle that one should only act on maxims that can at the same time be willed as universal law.[39] In the discussion of this and the following further formulations of the categorical imperative, especially the principle of humanity as an end in itself[40], Kant continues to emphasize that the principle of morality is not "a subjective principle on which we might act if we have the propensity and inclination", thus not a principle prescribing our happiness, but an "objective principle on which we would be directed to act even though every propensity, inclination, and natural tendency of ours were against it"[41], thus a principle that apparently ignores all reference to our own happiness. Kant stresses that the categorical imperative abstracts from all "subjective ends", and is thus formal rather than material[42]; but since human beings cannot act without an end at all, he elevates humanity into "an end in itself", "which is the supreme limiting condition of the freedom of action of every human being", "an objective end that, whatever ends we may have, ought as law to constitute the supreme limiting condition of all subjective ends"[43]. Thus, Kant insists – and insists that we will all come to recognize this readily by reflection on concepts that we already acknowledge such as those of the good will, duty, and the categorical imperative – the end of morality is not happiness, the satisfaction of our particular, subjective material needs and inclinations, but is rather something else, humanity as such, which is a limiting condition on the pursuit of happiness. This is not the result that we would get by induction from actual examples of human motivation, even if we were to dignify such an induction with the name of philosophy, but is the result that we get from reflection on the pure concepts of a metaphysics of morals that is in fact accessible to each of us.

Now at the height of the polemic against founding a principle of morality on the object of happiness in *Groundwork* II, Kant goes so far as to say not merely that "all objects of the inclinations have only a conditional worth", but also that "the inclinations themselves, as sources of needs, are so far from having an absolute worth so as to make one wish to have them, that it must instead be the universal wish of every rational beings to be altogether free from them"[44]. However, if this suggests that human beings either could or should eradicate all inclinations in themselves, thus eradicating everything the satisfaction of which could produce happiness, and that the goal of morality could or should be pursued by means of such a mass extinction of inclination, then it radically misrepresents what will become the considered position of Kant's moral philosophy. As Kant makes clear in *Religion within the Limits of Mere Reason*, we are not evil because we have sensuous inclinations, but because of the attitude we adopt toward them as our fundamental maxim. We are not evil simply because we have such inclinations, first because we "cannot presume ourselves responsible for their existence"[45], but even more because "predispositions in the human being" are "original", that is, "they belong to the possibility of human nature", and – certainly on the teleological view of nature which Kant had long assumed should regulate our reflection on our natural endowments[46] – they must therefore be assumed to be "not only (negatively) good (they do not resist the moral law) but they are also predispositions to the good (they demand compliance with it)"[47]. Further, Kant writes,

> "Considered in themselves natural inclinations are good, i. e., not reprehensible, and to want to extirpate them would not only be futile but harmful and blameworthy as well; we must rather only curb them, so that they will not wear each other out but will instead be harmonized into a whole called happiness."[48]

Other things being equal, the fulfillment of human inclinations can be assumed to be a part of what is good for human beings, which we represent to ourselves by conceiving of it as part of what nature intends for us. We realize our radical possibility for evil only if we "reverse the moral order of [our] incentives in incorporating them into [our] maxims", by placing the satisfaction of all of our own inclinations ahead of our obedience to the moral law. "Whether the human being is good or evil must not lie in the difference between the incentives that he incorporates into his maxim (not in the material of his maxim) but in their subordination (in the form of the maxim): which of the two he makes the condition of the other".[49] We are not evil simply because we satisfy natural inclinations, but only if we make the satisfaction of our own inclinations the sole condition under which we will comply with the moral law rather than making the possibility of our complying with the moral law the sole condition under which we will find it permissible to satisfy our natural inclinations (those of ourselves and of others whom we can affect by our actions).

On Kant's view, then, there is one sense in which it is natural to place our own happiness before all else and to try to dignify this into a moral principle by purporting to philosophize from actual examples of human conduct, but another sense in which the existence of inclinations the fulfillment of which would bring happiness is entirely natural and in itself a predisposition to the good rather than to evil. If this is so, then inclinations and happiness as their satisfaction cannot simply be banished from our conception of ourselves as moral agents, but must be given their proper place. This is what Kant suggests in highly abstract form by arguing in the *Religion* that being good lies not in eradicating but in subordinating natural incentives to the moral law, and expresses more concretely in his doctrine of the highest good, the exposition of which is found not only in the summation of each of Kant's three critiques but also in the Preface to the *Religion* itself[50] – a fact which cannot but suggest the absolute centrality of this doctrine for Kant. As Kant expounds this doctrine in the *Religion*, human beings cannot determine their wills to action except by the representation of some particular ends to be achieved by acting. That is, in order to act we must have something specific we intend to do, which can only be some particular action proposed as a way to fulfill some human need or inclination. Morality as "the supreme limiting condition of the freedom of action of every human being"[51] needs proposed particular courses of action to limit. Or as Kant puts it in the *Religion*, while the motivation to act – respect for duty – and a formal specification of the condition on all maxims of action – the fundamental principle of morality – can be acknowledged by us independently of "the representation of an end which would have to precede the determination of the will", morality must still have "a necessary reference to such an end" because without it we would be "instructed indeed as to how to operate but not as to the whither"[52] – that is, we wouldn't actually have anything particular to do. Particular things to do can only be suggested by nature, not by the pure rational idea of morality itself, and this means that such particular ends of action must be suggested by the various needs and inclinations that we all actually have. What morality imposes is not the eradication of such natural occasions for action, then, but

> "only the idea of such an object that unites within itself the formal condition of all such ends as we ought to have (duty) with everything which is conditional upon ends we have and which conforms to duty (happiness proportioned to its observance), that is, the idea of a highest good in the world"[53].

Such a happiness proportioned to duty is not just one's own happiness pursued without regard to any constraints – that would be a goal liable to be incoherent both in itself and with the happiness of others – but is rather the conjoint satisfaction of the naturally good inclinations of oneself and others insofar as that is both licensed by and indeed also prescribed by the goal of adopting maxims that are also fit to be universal law.

Section II of the *Groundwork* thus initiates Kant's complex argument about happiness. The satisfaction of our inclinations, and thus the attainment of happiness, is a natural goal of human beings. Unfortunately, the disposition to place above all else the attainment of our own, individual happiness – or, even more precisely, the attainment of what seems to us at a given moment the means to our own individual happiness – is also a natural tendency of human beings, and one which tries to dignify itself by co-opting an empiricist approach to philosophizing in order to dignify the actual conduct of human beings with an air of necessity. That tendency has to be resisted, but it cannot be resisted simply by extirpating all our natural inclinations. That would be both impossible and also incoherent, for it would leave us with no actions to undertake at all. Instead, we must combat our tendency to subordinate morality to our own happiness and to dignify this with the name of (popular) philosophy with a sounder philosophy and the proper subordination of happiness to duty that this philosophy prescribes – as we have always known. We misunderstand the conditions and requirements of our own agency both by subordinating morality to our inclinations but also by proposing to extirpate all our inclinations; we properly understand both our nature and our duty when we condition our pursuit of both our own happiness and that of others by the fundamental principle of morality, as is dictated by the concept of the highest good as the object of morality.

III

The other great mistake that we would make if we were to draw our moral principles solely from the observation of actual human conduct, and to rationalize such a restriction by elevating our actual conduct into a (popular) moral philosophy, would be to adopt the view that human actions are always entirely and solely determined by previous actions and events, leaving us no freedom of choice when faced with a particular moral issue. Such a view of the limits of human action would damage our original disposition to morality by transforming what we so often observe, namely human behavior falling short of the demands of morality because of frailty, impurity or depravity[54], into a necessity of human nature, which would then lead us – quite reasonably once the first step down this path has been taken – to cut and trim our original recognition of the stringent requirements of morality to whatever weaker principle might seem compatible with such a view of the limitations of human nature. If the actions commanded by morality seem to be "actions of which the world has perhaps so far given no example, and whose very practicability might be very much doubted by one who bases everything on experience", "then nothing can protect us against falling away completely from our ideas of duty and can preserve in our soul a well-grounded respect for its law"[55]. A revision of the principle of morality to reflect the limitations of what human beings can actually do would indeed be the only reasonable response to such limitations, on the principle of rationality that Kant always assumes we all share, that "duty commands nothing but what we can do"[56]. On this principle, if we cannot do an action, then the principle of morality cannot command it, so the principle of morality must reflect what we can do.

Kant clearly must limit the damage that could be done to morality by the all too common examples of human frailty and the philosophy of determinism that dignifies such examples with the air of necessity. But, as in the case of happiness, he cannot deal with the threat of frailty and its philosophical expression in the doctrine of determinism simply by "extirpating" or refuting this doctrine. For determinism is the keystone of Kant's own theoretical philosophy: the condition of the possibility of understanding nature, and of understanding ourselves as creatures in nature, is nothing less than the universal validity of the principle that every event in nature is determined to occur when it does in accordance with a law linking it to a prior occurrence that necessitates what follows. Determinism is not merely a natural attitude for us, but the condition of the possibility of an understanding of nature itself. Thus, just as Kant's normative moral philosophy must deal with the natural interest in happiness not by eradicating it but by assigning it its proper place in the complete object of morality, so his account of the conditions of the practicability of the stringent principle of morality must still find a place for a doctrine of determinism. In Kant's own words, "Philosophy must therefore assume that no true contradiction will be found between freedom and natural necessity in the very same human actions, for it cannot give up the concept of nature any more than that of freedom"[57].

It is hardly necessary here to go into the details of Kant's way of assuring that there is "no true contradiction" between "freedom and natural necessity": every reader will know that Kant argues that determinism is a necessary condition of assigning a determinate order to events as they occur in time, but that since time itself is a feature only of the appearance of things, not of those things as they are in themselves, it is entirely possible that the real agents of our actions are not – contrary to appearance – situated in time at all, and therefore are not subject to the condition of determinism, and so are instead free to act as morality requires regardless of what past experience might predict. Nor do I here want to canvass the well-worn objections to this reconciliation of freedom and determinism. What I do want to emphasize is that it is part of Kant's view of our own self-understanding, thus of what must be reflected by a proper philosophy, that certainty of our freedom is just as readily and naturally accessible to every normal human being as confidence in determinism is: the "rightful claim to freedom of will" is "made even by common human reason"[58]. The assignment of determinism into its proper place in the more complex doctrine of transcendental idealism is not merely the speculative replacement of unsound philosophy by sound philosophy; it is, in Kant's view, itself the proper expression of ordinary human self-understanding.

It might not seem surprising to say this about Kant's defense of freedom in the *Critique of Practical Reason*, where Kant argues precisely that everyone immediately infers his freedom to act as the moral law requires directly from "the moral law, of which we become immediately conscious (as soon as we draw up maxims of the will for ourselves)"[59]. On this account, "practical reason," starting from an indubitable consciousness of what the moral law demands of us, infers our freedom always to do what the law demands by the principle that ought implies can, and then imposes the fact of freedom on "speculative reason", which has as it were no choice of its own but to secure (if not explain) at least the possibility of freedom.[60] But, at least on one standard interpretation, the *Groundwork* reconciles freedom and determinism by a more theoretical or speculative route than the *Critique of Practical Reason*: the *Groundwork* argues that the distinction between appearances and things in themselves is one that is introduced in theorizing about the nature of knowledge, and then carried over to reflection on practical reason, where it can directly establish the fact of our freedom from which in turn the validity of the moral law can be inferred.[61] But theorizing about the conditions of the possibility of knowledge can easily look like the furthest thing from an activity of "common human reason", and thus it might well seem surprising to claim that Kant's defense of freedom in the *Groundwork* is intended to be a proper expression of ordinary human self-understanding.

But even in the *Groundwork* Kant claims precisely that "no subtle reflection" is required to make the distinction between appearances and things in themselves, rather "one may assume that the commonest understanding can make it, though in its own way, by an obscure discrimination of judgment which it calls feeling". Even this commonest human understanding, Kant alleges, is aware of the difference "between representations given us from somewhere else and in which we are passive, and those that we produce simply from ourselves and in which we show our activity"; and this is enough to "yield a distinction, although a crude one, between a world of sense and the world of understanding", a distinction which will in turn allow anyone to conceive of the difference between the appearance of objects and their states that are fully governed by deterministic laws of nature and the spontaneous actions of things as they are in themselves that can only be governed by laws of reason rather than sensibility.[62] The *Critique of Practical Reason* may infer the fact of our freedom from our prior acknowledgment of our obligation under the moral law, while the *Groundwork* may infer our obligation under the moral law from the fact of our freedom, which is in turn inferred from the basic structure of human cognition, but the epistemological status of both arguments is intended to be precisely the same: each argument assumes that what it characterizes as the sufficient ground for knowledge of our freedom is just as available to every human being, just as much a part of our self-understanding, as is the basis for the belief in determinism. In both arguments, Kant's philosophical reconciliation of freedom and determinism is supposed to be the expression of common human self-understanding.

This result leads to one last conclusion, which can tie together Kant's apparently optimistic moral writings of 1785 and 1788 with the apparently pessimistic *Religion* of 1793. If transcendental idealism with its reconciliation of freedom and determinism is really the proper expression of ordinary human self-understanding, then the belief in the philosophical doctrine of determinism could not possibly be due to an academic philosophical misunderstanding alone, any more than the elevation of one's own happiness into the unrestricted principle of morality could be the product of a merely speculative misunderstanding alone: the sounder philosophy which reconciles freedom and determinism, just like the sounder philosophy that subordinates but at the same time incorporates happiness into the complete object of morality, Kant has insisted, is just as available to common human reason as the one-sided philosophies are. Instead, the adoption of the one-sided "worldly wisdom" that would undercut our recognition that happiness is not the sole object of morality and human frailty not an excuse for trimming the demands of morality could only be the product or expression of the human possibility to be evil instead of good, not the cause of this evil. If the proper understanding of our own agency is always available to us, then misunderstanding the possibilities of our agency cannot simply be imposed upon us, but must be self-imposed. We cannot blame philosophy for our own failings, Kant must hold, for the philosophy that can save us from these failings is always already available to us.

Notes

1 "The Concept of Moral Insight and Kant's Doctrine of the Fact of Reason", in: D. Henrich, *The Unity of Reason: Essays on Kant's Philosophy*, ed. R. Velkley (Cambridge, Mass.: Harvard University Press, 1994), pp. 55–87, at p. 66; originally "Der Begriff der sittlichen Einsicht und Kants Lehre vom Faktum der Vernunft", in: *Die Gegenwart der Griechen im neueren Denken: Festschrift für Hans-Georg Gadamer*, ed. D. Henrich, W. Schulz, and K.-H. Volkmann-Schluck (Tübingen: J. C. B. Mohr, 1960), pp. 77–115.
2 This is, after all, why Kant always treats the proponents of the dialectically opposed theses and antitheses of his antinomies, Leibniz and Wolff or Locke and Hume, with the utmost respect, rather than dismissing them as fools: they are only giving voice to natural illusions of human reason which cannot fully be dispelled until the nature and conditions of the use of human reason are fully understood.
3 Passages from Kant's writings will be first cited with the volume in Roman numerals and page number of the Academy edition (= Akademie-Ausgabe [AA]), *Kant's gesammelte Schriften*, edited by the Royal Prussian (later German) Academy of Sciences (Berlin: Georg Reimer (later Walter de Gruyter), 1900 ff.). The second reference following the German title or an abbrevation for the work cited is to the pagination of the first (A) and where relevant second (B) original editions of the work. Translations from the *Groundwork* are from Immanuel Kant, *Practical Philosophy*, ed. and trans. M. J. Gregor (Cambridge: Cambridge University Press, 1996). Since this and other volumes in *The Cambridge Edition of the Works of Immanuel Kant* include the pagination of the Academy edition, the pagination of the translation has been omitted.

4 AA IV 389, *Grundlegung der Metaphysik der Sitten* [in what follows *Grundlegung*] A IX f. [trans. cf. note 3].
5 AA IV 405, *Grundlegung* A 23.
6 Cf. AA IV 402, *Grundlegung* A 17.
7 Cf. *Religion within the Boundaries of Mere Reason*: AA VI 49 f. note, *Die Religion innerhalb der Grenzen der bloßen Vernunft* B 58, Anm. [trans. cf. note 45].
8 Henrich has, of course, discussed the vexed issue of the relation between Kant's treatment of freedom in the *Groundwork* and in the second *Critique* in his famous paper "Die Deduktion des Sittengesetzes: Über die Gründe der Dunkelheit des letzten Abschnittes von Kants *Grundlegung zur Metaphysik der Sitten*", in: *Denken im Schatten des Nihilismus: Festschrift für Wilhelm Weischedel*, ed. A. Schwan (Darmstadt: Wissenschaftliche Buchgesellschaft, 1975), pp. 55–110. An English translation of most of this paper appears, for the first time, in *Kant's Groundwork of the Metaphysics of Morals: Critical Essays*, ed. P. Guyer (Lanham: Rowman & Littlefield, 1998), pp. 303–41. In the present paper, I will assume that Kant's transcendental idealist conception of freedom is the same in both works, although the arguments by which he introduces it are different; and even then, I will suggest below, there is a crucial structural similarity between the two work's arguments for transcendental idealism, as Kant tries to argue that the transcendental idealist understanding of freedom is in fact just as natural to us as the natural theory of determinism which is the internal threat to morality that a fuller self-understanding must resolve.
9 AA IV 391, *Grundlegung* A XIII.
10 Cf. AA IV 398, *Grundlegung* A 11.
11 Cf. AA IV, 421 ff. and 429 f., *Grundlegung* A 52 ff. and A 66 f.
12 AA V 8, *Kritik der praktischen Vernunft* A 14 [trans. cf. note 3].
13 AA IV 397, *Grundlegung* A 8.
14 AA IV 402, *Grundlegung* A 17.
15 AA IV 403, *Grundlegung* A 20.
16 Cf. AA IV 397, *Grundlegung* A 8 f.
17 AA IV 399 f., *Grundlegung* A 13.
18 AA IV 400, *Grundlegung* A 14.
19 Cf. AA IV 397, *Grundlegung* A 8 f.
20 AA IV 398, *Grundlegung* A 10.
21 AA IV 402, *Grundlegung* A 17.
22 AA IV 403, *Grundlegung* A 19.

23 Cf. AA IV 402 and 403, *Grundlegung* A 18 and 19.
24 AA IV 404, *Grundlegung* A 21.
25 AA IV 404 f., *Grundlegung* A 23.
26 Cf. K. Cramer, "Metaphysik und Erfahrung in Kants Grundlegung der Ethik", in: *Kant in der Diskussion der Moderne*, ed. G. Schönrich and Y. Kato (Frankfurt a. M.: Suhrkamp, 1996), pp. 280–325; originally published in *Metaphysik und Erfahrung: Neue Hefte für Philosophie* 30–31 (1991), pp. 15–68.
27 AA IV 408, *Grundlegung* A 29. Cf. also Kant's discussion of Christ as a model for our own morality in *Religion within the Boundaries of Mere Reason*: AA VI 62–64, *Die Religion innerhalb der Grenzen der bloßen Vernunft* A 70–77/B 76–83.
28 AA IV 406 f., *Grundlegung* A 25 f.
29 Cf. AA IV 407, *Grundlegung* A 26.
30 AA IV 410, *Grundlegung* A 32.
31 AA IV 409, *Grundlegung* A 31.
32 AA IV 412, *Grundlegung* A 36.
33 AA IV 410, *Grundlegung* A 31.
34 D. Hume, *An Enquiry concerning the Principles of Morals*, Section IX, Part I; in the second edition of Hume's *Enquiries*, ed. L. A. Selby-Bigge (Oxford: Clarendon Press, 1902), p. 268 (the pagination remains the same in the third edition of Selby-Bigge, revised by P. H. Nidditch in 1978).
35 Cf. AA IV 413 f., *Grundlegung* A 37 f.
36 AA IV 415, *Grundlegung* A 42.
37 Cf. AA IV 418, *Grundlegung* A 46 f.
38 Cf. AA V 28, *Kritik der praktischen Vernunft* A 50 [trans. cf. note 3].
39 Cf. AA IV 421, *Grundlegung* A 52.
40 For the classical exposition and discussion of the various formulations of the categorical imperative, cf. H. J. Paton, *The Categorical Imperative* (London: Hutchinson University Library, 1947). There has been much recent discussion of this subject; for my own approach, as well as references to much of the recent literature, see my "The Possibility of the Categorical Imperative", in: *Philosophical Review* 104 (1995), pp. 353–85.
41 AA IV 425, *Grundlegung* A 60.
42 AA IV 428, *Grundlegung* A 65.
43 AA IV 431, *Grundlegung* A 70.
44 AA IV 428, *Grundlegung* A 65.
45 AA VI 35, *Die Religion innerhalb der Grenzen der bloßen Vernunft* B 31 f./A 27 f.; translation by G. Di Giovanni, from: Immanuel Kant, *Reli-*

gion and Rational Theology, ed. and trans. A. W. Wood and G. Di Giovanni (Cambridge: Cambridge University Press, 1996).
46 Of course, at the time of writing the *Religion* Kant had already defended the adoption of a *regulative* interpretation of a teleological view of nature as a single system directed to our own moral fulfillment in the *Critique of Judgement* (cf. especially §§ 83–4). But the view that we should conceive of every natural faculty and disposition of our own nature as having a proper and indeed properly moral use was hardly new to the third *Critique*; it is clearly expressed in the 1784 essay "Idea for a Universal History from a Cosmopolitan Point of View", Proposition One (AA VIII 18, "Idee zu einer allgemeinen Geschichte in weltbürgerlicher Absicht", Erster Satz), and in the *Groundwork* itself (AA IV 395 f., *Grundlegung* A 6 f.).
47 AA VI 28, *Die Religion innerhalb der Grenzen der bloßen Vernunft* B 19/A 17.
48 AA VI 58, *Die Religion innerhalb der Grenzen der bloßen Vernunft* B 69/A 63.
49 AA VI 36, *Die Religion innerhalb der Grenzen der bloßen Vernunft* B 34/A 30.
50 In the *Critique of Pure Reason*, in the "Canon of Pure Reason": AA III 522–531, *Kritik der reinen Vernunft* A 804–19/B 832–47; in the *Critique of Practical Reason*, in the "Dialectic of Pure Practical Reason", especially: AA V 110–13, *Kritik der praktischen Vernunft* A 198–203; in the *Critique of Judgement*, especially in "the moral proof of the existence of God", § 87: AA V 447–53, *Kritik der Urtheilskraft* B 418–429/A 414–423; and in the Preface to *Religion within the Boundaries of Mere Reason*: AA VI 4–6, *Die Religion innerhalb der Grenzen der bloßen Vernunft* BA VI ff.
51 AA IV 430 f., *Grundlegung* A 69.
52 AA VI 4, *Die Religion innerhalb der Grenzen der bloßen Vernunft* A VI.
53 AA VI 5, *Die Religion innerhalb der Grenzen der bloßen Vernunft* A VII.
54 Cf. AA VI 30, *Die Religion innerhalb der Grenzen der bloßen Vernunft* B 23/A 21.
55 AA IV 407 f., *Grundlegung* A 27.
56 AA VI 47, *Die Religion innerhalb der Grenzen der bloßen Vernunft* B 54/A 51. Kant repeatedly asserts the principle that we must be *able* to do what we *ought* to do in the *Religion*, e. g.: AA VI 62 f., *Die Religion innerhalb der Grenzen der bloßen Vernunft* B 76 f./A 70 f.
57 AA IV 456, *Grundlegung* A 115.
58 AA IV 457, *Grundlegung* A 117.
59 AA V 29, *Kritik der praktischen Vernunft* A 53.
60 Cf. AA V 30, *Kritik der praktischen Vernunft* A 53 f.
61 Cf. AA IV 451–53, *Grundlegung*, A 106–110.
62 Cf. AA IV 450 f., *Grundlegung* A 104 ff.

Helmut Fahrenbach

Meinen, Wissen, Glauben
Über die Notwendigkeit der Kantischen Differenzierung von „Weisen des Fürwahrhaltens" für eine jede Philosophie, die als Metaphysik soll auftreten können*

I
Ist eine spekulative „Metaphysik des Abschlusses" wirklich notwendig – und welchen Geltungs- und Gewißheitsmodus könnte sie haben?

Die einleitende Frage lautet: Ist es für ein „bewußtes Leben" und dessen philosophische Reflexion wirklich notwendig, das „Grundverhältnis" des Menschen zur Welt und zu sich selbst auf einen „Grund jenseits seiner" und eine „All-Einheit" hin spekulativ zu überschreiten, weil erst in einer „letzte Gedanken" erörternden „Metaphysik des Abschlusses" Sinn und Einheit für Leben und Denken erschlossen werden können? Oder kann und muß man nicht vielmehr das mit der menschlichen Existenz gesetzte Grundverhältnis „immanent", d. h. von seinen anthropologisch-strukturellen Bedingungen her und in seinen geschichtlich-innerweltlichen Perspektiven auslegen und innerhalb der menschlichen Lebenswelt die Sinngebung suchen. Denn ist sie hier nicht zu finden, dann kann auch ein transzendenter Sinn-Grund die konkrete Existenz und das Sich-Verstehen in ihr nicht sinnvoll oder sinnvoller machen; ganz abgesehen davon, daß eine spekulative Metaphysik des Abschlusses auch theoretisch mehr Probleme aufwirft, als sie zu lösen verspricht.

Nun ist eine solche grundsätzliche Alternative und die ihr zugrunde liegende primäre Frage nach der Notwendigkeit und dann auch der Möglichkeit einer Metaphysik erfahrungstranszendenter, abschließender und einheitgebender Grundbezüge (nicht: transzendental elementarer Grundlagen) natürlich nicht kurzerhand und direkt zu beantworten. Eine für die Klärung der Problemsituation entscheidende Frage ist jedoch die nach den für derartige metaphysische Problemstellungen, Annahmen und Aussagen überhaupt möglichen Weisen und Ansprüchen des Wahrheits- und Geltungssinnes, wie der Gewißheits- und Mitteilungsart. Eine solche geltungstheoretische Reflexion ist ohnehin die notwendige Aufgabe eines jeden nicht dogmatisch, sondern methodisch reflektiert verfahrenden metaphysischen Denkens, zumal ihm in einem weitgehend „nachmetaphysischen" Zeitalter verstärkt die Beweislast zufällt. Sie ist aber auch ein Mittel und Maßstab der Metaphysikkritik angesichts unterschiedlich möglicher Geltungsansprüche spekulativen metaphysischen Denkens und darum eine wesentliche Voraussetzung für die jeweils sachlich angemessene Auseinandersetzung.

1. Gemäß seiner Absicht, im spekulativen, metaphysischen Denken „Kritik und Integration" zu verbinden, hat Dieter Henrich denn auch immer wieder auf die Verschiedenheit der „Wissensart" der aus einer Reflexion des „bewußten Lebens" und des Selbstbewußtseins spekulativ zu entwickelnden „letzten Gedanken" von beweisfähiger Wissenschaft und „alltäglichen Meinungszuständen" hingewiesen. Und er hat darüber hinaus die Notwendigkeit einer „Epistemologie der All-Einheitslehre" und einer darin eingeschlossenen „Lehre von der Abfolge und Aufstufung von in sich geschlossenen Weisen des Meinens und des Wissens" betont.[1]

Es ist allerdings bislang bei thematisch eingebundenen Hinweisen auf jene „epistemologischen" Unterschiede, Ansätzen zu Differenzierungen und dem programmatischen Verweis auf eine „epistemologische Lehre" geblieben, ohne daß es zu einer grundsätzlichen geltungs- und gewißheitstheoretischen Reflexion und Strukturierung gekommen wäre. So konnte Henrich im Rahmen eines zu weit gefaßten und unbestimmt bleibenden Begriffs des „Wissens" scheinbar problemlos auch das spekulative Denken ansiedeln, ja es sogar als eine ausgezeichnete und höhere Art des integrativen und auf letzte Einheit und Ganzheit zielenden Wissens ansehen.

Der entscheidende Mangel dabei ist, daß Henrich die Frage nach den unterschiedlichen „Gewißheitsmodi" der „Wissensarten" nicht stellt und sie darum alle als Arten des „Wissens" ansehen kann, obwohl differenzierende Begriffe wie „Vergewisserung", „Überzeugung", „Einsicht" zur Verfügung stünden und auch genannt werden. Auch wird, soweit ich sehe, gewißheitstheoretisch nicht zwischen Meinung und Wissen unterschieden. Auf diese Art kann aber die notwendige kritische Frage nicht aufkommen, ob es denn überhaupt möglich und sinnvoll ist, Annahmen und Aussagen einer spekulativ metaphysischen Grund- und Einheitslehre des Wirklichen, die kritisch und integrativ zugleich sein will, mit dem Wahrheits- und Geltungsanspruch eines implizit allgemeingültigen oder zumindest allgemeinverbindlichen „Wissens" (und einer „Lehre" oder Theorie) zu belegen und zu belasten, anstatt ihren „Erwägungen" und „Erkundungen" Geltungs- und Gewißheitsmodalitäten subjektiv möglicher, existentiell motivierter und individuell einsichtiger Annahmen, Glaubens-Überzeugungen und deren Vergewisserung zuzuordnen und sie dadurch in ihrer begrenzteren, aber auch konkreteren Bedeutung für die individuelle Welt- und Existenzdeutung, die Henrich selbst ja auch immer im Blick behält, zu bestärken.

Die angesprochene Problematik erfordert, wie gesagt, eine grundsätzliche geltungstheoretische Reflexion in Form einer differentiellen und strukturierenden Analyse der Wahrheits-, Geltungs- und vor allem der Gewißheitsarten, bzw. der Weisen des „Fürwahrhaltens" (Kant), und vielleicht auch einer „Lehre von der Abfolge und Aufstufung von Weisen des Meines und Wissens" (Henrich) und Glaubens (Kant, Jaspers), um den geltungstheoretischen Ort eines spekulativen metaphysischen Denkens bestimmen zu können.

2. Mein Beitrag zu der bezeichneten Problemlage und Aufgabe ist nun allerdings eher von indirekter Art. Denn ich versuche für die bei Henrich unentwickelte bzw. programmatisch bleibende geltungstheoretische oder epistemologische Reflexion spekulativer Metaphysik aufzuzeigen und zur Geltung zu bringen, was vor allem Kant, aber auch Jaspers zu dieser Sachlage methodisch-systematisch zu sagen haben. Dieses indirekte Verfahren – durch Bezug auf Kant (und Jaspers) einen relevanten Beitrag zur Sache zu leisten – ist

andererseits nicht weit hergeholt. Denn Kant ist für Henrich ja zweifellos von besonderem Gewicht, und Jaspers hätte ein stärkeres verdient, schon aufgrund mancher Parallelen u. a. mit Bezug auf Kant und M. Weber. Die Bedeutung Kants für die in Frage stehende Reflexionsthematik ist von Henrich jedoch nicht wahrgenommen, jedenfalls nicht in Anspruch genommen worden.

Obwohl Henrich die epochale Bedeutung Kants durch eine Fülle profunder Untersuchungen zur theoretischen und praktischen Philosophie neu erschlossen und unter Beweis gestellt hat, ist er der Kantischen Modallehre der Gewißheitsarten bzw. der Weisen des Fürwahrhaltens und ihrer methodisch-systematischen Bedeutung, die durch ihren Ort in jeder der drei Kritiken bezeugt wird, nicht nachgegangen. (Diesen blinden Fleck teilt er übrigens, soweit ich sehe, mit nahezu der gesamten Kant-Forschung.) Die Nichtbeachtung dieses Kantischen Lehrstücks war natürlich z. T. durch die spezifische Thematik seiner Kant-Untersuchungen bedingt. Aber wenn Henrich selbst dort, wo er die Kantischen Vernunftideen in den Kreis der „Metaphysik des Abschlusses" (und deren Wissensart) einbezieht[2], nicht darauf zu sprechen kommt, daß der Gewißheitsmodus ihrer Realitätsannahme nur der eines subjektiv gewissen reinen praktischen Vernunftglaubens ist – also nicht einmal der des vorausgesetzten moralisch-praktischen „Wissens", von einem theoretisch-spekulativen ganz zu schweigen –, dann ist das eine problematische Unterlassung.

Darum ist es auch nicht überraschend, daß die Unterscheidung der „Gewißheitsarten", die der Kantianer Jaspers vornimmt und in seiner Kritik der Wissensansprüche traditioneller Metaphysik und für die davon befreite Wahrheitsgeltung seiner Chiffern-Metaphysik der Transzendenz aus „philosophischem Glauben" zur Geltung bringt, bei Henrich keine Beachtung findet, zumal er von der Jaspersschen Philosophie ohnehin nur ein reduziertes und unangemessenes Bild hat. Denn wenn er die Existenzphilosophie als ein bloß „korrektives und nicht der Selbstbewegung fähiges Denken" charakterisiert, das „zu einer Integration, die Theorie ist, gar nicht gelangen kann"[3], dann ist das Jaspers gegenüber, zumal im Blick auf dessen Entwicklung zur Philosophie von *Vernunft und Existenz*[4], absolut unzureichend.

Denn Jaspers hat die von den „existentiellen" und „metaphysischen" Erhellungen methodisch strikt zu unterscheidenden strukturell-formalen „transzendentalen Erhellungen" der philosophischen Logik zu einem im Prinzip allgemeingültigen „philosophischen Grundwissen" kommunikativer Vernunft strukturiert, das als Vernunftdenken durch die notwendigen Differenzierungen (der Seins-, Bewußtseins-, Wahrheits-, Geltungs- und Mitteilungsweisen) hindurch die Verweisungszusammenhänge und eine offene (nicht nivellierende) Einheit sucht und dergestalt durchaus als eine kritische, differentielle und integrative (aber weder deduktive noch holistische) Theorie verstanden werden kann.[5] Und zum „methodologischen Bewußtsein" dieses transzendentallogischen Grundwissens gehört wesentlich auch die geltungstheoretische Differenzierung und Verbindung der „Gewißheitsarten". Dies alles müßte für Henrich eigentlich von Interesse sein.

So hoffe ich denn, über meine Distanz zur Metaphysik hinweg, durch die Interpretation der methodisch-systematischen Bedeutung der Kantischen Lehre von den Weisen des Fürwahrhaltens (und die Hinweise auf die analoge Thematik bei Jaspers) doch einen Beitrag zu den notwendigen geltungstheoretischen Reflexionsbedingungen einer kritischen Metaphysik und damit auch zu den spekulativen Intentionen von Dieter Henrich leisten zu können (cf. u. III. 3.). Das ist um so eher möglich, als Kant und Jaspers ihre geltungstheoretischen Reflexionen ihrerseits – zu meinem Leidwesen – zur methodisch-kritischen Klärung und Sicherung des auch von ihnen für notwendig gehaltenen, wenn auch des Wissens- und Theorieanspruchs entkleideten, metaphysischen Denkens genutzt haben. Könnte Henrich die von Kant und Jaspers vollzogene Restriktion eines allgemeingültigen Wissens-Anspruchs der Metaphysik zugunsten eines subjektiv-moralisch, bzw. ethisch-existentiell gewissen (glaubenden) Fürwahrhaltens metaphysischer Annahmen im Prinzip akzeptieren, dann hätte er Kant und Jaspers auf seiner Seite; wenn nicht, nicht.

Für ein im Sinne einer Transzendenz-Metaphysik nach- bzw. nicht-metaphysisches Denken, das lediglich (mit Bloch, Sartre, Marcuse u. a.) eine innerweltlich-geschichtliche, also „immanente Transzendenz" bzw. ein „Transzendieren ohne Transzendenz" (Bloch) in

Anspruch nimmt, wäre jedenfalls eine auf individuelle (bzw. existentiell „unbedingte") Gültigkeit reduzierte Metaphysik tolerabel. Denn es bestreitet nicht die existentielle Möglichkeit einer metaphysisch transzendenzbezogenen Seins- und Existenzdeutung, sondern nur deren Allgemeinheits- oder Notwendigkeitsanspruch. Sollten solche Ansprüche allerdings inkonsequenterweise auch bei Kant und Jaspers auftreten, dann wären auch sie entsprechend zu kritisieren.

II
Kants Unterscheidung der Weisen des Fürwahrhaltens und ihre geltungstheoretische Bedeutung für die kritische Philosophie und ihre Metaphysik des Vernunftglaubens

1. Die theoretischen Modi: Wissen und Meinen

a) Es ist ein merkwürdiger Tatbestand, daß die ja nun wahrlich nicht dürftige Kant-Forschung Kants Differenzierung der Modi des Fürwahrhaltens – über die Behandlung in den Kommentaren und über thematisch begrenzte Zusammenhänge hinaus – in ihrer methodisch-systematischen Bedeutung nicht zum Gegenstand entsprechend angemessener Interpretation gemacht hat.[6] Das ist um so unverständlicher, als es sich dabei ja nicht nur um ein Lehrstück der *Logik* handelt, sondern um die geltungslogische Strukturierung möglicher Erkenntnis, die in allen drei Kritiken (zumeist in der Methodenlehre) und anderen Schriften ausgeführt und in methodisch-systematisch wichtiger Funktion eingesetzt wird. Bedenkt man, daß die Differenzierung der Gewißheitsmodalitäten (und die Bestimmung des „Glaubens") von größter geltungstheoretischer Bedeutung für die Frage ist, ob und wie denn nach der Kritik der theoretischen Vernunft überhaupt noch eine Metaphysik möglich sein kann, dann dürfte die Notwendigkeit, die kantische Gewißheitslehre zu untersuchen, für eine angemessene Kant-Interpretation und -Vergegenwärtigung wohl außer

Frage stehen. Angesichts der Leerstelle in der Kant-Forschung bedarf es hier zunächst einmal der bloßen Darstellung.

b) In der *Logik* entwickelt Kant (unter den „besonderen logischen Vollkommenheiten des Erkenntnisses") die Weisen des Fürwahrhaltens als die der „Modalität" (Gewißheit) der Erkenntnis neben und nach denen der „Quantität" (Größe, Umfang, Horizont), der „Relation" (Wahrheit) und der „Qualität" (Klarheit, Deutlichkeit).

Nun scheint es naheliegend, zwischen Wahrheit und Gewißheit eine besonders enge Verbindung anzunehmen, ohne daß etwa Klarheit und Deutlichkeit, an denen die elementare Voraussetzung der Bestimmtheit der Vorstellungen und Urteilsgegenstände hängt, als nebensächlich gelten könnten. Aber Kant setzt nicht nur eine (berechtigte) Unterscheidung, sondern – zumindest thematisch – eher eine Trennung zwischen „Wahrheit" und „Gewißheit", wenn er definiert:

> „Wahrheit ist *objektive Eigenschaft* der Erkenntnis; das Urteil, wodurch etwas als wahr *vorgestellt* wird – die Beziehung auf einen Verstand und also auf ein besonderes Subjekt – ist *subjektiv* das ‚*Fürwahrhalten*'."[7]

Die inneren Beziehungen zwischen Wahrheit und Gewißheit werden jedoch nicht eigens thematisiert, obwohl doch Wahrheit als objektive Eigenschaft der Erkenntnis für den Erkennenden nicht objektiv oder an sich vorgegeben ist, sondern erst über Prozesse der Vergewisserung in den subjektbezogenen Modi des Fürwahrhaltens und der intersubjektiven Mitteilung für das Urteil anderer (als „Probierstein" der Wahrheit) zugänglich, erschlossen und feststellbar wird. Aus der Kantischen Unterscheidung und dem Blick auf die Beziehungen zwischen Wahrheit und Gewißheit läßt sich indessen die Berechtigung ziehen, die Reflexion der Weisen des Fürwahrhaltens bzw. der Gewißheitsmodalitäten als eine gegenüber der Wahrheitstheorie eigenständige Problemstellung aufzufassen und anzugehen und ihr unter geltungstheoretischen Gesichtspunkten sogar einen methodischen (heuristischen) Vorrang vor einer davon abgelösten und verselbständigten Wahrheitstheorie einzuräumen. Unbestreitbar ist im übrigen die Verschränkung von Geltung und Gewißheit. Denn Geltung gibt es nur für und durch ein artikulierendes Bewußtsein, und die Differenzierung von Geltungsmodi muß sich in entsprechenden Gewißheitsmodi spiegeln. Darum wird im folgenden Kants Gewißheitslehre zugleich als Geltungstheorie gefaßt.

Indem Kant die Problemstellung als Analyse der Modi des *Fürwahrhaltens* (und nicht direkt der Gewißheit) anlegt, wird die Untersuchung in ein weiteres und offeneres Feld gestellt, das auch das „Meinen" einzuschließen erlaubt, als wenn sie von vornherein auf den engeren Bezirk der Gewißheitsthematik und gar noch auf die (reduktive) Dominanz einer bestimmten Gewißheits- oder Wissensart ausgerichtet worden wäre. In diesem weiteren Rahmen sucht Kant eine prinzipiell umfassende bzw. „vollständige", aber auch differentiell strukturierte Typologie der möglichen Grundweisen des Fürwahrhaltens aufzustellen – und aus den verkürzten oder zu allgemeinen und geltungslogisch unklaren Bestimmungen über Gewißheits-, Wissens-, Glaubens- und Wahrscheinlichkeitsmodi des Erkennens, wie sie seit Descartes, Spinoza und dann insbesondere Locke, Hume, Leibniz (und anderen) auftraten, herauszukommen. Die Lehre von den Modi des Fürwahrhaltens ist in gewisser Weise Kants originäre Antwort auf die Gewißheitsreflexionen insbesondere der neuzeitlichen Philosophie, die er zum einen thematisch erweitert – nicht zuletzt auch um die Konzeption des „Vernunftglaubens" – und denen er zum anderen erst eine methodisch-systematisch strukturierte und präzisierte Form gegeben hat. Innerhalb des erweiterten und bestimmteren Rahmens bleibt freilich auch für Kant das Gewißheitsthema zentral und der Begriff der Gewißheit, trotz terminologischer Schwankungen, eine wesentliche Scheidemarke für die Weisen des Fürwahrhaltens. Denn das „Fürwahrhalten überhaupt ist von zwiefacher Art, ein *gewisses* oder ein *ungewisses*"[8]. Dabei rangieren Meinen, Glauben, Wissen der Gewißheitsart (nicht dem Gewißheitsgrad) nach in einer Stufenfolge vom objektiv und subjektiv ungewissen Fürwahrhalten des Meinens über das zwar objektiv unzureichende, aber subjektiv gewisse des Glaubens zum objektiv und subjektiv gewissen des Wissens.[9]

c) Dieser Stufenfolge entsprechend spricht Kant prinzipiell nur dem *Wissen* den vollen Modus der Gewißheit zu und identifiziert in dieser

Hinsicht Wissen und Gewißheit. Denn das „Fürwahrhalten aus einem Erkenntnisgrunde, der sowohl objektiv als subjektiv zureichend ist", ist Wissen „oder die Gewißheit"[10] und gründet „objektiv zulängliche Gewißheit (für jedermann)", im Unterschied zur subjektiv zulänglichen „Überzeugung (für mich selbst)"[11]. Die Terminologie hinsichtlich „Überzeugung" und „Gewißheit" ist jedoch nicht konsistent. In der *Kritik der reinen Vernunft* wird das objektiv begründete Fürwahrhalten auch „Überzeugung" genannt: d. h. es gibt einen doppelten Gebrauch des Ausdrucks „Überzeugung" in objektiver (logischer) und subjektiver (praktischer) Beziehung und Bedeutung.[12]

Die Bestimmung des Wissens bzw. objektiver Gewißheit oder Überzeugung als objektiver, allgemeingültiger und an jedermann überzeugungskräftig mitteilbarer Erkenntnis bezieht sich sowohl auf rationale als auch auf empirische Erkenntnis bzw. Wahrheit und also „auf die beiden Quellen, woraus unser gesamtes Erkenntnis geschöpft wird: die *Erfahrung* und die *Vernunft*"[13]. Demgemäß sind auch Wissen und Gewißheit zweifach „entweder empirisch oder rational, je nachdem sie entweder auf *Erfahrung* – die eigene sowohl als die fremde mitgeteilte" (auch historische) – „oder auf *Vernunft*" sich gründet.[14]

Auch wenn empirische und rationale Gewißheit (bei der Kant noch zwischen philosophisch-diskursiver und mathematisch-intuitiver unterscheidet) als Wissen der Gewißheitsart nach gleich sind (zumal gegenüber Meinen und Glauben), sind sie doch dem (objektiven) Gewißheitsgrad nach verschieden. Denn während rationale Gewißheit „durch das Bewußtsein der Notwendigkeit des für wahr Gehaltenen" eine apodiktische Gewißheit (mit entsprechenden apodiktischen Urteilen) darstellt, führt das empirische Wissen nur eine „assertorische Gewißheit" bei sich, die folglich auch nur zu assertorischen Urteilen berechtigen dürfte.[15]

Allerdings gibt es hinsichtlich der differentiellen Bestimmung der Gewißheitsgrade des Wissens und der entsprechenden Urteilsformen gewisse Überschneidungen, sofern auch für die Erkenntnis von „Gegenständen der Erfahrung [...] die Gewißheit davon doch empirisch und rational zugleich sein kann"[16]. Andererseits zeigen sich Konvergenzen zwischen den assertorischen Urteilsweisen des empirischen

Wissens und des praktischen Glaubens. So heißt es zu Beginn des Gewißheitskapitels der *Logik*-Einleitung zunächst mit Bezug auf das Wissen: „das gewisse Fürwahrhalten oder die Gewißheit ist mit dem Bewußtsein der Notwendigkeit verbunden; das ungewisse dagegen oder die Ungewißheit" – in Meinen und Glauben – „mit dem Bewußtsein der Zufälligkeit oder der Möglichkeit des Gegenteils"[17]. Die „Arten oder Modi des Fürwahrhaltens: Meinen, Glauben und Wissen" werden aber dann für die Urteilskraft und dem Urteilsmodus nach durch ein *problematisches* Urteilen (im Meinen), ein *assertorisches* (im Glauben) und ein *apodiktisches* (im Wissen) differentiell bestimmt. „Denn was ich bloß meine, das halte ich im Urteilen, mit Bewußtsein nur für problematisch; was ich glaube, für *assertorisch*, aber nicht als objektiv, sondern nur als subjektiv notwendig (nur für mich geltend); was ich endlich weiß, für *apodiktisch* gewiß, d. i. für allgemein und objektiv notwendig (für alle geltend); gesetzt auch, daß der Gegenstand selbst, auf den sich dieses gewisse Fürwahrhalten bezieht, eine bloß empirische Wahrheit wäre"[18]. Gewisse logische Konvergenzen zwischen assertorischen Urteilen empirischen Wissens und praktischen Glaubens ergeben sich daraus, daß in beiden etwas als wirklich angenommen wird, während die Differenzen den Gewißheitsmodus und die Sachbezüge betreffen: subjektiv und objektiv gewisses empirisches Wissen von Erfahrungsgegenständen – subjektiv gewisser, aber nicht beweisfähiger Glaube an die erfahrungstranszendente Realität von Vernunftideen.

Für Kants Wissens- und Wissenschaftstheorie bleibt die interne Differenzierung zwischen assertorischem Erfahrungs- und apodiktischem Vernunft-Wissen in Geltung und wichtig[19]: Im Blick auf die Unterscheidung der Modi des Fürwahrhaltens bilden sie aber zusammengehörige Weisen des Wissens, die durch die subjektiv und objektiv begründete Allgemeinheit und Gewißheit und die empirische oder rationale „Notwendigkeit" ihrer Erkenntnisurteile klar und strikt vom Meinen und Glauben zu scheiden sind.

d) Zum Verständnis dessen, daß und wie Kant das *„Meinen"* als objektiv und subjektiv unzureichendes, ungewisses Fürwahrhalten bestimmt, ist zunächst zu beachten, in welchem Sinn Kant den Begriff des Meinens faßt und verwendet. Er gebraucht ihn nicht einfach in dem seit der platonischen Diskussion über Meinen und Wissen *(doxa* und *episteme)* traditionellen Sinn des Meinungen bzw. Ansichten über etwas haben, die trotz ihres ungeprüften und unbegründeten Status für wahr gehalten und mit einem (zumindest impliziten) Wissensanspruch geäußert werden. (Dieser Komplex undurchschauter und Objektivität beanspruchender Ansichten, die grundsätzlich gefaßt als „Vorurteile" fixiert werden, würde für Kant am ehesten in den Kontext der Selbst-„Überredung" gehören.[20]) Demgegenüber faßt Kant den Begriff des Meinens in einem ausdrücklich reflexiven Sinn, nämlich als den seiner selbst als eines unzureichenden, ungewissen und problematischen Fürwahrhaltens „bewußten" Modus. „Meinen ist ein mit Bewußtsein sowohl subjektiv als objektiv unzureichendes Fürwahrhalten"[21]; und „Meinung [...] eine ungewisse Erkenntnis [...], *sofern sie für ungewiß gehalten wird*"[22].

Nur ein solches sich selbst in seinem wahrheits- und geltungstheoretischen Defizit als eines ungewissen, problematischen Fürwahrhaltens durchsichtiges Meinen kann eine bestimmte Stellung unter den „logischen Vollkommenheiten der Erkenntnis" im Hinblick auf mögliche Gewißheit einnehmen. Denn nur so vermag es, die Differenz zur bloßen „Überredung" wie zu den überzeugungskräftigen und gewißheitsfähigen Weisen des Fürwahrhaltens bewußt zu halten und als ein bewußt „vorläufiges Urteilen" die Irrwege zum Wahrheitsanspruch nur „privatgültiger" Selbst-„Überredung", fixierter „Vorurteile" und zum Dogmatismus zu verlegen und damit eine Anfangs-„Stufe" auf dem selbstkritischen Weg zu einem differenzierten Geltungs-, Gewißheits- und Wahrheitsbewußtsein zu bilden. Diese (mögliche) Funktion eines selbstbewußten Meinens für den Erkenntnisprozeß betont Kant ausdrücklich, auch wenn im begrenzten Feld der für uns möglichen Erfahrung ein Bereich von „Sachen des Meinens" bestehen bleibt, die sich nicht einfach in solche des Wissens und schon gar nicht des Glaubens überführen lassen[23].

„Vom Meinen fangen wir größtenteils bei allem unserem Erkennen an. [...] Das Meinen [...] kann als ein *vorläufiges* Urteilen (sub conditione suspensiva ad interim) angesehen werden, dessen man nicht leicht entbehren kann. Man muß erst meinen, ehe man annimmt und behauptet, sich dabei aber auch hüten, eine Meinung für etwas mehr als eine bloße Meinung zu halten."[24]

Die mögliche innovative Bedeutung des Meinens im und für den Prozeß der Erkenntnisgewinnung ist auch darin begründet, daß sich das in bewußt vorläufigen und problematischen Urteilen artikulierende Meinen an ein jeweils vorausgesetztes Wissen anschließen muß und sich eben dadurch von beliebiger Phantasterei unterscheidet und erkenntnis- und wahrheitsrelevant wird.

„Ich darf mich niemals unterwinden, zu *meinen*, ohne wenigstens etwas zu *wissen*, vermittels dessen das an sich bloß problematische Urteil eine Verknüpfung mit Wahrheit bekommt, ob sie gleich nicht vollständig, doch mehr als willkürliche Erdichtung ist. Das Gesetz einer solchen Verknüpfung muß überdem gewiß sein."[25]

Das für ein Meinen (implizit) in Anspruch genommene Wissen kann jedoch als solches keinen zureichenden Grund für eine objektiv oder subjektiv gewisse Annahme abgeben und die Ungewißheit des problematischen Fürwahrhaltens und damit das Meinen selbst nicht aufheben. Das wäre nur durch eine „Ergänzung" aus einer Art von (objektiven) Gründen möglich, die das Meinen in ein Wissen überführen könnten[26]. Aber das würde einen Wechsel im Modus des Fürwahrhaltens bedeuten und nicht etwa eine legitime Mischform zweier Modi darstellen. Zwar gibt es gewisse Zwischenformen, die aber als solche in sich klar und bestimmt sein müssen, wie etwa die „*Wahrscheinlichkeit*" bzw. die „Erkenntnis des Wahrscheinlichen", die als eine „Annäherung zur Gewißheit" „zur Lehre von der Gewißheit unsers Erkenntnisses gehört"[27]. Wahrscheinlichkeitsurteile artikulieren zwar einerseits auch nur „ein Fürwahrhalten aus unzureichenden Gründen" und bleiben vom Wissen unterschiedene problematische Urteile; sie sind aber andererseits dadurch spezifisch charakterisiert, daß mehr Gründe für die fragliche Annahme sprechen als gegen sie, so daß gegenüber der Ungewißheit und Unentschiedenheit des Meinens ein größeres Gewicht auf eine bestimmte (wahrscheinlichere) Annahme fällt. Das bedeutet „eine Annäherung zur Gewißheit", ohne daß diese doch erreicht würde. So bleibt das wahrscheinliche Fürwahrhalten bzw. die „Erkenntnis des Wahrscheinlichen" vom Wissen und der Glaubensgewißheit unterschieden und graduell auch vom Meinen, mit dem sie zwar den Sachbereich möglicher Erfahrung teilt[28], demgegenüber sie aber doch einen Schritt zur Überführung in ein mögliches Erfahrungswissen darstellt – ähnlich wie die Hypothesen bzw. hypothetischen Erklärungen.[29]

2. Das praktische Fürwahrhalten: Der moralisch-metaphysische Vernunftglaube

a) Mit dem Begriff des *Glaubens* wird gewiß die originärste und für Kant wohl auch gewichtigste Thematik innerhalb der geltungstheoretischen Reflexion und Strukturierung der Modi des Fürwahrhaltens bezeichnet, die darum auch etwas ausführlicher behandelt werden muß. Die Besonderheit wird schon daran ersichtlich, daß und wie Kant mit seiner Fassung und Einfügung des Vernunft-Glaubens in die Gewißheitsmodalitäten die traditionellen Vorgaben hinter sich läßt; indem er ihn 1. der überlieferten Zweiteilung bzw. Entgegensetzung von Meinen und Wissen als einen davon strikt unterschiedenen und selbstständigen Gewißheits- und Überzeugungsmodus hinzufügt, ohne ihn, wie insbesondere der Empirismus (zumal Humes „belief") als eine abgeschwächte Form von „Wissen" im Kontext empirisch bedingter Wahrscheinlichkeits-Erkenntnis bzw. eingewöhnter Annahmen anzusiedeln; und indem er ihn 2. aus der theologischen Dualität von Vernunft- und Offenbarungsglauben herauslöst und ihm eine geltungslogisch eigenständige und methodisch-systematisch zentrale Funktion innerhalb der (praktischen) Vernunftphilosophie gibt.

Für Kants Bestimmung des Glaubens ist zunächst charakteristisch, daß er ihn grundsätzlich in einen praktischen Kontext und Begründungszusammenhang rückt. Während Meinen und Wissen eindeutig in einem theoretisch-epistemischen Funktionszusammenhang verstanden werden, wird das Glauben – ohne als ein „besonderer Erkenntnisquell" zu fungieren[30] – sowohl hinsichtlich der für es zureichenden subjektiven Gründe als auch im Blick auf seine Gewißheits- und Wahrheitsfunktion in einem anthropologisch-praktischen Rahmen und von Gewißheitserfordernissen des Handelns her bestimmt.

„Es kann aber überall bloß in praktischer Beziehung das theoretisch unzureichende Fürwahrhalten Glauben genannt werden. Diese praktische Absicht ist nun entweder die der Geschicklichkeit oder die der Sittlichkeit, die erste zu beliebigen und zufälligen, die zweite aber zu schlechthin notwendigen Zwecken".[31]

Die erste führt zum „pragmatischen", die zweite zum „moralischen" Glauben. Natürlich wird auch im pragmatisch oder moralisch motivierten Glauben – als einer Weise des Fürwahrhaltens – etwas für wahr gehalten, d. h. es werden bestimmte Existenz- oder Sachverhalts-*Annahmen* gemacht und in entsprechenden „assertorischen Urteilen" formuliert, von deren Wahrheit der Glaubende subjektiv überzeugt ist. Aber diese „Annahmen" und „Voraussetzungen" des Glaubens sind durch praktische Absichten und Bedingungszusammenhänge erforderlich gemacht und motiviert, im Falle des moralischen Glaubens sogar „notwendig", „weil eine objektive praktische Regel des Verhaltens, als notwendig, zum Grunde liegt".[32]

Nun hat Kant allerdings neben dem *pragmatischen* Glauben, der sich auf subjektiv möglichst gewisse Annahmen für empirische, zufällige Zwecksetzungen bezieht, und dem *moralischen* Glauben, der es mit der Gewißheit über Voraussetzungen für notwendige und letzte Zwecke der praktischen Vernunft zu tun hat, auch noch den Begriff eines *„doktrinalen Glaubens"* gefaßt, der sich der praktischen Grundbeziehung des Glaubens „in strenger Bedeutung" nicht fügt, sondern ein rein theoretisch motiviertes Annehmen ist.[33] Der doktrinale Glaube bezieht sich vor allem auf die Voraussetzung des Daseins einer „höchsten Intelligenz" als Bedingung der möglichen Erklärung und regulativen „Leitung" für die Erforschung der „zweckmäßigen Einheit der Natur". Dieses Fürwahrhalten in einem „theoretischen Verhältnis" hat weder den Charakter eines beweisbaren theoretischen Wissens, ja nicht einmal den einer „Hypothese"[34], noch den eines ungewissen Meinens, sondern als „Festigkeit des Zutrauens in subjektiver Absicht" den eines (doktrinalen) Glaubens. Dieser ist aber nur Bedingung einer nicht notwendigen, sondern „zufälligen", wenn auch „nicht unerheblichen Absicht" (über die Einheit der Natur urteilen zu wollen) und hat „etwas Wankendes in sich".[35]

b) Demgegenüber ist der „*moralische Glaube*" als Exponent eines praktisch begründeten Vernunft-Glaubens von „ganz anderer" Art, Bewandtnis und auch von größerer Festigkeit. „Denn da ist es schlechterdings notwendig, daß etwas geschehen muß, nämlich daß ich dem sittlichen Gesetze in allen Stücken Folge leiste." Der Zweck – „das höchste Gut" – und seine Beförderung

> „ist hier unumgänglich festgestellt, und es ist nur eine einzige Bedingung nach aller meiner Einsicht möglich, unter welcher dieser Zweck mit allen gesamten Zwecken zusammenhängt, und dadurch praktische Gültigkeit habe, nämlich daß ein Gott und eine künftige Welt sei [...], und ich bin sicher, daß diesen Glauben nichts wankend machen könne, weil dadurch meine sittlichen Grundsätze selbst umgestürzt werden würden".[36]

Hier formuliert Kant allerdings (noch) eine unhaltbare Abhängigkeit der (praktischen) Gültigkeit des moralischen Zwecks und sogar der „sittlichen Grundsätze selbst" vom moralischen Glauben, ohne den „die moralischen Gesetze als leere Hirngespinste anzusehen" wären.[37] Die Unhaltbarkeit dieses (verkehrten) Abhängigkeits- und Begründungsverhältnisses, das der autonomen Geltung des moralischen Gesetzes widerstreitet und in eine gläubige Heteronomie führen würde, hat Kant später klar gesehen und (in der *Kritik der praktischen Vernunft* und der *Kritik der Urteilskraft*) die Verkehrung beseitigt.[38] Es ist

> „ein Bedürfnis der reinen *praktischen* Vernunft, auf einer *Pflicht* gegründet, etwas (das höchste Gut) zum Gegenstand meines Willens zu machen, um es nach allen meinen Kräften zu befördern; wobei ich aber die Möglichkeit desselben, mithin auch die Bedingungen dazu, nämlich Gott, Freiheit und Unsterblichkeit voraussetzen muß, weil ich diese durch meine spekulative Vernunft nicht beweisen, obgleich auch nicht widerlegen kann. Diese Pflicht gründet sich auf einem, freilich von diesen letzteren Voraussetzungen ganz unabhängigen, für sich selbst apodiktisch gewissen, nämlich dem moralischen Gesetze, und ist, so fern keiner anderweitigen Unterstützung durch theoretische Meinung von der inneren Beschaffenheit der Dinge, der geheimen Abzweckung der Weltordnung, oder eines ihr vorstehenden Regierers, bedürftig, um uns auf das vollkommenste zu unbedingt-gesetzmäßigen Handlungen zu verbinden."[39]

Es wäre darum grundfalsch zu denken,

> „daß die Annehmung des Daseins Gottes, *als eines Grundes aller Verbindlichkeit überhaupt*, notwendig sei (denn dieser beruht, wie hinreichend bewiesen worden, lediglich auf der Autonomie der Vernunft selbst)"[40].

Im moralisch-praktischen Vernunft-Glauben (und seinen Existenz-Postulaten: Gott und Unsterblichkeit) geht es also auf gar keinen Fall um Begründungsvoraussetzungen für die Moral, vielmehr fungiert umgekehrt das moralische Gesetz als Voraussetzung für den moralischen Glauben. Die metaphysischen Annahmen des moralischen Glaubens sind (nach Kant) jedoch nötig, weil die reale Möglichkeit des höchsten Gutes und der in ihm gedachten Zusammenstimmung von Tugend, Moralität und Glückseligkeit, „nicht in unserer Gewalt" ist, und in „Ergänzung unseres Unvermögens"[41] nur unter der Voraussetzung der Existenz Gottes als des „moralischen Welturhebers" und eines künftigen Lebens als praktisch gesichert angenommen werden kann.

Glaubenspostulate im strikten Sinn sind: Existenz Gottes und Unsterblichkeit der Seele, aber nicht eigentlich die Freiheit. Sie wird zwar auch unter den Postulaten aufgeführt, aber kaum als solches und eigens behandelt. Auf jeden Fall nimmt sie eine Sonderstellung in diesem Komplex ein. Einige Texte nehmen sie der Sache nach denn auch aus dem Status der Glaubenspostulate heraus, auch wenn sie natürlich dem intelligiblen Bereich der Vernunftideen zugehörig bleibt und theoretisch weder beweisbar noch widerlegbar ist. Die Differenz zu den eigentlichen Postulaten des Vernunftglaubens ist 1. darin begründet, daß Freiheit in einem inneren und notwendigen Bedingungszusammenhang mit dem moralischen Gesetz und der Moralität selbst steht, sofern intelligible Freiheitsmöglichkeit und Freiheitsbewußtsein (über die Verbindung von *ratio essendi* und *ratio cognoscendi*) eine durch das moralische Gesetz selbst beanspruchte notwendige Bedingung seines Sinnes und seiner Verbindlichkeit darstellt – während Gott und Unsterblichkeit demgegenüber erst und nur als „äußere" Bedingungen der Ausführbarkeit des moralischen Endzwecks postuliert werden müssen.[42] Diese im basalen Grundverhältnis von Moralität und Freiheit gelegene Differenz zeigt sich 2. im spezifischen und differenten Gewißheitsmodus der Freiheit bzw. des Freiheitsbewußtseins, sofern Kant der praktischen Idee der Freiheit eine bestimmte Erfahrbarkeit zuspricht,[43] ja sie sogar zu den „Tatsachen" des Wissens zählt und sie damit jedenfalls näher an den Sachbereich des (praktischen) „Wissens" als an den der „Glaubenssachen" heranrückt, die, als auf theoretisch „transzendent" bleibende Vernunftideen bezogen, sowohl von den „Tatsachen" des Wissens als auch von den möglichen Erfahrungssachen des Meinens und der Erkenntnis des Wahrscheinlichen geschieden sind.[44]

> „Was aber sehr merkwürdig ist, so findet sich sogar eine Vernunftidee (die an sich keiner Darstellung in der Anschauung, mithin auch keines theoretischen Beweises ihrer Möglichkeit, fähig ist) unter den Tatsachen; und das ist die Idee der Freiheit, deren Realität, als einer besonderen Art der Kausalität (von welchem der Begriff in theoretischem Betracht überschwenglich sein würde), sich durch praktische Gesetze der reinen Vernunft, und, diesen gemäß, in wirklichen Handlungen, mithin in der Erfahrung, dartun läßt. – Die einzige unter allen Ideen der reinen Vernunft, deren Gegenstand Tatsache ist, und unter die *scibilia* mit gerechnet werden muß."[45]

Diese in der Tat „merkwürdige" These wird freilich verständlicher, wenn man bedenkt, daß sich der moralische Vernunft-Glaube mit seinen Postulaten – im Unterschied zum pragmatischen, aber auch zum doktrinalen Glauben – auf einer apodiktisch gewissen Basis erhebt, nämlich der „gewissen Erkenntnis" der moralisch-praktischen Gesetze. Sofern die Freiheit als „übersinnliches Prinzip in uns selbst" im Unterschied zu den Postulaten wesentlich zum moralisch-praktischen Basis-Wissen gehört, kann sie zu den Gegenständen des praktischen Wissens gezählt werden, auch wenn damit Probleme verbunden sind, wie zum Beispiel das der „Beweisbarkeit" dieser „Wissens-Tatsache" Freiheit.

> „Eben solche gewisse Erkenntnisse" – wie im theoretischen Bereich – „und zwar gänzlich a priori haben wir in praktischen Gesetzen; allein diese gründen sich auf ein übersinnliches Prinzip (der Freiheit) und zwar *in uns selbst*, als ein Prinzip der praktischen Vernunft".[46]

Die Basisgewißheit des moralischen Wissens bildet nun zwar die Grundlage, nicht aber die Begründung für die Postulate des Vernunftglaubens, so daß diese zu Gehalten des praktischen Wissens werden könnten. Der Modus des Fürwahrhaltens der den Vernunftideen Gott und Unsterblichkeit aus moralisch-praktischen Gründen zugesprochenen Realität bleibt vielmehr ein nur subjektiv gewisser reiner praktischer Vernunft-*Glaube*, auch wenn ihm (gegenüber dem pragmatischen und doktrinalen Glauben) praktisch notwendige Vernunft-Zwecke, -Interessen und -Bedürfnisse zugrunde liegen und ihm eine größere subjektive Sicherheit und Festigkeit eignet, die sogar die des Wissens übertreffen kann.[47]

c) Um falsche Erwartungen und „Mißdeutungen", die sich „bei dem Gebrauche eines noch so ungewohnten Begriffes, als der eines reinen praktischen Vernunftglaubens ist", leicht einstellen, zu verhüten[48], kommt es Kant besonders darauf an, dessen Gewißheits- und Geltungsmodus möglichst genau zu bestimmen und einzugrenzen. Die Eingrenzungen betreffen vor allem drei Punkte: α) der moralische Glaube muß explizit als ein „freies Fürwahrhalten" verstanden werden; β) ihm ist eine subjektive moralische Gewißheit (und Gesinnung) eigen, deren Überzeugung nur in der ersten Person (Ich-Form) zum Ausdruck gebracht werden kann; und es ist γ) keine allgemeine „Mitteilung" bzw. Vermittlung dieser Glaubens-Überzeugung und ihrer Gehalte an andere möglich.

α) Daß der moralische Glaube als ein „freies Fürwahrhalten" oder „Annehmen" bestimmt wird, bedeutet natürlich nicht nur, was ohnehin klar ist, daß hier kein apodiktisch gewisses oder demonstrativ „erzwingbares" Fürwahrhalten vorliegt, sondern daß er auch nicht moralisch „geboten" bzw. selbst als eine allgemeingültige „Pflicht" verstanden werden kann. Denn „es kann gar keine Pflicht geben, die Existenz eines Dinges anzunehmen (weil dieses bloß den theoretischen Gebrauch der Vernunft angeht)"[49], und „ein Glaube, der geboten wird, ist ein Unding"[50]. Nur „ein freies Fürwahrhalten" ist zudem „als ein solches mit der Moralität des Subjekts vereinbar"[51] und hat „in moralisch praktischer Rücksicht auch an sich einen moralischen Wert"[52].

Die Freiheit bzw. Freigabe des moralischen Glaubens ist also in mehrfacher Hinsicht und Motivation praktisch notwendig. Zum einen stützt sich der moralische Glaube auf die Freiheits-Prinzipien und -Gesetze der Moral und ihre höchste Zweckbeziehung (die Beförderung des höchsten Gutes in der Welt); zum anderen aber ist der moralische Glaube mit seinen Postulaten keine direkte und zwingende Konsequenz aus dem moralischen Wissen, sondern nur als ein von solcher (epistemischen) Notwendigkeit freies und selbstbestimmtes Fürwahrhalten aus moralischer Gesinnung möglich; und schließlich besteht innerhalb der praktischen Nötigung, die Frage nach den Realisationsbedingungen der höchsten Zweckbestimmung des moralischen Willens stellen und beantworten zu müssen, auch noch der Freiheitsspielraum einer *Wahl, wie* sie zu beantworten sei, d. h. worein Glaube und Hoffnung auf Erfüllung des höchsten Gutes zu setzen seien. Denn „*die Art, wie* wir uns eine solche Harmonie der Naturgesetze mit denen der Freiheit denken sollen, hat etwas an sich, in Ansehung dessen uns eine Wahl zukommt"[53], nämlich zwischen den Möglichkeitsbedingungen: aus „allgemeinen Naturgesetzen, ohne einen der Natur vorstehenden weisen Urheber, oder nur unter dessen Voraussetzung"[54].

Angesichts dieser (metaphysischen) Alternative – in der allerdings die geschichtliche Praxis und die geschichtsphilosophische Dimension gar nicht in den Blick genommen werden, obwohl es doch um „die Beförderung des höchsten Gutes in der Welt" gehen soll – meint, vielmehr glaubt Kant selbst, daß aus dem „freien Interesse der praktischen Vernunft" die Entscheidung „für die Annahme eines weisen Welturhebers" zu fallen habe.[55]

β) Die Freiheits- und Entscheidungslage der objektiven Unbestimmtheit und der nur subjektiv möglichen, aber auch nötigen Selbst-Bestimmung des moralischen Glaubens kommt nun auch in seinem spezifischen Gewißheits- und Urteilmodus zum Ausdruck. Dabei verstärkt Kant den für alle Glaubensweisen charakteristischen Modus des nur subjektiv zureichenden Fürwahrhaltens für den moralischen Glauben derart, daß dessen Subjektivitätsbeziehung in der Subjektform einer geradezu existentiell unbedingten Weise alleiniger Selbstgewißheit des „ich bin gewiß, daß ..." hervortritt, obwohl sich doch das moralische Fürwahrhalten auf eine subjektiv stärkere (moralische) Gewißheits-Basis stützen und einen höheren Gewißheitsgrad erreichen kann als der pragmatische und der doktrinale Glaube.

„Das komplette Fürwahrhalten aus subjektiven Gründen, die in *praktischer Beziehung* so viel als objektive gelten, ist aber auch Überzeugung, nur nicht logische, sondern *praktische* (ich bin gewiß). Und diese praktische Überzeugung oder dieser *moralische Vernunftglaube* ist oft fester als alles Wissen. Beim Wissen hört man noch auf Gegengründe, aber beim Glauben nicht, weil es hierbei nicht auf objektive Gründe sondern auf das moralische Interesse des Subjekts ankommt."[56] Und sofern „die *moralische* Gewißheit [...] auf subjektiven Gründen (der moralischen Gesinnung) beruht, so muß ich nicht einmal sagen: *es ist* moralisch gewiß, daß ein Gott sei etc., sondern *ich bin* moralisch gewiß etc."[57]

γ) An diesen wesentlichen (existentiellen) Subjektivitätsbezug der moralischen Glaubensgewißheit schließt nun direkt die These an, daß sich diese nicht „mitteilen", d.h. in einer allgemeinen Weise an andere übermitteln lasse.

„Ich kann also nur sagen: Ich sehe mich durch meinen Zweck nach Gesetzen der Freiheit genötigt, ein höchstes Gut in der Welt als möglich anzusehen, aber *ich kann keinen anderen durch Gründe nötigen* (der Glaube ist *frei*)."[58] „Nur solche Gegenstände sind Sachen des Glaubens, bei denen das Fürwahrhalten notwendig frei, d. h. nicht durch objektive, von der Natur und dem Interesse des Subjekts unabhängige, Gründe der Wahrheit bestimmt ist. Das Glauben gibt daher auch wegen der bloß subjektiven Gründe keine Überzeugung, die sich mitteilen läßt und allgemein Beistimmung gebietet, wie die Überzeugung, die aus dem Wissen kommt. *Ich selbst* kann nur von der Gültigkeit und Unveränderlichkeit meines praktischen Glaubens gewiß sein".[59]

Diesen Aussagen über die „Nichtmitteilbarkeit" des existentiell zu vollziehenden moralischen Glaubens liegt nun allerdings ein sehr enger Begriff von (Wissens- bzw. Wahrheits-) Mitteilung zugrunde, nämlich das Muster einer direkten und zwingend überzeugenden Übermittlung von Erkenntnissen, die jedermann (qua Verstandes- und Vernunftwesen) als objektiv wahr und allgemeingültig gewiß anerkennen muß. Eine solche Art der Mitteilung ist aber nur bei einem Wissen möglich, das auf Grund seiner objektiven Begründung und Demonstrierbarkeit alle zur gleichen (apodiktischen oder empirischen) Gewißheit führen und zur „Beistimmung nötigen kann". Daß diese Form der Mitteilung zwar bestenfalls für das moralisch-praktische Wissen als Ausgangspunkt des moralischen Glaubens in Frage kommt, aber nicht für diesen selbst, ist klar, zumal wenn man die zugehörigen Momente der Wahl und Entscheidung bedenkt, die am wenigsten durch eine allgemeine und direkte Mitteilung erreicht und bestimmt werden können. Aber dies muß ja nun keineswegs bedeuten, daß es in der von Kant klar gesehenen – wenn auch natürlich nicht so genannten – existentiellen Dimension moralisch-metaphysischer Glaubensfragen und Annahmen keine sinnvoll mögliche Mitteilung, Kommunikation und Auseinandersetzung geben könne, ja müsse, zumal angesichts differenter Einstellungen und „ethisch-existentieller" Überzeugungen der anderen, die auch auf dieser Ebene zum „Prüfstein" der eigenen werden können und sollten, auch wenn es dabei nicht zu „Beistimmungen" und allgemeinen Übereinstimmungen kommt. Kierkegaard und Jaspers haben die Mitteilungsprobleme auf der ethisch-existentiellen Ebene reflektiert und durch Formen „indirekter Mitteilung" und eines an Freiheit „appellierenden", existenzerhellenden Denkens kommunikativ zu erschließen gesucht.

Bei Kant selbst hätte u. a. die Analogie zur Mitteilbarkeit des ebenfalls nur subjektiv notwendigen (ästhetischen) Geschmacksurteils die Verengung auflösen und in der Sache weiterführen können[60]; zumal das (moralische) Interesse am Glauben „für jedermann" gelten soll[61] und also auch subjektiv allgemein ansprechbar sein muß. Außerdem besagt eine Reflexion[62] zu Recht, daß es beim Glauben zwar keine „Beweise", wohl aber „Argumente" gebe. Kant bewegt sich denn auch denkend und argumentierend, also zumindest indirekt mitteilend, selbst auf der existentiellen Ebene des moralischen Glaubens; und dies nicht nur im Sinne einer formalen geltungslogischen Strukturanalyse, sondern auch, indem er für die metaphysischen Postulate des moralischen Glaubens seiner „Wahl" argumentativ plädiert, also selbst Partei ergreift und ist. Durch seine geltungs- und gewißheitstheoretische Bestimmung des moralischen Glaubens als eines existentiell-subjektiv motivierten freien (gewählten) Fürwahrhaltens hatte Kant selbst die existentielle Problemsituation aufgedeckt, die aber nicht nur eine existentiell-subjektive, sondern auch eine existentiell-intersubjektive Situierung bedeutet. Denn in ihr treten nun auch die existentiellen Gegenmöglichkeiten zum moralisch-metaphysischen Glauben bzw. zu dem von Kant für nötig befundenen und gewählten Vernunftglauben auf den Plan, die dem freien Fürwahrhalten der metaphysischen Postulate – ohne Abstriche an der Moralität – eine ethisch-existentiell motivierte „freie Ablehnung" entgegensetzen können und entgegensetzen.

Mit dieser intersubjektiv-existentiellen Problemsituation ethisch-existentieller Gegenmöglichkeiten und Gegenentwürfe zu dem von ihm selbst für nötig gehaltenen moralisch-metaphysischen Glauben hätte sich Kant, gerade auch im Blick auf das Mitteilungsproblem, ernsthaft auseinandersetzen müssen. Eine solche Auseinandersetzung und kritische Kommunikation mit den möglichen Gegenpositionen eines atheistisch-innerweltlichen und geschichtlich-praktischen Glaubens und Hoffens ist jedoch nicht bzw. nur in dürftiger und fragwürdiger Weise erfolgt. Kant erwähnt zwar die Gegenmöglichkeit des „moralischen Unglaubens" bzw. des „moralisch Ungläubigen", „welcher nicht dasjenige annimmt, was zu wissen zwar *unmöglich*, aber voraus zu setzen *moralisch notwendig* ist"[63]. Aber zum einen bezichtigt Kant den „Unglauben" der *Dogmatik*, sofern den Vernunftideen die Gültigkeit bestritten wird, „weil es ihnen an *theoretischer* Begründung ihrer Realität fehlt"[64], als ob dies der wesentliche, einzige oder auch nur der vorherrschende und naheliegendste Grund für den Unglauben hinsichtlich der metaphysischen Gegenstände (Gott und Unsterblichkeit) wäre oder sein könnte, da es hier ohnehin kein (positives oder negatives) Wissen gibt. Zum anderen suggeriert Kant, daß die Annahme, „es sei kein Gott", einer Selbst-„Überredung" entstamme[65] und also keine „Überzeugung" sei und sein könne. Und was er dann positiv gegen den „Zweifelglauben"[66] ins Feld führt, sind – abgesehen von den Argumenten zugunsten eines praktischen Fürwahrhaltens, die ja nicht wirklich überzeugungskräftig sein können – letztlich moralische Qualifikationen bzw. Diskreditierungen. Kant zeiht den „Ungläubigen" zwar nicht der Unmoralität, was nach seinen eigenen Prinzipien auch unmöglich wäre, aber doch des „Mangels an moralischem Interesse" und zureichender „moralischer Gesinnung"⁶⁷. „Je größer die moralische Gesinnung eines Menschen ist: desto fester und lebendiger wird auch sein Glaube sein an alles dasjenige, was er aus dem moralischen Interesse in praktisch notwendiger Absicht anzunehmen und voraus zu setzen sich genötiget fühlt."⁶⁸

So wird das kontroverse metaphysische Glaubensproblem in die Subjektivität der moralischen Gesinnung geschoben und in deren Homogenität mit dem Glauben aufgelöst, derzufolge es einen moralisch-metaphysischen Unglauben trotz oder gar aus moralischer Gesinnung nicht geben kann. Und wo Kant in die Nähe dieser Möglichkeit kommt, wie im Blick auf einen Atheisten, aber „rechtschaffenden Mann (wie etwa den Spinoza)"⁶⁹, da wird behauptet, daß dieser, trotz alles redlichen und uneigennützigen Bemühens, den letzten Zweck „als unmöglich aufgeben" oder sich zum Glauben bekehren müßte⁷⁰, als ob die „Beförderung des höchsten Gutes in der Welt" nicht primär eine innerweltliche (soziale) und geschichtlich-praktische Zweck-Verpflichtung wäre und bliebe, zumal wenn man eine erst jenseitige Erfüllung als illusionär und gegenstandslos ansieht und damit allerdings auch Kants Bestimmung des höchsten Gutes mit in Frage stellt.

Daß Kant die Auseinandersetzung mit der atheistischen bzw. innerweltlichen Gegenmöglichkeit eines ethischen Existenz- und Weltverständnisses im Grunde nicht vollzieht, hat seinen Grund letztlich jedoch nicht schon in der Auslegung des moralischen Glaubens, denn darin gibt es durchaus methodische Gegengründe gegen die angesonnene subjektive Allgemeinheit seiner „praktischen Notwendigkeit". Der eigentliche Grund liegt vielmehr in der metaphysischen Bedeutung, die dem reinen praktischen Vernunftglauben zukommt, angesichts des Unvermögens der theoretischen, spekulativen Vernunft, dem metaphysischen Interesse der Vernunft, ihren die Erfahrung transzendierenden Ideen objektive Realität zu sichern, Genüge zu tun.⁷¹

d) Diese besondere, ja einzigartige Funktion des moralischen Glaubens und seiner Postulate für die Möglichkeit einer „praktisch dogmatischen Metaphysik" markiert Kant sehr deutlich auch im Rahmen der strukturellen Differenzierung der den Weisen des Fürwahrhaltens je spezifisch zugehörigen Gegenstands- oder Sachbereiche. Im § 91 der *Kritik der Urteilskraft* heißt es zunächst zur grundsätzlichen Differenzierung: „*Erkennbare Dinge* sind nun von dreifacher Art: *Sachen der Meinung* (opinabile), *Tatsachen* (scibile), und *Glaubenssachen* (mere credibile)"[72].

Entgegen unserem Sprachgebrauch, demgemäß sich das *Meinen* gerade auch auf theoretisch nicht entscheidbare spekulative Fragen und nicht beweisbare Annahmen über metaphysische „Gegenstände" erstrecken kann, lehnt Kant eine solche extensive und im Prinzip auf alle möglichen ungewissen Fragen oder Sachen beziehbare Auffassung des Ausdrucks ab. Für Kant ist vielmehr das Meinen als der bewußte Modus des objektiv und subjektiv unzureichenden, vorläufigen Fürwahrhaltens strikt auf den Gegenstandsbereich einer im Prinzip – wenn auch nicht aktuell faktisch – „möglichen Erfahrung" und empirischen Erkenntnis bezogen und begrenzt.

> „Das bloße Meinen [...] [findet] lediglich in empirischen Erkenntnissen" statt, aber nicht „in Wissenschaften, welche Erkenntnisse a priori enthalten; also weder in der Mathematik, noch in der Metaphysik, noch in der Moral"; hier „gilt es: *entweder zu wissen oder nicht zu wissen*"[73].

So kann man denn auch mit Bezug auf

> „Gegenstände der bloßen Vernunftideen, die für das theoretische Erkenntnis gar nicht in irgendeiner möglichen Erfahrung dargestellt werden können [...] nicht einmal *meinen*".[74]
> „*Meinungssachen* sind jederzeit Objekte einer wenigstens an sich möglichen Erfahrungserkenntnis (Gegenstände der Sinnenwelt), die aber, nach dem bloßen Grade dieses Vermögens, den wir besitzen, *für uns* unmöglich ist (wie der Äther der neueren Physiker oder die Frage, ob ‚vernünftige Bewohner anderer Planeten anzunehmen' sind)."[75]

Der Gegenstandsbereich des *Wissens* wird durch den Bezug auf Tatsachen als Sachgehalte eines allgemeingültig und gegenständlich ausweisbaren Wissens definiert. Diese (nicht unproblematische) Bestimmung soll zwar durch Erweiterung des Begriffs der Tatsache von „wirklicher" auch auf bloß mögliche Erfahrung[76] der Reduktion auf bloßes empirisches Tatsachenwissen entzogen werden und die rationale Erkenntnisart mit umfassen, sie bleibt aber doch grundsätzlich auf gegenständliche Erkenntnis bzw. ein gegenständlich ausweisbares Wissen bezogen und eingeschränkt. Denn Tatsachen (res facti) sind

„Gegenstände für Begriffe, deren objektive Realität (es sei durch reine Vernunft, oder durch Erfahrung, und, im ersteren Fall aus theoretischen oder praktischen Datis derselben, in allen Fällen aber vermittels einer ihnen korrespondierenden Anschauung) bewiesen werden kann"[77].

Ein solcher Begriff gegenstandsbezogenen Tatsachen-Wissens wirft (trotz des programmatischen Einschlusses der rationalen Erkenntnis) u. a. das Problem auf, ob und wie in ihn auch das transzendentale Reflexions- bzw. Rekonstruktionswissen der apriorischen Bedingungen möglicher Gegenstandserkenntnis angemessen zu integrieren sei. Diese Frage, die in die weiterreichende Problematik der methodischen Selbstreflexion der Transzendentalphilosophie führt, muß und kann hier dahingestellt bleiben. Kant-immanent unstrittig ist indessen, daß mit der gegebenen Bestimmung des Wissens (in der Konsequenz der „Kritik der reinen Vernunft") die (metaphysischen) Gegenstände der Vernunftideen – bis auf den „merkwürdigen Fall" der Freiheitsidee[78] – als für die theoretische Vernunft „überschwenglich" aus dem Gegenstandsbereich des (rationalen) Tatsachen-Wissens ausgeschlossen sind und bleiben.

Und eben diese metaphysische Sphäre der Vernunftideen (Gott, Unsterblichkeit) und die Frage ihrer objektiven Realität macht nun den eigentlichen Bereich der *Glaubenssachen* (eines reinen praktischen Vernunftglaubens und seiner Postulate) aus.

„Nur Gegenstände der reinen Vernunft können allenfalls Glaubenssachen sein, aber nicht als Gegenstände der bloßen reinen spekulativen Vernunft."[79] „Gegenstände, die in Beziehung auf den pflichtmäßigen Gebrauch der reinen praktischen Vernunft (sei es als Folgen, oder als Gründe) a priori gedacht werden müssen, aber für den theoretischen Gebrauch derselben überschwenglich sind, sind bloße *Glaubenssachen*."[80]

Daß jene Vernunftideen, „denen man die objektive Realität theoretisch nicht sichern kann"[81], nur als praktisch notwendige Postulate des moralischen Glaubens eine Sicherung erfahren können, bedeutet natürlich auch, daß diese strikt unter den Bedingungen der Gewißheitsmodalität des Glaubens, d. h. als ein subjektiv zureichendes und gewisses „Fürwahrhalten in reiner praktischer Absicht, [...] das nichts für das theoretische [...] reine Vernunfterkenntnis beweiset"[82], stehen und gehalten werden müssen. Denn das Glauben

> „bezieht sich auf Gegenstände, in Ansehung deren man nicht allein nichts wissen, sondern auch nichts meinen, ja auch nicht einmal Wahrscheinlichkeit vorwenden, sondern bloß gewiß sein kann, daß es nicht widersprechend ist, sich dergleichen Gegenstände so zu denken, wie man sie sich denkt. Das übrige hierbei ist ein *freies* Fürwahrhalten [...] dessen, was ich aus moralischen Gründen annehme"[83]. „Auf solche Weise bleibt uns, nach Vereitelung aller ehrsüchtigen Absichten einer über die Grenzen aller Erfahrung hinaus herumschweifenden Vernunft, noch genug übrig, daß wir damit in praktischer Absicht zufrieden zu sein Ursache haben."[84]

Damit ist wohl hinreichend belegt und durch (z. T. kritische) Interpretation verdeutlicht worden, welche systematische und methodischkritische Bedeutung dem moralischen Vernunftglauben für das nach Kant auch innerhalb der kritischen Philosophie unabweisliche metaphysische Venunftinteresse und seine allein noch moralisch-praktisch mögliche Einlösung zukommt. Da die Möglichkeit einer „praktisch-dogmatischen Metaphysik" auf dem Boden der kritischen Philosophie aber streng an die geltungslogische Eingrenzung ihrer Annahmen als praktisch-notwendiger Glaubens-Postulate gebunden ist, und die Geltungs- und Gewißheitsart von Glaubens-Annahmen nur im Rahmen einer differentiellen Bestimmung der möglichen Modi des Fürwahrhaltens spezifisch bestimmt werden kann, ist auch die Wichtigkeit dieser geltungstheoretischen Reflexion für eine zentrale Problematik der Kantischen Philosophie erwiesen. Daß ihre Bedeutung noch weiter reicht und das methodisch-systematische Ganze der kritischen Philosophie durchdringt, soll zusammen mit einigen kritischen Überlegungen zum Abschluß der Kant-Interpretation wenigstens noch angedeutet werden.

3. Zur methodisch-systematischen Bedeutung von Kants Differenzierung der Gewißheitsarten für die kritische Philosophie

a) Die Bedeutung der geltungslogischen Strukturierung der Weisen des Fürwahrhaltens für das methodisch-systematische Ganze der Kantischen Philosophie kann im Zusammenhang mit dem bisher Erörterten in drei Hinsichten ergänzt werden:

α) im Hinblick auf ihre Stellung im „Kanon der reinen Vernunft"; β) mit Bezug auf die Abgrenzung des „Kritizismus" von „Dogmatismus" und „Skeptizismus"; und γ) für die Erfüllung des höchsten Begriffs der Philosophie in ihrer „weltbürgerlichen Bedeutung" und die dafür maßgebenden Grundfragen.

α) Die Differenzierung der Modi des Fürwahrhaltens (Meinen, Wissen, Glauben) wird in der „transzendentalen Methodenlehre" der *Kritik der reinen Vernunft* im Rahmen des „Kanons der reinen Vernunft" eingeführt und abgehandelt. Der „Kanon" „soll die Grundsätze a priori des richtigen Gebrauchs gewisser Erkenntnisvermögen überhaupt"[85], hier also der reinen Vernunft, klären und festlegen. Nachdem die Kritik als „Disziplin", d. h. Selbstdisziplinierung der reinen Vernunft den theoretischen Vernunftgebrauch in spekulativer Absicht als haltlos dialektisch und kognitiv nichtig erwiesen und entsprechend diszipliniert hat, kann ein richtiger, d. h. der „Endabsicht" der reinen Vernunft angemessener und rechtfertigungsfähiger Vernunftgebrauch hinsichtlich der Annahmen über die Realität der Vernunftideen nur noch auf dem Boden des reinen praktischen Vernunftgebrauchs (und seiner Glaubenspostulate) gefunden und vollzogen werden. Zu dessen Kanon und Grundsätzen aber gehört wesentlich die Klärung der prinzipiell möglichen Gewißheitsmodi des Fürwahrhaltens und die erst in ihrem Rahmen mögliche und nötige geltungslogische Abgrenzung und Rechtfertigung des Vernunftglaubens gegenüber Wissen und Meinen.

β) Die von Kant gegen „Dogmatismus" und „Skeptizismus" aufgerichtete Position des „Kritizismus", die von ihm als drittes und letztes Stadium in der Entwicklungslogik der Philosophie reklamiert wird[86], ist methodisch durch eine vorgängige kritische Prüfung der Möglichkeiten und Grenzen des Erkenntnis- und Vernunftvermögens definiert, die wesentlich auch die geltungslogische Bestimmung der Modi des Erkennens und Fürwahrhaltens einschließt. Demgegenüber beruht der *Dogmatismus* der traditionellen Metaphysik und ihres Anspruchs einer theoretisch-spekulativen Erkenntnis des Übersinnlichen auf einem ungeprüften, naiven Zutrauen in die höchste Erkenntnis- und Wissensfähigkeit der Vernunft; während der *Skeptizismus* zwar die nötigen Zweifel in Gang bringt – und von Kant auch als Vorstadium und in der Form „skeptischer Methode" als eigenes Element des Kritizismus verstanden wird[87] –, aber seinerseits den Zweifel zur Negation oder Infragestellung der Erkenntnis- und Wissensmöglichkeit überhaupt hypostasiert, weil er es methodisch versäumt, die Wahrheitsansprüche, Geltungsmodi und Gewißheitsarten möglicher Erkenntnis geltungslogisch zu differenzieren und entsprechend differentiell zu bewerten. Dies leistet erst der erkenntnis- und geltungskritisch reflektierte Kritizismus, wodurch er die Überwindung von Dogmatismus und Skeptizismus vollzieht.[88]

γ) Die höchste Sinnbestimmung der Philosophie nach ihrem „Weltbegriff" bzw. ihrer „weltbürgerlichen Bedeutung" artikuliert Kant in Grundfragen, die – im Unterschied zu „schulphilosophischen" Problemstellungen – „jedermann interessieren müssen"[89], nämlich: Was kann ich wissen, was soll ich tun, was darf ich hoffen?[90]; und in der *Logik* um die integrierende Frage ergänzt: Was ist der Mensch[91], im Sinne seiner „Bestimmung"[92]? Das Verständnis des Sinnes dieser Fragen und der auf sie möglichen Antworten erschließt sich erst im Rahmen der Modi des Fürwahrhaltens. Das ist offensichtlich für die ersten beiden Fragen, deren erste auf theoretisches Wissen zielt und deren zweite praktisches Wissen impliziert, und es ergibt sich für die dritte aufgrund des wesentlichen Zusammenhangs von Hoffen und Glauben und für die vierte im Blick auf ihren integrativen Status.[93] Die Verflechtung von Hoffen und Glauben wird von Kant in der *Kritik der reinen Vernunft* zwar nicht eigens erörtert, sie ist aber strukturell offenkundig.[94] Die „zugleich theoretische und praktische" Frage des Hoffens[95] zeigt, zumal im Blick auf die Kantische Geschichtsphilosophie, daß das Hoffen in engerem Kontakt zur geschichtlichen Praxis steht und einen stärker innerweltlich bezogenen Glauben impliziert, der ein gewisses praktisches Korrektiv zur Dominanz des moralisch-metaphysischen Glaubens abgeben könnte. (Hier schließt Blochs Philosophie der Hoffnung an.)

b) Der systematisch zentrale Problempunkt der dargestellten Position Kants liegt, wie bereits angedeutet, in der möglichen Konfliktspannung, die aus der methodischen Funktion der erkenntnis- und geltungskritischen Reflexion für die Klärung, Ermöglichung und Rechtfertigung einer praktischen Metaphysik des Vernunftglaubens als Erfüllung des metaphysischen Interesses der Vernunft erwächst. Dieser funktionale Zusammenhang führt leicht zu Konflikten und Inkonsequenzen zwischen dem festgestellten Geltungsmodus des moralischen Glaubens und einer darüber hinausführenden Aufwertung im metaphysischen Interesse. Eine wesentliche Voraussetzung für die Problematik ist Kants Annahme eines unausweichlichen „Bedürfnisses", ja einer „nicht zu dämpfenden Begierde" der Vernunft[96], die „von einem Hang ihrer Natur getrieben" werde[97], die Grenzen der Erfahrung ins Feld des Übersinnlichen zu überschreiten, um darin den notwendigen Vernunftideen (Gott, Freiheit, Unsterblichkeit) Realitätsgehalt zu verschaffen und so die Endabsicht der Vernunft zu erfüllen, was freilich nur noch auf dem Wege der reinen praktischen Vernunft möglich ist.[98] Sofern nun das metaphysische Bedürfnis und Interesse zu einer allgemeinen strukturlogischen Notwendigkeit der Vernunft erklärt wird, die letztlich auch dem Vernunftglauben voraus- und zugrundeliegt (ohne freilich dessen Realitätsannahmen dadurch begründen zu können), kann der moralisch-metaphysische Glaube ebenfalls das Ansehen bzw. den Anschein eines subjektiv-allgemeinen Geltungsanspruchs und d. h. einer für jedes moralische Subjekt (Person) verbindlichen und subjektiv notwendigen Gültigkeit gewinnen.

Das aber gerät in Widerspruch oder zumindest in Konflikt mit dem von Kant selbst herausgestellten Geltungsmodus des nur subjektiv, besser: individuell gewissen und existentiell motivierten moralisch-metaphysischen Glaubens, der maßgebend und kritisch begrenzend bleiben muß gegen alle aus metaphysischem Interesse überziehenden, „überschwenglichen" Interpretationen. Dies um so mehr, als Kant auch das praktisch metaphysische Bedürfnis der Vernunft nur als „subjektiven Grund" gelten läßt, „etwas vorauszusetzen und anzunehmen, was sie (die Vernunft) durch objektive Gründe zu wissen sich nicht anmaßen darf"[99], und er nicht nur von den Begriffen des Zwecks und Endzwecks, sondern auch von den Vernunftideen sagt, das wir sie uns jederzeit (a priori) „selbst gemacht" und nicht von irgendwelchen idealen Objekten entlehnt haben.[100]

Wird dagegen der Geltungsmodus des moralisch-metaphysischen Glaubens strikt eingehalten, dann erscheint er als eine (ethisch-)existentiell motivierte Möglichkeit des Existenz- und Weltverständnisses neben anderen (also auch der atheistisch bzw. innerweltlich sich verstehenden Gegenmöglichkeit), die sich Möglichkeit, Sinnmotivation und subjektive Berechtigung ihrer differenten Einstellungen, Lebensdeutungen und Wertüberzeugungen wechselseitig zuerkennen können und müßten. Durch die erkenntnis-anthropologisch einzig angemessene Zurückführung und Relativierung der differenten Möglichkeiten des Seins- und Selbstverständnisses in die subjektiv-existentielle Dimension – die weder die existentielle „Unbedingtheit" (Jaspers) noch gar die Allgemeinverbindlichkeit moralischer Verpflichtung aufhebt – würde auch erst die Ebene erreicht, auf der die mögliche und nötige Auseinandersetzung über die ethisch-existentiellen Differenzen geführt werden kann. Darin geht es weder um objektiv entscheidbare Wissensfragen noch um letztlich beliebige und gleichgültige Meinungen, sondern um Differenzen und Gegensätze zwischen Anschauungen, Wertungen, Glaubens-Überzeugungen, die für ein jeweils individuelles Existenzverständnis und -verhältnis maßgebend und tragend sind. Die hier erforderliche existentiell-kritische Kommunikation kann im Horizont wechselseitigen Motivationverstehens zu Infragestellungen, Selbstprüfungen, Modifikationen oder auch Bestärkungen der jeweiligen Einstellungen und Differenzen führen.

Auf dieser Ebene nicht demonstrativer, sondern explikativer Mitteilung und Diskussion hätte jedoch der aus seiner als subjektiv notwendig deklarierten Gesinnungsevidenz herausgesetzte moralisch-metaphysische Glaube (Kants) keine Prärogative gegenüber einem atheistischen und innerweltlichen, aber gleichwohl ethischen

Selbstverständnis individueller und gesellschaftlicher Praxis – aber natürlich auch nicht umgekehrt. Beide wären gleichermaßen genötigt, argumentativ zu explizieren, was für ihr Verständnis spricht, und hätten sich dem zu stellen, was gegen es vorgebracht wird, und ihre Überzeugungskraft der Kommunikation und Auseinandersetzung zu überlassen.

III
Zur gegenwärtigen Relevanz der Kantischen Differenzierung der Gewißheitsmodi – besonders im Blick auf Karl Jaspers und Dieter Henrich

1. Die Erörterung der Frage nach der gegenwärtigen Relevanz der Kantischen Lehre von den Weisen des Fürwahrhaltens müßte eigentlich mit Explikationen zur Problemgeschichte der thematisch entsprechenden Reflexionen, zumal der nachkantischen, eingeleitet oder zumindest verbunden werden. Das ist aber hier nicht möglich. Schon die „Vorgeschichte" seit Platon und Aristoteles über Skepsis, Stoa, Augustinus, Thomas, Duns Scotus und die Angelpunkte zur Neuzeit (Cusanus, Descartes, Pascal) bis hin zum Rationalismus (Leibniz, Wolff) und Empirismus (Locke, Hume), bzw. Dogmatismus und Skeptizismus vor Kant ist höchst komplex.

Noch vielschichtiger ist die Problemgeschichte seit Kant, die nur zum Teil auch eine Wirkungsgeschichte der Kantischen Reflexionen ist, wie etwa auf der Linie über Jacobi, Fichte, Hegels Kritik, Fries bis hin zum Neukantianismus und, besonders nahe, Jaspers mit seiner Theorie der „Gewißheitsarten" (cf. u.). Daneben verlaufen andere Linien: von Peirce aus innerhalb und im Umkreis des Pragmatismus, der „Wahrheitstheorie" von Habermas[101], mit der allerdings eher sekundären Rolle von „Gewißheitserlebnissen" (Verstehen, Wissen, Überzeugung, Glauben); dann im Rahmen der Gegenstandstheorie von Meinong, der Phänomenologie und ihrer Evidenzthematik (Brentano, Husserl u. a.), der Unterscheidung von „Wissensformen" in der Wissenssoziologie (Scheler); und schließlich in der analytischen Philosophie durch Russell, Wittgenstein („Über Gewißheit"), die Knowledge-Belief-Diskussion und die Ausbildung einer „epistemischen Logik" (seit Hintikka u. a.) und Wahrscheinlichkeitstheorie.

Diese nur selektiv bezeichnete Reflexionsgeschichte erbringt für die Relevanz-Beurteilung der Kantischen Theorie zweierlei. Zum einen gibt sie schon aufgrund ihrer eigenen Vielfältigkeit Anlaß, Einzelbestimmungen, Abgrenzungen, Differenziertheit und Umfang der Kantischen Lehre von den Modi des Fürwahrhaltens zu überprüfen und gegebenenfalls zu korrigieren. Kritische Fragen und korrektive Interpretationen liegen nahe etwa schon hinsichtlich einer Erweiterung des Begriffs des „Meinens", dann der Bestimmung bzw. Klärung des apriorischen und transzendentalen Wissens und der Ablehnung einer logischen Theorie der Wahrscheinlichkeit[102]; aber auch im Bedeutungs- und Funktionsbereich des Glaubensbegriffs gegenüber dessen fast ausschließlicher Besetzung durch den moralisch-metaphysischen Glauben unter weitgehender thematischer Ausschaltung nicht nur des pragmatischen, sondern vor allem auch eines geschichtlich-praktischen Glaubens (und Hoffens) sowie einer Erweiterung auf mögliche weitere existentielle Glaubensmotive und -bezüge (Jaspers). Naheliegend ist auch, neben dem Problem der Zuordnung des ästhetischen Urteils weitere Differenzierungen in dem von Kant aufgespannten Rahmen zwischen (rationalem und empirischem) objektivem Wissen und dem moralisch subjektiv gewissen Glauben zu erwägen und anzubringen, wie etwa: ideelle oder ethische, normative „Überzeugungen" (Jaspers, Habermas), Existenz- und Seins-„Vergewisserung" (Jaspers), Weisen der „Einsicht" oder verstehbarer Welt- und Lebens-„Deutung" (Henrich), die sich alle nicht einfach der Kantischen Auffassung von Wissen oder Glauben einordnen lassen.

Zum anderen und vor allem aber bietet die Problemgeschichte eine gerade aufgrund der verschiedenartigen Ansatzpunkte prinzipiell gewichtige Bestätigung und Bestärkung der Kantischen Problemstellung, d. h. der Notwendigkeit geltungs- und gewißheitstheoretischer Reflexion, wie auch ihrer Anlage und Grundgliederung für eine methodisch-kritisch reflektierte Philosophie. Elemente dieser Art von Reflexion haben zwar das philosophische Denken von Anfang an begleitet, aber sie sind doch nur selten in ihrer grundsätzlichen

Bedeutung und kritischen Konsequenz erfaßt und zur Geltung gebracht worden. Durch die kritische Philosophie Kants und seit ihr ist diese Reflexion jedoch methodisch-systematisch unausweichlich geworden und dies insbesondere und verschärft für eine Philosophie, die nach Kant und in Zeiten eines zumindest weitgehend „nachmetaphysischen Denkens" (Habermas) weiterhin als Metaphysik (nicht nur in „transzendentaler", sondern „transzendenter" Beziehung) meint auftreten zu können und zu müssen.

2. Fragt man nun, wo innerhalb der Philosophie des 20. Jahrhunderts die methodisch-systematische Relevanz der Gewißheitsreflexion Kants am deutlichsten vergegenwärtigt wurde, so ist in erster Linie, ja in gewisser Weise als einziger, *Karl Jaspers* zu nennen. Schon der methodisch-systematische Rahmen und Aufbau der materialen *Philosophie* von Jaspers[103] zeigt die grundlegende Kantische Prägung: mit der „philosophischen Weltorientierung" (bezogen auf die Bedingungen und Grenzen „zwingenden" Wissens von der Erfahrungs- und Erscheinungswelt), der das gegenständliche Wissen transzendierenden „Existenzerhellung" (als Vergewisserung der Existenz-, d. h. Freiheitsmöglichkeit des Menschen, freilich nicht nur gebunden an Moralität) und schließlich, vom „Boden" existentiellen Freiheitsbewußtseins aus, der „Metaphysik" (als der Glaubens-Vergewisserung der „Transzendenz" des eigentlichen umgreifenden Seins selbst, nicht nur im Sinne einer praktischen, sondern in Chiffren auch „spekulativen" Metaphysik). Sodann hat Jaspers im Zuge seiner Erweiterung der Philosophie zu der von *Vernunft und Existenz*[104] in seinem zweiten philosophischen Hauptwerk *Von der Wahrheit*[105] mit dem Entwurf der „transzendentalen Erhellungen" eines formal-strukturellen „philosophischen Grundwissens" der Seins-, Erkenntnis-, und Wahrheitsweisen eine neue Form von Transzendentalphilosophie entwickelt und der anfänglich beherrschenden Dualität von wissenschaftlichem Wissen und philosophischem Glauben ein transzendentalphilosophisches Wissen strukturell vorausgesetzt und zugrunde gelegt.[106]

Zur Strukturierung und methodisch-kritischen Funktion des (transzendental-logischen) Grundwissens der Vernunft gehört nun wesentlich eine Differenzierung der Wahrheits-, Geltungs- und Kommunikationsweisen, sowie der „Gewißheitsarten". Jaspers gliedert die Gewißheitsarten in *„Klarheit"* (des intentionalen Meinens und des Präsenthabens der Sache), *„zwingende Gewißheit"* (allgemeingültigen, beweisbaren Wissens empirisch wissenschaftlicher, mathematisch-logischer und kategorialer Art), ideelle *„Überzeugung"* (von geschichtlich-kulturell allgemeinverbindlichen Ideen des Geistes, Normen, Gestaltungen) und den existentiell-individuell unbedingten *„Glauben"*, in dem die das Selbstseinkönnen der Existenz tragenden Sinn- und Wahrheitsgehalte und letztlich der Transzendenz als des umfassenden Seinsgrundes vergewissert werden.[107]

Es ist offensichtlich, daß sich diese Differenzierung der Gewißheitsarten weitgehend von Kant herschreibt, auch wenn Jaspers das nicht direkt erwähnt und Unterschiede bestehen, die verschieden zu bewerten sind. So setzt Jaspers nicht beim Fürwahrhalten an und nimmt das Meinen nicht auf, während „Klarheit" zwar Medium und Bedingung von Gewißheit, aber keine eigene Gewißheitsart ist, und Kant recht hatte, sie nicht zu den Gewißheitsmodalitäten zu zählen (s. o.). Dagegen sind „zwingende Gewißheit" bzw. „Wissen", „Überzeugung" und „Glaube" genuine Gewißheitsarten, und es ist sinnvoll, daß Jaspers, gegenüber Kant, „Überzeugung" nicht nur im Sinne von „von etwas überzeugt sein" als Gewißheit und subjektive Vertretung von Wahrheit faßt, sondern als eigene Gewißheitsart, der nach Gehalt und Art der Gewißheit ein eigener Status zwischen Wissen und Glauben zukommt. Denn während die „zwingende Gewißheit" des (erfahrungswissenschaftlichen und logisch-analytischen) „Wissens" durch die Allgemeingültigkeit beweisfähiger Aussagen und die notwendige Anerkennung ihrer „zwingenden Richtigkeit" charakterisiert ist, gründet sich die Selbstgewißheit ideeller und normativer „Überzeugung" auf eine historisch-kulturell vermittelte, „allgemeinverbindliche" Gültigkeit und ist dadurch vom allgemeingültig zwingenden Wissen (in dessen Bereich auch die allgemeingültige Gesetzlichkeit des moralischen Sollens gehört) unterschieden, aber auch von der wesentlich dem Selbstseinkönnen des Einzelnen zugehörigen und entspringenden „Unbedingtheit" existentiell-transzendierenden „Glaubens" und seiner für das je eigene, individuelle Existenzverständnis unverzichtbaren, weil sinngebenden Gehalte.

Die Differenzen der Geltungs- und Gewißheitsarten, die sich natürlich auch in Unterschieden der jeweils entsprechend möglichen und nötigen Mitteilungs- und Kommunikationsweisen auswirken, bedeuten aber keine gegenseitige Isolierung und Trennung. Es bestehen vielmehr zwischen den verschiedenen Gewißheitsarten und ihren spezifischen Wahrheitsbezügen Bedingungszusammenhänge und Abhängigkeitsverhältnisse im und für das Ganze des „umgreifenden Seins, das wir selbst sind", als: Dasein/Leben – Bewußtsein überhaupt/Verstand – Geist – Existenz. Diese Bezüge aufzuzeigen und zur Geltung zu bringen, ohne die aufgewiesenen Differenzen zu verwischen oder gar aufzuheben, ist die Aufgabe und Leistung des „Orientierungswissens" der Vernunft und einer Philosophie der Vernunft und Existenz.[108] Das gilt auch und gerade für die für „Existenzerhellung" und „Metaphysik" zentrale geltungstheoretische Differenz von Glauben und Wissen. „Der philosophische Glaube, der Glaube des denkenden Menschen, hat jederzeit das Merkmal, daß er nur im Bunde mit dem Wissen ist. Er will wissen, was wißbar ist, und sich selbst durchschauen."[109]

Wie für Kant steht auch für Jaspers unter den Gewißheitsarten der (philosophische) Glaube, den er verschiedentlich auch Vernunftglauben nennt, im Mittelpunkt des existentiellen und philosophischen Interesses, zumal mit ihm die von der Erhellung der Existenz- und Freiheitserfahrung ausgehende Möglichkeit der Metaphysik verbunden ist. Die Erhellung der Existenzmöglichkeit, d. h. des freien Selbstseinkönnens des Menschen im Dasein und die glaubende Vergewisserung von deren alles Weltdasein transzendierender Unbedingtheit und ihres Grund-Bezuges zur Transzendenz bewegt sich allerdings in einem strukturell differenzierteren, existentiell konkreteren und spekulativ weiteren Horizont als Kants Metaphysik des moralisch-praktischen Vernunftglaubens. Und so geht denn auch die „Metaphysik" von Jaspers[110] thematisch über das hinaus, was in Kants Perspektive der „praktisch dogmatischen Metaphysik" noch möglich und sinnvoll hätte sein können. Andererseits reduziert Jaspers die theoretisch-kognitiven Ansprüche seines metaphysischen Denkens eher noch weiter als Kant die seiner Postulatenlehre. Denn nach Jaspers ist von der Transzendenz als dem allumgreifenden und grundgebenden Sein selbst aus den Erfahrungen der letztlich nicht aus sich selbst seienden und vollendbaren Existenz und der Ungeschlossenheit und Bodenlosigkeit der Welt nur in Chiffren und Symbolen zu sprechen, die für die je eigene existentielle Vergewisserung „in der Schwebe" bleiben und schlechterdings zu keinem objektiven und allgemeingültig verfügbaren Wissen führen.

Parallelen und Konvergenzen zwischen Jaspers und Kant zeigen sich auch im Blick auf besondere Probleme und problematische Züge ihrer Positionen. α) Auch bei Jaspers ergeben sich Schwierigkeiten, das (transzendental-)„philosophische Grundwissen" dem primär gegenstandsbezogenen Begriff des Wissens und seiner „zwingenden" Gewißheit zu integrieren bzw. es als eigene Wissensart zu fassen. Denn das transzendental rekonstruktive und strukturelle Grundwissen ist weder „gegenständlich" noch zwingend, obwohl im (wissenschaftsanalogen) Anspruch und Sinn allgemeingültig.[111] Dieser Entwurf eines philosophischen Grundwissens stellt m. E., neben der „Existenzerhellung", die bedeutsamste und für die Gegenwart wichtigste Leistung der Philsophie von Jaspers dar. β) Bei Jaspers und Kant wird das Metaphysikproblem in einem gewissen Maße strukturell vorentschieden: bei Kant über die Lehre von den Vernunftideen und das metaphysische Bedürfnis der Vernunft, bei Jaspers formal durch die quasi-ontologische („periechontologische") Bestimmung der „Transzendenz" als der das Umgreifendsein von Mensch und Welt noch umfassenden Grunddimension des Seins selbst und durch die ungedeckte Behauptung einer wesenhaften Beziehung von Existenz und Transzendenz (und damit von „Existenzerhellung" und „Metaphysik"). Und γ) (mit β) eng zusammenhängend): Auch Jaspers überzieht – und zwar erheblich stärker als Kant den moralisch subjektiven Glauben – die existentielle Glaubensgewißheit, sofern in ihr die Transzendenz sogar als Grund der Freiheit erfahren werden soll und Existenz (d.h. Freiheit) nur mit und durch Transzendenz ist und ohne sie nichtig wäre[112]; was von Kant aus über die moralisch-autonom begründete Freiheit niemals gesagt werden könnte. So ist es denn nicht verwunderlich, daß auch Jaspers, obwohl er den Transzendenz-Glauben als existentielle Möglichkeit faßt, ein atheistisches bzw. in „immanenter Transzendenz" sich haltendes (und also in seinem Sinne transzendenz- und glaubensloses), humanistisch-ethisches Existenzverständnis nicht als gleichrangige existentielle Möglichkeit anerkennen kann oder will, sondern sie als „nihilistisch" zerstörerisch zu diskreditieren sucht.

Was aber Jaspers mit Kant vereint und ihren Positionen über Differenzen und problematische Züge hinweg ihre gegenwärtige Bedeutung sichert, ist die grundsätzliche Erkenntnis, daß Philosophie, zumal wenn sie sich eine Transzendenz-Metaphysik als Aufgabe vorsetzt, der Forderung strenger erkenntnis- und geltungskritischer Reflexion zu genügen hat, um die in diesem Bezugsfeld überhaupt möglichen Weisen von Vergewisserung und Überzeugung nach ihrem Geltungs-, Gewißheits- und Kommunikationsmodus zu klären, zu bestimmen und gegenüber anderen, allgemeingültig wahrheitsfähigen Erkenntnis- und Wissensansprüchen abzugrenzen.[113]

3. Diese von Kant und Jaspers erhobene und erfüllte methodisch-kritische Forderung bleibt auch für ein spekulatives metaphysisches Denken gültig, das sich in einer von Kant und Jaspers unterschiedenen Argumentationsform, Darstellungsweise und Systematik vollzieht. Denn sie besteht notwendig für ein Denken, das kritisch zu sein beansprucht und gleichwohl die Welt- und Selbsterfahrung des Menschen auf einen transzendenten Grund und eine All-Einheit zu überschreiten sucht, also auch für *Dieter Henrichs* spekulatives Denken.

Nun ist Henrichs spekulatives metaphysisches Philosophieren mit der für es beanspruchten Verbindung von „Kritik und Integration"[114] gewiß ohne die kritische Philosophie Kants nicht zu denken, und es steht dadurch und durch einige weitere Züge auch in mancher Parallele zu Jaspers. Aber es ist natürlich, wie auch das von Jaspers, aus den Kant-Bezügen nicht schon hinreichend zu verstehen. Denn das alle drei verbindende metaphysische bzw. spekulative Interesse wird doch thematisch, systematisch und methodisch in jeweils unterschiedlicher Weise ausgelegt, angesetzt und durchgeführt. Der für Kant allein noch mögliche moralisch-praktische Weg zu einer Metaphysik des Vernunftglaubens wird weder von Jaspers noch von Henrich als der einzige anerkannt und beschritten. Beide bewegen sich vielmehr auch auf nach Kant ausweglosen spekulativen Pfaden, wenngleich auf unterschiedliche Art und mit spezifisch bestimmten (Henrich) oder explizit aufgehobenen Wissens-Ansprüchen (Jaspers).

Auch die Ausgangs- und Rückbindung metaphysischer Gedanken und Vergewisserungen an Grundgegebenheiten und -möglichkeiten der menschlichen Existenz ist zwar prinzipiell allen gemeinsam, aber die näheren Bestimmungen und konkreten Ansatzpunkte differieren. Denn während Kant von der grundlegenden moralischen Selbsterfahrung der Freiheit ausgeht, ist für Jaspers eine demgegenüber erweiterte und konkretisierte Erhellung existentieller Freiheitsmöglichkeit des Selbstseinkönnens im Dasein (in Grenzsituationen, unbedingtem Handeln, absolutem Bewußtsein, Kommunikation) der Angelpunkt für die Vergewisserung der Grund- und Glaubensbezüge zur Transzendenz, und für Henrich das „bewußte Leben", in dessen „Grundverhältnis" zur Welt „Selbstverhältnis" und „Selbstbewußtsein" zentrale, aber strukturell und begrifflich schwer faßliche Grundbestimmungen sind, deren philosophische Aufklärung im Sinne einer „Selbstverständigung des bewußten Lebens" nur aus einem „Grundverstehen" möglich wird, das spekulativ auf das Unbedingte, grund- und einheitgebende Absolute im Ganzen der Wirklichkeit ausgreifen muß.[115]

Vor allem aber unterscheiden sich Art und Form, in der das spekulative metaphysische Denken bei Jaspers und Henrich entwickelt wird. Jaspers vollzieht die Vergewisserung der Transzendenz aus philosophischem Glauben, indem er im Rahmen einer sachlich-perspektivischen und methodischen Strukturierung der Weisen und Möglichkeiten des Transzendierens die darin erschließbaren Bedeutungsaspekte und Sinnbezüge des letztlich umgreifenden und grundgebenden Seins der Transzendenz durch ein in Chiffren deutendes und umkreisendes Denken indirekt aufzuzeigen sucht. Henrich dagegen will durch einen bei der bezeichneten Ausgangsebene ansetzenden Gedankengang und in einer aufweisend, argumentierend und reflektierend verfahrenden Gedankenentwicklung Sinn und Notwendigkeit spekulativen Denkens und seiner metaphysischen Bezüge zum Unbedingten, All-Einen und zum Grund im Bewußtsein und Sein einsichtig werden lassen.

Dabei geht es Henrich – in zunächst wiederum ähnlicher Intention wie Jaspers – nicht zuletzt darum, die Philosophie der Vernunft als Kritik und Integration allererst wieder vor ihre eigentliche, höchste und letztlich spekulative Aufgabe zu bringen. Diese bestand und besteht in der „radikalen Nachfrage" und „Suche nach schlechtweg grundlegenden Einsichten"[116] bzw. „nach der Begründung von schlechtweg grundlegenden Annahmen"[117], die sich aber heute als „Verwahrung und Erkundung von Grenzfragen des Denkens" vollziehen[118] und die „gesicherten Bereiche des Wissens"[119] u. a. wissenschaftlicher Art ebenso überschreiten muß wie die „primären Verstehensweisen" des Grundverhältnisses und „das Wissen des common sense".[120] Freilich kann eine so verstandene Philosophie heute auch den traditionellen Anspruch der Metaphysik, ein erklärendes, deduktives und alle (anderen) Wissensweisen begründendes „Fundierungswissen" zu gewinnen und zu vermitteln, nicht aufrechterhalten.[121] Sie muß vielmehr, gerade um die spekulative Aufgabe und ihre mögliche Erfüllung überzeugend darstellen zu können, die von anderen Wissensarten unterschiedene eigene Wissensweise und Begründungsart eines auf das Ganze bezogenen (philosophischen) „Grundwissens" bzw. „Grundverstehens" klären und herausstellen.[122]

Indessen muß die schon in der Einleitung exponierte Frage erneut gestellt werden: ob denn Henrich die in Anspruch genommene besondere „Wissens- und Begründungsart" spekulativen Denkens wirklich hinreichend aufgeklärt und einsichtig gemacht hat, ja ob eine solche Differenzierung im Bereich des „Wissens" überhaupt der richtige Ansatz und Weg ist, um den hier erforderlichen geltungs- und gewißheitstheoretischen Reflexionen und Differenzierungen gerecht werden zu können. Diese kritische Frage verschärft sich noch, wenn und soweit man die beanspruchte spekulative Wissens- und Begründungsart durch die entwickelten Gedankengänge nicht als hinreichend erwiesen und bewährt ansehen kann, sofern sie trotz ihrer argumentativen Fassung nicht überzeugen konnten.

Nun ist es in der Tat so, daß ich von wesentlichen spekulativ metaphysischen Voraussetzungen und Überschritten nicht überzeugt (worden) bin. So etwa schon von der These, daß „das natürliche Selbstverständnis auf Metaphysik angelegt sei"[123], dann von der, daß die Selbstverständigung des bewußten Lebens und schon gar des Selbstverhältnisses nur mit Bezug auf die Gesamtwirklichkeit gewonnen werden könne[124] und deren „Grundverstehen" das Er-Denken eines Absoluten, Unbedingten, Einen erfordere. Abgesehen davon, daß solche „letzten Gedanken" oder Ideen ohnehin schwer zu erfüllenden, tragenden Gehalten eines realitätsbezogenen Welt- und Selbstverständnisses werden können, bin ich der Auffassung und Überzeugung, daß existentiell und philosophisch eine in anthropologisch-innerweltlicher Perspektive des Grundverhältnisses sich haltende und in diesem Sinne „transzendenzlose" Selbstverständigung nicht nur möglich ist, sondern auch ethisch-existentiell motiviert (um nicht zu sagen: begründet) werden kann. Darum muß ich mich gegen Henrichs Auffassung wenden, daß die Lehren der philosophischen Anthropologie über Mensch-Welt-Verhältnisse „schon im Ansatz zu kurz greifen"[125]; gerade im Ansatz ganz sicher nicht. Und mir leuchtet auch nicht ein, „daß es kein gelungenes Leben gibt ohne Metaphysik"[126]; entweder das Leben gelingt aus sich oder wenn nicht, dann auch nicht mit Metaphysik.

Und schließlich ist da noch eine gerade für die hier anstehende Auseinandersetzung prinzipiell wichtige These, der ich nicht zustimmen kann, nämlich, „daß das bewußte Leben eigentlich ganz und gar ohne Ernst" sein würde, wenn das „Wissen von der Vielzahl der Lebensmöglichkeiten und von der konfligierenden Natur der Lebensdeutungen" bestehen bliebe.[127] Ich meine im Gegenteil: Erst wenn dieses Wissen anerkannt und nicht durch ein vermeintlich übergreifendes spekulatives „Wissen" aufgehoben oder überholt wird, kann es eine ernsthafte, redliche und angemessene Auseinandersetzung in diesem ethisch-existentiellen Feld (einschließlich der metaphysischen Fragen) geben. (In all diesen Fragen glaube ich übrigens der Position M. Webers weit näher zu stehen als Henrich und Jaspers.)

Daß mich bestimmte spekulative Gedankengänge nicht überzeugt haben, ist gewiß nur ein subjektiver Tatbestand, und er wird hier natürlich auch nicht als „Wahrheitskriterium" oder gar „-beweis" angesehen und geltend gemacht, wohl aber als signifikant für die notwendige Frage, welcher Geltungs-, Gewißheits- und Mitteilungsmodi spekulativ metaphysischen Gedanken und Annahmen zuzusprechen sei. Daß es sich dabei nicht um ein (wenn auch in besonderer Weise) begründbares und argumentativ zu erzielendes spekulatives „Wissen" handelt, sondern weit eher um die Vergewisserung schon gehegter Überzeugungen, subjektiv für notwendig gehaltener letzter Annahmen (Postulate) und existentieller Entscheidungen und Einstellungen zum Leben und zur Welt, würde eine weitere Diskussion der angesprochenen Problempunkte, wie mir scheint, deutlicher zeigen.

Daß Henrich die letzten Gedanken einer Metaphysik des Abschlusses weiterhin mit dem Geltungsanspruch eines (besonderen) Begründens und Wissens versieht, ohne eine (möglicherweise wenigstens absichernde) prinzipielle geltungstheoretische Reflexion auf die überhaupt möglichen Wissens- und Gewißheitsarten bzw. Weisen des Fürwahrhaltens durchzuführen, bleibt, von den sachlichen Problemen abgesehen, bislang ein methodischer Mangel seiner spekulativen Philosophie. In diesem Punkt sind die Positionen von Kant und Jaspers überlegen, die diese Reflexion nicht zuletzt im Hinblick auf eine für kritische Philosophie noch mögliche Metaphysik nicht nur gefordert, sondern jeder auf seine und im Prinzip konvergente Weise vollzogen haben. Daß sie den Wissensbegriff aus dem Feld der metaphysischen Fragen verabschieden, scheint mir im Prinzip und um der Klarheit willen richtig. Seine Ersetzung durch geltungs- und gewißheitstheoretisch angemessenere Begriffe muß freilich nicht nur auf den Begriff des Glaubens und gar dessen eher zu enge (Kant) oder zu weite Fassung (Jaspers) führen oder bei ihm enden. Worauf es ankommt, ist vielmehr, daß die für existentiell-metaphysische Fragen (in Zustimmung oder Ablehnung!) wesentlichen subjektiv-existentiellen Geltungs- und Gewißheitsmodi möglicher Vergewisserung, Überzeugung und Entscheidung erreicht und gewahrt werden. Dann würde auch eine angemessene „philosophische Diskussion" möglich[128], die gerade zwischen metaphysisch transzendenzbezogenen und anthropologisch-weltlich immanent bleibenden und atheistischen Denkweisen geführt werden müßte. Die auf unterschiedliche Erfahrungen, Deutungen, Wertungen und Entscheidungen bezogenen und gestützten differenten Möglichkeiten und Weisen des Existenz- und Weltverständnisses ermöglichen und erfordern nämlich sehr wohl eine spezifisch „argumentative" Auseinandersetzung, d. h., in gewisser Analogie zur Diskussion „ästhetischer Urteile", „Streit", aber nicht wissenschaftlich entscheidbaren „Disput"[129]; denn, um Kant das letzte Wort zu geben, wenn auch nur im Telegrammstil einer Reflexion: in Glaubensfragen „ist Argument genug, darf nicht Beweis sein"[130].

Anmerkungen

* Ich möchte meinem Beitrag zu Ehren von Dieter Henrich eine persönliche Bemerkung beigeben, denn uns verbindet eine 45-jährige Bekanntschaft und kaum kürzere Freundschaft, die unser philosophisches Denken auch dort untergründig begleitet hat, wo es sich in unterschiedlichen Höhenlagen und Richtungen bewegte. Meine Bewunderung für die einzigartige Subtilität, mit der Henrich philosophiegeschichtlich bedeutsame Konstellationen – insbesondere zwischen Kant und Hegel – aufgeklärt und sachlich vergegenwärtigt hat, blieb ungebrochen, auch wenn ich ihm in manche Höhen und Tiefen nicht folgen konnte. Und dann war da ja immer noch Kant als gemeinsamer Ausgangs- und Rückgangspunkt, von dem aus die Wege allerdings auch in unterschiedliche Richtungen gingen. Denn während Henrich zum Idealismus weiter und höher stieg, freilich ohne Kant und die existentiellen Probleme hinter sich zu lassen, kam ich, auf dem Weg über Kierkegaard und die Existenzphilosophie zur philosophischen Anthropologie und marxistischen Praxisphilosophie, aus den anthropologischen und innerweltlichen Niederungen nicht heraus. Aber Kant blieb und bleibt doch stets unser Kreuzungs- und Treffpunkt, so auch hier.

1 Cf. „Dunkelheit und Vergewisserung", in: *All-Einheit. Wege eines Gedankens in Ost und West*, ed. D. Henrich, Stuttgart 1985, S. 33 ff.; *Fluchtlinien. Philosophische Essays*, Frankfurt 1982, S. 125 ff.

2 „Warum Metaphysik", in: *Metaphysik nach Kant?*, ed. D. Henrich, Stuttgart 1988, S. 95.

3 *Fluchtlinien* (cf. Anm. 1), S. 131.

4 Cf. K. Jaspers, *Vernunft und Existenz*, München 1935.

5 Cf. H. Fahrenbach, „Das ‚philosophische Grundwissen' kommunikativer Vernunft. Ein Beitrag zur gegenwärtigen Bedeutung der Philosophie von Karl Jaspers", in: *Karl Jaspers. Philosoph, Arzt, politischer Denker*, ed.

J. Hersch, München 1986; sowie id., „Kommunikative Vernunft – ein zentraler Bezugspunkt zwischen K. Jaspers und J. Habermas", in: *Karl Jaspers. Zur Aktualität seines Denkens*, ed. K. Salamun, München 1991.

6 Eine beachtliche Ausnahme ist neuerdings die Untersuchung von H. Leitner, *Systematische Topik. Methode und Argumentation in Kants kritischer Philosophie*, Würzburg 1994. Cf. aber auch R. Nimmer, *Kants kritische Religionsphilosophie*, Berlin 1990, § 5.

7 Im folgenden wird Kant an erster Stelle nach *Kant's gesammelten Schriften*, herausgegeben von der Deutschen (vormals Königlich Preußischen) Akademie der Wissenschaften (= Akademie-Ausgabe [AA]), Berlin 1900 ff. mit der Bandangabe in römischen Ziffern und der Seitenangabe in arabischen Ziffern zitiert. An zweiter Stelle erfolgen nach der Anführung des Titels (bzw. geg. eines Kurztitels) Seitenangaben der Originalausgabe(n) (A bzw. B); hier: AA IX 65 f., *Immanuel Kants Logik* [in der Folge: *Logik*] A 99.

8 AA IX 66, *Logik* A 99.

9 Cf. ibid. sowie AA III 533, *Kritik der reinen Vernunft* B 851.

10 AA IX 70, *Logik* A 107.

11 AA III 533, *Kritik der reinen Vernunft* B 850.

12 Cf. AA III 532, *Kritik der reinen Vernunft* B 848, sowie AA IX 72, *Logik* A 110.

13 AA IX 70, *Logik* A 107.

14 Ibid.

15 AA IX 71, *Logik* A 108, sowie AA IV 468, *Metaphysische Anfangsgründe der Naturwissenschaft* A V.

16 AA IX 71, *Logik* A 108.

17 AA IX 66, *Logik* A 99.

18 Ibid.; cf. § 30 über die „Modalität der Urteile": Problematische – Möglichkeit, assertorische – Wirklichkeit, apodiktische – Notwendigkeit, AA IX 108, *Logik* A 169.

19 Cf. AA IV, 467–479, *Metaphysische Anfangsgründe der Naturwissenschaft* A III–XXIV (Vorrede).

20 Cf. AA IX 72 u. 76, *Logik* A 111 f. u. 116 f. sowie AA V 457, *Kritik der Urtheilskraft* B 437.

21 AA III 533, *Kritik der reinen Vernunft* B 851.

22 AA IX 73, *Logik* A 113.

23 Cf. AA V 467, *Kritik der Urtheilskraft* B 454.

24 AA IX 66 f., *Logik* A 100; cf. auch AA IX 75, *Logik* A 116.

25 AA III 533, *Kritik der reinen Vernunft* B 850.

26 AA VIII 141, *Was heißt: Sich im Denken orientieren?* A 318.
27 AA IX 81, *Logik* A 127.
28 AA III 505, *Kritik der reinen Vernunft* B 803.
29 AA IX 84 ff., *Logik* A 132 ff.
30 AA IX 67 Anm., *Logik* A 102 Anm.
31 AA III 533, *Kritik der reinen Vernunft* B 851; cf. auch AA IX 67 Anm., *Logik* A 102 Anm., sowie AA VIII 141 f., *Was heißt: Sich im Denken orientieren?* A 319 f.
32 AA XX 297, *Welches sind die wirklichen Fortschritte, die die Metaphysik seit Leibnitzens und Wolf's Zeiten in Deutschland gemacht hat?* [in der Folge: *Preisschrift: Fortschritte der Metaphysik*] A 113.
33 AA III 535, *Kritik der reinen Vernunft* B 854.
34 AA III 535 f., *Kritik der reinen Vernunft* B 855.
35 AA III 536, *Kritik der reinen Vernunft* B 855.
36 AA III 536, *Kritik der reinen Vernunft* B 856.
37 AA III 526, *Kritik der reinen Vernunft* B 839.
38 Cf. D. Henrich, „Der Begriff der sittlichen Einsicht und Kants Lehre vom Faktum der Vernunft", in: *Die Gegenwart der Griechen im neueren Denken*, ed. D. Henrich, Tübingen 1960, S. 205 ff.
39 AA V 142 f., *Kritik der praktischen Vernunft* A 257; cf. AA V 131 f., *Kritik der praktischen Vernunft* A 237 f.; AA V 450 f., *Kritik der Urtheilskraft* B 425; AA IX 68 f. Anm., *Logik* A 103 ff. Anm.
40 AA V 125 f., *Kritik der praktischen Vernunft* A 226.
41 AA V 119, *Kritik der praktischen Vernunft* A 215.
42 Cf. AA V 472, *Kritik der Urtheilskraft* B 463.
43 Cf. AA III 521 f., *Kritik der reinen Vernunft* B 831 f.
44 Cf. weiter unten sowie AA V 467 ff. (§ 91), *Kritik der Urtheilskraft* B 454 ff.
45 AA V 468, *Kritik der Urtheilskraft* B 457; cf. AA V 473 f., *Kritik der Urtheilskraft* B 466 f.
46 AA IX 68 Anm., *Logik* A 102 Anm.; cf. AA V 472 u. 474, *Kritik der Urtheilskraft* B 463 u. B 467.
47 AA IX 72, *Logik* A 110 f.
48 Cf. AA V 144, *Kritik der praktischen Vernunft* A 259 f.
49 AA V 125, *Kritik der praktischen Vernunft* A 226.
50 AA V 144, *Kritik der praktischen Vernunft* A 260.
51 AA V 469 Anm., *Kritik der Urtheilskraft* B 458 Anm.
52 AA XX 298, *Preisschrift: Fortschritte der Metaphysik* A 115.
53 AA V 144 f., *Kritik der praktischen Vernunft* A 261.
54 AA V 145, *Kritik der praktischen Vernunft* A 262.

55 AA V 145 f., *Kritik der praktischen Vernunft* A 262.
56 AA IX 72, *Logik* A 110 f.
57 AA III 536 f., *Kritik der reinen Vernunft* B 857.
58 AA IX 69 Anm., *Logik* A 104 Anm.
59 AA IX 70, *Logik* A 107.
60 Cf. AA V 236 passim, *Kritik der Urtheilskraft* §§ 18–22, 29, 39, 40, 59.
61 AA XVI, 391 f. u. 393 f., *Kant's handschriftlicher Nachlaß* (Bd. III), *Reflexionen zur Logik* Refl. 2489, 2495.
62 AA XVI 386, *Kant's handschriftlicher Nachlaß* (Bd. III), *Reflexionen zur Logik* Refl. 2475.
63 AA IX 70, *Logik* A 107.
64 AA V 472, *Kritik der Urtheilskraft* B 464.
65 AA V 451, *Kritik der Urtheilskraft* B 426.
66 AA V 297, *Kritik der Urtheilskraft* B 164.
67 AA IX 70, *Logik* A 107.
68 Ibid.; cf. AA V 473, *Kritik der Urtheilskraft* B 465; AA V 145, *Kritik der praktischen Vernunft* A 262; AA III 537 f., *Kritik der reinen Vernunft* B 858 f.
69 AA V 452, *Kritik der Urtheilskraft* B 427.
70 AA V 453, *Kritik der Urtheilskraft* B 429.
71 AA V 469, *Kritik der Urtheilskraft* B 458 f.
72 AA V 467 (cf. § 91), *Kritik der Urtheilskraft* B 455.
73 AA IX 67, *Logik* A 100.
74 AA V 467, *Kritik der Urtheilskraft* B 454 f.
75 AA V 467, *Kritik der Urtheilskraft* B 455.
76 Cf. AA V 468 Anm., *Kritik der Urtheilskraft* B 457 Anm.
77 AA V 468, *Kritik der Urtheilskraft* B 456.
78 AA V 468, *Kritik der Urtheilskraft* B 457.
79 AA V 469, *Kritik der Urtheilskraft* B 459.
80 AA V 469, *Kritik der Urtheilskraft* B 457.
81 AA V 469, *Kritik der Urtheilskraft* B 459.
82 AA V 470, *Kritik der Urtheilskraft* B 459.
83 AA IX 67, *Logik* A 102; cf. AA V 471, *Kritik der Urtheilskraft* B 462.
84 AA III 536, *Kritik der reinen Vernunft* B 856.
85 AA III 517, *Kritik der reinen Vernunft* B 824.
86 Cf. AA XX 261 ff., *Preisschrift: Fortschritte der Metaphysik* A 15 ff.
87 Cf. AA III 292, *Kritik der reinen Vernunft* B 451; AA III 348, *Kritik der reinen Vernunft* B 535; sowie AA IX 83 f., *Logik* 130 f.
88 Cf. AA IX 83 f., *Logik* A 130 f.; AA VIII 415 ff., *Verkündigung des nahen Abschlusses eines Tractats zum ewigen Frieden in der Philosophie* A 490 ff.;

AA III 552, *Kritik der reinen Vernunft* B 884; AA VIII 226 ff., *Über eine Entdeckung, nach der alle neue Critik der reinen Vernunft durch eine ältere entbehrlich gemacht werden soll* BA 77 ff.
89 AA III 543 Anm., *Kritik der reinen Vernunft* B 867 Anm.
90 AA III 522, *Kritik der reinen Vernunft* B 833.
91 AA IX 25, *Logik* A 26.
92 Cf. AA III 543, *Kritik der reinen Vernunft* B 868.
93 Cf. H. Fahrenbach, *Zur Problemlage der Philosophie. Eine systematische Orientierung*, Frankfurt 1975 und „Philosophie in weltbürgerlicher Bedeutung', Kants höchste Sinnbestimmung der Philosophie nach ihrem Weltbegriff", in: *Würde und Recht des Menschen*, ed. H. Bielefeld, Würzburg 1992.
94 Cf. J. Schwartländer, *Der Mensch ist Person. Kants Lehre vom Menschen*, Stuttgart 1986, S. 248 ff.
95 AA III 522 ff., *Kritik der reinen Vernunft* B 833 ff..
96 AA III 517, *Kritik der reinen Vernunft* B 824.
97 AA III 518, *Kritik der reinen Vernunft* B 825.
98 Cf. AA VIII 136 ff. u. 140, *Was heißt: Sich im Denken orientieren?* A 309 ff. u. A 318; AA V 119 ff., *Kritik der praktischen Vernunft* A 215 ff.; AA III 440 ff., 452, 517 ff., *Kritik der reinen Vernunft* B 694 ff., 714, 823 ff.
99 AA VIII 137, *Was heißt: Sich im Denken orientieren?* A 311.
100 AA XX 294 f., *Preisschrift: Fortschritte der Metaphysik* A 106 f.
101 Cf. J. Habermas, „Wahrheitstheorien", in: *Vorstudien und Ergänzungen zur Theorie des kommunikativen Handelns*, Frankfurt 1984.
102 AA IX 82, *Logik* A 129.
103 Cf. K. Jaspers, *Philosophie*, 3 Bde., Berlin 1932.
104 Cf. *Vernunft und Existenz* (cf. Anm. 4).
105 Cf. K. Jaspers, *Von der Wahrheit*, München 1947.
106 Cf. hierzu H. Fahrenbach, „Das ‚philosophische Grundwissen' kommunikativer Vernunft" (cf. Anm.5).
107 Cf. *Von der Wahrheit* (cf. Anm. 105), S. 462 ff., 640 ff. u. ö.
108 Cf. loc. cit., S. 470 ff.; 675 f.
109 Cf. *Der philosophische Glaube*, München 1948 ff., S. 13; cf. auch *Philosophie* (cf. Anm. 103) Bd. I, S. 303 f.
110 *Philosophie* (cf. Anm. 103) Bd. III.
111 Cf. *Vernunft und Existenz* (cf. Anm. 4), S. 147; *Der philosophische Glaube angesichts der Offenbarung*, München 1962, S. 147 ff., 307 f.
112 Cf. *Philosophie* (cf. Anm. 103) Bd. II, S. 198; Bd. III, S. 6; cf. auch *Von der Wahrheit* (cf. Anm. 105), S. 110.

113 Besonders deutlich schon in *Philosophie* (cf. Anm. 103) Bd II, S. 117.
114 Cf. Henrich, *Fluchtlinien* (cf. Anm. 1), S. 125 ff.
115 Cf. loc. cit, S. 152 ff.
116 Loc. cit., S. 45 ff.
117 Loc. cit., S. 125 ff.
118 „Warum Metaphysik" (cf. Anm. 2), S. 87.
119 Loc. cit., S. 85.
120 Cf. *Fluchtlinien* (cf. Anm. 1), S. 159 ff., 169 ff., 174 ff.
121 Cf. „Warum Metaphysik" (cf. Anm. 2), S. 85 ff.; cf. auch „Dunkelheit und Vergewisserung" (cf. Anm. 1), S. 50.
122 Cf. „Warum Metaphysik" (cf. Anm. 2), S. 85, 87, u. ö.
123 *Fluchtlinien* (cf. Anm. 1), S. 162.
124 Cf. loc. cit, S. 141, 153.
125 Loc. cit., S. 141.
126 Loc. cit., S. 23.
127 Loc. cit., S. 54.
128 Wie sie Jaspers auf der Ebene der Existenzerhellung umrissen hat, in *Philosophie* (cf. Anm. 103) Bd. II, S. 111 ff.
129 AA V 338, *Kritik der Urtheilskraft* B 233 ff.; cf. zum moralischen Gottes-„Beweis" bzw. „Argument" AA V 450, *Kritik der Urtheilskraft* §§ 87–90, bes. B 424 Anm.
130 AA XVI 385, *Kant's handschriftlicher Nachlaß* (Bd. III), *Reflexionen zur Logik* Refl. 2474.

Vincenzo Vitiello

Epistemische Zeit
und historische Zeit

I
Endlichkeit der historischen Erkenntnis
und Unendlichkeit der Zeit

August Boeckh – den die moderne Philologie zu ihren Meistern zählt – bemerkte einmal, daß allein die gebildeten Völker und Individuen, die eine Vergangenheit zu bewahren und zu überliefern haben, das Bedürfnis zu *philologein* empfänden. Die nicht-gebildeten Völker und Individuen hingegen, d. h. diejenigen, die keine Tradition hätten, seien allein zu *philosophein* imstande. Wahrscheinlich dämpft die verschleierte Ironie die Besserwisserei dieses fast schon zu sehr gebildeten Bewahrers der Vergangenheit, aber sie verdeckt die Inkohärenz seiner Argumentation nicht. Nachdem Boeckh das ursprüngliche Wissen der Philosophie von der „Erkenntnis des Erkannten", der Philologie und der Historie, unterschieden hat – er sagt: „Die Philosophie erkennt primitiv, γιγνώσκει, die Philologie erkennt wieder, ἀναγιγνώσκει"[1] –, ist es schwer zu verstehen, wie er sich auf die tiefe Intuition Platons berufen und behaupten konnte, daß alle Erkenntnis (γνῶσις), darum auch die philosophische, ein Wiedererkennen (ἀνάγνωσις) sei. Um dem Widerspruch, in den er verfallen war, zu entfliehen, nahm er die Idee des Zirkels in Anspruch:

> „Philologie und Philosophie bedingen sich wechselseitig; denn man kann das Erkannte nicht erkennen, ohne überhaupt zu erkennen, und man kann auch nicht zu einer Erkenntnis schlechthin gelangen, ohne, was Andere erkannt haben, zu kennen."[2]

Aber dieses zirkuläre Verhältnis zwischen den beiden Erkenntnisformen schließt die Möglichkeit eines ursprünglichen Wissens aus. Übrigens hat die zeitgenössische philosophische Hermeneutik nichts so nachdrücklich und mit so vielen Argumenten bestritten wie die Idee, daß ein reiner, unbedingter Blick auf die Welt möglich sei. Das *thaumazein*, das Wundern vor dem ersten Morgen der Welt, ist keine Erfahrung eines Menschen: Unser geistiges Auge sieht immer von einem bestimmten Standpunkt aus; von jenem, in den es von der Zeit, der Vergangenheit, der Tradition, kurz: von der Geschichte gesetzt wird, so wie das körperliche Auge, das von dem Raum – dem Ort, an dem es sich befindet – seine Perspektive erhält. Der Unterschied zwischen den Gebildeten und Ungebildeten – Völkern oder Individuen – besteht nur in dem kritischen Bewußtsein der eigenen zeitlichen, geschichtlichen Bedingtheit, da wir alle – die Nichtgebildeten sowie die Gebildeten – schon immer den Garten Eden verlassen haben. Niemand kann die Welt am noch jungen Morgen sehen, weil dieser Morgen eine Vergangenheit ist, die niemals Gegenwart war.

Die zeitgenössische philosophische Hermeneutik hat besonders auf der Bedingtheit und mithin der Endlichkeit der menschlichen Erkenntnis bestanden, die deshalb geschichtlich ist, weil sie immer von Vor-Urteilen bestimmt ist, nämlich von der Vergangenheit bzw. von der Tradition, die das *wahre* Subjekt ist, bevor sie das mögliche Objekt der historischen Analyse wird. Sie ist das Thematisierende, bevor es das Thematisierte sein kann. Aber was zunächst als die Grenze des Erkennens erscheint, hat die Hermeneutik sogleich in einen Vorzug verwandelt: Die Zeit – so hat man hervorgehoben – macht die Kategorie, durch die wir erkennen, reicher und bedeutungsvoller, deutlicher und tiefer. Je größer die zeitliche Distanz ist, die uns von der Vergangenheit scheidet, desto größer ist die Möglichkeit, sie zu verstehen; so daß gerade das wissenschaftlich-erklärende Ideal, insofern es darin besteht, die Vergangenheit dem Interpreten gleichzeitig zu machen, die Interpretationskraft vermindern würde, wenn es sich durch ein Überspringen der Zeit verwirklichen ließe. Die Vergangenheit ist kein an sich vollständiges, vollkommenes *(perfectum)* Objekt, keine glatte Oberfläche, sondern vielmehr ein tiefer Brunnen. Sie ist nicht, sondern zeitigt sich. Sie „verzeitlicht" sich, „vergeschichtlicht" sich. Die Wahrheit der Vergangenheit lebt allein in der Zukunft.

Es ist nicht schwierig, die *Aporie* der zeitgenössischen philosophischen Hermeneutik zu erfassen. Sie gründet ihre Behauptung der Endlichkeit der geschichtlichen Erkenntnis in einer Voraussetzung, die ihr widerspricht: in der These der Unendlichkeit der Zeit, mithin der Vergangenheit bzw. der Tradition. Aber der historische Empirismus, der in der gegenwärtigen Hermeneutik und in einem großen Teil der Reflexion über die Hermeneutik waltet, zeigt sich nicht imstande, diese Aporie zu überwinden. Er ist so tief in ihr verwurzelt, daß er die Frage, die auf die Behauptung der Unendlichkeit der Zeit notwendig folgt, nicht mehr wahrnimmt, jene Frage, die Spengler mit aller nötigen Klarheit und strengen Einfachheit stellte:

„Gibt es eine Logik der Geschichte? Gibt es jenseits von allem Zufälligen und Unberechenbaren der Einzelereignisse eine sozusagen metaphysische Struktur der historischen Menschheit, die von den weithin sichtbaren, populären, geistigpolitischen Gebilden der Oberflächen wesentlich unabhängig ist? Die diese Wirklichkeit geringeren Ranges vielmehr erst hervorruft? Erscheinen die großen Züge der Weltgeschichte dem verstehenden Auge vielleicht immer wieder in einer Gestalt, die Schlüsse zuläßt?"[3]

Diese Frage ließe sich naheliegenderweise auf verschiedene Arten und Weisen beantworten, und man hat auch tatsächlich sehr unterschiedlich auf sie geantwortet. Was der Empirismus jedoch nicht einzuholen vermag, ist, daß, wenn die Frage eine *metaphysische* ist, auch die Antwort solcher Art sein muß. Der Deutlichkeit halber: Dieser Frage entgegenzustellen, daß, auch wenn unsere Forschungen noch so sorgfältig wären, wir den Sinn des Weltwerdens deshalb nicht erfassen können, weil allein ein kleinster Teil dieses Werdens bedeutungsvoll ist; sowie ihr zu entgegnen, daß die „Kultur", d. h. die sinn- und bedeutungsreiche, von den Menschen hervorgebrachte Welt nur ein endlicher Abschnitt der sinn- und bedeutungslosen Unendlichkeit des Weltwerdens ist – jener Frage also alles dieses entgegenzustellen bedeutet, schon über die Endlichkeit jenes Wissens hinauszugreifen, das vom Baum der Erkenntnis gegessen zu haben annimmt. („Schlecht gegessen!" würden wir sagen, wenn dieses Wissen nicht imstande ist, die *Hybris* seiner nur scheinbaren Bescheidenheit wahrzunehmen). Wo man von der Unendlichkeit des

Weltwerdens spricht, ist sein Sinn schon erfaßt – wenn auch als Chaos und Nicht-Sinn.

Man überwindet die philosophische Blindheit des Empirismus und Historismus jedoch nicht durch die einfache Feststellung der Unausweichlichkeit der metaphysischen Frage. Selbst Spengler scheint der Frage, die er so klar gestellt hatte, nicht gewachsen gewesen zu sein, wenn er, der sich der Grenzen der Geschichtsphilosophie bewußt war, eine Morphologie der historischen Epoche erarbeitete, ohne die traditionellen Begriffe der Zeit und des Raumes grundlegend in Frage zu stellen. In der Tat übernahm er diese Begriffe vielmehr passiv aus der Tradition.

II
Hegel und der transzendentale Zeithorizont

In einer bekannten, aber weniger verstandenen als kritisierten Passage seiner *Phänomenologie des Geistes* behauptet Hegel:

> „Die *Zeit* ist der *Begriff* selbst, der *da ist*, und als leere Anschauung sich dem Bewußtsein vorstellt; deswegen erscheint der Geist notwendig in der Zeit, und er erscheint so lange in der Zeit, als er nicht seinen reinen Begriff *erfaßt*, d. h. nicht die Zeit *tilgt*."[4]

Was ist die Bedeutung dieses „Zeittilgens"? Welche Zeit hat der Begriff zu *tilgen*?

Die Zeit, die *da ist*, die äußere Zeit der Anschauung – wie Hegel unzweideutig formuliert. Dies besagt: die Zeit als bloßes Vorbeigehen und „Verlaufen". Diese selbst den Erscheinungen *(Phänomenen)*, die sie verbraucht und verzehrt, äußerliche Zeit muß der Begriff tilgen. Aber nicht, um sich in den reinen Äther des Geistes zu bringen, wo es keine Zeit mehr gibt – wie der vulgäre Anti-Hegelianismus sagt –, sondern gerade im Gegenteil: um den Ort zu erreichen, an dem die wirkliche Zeit, die Weltzeit bzw. die Zeit der Geschichte oder der geschichtlichen Phänomene sich offenbart; um den Ort des reinen Begriffs zu erreichen, nämlich des Begriffs, der sich als Begriff weiß. Insofern nunmehr von der Geschichte die Rede ist, empfiehlt es sich, Hegels hierfür einschlägige Bemerkungen über die Geschichte und geschichtliche Erkenntnis einzubeziehen.

Am Schluß seiner die Philosophie der Geschichte einleitenden methodologischen Reflexionen behauptet Hegel, es habe den Anschein, als sollte sich der Historiker der Vergangenheit zuwenden, in Wahrheit aber betrachte er immer die Gegenwart, das *Jetzt.* Der Gegenstand seiner Betrachtung ist jedoch nicht die Gegenwart, die vergeht, sondern das Jetzt, das *ist* und allein *ist,* d. h. das aionische *„es ist",* das in sich Vergangenheit, Gegenwart und Zukunft enthält. Gemeint ist jenes *„es ist",* das die Ordnung der Zeit selbst ist – nicht die Ewigkeit (um auf Platon zu rekurrieren, an den Hegel sicher dachte, als er die hier ins Auge gefaßten Passagen niederschrieb), die ἐν ἑνί, d. h. in jener unterschiedslosen (ἀίδιος) Einheit verbleibt, die keine Gestalten (εἴδη) und Teilungen (μέρη) der Zeit kennt, sondern vielmehr die geteilte und mannigfaltige, die immerseiende *(aionische:* ἀεὶ ὄν) Ewigkeit, in der das „es war", das „es ist" und das „es wird" statthaben.[5] Die Rede ist also nicht von der verlaufenden Zeit, sondern von jener, in der alles Verlaufen sich ereignet und durch die es sich ereignen kann: die Himmel-Zeit, in der die Tage und Nächte, die Monate und Jahre aufeinanderfolgen. Diese ist die Zeit des Begriffs, der sich als Begriff weiß, mithin des Begriffs, der nicht das Fließen, sondern die Zeit als bloßes Fließen tilgt; denn es gibt kein Fließen außer in einer *Ordnung.* Dies ist die Zeit als die Ordnung selbst.

Hegel greift hier – wie bereits angemerkt – auf Platons Lehre der Zeit zurück, bezieht sich jedoch nicht weniger auf Kants Theorie, derzufolge nicht die Zeit verläuft, sondern die Phänomene in ihr.

„Wollte man der Zeit selbst eine Folge nach einander beilegen, so müßte man noch eine andere Zeit denken, in der diese Folge möglich wäre."[6]

Dennoch *kritisiert* Hegel Kant. Die Kritik liegt schon in der Bestimmung der Zeit als Begriff, der *da ist,* der als bloße Gegebenheit, d. h. als *leere Anschauung* angenommen ist. Hegel zielt darauf ab, die *Gegebenheit* der Zeit-Ordnung aufzuheben (aufzuheben, nicht: zu *tilgen),* weswegen er sich die Aufgabe stellt, sie zu begründen (λόγον διδόναι). Etwas begründen bedeutet, nach Hegels Auffassung, seine innere Geschichte bzw. die Geschichte seiner inneren Gliederungen wiederzugeben. Es handelt sich allerdings um eine Geschichte, die scharf von jener der Individuen und Institutionen zu unterscheiden ist, und die darum vielleicht besser *Genealogie* genannt werden sollte. Kurz, Hegel zielt darauf ab, in das Fließen der Zeit hinein die Zeit-Ordnung selbst einzuordnen.

Aber zu diesem Punkt gibt es noch einiges hinzuzufügen. Beachten wir daher zunächst, was den oben zitierten Passagen der *Phänomenologie des Geistes* folgt:

„Die Zeit erscheint daher als Schicksal und die Notwendigkeit des Geistes, der nicht in sich vollendet ist, – die Notwendigkeit, den Anteil, den das Selbstbewußtsein an dem Bewußtsein hat, zu bereichern, die *Unmittelbarkeit des Ansich* – die Form, in der die Substanz im Bewußtsein ist, – in Bewegung zu setzen oder umgekehrt, das Ansich als das *Innerliche* genommen, das was erst *innerlich* ist, zu realisieren und zu offenbaren, d. h. der Gewißheit seiner selbst zu vindizieren."[7]

Dieser Abschnitt besagt, daß die Zeit-Anschauung der transzendentalen Ästhetik Kants erst das „Ansich" des Begriffs sei, nämlich der Begriff als ein *Gegebenes*, der als solcher zum „Für-sich", d. h. zu einem seiner selbst bewußten Begriff, werden muß. Die Veränderung der Perspektive Hegels ist offensichtlich: Jetzt geht es nicht mehr um eine *Genealogie*, d. h. um die Geschichte der inneren Gliederungen der Zeit-Ordnung, sondern um die Geschichte des Sichbewußtwerdens dieses *ordo temporum*. Aus diesem Grund behauptet Hegel in ebenderselben Einleitung zu den *Vorlesungen über die Philosophie der Geschichte*, in der er (wie oben angemerkt) erklärte, daß der Geschichtsforscher der ewigen, *aionischen* Gegenwart und nicht dem vorbeigehenden Jetzt seinen Blick zuwendet, daß der Begriff, den sich der Geist von sich selbst macht – der Begriff jener Gegenwart, die nie untergeht, also der Begriff des *ordo temporum* (man beachte: der Begriff der Gegenwart und nicht: die Gegenwart) – das Resultat der Anstrengungen von sechstausend Jahren sei.

Daß Hegels These selbst aporetisch ist, kann man schwerlich bestreiten, denn die zwei verschiedenen Perspektiven, zwischen denen er sich bewegt, werden von ihm nicht unterschieden. Gewiß ist die

„Gegebenheit" der Zeit-Ordnung nicht als etwas Letztes und Unproblematisches anzunehmen. Auch sie, wenn nicht vor allem sie, muß thematisiert werden. In jedem Falle aber kann der *ordo temporum* niemals durch seine Einordnung in die Bewegung der Substanz, die zum Subjekt wird, begründet werden, denn hierdurch wird das Problem nur verlagert, nicht gelöst. Selbst die Bewegung von der Substanz zum Subjekt ist eine *Ordnung*, die es zu begründen gilt, will man kohärent sein. Ein *regressus in infinitum* scheint unausweichlich. Wenn man jedoch nun die Frage nach dem Ursprung der Ordnung in jene weitere Frage nach dem Sichbewußtwerden desselben übersetzt, um sich solcher schlechten Unendlichkeit zu entziehen, wird genau das ursprüngliche Gegebene – das Dasein der Ordnung – unkritisch angenommen.

Es scheint an diesem Punkt unumgänglich, nach dem Grund der Gegebenheit des *ordo temporum* zu fragen – Anlaß genug, sich dem Philosophen zuzuwenden, der diese Gegebenheit ins Zentrum seiner Reflexion gestellt hat, Kant.

III
Die Gegebenheit der Zeit bei Kant

Man sollte sich zunächst vergegenwärtigen, daß der Begriff der „Gegebenheit" bei Kant verschiedene Bedeutungen besitzt. *Gegeben* im Sinne der Nichtableitbarkeit von Anderem sowie der Sinnlosigkeit der Frage „Warum sie und nicht die anderen?" sind ebenso die reinen sinnlichen Anschauungen wie auch die Verstandesbegriffe a priori. Während erstere jedoch nur einer einfachen Erörterung, nämlich der Darstellung dessen bedürfen, was zu ihnen gehört, bedürfen letztere vielmehr einer Deduktion, des Beweises, daß sie auf die Erscheinungen anwendbar sind. Tatsächlich gibt es keine Vorstellung von sinnlichen Phänomenen – etwa einer Reihe von farbigen Punkten oder Bildern – außer im Raum und in der Zeit. Dagegen ist es möglich, sich etwa eine Beziehung vorzustellen, die nicht kausal ist, z. B. eine bloß zeitliche Aufeinanderfolge.

Aber dieser Unterschied nimmt nicht auf die Erscheinungen Bezug. Er gehört zur Methode der transzendentalen Analyse, die das Phänomen in seine Bestandteile zergliedert, um es in der Folge wieder zusammenzusetzen. Deshalb ist er dazu bestimmt, zu verschwinden. Keine Vorstellung ist wirklich möglich – auch nicht die einfachste, wie die einer geraden Linie – die nicht von der Einheit der transzendentalen Apperzeption begleitet wäre. Und diese operiert bekanntlich allein durch die Verstandeskategorie.[8] Deswegen gibt es niemals eine bloße raum-zeitliche Aufeinanderfolge, sondern immer eine kausale, oder besser: eine raum-zeitlich-kausale Verkettung – wie Kant in den *Analogien der Erfahrung* erläutert. Wenn einmal die erste, niedere Forschungsstufe der Ästhetik überwunden und die zweite, gegliedertere und intrikatere Stufe der Analytik erreicht ist, ist nicht zufällig der Unterschied zwischen „Erörterung" und „Deduktion" aufgehoben: Eine *Deduktion* auch bezüglich des Raumes (und infolgedessen der Zeit), d. h. also eine *Rechtfertigung* seiner Anwendbarkeit allein auf die sinnlichen Phänomene, wird notwendig. Dieses deshalb, weil die Begriffe, die über die sinnliche Erfahrung hinauszugehen vermögen, den Raum jenseits der Grenzen der Sinnlichkeit gebrauchen können.[9]

Das Gesagte beseitigt nicht die Ästhetik zugunsten der Analytik und bringt Raum und Zeit nicht einmal auf die Stufe der Begriffe; es bestätigt im Gegenteil den Vorrang der Sinnlichkeit insofern, als es zeigt, wie die ganze phänomenale Ordnung, der Horizont der Offenbarkeit des Seienden überhaupt, *gegeben* ist. „Vorrang der Sinnlichkeit" besagt: Vorrang der Rezeptivität. Offensichtlich ist, daß diese Rezeptivität, die auf die reine phänomenale Ordnung Bezug nimmt, nicht *empirisch,* sondern *transzendental* ist. Hieraus erklärt sich die deutliche Verschiedenheit des Kantischen Begriffs der „Deduktion" von dem idealistischen. Die Kantische Deduktion, so sie darauf abzielt, den Gültigkeitsanspruch der Begriffe (aber jetzt können wir sagen: der Begriffe und der Anschauungen) im Bereich des Sinnlichen zu rechtfertigen, setzt die Grenze nicht nur des Verstandes, sondern auch der Vernunft überhaupt fest, insofern sie allen Anspruch, Begriffe und Anschauung zu begründen, verwirft. Wenn auch die Aufgabe der transzendentalen Deduktion deswegen eine *positive* ist, weil sie dazu dienen soll, die objektive Gültigkeit der Begriffe zu begründen, so ist die Funktion der *metaphysischen* Deduktion demgegenüber *negativ,* denn sie muß die Grenze des Denkens überhaupt ausmachen, d. h. die Unmöglichkeit der Begründung des Horizontes der Offenbarkeit des Seienden im Ganzen zeigen. Es ist nicht möglich, durch die Kategorien, die dem Verständnis dessen dienen, was innerhalb des Horizontes ist, selbst den Horizont zu begründen.

„Daher kann man nicht fragen: warum hat sich die Vernunft nicht anders bestimmt?, sondern nur: warum hat sie die *Erscheinungen* durch ihre Kausalität nicht anders bestimmt?"[10]

Damit ist die Frage nach dem *Ursprung* der Ordnung jedoch nicht beseitigt – sondern nur ihr Sinn und unsere Erwartung verschoben. Von hier aus ist jedoch nunmehr ein weiteres Problem zu betrachten.

IV
Der Zeitraum als Verhältnis zwischen dynamischen Zentren

Die Zeit bleibt und wechselt nicht – so lautet ein bekannter Satz Kants. Aber die Frage stellt sich: Welche Zeit? Die Zeit als Horizont der Phänomene, d. h. selbst jener Phänomene, die Epochen ausmachen, also jener *endlichen*, begrenzten Zeiten, deren Entstehung und Untergang wir erkennen und beschreiben. Was bleibt und nicht wechselt ist allein die nicht-endliche, nicht-begrenzte Zeit, die Rahmen-Zeit aller besonderen Zeit, d. h. die Ordnungs-Zeit: der *ordo temporum*. Aber von dieser Zeit haben wir keine Wahrnehmung: *„Nun kann die Zeit für sich nicht wahrgenommen werden."*[11] Die Möglichkeitsbedingung aller Wahrnehmungen und Vorstellungen kann niemals Objekt des Wahrnehmens oder Vorstellens werden. Die Hand kann sich nicht selbst ergreifen.

Aber was läßt uns die Horizont-Zeit – oder, wie Kant sagt, die Zeit „als das beständige Correlatum alles Daseins der Erscheinungen" – verstehen?

Es ist das, was in den Erscheinungen selbst, wie die Zeit, bleibt und nicht wechselt: die *Substanz*. Damit die Veränderung einer Erscheinung (eines Gegenstandes) – z. B. der Aufgang und der Untergang der Sonne – wahrgenommen werden kann, ist es notwendig, daß es in der Erscheinung selbst, die sich verändert, „etwas" gibt, das mit sich identisch bleibt und auf das die Veränderung bezogen wird (in unserem Beispiel ist es die Sonne). Würde sich auch der Beziehungspunkt verändern – würde das Aufgehen sich auf die Sonne beziehen und das Untergehen auf den Mond – gäbe es keine Veränderung, sondern nur zwei verschiedene Zustände. Es scheint paradoxal zu sein, hebt Kant hervor, aber

> „nur das Beharrliche (die Substanz) wird verändert; das Wandelbare erleidet keine Veränderung, sondern einen *Wechsel*, da einige Bestimmungen aufhören und andre anheben."[12]

Kant nimmt auch terminologisch, vermittels des mittelalterlichen Latein, eine Unterscheidung wieder auf, die auf Aristoteles zurückgeht, nämlich diejenige zwischen Substanz und Akzidentien; diese als die wandelbaren Erscheinungen jener. Aber wie kann das Wandelbare die Erscheinung dessen, was beharrlich ist, das Verschiedene also, Offenbarung des Identischen sein? Die Substanz als das immer identische Substrat aller wandelbaren Phänomene kann *„weder vermehrt noch vermindert werden"*[13], so daß sie, insofern sie eine feste Größe ist, alle mögliche Veränderung in sich enthalten muß. Wie? Als Möglichkeit, *Kraft*, *dynamis* aller Veränderungen, d. h. aller ihrer möglichen Erscheinungen.

> „Wo Handlung, mithin Tätigkeit und Kraft ist, dort ist auch Substanz, und in dieser allein muß der Sitz jener fruchtbaren Quelle der Erscheinungen gesucht werden."[14]

Kant bezeichnet das *Substrat* oder „die Substanz in der Erscheinung" als das *Reale*. Das *Reale* ist nicht das Wirkliche, das Dasein, sondern das, was zum Wesen des Dinges *(res)* gehört. Im Begriff der Realität *(realitas)* eines Körpers ist die Ausdehnung mit enthalten – unabhängig von dem Dasein des Körpers. Es ist offensichtlich, daß sich das Dasein des *Realen* nicht von seiner Realität entfernen kann. Diese Realität ist allerdings *in einer Hinsicht* insofern „weniger" als das Dasein, als nicht all das, was *real* in dem Sinne der *realitas* ist, wirklich ist, da ist. (Eine nur potentielle Existenz zu haben ist etwas ganz anderes als eine wirkliche Existenz, wie Kants Beispiel der Taler hinreichend verdeutlicht). *In anderer Hinsicht* ist die *realitas* „mehr" als das Dasein, insofern sie nämlich die Möglichkeitsbedingung der Wirklichkeit ist.

Die Auffassung der Substanz als *dynamis* und die Auslegung derselben als *Kraft* bringen die tiefe Verbindung ans Licht, die ungeachtet der in der *Kritik der reinen Vernunft* gegen den „Intellektualphilosophen" der *Monadologie* entwickelten Einwände zwischen Kant und Leibniz besteht. Insbesondere im Anhang der Analytik über die „Amphibolie der Reflexionsbegriffe" verwirft Kant die Leibnizsche These der Substanz als „etwas Innerem", das „von allen äußeren Verhältnissen frei ist"[15], und behauptet, daß es kein Schlechthininnerliches gibt, da die *substantia phaenomenon* (die Materie) nichts als der Inbegriff der Verhältnisse ist, die sie mit den anderen Substanzen hat.

„Was wir auch an der Materie kennen, sind lauter Verhältnisse (das, was wir innre Bestimmungen derselben nennen, ist nur komparativ innerlich)."[16]

Wahr ist aber, daß es nicht möglich ist, den ganzen Substanzbegriff auf einen Bund von Verhältnissen mit dem Äußerlichen zu reduzieren, da die Substanz *an sich* wenigstens die „Möglichkeit" bzw. die *Kraft (dynamis)* dieser Verhältnisse ist. Als solche, d. h. als Kraft aller Verhältnisse, ist die Substanz das, was Zeit und Raum hervorbringt; jedoch nicht die Zeit und den Raum der Ästhetik, d. h. die Zeit als bloße Aufeinanderfolge und den Raum als leere Ausdehnung; sondern die der Analytik: die Zeit als kausale Folgerung (2. Analogie) und Zugleichsein (3. Analogie), das, als Wechselwirkung oder Gemeinschaft, die einheitliche *raum-zeitliche* Struktur des Offenbarkeitshorizonts des Seienden im Ganzen, d. h. den *ordo rerum, ad oculos* zeigt.

Aus der Analyse der Analogien ergibt sich, daß die raum-zeitliche Ordnung innerlich bewegt ist; daß das Fließen der Erscheinungen *(Phänomene)* keine bloße Zugabe zu dem festen und beharrlichen phänomenalen Horizont ist. Das Beharrliche ist vielmehr die Kraft, die die Bewegung, das Geschehen und die Verknüpfung der Erscheinungen hervorbringt. Das Beharrliche, die Substanzen-Kräfte, sind *gegeben*, ebenso wie der Horizont. Über diese Substanzen-*Kräfte* kann man nur sagen, daß sie weder entstehen noch vergehen. Sollten sie entstehen oder verschwinden, so

> „würde [das] selbst die einzige Bedingung der empirischen Einheit der Zeit aufheben, und die Erscheinungen würden sich alsdenn auf zweierlei *Zeiten* beziehen, in denen neben einander das Dasein verflösse, welches ungereimt ist. Denn es ist *nur Eine* Zeit, in welcher alle verschiedene Zeiten nicht zugleich, sondern nacheinander gesetzt werden müssen."[17]

Der *ordo temporum*, der Zeit-Raum, ist also innerlich bewegt, insofern er aus *dynamischen Kräften* besteht, die untereinander in Beziehung stehen. Es liegt nahe, danach zu fragen, ob diese Kräfte als mannigfaltige nicht einen kontinuierlichen Raum voraussetzen, in welchem sie sich bewegen und wirken können; einen Raum – um den „gründlichen Archetypus", das von René Thom evozierte Urbild der Räumlichkeit[18] zu verwenden –, der dem diskreten, aus den Substanzen-Kräften hervorgebrachten Raum unterliegt. Aber ist der Raum als eine reine, leere Ausdehnung denkbar, in der einige Kraft-Punkte, einige „Organisierungszentren", wie Sterne strahlen und ihn dadurch verändern können, daß sie ihn diskret machen? Als eine kontinuierliche Weite, um noch ein Beispiel Thoms anzuführen, in der „ein Embryo sich entwickelt und, nachdem er erwachsen geworden ist, sie erforscht, um darin das Ei abzulegen, in dem er fortleben wird"? In Wahrheit ist der Raum als solcher jeweils schon „kontinuierlich" und „diskret". Er ist ausschließlich jener, den die Substanzen-Kräfte hervorzubringen imstande sind. Es gibt keinen Raum vor den Substanzen-Kräften. Aber hieraus folgt nicht, daß diese Substanzen nichts voraussetzten. Allein, was sie voraussetzen ist nicht so etwas wie ein Raum. Ihre Voraussetzung ist die *transzendentale Materie* – auf die die *realitas phaenomenon* zurückzuführen ist; die transzendentale Materie, die weder Raum noch Mannigfaltigkeit ist. Sie ist jenseits, oder besser diesseits von diesem und jenem. Hieraus folgt, daß es in der Substanz, bzw. in der Kraft selbst etwas gibt, das weder Substanz noch Kraft ist; daß es im Raum und in der Zeit etwas gibt, das kein Raum und keine Zeit ist. Alle Analyse des Zeithorizontes, die dieses „Diesseits" nicht in Betracht zieht, ist – philosophisch – unzureichend.

Meiner Meinung nach hat die Philosophie heute die Aufgabe, eine Logik zu erarbeiten, die sich nicht darauf beschränkt, die innerlichen Strukturen des Offenbarkeitshorizontes des Seienden überhaupt (was ich „topoi" nenne) zu bestimmen, sondern die jenseits dieser Strukturen zu blicken versteht, ohne damit zu beanspruchen, diese aus dem, was jenseits liegt, ableiten zu können. Von diesem Standpunkt aus den Blick jenseits des Horizontes zu werfen bedeutet, die Grenze der Logik – der Topo-Logik – auszumachen, ohne sie zu überschreiten. Das aber heißt: die Endlichkeit als Endlichkeit zu denken; eine schwierige, jedoch – wie ich hoffe – nicht unmögliche Aufgabe.

Anmerkungen

1 A. Boeckh, *Encyklopädie und Methodologie der philologischen Wissenschaften*, ed. E. Bratuscheck, Leipzig 1877, S. 16.
2 Loc. cit., S. 17.
3 O. Spengler, *Der Untergang des Abendlandes*, München 1923, S. 3.
4 G. W. Fr. Hegel, *Phänomenologie des Geistes*, ed. J. Hoffmeister, Hamburg 1952, S. 558.
5 Cf. Platon, *Timaios* 37 d f.
6 *Kritik der reinen Vernunft* A 183, B 226.
7 Loc. cit., S. 558 f.
8 Cf. *Kritik der reinen Vernunft*, Die Analytik der Begriffe, §§ 15–17.
9 Cf. *Kritik der reinen Vernunft* A 87–89, B 119–121.
10 *Kritik der reinen Vernunft* A 556, B 584.
11 *Kritik der reinen Vernunft* B 225 (Herv. v. Verf.)
12 *Kritik der reinen Vernunft* A 187, B 230.
13 *Kritik der reinen Vernunft* B 225 (Herv. v. Verf.).
14 *Kritik der reinen Vernunft* A 204, B 250.
15 *Kritik der reinen Vernunft* A 274, B 330.
16 *Kritik der reinen Vernunft* A 285, B 341.
17 *Kritik der reinen Vernunft* A 188 f., B 231 f.
18 R. Thom, *Modèles mathématiques de la morphogenèse*, Bourgois, Paris 1980, § 8. 7.

Michael Dummett

The Metaphysics of Time

The present is real: there is no doubting that. We may be mistaken in what we suppose to be happening now; but that there is some fact of the matter about what is happening now cannot be doubted. There appear, then, to be four possible views about time:

(1) *Only* the present is real. All that reality consists in is what is happening *now*. The past *was* part of reality, but has ceased to be: it has passed away. The future *will be* part of reality, but has not yet come into existence. Generalized, that is to say that all that reality consists in at any one time is what is happening at that time. Reality – what there is – continually changes.

(2) The past is part of reality, the future is not. The future has not yet come to be; it does not yet exist. We therefore cannot *know* anything of it, because there is nothing to make a proposition about it true or false. Certainly we may entertain propositions about the future, and with good reason assign them high or low probability: but, however high the probability of some belief of ours about the future, that belief cannot be *knowledge*, because, so long as the belief continues to be *about the future*, the possibility will always remain open that the belief will be overturned, namely by things' not happening in accordance with it. The past, on the other hand, is a constituent of reality. Once something has happened, it has happened, and nothing can overturn our knowledge of its having happened. The passage of time is, as C. D. Broad maintained[1], a continual growth in the sum total of reality. When a moment that was future becomes present, a new layer of reality springs into being and is laid down to be for ever part of reality.

(3) The future is real, but the past is not. The future is accessible:

we have only to wait to see what it holds, which is what it has always held. The past, on the other hand, is inaccessible. It has left traces, indeed, including our own memories: but those traces, which are part of the present, are all there is of the past: they constitute it. As John Wheeler has remarked, "the past has no existence except as it is recorded in the present"[2]: it has no independent reality.

(4) Past and future are both real. They are simply regions determined, at any given time, by our temporal perspective, as it is at that time. There is no distinction between past and future in reality; there is no *now* in reality. Time is merely one of the dimensions along which reality varies, as it does along any of the three spatial dimensions; it is distinguished for us only by its special relation to our experience and our knowledge. Reality is four-dimensional.

How are we to decide which of these models is correct?

At first glance, model (1) simply describes reality as we experience it and know it to be: it just *does* continually change. The present is the substance of the world: the past consists of what *has been* present, the future of what *will be* present. All there *is* now is what is now present. But model (1) in effect denies that any propositions about the past can be true: for a proposition can be true only if there is something in virtue of which it is true, and, according to model (1), there simply is nothing in virtue of which a proposition about the past can be true. But this contradicts what memory vouchsafes: of things which we remember, we *know* that they happened, that memory tells us truly. But, if so, the past must in some sense exist, that is, must be part of reality, to render those memories true.

Model (1) also founders upon a difficulty raised by St. Augustine.[3] The present has no duration: it is a mere boundary between past and future. But the existence of a boundary depends upon the existence of the regions that it bounds. Suppose that one part of a surface is coloured red, and the rest yellow. There is a clean boundary between them: there is no gradation of colour, nor any colour separating the red and yellow regions, which abut on one another. Then the boundary between those regions exists, as a straight line or a curve, because the regions exist and are disposed as they are: it would make no sense to try to imagine the boundary as existing, but there being no regions which it bounded. How, then, can the present be all that there is?

Model (3) does not face exactly the same difficulty about the truth of propositions about the past as did model (1). It does not deny that there is anything to make such propositions true: it merely asserts that whatever makes them true lies in the present. But the thesis resists generalization. Suppose that we observe an event S occurring now; we can say for sure that the proposition "S is now happening" is true. Then the undeniable links between the truth-values of differently tensed propositions uttered at different times imply that, in a year's time, the proposition "S happened a year ago" will then be true. But it may well be that, in a year's time, every trace of S will have dissipated: there will be nothing in the way things are in a year's time to witness to the previous occurrence of S. If we try to generalize our thesis from the present to what will in a year's time be the present, we shall find ourselves holding that the proposition "S happened a year ago", considered as uttered or entertained a year hence, will be devoid of truth-value. But we previously decided that it would be true. How can this antinomy be evaded?

The only way which the proponent of model (3) can evade it is to immerse himself in time even more thoroughly than the proponent of model (1). It is common ground that the utterance of a sentence containing an indexical adverb such as "now" or "a year ago" must be considered as uttered at a particular time in order to assign it a truth-value; but, in accordance with model (3), even when that has been done, the assignment of the truth-value, or lack of one, must itself be relativized to the time at which the truth-value is assessed. It *now* holds good that the statement "S occurred a year ago", considered as uttered a year hence, will be true; but, in a year's time it will hold good that that statement, considered as uttered then, will lack a truth-value. As time passes, not only does the present change, on this model: the past changes as well.

Such a view is not formally incoherent; but it runs contrary to all our inclinations. Once we have fixed the time at which we are envisaging a statement as being uttered, we have done, we are disposed to think, all the relativization that is needed: the predicate "is true" does not need further relativization to the time at which it is applied, but is absolute. It is *what happened in the past*, and not the present traces of it, that renders our statements about the past true or false: *that* is the metaphysical principle that the truth-value links enshrine. It is not enough to say that what is happening now will render true a statement made in a year's time about what happened a year before, in the sense that the word "true" *now* has. That sense must remain constant; its constancy rules it out that it will be correct to say, in a year's time, that it is what *then* exists that renders what is then said about what happened a year before true or false, or lacking in truth-value, in the senses that "true" and "false" will then have. In a year's time, adherents of model (3) may formally recognize the truth-value link by agreeing that it is what happened a year before that renders what they say about what happened a year before true or false; but they will be honouring it only with their lips if, as they use the phrase, "what happened a year ago" proves to mean "what year-old events there are present traces of".

The trouble is that this objection to model (3), if sound, serves equally well to dismantle the far more generally palatable model (2). According to model (2), our statements about the future may carry probability values, depending on the degree to which they accord with present tendencies, but, so long as they remain statements about the future, are not either true or false, since the future has not yet come into existence to render them true or false. But, since S is happening now, the truth-value link demands that the statement, "S will happen a year from now", considered as uttered a year ago, was true: it was made true by what is happening now. It is *what happens in the future* that renders our statements about the future true, when they are true, and certainly not the tendencies discernible in the present. A proponent of model (2) may reply that the statement, as made a year ago, has now acquired a truth-value by the occurrence of S at the time it foretold: that statement, being about the future, was rendered true by what subsequently happened. But the conception of a future-tense statement's *acquiring* a truth-value is no more compatible with the constancy of truth than that of a past-tense statement's being deprived of the truth-value it formerly had. If truth and falsity are not to be relativized to the time at which truth-value is assessed, any statement, considered as uttered at a particular time, which is rightly judged at any time to be true must be or have been true at any other time.

We feel model (2) to be more palatable than model (3) because we think that the past has only the truth-value link to protect it. The future can look after itself. Even if it is now indeterminate, so that statements about it lack definite truth-values, it will eventually arrive in a determinate form; and that is all the reality that the future needs to have. We need not credit statements about the future, made now, with a determinate truth-value which they presently possess: they *will* be rendered true or false when the time comes, and that is enough to give the future tense the sense that we ascribe to it. With the past, it is different. It is not enough to concede that a statement about the past *was* rendered true or false at the time to which it relates: if the past does not continue to possess some present reality, so that our statements about the past do not necessarily now possess the truth-values they fleetingly had at, and soon after, the time to which they relate, the past tense cannot bear the sense we believe ourselves to have conferred upon it. A statement about the past must *still* be true or false, according to what happened at the time to which it relates; otherwise it has no substance.

This is a very natural reaction. The difficulty is to show that it is not mere rhetoric: that it really does point to some relevant difference between the objection to model (3) and the precisely analogous objection to model (2). It is a very common fallacy to argue about time by the use of loaded terminology; that is to say, to attempt to demonstrate an intrinsic difference between past and future by using terms explicable only in a temporally asymmetric manner. By such means, no genuine asymmetry has been shown to obtain, only an asymmetry in how we are disposed to talk about the matter.

Model (4) claimed that time is only one dimension of a four-dimensional reality, a fact which we fail to apprehend because of our special relationship, experiential and epistemological, to that dimension. What is this special relationship? According to model (4), we are rather curiously shaped four-dimensional creatures: to visualize our special relationship to the temporal dimension, we must imagine a static three-dimensional world. In this world, there are a number of roughly tubular objects; let us call them 'Tubes', and let us suppose that the dimension along which their length may be measured corresponds to the temporal dimension in the real world. We may call this particular spatial dimension 'pseudo-time'; and we may suppose that all the Tubes are smaller at an end of them that lies in the same pseudo-temporal direction. Let us call the smaller end of each Tube its 'left-hand end'. Investigation reveals that it is impossible to attribute either experience or knowledge to the Tubes in themselves; but both experience and knowledge can be attributed to two-dimensional cross-sections of them orthogonal to pseudo-time. (It is unnecessary to envisage the researches needed to establish this strange fact.) The experiences of a cross-section of a Tube depend only on what impinges on that cross-section; the knowledge of the world the Tubes inhabit that is possessed by any cross-section of one relates only to that part of the world that lies closer to its left-hand end; of that part lying in the opposite direction, it makes some well-founded guesses but has no knowledge.

It may be objected to this picture that it makes the distinction between the left-to-right direction along the pseudo-temporal dimension and the right-to-left direction depend only on the curious experiential and epistemological relation to that dimension of the cross-sections of the Tubes: nothing has been said about any asymmetries between the two directions observable in our imaginary world otherwise than in the Tubes. But the asymmetry for us consists in more than our experiencing only the present, or, rather, what we are presently in receipt of signals from, and in our having non-inferential knowledge of the present, in experience, and of the past, in memory, but having no non-inferential knowledge of the future. It lies in the fact that we form intentions to act in certain ways in the future, but can form no intentions to have acted in a particular way in the past; and also in the fact that we can bring it about that certain events shall later occur, but cannot bring it about that anything should have previously happened.

This latter asymmetry is connected, we may think, with an asymmetry we observe in external nature. We explain things by what led up to them, not by what follows them. More accurately, we take certain processes as not needing explanation for why they continue, but only why they deviate from some norm or other; they deviate because of some force that affects them. For example, we explain why a stone thrown by a small boy does not proceed indefinitely into space, but, if it does not hit anything, descends in a parabola to earth, by the force of gravity acting upon it. But we explain why the process occurs at all by what initiated it; we explain the stone's path by its having been launched upon it by the boy, not by what brings its flight to an end, its hitting a wall, say. These facts about what we require of an explanation, and what we do not normally accept as explaining anything, might be merely the result of our own cognitive asymmetry; but it appears to correspond to asymmetries we observe in nature. If the stone lobbed by the boy falls into a pond, it makes a splash from which concentric ripples emanate, and all this can be satisfactorily explained. But we never observe the reverse. We never observe concentric ripples converging on a spot on the pond from which first a jet of water emerges and then a stone that falls neatly into the hand of a boy standing by. Not just our style of causal explanation, but causality itself, appears to be temporally asymmetric.

It might be argued that, were it not for this asymmetry, we *could* act to bring it about that something had previously occurred; conversely, that because it is nonsensical to suppose that we could do so, causality must necessarily be temporally asymmetric. The latter direction of argument is, to most people, more appealing. For the absurdity of doing something in order to make it more likely that something should previously have happened is urged in cases when *causality* is not in question. The action that people are most likely to take in order to affect what has happened is prayer. Doubtless people sometimes pray for a miracle, but I am not speaking of this. The idea of affecting the past need not be that of making what has happened not have happened, any more than that of affecting the future is that of making what it was true to say would in fact happen not happen. I am, then, not speaking of someone's praying that something should have happened when he knows, or thinks he knows, that it has not: only of someone's praying that something should have happened when he does not know whether it has or not. Nevertheless, many people consider that this is an absurd, or even blasphemous, activity. Why?

There is a simple argument which convinces many people of the absurdity of doing something in order that some event, say P, should previously have happened. It runs like this:

> Either P has happened, or it has not.
> If it has happened, it is superfluous to do anything to bring about its previous occurrence.
> If it has not happened, it is futile to do anything to bring about its previous occurrence.
> If your action was superfluous, you will not have brought it about that P occurred.
> If your action was futile, you certainly will not have brought it about that P occurred.
> Hence in no case can you bring it about that P occurred.

This argument strikes many people as compelling. But what they fail to notice is that it is the precise dual of an argument that almost everyone would reject, namely the argument for fatalism. When you propose to do something in order that an event F should later occur, the fatalist argues that it is useless, as follows:

> Either F will happen, or it will not.
> If it is going to happen, it is superfluous to do anything to bring about its subsequent occurrence.
> If it is not going to happen, it is futile to do anything to bring about its subsequent occurrence.
> If your action is superfluous, you will not have brought it about that F occurs.
> If your action is futile, you certainly will not have brought it about that F occurs.
> Hence in no case can you bring it about that F occurs.

The two arguments are formally entirely analogous; hence, if either is valid, the other must be. If this is pointed out to a supporter of the former argument, he is likely to object, "But P has *already* either occurred or not occurred". This is of course only to reiterate that P is a past event, whereas F is a future event, and hence sophistically to assume what was to be demonstrated: it is a prime example of the use of temporally asymmetrical terminology to prove a temporal asymmetry. The sophistry may be carried further, by saying that it is senseless to try to bring about an event whose occurrence or non-occurrence is already determined; "determined" is then explained by saying that an event is determined if either it is an inescapable causal consequence of some past or present state of affairs or it has already happened: this is what the first of the two arguments shows, whereas the argument for fatalism fails since the future event F may not be determined. Or the petitio principii may be more blatant yet. The fallacy in the argument for fatalism lies in the fact that it may be only as an effect of the proposed action that the event F is going to occur, whereas the past event P cannot have occurred as an effect of the proposed action. If "effect" is *defined* in such a way that one event cannot be the effect of a later one, the objection becomes irrelevant; if not, the question has simply been begged.

There is a more sophisticated argument against the possibility of affecting the past, namely the falsification challenge. Someone who believes that an action Q will bring it about that a previous event P has occurred is challenged to perform Q on an occasion when he knows that P has not occurred. If he does so, this shows that Q is not a sufficient condition for the previous occurrence of P; if he fails, this shows that he was not free to perform Q when he chose, so that the occurrence of P might have been a causally necessary condition for performing Q. A similar challenge cannot be issued to one who believes that, by performing an action E, he can bring it about that a subsequent event F occurs, because, given such a belief, he cannot, independently of his intentions, identify an occasion on which F is not going to occur. This shows the connection between this asymmetry and that concerning our knowledge.

The falsification challenge is powerless when either:

(i) ignorance about whether P has occurred is taken to be integral to what makes the past event P more probable; or

(ii) it is impossible to know at the time of performing Q whether P has occurred or not.

Case (i) holds good when the action Q consists in praying that P may not have occurred; and yet many would consider this to be a senseless way to act. They cannot do so on the strength of the falsifying challenge: they must do so solely on the strength of the argument analogous to the argument for fatalism.

Even when it is applicable, the falsifying challenge is not as conclusive a refutation as may at first appear. For it to be reasonable to do Q in order that P may have happened, it is not necessary to believe Q to be a totally sufficient condition of P: it is enough that it makes it more probable that P should have happened, just as an action E may be done in order that the subsequent event F should happen even though E does no more than make it more probable that F will happen. So a certain number of 'falsifications' will not destroy the motive for performing Q. A failure to perform Q when P has not occurred will not always show that the agent was not free to perform it: it may be explained on some other ground, for instance by the house's catching fire at the crucial moment. Of course, this sort of thing is liable to happen when magic is involved; but we are not here supposing that other than natural agencies are at work. Finally, information is not always reliable: on some occasions when the agent intends to meet the challenge, it may later turn out that he had been mistaken in supposing that P has not occurred. But, if this were to happen often, and if we really had strong grounds for believing the action Q to make the previous occurrence of P more probable, we should come to lose the presupposition that we could identify cases in which P had not occurred, independently of our intention whether or not to perform Q. The challenge would lose its power to shake our belief in the efficacy of Q; and the connection between the asymmetry of causative action and that of knowledge would be strengthened by weakening both asymmetries.

The asymmetry between past and future embodied in model (2) is of course strongly connected, not only with the asymmetry of knowledge, but also with the asymmetry of causation. The future is indeterminate, in the view of the proponent of model (2), not only because we can know the past independently of our intentions, but cannot know the future independently of our intentions, and, moreover, cannot genuinely be said to *know* it even taking our intentions into account, but also because we can affect the future but cannot affect the past. Determinism is often thought to preclude our freedom of action. My being free to do or not to do something is usually expressed as my being able to do it if I choose, and not to do it if I choose not to. Arguments about free will then often turn on the question how free I am to make the choices that I do. This question is irrelevant to the falsifying challenge: all that is relevant is my freedom to do as I choose. But this freedom to perform an action of a given type A is closely linked to causation. It can be empirically established by my never having the experience of deciding to do A and unaccountably failing, or of determining not to do A and unaccountably finding myself doing it; but the adverb "unaccountably" here alludes to what is causally explicable. My freedom to do A is not impugned by interruptions that can readily be explained independently of my intention; my freedom not to do it is not impugned by changes of mind on reasonable grounds, nor by accidents that result in my doing A unintentionally. If, however, there should prove to be some prior or concomitant circumstance strongly correlated with events that prevent my carrying out my intention to do A, the suspicion may arise that it is the absence of such a correlated circumstance that renders me able to do A; the suspicion may be strengthened by experiment, and hardened to a likelihood if some causal explanation of the correlation is found. Similarly, if some concomitant circumstance is found to be strongly correlated with my doing A, whether intentionally or accidentally, a suspicion may arise that it is this circumstance that causes me to do A; the suspicion will be strengthened if the mechanism of such a causal link can be propounded. Freedom of action is very closely bound up with causal explanation.

The outcome of our discussion is that the epistemological asymmetry of past and future is matched by a causal asymmetry in nature. Contrary to what is usually supposed, the idea of doing something to bring it about that something should have previously occurred is not, indeed, an intrinsic conceptual absurdity; nor, therefore, is the idea that our knowledge of the past might be subject to our present intentions. But the way things happen in nature is not such as to provide us with any causal means of bringing about the past, and hence of realizing these ideas. It cannot be said absolutely that there are no instances of time-reversed causation in nature; but there are none that we are able to employ in order to determine what has previously happened. This is because there are no such instances in which it is possible for us to discover at the time of performing the action whether the prior event has occurred or not; it follows that there is no event of such a kind that we can, within a given interval, on occasion discover its prior occurrence, and whose occurrence we could on other occasions bring about retrospectively within that interval.

In view of the causal asymmetry between past and future, the future may indeed rightly be said to be open, as proponents of model (2) maintain, in so far as it is not constrained by deterministic laws. This conclusion is, however, insufficient to vindicate model (2). The fact that a proposition about the future is open in this sense, i. e. that its truth is not determined from present circumstances by exceptionless causal laws, has no tendency to show that it is devoid of truth-value: the arguments that we have considered for denying a truth-value to a statement about the future are no more cogent than arguments for denying one to a statement about the past. Model (4) wins the debate.

Does it follow that we ought to adopt model (4) without further ado? Not at all. The whole discussion in this paper has been conducted on the basis of a classical or realist conception of truth: that according to which truth and falsity are independent of what knowledge we possess or are capable of obtaining. There is an alternative conception: the justificationist conception of meaning and of truth according to which the truth of a proposition depends upon the possibility of our knowing it. It is evident that the adoption of a justificationist conception of truth must alter the whole debate between the rival models of time. All that I hope to have established in this discussion is that anyone who cleaves to a realist conception of truth must adopt model (4).

Notes

1 Cf. C. D. Broad, *Scientific Thought* (London: Routledge, 1923), pp. 53–85.
2 Cf. J. A. Wheeler, "The 'Past' and the 'Delayed Choice' Double-Slit Experiment", in: *Mathematical Foundations of Quantum Theory*, ed. A. Marlow (New York: Academic Press, 1978) pp. 9–48; here p. 41.
3 Cf. Augustine, *Confessions* XIV, 17 f.

Michael Theunissen

Rekonstruktion der Realität
Hegels Beitrag zur Aufklärung von Reflexionsbestimmungen*

Die folgenden Überlegungen wollen eine Philosophie, die wie keine andere „in synthetischer Absicht" betrieben wurde, auf eine bestimmte Synthetisierungsleistung hin prüfen. Sie fragen nach den Erfolgsaussichten des von Hegel unternommenen Versuchs, aus seinem Neuansatz ganz neu entwickelte Terme an die von Platon bis Kant geleistete Begriffsarbeit anzuschließen. Damit zielen sie weder auf eine rein immanente Interpretation noch auf eine bloß äußerliche Applikation.

Eine Verständigung über Hegels Beitrag zur Aufklärung der Begriffe, die bei ihm Reflexionsbestimmungen heißen, muß sich zwar an der aufzuklärenden Sache orientieren. Sie hält aber von einer über das Logische schlechterdings *hinaus*führenden Deutung kaum weniger Abstand als von einer tiefer ins Logische *hinein*führenden. Der absichtlich allgemein gehaltene, auch von Hegel variabel eingesetzte Terminus *Realität* umschreibt den Ort, auf den hin eine für sich genommen rein logische Theorie durch ihre geschichtliche Selbstvermittlung von sich aus über sich hinauswill.

Das Projekt hat seine eigenen Schwierigkeiten. In der Logik der Reflexion selbst ist Hegel bei sich, im Fortgang zu den Reflexionsbestimmungen geht er zugleich auf die Tradition zu. Relativ leicht einschätzen läßt sich der Wert seiner an der traditionellen Metaphysik und Logik geübten Kritik.[1] Schwerer zugänglich ist der Sachgehalt seiner eigenen Position. Wohl nicht zufällig existiert außer einem auf den Kantbezug eingeschränkten Buch Michael Wolffs[2] keine Studie, die Auskunft über die von Hegel erzielten Erkenntnisfortschritte gäbe. Daran mag seine Theorie mit schuld sein. Zum einen präsentiert sie sich in einer Sprache, in welcher der Gegenstand sonst nicht verhandelt wird. Zum anderen ist sie unlösbar ins System eingebunden und zumal von der sie fundierenden Reflexionslogik vorgeprägt. Das eine droht sie kommunikationsunfähig zu machen, das andere belastet sie mit Prämissen, die jeden Versuch behindern, von außen einen Zugang zu ihr zu finden.

Insbesondere ihre Abhängigkeit von der basalen Reflexionslogik erregt den Verdacht, daß sie sich vom allgemeinen Diskurs löst. Hegel setzt die fünf von ihm behandelten Reflexionsbestimmungen – Identität und absoluten Unterschied, Verschiedenheit, Gegensatz und Widerspruch – in ein künstlich anmutendes Verhältnis zur Ausdifferenzierung der Reflexion in setzende, äußere und bestimmende.[3] Sie sollen allesamt der bestimmenden Reflexion zugehören, als das, wozu diese sich bestimmt, aber so, daß sie die Differenz von setzender, äußerer und bestimmender Reflexion auf deren Boden erneuern: Identität und Unterschied sind Produkte der bestimmenden als setzender Reflexion, Verschiedenheit resultiert aus einer bestimmenden Reflexion, die zur äußeren tendiert, der Gegensatz entspricht einer bestimmenden Reflexion, die zu sich selbst kommt, und der Widerspruch wandelt sie zu einer ausschließenden ab.[4] Besteht auch nur die geringste Aussicht, mit einer solchen Konstruktion den Phänomenen gerecht zu werden? Darf Hegel überhaupt erwarten, von einer eigenwillig zum Ursprung von allem erklärten Reflexion aus die erwähnten Begriffe als deren Bestimmungen erfassen zu können? Konkreter gefragt: Hat er eine Chance, die diesen Begriffen einwohnende Negativität, die für Wolff die reflexionslogische schlechthin ist[5], so als gäbe es keine andere, aus der *absoluten* Negativität abzuleiten, welche die ursprüngliche Reflexion kennzeichnet? Die absolute Negativität ist die einer Reflexion, die reine Selbstnegation ist. Demgegenüber liegt die reflexionslogisch genannte darin, daß jene Begriffe sich als Relationen von Relaten darstellen, von denen jedes nicht ist, was das andere ist, und in diesem Sinne das Negative des anderen darstellt. Ist es möglich, die besondere Struktur dieser Negativität aus der Verfassung der absoluten zu entwickeln?

Mit einer Antwort sollte man sich nicht übereilen. Es scheint, als mache Hegel im Übergang von der absoluten zur relationalen Negativität einen Sprung. Aber auch die Gestalten der relationalen Negativität selber vermag er nicht bruchlos miteinander zu verbinden. Unmittelbares Thema soll im folgenden dieser Bruch im Gefüge der Reflexionsbestimmungen sein. Von ihm her läßt sich jene Frage wenigstens mittelbar beantworten. Er trennt nämlich die eigentlichen Reflexionsbestimmungen von einer Identität und einem Unterschied, die im Grunde nur Manifestationen der reinen Reflexion sind. Zugleich zeigt er die Schwierigkeiten an, die Hegel damit hat, seinen innovativen Ansatz an die Tradition zurückzubinden. Um den Bruch auch nur wahrnehmen zu können, müssen wir die Logik der Reflexionsbestimmungen in eine geschichtliche Perspektive rücken. Das zweite Kapitel der Wesenslogik antwortet auf das zehnte Buch der aristotelischen *Metaphysik*, das größtenteils dieselben Begriffe behandelt. Hegels noch nie gebührend beachtete[6] Replik auf den einzigen Text, der nach Platons *Sophistes* ein vergleichbares Unternehmen gestartet hat, wird aber mehr enthüllen als einen Bruch. In geschichtlicher Perspektive offenbart sich darüber hinaus dessen Fruchtbarkeit. Die Prüfung des antiken Konzepts und die Analyse seiner Transformation durch Hegel sollen die Voraussetzungen für den Versuch schaffen, an dessen Gegenentwurf eine Sachhaltigkeit aufzudecken, durch die er über seine immanente Rationalität hinausweist.

I

In methodischer Hinsicht unterscheidet sich Aristoteles von Hegel vor allem dadurch, daß er, auch in *Metaphysik* Iota, *ab ovo* anfängt. Und zwar macht er den Anfang mit dem Einen oder Eins (ἕν), das sich ihm durch seine Unteilbarkeit als Anfang empfiehlt, aber auch wegen seiner Bestimmtheit. Eine Rechtfertigung für den Anfang mit ihm gibt das Buch Gamma, demzufolge alles Denken und Sprechen damit anhebt, etwas Bestimmtes zu bezeichnen.[7] Dementsprechend ist das aristotelische Eins primär das je so oder so bestimmte Einzelne und sekundär das wiederum bestimmte Wesenswas, das davon ausgesagt wird. Der Anfang mit ihm opponiert der vermeintlich alle Bestimmtheit auflösenden Alleinheitslehre. Seine Konsequenz ist aber, daß Aristoteles ihn gewissermaßen wiederholen muß, nämlich mit der Frage nach dem Verhältnis des Einen zum Vielen. Nach der Exposition der Grundbestimmung macht der Verfasser von *Metaphysik* Iota einen Neuansatz mit den Folgebestimmungen des Einen und Vielen, mit dem Identischen, Ähnlichen, Gleichen auf der einen, dem Differenten, Unähnlichen, Ungleichen auf der andern Seite. Genötigt wird er dazu durch die Einsicht, daß er eigentlich immer schon die Vielheit des Einzelnen zum Ausgangspunkt genommen hat. Noch diskontinuierlicher wird seine Darstellung durch eine weitere Zäsur, nämlich die zwischen den Folgebestimmungen und dem Unterschied, der sich nicht einfach auf die eine oder die andere Seite verrechnen läßt. Die Diskontinuitäten setzen sich in die Folgebestimmungen des Unterschieds hinein fort. Aristoteles muß einen zweifachen Gegensatz annehmen, einen, der zwischen dem Einen und dem Vielen besteht, und einen durch den Unterschied hindurchgegangenen.[8] In den Kontext des letzteren arbeitet er den Widerspruch ein, der aber merkwürdig ortlos bleibt. Die Hauptuntersuchung über den Widerspruch lagert er ins vierte Buch aus, ohne daß klar würde, wie die dort sprachlogisch aufgefaßte Figur mit der in die Ontologie hineingezogenen Randerscheinung gleichen Namens zusammenhängt.

Zu den systematischen, die Anordnung der Begriffe betreffenden Problemen kommen interne Aporien in den Begriffen selbst hinzu. Das Eins ist faktisch bereits als etwas Identisches in Anspruch genommen, als das mit sich Identische, und umgekehrt gilt dieses, wie auch das mit anderem Identische, für Eins. Im übrigen bleibt offen, was das Identische, als zweistelliger Begriff mit dem einstelligen Eins in Wahrheit nicht zu verwechseln, *primär* sein soll, das mit sich Identische, als ein gegenüber der Fremdidentität stärkerer Fall von Einssein, oder das mit anderem Identische, von dem Selbstidentität nur ein Sonderfall wäre. Auf der Gegenseite erscheint das Differente noch mehrdeutiger. Es umfaßt, ein verleugnetes Erbe platonischer Anderheit, das bestimmte Andere (τὸ ἄλλο), das dem Identischen gegenübersteht, und das unbestimmt Verschiedene (τὸ ἕτερον) als eines unter den vielen anderen sowie auch die anderen insgesamt (τὰ ἄλλα). Soweit Aristoteles das bestimmte Andere unter diese Pluralität subsumiert, kann er es nicht wirklich gegen das Unterschiedene abheben, obwohl er es als Mittel zu dessen Abgrenzung vom *Ver*schiedenen benutzt: δια ορὰ δὲ καὶ ἑτερότης ἄλλο, *Unterschied und Verschiedenheit sind anderes.*[9] Ein weiteres Problem taucht bei der Definition des Unterschiedenen selbst auf. Es zeichnet sich vor dem bloß *Ver*schiedenen durch das Identische aus, worin etwas sich von etwas unterscheidet. Die zum Unterschied gehörige Identität fügt sich aber schwerlich dem eingeführten Identitätsbegriff. Aristoteles bringt eine nicht eingeführte Identität ins Spiel, die der Art oder Gattung. Ebenso wesentlich wie für den Unterschied ist die art- oder gattungsmäßige Identität für den aus ihm entwickelten Gegensatz. Dem Gegensatz hängt zudem die eigene Schwierigkeit an, daß Aristoteles sich nicht entscheiden kann, ob er ihn nur innerhalb einer Gattung oder auch zwischen Gattungen zulassen soll. Seine für die Kommentatoren so bedenkliche Unschlüssigkeit in dieser Frage ist aus der Sicht Hegels freilich kaum noch von Belang, da Aristoteles die Sache aus dieser Sicht schon dadurch verfehlt, daß er die gegensatzimmanente Identität mit den Begriffen von Art und Gattung regionalontologisch klassifiziert.

Wie geht nun Hegel mit seiner Vorlage um? Einer seiner Einwände gegen die Tradition lautet, die für Axiome ausgegebenen Sätze, vom Satz der Identität bis zum Satz des Widerspruchs, hätten, so die Anmerkung zum Ganzen, „die schiefe Seite, *das Sein, alles Etwas,* zum Subjekte zu haben" (Anm. 5. 1).[10] Ob nicht auch Hegel selbst an einem solchen Subjekt festhalten muß, wird noch zu fragen sein. Jedenfalls will er nicht mehr bloß *das* Identische, *das* Andere, *das* Unterschiedene usw. begreifen, sondern Identität, Anderheit, Unterschied. Hinter dieser Absicht steckt mehr als nur der Anspruch, die Reflexionsbestimmungen allererst auf den Begriff zu bringen, die Reflexionsbestimmung als solche und alle einzelnen Reflexionsbestimmungen. Der im Verhältnis zur Seinslogik fortgeschrittene Status der Wesenslogik verlangt, das vom Sein Übriggebliebene in den Reflexionsbestimmungen selbst zu suchen. Bei der Revision der Aufgabe operiert Hegel freilich nicht nur *gegen*, sondern auch *mit* Aristoteles. Die veränderte Aufgabenstellung ist vorgebildet in der aristotelischen Unterscheidung von zwei Fragen, der Frage nach den Dingen, die man Eins nennt, und der nach dem Einssein selber und dem Begriff des Eins.[11] Darüber hinaus entnimmt Hegel dem Buch Iota einen Hinweis auf das Gesuchte. Auch *sein* Interesse zielt auf Bestimmtheit. Nur ist es sein Programm, die Option des Aristoteles für Bestimmtheit mit der Philosophie zu versöhnen, gegen die sie gerichtet war, nämlich mit der Alleinheitslehre.

Das Programm steckt den Rahmen ab, in welchem Hegel erstens das Verhältnis der Reflexionsbestimmungen zueinander und zweitens diese selbst umorganisiert. Die von Aristoteles diskontinuierlich angeordneten Begriffe bilden für Hegel einen denknotwendigen Zusammenhang, in welchem ein absolut erster den nachfolgenden und jeder weitere den nächsten aus sich hervortreibt, weil er ihn bereits in sich enthält. Indessen kann die „Umschmelzung" des aristotelischen Konzepts, die Hegel in seinen philosophiegeschichtlichen Vorlesungen fordert,[12] ebenfalls daran anknüpfen. Punktuell nimmt Aristoteles selbst sie schon vor, mit seiner von Hegel wörtlich übernommenen These, daß der Gegensatz der vollendete Unterschied sei, und generell ermutigt er zu ihr mit seinem Ansatz bei der Bewegung. Seine Einheitslehre ist orientiert an einheitlicher Bewegung und an einem einheitlichen Denkvollzug, den er seinerseits als Bewegung deutet. Hegels Vorhaben, alle Begriffe in eine sie übergreifende Gedankenbewegung aufzulösen, läßt sich als Konsequenz aus diesem Ansatz auffassen. Die derart universalisierte Bewegung kommt aber programmgemäß dadurch zustande, daß jede Reflexionsbestimmung, noch vor ihrer Auffüllung durch etwas Bestimmtes außerhalb ihrer, selbst in einer Weise bestimmt ist, die ihre Ergänzung durch eine bestimmte andere fordert und so einer Einheit zustrebt, die in ihr zunächst verloren scheint.

Dem Programm widerspricht nur scheinbar, daß Hegel Einheit aus der Reihe der in *Metaphysik* X untersuchten Begriffe streicht. Abgesehen davon, daß die Einheit, um die es ihm geht, unter der Herrschaft der Reflexionsbestimmungen eben verloren scheint, ist ja auch die aristotelische, als einstelliger Begriff, keine Reflexionsbestimmung. So fängt Hegel mit der Identität an, allerdings mit einer, die er als Kontrastfigur zur aristotelischen anlegt. Die aristotelische, herabgesetzt zur abstrakten, kommt fast nur in Anmerkungen zu unserem Kapitel vor, als Objekt der Kritik. Gleichwohl läßt sich allein aus der abstrakten Identität zureichend erklären, wieso das Kapitel bei einer vermeintlich konkreten ansetzt. Aus dem Rückbezug der Reflexionslogik auf die Seinslogik mag der Anfang mit ihr verständlich sein. Als Identität reformuliert Hegel ja die seinslogische Anfangsbestimmung, das reine Sein. Aber nach den Kriterien der Reflexionslogik selber verdient die Identität den Primat nicht. Resultiert doch die Gleichheit des Wesens mit sich, deren Nachfolge sie antritt, erst aus dessen Grundverfassung, der absoluten Negativität, die sich zum absoluten Unterschied fortbestimmt.

Hegels Hauptaugenmerk richtet sich denn auch auf Differenz, nicht auf Identität. Seine Logik der Reflexionsbestimmungen hat ihren Schwerpunkt insofern da, wo sie nach ihrem Selbstverständnis mit *Metaphysik* X übereinkommt. Der absolute Unterschied markiert nämlich die Stelle, an der sie in die von Aristoteles eröffnete Bahn einbiegt. Zur Vorlage greift Hegel an dieser Stelle allerdings aus Schwäche. Der als Herzstück gedachte Abschnitt über den absoluten Unterschied (B.1) gerät zur lockeren Klammer. In der Sache zusammengehörig mit dem Identitätsabschnitt (A), dient er nur als Absprungsbasis für die Analyse der weiteren Differenzbestimmungen (B.2 und B.3). Zu seiner Klammerfunktion verhilft ihm Aristoteles. Der Abschnitt kreist um Sätze, die gar nicht vom *absoluten* Unterschied handeln: „*Darin*, drückt man sich aus, sind zwei Dinge *unterschieden*, daß sie [usw.] – *Darin*, d. h. in einer und derselben Rücksicht, in demselben Bestimmungsgrunde" (B.1.1.6–7). Die Sätze zitieren *Met.* X,3: „Das Differente differiert von etwas durch etwas, so daß es etwas Identisches geben muß, worin sie differieren."[13] Diese Art von Differenz wird Hegel unter seinen Begriff des Unterschieds überhaupt subsumieren, das *überhaupt* so auslegend, daß es das Gemeinsame von Verschiedenheit und Gegensatz anzeigt. Daß jene Differenz auch auf die Verschiedenheit übergreife, behauptet Hegel freilich ohne Rückendeckung durch Aristoteles. Einer seiner folgenreichsten Eingriffe in die aristotelische Konzeption ist, daß er die Verschiedenheit, die ἑτερότης, unter die Botmäßigkeit des Unterschieds bringt. Während Aristoteles Unterschied in Verschiedenheit fundiert, macht Hegel umgekehrt die Verschiedenheit vom Unterschied abhängig. Man muß, so sein unausgesprochenes Argument dafür, immer schon verstanden haben, was Unterschied bedeutet, um Verschiedenheit verstehen zu können. Mit dieser Einsicht kehrt sich in Wirklichkeit auch seine Philosophie der Differenz von der Vorlage ab. Die gegen die Verschiedenheit abgehobenen Differenzbestimmungen, Gegensatz und Widerspruch, begreift Hegel geradezu in Opposition zu Aristoteles.

Hegels Gegensatz hat mit dem, den auch Aristoteles aus dem Unterschied ableitet, mit der ἐναντίωσις, sonst wenig zu tun und so gut wie gar nichts mit dem anders verfaßten, an der Beziehung des Einen zum Vielen abgelesenen Gegensatz, der uns bei dem Verfasser von *Metaphysik* X fast nur in Verbform begegnet, als ἀντικεῖσται, *einander gegenüberliegen*. Der davon später durch den Zusatz *konträr* abgehobene Gegensatz, der zwischen seinen beiden Extremen ein Mittleres hat, liegt unter dem Niveau einer Theorie, derzufolge wirklich entgegengesetzte Pole eine vollständige Disjunktion bilden: Das Positive ist identisch mit dem Nicht-Negativen, das Negative identisch mit dem Nicht-Positiven.[14] Hegel setzt die ἐναντίωσις auf die Stufe äußerster Verschiedenheit herab und erklärt den Gegensatz, der seinen Namen verdient, aus einer sozusagen zugespitzteren Lage. Daran zu erinnern, muß im Rahmen eines Vergleichs mit Aristoteles genügen. Hegels Gegensatzkonzeption wird noch ausführlich darzustellen sein. Für eine Interpretation, welche die Logik der Reflexionsbestimmungen auf ihren Sachgehalt befragt, ist sie von besonderem Interesse.

Auch hinsichtlich des Widerspruchs reicht vorläufig ein Wort zum Wandel des Theoriegefüges aus. Daß Hegel mit seinem berüchtigten Ja zum Widerspruch nicht einfach dasselbe affirmiert, das Aristoteles negiert, dürfte ohnehin klar sein. Aber vor aller Neubestimmung des Begriffs weist er ihm bereits einen anderen Ort an. Während Aristoteles den Widerspruch tendenziell von den in Iota thematischen Begriffen abtrennt, möchte Hegel ihn zunächst einmal in die umgeordnete Reihe dieser Begriffe hineinverlegen. Er beraubt ihn zwar keineswegs jeder Eigenständigkeit. Aber was er ihm noch für sich zugesteht, über die ihm vorgelagerten Reflexionsbestimmungen hinaus, ergibt sich selbst erst aus der Rolle, die er in der Logik dieser Bestimmungen von Anfang an spielt.[15] Basal ist er erstens einer, der im Begriff der Reflexionsbestimmung überhaupt liegt, und zweitens der jeder einzelnen. Allen Reflexionsbestimmungen ist nach Hegel gemeinsam, daß in ihnen ein „Gesetztsein" mit einer „Reflexion-in-sich" zusammentrifft, die es zu dementieren scheint. Hängen nämlich die Relate der Relationen, die sie bilden, als gesetzte von der sie setzenden Reflexion ab, so beanspruchen sie als ihrerseits in sich reflektierte, auf sich zurückgebeugte Unabhängigkeit. Zum Programm der ihnen gewidmeten Logik gehört, diesen latenten Widerspruch durch eine Bereinigung seiner Quelle, der Reflexion-in-sich, aufzulösen. Dafür ist aber erforderlich, jede einzelne Reflexionsbestimmung zuvor in den ihr immanenten Widerspruch zu treiben. Von ihrem Übergehen in die nächsthöhere ist ein Übergehen zweiter Potenz zu unterscheiden, das in den Widerspruch. Der hat eine je besondere Gestalt. Das potenzierte Übergehen braucht sich nicht in und mit dem Übergang in die nächsthöhere Bestimmung zu vollziehen. Der unter den basalen Widerspruchsformen härteste Widerspruch, der im Gegensatz, dessen nächsthöhere Bestimmung ja der Widerspruch selbst ist, muß schon darum eine andere Struktur aufweisen. Der für die Verschiedenheit kennzeichnende Widerspruch entsteht gar nicht durch Progression, sondern gewissermaßen durch Regression, nämlich in die abstrakte Identität, auf welche die Beachtung des von Aristoteles über ihn verhängten Verbots zurückführt. Progressiv ist eigentlich nur das In-den-Widerspruch-Übergehen der Identität. Es fällt damit zusammen, daß die Identität in den absoluten Unterschied umschlägt, weil sie sich gegen ihn bloß abstrakt und damit nicht wirklich festhalten läßt.

II

Mit alledem wurde die Theorie Hegels erst nur auf ihren aristotelischen Hintergrund abgebildet. Wie steht es aber um ihren Sachgehalt? Die Frage zielt allem voran auf den Punkt, der Hegels Ausgangspunkt war und auf den wir bei der Suche nach dem Ort des Widerspruchs zurückgekommen sind: die These, daß Identität, in seiner Sprache ausgedrückt, ihre Wahrheit im absoluten Unterschied habe.

Da stellt sich uns jedoch sogleich ein Hindernis in den Weg. Wenn zutrifft, daß Hegel in der Konsequenz seines vorgängigen Ansatzes bei der Reflexion mit dem Unterschied anfangen müßte, dann verheißt der gemeinten Identität nur ein solcher Anfang logische Wahrheit. Die gemeinte Identität besteht allein darin, daß die Reflexion als selbstbezügliche Negativität *ist*. Demzufolge gibt es sie nicht ohne den für die Reflexion einstehenden Unterschied. Daß *Hegels* Identität sich in ihrem Gegenteil wiederfindet, leuchtet also ein. Aber ist damit auch einsichtig, daß wir *alle* Identität so zu denken haben? Hiervon müßte uns Hegel in der den Reflexionsbestimmungen selbst gewidmeten Logik überzeugen. Tatsächlich unternimmt er, folgerichtig ausgehend von der Identität als abstrakter, den Versuch, Überzeugungsarbeit zu leisten, allerdings nicht im Haupttext, sondern in einer Anmerkung, in der zweiten zur Identität.

Daß diese Anmerkung als einzige in den Haupttext übergeht[16], verweist auf ihre paradigmatische Funktion. Fast alle Anmerkungen zum Haupttext sind den Sätzen gewidmet, in denen die Tradition Reflexionsbestimmungen formuliert, dem Satz der Identität, dem Satz der Verschiedenheit, den Hegel aus Leibniz herausliest, dem Satz des Gegensatzes, als den er den vom ausgeschlossenen Dritten deutet, und schließlich dem Satz vom Widerspruch, der für ihn nur die Kehrseite des Identitätssatzes ist. Hegels Traditionskritik hat vornehmlich die Form einer Kritik dieser Sätze. Als solche kann sie die Sache in einer Außenperspektive zugänglich machen, weil sie ihr im Kritisierten selbst auf die Spur kommt, indem sie den Sätzen einen nicht intendierten Sinn gibt. Gegen die Intention der Sätze spielt sie aus, was wir als deren Sprecher faktisch tun. Der so geborgene Gehalt ist natürlich nicht der des logisch Wahren, das die Theorie in ihrem Darstellungsgang entfaltet. Er ist ein Erfahrungsgehalt. Und zwar liegt er in der Erfahrung, die wir im Sprechen mit der Sache machen. Dies möchte Hegel beispielhaft am Identitätssatz demonstrieren.

Anders als im Haupttext schiebt Hegel die abstrakte Identität in der Anmerkung zu diesem Satz nicht umstandslos beiseite. Zwar versteht er unter ihrer Abstraktheit auch hier ihr Getrenntsein vom Unterschied. Aber darüber hinaus traut er ihr zu, in der Trennung vom Unterschied ihre Einheit mit ihm zu realisieren. Zutrauen zu ihr gewinnt er deswegen, weil er sie an Erfahrung anschließt, wenn auch nur an eine reduzierte. Konkrete Identität entsteht in jedem Sprechakt aus einem Erfahrungs*prozeß*. Es ist dieser Prozeß, der sie zu einer vollgültig wirklichen, lebendigen macht. Die abstrakte Identität hingegen ist starr und leer, weil sie Dinge so zurückspiegelt, wie sie sich einer stationären Erfahrung darstellen. Dies glaubt Hegel an dem über sie aufgestellten Satz selbst ablesen zu können. Die Pointe seiner Kritik ist, daß der Identitätssatz seinerseits von Sätzen abgezogen ist, aber nicht von normalen, die einem Subjekt ein Prädikat beilegen, sondern von solchen, die ihr Subjekt nur durch es selbst bestimmen und darum defizitär sind. In der Rumpferfahrung, die im Dahersagen von Tautologien übrigbleibt, ist aber, gerade weil sie auf der Stelle tritt, die Defizienz miterfahren, dies, daß „*nichts* gesagt ist" (A. Anm. 2.5.2). Das Nichts enthält eine Anzeige auf den Mangel isolierter Identität und so indirekt auf deren „Hinausgehen über sich in die Auflösung ihrer selbst" (A. Anm. 2.6.3). Im Gedanken an das Hinausgehen reproduziert der Sprecher das Übergehen der Identität in einen Unterschied, der als absoluter das Übergehen *ist*, weil er, mehr als nichts, sich dennoch nicht in etwas festsetzt. Die abstrakte Identität wird so zum Beweis dessen, wogegen das Verstandesdenken sie mobilisiert.

Selbstverständlich möchte Hegel mehr liefern als einen der äußeren Reflexion anvertrauten Beweis. Auch im strengen Darstellungsgang des *Corpus* seiner Theorie deckt er einen intersubjektiv vermittelbaren, nicht bloß systemimmanenten Sachverhalt auf. Dessen können wir uns jedoch nur auf einem Umweg vergewissern, über die Besinnung auf eine Schwierigkeit, welche die Theorie mit sich selbst hat. Wir müssen den Subtext freilegen, der sich unter der Textoberfläche verbirgt. Eine augenscheinlich theoriekonstitutive Schwierigkeit tut sich uns auf, sobald wir die Zweitlektüre, die wir mit der von *Corrolarien* angeleiteten Lesung des Anfangs aufgenommen haben, in Orientierung am Haupttext fortsetzen und fürs erste auf die Verschiedenheit ausdehnen. Da nämlich ereignet sich so etwas wie eine unbedachte Wiederkehr des Aristoteles. Durch die im ganzen homogenisierte Theorie geht ein Riß, der den basalen Bruch im immer wieder neu ansetzenden Original reproduziert. Die Hoffnung, der Wahrheitsgehalt der Theorie werde sich ihrer Innenansicht erschließen, gründet sich indes auf den guten Sinn, der durch den Riß hindurchscheint.

Die Reihe der Widersprüche, in welche die einzelnen Reflexionsbestimmungen auf je besondere Weise geraten, wird durch einen tiefen Einschnitt unterbrochen. Hegel selbst unterteilt die Reihe in einen nur an sich bestehenden und einen gesetzten Widerspruch. Der Widerspruch an sich belastet schon die ursprüngliche, in den absoluten Unterschied umschlagende Identität. Der gesetzte Widerspruch reicht seinerseits weit hinter den Endpunkt der Entwicklung zurück. Er ist der, von dem Hegel im Rückblick sagt, daß er bereits „an der Entgegensetzung hervortritt" (C. Anm. 3.1.2). An der Entgegensetzung tritt aber ein Widerspruch hervor, der zutiefst in der Verschiedenheit wurzelt, darin, daß entgegengesetzte Seiten zugleich verschiedene sind. Nun ist er ein Indiz dafür, daß der Prozeß der Bewahrheitung jedes Begriffs durch den höheren zwischen dem absoluten Unterschied und der Verschiedenheit aussetzt. Das die einzelnen Reflexionsbestimmungen umschlingende Band ist an dieser Stelle verknotet. Hat die Identität ihre Wahrheit im absoluten Unterschied, so die Verschiedenheit die ihrige im Gegensatz, dem sie schon in sich, durch eine Verwandlung der diffusen in eine *„bestimmte"* (B.2. Anm. 3.2), zuneigt. Aber die Verschiedenheit ist nicht ihrerseits die Wahrheit des absoluten Unterschieds. Hegel entwickelt sie denn auch nicht aus ihm. Ja, er entwickelt sie überhaupt nicht. Er nimmt sie als ein Zerfallsprodukt hin, als das Residuum eines Zerfalls der Identität, den er mehr voraussetzend als setzend an den Anfang ihrer Analyse stellt: „Die Identität *zerfällt* an ihr selbst in Verschiedenheit..." (B.2.1.1.1). Daß er, wie vorhin erwähnt, den von Aristoteles angenommenen Vorrang der Verschiedenheit vor dem Unterschied in dessen Priorität umdeutet, heißt keineswegs: Er leitet Verschiedenheit aus dem absoluten Unterschied ab. Dies heißt nur: Er depotenziert sie. Immerhin bereitet er seiner Theorie eben dadurch einen neuen Boden, den, auf den die Identität durch ihren Zerfall abgleitet. Die Wiederkehr des Aristoteles besteht in dieser Doppelbödigkeit der Theorie. Setzt Aristoteles nach dem Ansatz beim Eins mit dessen Vielheit neu an, so Hegel nach dem

Ansatz bei der Identität mit der Verschiedenheit, die er, vermutlich in Erinnerung an Aristoteles, „die bloße Mannigfaltigkeit der Vorstellung" (C. Anm. 3.7.5) nennt. Dementsprechend spaltet sich die eine Reihe in zwei Reihen, in eine Reihe eigentlicher und eine Reihe uneigentlicher Reflexionsbestimmungen. Die, wie Hegel im Vorspann des Kapitels sagt, „eigentliche Bestimmung" eines Unterschieds, der Verschiedenheit und Gegensatz umfaßt, spaltet sich von den uneigentlichen Bestimmungen der Identität und des absoluten Unterschieds ab.

Allerdings hat es mit jener Mannigfaltigkeit bei Hegel etwas durchaus Unaristotelisches auf sich. Aristotelisch gedacht, wäre sie weltliche Realität, eine Pluralität von Dingen. Die Identität zerfällt aber mit ihrem Zerfall in die Verschiedenheit nicht wirklich in die vielen Dinge, sondern wiederum in Gedankenbestimmungen, in die, zu denen sie selbst und der Unterschied, im Verlust seiner Absolutheit, werden. Der Zerfall liegt darin, daß Identität und Unterschied sich einander entfremden. Aus der Identität wird eine Gleichheit, die nicht auf Ungleichheit bezogen ist, aus dem Unterschied eine Ungleichheit, die ihre Beziehung auf Gleichheit verleugnet. Die Substitution des Zerfalls in Dinge durch einen Zerfall von Begriffen entspringt freilich keiner *directio recta*, sondern der Rücknahme einer Intention. Daß die Mannigfaltigkeit von Dingen zunächst intendiert war, verrät die Inanspruchnahme des weltlichen Daseins als „Anundfürsichsein" (B.3.2.2). Insofern kann man die Substitution sicherlich kritisch beurteilen und aus ihr schließen, daß Hegel die „im Plural der Dinge" (B.2. Anm. 3.1) bestehende Realität nicht erreiche. Wasser auf die Mühle einer solchen Kritik wäre, daß Hegel die Sphäre der Verschiedenheit, so als wäre sie kein Ensemble von Verschiedenem, auf ein gegenüber Gleichheit und Ungleichheit Drittes reduziert, das dem anderen Dritten, dem nach Gleichheit und Ungleichheit vergleichenden Subjekt, kompakt gegenübersteht; es bildet für dieses ein unerreichbares Jenseits. In der Rücknahme der Intention läßt sich aber ebensowohl ein bewußter Akt der Exterritorialisierung sehen. Diese Alternative ergreife ich. Nur begnüge ich mich nicht mit der Rechtfertigung der Operation aus dem System, das an dieser Stelle verlangt, zwar den Sprung vom Sein und Nichts zum Dasein zu wiederholen, aber eine Regression in pure Seiendheit zu vermeiden.

Über die systemimmanente Legitimation hinaus möchte ich die Ausbürgerung des Aristoteles geschichtlich begründen.

Von der angedeuteten Exterritorialisierung aus zeigt sich der affirmative Aspekt des Bruchs, der, oberflächlich betrachtet bloß ein von Aristoteles geerbter, im Grunde ein Bruch *mit* Aristoteles ist. Die Verschiedenheit entzweit sich bei Hegel mit sich selbst. Hegel arbeitet mit zwei Termen von Verschiedenheit. Schon vor der Einführung des auf die Mannigfaltigkeit der Dinge zielenden Begriffs hat er mit einem anderen operiert, der die Verschiedenheit in eine bestimmte, durch Gleichgültigkeit gekennzeichnete Relation von Denkbestimmungen setzt, in die Fremdheit, die sich in der Beziehung von Identität und Unterschied einnistet, sobald sie zur eigentlichen Bestimmung eines ganz anders verfaßten Unterschieds werden. Wieso aber orientiert sich Hegel ursprünglich an einem Begriff, der selbst begriffliche Verhältnisse zum Gegenstand hat? Auf eine Antwort deutet die Herkunft des introvertierten Begriffs aus der modernen Philosophie. Hegel setzt voraus, daß er die Realität, die sich ihm als die des antiken Realismus entzogen hat, in der Moderne nur durch den Nominalismus hindurch zurückgewinnen kann. Letztlich ist seine Hoffnung, sie möge in den Begriffen selbst wiederauferstehen. Dazu muß er die Begriffe so aufnehmen, wie der Nominalismus sie zugerichtet hat, als einander entfremdete. Letztlich geht es in seiner Logik der Reflexionsbestimmungen um eine Rekonstruktion der Realität in der Form einer begrifflich vermittelten. Eben deswegen hat die Analyse der eigentlichen Bestimmung bei der in die Begriffsverhältnisse eindringenden Verschiedenheit anzusetzen. Nur von da aus kann Hegel zu einem Gegensatz gelangen, der Realität zu seinem eigenen Implikat hat.

III

Die spekulativ-dialektische Gegensatztheorie ist nicht so sehr von Aristoteles beeinflußt als vielmehr durch Kants Lehre von einer realen Opposition. Kant gibt ihr einige der Mittel an die Hand, die sie für die Suche nach der verlorengegangenen Realität einsetzt. Da sie gleichwohl stark von der Lehre Kants abweicht, erscheint sinnvoll, mit ihr selbst zu beginnen und ihre modernen Prämissen erst im nachhinein aufzudecken. Ein solches Vorgehen empfiehlt sich um so mehr, als sie durchsichtig aufgebaut ist und keiner historischen Erklärung bedarf. Hegel exponiert zunächst den *Begriff* des Gegensatzes und beschreibt sodann dessen *Formen.* Diese sind Realisationsformen. Damit ist ihr Verhältnis zum Begriff bezeichnet. Die Formen des Gegensatzes gehen über dessen Begriff hinaus, aber nur in dem, was durch Realisierung hinzukommt. Dennoch verändert sich vornehmlich mit ihnen die von Kant vorgegebene Lage. Die im Anschluß an die Gegensatzformen zu umreißende Umbildung des Kantischen Ansatzes durch Hegel wird uns schließlich in dessen Widerspruchskonzeption hinüberleiten, mit der er sich, wiewohl mit Kant beginnend, vollends von Kant trennt.

Seinem Begriff nach ist der Gegensatz für Hegel eine Relation von Relaten, die einander enthalten und zugleich ausschließen. Sowohl die Bestimmtheit der Relation als Doppelverhältnis von Implikation und Exklusion wie auch die Bestimmtheit der Verhältnisglieder weisen den Gegensatz als einen Unterschied aus, der die für ihn konstitutive Identität auf dem Boden der Verschiedenheit wiedergewinnt. Seine Pole sind einerseits *unterschiedliche* Seiten, die von einer übergreifenden Identität getragen sind und von denen darum jede die andere als Moment in sich selbst hat. Andererseits sind sie bloß *verschiedene* Seiten, die nebeneinander, Hegel sagt: „gleichgültig", bestehen und sich darum ausschließen. Das im Text maßgebliche Verständnis des Gegensatzes setzt aber voraus, daß beide Relate nicht nur vermöge ihrer wechselseitigen Implikation, sondern auch dank ihrer Exklusion sein können, was sie sind. Jedes ist, was es ist, erstens dadurch, daß das andere in ihm als Moment aufgehoben ist, und zweitens deshalb, weil das andere unaufgehoben mit ihm koexistiert.[17]

Worauf Hegel hinauswill, zeichnet sich bereits in den nicht eigens begründeten Namen für die Relate ab: Abweichend von seiner für die früheren Bestimmungen gewählten Sprache, die solche Vergegenständlichungen vermieden hat, tituliert Hegel das eine als *das* Positive, das andere als *das* Negative. Auch die so markierte Bestimmtheit der Relate erinnert an die Herkunft des Gegensatzes aus der Verschiedenheit. Das Positive tritt die Nachfolge der Gleichheit an, das Negative die der Ungleichheit. Aber Gleichheit und Ungleichheit nehmen als Bestimmungen des Gegensatzes einen anderen Sinn an. Auf ihren Wandel deutet die Ernennung des Positiven und Negativen zu *selbständigen* Reflexionsbestimmungen. Deren Selbständigkeit gehört zum Begriff des Gegensatzes, wenn sie auch als begriffsimmanente erst nur auf Einschließung beruht, noch nicht auf Ausschließung. Das Positive und Negative gelten gewiß auch insofern für selbständig, als sie eigene Reflexionsbestimmungen sind, nicht bloß Bestandteile der Reflexionsbestimmung Gegensatz. Aber ihre Selbständigkeit definiert vor allem den Gegensatz. In diesem elementaren Sinne besagt sie, daß Gleichheit und Ungleichheit, in der unbestimmten Verschiedenheit mit anderem, als Seiten des Gegensatzes zur Gleichheit beziehungsweise Ungleichheit mit sich selbst werden. Begriffskonstitutiv ist diese ihre Reflexion. Der Gegensatz etwa, den Hegel zwischen Natur und Geist aufmacht, läßt sich nur so denken, daß der Geist trotz aller Ungleichheit gleich mit sich, die Natur trotz aller Gleichheit ungleich mit sich ist.

Hinter Hegels reflexiver Fassung von Gleichheit und Ungleichheit verbirgt sich ein erster Schritt auf Realität zu. Dem Gedanken einer Gleichheit oder Ungleichheit von etwas mit etwas anderem bleibt beides äußerlich. Ein Vergleich „geht weder das eine noch das andere an" (B.2.2.3.4). Hingegen ist in der Selbstgleichheit, der positiven und auch der negierten, das mit sich Gleiche oder Ungleiche mitzudenken. Selbstverhältnisse schließen das, was sich zu sich selbst verhält, mit ein. Leicht ontologisierend ausgedrückt: Gleichheit und Ungleichheit mit sich sind Verfassungen von solchem, das so *ist*, daß es gleich oder ungleich mit sich ist. Natürlich handelt es sich da um keine denkunabhängigen Entitäten und nicht einmal schon um die begrifflich vermittelte Realität, auf die Hegel abzielt. Die Bestimmtheit des Positiven und Negativen bildet lediglich den Anknüpfungspunkt für Realität im Begriff selbst. Hegel erläutert die rein implikative, in den Begriff fallende Selbständigkeit so, daß Positives und Negatives Funktionen eines Ganzen seien. Das Ganze ist im Denken gesetzt. Um beispielsweise Natur und Geist einander entgegensetzen zu können, müssen wir sie in das Verhältnis setzen, in welchem mit der Selbstungleichheit der Natur auch die Selbstgleichheit des Geistes allererst denkbar wird. Insofern ist jene Selbständigkeit in dem genauen Sinne dialektisch, daß sie ihr Gegenteil, die Unselbständigkeit, umfaßt. Hier bahnt sich eine Dialektik an, die sich verschärfen wird.

Vom Gegensatz*begriff* aus betrachtet Hegel, wie gesagt, die Gegensatz*formen*. Er unterscheidet zwei und, was gegen andere Interpretationen geltend zu machen ist, *nur* zwei Formen.[18] Die beiden Formen sind Hauptstationen auf dem Weg der Realisierung des Begriffs. Der Weg verläuft von einem unvollkommen zu einem vollkommen realisierten Begriff. Den vollkommen realisierten Gegensatz charakterisiert Hegel als einen, dessen Seiten als selbständige *gesetzt* sind, worin unausgesprochen die Annahme liegt, daß es im unvollkommen realisierten noch keine gesetzte Selbständigkeit gebe. Die Annahme bedarf der Erläuterung. Nicht die implikative Selbständigkeit ist unrealisiert. Unrealisiert ist vielmehr die exklusive, und zwar als Element der Gegensatzstruktur. Sie ist durchaus vorhanden, aber nur als gleichgültiges Bestehen. Der unvollkommen realisierte Gegensatz ist so ein in den Boden dinghafter Verschiedenheit bloß eingepflanzter Unterschied.

Darin ist seine Doppeldeutigkeit begründet. Der Schein, als hebe Hegel drei Formen gegeneinander ab, entsteht deshalb, weil die erste Form sich in zwei komplementären Perspektiven darbietet, in denen einer setzenden und einer äußeren Reflexion. Setzende und äußere Reflexion sind zwar in der bestimmenden vereint, aber bloß dadurch, daß jede, mit Husserl zu reden, in dem ihr unmittelbar präsenten Objekt das der anderen appräsentiert. Unvollkommen realisiert ist der so wahrgenommene Gegensatz, weil er nicht nur in jeder der beiden Perspektiven unvollständig bestimmt ist, sondern auch in beiden zusammengenommen hinter sich selbst zurückbleibt. Die setzende Reflexion hat primär die Unterschiedskomponente im Gegensatz vor sich, also Seiten, die als Momente ineinander reflektiert und im übrigen gegeneinander negativ sind. Die äußere Reflexion hebt auf die Verschiedenheitskomponente im Gegensatz ab, also auf Seiten, die als gleichgültig bestehende in sich reflektiert sind. Weil die

Seiten in sich reflektiert sind gemäß ihrer jeweiligen Bestimmtheit, kann die äußere Reflexion eine als positiv, eine andere als negativ bestimmt gelten lassen. Weil aber die Reflexion-in-sich zugleich aus der Gegensatzstruktur herausfällt, können Positives und Negatives, wie Hegel sagt, „verwechselt" (B.3.7.2), das heißt: ausgetauscht, werden. Darin betätigt und bestätigt sich die äußere Reflexion als Komplement einer setzenden, die als eine aus der Einheit mit der bestimmenden tendenziell heraustretende anders als die ursprüngliche nur subjektiv setzend ist. Das Subjektive, das Hegel lieber verschweigt, kennzeichnet das in die erste Gegensatzform eingehende Gesetztsein in Wahrheit ebenso wie das Äußerliche die gegensatzexterne Reflexion-in-sich.

Hegels Schweigen über das Subjektive am Gesetztsein des noch unvollständigen Gegensatzes entspringt einem Selbstmißverständnis. Der Rückgang auf eine absolute, präsubjektive Reflexion sollte ja die subjektive begründen und nicht beseitigen. Nach Hegels eigener Einsicht kommt die subjektive ins Spiel, sobald Identität in Verschiedenheit zerfällt; eine Reflexion, die verschiedene Dinge vergleicht, wird „ein subjektives, außerhalb ihrer fallendes Tun" (B.2.3.4.4). Und sie bleibt notwendigerweise im Spiel, solange die Verschiedenheit gegenüber der Unterschiedskomponente des Gegensatzes ihr Eigenrecht behauptet. Wer darüber hinwegsieht, überblickt auch nicht die weiteren Schritte auf dem Weg einer Wiedergewinnung der als Mannigfaltigkeit von Dingen verlorengegangenen Realität. Diese erschließt sich nämlich in dem Maße, in welchem das Produkt eines endlichen Subjekts auf das tieferliegende Gesetztsein hin transparent wird, zu dem das absolute, reflexionslogisch als Wesen gedachte Subjekt sich macht. Aber die Vernachlässigung des endlich-subjektiven Faktors muß auch zur Blindheit für das führen, was an der elementaren Gegensatzform selbst alles Subjektive übersteigt. Das auf die Mitwirkung eines endlichen Subjekts angewiesene Gesetztsein und das äußere Vorhandensein der Seiten korrelieren auf dem Grunde eines Dritten, das für eine subjektiv setzende und für eine äußerlich aufnehmende Reflexion gleichermaßen erforderlich ist. Sie verlangen beide ein Substrat. Zwar kann das Substrat für die Bestimmungen kein selbst unbestimmter Träger sein. Da jeder Gegensatz durch eine an sich bestimmende Reflexion konstituiert ist, müssen die Seiten schon des unvollständig konstituierten Bestimmungen sein, denen ein seinerseits *bestimmter* Gegenstand zugrunde liegt. Nur ist im Falle der ersten Form die Bestimmtheit des bestimmten Gegenstands nicht die seiner Bestimmungen, also keine positive oder negative, sondern Bestimmtheit überhaupt. So ist das für die erste Gegensatzform unabdingbare Substrat zu definieren, und da das Schicksal des Substrats für Hegels Projekt einer Wiedergewinnung bestimmter Realität entscheidend ist, sollte die Definition festgehalten werden. Festzuhalten ist aber auch: Mit dem Entwurf des substratabhängigen Gegensatzes tut Hegel durchaus einen weiteren Schritt auf Realität zu, den nach der Reflexivierung von Gleichheit und Ungleichheit zweiten. In einem vollgültigen Sinne kann man zwar nicht sagen, daß es diesen Gegensatz in der Realität gebe. Ist er doch subjektiv gesetzt. Aber es gibt in der Realität außer dem Substrat des unvollständig konstituierten Gegensatzes auch die verschiedenen Seiten, die als entgegengesetzte gesetzt sind.

Wenden wir uns jetzt der zweiten Gegensatzform zu! In ihr nehmen die Relation und die Relate eine neue Gestalt an. Die neue Gestalt der Relation versucht Hegel, mehr bildlich als begrifflich, mit der Feststellung zu treffen, das Gesetztsein der Relate sei „in jedes *zurückgenommen*" (B.3.8.1).[19] In eine Metapher flüchtet er, weil er in der Konsequenz seines Schweigens über das Subjektive am bisher betrachteten Gesetztsein darauf verzichtet, das jetzt thematische als ein objektives zu kennzeichnen. Das Gesetztsein der Relate ist in beide zurückgenommen, weil beide so in den Gegensatz eingehen, wie sie objektiv gesetzt sind. Dem entspricht die neue Gestalt der Relate selbst. Sie sind das *an ihm selbst* Positive und Negative, in dem Sinne, daß die Bestimmtheit, die jedes an ihm selbst hat, in die Gegensatzstruktur integriert ist. Hegel sagt in der Sache dasselbe, wenn er jedes der Relate als „selbständige, für sich seiende Einheit" (B.3.9.1) anspricht. Die Selbständigkeit der Seiten ist nun gesetzt. Dies bedeutet primär: Die Relate sind selbständig in der Weise eines gegensatzinternen Fürsichseins. Im zweiten Gegensatz kommt zu Gesetztsein und Reflexion-in-sich nichts anderes hinzu, sondern nur eine andere Form der Bestimmtheit von beidem. Was die Reflexion-in-sich betrifft, so tritt an die Stelle der äußerlich vorhandenen eine begrifflich vermittelte. Gegensatzspezifisch realisiert wird damit über die *in*klusive Selbständigkeit hinaus ebensowohl die *ex*klusive. In der gesetzten Selbständigkeit liegt aber auch: Objektiviert ist zugleich die Reflexion der Seiten ineinander, dies, daß sie sich wechselseitig als Momente enthalten. Von der ersten Form her, aus der Sicht der subjektiv setzenden Reflexion, definiert Hegel das ins Positive und Negative zurückgenommene Gesetztsein als „die Beziehung auf das Andere in einer Einheit, die nicht sie selbst sind" (B.3.8.1). Durch die Rücknahme des Gesetztseins geht das Ineinander-Reflektiertsein des Positiven und Negativen in eine Einheit ein, die sie selbst sind. Auch als ineinander reflektierte sind sie objektiv gesetzt. Das subjektive Setzen kann dann nur noch der Nachvollzug eines Gegensatzes sein, in dem sie nach beiden Hinsichten, der Reflexion in sich und der Reflexion ineinander, an ihnen selbst bestimmt sind.

Mit alledem tut Hegel einen dritten Schritt auf seinem Wege einer Wiedergewinnung von Realität, den, mit dem er zwar noch nicht ans Ziel, aber bei der Realität ankommt, die immerhin ausgezeichnete innerweltliche Gegensatzverhältnisse haben. Während im unvollendeten Gegensatz nur seine Bestandstücke real waren, existiert der vollendete in dem starken Sinne, daß er selbst Realität besitzt. Eben deswegen verschwindet das Substrat. Die Existenz eines Substrats schließt gesetzte Selbständigkeit und gesetzte Selbständigkeit schließt die Existenz eines Substrats aus. Wenn Entgegengesetztes sowohl als Gesetztsein wie als Reflexion-in-sich die Realität durchdringt, dann bleibt für eine „tote Grundlage" (B.3. Anm. 2.1) nichts mehr übrig. Erhalten bleibt zwar ein bestimmter Gegenstand. Aber die Bestimmtheit des Gegenstands ist nicht mehr verschieden von der seiner Bestimmungen. Obwohl diese nicht in ihm aufgehen, machen sie seine eigene, einerseits positive, andererseits negative Bestimmtheit aus.

An dieser Stelle ist ein distanzierendes Wort über die von Michael Wolff vorgeschlagene Deutung des beschriebenen Sachverhalts unumgänglich. Wolff hat breite Zustimmung für seine These gefunden, daß in der zweiten Form – er zählt sie als die dritte – der Gegensatz einer zwischen den beiden Bestimmungen und dem Substrat werde.[20] Danach bilden das ehemalige Positive und Negative zusammen ein Negatives höherer Stufe, dem das Substrat als gleichfalls höherstufiges Positives, sagen wir: als P2, gegenübertritt. Offenkundig läßt sich diese Deutung mit der hier zur Diskussion gestellten nicht vereinbaren. Wolff kann sich aber auf bedeutsame Aussagen über das an ihm selbst Positive und Negative berufen. Ihnen zufolge ist dieses „das für sich bestehende Entgegengesetzte" oder „der auf sich beruhende *ganze Gegensatz*" (B.3.10.3), jenes „das *Nichtentgegengesetzte*, der aufgehobene Gegensatz, aber als Seite des Gegensatzes selbst" (B.3.9.3). Was liegt näher als das zum ganzen Gegensatz gewordene Negative auf +a und −a zu beziehen, das als Nichtentgegengesetztes zur Gegensatzseite gewordene Positive auf das ὑποκείμενον |a|? Eine solche Art der Zuordnung ist von der Anmerkung angeregt, in der Hegel versucht, seine Lehre von den zwei Formen auf die Arithmetik abzustützen. Allerdings bemüht die Anmerkung das Substrat, in der Terminologie der heutigen Mathematik den absoluten Betrag, gerade für die erste Form, während sie die zweite auf ein angeblich „qualitatives" Zahlenverhältnis (B.3. Anm. 11.2) abbildet, aus dem sie – bezeichnenderweise ohne Erfolg – ein Analogon zur Relation des an ihm selbst Positiven und Negativen konstruieren möchte. So scheint geboten, den in eine Beziehung von Nichtentgegengesetztem und für sich bestehendem Entgegengesetztem übergegangenen Gegensatz ohne Zuhilfenahme eines Substrats plausibel zu machen. Ich sehe dazu keine andere Möglichkeit als die, jene Aussagen schlicht als Hinweise auf die Dialektik in den Gedanken eines an ihm selbst Positiven und eines an ihm selbst Negativen zu lesen. Ein an ihm selbst Positives ist so zu denken, daß es als Poniertes Seite eines Gegensatzes ist, den es als Fürsichseiendes zugleich übersteigt, und ein an ihm selbst Negatives läßt sich nicht anders begreifen als so, daß es sein Sein in einem Gegensatz hat, den es ganz in sich aufnimmt. Zugegebenermaßen brauchte Hegel dies nicht so scharf zu formulieren. Die Schärfe der Formulierung erklärt sich aus seiner Absicht, den Gegensatz bereits auf den Widerspruch auszurichten. Nicht zufällig werden wir auf die zitierten Sätze bei der Auslegung des Schlußabschnitts über den Widerspruch zurückkommen müssen.

An Überzeugungskraft gewinnen dürfte die vom vollendeten Gegensatz gegebene Deutung, die ohne ein Substrat auskommen möchte, durch die zurückgestellte Ausleuchtung des Kant-Hintergrunds.[21] Denn die Verabschiedung des Substratdenkens gehört wesentlich mit zu den Strategien, von denen Hegel sich auch für seine Gegensatztheorie eine über Kant hinausführende Position verspricht. In seiner das Konzept einer realen Opposition entwickelnden Schrift von 1763 hatte Kant als eine notwendige Bedingung einer solchen Opposition gefordert, daß deren Pole „in eben demselben Subjekte"[22] verbunden sind. ‚Subjekt' meint da: Substrat. Soweit Kant nicht geradezu von einem Ding spricht, stellt er sich das Subjekt nach Art eines Dings vor. Gegen eine Interpretation wie die Wolffs regt sich der Verdacht, daß sie dies umstandslos auf Hegel überträgt. Damit verfremdet sie ihren Gegenstand um so mehr, als Hegel die Lehre von der realen Entgegensetzung in der Version aufnimmt, in der sie in die Besinnung der ersten Kritik auf die Amphibolie der Reflexionsbegriffe eingegangen ist. Im Rahmen eines kleinformatigen Aufsatzes muß unausgeführt bleiben, wie er das Konzept der Reflexion sowie der Reflexionsbegriffe abwandelt und zudem die Idee der Amphibolie dahingehend verändert, daß die äußere Reflexion, wenn sie sich von der bestimmenden trennt, einen Schein erzeugen kann, mit dem die Verwechslung von Erscheinung und Ding an sich als Verwechslung der Bestimmungen mit Substraten wiederkehrt.[23] Zu notieren ist wenigstens, daß die von Hegel intendierte Realität Züge der *realitas phaenomenon* trägt, auf die Kant die mit dem Widerstreit behaftete im Anhang zur transzendentalen Analytik einschränkt. Wiewohl ohne Anschaulichkeit, ist sie als begrifflich vermittelte nachkantisch durch Konstitutionsleistungen erschlossen, so wie umgekehrt die phänomenale vorhegelisch als „Inbegriff von lauter Relationen"[24] gedacht war. Im übrigen sollten wir uns jedoch an die frühe Schrift halten, weil nur sie die Gegensatzlehre so reich entfaltet, daß die weiteren Punkte sichtbar werden, an denen sie dem Nachfolger zum einen Anschlußstellen, zum andern Absprungsbasen bot.

Zunächst zu den Anschlußstellen. Die befremdliche Selbstverständlichkeit, mit der Hegel Positives und Negatives in Ansatz bringt, ist wohl nicht zuletzt in der Verbindlichkeit begründet, die Kants Begriff positiver und negativer Größen für ihn hatte. Schon bei Kant sind die real opponierenden Seiten in dem genauen Sinne Bestimmungen, daß auch das Negative etwas Bestimmtes ist. Das in eine Realopposition eingehende Negative hat eine gänzlich andere Verfassung als die in der logischen Opposition stattfindende *Negation* des Positiven. Weil Hegel dem beipflichtet und zugleich keine andere Oppositionsart berücksichtigt, muß er nach der Abweisung des konträren Gegensatzes auch dem kontradiktorischen den Zugang zu seiner Theorie verwehren. Von Kant vorgedacht ist außer dem Positiven und Negativen selbst ebensowohl die Negativität, in der sie sich zusammenschließen, eine relationale, in der beide Relate, auch das positiv bestimmte, gegeneinander negativ sind.

Hier bringt Hegel allerdings, nach der Berichtigung des Substratdenkens, eine zweite Korrektur an. In der Schrift von 1763 kommt zwar faktisch auch ein Negatives „im metaphysischen Verstande"[25] vor, beispielhaft das Finstere, das negativ ist, obwohl es in der Entgegensetzung zum Nichtfinsteren positiv ausgedrückt wird. Das metaphysisch Negative hat jedoch in einer Konzeption, die bei einer rein relationalen Negativität stehenbleibt, keinen Ort. Daß Kant die relationale Negativität nicht überschreitet, liegt an dem Gebrauch, den er von der Mathematik macht. Weil er das Verhältnis, in dem positive und negative Zahlen zueinander stehen, auf alle Realoppositionen ausdehnt, kann er das, was er unter dem Titel des metaphysisch Negativen selbst anerkennt, nicht wirklich *er*kennen. Ihm entgehen Realitäten, die in der Entgegensetzung als die negativen erfaßt werden, die sie schon zuvor waren. Diesen Mangel behebt Hegel mit seiner Theorie der vollendeten Gegensatzform. Sein Begriff von einem an ihm selbst Negativen weist dem Negativen „im metaphysischen Verstande" einen Platz an. Daß er gleichwohl beide Formen in der Arithmetik unterbringen möchte, verschuldet eine trotz besserer Einsicht fortbestehende Anhänglichkeit an Kant. Das Mißlingen seines Versuchs, auch die zweite Form zu mathematisieren, verrät, wie sehr er da gegen sich selbst argumentiert. In Wirklichkeit schwebt ihm denn auch vage ein anderes Modell der Beziehung von Metaphysik und Mathematik vor als das Kantische, eines, in dem Zahlenverhältnisse nicht so sehr Vorbild relationaler Realität sind als vielmehr deren schwaches Abbild.

Noch folgenreicher indessen als alle Modifikationen sind an Hegels Umgang mit Kant gewisse Radikalisierungen. Kant hat, wie bereits seine Rede von einer Realrepugnanz bezeugt, eine dynamistische Gesamtsicht. Im Widerstreit sieht er Kräfte, die so aufeinander wirken, daß sie wechselseitig ihre Folgen aufheben. Sicherlich revidiert Hegel die Sprache des Kantischen Dynamismus. Er spricht weder von Kräften noch von den Gründen, als die Kant die aufeinander wirkenden Ursachen bezeichnet, noch von den Folgen, die sie haben. Doch das verbale Nein zum Dynamismus ist in der Sache ein ihn bekräftigendes Ja. Nicht bloß Folgen sollen einander aufheben, sondern die Opponenten selbst. Genaugenommen sollen sie sich auch nicht bloß aufheben, sondern ausschließen. Vor allem verschärft sich ihr Widerstreit dadurch noch, daß zu ihrer Exklusion hinzukommt, was es bei Kant gar nicht gibt, worauf aber bei Hegel ein schweres Gewicht fällt: ihre gleichermaßen gegenseitige Implikation.

Nun findet die Radikalisierung des vorgegebenen Dynamismus ihren schärfsten Ausdruck darin, daß der Wider*streit* auf einen Wider*spruch* hinausläuft. Hegel ersetzt Kants noch aristotelesnahe Privation durch Negation. Damit überschreitet er die Grenze, die Kant dem realen Antagonismus zieht. Mit einem Wider*spruch* haben ja nach Kant nur die anderen Oppositionsarten zu tun, die dialektische mit einem scheinbaren, die logische mit einem wirklichen. Hegel hingegen führt den Widerstreit selbst auf einen Widerspruch zurück. Damit provoziert er die Frage, wie er sich dessen Verhältnis zum Gegensatz denkt. Schon ein flüchtiger Blick in die den beiden letzten Bestimmungen gewidmeten Textstücke zeigt, daß es zu dieser Frage reichlich Anlaß gibt. Einerseits finden wir bereits unter dem Titel *Gegensatz* Aussagen, die wie die vorhin angeführten faktisch Widersprüchliches zur Sprache bringen und dementsprechend unter dem Titel *Widerspruch* mehr oder weniger wörtlich wiederkehren. Andererseits bleibt der so betitelte Schlußabschnitt in den beiden ersten seiner drei Unterabschnitte beim Gegensatz. Aber dessen Zuspitzung zum Widerspruch stellt auch die hier aufgestellte Realitätsthese in Frage. Ist doch die Negation, in die Hegel den Antagonismus hineintreibt, das Gegenteil von Realität. Die für die spekulative Logik im ganzen kennzeichnende Doppelstrategie einer Enthüllung von Wahrheit und einer Auflösung von Schein[26] macht die Logik der Reflexionsbestimmungen zu einem besonders zwiespältigen Unternehmen, weil, so Hegel am Schluß der Einleitung in sein Werk, dieselben Bestimmungen, deren „System" eine für sich schon wahrheitshaltige Vorstufe des Begriffs bildet, Vehikel einer scheinerzeugenden Metaphysik sind.[27] Die These über die Wiedergewinnung der Realität in der Gegensatztheorie hat diese ganz und gar unter dem Aspekt ihres Wahrheitswerts betrachtet. Dem Einwand willkürlicher Einseitigkeit entgeht sie nur unter der Voraussetzung, daß Hegel Wahrheit und Schein, Realität und Realitätsverschleierung gewissermaßen auf Gegensatz und Widerspruch verteilt. Wenn jedoch der Widerspruch schon im Gegensatz aufbricht und der Gegensatz noch den Widerspruch fundiert, dann kann die Verteilung nicht komplett sein. Dann muß der Gegensatz scheinanfällig und der Widerspruch wahrheitsfähig sein. Im vorgezeichneten Interpretationshorizont richtet sich das Hauptinteresse auf die Wahrheit des Widerspruchs. Es läßt sich freilich erst in einer Analyse des Schlußabschnitts befriedigen. Zunächst ist zu sehen, wie der Widerspruch in den unter seinem eigenen Namen auftretenden Gegensatz gerät und damit die Möglichkeit mit sich bringt, daß die wiedergewonnene Realität scheinhaft wird.

Der in alledem gemeinte Widerspruch ist, nach der Sprachregelung Hegels, der *gesetzte*, nicht bloß der Widerspruch *an sich*. Der nur an sich seiende läßt sich durch eine einfache Unterscheidung von Hinsichten auflösen, der gesetzte nicht. Der gesetzte fällt also – was seine Strenge, nicht was seine Struktur betrifft – mit dem von Aristoteles für unmöglich erklärten zusammen. Gleich allen früheren Reflexionsbestimmungen ist auch der Gegensatz an sich oder latent widersprüchlich. Dies ist der Fall, sofern seine Seiten einander wechselseitig enthalten und trotzdem ausschließen. Der darin lauernde Widerspruch bleibt im Untergrund, solange die eine Seite auf die andere nicht nur in je anderer Weise bezogen ist, als sie einerseits in sich enthaltende, andererseits sie aus sich ausschließende, sondern sich eben damit auch auf anderes an ihr bezieht, sie enthält als Moment und ausschließt als fürsichseiende Einheit. Aber das Ausschließen selbst ist mit einem Widerspruch behaftet, und der muß sich seiner Auflösung durch die Identifizierung verschiedener Hinsichten entziehen. Bisher hat die Interpretation vorausgesetzt, daß die Ausschließung für das Ausschließende eine konstitutive Funktion habe, daß sie es in seinem Sein ermögliche. Auch Hegel macht diese Voraussetzung. Dessenungeachtet nimmt er jedoch auch das Gegenteil an, ein Ausschließen mit vernichtender Wirkung. Wenn er sagt, der Widerspruch, und zwar der gesetzte, trete schon *am* Gegensatz hervor, so zielt er wahrscheinlich auf den, der hieraus resultiert. Die selbst einander entgegengesetzten Voraussetzungen können miteinander konkurrieren, weil sie sich beide auf denselben Begriff stützen, aufs ‚Nichtsein'. Wo damit nicht einfach das je andere gemeint ist, als das, was das eine nicht ist, da hat Hegel entweder ein das Fürsichsein negierendes Nichtsein im Sinn, zu dem jedes Relat als ein zum Moment im anderen herabgesetztes wird, oder das die Existenz negierende Nichtsein der fürsichseienden Einheiten selber. Nach der letzteren Bedeutung ist das im einen als Moment enthaltene andere als Fürsichseiendes „auch das Nichtsein dessen, in welchem es nur als Moment enthalten sein soll" (B.3.5.7). Daran wird der Schlußabschnitt anknüpfen. Nicht von ungefähr zieht Hegel aus dem Nichtsein des Ausschließenden, in gewollter Annäherung an das aristotelische *principium contradictionis,* das Fazit: „Jedes ist daher nur, insofern sein *Nicht*sein *ist,* und zwar in einer identischen Beziehung" (B.3.5.8). Soll die Behauptung einer Identität der Beziehung zutreffen, so kann nicht bloß gemeint sein: Jedes ist nur dadurch, daß auch ist, was es nicht ist. Dann muß der Sinn des Satzes sein: Jedes ist nur unter der Bedingung seines eigenen Nichtseins.

Auf den ersten Blick sieht es so aus, als ginge der am Gegensatz hervortretende Widerspruch auf das Konto Hegels. Ist es doch Hegel selbst, der das Ausschließen widersprüchlich deutet. Indessen ist durchaus möglich, daß er sich mit seiner negativen Deutung des Ausschließens, welche die kantische Perspektive auf eine destruktive Dynamik in seine Theorie einbringt, auf den Standpunkt eines Verstandesdenkens stellt, das in seiner Sicht für ruinöse Widersprüche verantwortlich ist. Wie wir uns dies des näheren vorzustellen hätten, dokumentiert ein schlichter Textbefund. Negativ gedeutet ist das Ausschließen allein in der Exposition des Gegensatz*begriffs*; bei der Beschreibung der Gegensatz*formen* tritt das vernichtende Ausschließen vollständig zurück. Nun waren ja die Formen die der bestimmten Gegensatzverhältnisse, die in der Welt realisiert sind. Daraus läßt sich die Hypothese ableiten, daß die negative Deutung des Ausschließens einem Denken entspringt, welches innerweltliche Gegensatzverhältnisse mit einem Widerspruch belastet, der in der Welt keinen Ort hat. Ein solches Denken erzeugt Schein, indem es Implikationen, die im Gegensatzbegriff liegen, auf eine ihnen fremde Realität projiziert. Nichts Einzelnes in der Welt ist so, daß es nur sein Nichtsein wäre. Dies bedeutet allerdings keineswegs, daß es ein derart seiendes Nichtsein überhaupt nicht gäbe. Mit einem seienden Nichtsein könnte uns das Ganze der Welt konfrontieren. Gewiß, die Hypothese kann sich nicht auf Verlautbarungen Hegels stützen. Hegel selbst hat, wie seine Anmerkungen zeigen, das Problem nicht hinreichend durchdacht. Die Hypothese trägt zudem unhegelsche Begriffe an den Text heran. Hegel arbeitet nicht mit dem Weltbegriff; und das Ganze, mit dem er operiert, das, welches jede Reflexionsbestimmung für sich beansprucht[28], meint nicht das Ganze der Welt. Aber für eine Hypothese, welche die Lektüre des Schlußabschnitts lediglich anleiten soll, erscheinen theorieexterne Begriffe durchaus angemessen. Im Schlußabschnitt wird Hegel das Ganze der Welt in seiner eigenen Sprache formulieren. Dabei untersucht er den Widerspruch auch auf seinen Realitätsgehalt. Im Hinausgehen über den Gegensatz geht er zugleich auf dem Weg weiter, auf dem er sich schon in der Reflexion des Gegensatzes selbst der Realität wiederanzunähern versuchte. Ja, er gelangt erst da an sein Ziel. Nur ist die Realität, die er findet, in sich nichtig, die Realität des Scheins, den das im Irrealen sich bewegende Denken durch Projektion verdoppelt.

IV

In seiner Logik des Widerspruchs knüpft Hegel an die vollendete Gegensatzform an. Er tut dies zum einen, weil die Seiten des vollendeten Gegensatzes, das an ihm selbst Positive und das an ihm selbst Negative, ein Vorschein des Ganzen sind, auf das der Gedanke hinauswill, zum andern aber auch, weil ihre gesetzte Selbständigkeit auf der wechselseitigen Ausschließung beruht, deren Dialektik zu vertiefen ist. Jede Seite des vollendeten Gegensatzes kann sich nur so setzen, daß sie die je andere aus sich ausschließt. Da sie aber in der anderen enthalten ist, schließt sie damit sich selbst aus derart, daß ihr Sich-Setzen in ein Setzen der anderen umschlägt. Das Neue an dem Widerspruch, dem Hegel einen eigenen Abschnitt widmet, ist die Verbalisierung der ihrem Begriff nach destruktiven Selbstausschließung. In ihr ist begründet, daß der separat abgehandelte Widerspruch im Verhältnis selbständiger Reflexionsbestimmungen ein rein negatives Resultat oder vielmehr gar kein Resultat hat. Hegel verfolgt zwar anfangs nur die drei Schritte von Ausschließen des anderen, Sich-selbst-Ausschließen und Setzen des anderen. Weil jedoch das Schicksal des einen auch das des anderen ist, muß er nachtragen, daß beide sich zugrunde richten. Sie richten sich wechselseitig zugrunde, indem jedes sich selbst zugrunde richtet. Rastlos verschwinden sie ineinander und zugleich in ihnen selbst.

So sind das Positive und das Negative, in der vollendeten Gegensatzform zu selbständigen Einheiten geworden, der gesetzte Widerspruch, auch in dem Sinne, daß dieser aus ihrem Sich-Setzen hervorgeht. Allerdings handelt es sich vorerst tatsächlich nur um die Widersprüchlichkeit ihres Verhältnisses zueinander. Hegel führt den gesetzten Widerspruch als einen relationalen ein. In seiner Sprache besagt dies, daß er mit der einen, durch beide Relate hindurchgehenden Reflexion beginnt, der ausschließenden, zu der die bestimmende sich im Widerspruch modifiziert. Die Erkenntnis, daß der beschriebene Widerspruch in der übergreifenden Relation situiert ist, bildet eine unabdingbare Voraussetzung für die Einsicht in seinen Status. Seine Relationalität gehört damit zusammen, daß die sich widersprechenden Seiten selbständige und doch nur im Verhältnis zueinander bestehende Reflexionsbestimmungen sind. An der ausschließenden Reflexion ist ein reflektierender Verstand beteiligt, der die nachgezeichnete Dialektik durch die ihn kennzeichnende Fixierung der Bestimmungen allererst in Gang setzt.

Hegel geht jedoch über den relationalen Widerspruch hinaus, mit der Konsequenz, daß er am Ende die Reflexionsbestimmungen selber hinter sich läßt. Der Abschnitt C ist zwar so aufgebaut, daß C.1

noch an den Reflexionsbestimmungen festhält und erst C.2 den Zusammenbruch ihrer Selbständigkeit konstatiert. Den Zusammenbruch konstatiert C.2 aber retrospektiv; das eigene Thema von C.2 ist seine Kehrseite, die Entstehung einer Selbständigkeit, die nicht mehr die der Reflexionsbestimmungen ist. An den Reflexionsbestimmungen deckt Hegel im ersten Gang eine Struktur auf, die den ihnen vorgegebenen Rahmen sprengt, und dabei stößt er auf etwas, dessen noch verborgene Selbständigkeit er im zweiten Gang gegen die der Reflexionsbestimmungen geltend macht und als die ihr gegenüber wirkliche behauptet. Demzufolge kann sich die Interpretation im wesentlichen auf den ersten Gang beschränken. Was C.2 betrifft, so genügt eine kritische Bemerkung über das darin angewandte Verfahren, und die kurze Schlußpassage C.3 kann gänzlich unberücksichtigt bleiben, weil sie bereits den Übergang in den Grund vollzieht und die widersprüchliche Konstellation kategorial überformt.[29]

Den internen Aufbau des Basistextes regelt die das gesamte Kapitel anleitende Differenzierung von Widerspruch an sich und gesetztem, realisiertem Widerspruch. Mit dem schon früher erwähnten, gleich noch zu erläuternden Begriff des Unterschieds überhaupt, in welchem der bloß an sich seiende Widerspruch ursprünglich liegen soll, greift der Text bis auf die ersten Schritte des Kapitels zurück, um das Ende mit dem Anfang zu verknüpfen. Zugleich soll aber die Binnendifferenzierung des Widerspruchs den weiteren Weg einteilen. Den gesetzten Widerspruch sucht Hegel zunächst in dem Verhältnis, in welchem die selbständigen Reflexionsbestimmungen stehen. Er identifiziert ihn also mit dem relationalen, an dem beide Bestimmungen teilhaben. Sodann belastet er gleichwohl allein das Negative mit dem gesetzten, während er im Positiven doch wieder nur einen an sich seienden Widerspruch sieht. Die scheinbare Unstimmigkeit erklärt sich daraus, daß Hegel inzwischen über den rein relationalen hinausgegangen ist. Der Gedanke ist vom relationalen zu dem Selbstwiderspruch fortgeschritten, in den das Positive und das Negative je für sich verstrickt sind. Dieser für absolut ausgegebene Widerspruch ist es, der im Positiven ein lediglich an sich seiender und im Negativen gesetzt ist. Darum zielt der Weg, der vom Widerspruch im Verhältnis des Positiven und des Negativen zum Selbstwiderspruch beider führt, in gewisser Weise noch darüber hinaus, auf eine äußerste Selbstwidersprüchlichkeit, der das Negative und nur das Negative anheimfällt. Der Überstieg über den relationalen Widerspruch erfordert auch noch den über das Positive, weil er selbst erst im Negativen an sein Ziel kommt. Bei der Darstellung des Selbstwiderspruchs betrachtet Hegel fürs erste das Positive und in einem zweiten Ansatz das Negative für sich. Wenn er dies in der Meinung tut, die Sache zuzuspitzen, so deshalb, weil die nur tentativ isolierende Betrachtung des Positiven von dessen Außenbezug zu seinem Gegenpol noch nicht absehen kann, während erst die isolierende Betrachtung des Negativen dessen vormals externen Bezug zum Positiven vollständig internalisiert.

Das Positive ist das mit sich Gleiche. Als solches gerät es in einen Widerspruch zu seinem eigenen Gesetztsein, das, wie Hegel hervorhebt, die Ungleichheit selbst ist. Der Begriff des Positiven verlangt, ihm ein Fürsichsein zuzusprechen und es damit als das Gegenteil dessen zu denken, was ebenfalls in seinem Begriff liegt: daß es ein Poniertes ist. Diesem Widerspruch verfällt das Positive bloß an sich, weil seine Identität mit sich, in die der Text seine Selbstgleichheit übersetzt, nur das Andere des Gesetztseins ist, eine Gegeninstanz, die aus dem Gesetztsein gewissermaßen herausfällt. Darum sind die Hinsichten unterscheidbar, nach denen Positives einerseits mit sich identisch, andererseits nur gesetzt ist. Hegel knüpft hier an die bei der Analyse der vollendeten Gegensatzform gegebene Bestimmung des an ihm selbst Positiven an, derzufolge es „Gesetztsein als aufgehobenes" ist, „das *Nichtentgegengesetzte*, der aufgehobene Gegensatz, aber als Seite des Gegensatzes selbst". Nur mobilisiert er jetzt die Dialektik eines Ausschließens, durch welches das Ausschließende zum Ausgeschlossenen wird. Was für die Vertikale des Gesetztseins gilt, für die Beziehung zum Setzenden, das trifft auch in der Horizontale zu, hinsichtlich der Beziehung zum Mitgesetzten.[30] In seinem Fürsichsein drängt das an ihm selbst Positive seinem Begriff nach auf die Ausschließung des Negativen, welches es aber nur so ausschließen kann, daß es sich zum Anderen des Negativen macht, also zum ausgeschlossenen Negativen. Auch für sich betrachtet zeigt es sich als das, was es ist, allein in der Relation zum Negativen.

Das Negative seinerseits ist das mit sich Ungleiche. Diese ebenfalls schon im Umgang mit dem Gegensatz gewonnene Einsicht bildet die Grundlage, auf der Hegel die Selbstwidersprüchlichkeit des Negativen entwickeln möchte. Indessen verrät eine merkwürdige Uneinheitlichkeit oder Gebrochenheit der Gedankenentwicklung, daß hinter der Fassade einer Symmetrie der dem Positiven für sich und dem Negativen für sich gewidmeten Betrachtungen ein radikaler Strukturwandel stattfindet. Hegel macht in seiner isolierenden Betrachtung des Negativen zwei Anläufe. Im ersten faßt er das mit sich Ungleiche als das in seine Ungleichheit Reflektierte, um diese Reflexion in die Figur einer selbstbezüglichen Negation einzuschreiben: Sie ist die Beziehung des Ungleichen auf sich. Im zweiten Anlauf bringt er das reflexionslogisch zu denkende Negative, um das es hier zu tun ist, in eine Beziehung zum qualitativ bestimmten, in der Seinslogik abgehandelten. Dabei bleiben aber die beiden Anläufe unverbunden. Die eigentlich geforderte Herstellung einer Verbindung ersetzt Hegel schlicht durch einen Gedankenstrich. Ebensowenig rechtfertigt er den Rückgriff auf die Seinslogik, geschweige denn, daß er sagte, wieso er von dem Rückgriff Hilfe für die Auflösung einer reflexionslogischen Problemlage erwartet.

Der Versuch einer Freilegung der geheimen Argumentation muß von der Stellung des ersten Anlaufs innerhalb des ganzen Beweisprogramms ausgehen. Die Selbstbeziehung, die das Resultat des ersten Anlaufs war, stiftet eine Identität, mit der das Negative sich das Positive zueignet. Als Beziehung des Negativen auf sich kann das Positive nicht mehr das ihm opponierende sein. Es ist ein Implikat des Negativen selbst geworden. Der erste Anlauf ist also ein erster Schritt zur endgültigen Internalisierung des vormals relationalen Widerspruchs. Das Negative erweist sich als gesetzter Selbstwiderspruch, weil seine eigene Identität, zu der das Positive wird, in sein Gesetztsein aufgenommen ist: In seiner Ungleichheit ist das Gesetztsein selbst in die Ungleichheit mit sich reflektiert. Aber ein Negatives, das im Positiven keinen Gegenpol findet, fungiert auch selbst nicht mehr als Pol. Wie das Positive, so verändert auch das Negative seinen Ort. Der Rückgriff auf die Seinslogik dient dazu, dem Negativen seinen neuen Ort anzuweisen. Das selbstbezügliche Gesetztsein ist nicht mehr bloß das auch subjektive, das in die unvollkommene Gegensatzform einging, und es ist darüber hinaus noch mehr als das objektive der in der vollkommenen Gegensatzform in ihrer Selbständigkeit gesetzten Bestimmungen. Es ist das Gesetztsein, das die Wahrheit des Daseins ausmacht.[31] Die Erinnerung an die Seinslogik verweist darauf. Das Negative als solches, zu dem der Text das reflexionslogische spezifiziert, ist das Gesetztsein selbst, das qualitativ bestimmte Negative, als Qualität oder unmittelbare Bestimmtheit, ist Dasein.

Freilich gibt die Ortsanweisung noch keine Begründung dafür, daß das Negative den ihm angewiesenen Ort wirklich einnimmt. Zu einem Argument dafür wird der Rückgriff erst durch seine kontextuelle Funktion. Dem bisher thematischen Gesetztsein stückt Hegel nicht einfach ein anderes an. Er will vielmehr zeigen, daß das Negative erst als das Gesetztsein, zu dem das Wesen sich macht, den Begriff erfüllt, unter dessen Anspruch es von vornherein steht. Wir müssen, so lautet seine These, die Ungleichheit des Negativen mit sich letztlich als Ungleichheit des qualitativ bestimmten und des in seiner Negativität realisierten Negativen denken. Dementsprechend argumentiert er: Zwar ist dieses mit jenem, formal gesehen, identisch. Sofern jenes aber ein Unmittelbares ist, kann es im Grunde seines Daseins kein Negatives sein; denn „das Negative ist überhaupt nicht ein Unmittelbares" (C.1.6.5). Folglich stehen die beiden wesentlich im Verhältnis der Nichtidentität. Das als Gesetztsein in metaphysischem Sinne identifizierte Negative ist das Nichtidentische schlechthin. Von daher klärt sich auch auf, wie der zweite Anlauf mit dem ersten zusammenhängt. Er antwortet auf dessen Ungenügen. Der erste Anlauf macht einen zweiten erforderlich, weil er für sich genommen eine Identität vortäuscht, die nicht die des Nichtidentischen sein kann. Die Identität eines Nichtidentischen ist notwendigerweise selbst von Nichtidentität tangiert. Das Negative bezieht sich so auf sich, daß es sich selbst ausschließt. Es schließt sich aus als qualitativ bestimmtes, mithin als das Dasein, an dessen Stelle es sich setzt. Die hierin enthaltene Selbstbeziehung besteht allein in dem Umstand, daß das Ausgeschlossene mit dem Ausschließenden zusammenfällt. Ob das Negative sich noch auf andere Weise auf sich bezieht, ist an seiner gegenwärtigen Gestalt nicht zu sehen.

Das neu verortete Negative scheint den Platz einzunehmen, den Wolff dem Substrat des vollendeten Gegensatzes zuweist: P2 wäre durch N2 zu ersetzen. Ist aber schon der bestimmte Gegenstand, der die in ihrer Selbständigkeit gesetzten Reflexionsbestimmungen umschließt, kein Substrat mehr, so das dem Wesen überantwortete Gesetztsein erst recht nicht. Als das sich selbst Widersprechende löst es sich in seinem Sein auf. Ebensowenig läßt es sich als Träger von Bestimmungen denken. Obwohl Hegel die Fiktion von Reflexionsbestimmungen noch aufrechterhält, hat er sie mit dem Übergang vom relationalen Widerspruch zur Selbstwidersprüchlichkeit des Negativen faktisch bereits untergraben. Denn N2 *ist* die Selbstbeziehung, zu der in diesem Übergang P1 wurde, und es *ist* die Selbstausschließung, zu der N1 sich gewandelt hat. Der im Hinausgehen über den vollendeten Gegensatz erzielte Fortschritt im Prozeß der Überwindung von Substraten ist unverkennbar: Statt daß die Bestimmtheit des bestimmten Gegenstands bloß mit der seiner Bestimmungen zusammenfiele, fallen P1 und N1 mit ihm selbst zusammen. Eine angemessene Auseinandersetzung mit Hegels Affirmation des Widerspruchs ist nur auf Grund der Einsicht in diese Struktur möglich. Eine Kritik wie die Poppers[32] tut so, als erkläre Hegel für möglich, was nach dem aristotelischen Satz vom verbotenen Widerspruch unmöglich ist: daß dasselbe demselben in derselben Hinsicht zukommt und auch nicht zukommt. In Wirklichkeit markiert Hegel nur die Grenze der durchaus anerkannten Geltung dieses Satzes. Der Satz hat dort keine Gültigkeit mehr, wo Sätze überhaupt nicht mehr so beschaffen sein können, wie er es voraussetzt. Ist der Gegenstand kein Substrat, dem irgendwelche Bestimmungen zugrunde lägen, so kann er auch nicht als ein Subjekt zur Sprache kommen, dem Prädikate beizulegen wären. Der von Aristoteles verbotene Widerspruch erneuert sich bei Hegel nur im Kollaps der Struktur des Satzes und damit auch des Satzes von ihm. Hegel leugnet nicht eigentlich das Recht des Verbots, sondern die unbeschränkte Reichweite der darin implizierten Ontologie.

Nun regt sich freilich gegen die These über die Selbstwidersprüchlichkeit des Negativen ein Verdacht. Kann eine Ausschließung, in der das Negative sich auf sich zurückwendet, noch die sein, die sie im relationalen Widerspruch war, die, welche aus dem Umschlag der Ausschließung des Anderen resultierte? Büßt sie nicht damit, daß sie reflexiv wird, die zerstörerische Kraft ein, die der relationalen innewohnte? Hegel wird sie tatsächlich in eine durch Negation nur vermittelte Selbstbeziehung integrieren. Dies tut er aber erst im Hinausgehen über das Negative. Das Negative selbst, so wie es sich ergeben hat, ist mit einem Selbstwiderspruch belastet, der sich im Widerspruch von Selbstbeziehung und Selbstausschließung spiegelt. Zieht es die Bestimmungen in sich ein, als die das Positive und das Negative auftraten, dann auch den Widerspruch, der zwischen ihnen herrschte. So ist es dies, *„gegen die Identität identisch mit sich* zu sein" (C.1.7.3). Die Identität mit sich, die das Negative als sich auf sich beziehendes hat, ist eine *gegen* die Identität, weil es die des Nichtidentischen ist. Die übliche Kritik am Identitätsdenker Hegel reicht an diese Problemlage gar nicht heran. Sie verfehlt ihr Objekt infolgedessen genauso wie die an Hegel als Widerspruchsdenker. Billigt sie doch dem Kritisierten höchstens zu, daß er Identität als Identität von Identität und Nichtidentität auffasse. Aber schon am Anfang der Logik der Reflexionsbestimmungen steht keine Identität, die über ihr Gegenteil übergreifen könnte, sondern eine, die sich unversehens als ihr Gegenteil wiederfindet[33], und am Ende kommt eine heraus, die als Identität gegen die Identität eine in sich selbst widersprüchliche ist.

Eben hieran knüpft Hegel im Hinausgehen über das Negative an. Widerspruchsfrei läßt sich eine Identität gegen die Identität, so seine These, nur unter der Bedingung denken, daß das Negative seine Identität in dem Anderen hat, welches sich zu ihm, zum Gesetztsein macht, also in dem als Wesen bestimmten Absoluten. Unter dieser Bedingung wird die Selbstbeziehung des Negativen zu einer, in der es das Wesen ist, das sich auf sich bezieht. Zugleich löst sie sich von seiner Selbstausschließung ab, jedoch so, daß sie sie in sich aufnimmt. Die Selbstausschließung des Negativen enthüllt sich als die des Absoluten. Indem das Wesen sich im Negativen auf sich bezieht, bezieht es sich negativ auf sich. Es setzt sich im Negativen so, daß es sich von sich ausschließt. Diesen Schritt vom Gesetztsein zum Setzen vollzieht Hegel ausdrücklich erst im zweiten Gang. Aber schon im ersten bereitet er ihn vor, indem er noch in der Analyse des Negativen den begrifflichen Rahmen für die es übersteigende Operation ausspannt. Es zeichnen sich da allerdings auch bereits Schwierigkeiten ab, die bei der Durchführung der Operation an den Tag treten. Sie machen sich zunächst in Doppeldeutigkeiten der den Rahmen bildenden Begriffe bemerkbar, die das Negative umschreiben.

Nach dem Schluß von C.1 ist das selbstwidersprüchliche Negative „die ganze, als Entgegensetzung auf sich beruhende Entgegensetzung, der absolute sich *nicht auf Anderes beziehende* Unterschied" (8.1). Eine erste Irritation entsteht dadurch, daß Hegel Assoziationen mit seiner Bestimmung des Negativen im vollendeten Gegensatz wachruft, ohne Differenzen zu markieren, so wenig wie seine auf das korrelative Lehrstück zurückgreifende Explikation des selbstwidersprüchlichen Positiven das Neue eigens ausformulierte. Noch größere Unsicherheit ruft die Rede vom absoluten Unterschied hervor. Sie zitiert zweifellos das Wesen als die absolute Reflexion, die sich nur auf sich bezieht, aber in eins damit das Andere des Wesens, das in der Logik der Reflexionsbestimmungen die Stellung des absoluten Unterschieds einnimmt. Am schillerndsten aber ist der Begriff des Unterschieds überhaupt, der im Abschnitt über den Widerspruch offenbar vorzugsweise dazu dient, jenen Rahmen abzustecken. Nicht zufällig setzt der Abschnitt mit ihm ein. Der exponierende Absatz faßt alles Bisherige unter den Kategorien Unterschied überhaupt, Verschiedenheit und Gegensatz zusammen. Dabei scheint der Unterschied überhaupt den zu meinen, unter den der absolute und die Identität subsumiert werden, wenn es von ihnen heißt, sie seien „die Momente des Unterschieds innerhalb seiner selbst gehalten" (B.3.2.1). Spätestens die Stelle jedoch, die den Unterschied überhaupt auf einen Widerspruch an sich festlegt, greift auf den schon in den Abschnitt über den absoluten eingeschmuggelten Gebrauch des Begriffs zurück. Die im Unterschied überhaupt verborgene Widersprüchlichkeit begründet sie zweifach. Nach einer ersten Begründung ist er an sich widersprüchlich als „*Einheit* von solchen, die nur sind, insofern sie *nicht eins* sind", nach einer zweiten als „*Trennung* solcher, die nur sind als *in derselben Beziehung* getrennte" (C.1.4.1). Auf einen

Unterschied überhaupt, der den absoluten und die Identität übergreift, ist allein die erste Begründung zugeschnitten. Die zweite dehnt ihn auf den sogenannten bestimmten aus, auf die aristotelische διαφορά, die man dann einen Unterschied überhaupt nennen kann, wenn man annimmt, daß sie Verschiedenheit und Gegensatz umfaßt. Dementsprechend läßt sich schon der Anfang des Abschnitts so lesen, daß er Verschiedenheit und Gegensatz nicht von dem ihnen zuvorkommenden Unterschied distanziert, sondern so, daß er sie auf das ihnen Gemeinsame bezieht. Dadurch wird, nebenbei bemerkt, auch der Widerspruchsbegriff inflationär. Hegel kann zwar an der Verschiedenheit und am Gegensatz einen je eigentümlichen Widerspruch an sich aufweisen. Aber er vermag ihn nicht an dem bestimmten Unterschied zu demonstrieren, unter den er beide subsumiert. Daß Dinge in derselben Beziehung voneinander getrennt sind, ist kein Widerspruch, nicht einmal ein an sich seiender. Indessen ist die Inflationierung des Widerspruchsbegriffs nur eine Begleiterscheinung der Strategie, welche die ganze Bedeutungsverschiebung anleitet. Die Strategie zielt auf die abschließende Definition des Negativen. Sie suggeriert, daß der bestimmte Unterschied in den Gegensatz so übergeht, daß dieser seinerseits in den absoluten zurückgeht.

Die Kontaminationen sind schwerlich geeignet, Vertrauen in den Schritt zu wecken, auf den all dies vorausweist. Noch weniger vermag der in C.2 gewagte Schritt selbst zu überzeugen. Hegel meint dadurch an sein Ziel zu kommen, daß er die ausschließende Reflexion zunächst als setzende und sodann als eine bestimmende faßt, die sich als das Negative setzt, das sie auch aufhebt. Er wählt aber einen Ausgangspunkt, von dem aus kein Weg zum Ziel führt. Im Rückgang vom Gesetztsein aufs Setzen soll geschehen, was der titelartige Eingangssatz von C.2 verspricht: *„Der Widerspruch löst sich auf."* Thema sind im Widerspruchsabschnitt in Wirklichkeit drei untereinander sehr verschiedene Formen von Auflösung, entsprechend den drei Unterabschnitten. Die Anfangspassage läuft auf die noch anonyme Auflösung hinaus, die durch die Fundierung des vollendeten Gegensatzes im absoluten Unterschied ermöglicht wird, und die Schlußpassage expliziert dieselbe Auflösung mit anderen Mitteln, nämlich durch Antizipation der Kategorie des Grundes. In beiden ist der aufzulösende Widerspruch der, in den das Negative mit sich selbst gerät. Die mittlere Passage hingegen, also C.2, schickt sich an, den relationalen Widerspruch aufzulösen. Die ausschließende Reflexion begreift sie als die eine, durch das Positive und das Negative hindurchgehende. Fragwürdig ist nicht so sehr jener Doppelschritt als vielmehr der in ihm immer schon vorausgesetzte Subjektwechsel, der die Selbstbeziehung des Negativen und letztlich auch dessen Selbstausschließung an das Wesen delegiert. Ihn versucht Hegel im Zuge der Auflösung des relationalen Widerspruchs zu begründen. Nach seiner Auffassung entsteht das neue Subjekt daraus, daß die Relate die Selbständigkeit, die dem in ihrem Verhältnis zueinander herrschenden Widerspruch anheimfällt, gewissermaßen an die Relation übergeben. Faktisch kann er jedoch nicht mehr zeigen als dies, daß die Destruktion der Selbständigkeit in Wahrheit nur die ihres Gesetztseins sei. Daß sie in Gestalt einer Selbständigkeit, welche der übergreifenden Reflexion zuzuschreiben wäre, wiederauferstehe, bleibt leere Prätention. Als „fürsichseiende und in der Tat selbständige Einheit" (C.2.4.2) stiege die Relation nicht zum Wesen auf; sie fiele auf das Niveau ihrer Relate herab.

Aber zu monieren ist nicht erst, daß der Versuch, den Schritt zurück auf das Wesen als setzende Reflexion im Ausgang vom relationalen Widerspruch zu tun, mißlingt. Bedenklich stimmt bereits, daß Hegel einen solchen Versuch überhaupt unternimmt. Oder noch grundsätzlicher: Kritik fordert schon die Meinung heraus, der relationale Widerspruch ließe sich so auflösen, wie die Aufgabe einer Fundierung des Negativen im Wesen es anzeigt. Indem Hegel eine derartige Auflösung suggeriert, ebnet er die Differenz ein, die er in C.1 durch den Fortgang vom relationalen Widerspruch zum Selbstwiderspruch des Negativen herausgearbeitet hat. Es ist dies keine geringere Differenz als die von Schein und Realität. Auflösbar ist der relationale Widerspruch natürlich in dem Sinne, daß man den ihm anhaftenden Schein auflöst. Scheinhaft sind zwar nicht die in ihrer Selbständigkeit einander widersprechenden Reflexionsbestimmungen. Andernfalls würde das gesamte Gegensatzkonzept hinfällig, das ja gerade über ihre Selbständigkeit Zugang zur Realität gewinnt. Aber scheinhaft ist der Widerspruch, den der Verstand aus der Opposition fürsichseiender Seiten macht. Der Selbstwiderspruch des Negativen hingegen durchherrscht etwas Reales. Seine Auflösung kann darum nicht in der Leugnung der Realität des derart Widersprüchlichen bestehen. Im Gegenteil: Er muß dadurch sich auflösen, daß die Möglichkeitsbedingung der Realität des Negativen an den Tag kommt. Hierin und hierin allein liegt die Notwendigkeit des Schritts zurück auf das Wesen. Der Schritt ist notwendig, um zu erklären, daß das Negative, in seiner Widersprüchlichkeit nichtig, gleichwohl *ist*. Die in C.3 getroffene Feststellung, es sei „ein sich selbst Widersprechendes, das daher im Wesen als seinem Grunde bleibt" (2.6), meint: Nur unter der Voraussetzung, daß es im Wesen als seinem Grunde bleibt, kann es trotz seiner Widersprüchlichkeit existieren.

Auch als Widerspruchstheorie ist die Logik der Reflexionsbestimmungen demnach auf Wiedergewinnung von Realität angelegt. Sie fragt am Ende nach den Konditionen der Realität einer Welt, die durch ihre Widersprüchlichkeit über sich hinausweist oder vielmehr in sich hineinweist. Gewiß, diese Realität verharrt in den der ganzen Logik der Reflexionsbestimmungen gesetzten Grenzen. An die, welche die Logik schlechthin übersteigt, an die Realität der Realphilosophien, reicht sie ohnehin nicht heran. Und auch hinter der, zu der sie sich im weiteren Verlauf der Wesenslogik fortbestimmt, hinter der terminologisch streng gefaßten Wirklichkeit, bleibt sie weit zurück. In alle reicheren Realitätsbegriffe geht gleichwohl der Gedanke einer Welt ein, die nicht ist und dank des in ihr präsenten Wesens doch ist, gemäß dem Satz, mit dem das Kapitel schließt: „Das *Nichtsein* des Endlichen ist das *Sein* des Absoluten". In der Sprache der Daseinslogik, die in der Logik der Reflexionsbestimmungen aufgehoben ist, hält der Satz den Sachgehalt der spekulativen Metaphysik fest, in welche diese sich ihrerseits aufhebt.

Anmerkungen

* Die der Kategorie des Grundes voraufgehenden Kapitel der *Wissenschaft der Logik* bilden ein Stück spekulativen Denkens, in dessen Erschließung die philosophische Arbeit Dieter Henrichs sich in unserer gemeinsamen Heidelberger Zeit mit meinen damaligen Bemühungen traf. Henrich war in den siebziger Jahren mit Hegels Logik der Reflexion befaßt, und ich beschäftigte mich mit der auf ihr aufbauenden Logik der Reflexions*bestimmungen*. Allerdings verfolgten wir methodisch entgegengesetzte Ziele: Henrich hatte eine argumentanalytische Rekonstruktion im Sinn, während ich an der inhaltlichen Relevanz des Gedankens interessiert war, vor allem an seiner Relevanz für gesellschaftliche Verhältnisse. Sicherlich lag im Unterschied der Zugangsweisen ein Grund dafür, daß der eine seine Forschungsergebnisse in eindrucksvollen Schriften dokumentieren konnte (cf. Anm. 3), während der andere außer knapp sechs Seiten, die in einem auf Marx ausgerichteten Kurzreferat für Hegel abfielen (cf. Anm. 12), nichts Einschlägiges veröffentlicht hat. Jedenfalls versprach er sich von dem Versuch, Hegels Logik der Reflexionsbestimmungen für die Gesellschaftstheorie fruchtbar zu machen, bald keinen Erfolg mehr. So möchte er auch mit den hier vorzutragenden Überlegungen nicht in seiner früheren Bahn weitergehen. Statt dessen will er sich auf die Mitte zwischen den einstigen Extremen zubewegen. Immerhin greift er ein lange liegengelassenes Thema auch deshalb wieder auf, weil er testen möchte, inwieweit er sein früheres Ziel auf einem anderen Wege einholen kann.

1 Die Kritik identifiziert und expliziert zu haben ist, neben einer minutiösen Exegese des Textes, das Hauptverdienst von Chr. Iber, *Metaphysik absoluter Relationalität. Eine Studie zu den beiden ersten Kapiteln von Hegels Wesenslogik*, Berlin 1990. Cf. bes. loc. cit., S. 269–285, 362–369, 374–380, 501–518.

2 *Der Begriff des Widerspruchs. Eine Studie zur Dialektik Kants und Hegels.* Königstein/Ts. 1981. Cf. von Wolff auch „Über Hegels Lehre vom Widerspruch", in: *Hegels Wissenschaft der Logik*, ed. D. Henrich, Stuttgart 1986, S. 107–128.

3 Cf. D. Henrich, „Hegels Logik der Reflexion", in: ders., *Hegel im Kontext*. Frankfurt a. M. 1971, S. 91–156, und bes. „Hegels Logik der Reflexion. Neue Fassung", in: *Die Wissenschaft der Logik und die Logik der Reflexion*, ed. D. Henrich, Bonn 1978, S. 203–324; ferner ders., *Selbstverhältnisse*.

Stuttgart 1982. – Zu den drei Reflexionsformen vgl. loc. cit. (1978), S. 273–304.
4 Cf. dagegen H. Fink-Eitel, *Dialektik und Sozialethik. Kommentierende Untersuchungen zu Hegels „Logik"*, Meisenheim am Glan 1978, S. 124: „Dem Widerspruch korrespondiert keine der drei Reflexionen"; ähnlich Iber.
5 Cf. Wolff (1981, cf. Anm. 2), S. 106–109 et passim.
6 Der Hauptgrund dafür dürfte sein, daß Hegel in seinem Aristoteles-Kolleg auf *Met.* X nicht eigens eingeht. Vieles darin Gesagte läßt sich jedoch auf dieses Buch anwenden. Im übrigen besagt das Fehlen einer ausdrücklichen Bezugnahme wenig. Auch Kants Schrift über den Begriff der negativen Größen erwähnt Hegel nirgends, obwohl seine Beeinflussung durch sie auf der Hand liegt. – Zu seinem generellen Umgang mit der aristotelischen Metaphysik cf. u. a. Valerio Verra, „Hegel e la lettura logico-speculativa della *Metafisica* di Aristotele", in: *Rivista di Filosofia neo-scolastica* 85 (1993), S. 605–621.
7 Cf. M. L. Ross, „Aristotle on 'Signifying One' at Metaphysics I 4", in: *Canadian Journal of Philosophy* 25 (1995), S. 375–393.
8 Cf. O. N. Guariglia, *Quellenkritische und logische Untersuchungen zur Gegensatzlehre des Aristoteles*, Hildesheim 1978; F. Morales, *Antikeimena. Untersuchungen zur aristotelischen Auffassung der Gegensätze*, Frankfurt a. M. 1991.
9 *Methaphysik I* (Buch X), 3. 1054b, 23.
10 Bei Zitaten aus dem Kapitel über die Reflexionsbestimmungen verweisen im folgenden der Buchstabe (A, B oder C) auf den Abschnitt, die erste Ziffer gegebenenfalls auf den Unterabschnitt, die zweite (erste) auf den Absatz, die letzte auf den Satz. Für die Anmerkungen steht „Anm.".
11 Cf. *Metaphysik I* (Buch X), 3. 1052b, 3. Zu den beiden Fragen und zur Antwort des Aristoteles auf die zweite cf. D. Morrison, „The Place of Unity in Aristotle's Metaphysical Project", in: *Proceedings of the Boston Area Colloquium in Ancient Philosophy*, ed. J. J. Cleary et W. Wians, Bd. 9 (1993), S. 131–156, bes. 149–154.
12 Cf. V*orlesungen über die Geschichte der Philosophie*, in: Hegel, *Werke* Bd. 19, Frankfurt a. M. 1986, S. 241.
13 *Metaphysik I* (Buch X), 3. 1054b, 25–27.
14 Für Hegel gilt: „zwei Bestimmungen x und y verhalten sich negativ zueinander genau dann, wenn x mit nicht-y und y mit nicht-x identisch ist" (Wolff (1981, cf. Anm. 2), S. 108).
15 Dies ist auch gegen meine Thesen in „Krise der Macht. Thesen zur Theorie des dialektischen Widerspruchs", in: *Hegel-Jahrbuch 1974*, ed.

W. R. Beyer, Köln 1975, S. 318–329 (zu Hegel: S. 318–323), geltend zu machen; in ihnen wird der Widerspruch, wie Iber (1990, cf. Anm. 1), S. 447 Anm., mit Recht bemerkt, allzu scharf vom Gegensatz abgehoben.

16 Mit der Erinnerung an „das Nichts, das durch das identische Sprechen gesagt wird" (B. 1. 1), knüpft der Abschnitt über den Unterschied unmittelbar an sie an.

17 Hiermit relativiere ich den Satz in meiner achten These von 1975 (cf. Anm. 12): „Ist das Enthalten ein *Nieder*halten, so das Ausschließen ein Vernichten ...". In eingeschränkter Form nehme ich die These am Ende dieses Abschnitts auf.

18 Cf. Wolff (1981, cf. Anm. 2), S. 110–138, spricht von drei Stufen oder Arten, Iber (1990, cf. Anm. 1), S. 402–418, auf ihm fußend, von drei Formen, A. Schubert, *Der Strukturgedanke in Hegels „Wissenschaft der Logik"*, Königstein/Ts. 1985, S. 95 f., von drei Stadien. Nach dem zum Traditionsbezug Gesagten und noch zu Sagenden kann ich mich ebensowenig dazu verstehen, die Unterscheidung mit Fink-Eitel (1978, cf. Anm. 4), S. 116–124, und Schubert auf die überkommene Einteilung der Gegensätze in konträre und kontradiktorische abzubilden.

19 Die schon in die Analyse des ersten Gegensatzes eingeschobene Behauptung über das Positive und Negative, daß „jedes sein Gesetztsein an ihm selbst ist" (B. 3. 7.1), lese ich als Vorwegnahme der hiermit exponierten Bestimmung des zweiten. Iber (1990, cf. Anm. 1), S. 412, bezieht diese umgekehrt auf den ersten Gegensatz zurück.

20 Wolff (1981, cf. Anm. 2), S. 124 f. Cf. insbesondere Iber (1990, cf. Anm. 1), S. 411.

21 Cf. zu ihm die vorzüglichen Ausführungen im ersten Teil des Buches von Wolff (1981, cf. Anm. 2), S. 37–77.

22 *Versuch, den Begriff der negativen Größen in die Weltweisheit einzuführen* A 13.

23 In der äußeren Reflexion des Gegensatzes liegt m. E. nur die Möglichkeit des Scheins, nicht dessen Notwendigkeit, keine „unvermeidbare Amphibolie" (Iber (1990, cf. Anm. 1), S. 410). Die Verwechslung der Bestimmungen mit Substraten ist zu unterscheiden von der im Text thematisierten, die ja nur eine Vertauschung der Bestimmungen selbst meint. Die voreilige Identifizierung geht auf Wolff (1981, cf. Anm. 2), S. 116–123, zurück, für den der aus der Perspektive der äußeren Reflexion wahrgenommene Gegensatz der „amphibolische" ist. Ähnlich Schubert (1985, cf. Anm. 18), S. 95–98.

24 *Kritik der reinen Vernunft* B 321/A 265.

25 Loc. cit. (cf. Anm. 22) A 5.
26 Cf. vom Vf. *Sein und Schein. Die kritische Funktion der Hegelschen Logik*, Frankfurt a. M. 1978.
27 Cf. die „Allgemeine Einteilung der Logik" in der *Wissenschaft der Logik*, Hegel, *Werke* Bd. 5, S. 61f.
28 An ihm, an den konkurrierenden „Totalitäten", war meine Thesenreihe zur *Krise der Macht* ausgerichtet. Hier sehe ich weitgehend davon ab, nicht weil ich es irrelevant fände, sondern um die Tragfähigkeit einer Interpretation zu prüfen, die sich an die im Text stärker explizierte „für sich seiende Einheit" hält. Notwendigerweise fällt der Abstraktion der in der zehnten These vorgetragene Gedanke einer „Totalisierung des Enthaltens" zum Opfer, mit dem der Übergang vom Gegensatz zum expliziten Widerspruch rekonstruiert wurde.
29 Mit diesen Einschränkungen ist der Abschnitt über den Widerspruch, anders als alle vorhergehenden Abschnitte, gleichwohl *auszulegen*, weil nur eine Textexegese seine extreme Dunkelheit auflichten kann.
30 Die metaphorische Unterscheidung von Vertikale und Horizontale ist eine verräumlichende Abbreviatur für einen Sachverhalt, den Henrich, op. cit. (1978, cf. Anm. 3), S. 274, genauer so faßt: „‚Gesetztsein' ist Hegels Gegenbegriff zu ‚Ansichsein' und gegen diesen Gedanken durch zwei Eigenschaften unterschieden: (a) Was gesetzt ist, ist nicht selbständig; (b) ferner ist es im Unterschied zum undifferenziert an sich Seienden in Bestimmtheitsverhältnissen zu denken."
31 Schon die Theorie der bestimmenden Reflexion hatte konstatiert: *„Das Dasein ist nur Gesetztsein;* dies ist der Satz des Wesens vom Dasein" (6.32).
32 Cf. K. R. Popper, „What is Dialectic?", *Mind* 49 (1940), S. 403–426, bes. S. 407–411.
33 Dahingehend ist die dritte These in *Krise der Macht* (cf. Anm. 12) zu präzisieren. Hegel selbst tendiert am Anfang des Kapitels dazu, auf die erst als Grund denkbare Identität von Identität und Nichtidentität vorauszugreifen und damit den Widerspruch zu entschärfen.

IV.

Konzeptionen der Ethik
Orientierung des Lebens

Ethical Reasoning, Leading a Life

Gianni Vattimo

The Demand for Ethics and Philosophy's Responsibility

Today, there is in philosophical reflection no less than in common culture a demand for ethics that appeals to philosophy's responsibility. If there is an agreement amongst those who articulate this demand, it has to do with the expectation that here one comes across binding "principles". The question can be easily articulated in terms of "what (shall we have) to do?" The very term duty, perhaps the most frequent in every ethical discourse, seems to be meaningless other than in relation to some principles from which the response is "derived" as in a logical consequence, where to rise against it amounts to a revolt against reason – practical reason, not so easily distinguished from theoretical reason; so much so that for intellectualism dominant in much philosophical ethics, it is difficult to understand why someone would rise against rational action (that is, an action in conformity with principles). The explanations adduced for such an "irrational" behaviour are the passions, the interests, the stimuli belonging to the sphere of "concupiscence", an opponent of rationality, bound to the least noble part of the human being, the body destined to the decomposition of death, whereas the soul bears an essence similar to the eternal Ideas, where reason has its place.

Today, philosophical literature rarely begins a discourse on ethics in this fashion, and the reasons are evident. It is not a question of "principle", but a given: The argument based on principles, that is, on ultimate grounds that are established, recognized, intuited, and whose logical and practical implications would have to be drawn, is outmoded. The crisis of ethics lies in that the argument based on principles, which would be legitimized only by appealing to universally valid foundations, has been discredited. It is evoked as one of the elements, for some the principal one, of a scarce morality of public and private behavior. It is not difficult to see how the universality and ultimacy of principles amount to the same thing: An ultimate foundation is such that it cannot show the conditions that ground it. If it has no condition, it is unconditional; it can only present itself as an absolute truth, which none should be able to refute (except as a groundless refutation, as a pure irrational act). The claim to universality was discredited by nineteenth and twentieth century thought when the first principles were shown to be secondary, conditioned by something else (the ideological mechanism of false consciousness, the will to mastery, the scheme of removal in the play of the unconscious). The fact that they are discredited is not a demonstrative refutation of the principle, but rather a change of direction, which is contingent and full of exceptions; it can only be described with approximation and cannot be justified once and for all with binding arguments. It has to do with the affirmation of cultural pluralism that as a consequence of the changed political relationships between the West and other cultural worlds, which have moved from the state of colonies to the one of independent nations, has made visible the partiality of what for centuries European philosophy conceived as the essence of *humanitas*; it has to do with the Marxist critique of ideology, with Freud's discovery of the unconscious, and with the radical demythization to which Nietzsche subjected Western morals and metaphysics, included the very ideal of truth. All these "schools of suspicion" were not born out of pure theoretical elaborations, but accompanied, if not simply mirrored, deep social transformations. One cannot argue for their reasonableness, for their theoretical validity without recalling these historical circumstances and showing that when philosophy does without principles, or is born out of the theoretical recognition that thinking is groundless, it is the most appropriate – most attuned and most likely – response to the epoch of late-modern pluralism.[1]

To correspond to the epoch is a responsible form of commitment, too; thus a form of obligation is present here authorizing us to speak of rationality and the ethical life, that is, of a commitment to draw logical consequences and practical imperatives from certain principles (only as points of departure). If someone pointed out that this repeats the metaphysical scheme – recognize the principles, articulate them rationally, and draw their implications for action – he would be absolutely right. But here the metaphysical scheme is taken over and distorted according to the logic Heidegger recognized and theorized under the name of *Verwindung*, which repeats the logic of metaphysics while radically changing its meaning.

Metaphysical ethics, for example, falls fatally under the critique known as "Hume's law," according to which it is not legitimate to pass, as metaphysics does, from the description of a state of affairs to the formulation of a moral principle, without any explicit reason. If someone exhorts me to be a man, he does not really want me to be what I naturally am, but rather wants to recommend certain virtues that reflect (but why?) the essence of man. And so on. Now an ethics "responsible" for the epoch and not grounded on first principles does not fall under the critique of Hume's law, because the "fact" to which it seeks to correspond is very little objective; it is a multiple, cultural heritage, which can only be represented through a responsible act of interpretation, without giving rise to univocal imperatives.

If philosophy may still speak rationally about ethics, that is, in a responsible way on the face of the only reference it can grant itself – the epoch, the heritage, the provenance – it will be able to do so only by appropriating the groundless condition in which it is thrown today as its explicit point of departure, and not as its foundation.

The dissolution of the first principles and the affirmation of pluralism that cannot be unified constitute the provenance and the heritage which is presented as the dominant one, or deserves to be considered dominant (but preferable to what else?). Is it possible to articulate an ethical discourse – "principles" from which one might derive maxims of action, indications for modes of behaviour, hierarchies of "value" – on the basis of the "provenance" or the epochal condition, which is characterized by the dissolution of foundations? It may be that this dissolution is not only a given, a circumstance within which we think, or, since it is the situation in which the foundations have been outmoded, the dissolution itself becomes the only foundation – very *sui generis* and *verwunden* – at our disposal for formulating ethical arguments. Metaphysics does not leave us completely orphans: its dissolution (the death of God of which Nietzsche spoke) appears as a process endowed with its own logic from which one can also draw elements for a reconstruction. (I am speaking of what Nietzsche called nihilism: which is not only nihilism characterized by the dissolution of all principles and values, but also an active nihilism, the chance to begin a different history).

But what can one draw for ethics (maxims of action, modes of behaviour, hierarchies of "value"), from the recognition (an interpretation, which is full of responsible choices) of belonging to a tradition characterized by the dissolution of principles? The first feature of such an ethics can be recognized as the "step backward", to distance oneself from the choices and concrete options which are immediately imposed as binding by the situation. It is true that if there are no first, supreme, universal principles, only the imperatives dictated by a specific situation would seem to hold true; here, however, one must call attention to the difference between a postmetaphysical ethics and a pure and simple relativism (granted that such a state of affairs might ever be given): The observation that the first principles have dissolved and are no longer credible cannot lead to the assumption of our historical situation and our belonging to a community as the sole absolute. If the true world (the first principles) has become a fable, as Nietzsche writes in the *Twilight of Idols*, then the fable has been destroyed as well (thus it cannot be made absolute).

The situation to which we truly belong and for which we are responsible in our ethical choices is characterized by the dissolution of principles, by nihilism[2]; whereas to assume the most specific belonging (for example, racial, ethnic, familiar and of class) as the ultimate reference amounts to positing from the start an arbitrary limit to one's own perspective. Against this limit, one cannot appeal to the validity of an absolute imperative – which would repeat the metaphysical scheme of the first principles by positing a specific fable as the "true world" through an absolute ideological act; rather, one can only exhort to broaden one's own horizons. In other words, if you agree that the provenance is the only possible reference for ethics, I would ask you not to fail to consider its multiplicity.

The matter, however, is not even to "take account of everything", as if it were possible to make a complete inventory of the provenance, for which we are responsible. To characterize the provenance as the dissolution of principles – as nihilism – could never lead to the definition of a new, more valid, principle; rather, what is possible here is only the basis for a critical attitude on the face of everything that is presented as an ultimate and universal principle. Note that even this attitude cannot be thought to be universally valid, that is, as always valid and applicable to all. It recognizes to be appropriate for a certain situation – Heidegger calls it the epoch of the end of metaphysics, an end which does not want to be accomplished; Nietzsche calls it the death of God, of which nobody knows, and will require centuries for its consequences to fully unfold.

The modern philosophical tradition offers significant elements to support this thesis: not only Hume's law mentioned above, but above all, Kantian ethical formalism, with the imperative to adopt only the maxims that can be valid as universal norms (doing what you would expect others to do in the same situation). It is clear that here universality is not the positive predicate of a given content; rather, it only functions to remind us not to assume specific contents that are presented in specific circumstances (inclination, interest, etc.) as ultimate binding principles. So what do we draw in terms of maxims of action and hierarchies of value from assuming responsibility for the dissolution of principles? The risk of the step backward, distancing oneself from concrete alternatives is to give rise to a relativistic metaphysics, which could be called rightly metaphysics, since only from a stable position placed in a universal viewpoint could one look at multiplicity as multiplicity. One could say that relativism represents a (self-contradictory and impracticable) metaphysical stiffening of finitude. Only God could be an authentic relativist. If the step backward makes any sense, it is not because placing oneself in a superior and universal perspective is a possibility or duty, but rather because the situation itself, analysed without hasty metaphysical closures (interpreting it making an effort to understand its formally open character), requires to distance oneself from the alternatives which are falsely presented as ultimates.

In my view, today, a responsible philosophy can speak about ethics only if it wrestles with these complicated concepts. Are we demanding to appropriate too abstract an attitude, which is too remote from everyday experience? But would not a sensation of foreignness to the "concrete" alternatives in which we are thrown be itself constitutive of our everyday experience? Why should we accept this sensation as a pure individual, psychological fact, and not as a "discontent of civilization", which should not be put aside?

No matter how one proceeds on this line of argumentation, its stakes concern the assumption of the dissolution of principles as a point of departure for elaborating a non-metaphysical ethics, that is, one which no longer, not even surreptitiously, claims to construe its task as a practical application of a theoretical certainty about ultimate foundations. If relativism itself were to take the step backward as a pure and simple suspension of assent, resulting in an apology of the intellectual blasé, it would lapse into a metaphysics of principles inasmuch as it would claim to be stably placed in a universal point of view (there are many examples of this in contemporary philosophy, often arising from phenomenology as ethical applications of Husserl's *epoché*).

By contrast, if one really wants to correspond to the dissolution of principles, there seems to be no other way than constructing an ethics of finitude. But it may not be a finitude construed as the prelude to a leap in the infinite, nor as a definitive appropriation of the concrete alternatives presented in a situation (many religious outcomes in the twentieth century offer this argument: the recognition of finitude prepares the leap of faith, only a God can save us). An ethics of finitude woud seek to remain faithful to the discovery of its finite location in the provenance, which can never be overcome, without forgetting its pluralistic implications. As the old Italian proverb says, "sto coi santi in chiesa e coi fanti in taverna" (the English equivalent might be "when in Rome, do as the Romans do"). I could never deceive myself into thinking that I could be placed in a superior situation; even when I pronounce this sentence in the context of a philosophical discourse, I am placed in an other situation, which demands specific commitments, just as any other: I am placed in a particular situation as a philosopher, as an essayist, as a critic, but never as a Universal Man. What kind of ethics – maxims of action, hierarchies of values – can we draw from this awareness (which is very rare in contemporary disenchanted philosophy; think of the popularity of phenomenology or of philosophy's tendency to draw closer to the cognitive sciences)?

First of all, we can draw maxims and indications for critical modes of behaviour: "If anyone should come and tell you: 'Here is the Messiah or there he is', do not believe them"; even the Messiah announces himself above all (perhaps only) under the negative form of the critical ideal. Thus we take the step backward to help the work of nihilism, which has always already begun. Our duty is to clear the forest of metaphysical absolutes that present themselves under various disguises; perhaps, even the laws of the market.

Then, we have to listen to the ever renewed contents of the heritage, of the provenance. We could subsume all this under the name of alterity in order not to exaggerate the dimension of the past: the voice of the other, who is obviously our contemporary, and for whom we are responsible, constitutes the provenance, too. As in the case of the critical edition of a text, listening involves a number of "philological" choices; what can we actively retrieve, or expel from the core of ideas, values and "principles" of which we consider ourselves to be the heir and from which we are called? Such a core should be singled out with a responsible, interpretive act of recognition. It is a job for professional intellectuals, too. Yet the work of listening – as Heidegger would call it, or "deconstruction", as Derrida calls it – to the provenance cannot be thought to be the affair of a few professionals in contemporary society, characterized by the media that spread the substance of the Western cultural heritage and by now of other cultures as well. In Nietzschean words, today the one who does not become a superman (one capable of interpreting on his own), is destined to perish, at least to perish as a free individual. To deceive oneself into thinking that there is a proper "natural" core of man, which would be intelligible to anyone who has a healthy intellect, would be an error that, by now, can hardly be committed in good faith. The churches, I am thinking of the Catholic

Church, hold on to the idea that a "natural" metaphysics is intelligible for a healthy, human intellect (it is led, however, by the authoritative teaching of popes and priests; there is the presence of original sin; that is, in non-mythical language, historicity). Perhaps, this attitude is motivated by skepticism about the possibility of transforming everybody into *Übermenschen*, into interpreters. Yet, such a skepticism is precisely the main reason for destroying such a possibility.

Listening to the heritage does not only lead to the "devaluation of all values", but also to the retrieval and further elaboration of the specific inherited contents. An ethics of finitude would not suspend nor revoke many of the "rules of the game" that govern our society. A lot of them are the ones smuggled in by metaphysics or by the authoritarianism of the Churches as "natural norms". If they are recognized not as nature or essences, but rather as our cultural heritage, they can still be valid for us, though with a different cogency: as rational norms – recognized by a dis-cursus, *Logos*, reason, through a reconstruction of the way in which they have come to be – deprived of the violence characteristic of ultimate principles (and of the authorities that see themselves as their custodians). Whether these norms are still valid or not should be decided in the name of the leading thread we take, through a responsible interpretation, to be characteristic of what "really" belongs to the heritage to which we are committed. If we identify this main thread with nihilism, the dissolution of ultimate foundations and of their incontrovertibility – always a violent interruption of questioning – then the choice of what is valid or not with respect to the cultural heritage which we come from will be based on the criteria of the reduction of violence. It will be made in the name of a rationality construed as discursus-dialogue between finite positions that are recognized as such, and are not tempted by the idea of legitimately (legitimate with respect to the validation of first principles) imposing their perspective upon the others'. The main thrust of this ethics of finitude is the exclusion of every violence that construes itelf as legitimate, the exclusion of every form of violence – defined as the interruption of questioning and as the silencing of the other in the name of principles, if one wants to avoid metaphysical essentialism. As I mentioned above, many aspects of Kantian ethics are retrieved here as in much contemporary philosophical ethics. In particular, the categorical imperative formulated in terms of respect for the other: Consider humanity in yourself and in others always as an end, never as a simple means. These traits, however, are deprived of any dogmatic residual, still visible in Habermas's theory of communicative action and in Apel's thought. For the ethics of finitude, respect for the other is not even remotely associated with the idea that the human being is the bearer of human reason, which is the same for all. The positions mentioned a moment ago draw from the latter principle the authoritarian-pedagogical implication that one must listen to the other's reasons, but only after verifying and vouching that they are not "manipulated". Respect for the other is above all the recognition of the finitude that characterizes both of us; it excludes any definitive removal of opacity which each carries in oneself. One may note that here there are no positive reasons grounding respect, which is itself hardly defined. It is not grounded, for example, in the idea that we are all children of the same father, or that our lives depend upon others, etc. As soon as one makes such reasons explicit, they are shown to be vague and untenable: Only a familial prejudice could justify the commandment to love brothers; only a "specistic" egoism, the idea that I must respect the other because he is essentially like me; only a pure and simple egoism would appeal to the commandment to respect the other because our survival depends on him, and so on.

If we assume the nihilistic destiny of our epoch and recognize that we do not have access to an ultimate foundation, we withdraw any possible legitimation to the abusing violence against the other. Violence may still be a temptation – neither less nor more than in any other ethical position; the difference here is that violence would be deprived of any appearance of legitimation, an appearance characteristic of essentialist ethics or of disguised ones (included "communicative" ethics).

Yet, if the thread marking the dissolution of principles and of the reduction of violence is not "demonstrated", but rather interpretatively assumed (once again on the basis of rhetorical, likely arguments, and so on), is this ethics, then, merely exhortative discourse? Even a metaphysician like Aristotle recognized that the cogency of mathematical demonstrations and the persuasiveness of ethical discourses are not the same thing. If Hume's law has any validity, one cannot demonstrate ethics. And Hume's law articulates the condition of ethics, which can command, exhort and judge only if what shall be done, is not yet *done*, not yet a *factum*.

Notes

1 I have developed this thematics more in depth in *Beyond Interpretation: The meaning of Hermeneutics for Philosophy* (1994), translated by D. Webb (Cambridge: Polity Press, 1996). Cf. especially chapter 1 and appendix 1.
2 It is only in the epoch of the end of metaphysics, or of accomplished nihilism, that it makes sense to speak of the task of thinking in terms of cor-respondence to the epoch or as Reiner Schürmann put it *(Heidegger on Being and Acting: from Principle to Anarchy* (Bloomington, Ind., Indiana University Press, 1986)) in terms of accepting an injunction which comes from an economy of presencing, an aletheiological order, a normative reference to what in Heidegger's language would be called an 'opening' of Being, a specific sending (*Geschick*) which *bestimmt* (attunes or determines) the existence of a historical humanity. While Schürmann's analysis is by far among the best available in Heideggerian literature, it is guided by a kind of phenomenological prejudice which leads him to emphasize too much, in the context of a theoretical reflection that turns him astray (although he is faithful to the letter of Heidegger's thought), the primacy of Being over Dasein; it ends up not distinguishing itself from an objective consistence, which is not too different from metaphysical being. For example, consider the following passage: "As aletheiological and therefore systemic, any essential decision is necessarily non-human" and "precedes all human or voluntary decisions, all comportment" (p. 247). If, as Schürmann rightly observes, anarchy becomes possible only with the end of metaphysics, that is, with a departure from the world of *archai*, of metaphysical principles, of foundations, this happens also because of the unfolding of nihilism as the "epoch of the world-image", which is also an epoch of the IMAGES of the world that are in conflict with one

another. Nihilism only occurs as the conflict of interpretation, not as an objective event that Dasein could follow, accept or to which it could adapt itself. Schürmann conceives the departure from metaphysics as an entry into the event, which would mean being placed in an an-anarchical situation, that is, absolutely "without principal overdeterminations" (p. 273), the outcome of a transition "from the era of Janus to that of Proteus" (p. 274). This epoch, however, cannot be really considered epochal insofar as it tends to identify itself excessively with the condition prior to the origin of all the determinations of finite existing. "But it is obvious that this originary coming-about of an age just as the 'soundless play' without consequences differs from any inaugural founding deed." (p. 273) Such a condition can only be realized through a leap, it has no real historical location; rather, it is like a natural event, "suddenly it is autumn, the eighties, old age" (p. 273). In this light Schürmann reads Heidegger's emphasis on the "step backward" "through which Heidegger adopts and modifies the transcendental tradition" (p. 19), and above all his refusal to construct an ethics. It seems fair to speak here of a phenomenological prejudice insofar as it leads to the "naturalization" of history and of the destiny of being, and therefore does not cor-respond to Heidegger's still actual programme of the overcoming of metaphysics – who did not deny scientific objectivism only to lapse into Spengler's vitalism or phenomenology's transcendentalism.

Bernard Williams

Naturalismus und Genealogie*

I
Naturalismus

In der Ethik weckt der Ausdruck „Naturalismus" zwei verschiedene Arten von Assoziationen. Eine Assoziationskette entspringt der nicht sehr glücklichen Aneignung des Ausdrucks durch G. E. Moore in der Rede vom „naturalistischen Fehlschluß". Die andere Folge von Assoziationen geht mit der Verwendung des Ausdrucks in anderen Forschungsbereichen einher und kreist um den Satz, der Mensch sei Teil der Natur. Daß beide Assoziationsbereiche nicht deckungsgleich sind, wird deutlich, wenn man über die Ansicht nachdenkt, derzufolge moralische Forderungen Gebote Gottes sind: Im Sinne Moores mag eine solche Ansicht naturalistisch sein, d. h. damit einhergehen, den naturalistischen Fehlschluß zu begehen. In der zweiten Verwendungsweise ist diese Ansicht aber offensichtlich nicht-naturalistisch.

Moores Verwendungsweise des Ausdrucks soll mich hier nicht beschäftigen. Dennoch ist vielleicht von Nutzen, zu ihr noch eine weitere Anmerkung zu machen. Der naturalistische Fehlschluß wird heute oft im Rekurs auf die Beziehungen zwischen Tatsache und Wert erklärt: Man könnte sagen, daß der Fehlschluß auf dem irrtümlichen Versuch beruht, Werte auf Tatsachen zurückführen zu wollen. Für Moore selbst hingegen läge bei dem Tatsache-Wert-Paar eine Bestimmung über Kreuz vor: Tatsachen hinsichtlich von Werten sind eine Art Tatsache. Die Unterscheidung als solche zwischen Wert und Tatsache (oder, genauer gesagt, die weiteren Erklärungen, die man geben müßte, um eine solche Unterscheidung zu treffen) bietet (bzw. bieten) vielmehr einen Begründungsversuch dafür an, warum der naturalistische Fehlschluß ein Fehlschluß ist – falls er ein solcher ist.

Ich möchte mich mit jenem anderen, traditionelleren Verständnis von „Naturalismus" beschäftigen. Eine wohlvertraute, ganz systematische Schwierigkeit – die nichts im engeren Sinne mit Ethik zu tun hat – resultiert daraus, daß man den „Natur"-Gedanken so entwickeln möchte, daß die naturalistische Konzeption, auf welchem Gebiet auch immer, nicht trivialerweise wahr bzw. in einem solchen Grad und in einer solchen Weise unplausibel wird, daß sie uninteressant wird. Sofern „Natur" alles einschließt, was es gibt, ist der Naturalismus trivialerweise wahr. Im Gegenzug könnte man sagen, daß dasjenige, was der Naturalismus als Gegenstand anerkennt, schlechthin das ist, was die Wissenschaften – die Natur-Wissenschaften – als solchen anerkennen. Ist die Biologie aber eine Naturwissenschaft? Wenn die Biologie eine ist, gilt dies auch für die Ethologie? An diesem Punkt könnte man die Schraube weiterdrehen, wobei an den Naturalismus die Forderung gestellt wird, alle Gegenstände darzustellen, die er im Sinne der einen universell anwendbaren Naturwissenschaft, d. h. also der Physik, anerkennt. Das Projekt des Naturalismus wird so mit dem physikalischen Reduktionismus verknüpft. Der physikalische Reduktionismus für sich genommen ist aber ein gänzlich unplausibles Unterfangen. Die Zielsetzung eines naturalistischen Ansatzes in der Ethik etwa kann unmöglich in ihrem Kern an diesen Reduktionismus gekoppelt sein.

Wir sollten von der vornehmlichen Beschäftigung mit dem Reduktionismus loskommen. Unmöglich können die Überlegungen derjenigen, die den Menschen in ethischer wie auch anderer Hinsicht als Teil der Natur haben verstehen wollen, in ihrem Kern an die Aussichten für die *Enzyklopädie der Einheitswissenschaft* gekoppelt sein. Will man zu etwas Besserem kommen, ließe sich beispielsweise das „Leben" untersuchen. Wenn etwas Teil der Natur ist, dann sind es, so möchte man meinen, Lebewesen: Ihr Studium nennt (oder nannte man für gewöhnlich) „Natur-Geschichte". Wie aber konnte der Naturalismus in der Biologie überhaupt in Frage stehen? Anders gesagt: Auch wenn die Rolle der Physik und Chemie in der Biologie ein Diskussionsgegenstand sein mag, so stellt sich hinsichtlich des Naturalismus diese Frage nicht. Man ignoriert hierbei allerdings ein bedeutsames Stück Geschichte. Bis zu und noch in unserem Jahrhundert stellte der Vitalismus eine mögliche Option dar. Man war sich darin einig, daß es Lebewesen gab, es bestand jedoch große Unklarheit darüber, um was für eine Eigenschaft es sich bei *Leben* handelte. Insbesondere war unklar, in welcher Beziehung das Leben zu solchen Eigenschaften stand, die von den anderen Wissenschaften beschrieben wurden. Fraglich war insofern auch, ob das Leben Teil der Natur – damit war gemeint: der *übrigen* Natur – war. Heutzutage wird diese Frage bejaht, wobei sich das, was für Lebewesen charakteristisch ist, heute eindeutig in einer Weise verstehen läßt, die im Einklang mit der Biochemie steht. Wir sind in der Lage, mit Hilfe wissenschaftlicher Begriffe die Möglichkeit der Entstehung von Lebewesen nachzuvollziehen. (Ich hörte einmal, wie Peter Geach das Argument vorbrachte, daß Lebewesen nicht aus der Evolution hervorgegangen sein könnten, weil sich der Evolutionsbegriff nur auf Lebewesen anwenden ließe. Ich überlasse dieses Sophisma von geringer Anziehungskraft demjenigen, der sich dafür interessieren mag.)

Geht man hiervon aus, scheint es mir weder nötig zu behaupten, daß das Leben auf biochemische Phänomene „reduziert" worden ist, noch auch notwendig, dies zu leugnen: Die Frage hat sich schlichtweg verflüchtigt; sie ist von keinerlei Interesse mehr. (Möglicherweise gilt die allgemeine Regel, daß die Rede von Reduktion nur solange von Belang ist, als wir noch nicht verstehen, wie Dinge, Prozesse und Tatsachen auf der einen Ebene sich auf Entitäten der anderen Ebene beziehen und wie sie mittels ihrer erklärt werden können. Vielleicht ist mit dem Reduktionismus-Gedanken, so wie mit dem Gedanken der Supervenienz und dem der notwendigen synthetischen Wahrheit, immer eine Problemstellung markiert, jedoch keine Lösung gegeben.)

Fragen bezüglich des Naturalismus sind, wie etwa solche hinsichtlich des Individualismus in den Sozialwissenschaften[1], keine Fragen bezüglich einer Reduktion, sondern bezüglich einer Erklärung. Natürlich bin ich mir dessen bewußt, daß damit nahezu alles offen bleibt. Das muß aber auch so sein, denn die bedeutsamen und interessanten Fragen *sind* offen. Es geht darum, daß die Fragen das betreffen, was wir auf jeder Erklärungsstufe als Erklärung akzeptieren. Darüber hinaus haben wir keinen Grund zu glauben, daß auf jeder einzelnen Stufe das, was als Erklärung gelten soll – von der

Ebene der Naturbausteine, die nur mit physikalischen Begriffen beschreibbar sind, bis hin zum Menschen und seiner Kultur – gleicher Art ist. Ein (aber auch nur ein) Grund, auf dem die Differenz zwischen Naturalismus und Reduktionismus beruht, ist derjenige, daß „ist reduzierbar auf" eine transitive Relation ist, während „kann erklärt werden mittels" nicht transitiv ist. Die Frage hinsichtlich des Naturalismus lautet immer: Können wir – ausgestattet mit angemessenen und einschlägigen Erklärungskriterien – das fragliche Phänomen vermittels der *übrigen* Natur erklären? (Diese Position könnte man das „Sperrfeuer des Naturalismus" nennen.)

II
Der Mensch

Sobald wir zu den besonderen Eigenschaften des Menschen kommen, verschieben sich die Streitpunkte gegenüber dem vorausgehenden Diskussionsstand etwas. Das überwältigend Neue, das mit *homo sapiens* verbunden ist, ist die Bedeutung des Erwerbs von nicht angeborenem Wissen. Hierin kommt in erster Linie ein ethologisches Differenzkriterium zum Ausdruck. Jeder Spezies läßt sich eine ethologische Beschreibung zuordnen – *homo sapiens* bildet da keine Ausnahme. Was seinen Fall auszeichnet ist, daß man ausschließlich beim Menschen kein ethologisches Profil zeichnen kann, ohne seine Kultur mit einzubeziehen. (Man bedenke etwa, was unmittelbar mit der Frage einhergeht: „In welchen Behausungen leben sie?"). Folglich wird sich die Darstellung bei verschiedenen Menschengruppen wahrscheinlich erheblich unterscheiden, und zwar in einer Art und Weise, die typischerweise die Historie einschließt. Die Menschen, die beschrieben werden, werden sich in vielen Fällen – in unterschiedlichen Graden – dieser Geschichte auch bewußt sein. Dies alles ergibt sich aus dem besonderen ethologischen Charakter dieser Spezies.

Die einzelnen Mitglieder der Art müssen natürlich idealtypisch bzw. standardmäßig, zumindest aber in einem angemessenen Umfang über jene charakteristischen Merkmale verfügen, aus denen dieses ethologische Profil des Menschen hervorgeht, die ihm also das Leben in einer Kultur eröffnen. Folgefragen sind dann: Worin bestehen diese Charakteristika? Wie sieht deren beste, d. h. deren umfassendste und erklärungsmächtigste Beschreibung aus? Wie läßt sich, setzt man eine entsprechende Beschreibung voraus, die Entstehung dieser charakteristischen Merkmale erklären? Hinsichtlich einiger von ihnen wird man sich bei der Beantwortung schlechthin auf überlieferte soziale Einflüsse berufen, die auf den Menschen, der mit einer allgemeinen Lernfähigkeit begabt ist, einwirken. Einige andere (wie etwa die Lernfähigkeit selbst) hingegen müssen auf der Entwicklung von Erbanlagen beruhen, und die Folgefrage lautet dann zwangsläufig: Wie? Dies gilt offensichtlich für die Fähigkeit des Spracherwerbs.

Ein für uns interessanter Sonderfall ist eine bestimmte Fähigkeit, die Menschen in allen Kulturen auf die eine oder andere Weise unter Beweis gestellt haben, nämlich diejenige, ihr Leben Regeln und Werten zu unterwerfen und ihr Verhalten bis zu einem gewissen Grad an sozialen Erwartungen auszurichten, wobei diese Ausrichtung keiner unmittelbaren Überwachung und keiner direkten Kontrolle durch Strafandrohung und Belohnung unterliegt. Nennen wir dies die Minimalversion dessen, was es heißt, in einem ethischen System zu leben, auch wenn damit viele Fragen aufgeworfen werden.

In einem ethischen System zu leben erfordert eine bestimmte psychologische Verfassung. Wichtig ist indes, daß hieraus nicht folgt, daß alle ethischen Systeme dieselbe psychologische Struktur verlangen – die Moralpsychologie könnte einem Opportunismus folgen (ein Beispiel hierfür wäre der angebliche Unterschied zwischen einer Scham- und einer Schuld-Gesellschaft). Ebensowenig gilt, daß ein- und dasselbe ethische System eine identische psychologische Verfassung aller seiner Mitglieder verlangt. Variation könnte auf dieser Ebene nicht nur individuell, sondern, was von größerem Interesse ist, systematisch bedingt sein: Dies würde für unser bestehendes ethisches System gelten, falls Carol Gilligans Hypothese zutrifft, daß unterschiedliche psychologische Ausstattungen von Mann und Frau in ihm eine Rolle spielen.[2]

Geht man davon aus, daß es eine psychologische Verfassung oder deren mehrere geben muß, die jeglichem ethischen System zugrunde liegen, stellt sich die Frage: Wie müssen diese psychologischen Strukturen beschaffen sein? Was schließen sie ein? Unsere unmittelbare Frage lautet dann: Wie sieht eine Antwort auf diese Fragen aus, die den Forderungen des Naturalismus Rechnung trägt?

III
Konvention

Es lohnt sich, im Zuge des Versuchs, einen Rahmen für die zuletzt gestellte Frage abzustecken, den Konventionsbegriff zu betrachten. Zwischen Natur und Konvention besteht seit der Antike ein Gegensatz, so daß man glauben könnte, jemand würde sich mit der Annahme, daß „Konvention" die Natur und das Bestehen ethischer Systeme in einschlägiger Weise erklären könnte, einem Naturalismus bezüglich dieser ethischen Systeme widersetzen. Dem ist aber offensichtlich nicht so. Diejenigen, die ethische Systeme als „Konvention" betrachten, gehen normalerweise so vor, daß sie ihre Betrachtung als Teil eines naturalistischen Modells verstehen. Dies erklärt sich daraus, daß sie zwei Annahmen machen, von denen eine offensichtlich wahr ist, während die zweite zweifelhafter zu sein scheint. Die Annahme, die offensichtlich wahr ist, besagt – wie Plato (oder vielleicht schon Demokrit) als erster feststellte –, daß es zur Natur des Menschen gehört, sein Leben gemäß bestimmter Konventionen zu führen: Das ist gerade der Kern des Gedankens, demzufolge die Humanethologie die Beschreibung einer Kultur ist. Die zweite Annahme besteht darin, daß keine andere psychologische Verfassung als diejenige, die man dem Menschen *ohnehin* zuschreiben würde, dazu notwendig ist, um ein Leben gemäß bestimmter Konventionen zu führen. Diese Annahme ist zweifelhafter. Was nämlich könnte mit „ohnehin" gemeint sein?

Wir kommen zum Kern dieser Frage, wenn wir uns die Form der Frage des Naturalisten auf den vorausgegangenen Stufen nochmals vor Augen führen. Ein Naturalist behauptet, daß die Implikationen des menschlichen Lebens innerhalb ethischer Systeme sich auf kohärente Weise zur übrigen Natur in Beziehung setzen lassen. Was aber ist nunmehr die übrige Natur genau? Im Vitalismus waren die

Gegenstände der Natur bis hin zum Lebewesen gemeint; wo auch von Bewußtsein (das ich bislang unerwähnt gelassen habe) die Rede ist, meint man wohl alle Gegenstände einschließlich der Lebewesen bis hin zu Lebewesen mit Bewußtsein. Was also bedeutet „die übrige Natur" im vorliegenden Fall? Bedeutet es: alles – Lebewesen mit Bewußtsein bis hin zum Menschen einschließlich? Wenn das gemeint ist, rückt folgendes in den Brennpunkt der naturalistischen Frage: Steht die Fähigkeit des Menschen, in einem ethischen System zu leben, in enger Beziehung zu charakteristischen Eigenschaften anderer Arten, d. h. solcher Lebewesen, die nicht der menschlichen Spezies angehören? Läßt sich diese Fähigkeit und ihre Entwicklung mit Hilfe unseres Verständnisses anderer Arten erklären?

Die naturalistische Frage in der Ethik ist oft so formuliert worden. Einige derer, die die Frage in diesem Sinne diskutiert haben, haben sie negativ beantwortet. Es gab insbesondere solche, denen es sehr darum ging, die ethischen Fähigkeiten des Menschen mittels der Entgegensetzung zu anderen Tieren herauszustellen.

Andere haben die naturalistische Frage genau so verstanden, aber eine positive Antwort auf sie gegeben. Typischerweise sind dies Leute, die von der Soziobiologie beeindruckt sind und die Fähigkeit, die zum Leben in einem ethischen System erforderlich ist, beispielsweise den „Altruismus", in einem Sinn auffassen, demzufolge besagte Charaktereigenschaft durch Selektion in anderen Arten entstehen könnte. „Altruismus" läßt sich aber nicht von anderen Arten auf den Menschen übertragen, ohne die Unterschiede zwischen den Arten in Rechnung zu stellen, die einen wesentlichen Teil des Problems ausmachen.

Das Unausgegorene beider Ansätze, des negativen wie des positiven, legt nahe, daß die Form der naturalistischen Frage, die sie beide gemein haben – die Art und Weise, in der sie „die übrige Natur" interpretieren –, das Resultat einer Fehldeutung ist. Bevor man zu den psychologischen Strukturen kommt, die speziell von ethischen Systemen vorausgesetzt werden, muß man einräumen, daß sich die Kultur auf nahezu jeden Aspekt der menschlichen Psychologie auswirkt. Eine Betrachtung selbst der elementarsten instinktiven Triebe des Menschen, also derjenigen Triebe, die er offensichtlich in einem gewissen Sinn mit anderen Arten gemein hat, muß den Einfluß des

Kulturellen auf sie und ihre Ausdrucksformen mit ins Kalkül ziehen. Darin liegt schlicht die Anwendung einer – zugegeben weitreichenden – ethologischen Platitüde: Die Art und Weise, wie sich ein bestimmter Instinkt oder Trieb bei einer bestimmten Spezies manifestiert, hängt von der Form des Lebens dieser Art ab. Es ist kaum verwunderlich, daß sich das Fortpflanzungsverhalten des Rothirschs auf signifikante Weise von dem des Igels oder Stichlings unterscheidet, denn ihre Lebensweisen sind merklich verschieden. Wenn wir mit einem naturalistischen Begriffsinventar – oder auch ganz konträr dazu – über die psychologische Struktur des Menschen nachdenken, insofern sich diese unmittelbar auf sein Leben in ethischen Systemen bezieht, sollten wir an erster Stelle über die Beziehungen dieser psychologischen Verfassung zu anderen Aspekten der Psychologie *des Menschen* nachdenken.

Natürlich ist hier eine falsche Abstraktion im Spiel. Ich habe bereits gesagt, daß der Mensch in einer Kultur lebt, was aus der zentralen Bedeutung seiner Fähigkeit zum Erwerb nicht-angeborenen Wissens resultiert. Ich habe auch gesagt, daß – grob gesprochen – das Leben in einer Kultur einschließt, in einem ethischen System zu leben. Wenn das stimmt, ist es letztendlich unmöglich, das Leben in einer Kultur samt all der Wirkungen, die das auf andere Aspekte der menschlichen Psychologie hat, von dem zu trennen, was den Menschen befähigt, in einem ethischen System zu leben – was auch immer es ist. Mit Sicherheit können wir das letztlich nicht. Aber vielleicht wäre es zielführender, wenn wir die *gleichzeitige* Diskussion aller dieser Punkte verschieben würden.

Es lassen sich Gründe angeben, die es geraten erscheinen lassen, einen solchen Versuch zu machen. Für die Besonderheiten, die beim Menschen auftreten, ist ein Charakteristikum von ganz grundlegender Bedeutung, nämlich der Sprachgebrauch. Wir sollten also als erstes die Rolle der Sprache für andere Aspekte der menschlichen Psychologie ins Kalkül ziehen. Der Spracherwerb präsentiert sich darüber hinaus als etwas, das der naturalistischen Forderung genügen könnte. Insbesondere sind wir vielleicht in der Lage, eine Erklärung dafür zu geben, wie sich Sprache als solche entwickelt haben könnte.

Die Zusammenführung dieser beiden Überlegungen legt einen plausiblen oder jedenfalls vertrauten Gedanken nahe: Die Beziehung zumindest einiger grundlegender instinktiver Triebe im Menschen, auch wenn diese unweigerlich durch Sprache und Kultur modifiziert sind, zu funktional ähnlichen Trieben bei anderen Arten ist transparenter als die psychologischen Strukturen, auf die sich die ethischen Systeme stützen. Ein solcher Gedanke hat zweifellos dazu beigetragen, diejenigen zu ermutigen, die sich traditionell an dem Modell orientierten, daß der Mensch einen „animalischen Teil" hat, dem seine rationalen Fähigkeiten und ethischen Motivationen gegenüberstehen.

Setzt man diese Überlegungen voraus, läßt sich aus ihnen die naturalistische Frage bezüglich einer Ethik in etwa als Frage danach ableiten, wie eng die Beziehung der ethischen Motivationen und Praktiken zu anderen Aspekten der Humanpsychologie ist – zu, wie sich sehr vage und ungenau sagen ließe, der Art und Weise, wie der Mensch „ohnehin" beschaffen ist. Unter Berücksichtigung dieses besonderen Aspekts der sehr eigentümlichen Ethologie dieser Spezies nimmt die immer wieder artikulierte naturalistische Frage eine spezifische Gestalt an; wir haben die Frage dabei als solche identifiziert, die sich auch andernorts, beispielsweise gegenüber dem Leben als solchem, stellen läßt: In welchem rational nachvollziehbaren Verhältnis steht das fragliche Phänomen zur *übrigen* Natur; und insbesondere: Wie erklärt sich seine Entstehung? Man könnte sagen, wir fragen nach dem ethischen Leben des Menschen in seiner Beziehung zur übrigen Natur des Menschen.

Wenn wir einem Vorhaben Sinn abgewinnen können, demzufolge das Ethische mit Hilfe einer Darstellung des Menschen erklärt werden soll, die so weit wie möglich diesseits von Gedanken des Ethischen steht, so ist damit ein Projekt des ethischen Naturalismus formuliert, das intelligibel ist, nicht leerläuft und darüber hinaus keinem allgemeinen physikalischen Reduktionismus verpflichtet ist, der (milde ausgedrückt) zweifelhaft ist und ohnehin gesondert behandelt werden sollte.

IV
Geschichte

Der nächste Vorschlag, den ich machen möchte, hat seine Entsprechung in der zweiten Hälfte des Titels. Dieser Vorschlag besagt, daß ein im Hinblick auf eine Ethik entwickeltes naturalistisches Projekt dergestalt, wie wir es soeben entworfen haben, wohl am besten mit Hilfe bestimmter historischer oder quasi-historischer Untersuchungen vorangebracht werden kann. Mein bisheriger Vorschlag ist zu einem beträchtlichen Grad von diesen weiteren Überlegungen unabhängig. Zwar müßte eine naturalistische Darstellung der Ethik wohl diejenigen Bedingungen erfüllen, die ich zuvor entwickelt habe; aber sie muß nicht die besondere Gestalt annehmen, die ich jetzt vorschlage. Gleichwohl glaube ich, daß sich einige Gründe dafür anführen lassen, daß eine Darstellung der Ethik zum Teil wahrscheinlich doch eine solche Form annehmen wird. Die Gründe hierfür werden – bis zu einem gewissen Grad – im vorliegenden Fall wohl eher von selbst aufscheinen müssen, als daß ich für sie werde im Detail argumentieren können.

Der Vorschlag ist tatsächlich weit komplizierter, als ich bisher angedeutet habe. Zumindest im Hinblick auf unser eigenes ethisches Leben, das ethische Leben der Moderne, wird ein Teil der Darstellung aus realer Geschichte bestehen, die bis zu einem gewissen Grad, wie Foucault formulierte, „grau [...], ängstlich und geduldig [...] mit Dokumenten beschäftigt"[3] sein wird. Der Grund hierfür liegt darin, daß unsere ethischen Vorstellungen, im Gegensatz etwa zum ethischen Leben einer isolierten, nach festen, tradierten Normen verfaßten Gesellschaft, ein vielgestaltiger Bodensatz vieler verschiedener Traditionen, sozialer Kräfte usw. sind und daß unser ethisches Leben selbst durch die bewußte Reflexion auf diese Tatsachen bestimmt ist. (Damit soll nicht – wie dies bei einigen bedenklichen anthropologischen Ansätzen angenommen wurde – gesagt sein, daß Gesellschaften, die nach tradierten Normen verfaßt sind, keine Prägungen aus der Geschichte erfahren haben. Ihre Geschichte ist aber weniger komplex, einer geringeren Vielfalt von Einflüssen ausgesetzt, nicht durch reflexive Selbstdeutungen vermittelt und weitgehend unbekannt. Aus all dem lassen sich große Unterschiede für die Darstellung ableiten, die man von der Sache liefern kann, wie auch für das, was als Erklärung akzeptiert wird.)

Darüber hinaus trifft wahrscheinlich zu, daß – insbesondere, wenn wir uns an den eigenen Fall halten – der erhebliche Einfluß dieser historischen Prozesse bis zu einem gewissen Grad durch die Art und Weise verdeckt wird, wie das Resultat dieser Prozesse sich selbst wahrnimmt. Hierfür läßt sich mehr als ein Grund angeben, der allgemeinste jedoch besteht vielleicht darin, daß eine wahrheitsgemäße historische Darstellung einen gewissen Kontingenzgrad unserer geläufigen ethischen Modelle zutage fördern wird. Dies gilt sowohl hinsichtlich der Spezifität der Modelle als auch hinsichtlich des Umstands, daß die historischen Veränderungen, aus denen diese Modelle hervorgegangen sind, zu den ethischen Vorstellungen, die durch sie befördert wurden, nicht in einem offenkundigen Begründungsverhältnis stehen und unseren Glauben an diese ethischen Werte nicht schlechthin bestätigen oder bestärken. (Dies steht im Gegensatz sowohl zur hegelianischen als auch zur marxistischen Geschichtsteleologie.) Ein Aspekt solcher Kontingenz steht in einer gewissen Spannung zu einer Forderung des ethischen Systems selbst, nämlich derjenigen, die Autorität des Systems anzuerkennen. Die Spannung hierbei wird dadurch noch verstärkt, daß moderne ethische Systeme den Versuch machen, Autorität und Transparenz zu verbinden. Der hohe Stellenwert von Transparenz, der ein eigener Ausfluß dieser Systeme ist, trägt vermutlich dazu bei, den naturalistischen Impuls zu verstärken.

Mit all dem Gesagten ist der Gedanke verbunden, daß solche Darstellungen wohl etwas Ungefälliges, Respektloses oder Kritisches an sich haben. Wie wiederum Foucault sagte, „ist jeder Ursprung der Moral, sobald er nicht mehr verehrungswürdig ist [,][...] Quell der Kritik."[4] Ich werde auf diesen Gedanken noch zurückkommen.

Es geht hier allerdings nicht einfach um eine Frage der von mir so genannten realen Geschichte. Auch imaginäre Geschichte, eine fiktive Entwicklungsgeschichte, kann bei der Erklärung eines Begriffs, eines Wertes oder einer Institution eine Rolle spielen, indem sie Wege ihrer möglichen Entstehung unter vereinfachten Bedingungen aufzeigt, wobei unter diesen Bedingungen menschliche Interessen und Fähigkeiten auftreten, die – relativ zu dieser Geschichte – als gegeben angenommen werden. Ein Musterbeispiel hierfür sind Geschichten des Naturzustandes, die von den Ursprüngen des Staates handeln; ein weiteres Beispiel ist Humes Darstellung der künstlichen Tugend der Gerechtigkeit. Ein äußerst interessantes jüngeres Beispiel ist Edward Craigs sehr erhellende Darstellung des Erkenntnisbegriffs[5].

Interessant ist die Frage danach, wie es möglich ist, daß gänzlich fiktive Geschichten in der beschriebenen Weise irgend etwas erklären oder erhellen können. Ich kann dieser Frage hier nicht sehr weit nachgehen, aber ich werde eine Skizze entwerfen. Die Geschichten, die uns hier beschäftigen, beziehen sich auf Begriffe, Werte und Institutionen, und die besondere Aufgabe einer Geschichte ist es zu erklären, wie diese Dinge aufkommen und neue Handlungsgründe liefern können. Sie geht dabei von bestehenden Handlungsgründen als gegeben aus. Die Geschichte erfüllt eine besondere Funktion, weil die neuen Handlungsgründe in einer rationalen bzw. verständlichen Beziehung zu den ursprünglichen Gründen oder Motivationen stehen. Diese Beziehung ist nicht einfach instrumentell – sie ist zumindest insoweit nicht instrumentell, als sie den Individuen nicht Handlungsgründe liefert, die sich diese letztlich individuell aneignen könnten. Ein wichtiger Sonderfall liegt bei der Konstruktion von etwas vor, dessen intrinsischen Wert man anerkennen muß, sobald es einmal konstruiert worden ist.[6]

Man kann einiges aus fiktiver Geschichte lernen. Der Umstand, daß sie ohne bestimmte Quellen auskommt, legt u. U. nahe, daß es eine wirkliche, weit weniger geordnete Darstellung geben könnte, die auf solche Ressourcen ebenfalls verzichten könnte und selbstgenügsam wäre.[7] Darüber hinaus könnte so eine Geschichte bei der Skizze einer funktionalen Darstellung des Produkts von Wert sein, so daß wir in die Lage versetzt werden, das Explanandum in der realen Welt mit Hilfe eines Inventars von elementaren Eigenschaften zu interpretieren, sowie mit Hilfe einiger anderer, die das Resultat höherstufiger Überlegungen sind – wobei die reale Geschichte und die Sozialwissenschaften vermutlich einiges zur Identifizierung dieser verschiedenen Eigenschaften beitragen werden.

V
Nietzsche

Eine Darstellungsform, die die eine oder andere, oder typischerweise diese beiden Geschichten – die historische und die quasi-historische – vereint bietet, ist die Genealogie. Der Begriff zeigt natürlich an, daß die Gedanken, die ihn begleiten, Nietzsche sehr viel verdanken, dessen *Genealogie der Moral* der bekannteste und spektakulärste Beitrag seines Genres ist. Die *Genealogie der Moral* hat die Eigenschaft, auf Anhieb hochgradig überzeugend zu wirken, was vor allem daran liegt, daß sie vermeintlich etwas mit großer Genauigkeit trifft. Auf der anderen Seite ist sie in einer höchst ärgerlichen Weise vage. Sie entwickelt eine anschauliche Phänomenologie des Ressentiments, die bestimmte moralische Vorstellungen auf die geistige Kompensation eines Mangels an Macht zurückführt. Sie hat auch etwas mit Geschichte zu tun, ohne daß allerdings auch nur ansatzweise klar wäre, mit welcher Geschichte: Es treten einige vage verortete Herrenmenschen und Sklaven auf; des weiteren ein historischer Wandel, der etwas mit Juden und Christen zu tun hat; von einem Prozeß ist die Rede, der vielleicht in der Reformation, vielleicht in Kant kulminiert. Die Geschichte dauerte angeblich zweitausend Jahre an.[8]

Wir haben es hier mit einem Amalgam aus Psychologie und Geschichte zu tun, das Hegels Phänomenologie sicherlich einiges verdankt: Zwischen Vorstellungen, Grundanschauungen und Haltungen, die sich sowohl psychologisch als auch historisch artikulieren, besteht eine Reihe von Beziehungen, durch die zwischen den beiden Ausdrucksformen eine wesentliche Verbindung hergestellt wird. Wir müssen das insbesondere deshalb für unbefriedigend halten, weil dieses Amalgam mit Elementen des Hegelschen Idealismus durchsetzt ist, den Nietzsche selbst wie kein anderer zu desavouieren trachtete. Wenn wir es aber sozusagen zerlegen, kann es für uns immer noch von großem Nutzen sein.

Eine (und sicherlich nur eine) Art und Weise, wie dies mit Rücksicht auf einen Teil der Geschichte Nietzsches geschehen kann, ist folgende:

(a) Ein Aspekt unserer eigenen Grundanschauung, unserer Moralität, ist psychologisch und begrifflich zweifelhaft: der Wille oder, u. U., der freie Wille, verstanden als etwas, das aus einem Prozeß der ausschließlichen Selbstbegründung hervorgeht und erlaubt, Verbindungslinien zur Praxis der Zuschreibung von Schuld und Verantwortung, zur Praxis der moralischen Werte im Gegensatz zu den profanen usw. zu ziehen. Dies hat sich immer wieder als ein Problemfeld in Theorie und Praxis erwiesen, ein Ort für Grabenkämpfe und Brüche. Es existiert eine Geschichte, eine nüchterne, reale Geschichte dieser Schwierigkeiten.

(b) Es existiert eine nüchterne, reale Geschichte eines konkreten Gegenstücks zu diesen Vorstellungen: die Historie vorauffliegender Welten, in denen es diese Vorstellungen nicht gab. Zweifellos existieren auch andere Kontrastwelten; diejenigen aber, die uns in besonderer Weise angehen, sind jene Welten, die die Vorläufer der unsrigen sind.

(c) Es besteht eine ganze Reihe von moralischen Reaktionsweisen, die mit (a) und den damit assoziierten Praktiken verbunden sind; mit diesen Reaktionsweisen geht typischerweise ein hoher Grad von Affekt einher.

(d) Wir verfügen über eine weitere – oder hegen die Hoffnung auf eine künftige – nüchtern-reale Geschichte, die dabei behilflich ist, die Übergänge von jenen früheren Welten in unsere gegenwärtigen Verhältnisse nachzuvollziehen, und die dazu beiträgt, (c) zu erklären.

Bei der Geschichte, die uns nun Nietzsche selbst liefert, spielt eine zentrale Rolle, daß sie eine phänomenologische Darstellung ist, die allem Anschein nach einen psychologischen Prozeß angibt, der von früheren ethischen Verhältnissen zu so etwas wie den Grundanschauungen in den späteren ethischen Verhältnissen (dem Explanandum) führt. Würde es sich dabei um einen psychologischen Prozeß handeln, müßte man ihn am einzelnen Menschen identifizieren können. Ein realer Prozeß, der tatsächlich bis zum eigentlichen Explanandum führen würde, könnte jedoch nicht in einem Individuum statthaben, denn das Ergebnis dieses Prozesses besteht aus Überzeugungen, die gesellschaftlich begründet sind; diese Überzeugungen wiederum können nicht einfach die Summe individueller Phantasien sein. Vielmehr handelt es sich um einen gesellschaftlichen Prozeß, der in Wirklichkeit ohne Zweifel viele Stationen, viele Unterbrechungen und Zufälligkeiten aufweist. Dieser Prozeß – so lautet jedenfalls die Grundidee – läßt sich auf interessante Weise nachzeichnen, wenn man ihn nach dem Modell einer bestimmten psychologischen Strategie konstruiert. Nicht alle Genealogien ziehen m. E. eine solche phänomenologische Darstellungsform nach sich. Dieser zusätzliche Aspekt in Nietzsches besonderer Genealogie ist vielmehr ein Sonderfall dessen, was wir zuvor schon erkannt hatten, nämlich der Sonderfall

(e) einer fiktiven Geschichte, die einen neuen Handlungsgrund unter vereinfachten Bedingungen als Funktion von Motiven, Reaktionen und psychologischen Prozessen entwickelt, von denen auszugehen wohlbegründet scheint.

VI
Ein schlechter Ursprung

Wir waren zuvor auf den Gedanken gestoßen, daß eine Genealogie sich als schädlich oder ungefällig herausstellen könnte: Sie könnte einen schmachvollen Ursprung zutage fördern. Foucault war, wie wir sahen, der Meinung, daß eine Genealogie als faktische Geschichte fast zwangsläufig bis zu einem gewissen Grad kritisch sein muß. Der Grund hierfür liegt, so Foucault (und ich schließe mich an), nicht etwa darin, daß „die Vergangenheit [...] in der Gegenwart noch lebt und sie insgeheim belebt"[9]. Die Grundidee ist vielmehr, daß die Begriffe oder Werte, die erklärt werden sollen, wohl einen Autoritätsgrad für sich reklamieren, der nicht zuläßt, daß Zufälligkeiten auftreten, so daß sie sich dem Versuch widersetzen, überhaupt angemessen erklärt zu werden. Dies gilt allerdings für einige Werte und Institutionen in einem höheren Maße als für andere. Wie Nietzsche unbarmherzig feststellte, gilt dies in einem weit höheren Grad für das System der Moral als für einige andere ethische Gebilde, wobei der Grund hierfür in dessen verzweifeltem Zwang zur Autarkie in jeder Hinsicht liegt. Nicht alle ethischen Grundeinstellungen widersetzen sich gleichermaßen dem Versuch, durchsichtig gemacht zu werden. Andere Einstellungen könnten durchaus zulassen, von einem Bewußtsein ihrer Genese begleitet zu werden. Sie verfügen im Lichte einer genealogischen Erklärung über einen höheren Stabilitätsgrad.

Dies gilt in noch höherem Maße von fiktiven Entwicklungsgeschichten. Die entscheidende Frage ist hier, ob man das Explanandum mit Hilfe der fiktiven Geschichte verstehen und dennoch die Handlungsgründe, die das Explanandum liefert, (mehr oder weniger) in ihrer ursprünglichen Darstellungsform fortbestehen lassen kann. Im Falle der *Genealogie der Moral* läßt die phänomenologische Fiktion des Ressentiments dies nicht zu, wobei, um es noch einmal zu sagen, dies aus der besonderen Forderung an das Moralsystem resultiert, eines sein zu müssen, das von solchen Motiven unabhängig ist und über ihnen steht. Hierin kommt die tiefe Verwicklung mit dem zum Ausdruck, was Nietzsche den „Grundglaube[n] der Metaphysiker", nämlich den *„Glaube[n] an die Gegensätze der Werthe"*[10] genannt hat. (Ein wichtiges Merkmal eines solchen Falles ist, daß der Prozeß, den die Geschichte aufbietet, sogar in der Geschichte selbst unerwähnt bleiben müßte. Hierin liegt eine Spielart, und zwar eine besondere, derjenigen Eigenschaft, die, wie gesagt, allen diesen Geschichten eigen ist: Sie liefern die Darstellung eines Handlungsgrundes, der sich instrumentell nicht von einem Individuum ableiten läßt.) Andere fiktive Geschichten könnten ihr Explanandum allerdings auf eine Weise darstellen, die sich gegenüber einer solchen Reflexion als stabil erweist, was hier nicht der Fall ist. Bei einer Geschichte der Ursprünge des Staates etwa könnte das durchaus so sein. Man könnte in so einem Fall sagen, daß eine Genealogie eine Rechtfertigung lieferte.

Eine gute Frage ist diejenige, ob und weshalb es überhaupt von Bedeutung ist, daß ein Wert oder eine Institution im Lichte irgendeiner genealogischen Erklärung stabil ist. Eigentlich sind hier zwei Fragen im Spiel: Die eine bezieht sich auf fiktive Genealogien und ist ein Anwendungsfall der allgemeinen Frage danach, inwiefern eine Erklärung mittels einer fiktiven Geschichte überhaupt eine Erklärung sein kann oder inwiefern sie etwas zum Verständnis der wirklichen Geschichte beiträgt. Ich muß die Frage hier als solche stehen lassen und mich darauf beschränken zu sagen, daß in dem Maße, wie solche Geschichten einen Wert, der uns Handlungsgründe liefert, mit anderen Handlungsgründen, die (wie ich ganz grob formuliert habe) wir „ohnehin" haben, tatsächlich korrelieren – in diesem Maße also zugleich eine bestimmte Frage (man könnte auch sagen: ein einschlägiges Gedankenexperiment) aufkommen wird, nämlich ob wir – sobald wir die Wahrhaftigkeit einer solchen Geschichte eingesehen haben – dem abgeleiteten Wert weiterhin denselben Grad an Respekt zollen würden.

Die zweite Frage ist allgemeinerer Natur: Angenommen, ein bestimmter Wert stellt sich im Lichte der genealogischen Erklärung als instabil heraus. Natürlich folgt daraus nicht, daß wir ihn fallen lassen oder das Vertrauen in ihn verlieren. Wir könnten einfach aufhören, über ihn nachzudenken, uns nicht mit seiner Erklärung beschäftigen, den Gedanken aufgeben, ihn durchsichtig machen zu wollen. Ein einfacher Grund hierfür liegt darin, daß wir irgendwie weitermachen müssen, irgend etwas als Leitlinie im Leben brauchen und bei fehlender Alternative versuchen werden, das zu bewahren, was wir *de facto* haben, auch wenn es einer Untersuchung nicht standhält. Nietzsches Diagnose der Moderne war,
- daß wir uns in ebender Lage befinden, eine Moral zu besitzen, die in erheblichem Maße instabil ist, sobald sie einer genealogischen Erklärung ausgesetzt wird;
- daß wir (unter anderem gerade durch diese Moral selbst) dazu verpflichtet sind, sie uns durchsichtig zu machen; und
- daß wir über nicht viel verfügen, was als Alternative herhalten könnte.

Ich weiß nicht, inwieweit wir dieser Diagnose beipflichten wollen. Wenn wir solche Fragen erwägen, gibt es aber eine weitere Überlegung Nietzsches, die wir sicherlich bedenken sollten. Ob eine Alternative wirklich besteht oder nicht, ist nichts, was offen vor unseren Augen läge. Des weiteren ist es keine Frage der Willkür oder praktischen Vernunft, ob wir uns auf eine solche Alternative einlassen sollen. Die Frage geht vielmehr darauf, ob andere Formen des Lebens einschließlich anderer Formen, über das Leben zu denken, uns oder den Nachgeborenen helfen werden zu leben. Eine der wichtigsten Lehren Nietzsches geht dahin, daß Erwägungen dieser Art als *Kriterium* untauglich sind. Es geht nicht um die *Wahl* eines Konzepts oder Leitbilds, *weil* es uns helfen wird zu leben, d. h. nicht um eine Entscheidung *aufgrund* entsprechender *Erwägungen*. Es geht vielmehr darum, ob ein solches Leitbild uns *tatsächlich* helfen wird zu leben. Ob es das konnte, wird sich nur im nachhinein einsehen lassen, und zwar zunächst einmal, insofern wir den Eindruck haben, daß wir im und mit dem Leben zu Rande kommen; später dann, mit einem höheren Grad an Bewußtsein, vielleicht abermals mittels einer genealogischen Erklärung.

Anmerkungen

* Anmerkung des Herausgebers: Dieser Beitrag ist die für den vorliegenden Band vorgenommene Überarbeitung eines Vortrags, den Bernard Williams im Rahmen der „Werner Heisenberg Vorlesungen" der Bayerischen Akademie der Wissenschaften und der Carl Friedrich von Siemens Stiftung Ende 1996 in München unter dem Titel „Naturalism and Genealogy" hielt. Die Übersetzung besorgte Marcelo Stamm.

1 Cf. S. James, *The Content of Social Explanation*, Cambridge 1984.
2 Cf. C. Gilligan, *In a Different Voice: Psychological Theory and Women's Development*, Cambridge Mass. 1982.
3 M. Foucault, „Nietzsche, la généalogie, l'historie", in: *Hommage a Jean Hyppolite*, Paris 1971, S. 145; dt.: „Nietzsche, die Genealogie, die Historie", in: *Von der Subversion des Wissens*, ed. et trans. W. Seitter, Frankfurt 1987, S. 69.
4 Foucault, loc. cit. S. 152 [trans. M. Stamm, in Abweichung von W. Seitter (loc. cit. (cf. Anm. 3), S. 74). Orig.: „Toute origine de la morale, du moment qu'elle n'est pas vénérable [...] vaut critique."].
5 Cf. E. Craig, *Knowledge and the State of Nature*: *An Essay in Conceptual Synthesis*, Oxford 1990.
6 Es gibt mehr als einen Grund, warum ein Individuum den Schlußpunkt nicht auf instrumentellem Wege erreichen könnte. Ein Grund besteht –

wie in Humes Darstellung der Gerechtigkeit – darin, daß ein Koordinationsproblem gelöst werden muß. Ein weiterer Grund ist dort zu suchen, wo die Geschichte einen intrinsischen Wert konstruiert. Davon abgesetzt ist noch der Fall, in dem es überhaupt nicht möglich ist, den fraglichen Prozeß bewußt nachzuvollziehen, wie im Beispiel von Moral und Ressentiment, das unten in Abschnitt VI erörtert wird.

7 Das gilt sogar dann, wenn die Geschichte nicht nur fiktiv, sondern sogar unmöglich ist, was für die genealogischen Fälle zutrifft. In anderen Bereichen könnte eine fiktive Geschichte einen möglichen Mechanismus liefern, durch den ein bestimmtes Ergebnis zustande gekommen sein könnte. Sie zeigt auf diese Weise, daß eine bestimmte Form der theoretischen Erklärung möglich ist. Das ist die Pointe von „Genau-so-Geschichten" in der Evolutionsbiologie [Anmerkung des Hrsg.: cf. R. Kipling, *Genau-so-Geschichten*, trans. G. Haefs, München 1990, Orig.: *Just So Stories for Little Children*, London 1902, zu Zeiten eines der drei wichtigsten Vorlesebücher der englischsprachigen Welt. Das „Just So" des Titels meint hierbei nicht die spezifische Art der „Erklärung", die in den Geschichten aufgeboten wird, sondern die Authentizität des Wortlauts: Kipling schrieb im Dezember 1897 in einer Vorbemerkung zur Erstveröffentlichung einer der Geschichten, "How the Whale Got His Throat", der in den *Just So Stories* berühmte weitere (von "How the Leopard Got His Spots" bis "How the Alphabet Was Made") an die Seite gestellt sind: „Abends gab es Geschichten, bei denen Effie [Kiplings 1892 geborene Tochter, Anm. M. Stamm] einschlafen sollte, und da durfte kein einziges Wort abgeändert werden. Sie mußten *just so* erzählt werden, sonst wurde Effie wach und ergänzte den fehlenden Satz. Schließlich wurden sie beinahe zu Zaubersprüchen ..." (loc. cit., S. 225)].

8 Cf. Fr. Nietzsche, *Zur Genealogie der Moral*, in: *Werke: Kritische Gesamtausgabe*, ed. G. Colli et M. Montinari, Bd. VI 2, Berlin 1968, Erste Abhandlung, Abschnitt 7, S. 282: „der Sklavenaufstand in der Moral [...], welcher eine zweitausendjährige Geschichte hinter sich hat".

9 Foucault, loc. cit. S. 74.

10 Nietzsche, *Jenseits von Gut und Böse*, loc. cit., Bd. VI 2, Berlin 1968, Erstes Hauptstück, Abschnitt 2, S. 10.

Wolfgang Schluchter

Max Weber
am Ausgang eines Denkweges*

I

Dieter Henrich begann nicht aus Übermut zu philosophieren, wie er einmal sagte[1], sondern aus Not, die Nationalsozialismus und Krieg erzeugt hatten. Und er begann zu philosophieren nicht mittels der Explikation eines großen Philosophen, sondern eines großen Historikers und Soziologen, nämlich Max Webers, in dem freilich schon Karl Jaspers nicht einfach nur einen Fachwissenschaftler, sondern einen „existentiellen Philosophen" gesehen hatte.[2] Ein existentieller Philosoph war für Jaspers nicht ein bloß Erkennender, sondern ein Repräsentant seiner Zeit, und zwar in „substantiellster Weise".[3] Man kann vermuten, daß der junge Dieter Henrich nach der Befreiung Deutschlands durch die Alliierten Max Weber ähnlich sah. So widmete er ihm seine Dissertation, denn für den gerade Zwanzigjährigen repräsentierte Max Weber am glaubwürdigsten, worauf es ihm damals und fürderhin ankam:

> „Verständnis für die Grundsituation der Moderne, kritische Diagnose konkurrierender Heilslehren, Verteidigung der Rationalität, – aber nicht in der Beschränkung auf die Sicherheit parzellierter Forschung, sondern als Medium der Integration historischer und gelebter Erfahrung."[4]

Fügen wir Theorie hinzu, so haben wir, wie ich glaube, den Ausgang eines philosophischen Denkweges bezeichnet – eines Weges, auf dem die Orientierung an Max Weber, also auch an sozialwissenschaftlichen Fragen, wesentlich blieb.

Mit seiner Dissertation, einem genialischen Jugendstreich, suchte sich Dieter Henrich Max Weber allerdings vor allem dadurch zu nähern, daß er ihn zunächst von aller Fachphilosophie freisprach.

Julius Jakob Schaaf, ein heute vergessener Autor, hatte, wie mancher vor ihm und noch viele nach ihm, das Gegenteil getan. Er hatte die Grundbegriffe von Max Webers Aufsätzen zur Methodenlehre der Sozial- und Kulturwissenschaften mit denen der Kantischen Kritik zusammengelesen. Von solcher Identifikation, die Max Weber eine uneinlösbare Beweislast aufgebürdet und seine Originalität gerade verdeckt hätte, wollte der junge Autor den in seinen Augen großen Mann befreien. Gewiß, er sah klar, daß Max Weber sich in seiner „Wissenschaftslehre"[5] immer wieder auf philosophische Gewährsleute berief, insbesondere auf seinen Freund Heinrich Rickert. Und dessen Gedanken über die Grenzen der naturwissenschaftlichen und die Möglichkeiten der kulturwissenschaftlichen Begriffsbildung seien denn auch, so gestand er zu, überall in Webers Methodenlehre präsent. Aber weder folge Rickert Kant, noch teile Weber Rickerts erkenntnistheoretische Interessen. Einen Zugang zu seiner Methodenlehre finde nur, wer einsehe, „wie unbelastet von erkenntnistheoretischen Implikationen ihr Aufbau" sei.[6] Ihr liege, freilich unausgesprochen und unbewußt, eine andere Erkenntnislehre als die Rikkerts zugrunde. Diese entspreche zwar durchaus Kants Begriffen, werde in ihren methodologischen Konsequenzen aber am besten mit den Begriffen Hegels beschrieben, trotz der erklärten Gegnerschaft, in der Weber zu Hegel stand.[7] Denn Webers Methodenlehre liege eine Anthropologie zugrunde, ein Begriff vom Menschen als einem vernünftigen und freien Wesen, das aus dem „bloßen An-sich-sein zur für-sich-seienden Bewußtheit" gelangen könne.[8] Dies freilich nur in der Verstrickung in eine Realität, die immer auch vernunft- und freiheitsgefährdend sei. Im Zentrum von Webers Lehre stehe deshalb nicht die Funktion der Vernunft im Leben, sondern das Nachdenken darüber, wie man ein Leben aus der Kraft der Vernunft führen könne. Dieser Grundgedanke bilde das einheitsstiftende Prinzip seiner Methodologie. Diese sei eine Lehre möglicher Vernunft und Freiheit unter Bedingungen einer im Denken nie voll durchschaubaren und im Handeln nie voll beherrschbaren Wirklichkeit.[9]

Dem jungen Dieter Henrich erschien Max Weber also als ein illusionsloser Aufklärer, der nicht mehr der Macht der Vernunft huldigt, aber auch nicht in Nihilismus abgleitet. Folgerichtig sah er die Methodenlehre um eine Ethik komplettiert. Anders als die Erkenntnislehre, die den Begriffen Kants allenfalls entspreche, sei diese ein Stück Theorie, die der Philosophie Kants sehr viel verdanke. Und unser Autor macht unmißverständlich klar, daß Weber in seinen Augen eine normative Ethik vertrat. Dem stehe auch nicht die berühmt-berüchtigte Lehre von der Kollision der Werte entgegen. Denn diese komme unter anderem eben dadurch zustande, daß es eine Wertsphäre gebe, die „durch Imperative an das Gewissen des Einzelnen Forderungen stellt"[10]. Wie Kant formuliere auch Weber Postulate, die nur „als Appell an die Evidenz des Geforderten für vernünftige Wesen" verstehbar seien.[11] Die Einheit der „Wissenschaftslehre" Max Webers sei deshalb eine der Methodenlehre und der Ethik zugleich. Wie unausgeführt die letztere auch bleibe, in den Aufsätzen zur „Wissenschaftslehre" lasse sich durchaus der Ansatz zu einer wissenschaftlichen Moralphilosophie erkennen.[12] Sie sei eine Theorie der Evidenz, ähnlich wie bei Kant. Sie stehe der Romantik, aber auch der englischen Tradition, also dem Utilitarismus, ablehnend gegenüber.[13] Der Mensch könne nach Weber nicht nur sein Leben aus der Kraft der Vernunft führen, er solle dies auch tun.

Ich verzichte auf eine Rekonstruktion der gedanklichen Skizze, die sich in der Dissertation unter dem Titel „Die Grundlagen der Ethik" findet und die für meine eigenen Überlegungen auf diesem Gebiet richtungsweisend wurde.[14] Sie ist um die Begriffe Entscheidung, Glaube, Leidenschaft, vor allem aber um den Begriff Persönlichkeit zentriert. Für meine weiteren Überlegungen ist aber ein darin formulierter Zusammenhang wichtig: Der Mensch, der dem Gebot der Vernunft, sein Leben bewußt zu führen, folge, werde durch dieselbe Vernunft belehrt, *„daß das bewußte Leben nicht allein aus ihr geführt werden kann"*[15].

Sei erst einmal die Ungeschiedenheit des Erlebens überwunden, in meiner Terminologie: die axiologische Kehre vollzogen, so sei auch schon der Weg in die Paradoxie beschritten: Kollisionen entstünden im sittlichen Bewußtsein selber wie aus seiner Bezogenheit auf eine deutungsbedürftige und bedeutungsdurchherrschte Welt. Tatsächlich entfaltete Max Weber diese doppelte Kollision aus sinnkonsequenter Orientierung besonders eindrucksvoll in seiner Religionssoziologie, insbesondere in der „Zwischenbetrachtung", die in der Dissertation allerdings noch keine zentrale Rolle spielte. In diesem übrigens auch für Karl Jaspers zentralen Text zeigt Weber die religiöse Brüderlichkeitsethik innerlich in den Konflikt zwischen Gesinnungs- und Verantwortungsethik, äußerlich in den mit den übrigen Ordnungen der Welt und ihren Werten verstrickt. Paradoxe Situationen dieser Art, so lernen wir aus der Dissertation, entstehen aber deshalb, weil der Mensch ein vernünftiges Wesen ist, das unter dem Imperativ der Persönlichkeit steht. Und es sei deshalb geradezu *„ein Gebot der Moral, sich der Paradoxie auszusetzen"*[16] und sie auszuhalten, statt sich ihr durch Flucht ins Erlebnis, durch Flucht aus Vernunft und Freiheit heißt das, zu entziehen.

Ich möchte nun behaupten, daß diese frühe Einsicht für Dieter Henrichs eigene Ethik-Theorie maßgebend wurde, daß man diese jedenfalls als eine Entfaltung von Webers Ansatz lesen kann. Dafür lieferte freilich nicht dieser, sondern der deutsche Idealismus, insbesondere Kant, Fichte und Hegel, die begrifflichen Mittel. Diese für einen Nichtphilosophen vielleicht allzu vorlaute These wage ich auch deshalb, weil ich im Nachwort von Dieter Henrichs Ethik zum nuklearen Frieden lese, daß ihm, zumindest in Fragen der praktischen Philosophie, die klassische deutsche Philosophie und Max Weber sowie ihre sowohl gegenwärtige wie eigenständige Verwandlung, nicht zuletzt unter dem Eindruck der analytischen Philosophie, verbindlich geworden seien.[17] Ich möchte darlegen, in welchem Sinne ich als Sozialwissenschaftler Dieter Henrichs Ethik-Theorie als Entfaltung von Max Webers Unterscheidung zwischen Gesinnungs- und Verantwortungsethik lese und weshalb es neben theoretischen auch empirische Gründe gibt, in dieser Unterscheidung, ihm folgend, keine Alternative, sondern eine Folge zu sehen.

II

Bei meinem Versuch halte ich mich an die Ethik zum nuklearen Frieden, die sich ja an philosophische Laien wie mich richtet. Ich lese sie als Antwort der Ethik-Theorie auf eine allerdings gegenüber dem deutschen Idealismus und auch Max Weber radikal veränderte Situation. Sie ist durch Totalitarismus, industriellen Massenmord, vor allem aber durch Hiroshima und Nagasaki und die seitdem ständig gewachsene Möglichkeit der Selbstdestruktion der Menschheit gekennzeichnet. Zum Wissen um unsere kosmische Randstellung und unseren transitorischen Charakter als Gattung, das uns Kopernikus und die moderne Physik vermittelten, ist das Wissen um die Möglichkeit der Selbstdestruktion hinzugekommen, nicht nur von einzelnen oder Gruppen oder ganzer Völker, sondern der Menschheit. Eine solche Weltlage hatten sich weder Kant noch Weber ausgemalt, also auch nicht darauf reagiert. Dadurch wurden die nihilistischen Potentiale enorm gesteigert. Philosophie und Sozialwissenschaft müssen sich fragen, was sie beitragen können, um sie denkend und handelnd zu bändigen.

Gibt es also eine Ethik-Theorie, die solcher Weltlage gerecht wird? Wenn ja, dann muß dies eine Theorie möglicher Vernunft und Freiheit angesichts kontingenter, aber irreversibler Entwicklungen und damit verbundener Kollisionen sein. Eine solche Ethik-Theorie findet sich unter anderem in der Ethik zum nuklearen Frieden. Sie ist Teil einer Theorie der Verlaufsform des bewußten Lebens, einer Theorie des Geistes, der Unreduzierbarkeit von Selbstbewußtsein, die nicht die überkommenen dualistischen Prämissen wiederholt.[18]

Ich wage es, die Grundzüge dieser Ethik-Theorie in fünf Punkten zusammenzufassen:

1. Der kantische Ausgangspunkt: Das gewöhnliche sittliche Bewußtsein gebraucht eine auf Neutralität gegründete Primärregel zur Beurteilung von Handlungsweisen, die sich grundsätzlich von der Beurteilung der Folgen von Handlungsweisen unterscheidet. Diese von Kant besonders prägnant formulierte Primärregel ist weder leer noch tautologisch. Sie eignet sich allerdings nur für einfache, wenngleich durchaus wichtige Fälle und sagt in erster Linie aus, was nicht getan werden darf.

2. Die nachkantische Erweiterung: Die mittels der Primärregel gewonnenen Handlungsanweisungen sind nicht erschöpfend und des-

halb nicht zureichend. Das gewöhnliche sittliche Bewußtsein zeigt eine Tendenz zur Entfaltung und Vertiefung, für die es innere und äußere Gründe gibt. Die inneren haben mit den Spannungen zu tun, die in seinem Kern von Beginn an zwischen den Dimensionen Regel, Motiv und Ziel herrschen, die äußeren mit der Tatsache, daß es in eine Weltlage mit einer kosmischen und einer für uns fundamentalen historischen Dimension verflochten ist.

3. Die Stufentheorie: Kantischer Ausgangspunkt und nachkantische Erweiterung lassen sich mittels einer Stufentheorie verbinden. Der kantische Ausgangspunkt, die Primärregel, bleibt erhalten, aber sie wird mit sich entwickelnden Motiven und neu erkannten sittlichen Zielen zur Synthese gebracht. Das setzt voraus, daß sittliche Grundorientierung und Weltlage nichtreduktionistisch in eine sich wechselseitig stabilisierende Beziehung kommen. Dies wiederum verlangt Selbstbeschreibungen und Weltbilder, die einem Vernunftbegriff entsprechen, der das Wissen um Vernunft als Täuschung in sich aufgenommen hat.

4. Kern und Kontext: Die Stufentheorie läßt sich mit der Unterscheidung in Kern und Kontext verbinden. Auf der Primärstufe bilden sich Kern und Kontext gleichzeitig und vollständig aus. Auf der Sekundärstufe dagegen entwickeln sie sich relativ autonom, aber in Beziehung aufeinander. Für ein sich vertiefendes sittliches Bewußtsein sind beide konstitutiv.

5. Verfugung: Zur Stufentheorie und zur Kern-Kontext-Theorie tritt eine Theorie der Verfugung. Verfugt sind die beschriebenen Komponenten, weil keine von ihnen selbstgenügsam ist. Dies gilt für die Dimensionen des ethischen Kerns (Regel, Motiv, Ziel), für die Beziehung zwischen ethischem Kern und Weltlage, aber auch für die zwischen Ethik- und Wissens-Theorie.

Diese Stufentheorie der Ethik beginnt also mit dem kantischen Ausgangspunkt und zeigt die Notwendigkeit seiner Erweiterung und Vertiefung im Lichte unvermeidbarer interner und externer Kollisionen. Es handelt sich um eine philosophische Stufentheorie, die mit einer empirischen, wie etwa der psychologischen Stufentheorie von Lawrence Kohlberg, nicht verwechselt werden darf. Kohlberg ergänzt Kant zwar, doch er vermag ihn weder zu erweitern noch zu vertiefen. Wenn man so will, schreitet er nicht von Kant (und Rawls) zu Hegel fort. Doch wichtiger ist: Bei dieser philosophischen Stufentheorie liegt bereits die Primärstufe auf postkonventionellem Niveau, genauer: auf Kohlbergs Stufe 6. Auf Kohlbergs Stufe 6 ist, folgt man der philosophischen Stufentheorie, das sittliche Bewußtsein aber gerade noch nicht erweitert und vertieft. Es urteilt noch abstrakt, stellt den als richtig erkannten Imperativ hart der kontingenten Realität gegenüber und tendiert deshalb zur Selbstgerechtigkeit.[19] Auch sucht es die Dynamik, die aus seiner dilemmatischen Struktur stammt, zu unterdrücken oder in die Kasuistik abzuschieben. Erst das sich erweiternde und vertiefende sittliche Bewußtsein lernt, das Kontingente zu nobilitieren und sich seiner eigenen Dynamik zu öffnen und sich den Paradoxien auszusetzen, die aus seiner Verflochtenheit in eine Weltlage entstehen.

Dem sittlichen Bewußtsein der zweiten Stufe entspricht denn auch, anders als dem der ersten Stufe, ein eher schwacher Begriff von Vernunft und von Freiheit. Und doch kommt keine Ethik-Theorie ohne diese Begriffe aus. Auch in der Phase der dritten Reflektiertheit und der atomaren Bedrohung kann und soll der Mensch sein Leben führen, wenngleich er dabei – und gerade die nukleare Waffe macht dies überdeutlich – ohne institutionellen Schutz nicht auskommen kann. Dies führt zu schwierigen Problemen über das Verhältnis von Ethik, Recht und strategischem Handeln, aber auch von Handlung und Ordnung, die ich hier nicht weiter verfolge. Ich komme vielmehr auf Max Weber zurück.

Max Weber unterschied bekanntlich zwischen Gesinnungs- und Verantwortungsethik. Einmal sagt er, beide schlössen sich aus, wie Gott und Teufel, ein andermal, beide ergänzten sich. Das eine erschien mir schon immer genauso unbefriedigend wie das andere. Denn mit beiden Begriffen bezeichnet Weber ja Prinzipienethiken, beide verlangen Beurteilungen von Handlungsweisen auf postkonventionellem Niveau. Tatsächlich bin ich schon lange der Auffassung, sie stünden in einer Folge.[20] Aus Dieter Henrichs Ethik-Theorie kann man lernen, warum und wie.

Zunächst sollte ich noch ein Wort zur genaueren Charakterisierung dieser Unterscheidung sagen. Gesinnungsethisch nennt Max Weber eine Position, nach der der Eigenwert des ethischen Handelns allein zu seiner Rechtfertigung ausreicht, verantwortungsethisch aber eine, nach der „die Verantwortung für die als möglich oder wahrscheinlich vorauszusehenden Folgen des Handelns, wie sie dessen Verflochtenheit in die ethisch irrationale Welt bedingt, mit in Betracht zu ziehen ist"[21]. Mit in Betracht zu ziehen –, das heißt doch wohl, daß die Rechtfertigung durch den ethischen Eigenwert des Handelns schon erfolgt ist, daß die Primärregel bereits angewandt wurde. Liest man die Unterscheidung so – und ich bin davon überzeugt, man muß sie so lesen –, dann steht die Verantwortungsethik nicht im Gegensatz zur Gesinnungsethik, sie ist auch nicht deren bloße Ergänzung, sie läßt sich vielmehr, im Sinne der Ethik-Theorie von Dieter Henrich, als deren Erweiterung und Vertiefung verstehen.

Wählen wir, zur Überprüfung, Dieter Henrichs Hinweis, Kern und Kontext stünden auf den beiden Stufen in verschiedenen funktionalen Beziehungen zueinander. Trifft dies auf Webers Unterscheidung zwischen Gesinnungs- und Verantwortungsethik zu? Zweifellos, denn die beiden Ethiken unterscheiden sich in ihrer Weltbeziehung. Bei der Gesinnungsethik ist sie durch die Formel repräsentiert: Der Christ handelt recht und stellt den Erfolg Gott anheim; oder auch: Der vernünftige Mensch, der sein Leben bewußt führt, handelt recht und stellt den Erfolg dem Weltlauf anheim. Das aber heißt: Der Gesinnungsethiker bildet den Kontext gerade nicht in Beziehung auf eine Weltlage aus. Der Verantwortungsethiker dagegen tut dies. Für ihn ist die Verflochtenheit seines Handelns in die ethisch irrationale Welt mitentscheidend für seinen Handlungsplan. Dies verlangt ein welthaltiges sittliches Bewußtsein, das den Universalismus der Primärregel zu kontextualisieren vermag.

III

Mit Dieter Henrichs Ethik-Theorie läßt sich also Max Webers Unterscheidung zwischen Gesinnungs- und Verantwortungsethik als eine Folge explizieren, ja es scheint, als sei seine eigene Ethik-Theorie durch diese Unterscheidung mit motiviert. Aber es gibt noch eine andere überraschende Parallele zu sozialwissenschaftlichen Gedankengängen. Sie hat mit Veränderungen im Ansatz zu einer Psychologie der Moralentwicklung zu tun.

Dieter Henrich trennt seine Stufentheorie ausdrücklich von der Kohlbergs. Dafür gibt es den bereits genannten systematischen Grund. Nun veränderte aber Kohlberg in den letzten Jahren seines Lebens seine Position in einer für meinen Zusammenhang interessanten Weise. Dazu gebe ich einige Hinweise.

Kohlberg ist mit seiner Stufentheorie, die drei moralische Urteilsniveaus und, innerhalb dieser, jeweils zwei Stufen, also insgesamt sechs Stufen unterscheidet, in vielfältige Kritik geraten. Eine besonders herausfordernde stammt von seiner Schülerin Carol Gilligan. Sie bestritt den von Kohlberg behaupteten Universalismus der Moralentwicklung. Sie sah in dem seinem Stufenschema zugrunde liegenden dekontextualisierten Gerechtigkeitsdenken ein männliches Vorurteil. Dagegen suchte sie die andere Stimme, die der Frau, zur Geltung zu bringen. Anders als Männer dächten Frauen nicht so sehr in Kategorien abstrakter Gerechtigkeit als vielmehr konkreter Fürsorge, nähmen das Eingelassensein in konkrete Lebensverhältnisse und die Verantwortung für den Nächsten zum Maßstab bei der Lösung von Lebenskonflikten. Es gebe deshalb eine weibliche Moral der Fürsorge, die Kohlbergs männlicher Gerechtigkeitsmoral entgegengesetzt sei.[22]

Kohlberg verarbeitete nun diesen Einwand gegen seine Theorie zusammen mit anderen in interessanter Weise.[23] Ich greife drei Punkte heraus:

1. Kohlberg trennte danach schärfer zwischen Struktur und Inhalt und unterschied zwischen harten, weichen und funktionalen Stufen. Da er bereits seine ursprüngliche Stufentheorie als eine Theorie har-

ter Stufen verstanden wissen wollte, mußte er sein empirisches Material angesichts der gehärteten Kriterien erneut durchsehen, mit dem interessanten Resultat, daß Personen, die zuvor in Stufe 6 eingeordnet waren, nun in den Stufen 3 und 4 auftauchten, daß die Stufe 6 überhaupt leer blieb, also keinerlei empirische Bestätigung erfuhr. Folgerichtig definierte er sie jetzt als normativen Richtpunkt, der moralphilosophisch gerechtfertigt werden müsse. Diese Rechtfertigung suchte er freilich nach wie vor in erster Linie bei Kant und Rawls.

2. Kohlberg gab zu, daß das Gerechtigkeitsdenken, reduziert auf die beiden Gerechtigkeitsoperationen Gleichheit und Reziprozität, nur eine notwendige Bedingung für moralisches Handeln darstelle. Hinzu kämen weitere kognitive Komponenten, die einer Ethik der Fürsorge entstammten, sowie emotionale Komponenten. Folgerichtig suchte er jetzt die Gerechtigkeitsethik mit der Ethik der Fürsorge zu verknüpfen sowie die so erweiterte Urteils- mit einer Emotionstheorie.

3. Der Versuch, die Gerechtigkeitsethik für eine Ethik der Fürsorge zu öffnen, ohne den Universalismus aufzugeben – seine Antwort an Gilligan –, motivierte ihn dazu, für jede harte Urteilsstufe eine A- und B-Variante einzuführen. Die B-Variante bedeutet zunächst eine Ergänzung der A-Variante insofern, als zum Gerechtigkeitsdenken ein Verantwortlichkeitsdenken tritt. Kohlberg interpretierte es auch als Ausführungsdenken. Das Richtigkeitsurteil, das eine Handlungsweise als richtig oder unrichtig einstuft, wird durch ein Verantwortungsurteil komplettiert, das mir sagt, welche richtige Handlungsweise ich in einer gegebenen Situation auch ausführen soll.

Kohlberg interpretiert das Verantwortlichkeitsdenken also ausdrücklich als eine Ergänzung und damit auch als eine Erweiterung des Gerechtigkeitsdenkens. Stellt es auch eine Vertiefung dar? Hier bleiben Ambivalenzen. Einerseits scheint es die Aufgabe des Verantwortungsdenkens, das Gerechtigkeitsdenken zu kontextualisieren. Dies ließe sich als Vertiefung verstehen. Andererseits aber scheint das Gerechtigkeitsdenken selbstgenügsam. Dies deutet auf bloße Erweiterung hin. Tatsächlich erweckt Kohlberg am Ende den Eindruck, als bestehe das umfassende moralische Urteil aus zwei voneinander unabhängigen Teilurteilen: einem deontischen Richtigkeitsurteil und einem strebens- oder güterethischen Verantwortungsurteil. Hier hilft nun die philosophische Stufenethik weiter, die zeigt, daß der kantische Ausgangspunkt, das deontische Richtigkeitsurteil, nicht einfach nur ergänzt werden darf, sondern erweitert und vertieft werden muß. So gesehen, ließe sich dann Kohlbergs B-Variante, die er auch als Unterstufe bezeichnete, als Erweiterung und Vertiefung der A-Variante deuten, die zu dieser in einer Folge steht.

IV

Ich habe versucht, zwei sozialwissenschaftliche Gedankengänge mit Dieter Henrichs philosophischer Ethik-Theorie zusammenzuführen. Der eine, der sich bei Max Weber findet, kommt eher von innen, der andere, der von Kohlberg stammt, eher von außen. Doch die dargestellte Konvergenz scheint mir bemerkenswert. Philosophie und Sozialwissenschaft verhalten sich, wie sich daran zeigt, nicht substitutiv, sondern komplementär zueinander. Eine Philosophie, die sich von der Sozialwissenschaft isoliert, wird leicht leer, eine Sozialwissenschaft, die sich von der Philosophie isoliert, leicht blind.

Als Karl Jaspers daranging, seine *Großen Philosophen* zu schreiben, gewissermaßen als Gegenprogramm zu Hegels Vorlesungen über die Geschichte der Philosophie, dachte er natürlich auch an Max Weber. Für diesen sah er jetzt in seinem Band III einen Platz unter den Philosophen in der Forschung vor.[24] Zugleich erinnerte er daran, daß ein einzelner nicht alle Philosophen zugleich studieren könne, daß er vielmehr in dem ihm zugemessenen Leben auf viele verzichten müsse. Dann fuhr er fort: „Welche Philosophen er aber zuerst wählt, und welche er später ergreift, in welchen er Größe sieht, das sind für ihn folgenreiche Entscheidungen."[25] Dieter Henrich wählte vor gut 50 Jahren als einen der ersten Max Weber. Dies halte ich für einen glücklichen Umstand – für die Philosophie, für die Sozialwissenschaft und nicht zuletzt auch für mich selbst.

Wolfgang Schluchter

Anmerkungen

* Dieser Beitrag ist Dieter Henrich in langjähriger Verbundenheit gewidmet.
1   Cf. „Antrittsrede", in: *Jahrbuch der Heidelberger Akademie der Wissenschaften für das Jahr 1972* (Heidelberg: Carl Winter, 1973), S. 33.
2   K. Jaspers, „Max Weber. Eine Gedenkrede (1920)", in: ders., *Max Weber. Einführung* von D. Henrich (München: Piper, 1988), S. 36.
3   Ibid.
4   Op. cit. (cf. Anm. 1), S. 34.
5   Dieser Titel stammt bekanntlich nicht von Max Weber, sondern von seiner Frau Marianne. Max Weber sprach bescheidener von seinen methodologisch-logischen Aufsätzen und war sich keineswegs sicher, wo genau die Grenze zu seinen anderen Arbeiten zu ziehen sei. Die Herausgeber der Max Weber-Gesamtausgabe haben deshalb diesen Titel aufgegeben, was eine Kontroverse auslöste. Cf. dazu W. Schluchter, *Unversöhnte Moderne* (Frankfurt a. M.: Suhrkamp, 1996), S. 230, Fn. 18.
6   D. Henrich, *Die Einheit der Wissenschaftslehre Max Webers* (Tübingen: J. C. B. Mohr (Paul Siebeck), 1952), S. 2.
7   Cf. zum Verhältnis Rickert-Weber die Ausführungen in Henrich, *Wissenschaftslehre* (cf. Anm. 6), bes. S. 35, und zum Verhältnis Rickert-Kant-Hegel-Weber bes. S. 104, vor allem die Fn. 1.
8   So die hegelianisierende Formulierung ibid. Sie nimmt in gewissem Sinne vorweg, was die spätere Philosophie Henrichs kennzeichnet: die Analyse der Bewegung des bewußten Lebens mit begrifflichen Mitteln, die aus Kant und Hegel (und natürlich auch aus Fichte) entwickelt sind.
9   Die Momente der Nichtdurchschaubarkeit und Nichtbeherrschbarkeit sind im Begriff der Wirklichkeit als eines heterogenen Kontinuums mitgedacht, den Weber von Rickert übernimmt. Das Streben nach größtmöglicher Transparenz und Beherrschbarkeit verlangt mehr als nur die naturwissenschaftliche ‚Umbildung' dieses heterogenen Kontinuums. Henrich argumentiert: Die Notwendigkeit seiner kulturwissenschaftlichen ‚Umbildung' werde zwar zunächst, ganz im Sinne Rikkerts, logisch begründet, doch noch wichtiger sei die anthropologische Begründung: „Der Mensch ist wesentlich vernünftig. Er hat die notwendige Tendenz zur Aktualisierung seiner Vernunft in der Kultur." Cf. Henrich, *Wissenschaftslehre* (cf. Anm. 6), S. 83. Daraus erkläre sich der letztlich maieutische Charakter der verstehenden Kulturwissenschaft und

ihrer idealtypischen Begriffe, die Realexplikationen darstellten und sinnträchtige Wirklichkeitszusammenhänge in eine konsequente Form brächten, somit Denk- und Handlungsmöglichkeiten verdeutlichten, die immer auch Entwürfe des bewußten Lebens und seiner Gefährdung seien. Prägnant formuliert der junge Autor die Ambivalenz, die in Webers Vernunftbegriff steckt: Die ursprüngliche Vernünftigkeit des Menschen sei immer nur eine Tendenz. „Diese Tendenz zur Vernünftigkeit ist also für den empirischen Menschen notwendig mit der übermächtigen Gefahr der Unvernunft verbunden. Und nur deshalb kann es idealtypische Begriffsbildung geben." Ibid., S. 102 f. Aber ein freies und vernünftiges, ein bewußtes Leben sei möglich, wenn auch gebunden an niemals völlig durchschaubare und beherrschbare Bedingungen.

10 Henrich, *Wissenschaftslehre* (cf. Anm. 6), S. 118.
11 Loc. cit., S. 116.
12 Loc. cit., S. 117.
13 Cf. die Bemerkung auf S. 116, Fn. 1.
14 Cf. W. Schluchter, *Religion und Lebensführung* (Frankfurt a. M.: Suhrkamp, 1988), Band 1, Kap. 3.
15 Henrich, *Wissenschaftslehre* (cf. Anm. 6), S. 120.
16 Ibid.
17 D. Henrich, *Ethik zum nuklearen Frieden* (Frankfurt a. M.: Suhrkamp, 1990), S. 316.
18 Zu diesen schwierigen Fragen D. Henrich, *Fluchtlinien. Philosophische Essays* (Frankfurt a. M.: Suhrkamp, 1982), bes. S. 38 ff.
19 Henrich sagt über die Primärstufenmoral: „Diese Überzeugungen lassen sich zusammenfassen als die Gewißheit, daß man immer weiß, was zu tun richtig wäre, daß man sodann auch immer das Rechte zu wollen vermag, und daß, was dem Sieg des Rechten entgegensteht, nur mangelnder Mut und schwacher Wille der Menschen sein kann." *Ethik zum nuklearen Frieden* (cf. Anm. 17), S. 99 f.
20 Cf. W. Schluchter,. *Die Entwicklung des okzidentalen Rationalismus. Eine Analyse von Max Webers Gesellschaftsgeschichte* (Tübingen: J. C. B. Mohr (Paul Siebeck), 1979), S. 59 ff.
21 M. Weber, *Gesammelte Aufsätze zur Wissenschaftslehre* (Tübingen: J. C. B. Mohr (Paul Siebeck), 3. Aufl., 1968), S. 505.
22 Cf. C. Gilligan, *Die andere Stimme. Lebenskonflikte und Moral der Frau* (München: Piper, 1984).
23 Dazu bes. L. Kohlberg, *Die Psychologie der Moralentwicklung* (Frankfurt a. M.: Suhrkamp, 1996), S. 217 ff.

24 K. Jaspers. *Die großen Philosophen. Erster Band* (München: Piper, 1988), S. 48.
25 Loc. cit., S. 56.

Harry Frankfurt

On Caring, and a Certain Parallel

I

However productive and valuable the inquiries of political philosophers may be, the topics to which their work is typically addressed have only a rather limited bearing on the difference between a good society and a bad one. As political philosophy is ordinarily construed, it has to do mainly with issues concerning liberty, justice, rights, und the distribution of power and wealth. However, a society in which all of the problems connected with these issues are correctly and effectively resolved might still be a rotten place to live. What I have in mind is not that a society of impeccable political form and function might be miserably poor, or that it might be oppressed by external enemies or beset by natural afflictions that burden and diminish the lives of its people. My point is that the society might be a rotten place to live because it engenders or sustains endemic personal limitations and inadequacies among the people who inhabit it.

A prosperous and stable society, which is untroubled by any serious exogenous disturbances, and whose modes of political organization and behavior conform optimally to the most demanding structural and procedural ideals, might nonetheless be rather barbaric. Thus, it might promulgate among its members attitudes and ideas that are generally trivial, vulgar, and harsh. The pervasive ethos of the society, and the design and operation of its institutions, might encourage widespread indifference or even antipathy to the importance of maintaining conditions without which human beings are unlikely to find their lives satisfying or meaningful. Both the high culture of the society and its popular culture might be uninteresting and drab. Personal relations among the members of the society might tend generally to be superficial and coarse, with very little experience of intimacy or warmth. Life for everyone might be chronically tedious, lacking in refinement and imagination and depth, and more or less unpleasant.

I suppose that a good society is, roughly speaking, one that at the very least does not systematically discourage or obstruct the development among its members of what is best in them. By the same token, I suppose that a society is bad insofar as it systematically supports among its members lives that are shallow, colorless, and unrewarding. From this point of view, it seems clear that even a society that meets the highest of distinctively *political* standards might be very bad.

The problem in such a society would not be that its members are insufficiently dutiful to the precepts of morality. Just as the issues ordinarily addressed by political philosophy have only a limited bearing either upon the difference between good societies and bad ones, so the specific concerns of ethical philosophy have only a limited bearing either upon the difference between good and bad people or upon the difference between good and bad lives. The theory of ethics is devoted to understanding our various responsibilities and obligations; most particularly, it is concerned with how we are to order our relationships with other people. It inquires into the sources and the requirements of duty and into the design of virtuous character and conduct. But it can hardly be supposed that being virtuous, doing what duty requires, maintaining a scrupulous respect for others, and sincerely meeting whatever other demands the moral law may impose, are enough to make life even tolerably good. What I have in mind is not that an ethically irreproachable life may be ruined on account of poverty, or disease, or violence, or mistreatment, or tragic personal loss. My point is that a person may have a rotten life because of defects or deficiencies in his own beliefs, feelings, attitudes, and aspirations.

The most unequivocal realization of the highest ethical ideals is compatible, it seems to me, with crippling personal inadequacies and failures. It may be accompanied by a lack of understanding of one's own emotional needs, by a dismally meager vision of personal success, by an absence of ambition, and consequently by unremitting self-imposed frustration, aimlessness, and boredom. The life of a person who fulfills all the requirements of ethics may not be a life that is fulfilling for that person at all. I suppose that, roughly speaking, a good life is one that a reasonable, perceptive, and well informed person would be more or less satisfied to live. But a virtuous person may suffer endlessly from indecisiveness and narrowness of vision. His existence may be on the whole petty and without flavor, because he lacks an invigorating conception of what to do with himself. His life, notwithstanding that it is ethically unimpeachable, may be relentlessly banal and ungratifying.

What I have been saying is not meant as a complaint against the disciplines of ethics and of political philosophy or against their practitioners. It is intended rather as a reminder or caution against overlooking the fact that political and ethical criteria alone do not provide adequate guidance either for the design of the social order or for the conduct of our own lives. We need to appreciate the importance, both for societies and for individuals, of regulative personal ideals and conceptions of a good life. These ideals and conceptions have to do primarily neither with formal considerations of structure or procedure nor with any principles that could plausibly be represented as universally valid. They shape our conduct and affect the value to us of our lives in more intimate and more particular ways.

II

Many people believe strongly that forming a conception of a good life is strictly and inviolably a private matter. It is more or less generally accepted doctrine, indeed, that no one – and certainly no one armed with the massively coercive resources of the society or the state – may legitimately encroach upon the right of each individual to decide for himself what are to be his ideals. From this it does not quite follow, however, that the problem of establishing personal ideals belongs entirely outside the scope of public interest and concern. After all, the doctrine that individuals must be left free to arrive at their own ideas concerning how to live does not entail a wholesale indifference to whether people are actually in a position to exercise this freedom effectively. It surely cannot be presumed that if society and state remain fastidiously neutral, the problem of how individuals are to reach these ideas and decisions will then somehow take care of itself. A commitment to refrain from interfering does not require a repudiation of all responsibility for ensuring conditions that are essential if people are actually to be able to consider ideas of the pertinent kind and to make reasonable judgments and decisions about them.

Circumstances that are in one way or another subject to public influence may have a significant bearing upon whether and how individuals deal with these matters. Insisting that society must refrain from interfering with personal solutions to the problem of articulating a conception of a good life does not preclude allowing that it must also take some care to facilitate the efforts of individuals to arrive at these solutions. Surely it must be careful at least to avoid practices and arrangements that obstruct or that undermine those efforts.

Of course it cannot be assumed that even under the most auspiciously favorable political and social conditions, people will reliably arrive at conceptions of a good life that genuinely suit them. Granting that the criteria of suitability are strictly personal, it nonetheless cannot be presumed that people generally possess sufficient resources of intellect and imagination to be capable on their own of arriving at conceptions that meet these criteria. In many instances, they may need help in understanding how to develop and how to evaluate personal ideals and conceptions of a good life. It is important, therefore, for philosophers to see if they can find something useful to say about these things.

III

The problem of deciding what sort of life to lead is a problem of practical reason. Philosophical discussions of practical reason typically draw upon a theoretical repertoire that includes, among other items, the notions of desire and preference, the distinction between means and ends, and a presumption that the value of a means derives from the value of the end for the sake of which the means is to be employed. This repertoire needs to be revised, I believe, in at least two respects.

First, the recognition that we have desires and preferences, and that we take certain things as ends, must be supplemented by an appreciation that there are also things that we care about. These are distinct facts. It is obvious enough that we want many things that we do not actually pursue and that therefore do not figure among the ends at which our conduct aims. What must also be made clear is that pursuing something as an end does not entail caring about it. From the fact that a person aims at a certain end, it follows that the end is something that he wants to attain. It does not follow, however, that either the end or its attainment is something that he cares about.

Second, it is necessary to develop a more complex and perspicuous understanding of the respective values of means and ends. We do not desire to be competent, or to engage in instrumentally effective activity, only because competence and effective activity are useful. Precisely by virtue of their instrumental value, these things are important to us for their own sakes as well. Taking this into account requires certain alterations in our customary ways of thinking about means and ends.

IV

A conception of a good life consists in part of a set of personal ideals. These define criteria to which a person accords particularly significant authority in guiding and constraining his attitudes and his conduct. They identify certain things that he especially cares about and that he considers to be not simply important but important *to him*. But what does it mean for a person to care about something? How are we to understand this notion, or the more or less equivalent notion of what a person considers to be important to himself?

It is not at all satisfactory just to say, as I myself did in an essay written some time ago, that "the notion of what a person cares about [...] coincides in part with the notion of something with reference to which the person guides himself in what he does with his life and his conduct"[1]. This is perhaps too vague to be dismissed as unequivocally false. It is, however, unacceptably misleading. The trouble with it is that it does not apply exclusively to what people care about. It applies as well to anything that a person takes as a goal; indeed, it applies to anything that a person merely wants. Thus, it conflates questions concerning what a person cares about with questions concerning what the person wants and concerning the ends that he seeks to attain. But caring about something must not be confused with simply wanting it – not even with having a strong and enthusiastic preference for it over other things. Moreover, to care about something differs significantly from pursuing it as a goal – even as a goal or end that is valued for its own sake alone. I shall attempt to clarify these differences between what we want, what we seek as our ends, and what we care about.

V

While human conduct is often motivated and shaped by what the agent cares about, that is not always how things are. Behavior that is entirely voluntary, that has been carefully considered and meticulously planned, and that proceeds exactly as intended, may not be guided or constrained by anything that the agent considers to be important to him. For example, someone may seek to obtain some ice cream, for the sake of the intrinsically valuable pleasure that it will provide, without regarding either the ice cream or the pleasure as of any importance to him. On many occasions, people adopt and pursue goals that they do not care about at all. Their conduct on such occasions may nonetheless be quite thoughtful; it certainly need not be at all incoherent or arbitrary. There is no reason to suppose, when a person regards his goals as being of no importance to him, that what he does reflects some deficiency on his part of understanding or of control.

It goes without saying that people regard some of the goals that they pursue as more important to them than others; and, of course, they may have some goals that they consider to be of very little importance to them. What I am asserting, however, is not merely that people sometimes pursue goals about which they do not care very much. My point is that they sometimes engage voluntarily and intelligently in activities to which they attribute measurable instrumental or inherent value but which they do not care about at all. There are many things that we value and desire and seek to attain, but that we do not consider to be of any importance to us whatever.

In order to clarify this matter, let us consider the following scenario. Someone makes arrangements to attend a concert that is to be devoted to music that he especially appreciates and enjoys. Subsequently, he is asked by a close friend for a favor that would make it impossible for him to get to the concert. He agrees to do the favor; but he mentions to his friend that this means that he will have to change his plans. The friend then apologetically expresses a reluctance to take advantage of his good-natured readiness to forego the concert, and begins to withdraw the request. At this point, the person interrupts his friend, and says: "Don't be concerned. As a matter of fact, going to this concert is not at all important to me. I really don't care a bit about missing it."

There is a possibility here, of course, that the music-lover is not being altogether candid. It may not be true that missing the concert has absolutely no importance to him; perhaps he does care about missing it, but chooses to deny this in order to protect his friend from embarrassment. I assume that what the person says to reassure his friend may be the exact and literal truth. But what if it is not? Suppose that, despite his disclaimer, the person does care at least a bit about going to the concert. That would imply at least, it seems to me, that foregoing the concert will cost him something. And if it would cost him something, then it must be the case – even if doing the favor is far more important to him than doing as he planned – that attending the concert is something that he *still* wants to do. Under the circumstances, he is willing to give up the concert; but his desire to attend it persists, albeit with a lower priority than before.

Foregoing the concert will entail for him, accordingly, the cost of a certain degree of frustration or disappointment.

If the person truly does not care at all about going to the concert, on the other hand, there is *no* cost to him in doing instead something else that he wants to do at least as much. When he agrees to do the favor for his friend, he does not merely assign his desire to go to the concert a lower priority than it had before. He gives up this desire entirely. He may continue to recognize, of course, that going to the concert is something that he would enjoy. It is no longer, however, something that he actually wants. That is why he incurs no cost, in frustration or in disappointment, by foregoing it.

Whether the person cares about going to the concert is not a matter of how enthusiastic he is about going to it, or of the strength of his desire to attend it, or of the magnitude of the gratification that he believes he would derive from attending it. In fact, it does not pertain directly to anything that he feels or believes about the concert itself. Rather, it concerns his attitude towards himself or, more precisely, towards his desire to attend the concert. It is essentially a matter of whether he is committed to this desire or whether he is prepared to give it up.

Being committed to a desire is not equivalent to approving the desire or endorsing it. Commitment to a desire is a more active matter. It involves not merely a positive evaluation of the desire, and not merely a willingness to allow oneself to be moved by it. In addition, it involves a disposition to take steps to see to it that the desire continues. If a person cares about something, he may not actually pursue it as an end; after all, he may prefer to pursue other things that he cares about more. But he will be concerned that the desire for what he cares about be maintained; and, if the desire should threaten to disappear or tend to fade, he will be disposed to support its continuation. For a person to care about something, accordingly, involves his concern to ensure the stability and continuity of his own desires and interests.

Given that caring consists at least partly in this, it follows that it is of considerable importance to us that we care about things. If we cared about nothing, we would be creatures with no active interest in establishing and protecting any thematic continuity and order in our volitional lives. We would make no effort to maintain or to extend the duration of our aims and ambitions. The history of our desires and aims would be merely a succession of separated fragments, unconnected by any deliberate intent and manifesting no intentional unity or coherence. Our active lives would consist for us of discontinuous volitional episodes, in the definition and sequence of which we ourselves play no concerned or guiding role.

The importance to us of *caring* about something is manifestly not the same, then, as the importance to us of *what* we care about. Regardless of what it may be that we care about, it is important to us for its own sake that there *be* things that we consider to be important to us. Needless to say, it is better for us to care about what is genuinely important, and what is truly worth caring about, than to care about things that are inconsequential or harmful. But the value to us of the fact that we care about something does not derive simply from the value of the objects about which we care. Caring about things has inherent value, independently of whether its objects are appropriate or worthy, insofar as it provides an indispensably foundational unity to our active lives.

VI

Caring possesses an inherent value, which neither derives from nor depends upon the worthiness of its object. In this respect, the relationship between caring and its object is analogous to a certain generally overlooked aspect of the relationship between means and ends. Just as the importance to us of caring is not due simply to the importance to us of what we care about, so the importance to us of using means – that is, of engaging in instrumentally effective activity – is not simply tantamount to the importance to us of the ends that the use of those means enables us to obtain. To engage in instrumentally effective activity is important to us for its own sake. Working to achieve a goal is inherently valuable, even apart from the value of the goal to which it is designed to lead.

It is a mistake to suppose that the importance to us of having means is exhausted by the importance to us of attaining our ends. Activity that is intended to be instrumentally effective or useful involves figuring out what to do and making plans to do it. Without these exercises in practical reason, there would be no continuity to our active participation in our own lives. Our lives would be devoid of the elementary cohesion and meaning that the use of practical reason generates. It is not only for the sake of its product, then, that work is valuable to us. It is also valuable to us in itself, because it is inherently important to us that we bind ourselves to the temporality of our experience by having something useful to do.

Engaging in productive activity or work is instrumentally valuable, of course, but it is also valuable as an end in itself. By the same token, those ends or objects at which our work ultimately aims, and which we desire for the sake of the terminal value that is intrinsic to them, are not only valuable in themselves. They also necessarily have instrumental value. After all, there can be no productive activity or useful work for us to do unless we have goals or ends to pursue; so the latter are conditions for realizing the value that the former inherently possess. However dissonant or paradoxical it may sound, accordingly, the use of means has inherent value precisely because of its instrumental value; and final ends have instrumental value precisely by virtue of the terminal or inherent value that is attributed to them.

In a certain way, therefore, caring and working are similar. Each is by its very nature devoted to something other than itself, upon which it essentially depends; but, precisely by virtue of its relationship to an object, each possesses an intrinsic value that does not simply derive from or reflect the value with which its object is endowed. The relationship between the value of means and the value of the ends that the means enable us to attain parallels the relationship between the value to us of caring and the value to us of what we care about. Just as using means has an inherent value that is independent of the value of the ends for which the means are employed, so caring is inherently valuable regardless of the value of what is cared about.

The ends and objects to which working and caring are devoted are essential to them; without ends and objects, working and caring would be impossible. Therefore, these ends and objects serve as conditions or means. Considering them in this way offers a basis for applying to them the familiar and relatively unproblematic principle that a means is reasonably to be evaluated in terms of its usefulness in facilitating the attainment of its end. In general, it is reasonable to select those means that will most effectively enable us to attain the most valuable ends. Insofar as the objects of working and of caring are considered as means to working and to caring, it is reasonable for us to select or to endorse those that dictate or inspire modes of working or of caring that are inherently more valuable than the modes of working or of caring that would be dictated or inspired by others. In order to exploit this approach to the question of how final ends may be rationally chosen, however, it will be necessary to develop both a more penetrating understanding of why it is that working and caring are so fundamentally important to us in themselves and a fuller appreciation of what imbues one mode of caring or of working with greater inherent value than another.

Note

1 The essay, entitled "The Importance of What we Care About", appeared first in *Synthese* 53, no. 2 (1982), pp. 257–272. It was subsequently included in an eponymous collection of my essays published by Cambridge University Press in 1988.

Richard Wollheim

Emotion, the Malformation of Emotion, and J.-P. Sartre*

I

The background to this essay is a larger project on which I am engaged, which is an inquiry into the nature of the emotions. This inquiry makes the assumption that, in order to understand the emotions, we need to know two things. As with all mental dispositions, we need to know the role of the emotions, or the part they play in the life of the person. However, in the case of the emotions, we need additionally to know their history: that is to say, the characteristic way in which an emotion arises in the life-history of the individual.

My thesis is that the role of an emotion is to provide the individual with an attitude, where this contrasts with a picture of the world, which belief offers, or a target in the world, which is what desire provides us with. As to its history, an emotion standardly forms in the wake of the satisfaction or frustration of a desire, and the attitude, which lies at the core of an emotion, is the projection outwards, initially on to what is held to have satisfied or frustrated the desire, and then on to things found similar, of the experience of satisfaction or frustration.

Satisfaction and frustration must be understood broadly to include merely believed-in satisfaction and frustration, and imminent satisfaction and frustration.

(It should already be clear that nothing that I have to say about the emotions will be found intelligible without a psychologisation, or better a repsychologisation, of fundamental mental concepts: thus far, desire, and the satisfaction of desire. The former cannot be equated with a pattern of behaviour, nor the latter with the mere coming about of what is desired.)

II

Exactly how the attitude, in normal circumstances, arises out of the experience of satisfaction or frustration, and so how emotion standardly forms, is not a short story. But this essay is not concerned with normal circumstances. It is concerned with deviant cases, or when emotion malforms. And my contention, which will be explored rather than established, is that emotion malforms when the person is unable to tolerate satisfaction or frustration.

What the person is unable to tolerate is, let me make clear, not the fact of satisfaction or frustration. That is also possible, but it is another matter. When emotion malforms, what the person is unable to tolerate is the experience of satisfaction or frustration. Once this is so, then anxiety is experienced, and this causes the situation to be perceived afresh, an attitude appropriate to this new or adjusted perception arises, and an emotion that could never have been anticipated on the basis of the originating condition now forms.

There are a number of broadly discriminable situations in which this inability might manifest itself, and what follows is an incomplete inventory.

The fault may lie with the object of the desire, and how the person thinks of it. Guilt may attach to its attainment. Or the fault may lie with how the person stands to the desire itself: he may be too committed to it to tolerate being denied it, or too little committed to it to tolerate being granted it. Or the fault may lie with the pleasure that follows upon satisfaction of the desire or the unpleasure that follows upon its frustration. For these may be envisaged in such an extreme fashion that the person dreads their oncoming: they threaten to excite him beyond endurance or to numb him totally, to enflame him or to suffocate or stifle him. A related but more complex possibility is that the fault lies with a certain history that the person is led to ascribe to the pleasure or unpleasure he experiences. So the pleasure that is linked with satisfaction may be thought of as robbed or filched from another, whose anger is thereby provoked: or the unpleasure that is linked with frustration may be thought of as punishment for some unknown transgression, which will brand the person for ever.

III

In philosophy, we hear little of malformed emotion, but a fact that has escaped notice is that one of the most detailed discussions of the emotions to be found in the twentieth-century literature, Jean-Paul Sartre's *Sketch for a Theory of the Emotions*[1] confines its attention to these emotions. Not only does Sartre talk exclusively about malformed emotion, but he too traces malformed emotion to the person's inability to tolerate satisfaction or frustration.

However both these points need to be vindicated against other interpretations of what Sartre says, and that is because of three idiosyncrasies of his approach. First, he never concedes, even in the most roundabout way, that his essay has as its subject-matter anything other than the standard process by which the emotions form. Secondly, and as a direct consequence of the first, he calls the emotions whose formation he traces, not by the names they merit, but by the names of those emotions which they displace, or which would have formed, had satisfaction or frustration been tolerated. And, thirdly, Sartre assumes that all emotion is formed in this deviant way.

Sartre develops his theory around a few key examples of emotion, which occur in situations that he asks us to imagine.

First, there is a situation of danger, in which what Sartre calls fear arises. The second is a situation of loss, in which what Sartre calls sorrow arises. The third situation is one of good luck, or, more precisely, of imminent good luck, in which what Sartre calls joy arises. Sartre illustrates this third situation by two examples, one of a man who is about to receive a fortune, the other of a man who is about to meet someone whom he loves and has not seen for a long time. In the first two of these three situations, those of danger and loss, the man's desire is frustrated, actually frustrated: in the third, it is satisfied, though, in both examples, only imminently.

Sartre does not explicitly say of any of the three situations that the person finds the satisfaction or the frustration of his desire intolerable, or that this is how the emotion arises. What he says is that the emotion arises because the world becomes "difficult", unbearably difficult, for the person. Sartre's lack of explicitness makes it easy to think that he has another way, a way other than that which I might seem to foist upon him, of explaining what this means. It might be thought that how Sartre would explain why the world becomes difficult for the man is by pointing, in the first two situations, that of danger and that of loss, to the fact that his desire has been frustrated, rather than to his inability to tolerate the frustration, and, in the third situation, that of imminent good luck, to the fact that a desire so important for him has been only imminently, not actually, satisfied, rather than to his inability to tolerate any form of satisfaction.

These alternative explanations are closer to commonsense, and, without a doubt, they would account perfectly well for many people situated similarly to those whom Sartre asks us to consider. But they do not, I believe, hold for *them*, for Sartre's *dramatis personae*.

To justify my interpretation, I shall look more closely at one of Sartre's examples, and, since he is insistent that they have a common structure, I shall choose that about which he has most to say: the man who is about to be reunited with a mistress long absent.

The fundamental fact about this man is, we are told, that one of his deepest desires will soon be satisfied. He starts to reflect upon his position, and, as he does so, he comes up with various thoughts. First, he thinks that he has a further period of waiting in store for him, and that is something that he cannot bear. Then he thinks that, when that period of waiting is over, he will have to behave so as to bring himself and the woman he loves closer: he will have to try to please her, to make himself deserving of her love, to make her love him in return – and that is more of what he cannot bear. But what he can bear least of all is the thought that, when at last the moment of possession arrives, when at last she is his, then, through the very nature of human love, his possession of her can never be exclusive, or total, or sealed and delivered in a single moment of time.

It is at this stage that the world becomes "difficult" for the lover, and it is in direct response to this difficulty that he turns away from his situation, and he seeks to transform the world as he sees it, and to replace it with another world so pictured that whatever has proved difficult for him in this world is now negated. The impossible become possible. In this world, the lover can, Sartre tells us, gain possession of the desired one as "an instantaneous totality".

There are two elements in this story, both of which recur in Sartre's other examples, that best substantiate my claim that the emotion that he tells us of is emotion that is (one) malformed and (two) the product of a failure to tolerate satisfaction or frustration.

In the first place, there are the thoughts that the man rehearses as he waits for his desire to come true, and that form the prehistory of emotion. Are they the thoughts we should expect from someone with a simple commitment to his desire and its satisfaction? Satisfaction has been postponed, and that makes it natural for him to look into the future. But, when he does, what he sees in store for him is not pleasure, not some state of the world to which his desire has sensitized him, but the travail of surviving what he wants when he gets it. Sartre being the sort of thinker that he is, he proposes metaphysical rather than psychological reasons for the lover's inability to tolerate the satisfaction, the still merely prospective satisfaction, of his desire, but it is this inability that is the fundamental reason why the world turns out to be so difficult for him to live in, and why he flees the woman, and love, and ultimately the world itself. It is why he replaces the world as it is with another world that he wishes into existence.

And this brings us to the second element in Sartre's story that supports my interpretation: the so-called "transformation of the world", which is for him the core of emotion.

Of the transformation of the world Sartre says that it is a "magical" act, and the term "magic" covers various aspects of the act. In the first place, it captures how the person's picture of the world is changed: it is changed through the will, which is, in turn, a piece of thinking to which the person, even as he engages in it, attributes powers that mere mental activity couldn't have. What the person resorts to is more familiar to us through Freud's term, or the term he appropriated from his patient, the Ratman: "omnipotent thinking".

Secondly, "magic" conveys how the person stands to this change, once it is effected: he does not merely believe that it has occurred, he lives it. He cannot stand outside it. And, thirdly, the term implies that the transformation is global. It is not a mere alteration of the world at the empirical margin, so that the person gets rid of things that he doesn't like, replacing them with things more to his liking, while leaving all the general conditions of human desire and its pursuit – the adaptation of means to ends, the reliance upon trial and error, the need for causal knowledge – intact. The person who invokes magic to escape the difficulty of the world wills to transform the world out of all recognition.

It is supremely the global nature of the changes the person seeks that reveals his attitude to the satisfaction and frustration of desire. For someone who can accept satisfaction and frustration – though, all the while, as a human being must, preferring satisfaction to frustration, and satisfaction sooner to satisfaction later – will be someone who continues to act in, and to act upon, the world as he finds it, whereas someone who wills to abolish the world he inhabits and to substitute for it another in which gratification is immediate and total is someone to whom both satisfaction, normal satisfaction, and frustration of desire are alike intolerable. There is, in other words, no plausible story that runs forwards from the acceptance of satisfaction or frustration to the global transformation of the world, or that runs backwards from the invocation of a magical solution of life's difficulties to anything except the inability to tolerate satisfaction or frustration.

It might now be objected that, if I have shown that Sartre's account of emotion does indeed trace it to the failure to tolerate satisfaction or frustration, and hence is exclusively an account of, *in my sense of that phrase*, malformed emotion, I have not shown this for a more neutral sense of the phrase. I dispute this. The most basic way of understanding malformed emotion is as emotion that is an oblique, or an inapposite, response, to the circumstances in which the person believes himself to be. If that is so, then any emotion the history of which appeals to an adjusted perception of the world, let alone a wilfully adjusted perception of the world, must qualify as malformed.

IV

There is one deceptive element in Sartre's account of emotion, which might prevent the unwary reader from recognizing how starkly Sartre contrasts emotion as he sees it with an appropriate response to the world. We must go back a little.

Sartre, as we have seen, places at the centre of emotion the transformation of the world, which is fundamentally a change of consciousness. This change is induced through the will.

So a question to ask is: How does the will bring this about? What means – if we may allow ourselves a term that so obviously belongs to a more instrumental conception of acting upon the world – does the will employ? Sartre's answer is that the will employs behaviour: behaviour, which, like the will itself, now has magical powers attributed to it. As the world becomes difficult for us, so we engage in behaviour that Sartre calls "incantatory": it is incantatory of the world, wooing it to submit to the transformation willed upon it. The next question is: How is the behaviour selected? Or: What pairs behaviour to the emotion to which it gives rise? Now, without giving a general answer to this question, Sartre links each emotion – and this is the element I have called deceptive – with the specific behaviour that, not only is standardly associated with it, but owes this association to a rational link generally thought to hold between the two. Sartre, of course, rejects the rationality of the link. Instead he claims that what pairs the behaviour to the emotion is that the behaviour, in some primitive symbolic fashion, denies that aspect of the world which the person finds difficult.

The case of fear will illustrate the point. Sartre too insists on the familiar association of fear – or what he thinks of as one kind of fear, which he calls active fear – with flight. To the obvious objection that this goes against the view of emotion as a form of magic, Sartre's reply is that the profound error in ordinary thinking is to believe that the primary aim of the fleeing person is to put as much distance between himself and the danger as possible. He suggests that, to grasp the real link between fear and behaviour, we should start, not with active fear and flight, but with the other kind of fear, passive fear, and the behaviour with which it is associated: fainting. When a person faints in a situation of danger, he is doing two things. He is trying, first, to negate or annihilate the difficult character that the world has taken on, and, secondly, to induce, to induce magically, incantatorily, another, a different kind of, world. Once we have understood this, we can then turn back to the person who, in the grip of active fear, flees. For the two men are doing exactly the same thing, to which what the man who is gripped by passive fear does provides the clue. Flight is, in Sartre's words, "active fainting". By running away, the man who flees is at once denying that danger exists and conjuring into existence a world alternative to the present world, from which danger has been purged.

V

In claiming that Sartre implicitly offers us an account of malformed emotion, furthermore an account that gives malformed emotion an origin similar to that which I propose, I am not implying that Sartre gives us a full, or accurate, picture of how such emotion comes about. He does not. I shall now offer the outlines of an adequate account, using wherever possible, and refining as necessary, the materials that Sartre provides.

In the first place, an adequate account must explicitly identify the originating condition of malformed emotion. This, I have contended, is the inability to tolerate satisfaction or frustration of desire. Sartre specifies the condition only implicitly, and confuses the issue by assuming that we are looking for a metaphysical, not a psychological, condition.

Secondly, a mechanism of defence needs to be inserted between the failure of the person to tolerate satisfaction or frustration and how he then perceives the world. Examples of such mechanisms are projection, introjection, denial, splitting, and projective identification. It is this mechanism, initially triggered by anxiety, that brings about the next stage in the development of the emotion, and not, as Sartre claims, the will, embodied in incantatory behaviour.

Thirdly, this next stage, which Sartre calls "the transformation of the world" is better thought of as the content of a phantasy. In the case of a malformed emotion phantasy takes the place that is occupied, in the case of normally formed emotions, by an attitude. And, as to Sartre's insistence that the transformation is total, this is an exaggeration. All that it is necessary to maintain is that the phantasy tends to occlude any aspect of the world that would falsify the phantasy.

Fourthly, the account must say more about the content of this phantasy. In general what seems right to say is that the content of the phantasy is elaborated around whatever is believed to have made the experience of satisfaction or frustration intolerable.

Fifthly, once the function that Sartre attributes to behaviour is delegated to a mechanism of defence, the role that behaviour actually plays needs to be reconsidered. My suggestion is that much of the behaviour ordinarily associated with emotion is best thought of either as an expression of the emotion or as an acting-out of the core phantasy.

Finally, a revised account needs to correct the systematically misleading way in which Sartre bestows upon the malformed emotions the names of those quite different emotions for which they substitute themselves. Sartre, as we have seen, talks of fear, sorrow, and joy, when he would have done better to have talked of mania, melancholia, and envy. Better, but still not well. The truth is that malformed emotions necessarily resist a clear taxonomy, and that is because, in any given instance, the malformed emotion owes its content or character, partly to the situation to which the person now perceives himself to be responding, but partly to the mechanism of defence that accounts for the misperception. Malformed emotion is, in Freudian terminology, a compromise-formation. It is a compromise between the defensive agency, which introduces the new emotion and the old, or defended against, emotion.

At one point in his essay, Sartre makes a revealing admission. There is no work of literature that illustrates more succinctly what happens to our emotions when we repudiate our desires than Aesop's fable of the *Fox and the Grapes*. The fox cannot get what he wants because nature has put it out of his reach. Unable to accept frustration of his desire, he is led off on a path that, starting from denial of his desire, leads him, through scorn of its object, to envy. And Sartre tells us that this fable delivers to us the essence of emotion.

Notes

* I hope that this essay will be accepted by Dieter Henrich as a tribute to the breadth of his own philosophical interests.
1 Cf. J. P. Sartre, *Esquisse d'une théorie des émotions* (Paris: Hermann, 1939).

Ernst Tugendhat

Gedanken über den Tod

Kann die Philosophie etwas zum Todesverständnis beitragen? Montaigne hat seinen Essay I, 20 überschrieben *„Que philosopher, c'est apprendre à mourir"*. Dieser Satz geht, über Cicero, auf Platon zurück.[1] Hugo Friedrich[2] hat aber glaubhaft gemacht, daß Montaigne, zumindest in seinen späteren Versuchen, sich gegenüber dem Nutzen der Philosophie für das Sicheinstimmen auf den Tod eher skeptisch verhalten hat. Und man wird Montaigne darin gewiß zustimmen können, soweit man sich den Beitrag der Philosophie von einem eigenständigen Zugang, den die Philosophie zu dem Todesphänomen haben könnte, erwartete, wie es bei Platon der Fall war. Freilich, man könnte weitergehen und die Besorgnis zum Ausdruck bringen, daß die abstrakt begrifflichen Mittel der Philosophie schon als solche die Todeserfahrung in ihrer Konkretisierung und Variabilität verstellen. Zweifellos stammen von der Philosophie auch viele Sophismen über den Tod, wie z. B. der epikureische Gedanke, daß am Tod nichts zu fürchten sei, weil wir, wenn wir tot sind, nichts empfinden; als ob die Furcht vor dem Tod in der Furcht vor einem Zustand danach bestünde. Sollte man also nicht einfach sagen: Der Tod ist eben das Ende des Lebens, und wir wissen, daß, wenn auch nicht alle, so doch die meisten Menschen sich vor ihm fürchten, und basta? Wozu noch eine philosophische Klärung? Aber schon, daß wir hier sagen müssen „die meisten", zeigt, daß dieser Sachverhalt keineswegs eindeutig ist (Montaigne sagte (I,50): Cicero ängstigte sich vor dem Tod, Cato wünschte sich ihn, Sokrates war er gleichgültig). Außerdem ist unklar, wenn man von der Furcht vor dem Tod spricht, was es genau am Tod ist, wovor wir uns fürchten. Es scheint also ein Klärungsbedarf zu bestehen, und ist das nicht die klassische Ausgangssituation für eine philosophische Frage?

Viele Menschen haben nicht nur das eine oder andere Verständnis vom Tod, sondern leben in einem vortheoretischen Konzept, das sie sich zusammengezimmert haben; sie geben etwa Gründe an, warum sie sich vor ihm fürchten oder warum sie sich nicht vor ihm fürchten. So gibt es eine Vielfalt von Meinungen, die sich meist in Wörtern ausdrücken, die ihrerseits häufig vieldeutig oder unbestimmt sind. Damit ist die Frage, ob Philosophie hier etwas beitragen kann, nicht nur positiv beantwortet, sondern auch ein Weg, eine Methode vorgezeichnet. Es gibt, meine ich, keinen eigenständigen philosophischen Zugang, wir können nur von vorgegebenen Ansichten ausgehen, und die philosophische Zutat besteht erstens in Klärung und zweitens in Ergänzung von Einseitigkeiten. Hier wie in so vielen anderen Fällen philosophischer Klärungsbedürftigkeit gilt die Maxime, daß alle Ansichten berücksichtigt werden sollten, sei es, daß sie sich dann als falsch erweisen, sei es, daß sie mit anderen zu integrieren sind, sei es, daß Alternativen offen bleiben. So ergibt sich ein Vorgehen, das unvermeidlich einen subjektiven Ausgangspunkt hat und sich dann schrittweise als klärungs- und ergänzungsbedürftig erweist und allemal unabgeschlossen bleibt. Falls eine Art von Ansichten nicht berücksichtigt wird, liegt darin eine gewisse Willkür, die aber gemildert wird, wenn man sie explizit macht. Ich z. B. werde eine ganze Klasse von Ansichten über den Tod überhaupt nicht berücksichtigen, nämlich die, die eine der Varianten des Glaubens an ein Leben nach dem Tod voraussetzen. Ich bekenne, daß das eine subjektive Entscheidung ist. Ich meine, daß es gute Gründe gibt, einen solchen Glauben nicht zu haben, und daher interessieren mich diese Meinungen zu wenig.

Bevor ich mit einem mehr systematischen Versuch beginne, will ich, wie ich mir das angedeutete Hin und Her zwischen Ansichten und philosophischer Klärung vorstelle, an einem Beispiel illustrieren, das für mich – hierin zeigt sich der unweigerlich subjektive Ausgangspunkt – kein beliebiges ist, weil es eigentlich diese Begegnung war, die, ein oder zwei Jahre zurückliegend, mir den Anstoß für die folgenden Reflexionen gab. Ich war in einem Hafenstädtchen in Chile zufällig mit einem alten Mann, viel älter noch als ich, in ein Gespräch geraten. Vor einiger Zeit habe er sich in einer Krankheit befunden und sich gefürchtet, daß sie zum Tod führen könnte. Er habe gegenüber Gott ein Gelübde abgelegt, ihm eine Kirche zu bauen, falls er ihn errette und ihm noch einige Jahre schenke. Gott hatte ihn erhört, und hier war er also und baute. In diesem Fall handelt es sich nicht um eine Ansicht über den Tod, sondern um ein Verhalten, das eine bestimmte Ansicht impliziert, eine Ansicht freilich, die so trivial scheinen kann, daß man sich wundern könnte, warum sie mich aufhorchen ließ. Um das verständlich zu machen, muß ich einen Schritt zurückgehen und sagen, welches vor dieser Begegnung mehr oder weniger die Vorstellung gewesen war, die ich mir vom Tod zurechtgezimmert hatte. Ich hatte mir das Leben wie eine Wurst vorgestellt in zeitlicher Dimension, eine Wurst, die allemal ein Ende in der Zukunft hat, und ob sie nun etwas länger oder kürzer sei, das mache zwar einen Unterschied, aber keinen wesentlichen: Wurst bleibt Wurst. Wie kommt man zu so einer Auffassung? Sie legt sich nahe, wenn man sich klarmacht, daß das Leben *irgendwann* ein Ende findet; es ist nicht dieser Umstand als solcher, der uns ängstigt, ja es liegt nahe, daß uns, wie es Bernard Williams in einem Aufsatz vertreten hat,[3] das Gegenteil ängstigen würde: daß wir das Leben ohne Ende weiterführen müßten. Heißt das dann aber nicht, daß es uns außer in den Fällen, die man als tragisch zu bezeichnen pflegt, beim Tod eines jungen Menschen, der, wie man sagt, sein Leben noch vor sich hat, nicht so schrecklich erscheinen sollte, daß das Leben etwas kürzer statt etwas länger sei? Aber für meinen Alten in Chile war das offenbar der Fall, und was mich nach dieser Begegnung beunruhigte, war, daß seine Auffassung so natürlich wirkte. Aber warum? Worin genau lag der Unterschied zwischen seiner und meiner Auffassung? Seine Auffassung mag deswegen als so natürlich erscheinen, weil beim Leben wie bei allem mehr eben mehr ist als weniger. Doch das hatte ich nicht geleugnet; ich hatte nur gemeint, dieser quantitative Unterschied könne nicht so wesentlich sein. Angenommen, er wäre nicht alt gewesen, und, als er 27 war, hätte ihm eine *bruja*, wie man in Chile sagt, eine Wahrsagerin also, vorausgesagt, er werde 79 Jahre alt werden; hätte er auch dann ein so großes Gelübde abgelegt, damit Gott ihm noch ein paar zusätzliche Jahre schenke (über die 79 hinaus)? Das wäre nicht undenkbar, aber eher kurios, und gewiß hätte es mich nicht aufhorchen lassen. Jetzt wird deutlich, was mich an der Äußerung des Alten betroffen machte. Es war nicht die Bedeutung des Quantitativen, die ich übersehen hatte, sondern daß wir uns zum Tod immer von einem bestimmten Standpunkt aus verhalten, von einem Standpunkt innerhalb der Wurst: Wir sehen weder die Wurst noch ihr mögliches Ende von außen. Was mich also an dieser Geschichte beeindruckte, war die Wichtigkeit der angenommenen Nähe oder Ferne des Todes oder besser gesagt: der Unterschied zwischen der angenommenen Wahrscheinlichkeit oder Unwahrscheinlichkeit seiner Nähe. Mit Nähe möchte ich sagen, daß man glaubt, daß man *bald* sterben wird.

Ein solches Bewußtsein unterscheidet sich nicht nur auf der einen Seite von unserem gewöhnlichen, in dem der Tod uns fern scheint und es einen Phantasieaufwand erfordert, sich vorzustellen, er könnte uns jetzt oder bald treffen; es ist auch auf der anderen Seite zu unterscheiden von dem, was ich die vegetative Todesangst nennen will. Freilich gibt es hier keine scharfen Grenzen: Weder das Bewußtsein der Todesferne ist von dem der Todesnähe scharf unterschieden, noch ist das Bewußtsein von Todesnähe immer scharf unterschieden von der vegetativen Todesangst; aber auch wenn beide eng verbunden sind, meine ich, daß sie begrifflich unterschieden werden sollten. Von vegetativer Todesangst spreche ich, wenn man in einer bedrohlichen Situation zu sein glaubt, die zum Tod führen kann, aber nicht muß, z. B. wenn man verfolgt wird oder von einer Brücke heruntergestürzt oder sich in einem abstürzenden Flugzeug befindet usw. Wieder ein wenig anders ist es, wenn man in einer Krankheit im Sterben zu liegen glaubt; in diesem Fall kommt die Bedrohung von innen. Im Unterschied zu der bloßen Vorstellung, man werde bald sterben, sind für die vegetative Todesangst (ich sehe jetzt von dem eben genannten Krankheitsfall ab) bestimmte Ausdrucks- und physiologische Faktoren charakteristisch, die wir ähnlich an anderen Säugetieren wahrnehmen, z. B. Zittern, extrem erhöhte Herztätigkeit usw., wenn ein Kalb in einem Rodeo von Reitern bedrängt wird. Nicht zufällig sprechen wir bei der vegetativen Todesangst von Angst, weil das ein diffuser Zustand ist, der nicht, wie man in der Philosophie zu sagen pflegt, einen bestimmten intentionalen Gegenstand hat, während die Furcht, daß man bald sterben wird (trotz Heideggers abwegiger Rede von der

Angst vor dem Tod), die Furcht vor einem klar definierten Ereignis ist (das Ereignis ist natürlich nicht hinsichtlich seines Wann und Wo usw. definiert, aber das ist auch nicht erforderlich: Es ist klar definiert einfach dadurch, daß es das Ereignis ist, das darin besteht, daß einer aufhört zu leben). Während bei der vegetativen Todesangst uns nahestehende andere Tiere zwar nicht genauso, aber doch ähnlich reagieren wie Menschen, ist nicht anzunehmen, daß andere Tiere die Furcht, daß man bald sterben wird, kennen, weil man dafür die Sprache und ein Zeitbewußtsein braucht: man muß das Wort „bald" verstehen. So sehr sich beim Menschen beides verbinden kann, wäre es doch falsch anzunehmen, daß, was ich das vegetative Todesbewußtsein nenne, den Höhepunkt der Furcht vor dem baldigen Tod darstellt – etwa wie sich das „schon" zum „bald" verhält. Wir können uns den Unterschied der beiden Phänomene etwa an einer Person verdeutlichen, die ihrem Leben ein Ende bereiten will, und in dieser Hinsicht ganz unambivalent und ohne Furcht ist und gleichwohl Furcht vor der vegetativen Todesangst hat, die sie für die kurze Übergangszeit des gewaltsamen Sterbens (wenn sie sich z. B. ertränkt) voraussieht.

Für die Frage, was es denn ist, wovor genau wir uns fürchten, wenn wir uns vor dem Tod fürchten, scheint mir einiges gewonnen zu sein, wenn wir die Furcht vor der Todesnähe einerseits von dem Bewußtsein, daß wir irgendeinmal sterben werden bzw. daß wir jederzeit sterben können, unterscheiden und sie andererseits auch von der vegetativen Todesangst unterscheiden. Was mich an dem Gelübde meines Alten aufhorchen ließ, ist, daß es, ganz unabhängig davon, ob sich vegetative Todesangst damit vermischt oder nicht, beängstigend sein kann (nicht muß), daß man bald nicht mehr leben wird, obwohl man natürlich immer wußte, daß man irgendwann einmal nicht mehr leben wird, und einen das gewöhnlich so wenig affektiv berührt, daß man es als natürlich ansieht. Es kann einem entscheidend wichtig sein, jetzt, sagen wir mit 81, noch eine Weile weiterzuleben, obwohl einem dieselbe Verlängerung nach 81 früher, als man 27 war, gleichgültig gewesen wäre. Ist also, was man angesichts eines bevorstehenden Todes meist will, so etwas wie eine Galgenfrist, ein Aufschub? Wenn ja, warum? „Nur jetzt nicht sterben, sondern später": Das, meine ich, ist es, was in dem Gelübde des Alten zum Ausdruck kam.

Ich habe von dieser Begegnung erzählt, um an einem Beispiel zu zeigen, wie ich mir die Methode vorstelle, verschiedene Meinungen zu vergleichen, aneinander zu korrigieren, Zweideutigkeiten zu desambiguieren, und wie dazu, in einem so subjektiven Reflexionsbereich, auch die Berechtigung gehört, einige Aspekte zurückzustellen und andere verstärkt zu beleuchten, wenn man das nur explizit macht. Freilich ist dabei auch schon die Frage selbst ein Stück weit verdeutlicht worden. Es ist nicht so klar, was es ist, wovor wir uns fürchten, wenn wir uns vor dem Tod fürchten. Warum, so läßt sich jetzt fragen, fürchten wir uns, falls wir uns überhaupt vor ihm fürchten, nicht vor dem Tod als solchem, sondern wollen nur einen Aufschub?

Aber ich will jetzt etwas systematischer vorgehen. Freilich, nach dem, was ich anfangs sagte, kann das nur einen relativen Sinn haben. Der Ausgangspunkt ist unausweichlich subjektiv, von der begrenzten Optik des Reflektierenden abhängig. Es scheint mir aber jetzt vorteilhaft, von philosophischen Ansichten auszugehen, allerdings nur, wenn diese sich nicht, wie die platonisch-stoisch-epikureische Tradition, in einen Gegensatz zu vorphilosophischen Ansichten setzen, sondern sich als deren Interpretation verstehen, also „hermeneutisch", wie man es mit Heidegger nennen kann. Der methodische Vorteil besteht dann einfach darin, daß es das Vorgehen abkürzt: In einer philosophischen Ansicht treten uns meist vorphilosophische Ansichten schon gebündelt entgegen. Ich will nun – das ist wiederum ganz subjektiv – von zwei philosophischen Ansichten ausgehen, die als Ausgangspunkt den Vorteil haben, daß sie nicht nur entgegengesetzte Auffassungen darstellen, sondern gar nicht auf ein und dieselbe Frage antworten. Jede interessiert sich für etwas, was die andere nicht einmal erwähnt, wie zwei Schiffe, die in einem Fluß aneinander vorbeifahren, ohne voneinander Notiz zu nehmen. Ich meine erstens das Kapitel über das „Sein zum Tode" in Heideggers *Sein und Zeit* (1927) und zweitens Thomas Nagels Aufsatz „Death" (1970).[4]

Heidegger stellt eine Frage, die im christlichen Denken üblich war, aber er stellt sie, wie es wohl erst seit dem 19. Jahrhundert hie und da geschehen ist (ich bin kein Historiker), ohne den christlichen Jenseitsbezug, nämlich was es für das *Leben* bedeutet, des Todes ansichtig zu sein. Bei Nagel kommt diese Frage nicht vor. Seine Leitfrage ist die Frage, ob und wieso der Tod ein Übel ist. Diese Frage kommt wiederum bei Heidegger nicht vor. Das aber muß nun, wenigstens auf den ersten Blick, äußerst merkwürdig scheinen. Man müßte ja vielleicht nicht unbedingt, wie Nagel es tut, von einem *Übel* sprechen; vielleicht paßt dieses Wort auf den Tod nicht. Allerdings müßte man zeigen, warum nicht. Was jedoch Heidegger tut, nämlich behaupten, daß wir den Tod fürchten oder, wie er zu sagen vorzieht, uns vor ihm ängstigen, ohne zu sagen warum, und was es an ihm ist, was wir fürchten: das bedeutet, etwas als Faktum voraussetzen, statt es verständlich zu machen. Heidegger hat die Wörter „gut" und „schlecht" ganz allgemein in *Sein und Zeit* vermieden, wohl weil er das Normative vermeiden wollte, aber man mag das beurteilen, wie man will, allemal reicht die Verwendung dieser Wörter weit über den Bereich des Moralischen und überhaupt des Normativen hinaus, und ich meine, es handelte sich hier mehr um eine tiefsitzende Antipathie als eine durchdachte Position, wie so manches bei Heidegger. Nun könnte man vielleicht sagen, die Rede von Gütern und Übeln mußte für Heidegger allzu objektivistisch klingen, aber es gibt doch eine recht unschuldige Verwendung dieser Wörter, die durchaus subjekivistisch ist: Man nennt Übel diejenigen Dinge, die im allgemeinen vermieden werden wie Schmerzen, Freiheitsentzug, Verlust von Menschen, Verlust von Sachen und schließlich eben auch den Verlust des eigenen Lebens, und Güter diejenigen Dinge, die im allgemeinen erstrebt werden wie Schmerzlosigkeit, Freude, Freiheit, menschliche Beziehungen usw. und schließlich eben (scheinbar): zu leben. Vielleicht gibt es eine Möglichkeit, hier Heidegger näherzukommen, indem man solche objektiv klingenden Wörter wie „schlecht" und „Übel" durch subjektive Wörter wie Wünschen einerseits, Vermeidenwollen andererseits ersetzt. Aber irgendein Vokabular dieser Art ist unvermeidlich, um überhaupt verständlich zu machen, warum man Wörter wie „Angst" und „Furcht" verwendet und worauf sie sich im jeweiligen Fall speziell beziehen. (In dem Abschnitt über die Furcht gebraucht Heidegger immerhin den Ausdruck „Übel", aber nur, um Aristoteles zu zitieren.)

Heidegger gebraucht hier aber doch wenigstens *ein* Wort, das die angegebene Funktion zu erfüllen scheint. Nur ist es leider, ohne daß Heidegger darauf aufmerksam wird, zweideutig. Es ist das Wort „Worumwillen". Dieses etwas künstliche Wort (es ist sehr schwer, es in andere moderne Sprachen zu übersetzen) ist die Übertragung des selbst bereits etwas künstlichen, aber bewußt terminologischen Ausdrucks *to hou heneka* des Aristoteles. Aristoteles verwendet den Ausdruck für das, um willen wovon jemand etwas macht oder überhaupt handelt, also den Zweck, und da dieses Wort bei Aristoteles noch nicht zweideutig war, hatte er keine Hemmungen, es mit dem Guten (in einer bestimmten Verwendung des Wortes) gleichzusetzen. Nun ist die erste starke These in *Sein und Zeit*, daß der Mensch (oder „das Dasein", wie Heidegger zu sagen beliebt), sich so auf sein Sein (Leben) bezieht, daß es ihm um dieses geht[5], eine Formulierung, die Heidegger später so aufnimmt, daß für den Menschen (ich sage „den" statt „einen", um Heideggers Rede von „dem Dasein" näher zu bleiben) das eigene Sein sein letztes Worumwillen ist.[6] Heidegger hat das in einer bestimmten Umwandlung von Aristoteles übernommen. Aber er hätte nun dadurch, daß er das Worumwillen nicht einfach mit Zweck, dem Guten, dem Erstrebten gleichsetzte, der Möglichkeit Rechnung tragen können, daß wir gegebenenfalls den Tod dem Leben vorziehen können. Denn man könnte ja zustimmen, daß das Leben unser letztes Worumwillen ist, also worum es uns letztlich geht, aber doch gleichzeitig finden, daß wir gleichwohl mit Hamlet fragen können, ob es nicht besser ist, tot zu sein, als zu leben. Aber bei Heidegger kommt diese Frage nicht vor; ja, da man, um sie zu stellen, das Wort „besser" oder ähnliches braucht („whether 'tis nobler", sagt Shakespeare) und Heidegger solche Wertwörter nicht verwenden will, kann die Hamletsche Frage bei ihm gar nicht vorkommen. Daß es einem Menschen „um sein Sein" geht, erscheint daher bei Heidegger wie ein bloßes Faktum, über das sein Wille nicht hinausreichen könnte, wie er es aber doch offenkundig kann, wenn wir vorziehen, nicht mehr zu leben.

Das Wort „Worumwillen" ist zweideutig, weil es einerseits für die Zwecke im Leben steht und andererseits für den Lebensrahmen als solchen. Auch derjenige, der sich sein Leben nimmt, tut dies, weil es ihm um sein Leben geht; das Leben ist der äußerste Bezugspunkt alles seines Wollens. Jetzt läßt sich deutlich sehen, inwiefern sich jenes äußerste Worumwillen, das für uns das Leben ist, von jedem begrenzteren Worumwillen, von bestimmten Zwecken, unterscheidet. Wer einen bestimmten Zweck nicht mehr will, sieht von ihm ab, hat dann eben andere Zwecke; wer hingegen sein Leben nicht mehr will, will es nicht mehr, weil es so ist, wie es ist; er bleibt auch, indem er es zurückstößt, willentlich auf es bezogen. Das Verhältnis des Lebens als Worumwillen zu den übrigen Gütern ist daher nicht einfach hierarchisch. Was ich Heidegger vorwerfe, ist nicht, daß er das Leben nicht als gut bezeichnete, sondern daß er nicht, wenn er schon eine neue Begrifflichkeit entwickelte, der Möglichkeit Rechnung getragen hat, daß man es als „besser" ansehen kann, dem Leben ein Ende zu setzen. Es hätte, wenn Heidegger das Problem überhaupt erörtert hätte, gute Gründe geben können zu bestreiten, daß das Leben ein Gut ist, erstens weil alle Güter Güter nur sind innerhalb seiner und weil man es zweitens als schlecht, sogar als unerträglich ansehen kann. Aber dann beginnt natürlich auch die Auffassung vom Tod als Übel fragwürdig zu werden. Gewiß, auch das wird von Heidegger nicht gesagt, aber einfach deswegen nicht, weil er sowohl diese objektiv-wertende als auch eine subjektiv-wertende Terminologie vermeidet. Wieso also haben wir Angst vor dem Tod?

Hier führt Heidegger ein weiteres Wort ein, das eine Antwort auf diese Frage geben soll, aber es ist eine Scheinantwort. Es handelt sich um den Ausdruck „das Nichts" oder, wie Heidegger in *Sein und Zeit* noch vorsichtiger formulierte, das „Nicht" oder „die Nichtheit"[7]. Ist es denn aber evident, daß wir vor dem Nichthaften Angst haben? Fürchten wir uns davor, einzuschlafen? Im Gegenteil, wir wünschen häufig nichts sehnlicher, als zeitweise in dieses Nichts zu sinken. Aber eben vielleicht nur zeitweise? Nun ja, vielleicht ist das der Punkt, aber eben das ist doch vielmehr klärungsbedürftig. Jedenfalls ist es ein Fehlschluß zu sagen: Das Sein des Menschen ist sein Worumwillen, also fürchtet er sich davor, nicht mehr zu sein.

Auf die Frage, warum sich, seien es alle Menschen (so Heidegger), seien es die meisten (so fände ich es richtiger formuliert) vor dem Tod fürchten, erhalten wir also von Heidegger keine Antwort, und wir können keine erwarten, weil er die Terminologie, mit deren Hilfe sie zu beantworten wäre, verwirft, ohne eine andere, entsprechend differenzierte, an ihre Stelle zu setzen.

Was tut nun Nagel? Setzt man sich erst einmal über die Zweideutigkeit hinweg, die sich innerhalb der Rede von Gütern und Übeln zeigte, scheint er die richtige Ausgangsfrage zu stellen: Ist der Tod ein Übel, und wenn ja, inwiefern? Das könnte zu einer Antwort auf die Frage führen, was es am Tod ist, was wir fürchten, wenn wir uns vor ihm fürchten. Nagel verwirft zuerst mit Recht die Auffassung, daß das *Totsein* ein Übel ist, denn wenn ich tot bin, kann für mich nichts weder gut noch schlecht sein. (Allerdings setzt Nagel hier, ebenso wie ich es getan habe, die Auffassung voraus, daß es kein Leben nach dem Tod gibt, daß also der Tod wirklich ein Aufhören und nicht nur ein Wandel ist.) Das Übel scheint also nur darin bestehen zu können, daß mich der Tod, wie Nagel das zunächst formuliert, der Güter des Lebens beraubt. Diese Redeweise hat nun aber etwas Mißliches an sich, das auch viele andere Formulierungen haben, die bei der Beschreibung des Todes verwendet werden, wie wenn man sagt, im Tode verabschiede sich der Sterbende von der Welt. Alle solche Redeweisen implizieren, daß das Subjekt, das diese Tätigkeiten vollzieht (wie Abschiednehmen) oder diese Widerfahrnisse erleidet (wie der Güter beraubt zu werden), irgendwie erhalten bleibt, während es doch in Wirklichkeit aufhört zu existieren. Diese Schwierigkeit ist freilich eine in der Sprache tief verwurzelte: Auch wenn wir es mit etwas Nichtlebendigem zu tun haben, ergibt sich dieselbe Mißlichkeit, wenn wir sagen: „Es hat aufgehört", als ob noch von *ihm* zu reden wäre, wenngleich als einem nicht mehr Existierenden. Hier in fehlerhafte Vorstellungen zu geraten ist nur dadurch vermeidbar, daß das einzige Prädikat, das dem Gegenstand, nachdem er aufgehört hat, im Präsens oder Futur zusprechbar ist, eben das des Aufgehörthabens ist. Man kann also, wenn es sich um ein Lebendiges handelt, noch im Präsens sagen: Es ist gestorben, es ist tot. Freilich ist auch das nicht ganz ohne Schwierigkeit, weil immer noch ein Subjekt im Präsens erwähnt wird, aber wenigstens sagt man dann nichts weiter von diesem Subjekt, als daß es nicht existiert. Von Beraubtwerden, Abschiednehmen usw. kann jedoch nicht die Rede sein. Wenn also der Tod als Übel angesehen wird, kann dieses Übel nicht darin bestehen, daß man der Güter des Lebens verlustig geht, sondern nur darin, daß das Leben selbst zu Ende geht, und das könnte heißen, wenn doch der Tod ein Übel ist, daß das Leben selbst ein Gut ist. Nagel führt das nicht in dieser Weise ein, aber er behauptet es, und er befindet sich mit diesem Satz, daß es gut für einen ist zu leben, in einer edlen Tradition, wie sich eben an Aristoteles gezeigt hat. Nagel schreibt: Es gibt Dinge, die das Leben besser machen, andere, die es schlechter machen, aber der Wert des Lebens besteht nicht einfach in dem, was übrig bleibt, wenn man das eine vom anderen abzieht. Das Lebendigsein selbst – und d. h. gewisse Faktoren, sagt er, die das bewußte Lebendigsein als solches konstituieren wie Wahrnehmen, Wollen, Tätigsein und Denken – seien schon an und für sich „entschieden positiv"[8].

Bevor ich das problematisiere, will ich zwei Zusatzgedanken von Nagel erwähnen. Erstens macht er, wie ich finde zu Recht, darauf aufmerksam, daß dieser Wert des Lebens (wenn er denn besteht) offensichtlich ausschließlich nur eine Sache des Bewußtseins sein kann und sich nicht auf das organische Leben bezieht: „Fast jedermann", schreibt er, „wäre es egal, ob er auf der Stelle tot wäre, oder ob er nur in ein Koma fiele, das zwanzig Jahre später, ohne daß er je wieder erwacht wäre, mit dem Tod endete"[9]. Zweitens bemerkt er in einer Anmerkung: „Manchmal wird behauptet, es sei der Prozeß des Sterbens, den wir in Wirklichkeit fürchten. Aber ich hätte eigentlich nichts am Sterben auszusetzen, würde ihm nicht der Tod folgen."[10] Der letzte Satz ist gewiß eine Übertreibung, aber Nagel will hier die Furcht vor dem Aufhören von der vegetativen Todesangst ähnlich unterscheiden, wie ich es vorhin getan habe.

Zurück nun aber zu seiner These, daß das Leben im Sinn des Erlebens – er faßt die vorhin genannten Faktoren im Wort „experience" zusammen – unabhängig von allen einzelnen Gütern ein Gut sei. Er gibt, merkwürdigerweise, keine Gründe an und keine näheren Erklärungen, und sein Wort „emphatisch" ist gewiß verdächtig. Man benützt es, wenn man sich in Wirklichkeit seiner nicht so sicher ist. Man pflegt nicht zu sagen, man sei emphatisch der Meinung, daß $2 + 2 = 4$ ist. Vielleicht meinte Nagel, die These vom Leben als Gut folge aus dem Faktum der Furcht vor dem Tod. Aber das wäre ähnlich zirkulär, wie wenn Heidegger die Angst vor dem Tod einfach als Faktum voraussetzt. Auf den naheliegenden Einwand freilich, den man hier gegen Nagel machen könnte: daß es Menschen gibt, die den Tod nicht fürchten, und andere, die ihn sogar suchen, hätte er eine leichte Antwort. Er könnte sagen: Wenn die Übel im Leben ein gewisses Maß überschreiten, können sie das Gut, das im Leben selbst liege, überwiegen. Dies also wäre kein Einwand. Aber ein ausreichender Einwand bestünde doch darin, daß, solange keine Begründung angegeben wird, Nagels These eine bloße Behauptung ist und viele Menschen es umgekehrt sehen. Sie würden entgegnen: „Nein, das bewußte Leben ist als solches neutral. Wieso soll das bloße Bei-Bewußtsein-Sein schon als solches positiv sein?" „Und wir", so könnte weiter argumentiert werden, „können das Phänomen, daß die meisten sich vor dem Tod fürchten, durchaus einfacher erklären, nämlich so: du, Nagel, hast ja eben zugegeben" (das habe freilich nur ich für ihn getan, aber nehmen wir an, er habe es zugegeben), „daß die Übel im Leben den Wert des Lebens überwiegen können; ist es dann nicht näherliegend, von diesem fragwürdigen Wert des Lebens an sich abzusehen und einfach die Übel mit den Gütern zu vergleichen?" Wer so denkt, braucht nicht den vorhin genannten semantischen Fehler zu begehen, daß, wovor man sich fürchtet, darin bestünde, von den Gütern des Lebens beraubt zu sein; wovor wir uns fürchten, kann aus logischen Gründen zwar immer nur das Aufhören des Lebens sein, nicht das Beraubtwerden der Güter. Aber der Grund, warum einer nicht will, daß das Leben aufhört, kann durchaus eben darin bestehen, daß er meint, daß die Güter im Leben die Übel überwiegen.

Man scheint es also so sehen zu können oder auch so, wobei freilich Nagel den Nachteil hat, den jeder hat, der eine unbewiesene und von anderen als uneinsichtig erklärte Annahme macht. Welche Partei hätte mein chilenischer Alter in diesem Streit ergriffen? Betete er um noch ein paar Jahre unter der Voraussetzung, daß in ihnen die Güter die Übel überwiegen würden? Diese Annahme wirkt gerade bei einem alten Mann merkwürdig. Ging es ihm also, wie Nagel nahelegt, lediglich um die Lebensverlängerung als solche? Aber warum? Weil, wie Nagel behauptet, das Leben ein Gut ist, und wenn es länger dauert, ein größeres? Klingt das nicht unwahrscheinlich? Erinnern wir uns, daß die Geschichte des Alten zu einem Phänomen führte, von dem wir bei Nagel nichts hören, die besondere Relevanz der Todesnähe, genauer natürlich: der angenommenen Todesnähe.

Nun scheint mir, daß die beiden eben referierten Auffassungen, die von Nagel und die eines von mir fingierten Gegners, in gleicher Weise etwas im unklaren lassen oder sogar falsch sehen, nämlich das Verhältnis zwischen dem Leben einerseits und den Übeln und Gütern andererseits. Beide Parteien scheinen vorauszusetzen, daß das Leben wie ein Behälter oder eine Unterlage ist, sei es, daß es einen eigenen Wert hat oder – nach der anderen Auffassung – keinen. Dem steht eine verbreitete Lebenserfahrung entgegen, die die übrigen Tiere wohl nicht kennen, die die Menschen jedoch häufig befällt und häufig lange erfüllt, nämlich die der Leere, des Überdrusses. Das Leben kann, ohne positive Übel, gleichwohl unerträglich erscheinen, und zwar so unerträglich, daß viele sich gerade deswegen (andere freilich aus anderen Gründen) den Tod *wünschen*. Dieses Phänomen dürfte es nach Nagel, also wenn das bewußte Lebendigsein schon als solches wünschenswert (oder „ein Gut") ist, gar nicht geben, ja nicht einmal geben können; nach der anderen Auffassung natürlich noch weniger, da es dort nicht einmal vorkommt, außer als Behälter, also quasi als Tablett: für angenehme Klötzchen einerseits, unangenehme andererseits. In Wirklichkeit scheint jedenfalls ein Teil dessen, was man die Lebensgüter nennt, sich in seinem Gutsein-für-mich gerade auf das Leben zu beziehen, in einer Weise, die häufig so zum Ausdruck gebracht wird, daß man sagt, daß diese Güter – es sind meist Tätigkeiten, Weisen des Bezogenseins auf andere, aber auch einfach Erlebnisse – es – das Leben – „erfüllen",[11] ihm, wie man auch sagt, „Sinn" geben; anderenfalls erscheint es eben als „leer", „sinnlos". Es gibt Güter, die den negativen Gegenpart zu Übeln bilden, z. B. Freiheit gegenüber Freiheitsentzug, aber diejenigen Güter, die dem Leben Sinn geben – es sind wohl immer Verhaltensweisen –, sind nicht von dieser Art, sie haben eine andere Metrik. Ein Unterscheidungsmerkmal scheint zu sein, daß das, was dem Leben Sinn gibt, nie nur, aber immer auch von mir abhängt. Ich erlange z. B. ein Gut,

Freiheit, wenn ich aus dem Gefängnis entlassen werde, aber ob das meinem Leben Sinn geben wird, hängt davon ab, ob und was ich mit dieser Freiheit mache.

Was folgt daraus für Nagels These vom Eigenwert des Lebens? Erst einmal dasselbe wie vorher, nur mit diesem anderen Begriff. Während Nagel sagt, das Leben als solches sei emphatisch positiv, meine ich, daß das Leben als solches neutral ist, es ist an und für sich ohne Sinn, es kann mir ebensowohl als erfüllt wie auch als leer erscheinen, das aber hängt jetzt auch von mir ab: Ich kann ihm Sinn geben. Und wenn mir das nicht gelingt, finde ich das Leben häufig (nicht notwendigerweise, wie sich zeigen wird) unerträglich: Manche wollen dann lieber tot sein. Das soll natürlich nicht heißen, daß ich in dieser Sinngebung etwas aus nichts schüfe, frei nach Sartre. Wenn ich z. B., wie vorhin, aus dem Gefängnis entlassen werde, ist mir die Freiheit vorgegeben, aber das ist noch nicht an und für sich sinnvoll, und es ist uns natürlich sehr viel mehr vorgegeben, z. B. haben die meisten von uns zwei Beine, aber wir müssen sie in Bewegung setzen, und wir finden Menschen um uns vor und z. B. auch Musik und schöne Kunst usw., aber: usw. Wir befinden uns also in einer bestimmten, günstigeren oder ungünstigeren Umgebung und sind mit Dispositionen ausgestattet, in der Jugend meist mehr als im Alter, aber wir müssen die Dispositionen betätigen, und, wenn das in der Weise befriedigen soll, daß es das Leben erfüllt – und das muß es scheinbar, wenn wir das Leben nicht als leer empfinden sollen –, müssen wir sie in einer bestimmten Weise betätigen, aber wie, darauf ist wohl nicht generell zu antworten, weil es eine Frage ist, die sich jedem einzeln stellt.

Diese Kritik an Nagel verweist natürlich schon auf eine existenzphilosophische Auffassung. Aber bevor ich zu Heidegger zurückkehre, muß ich sagen, wie aus der jetzigen Perspektive Nagels Frage zu beantworten ist. So wie Nagel es darstellt, wäre der Tod schon an und für sich ein Übel, wie das Leben an und für sich ein Gut ist. Man müßte es dann auch vorziehen, daß das Leben gar kein Ende hätte. Daß dies erstens für Wesen, wie wir es sind, deren Bewußtsein im Unterschied zu dem von anderen Tieren auf das Leben selbst bezogen ist, attraktiv wäre, und daß dies zweitens, zeitlich, einem todlosen

Gedanken über den Tod

Leben (wenn wir denn die Option hätten) vorzuziehen wäre, ist zumindest umstritten;[12] es liegt eher nahe zu sagen, daß wir dann noch in der einen oder anderen Tätigkeit Sinn finden könnten; aber was wäre dazwischen? Hätte das *Leben* Sinn? Es scheint sich jedenfalls das, was ich anfangs nahelegte, zu bestätigen, nämlich daß wir uns nicht vor dem Tod im allgemeinen – daß wir einmal sterben werden – fürchten, sondern jeweils jetzt; das heißt: Es wäre jetzt ein Übel; aber warum? Nur weil man länger leben will? Vielleicht, aber nun nicht mit Nagels Begründung, denn das Leben ist nicht an und für sich ein Gut. Hingegen ließe sich jetzt sagen: Das Übel bestünde darin, daß ich jetzt durch den Tod die Chance – die letzte Chance – verliere, meinem Leben Sinn – oder mehr Sinn – zu geben. Das würde erklären, warum der baldige Tod uns erschreckt, warum wir einen Aufschub wollen. „Nur nicht jetzt, nur nicht in dieser Sinnlosigkeit sterben". Das gäbe zumindest eine Antwort auf die Frage, was am jetzt bevorstehenden Tod das Übel ausmacht. Ich sage nicht, daß es die einzige Antwort ist; sie enthielte aber zugleich eine Erklärung, wieso das Bevorstehen dieses Übels als Herausforderung erlebt wird.

Es ist diese Antwort, die zu Heidegger zurückführt. Es ist der Aspekt der Herausforderung, den er im Auge hat. Aber was bedeutet diese Herausforderung bei ihm, denn sie ist offenbar nicht einfach identisch mit dem, was sich eben zeigte? Bei Heidegger sieht es so aus, daß der Mensch, weil es ihm um sein eigenes Leben geht, Angst vor dem Tod hat, haben muß (wenn er nicht uneigentlich existiert), aber wir haben schon gesehen, daß das falsch ist. Diese Auffassung ist die Folge davon, daß Heidegger die Zweideutigkeit im Begriff des Worumwillens nicht gesehen hat und daß er den Wertwörtern ausweicht (Hamlets „ob es besser ist" ist bei ihm kein möglicher Gedanke). Er hätte sonst seine These so erläutern müssen, daß das Leben das höchste Gut ist, und wir haben eben in der Auseinandersetzung mit Nagel gesehen, daß das nicht stimmt: Das Leben ist nicht ein Gut, sondern es kann, teils durch glückliche Umstände, teils immer auch durch uns, Sinn gewinnen; kann, muß nicht. Die Erfahrung der Leere ist immer die andere Seite für ein Bewußtsein, das sich zeitlich zu seinem Leben verhält. Der eigentliche Kern von Heideggers Gedanke, daß das letzte Worumwillen jedes Menschen sein eigenes Leben ist,

ist, daß wir voluntativ nicht nur auf einzelne Inhalte bezogen sind, Zwecke und Tätigkeiten, sondern immer auch auf das eigene Leben, aber auf dies beides, das eigene Leben und die Inhalte, nicht nebeneinander, so daß wir auf das eine und auch auf das andere voluntativ bezogen wären, sondern – wie ich das in der Kritik an Nagel zu zeigen versuchte – so, daß wir durch die Inhalte (und natürlich nur durch sie) dem Leben Sinn geben können oder auch nicht. Es ist freilich nicht abzustreiten, so gibt Heidegger selbst zu, daß wir das Leben als solches vergessen und uns an die Inhalte, die begrenzten Zwecke, gewissermaßen verlieren können. Es ist das, was Heidegger mit dem Wort „Verfallen" meint. Wenn das aber eine offensichtliche Möglichkeit ist – wir gehen zumeist in isolierten Tätigkeiten, Zielsetzungen und der Vermeidung von Übeln auf –, dann stellt sich die Frage, ob die These von dem voluntativen Bezug auf das Leben als solches vielleicht nur eine philosophische Erfindung ist. Ist er überhaupt phänomenal ausweisbar? Darauf lautet Heideggers Antwort: gerade durch die Angst vor dem Tod. Wenn die Furcht vor dem Tod, wie es sich vorhin in der Kritik an Nagel nahelegte, so verstanden werden kann, daß ich angesichts der Möglichkeit des Nichtmehrseins davor erschrecke, daß mein Leben leer war – jetzt auch in dem Sinn, daß ich mich an belanglose Inhalte verloren habe –, dann heißt das, daß der Tod mich daran erinnert, daß ich nicht nur dies und das verfolge und befürchte, sondern eben – in all dem – *lebe.* Im Verhalten zum Tod – dem Ende meines *Lebens* – werde ich meines Lebens ansichtig.

Ich meine nun aber – in der Auseinandersetzung mit Nagel wurde es offensichtlich –, daß es nicht nur die Nähe des Todes ist, die uns auf das Leben als solches aufmerksam machen kann. Man kann hier auf die Verzweiflung hinweisen, so wie Kierkegaard sie beschreibt, das Verzweifeln am Leben, weil unsere begrenzten Ziele scheitern oder weil sie uns ausgehen; dann erscheint, gewissermaßen hinter den begrenzten Zielen, das Leben selbst, und dann stößt unser Wollen, wenn wir es so definiert haben, daß es sich an den begrenzten Zielen erschöpft, ins Leere. Das ist nicht die Leere des Todes, sondern des Lebens, und was uns unerträglich scheint, ist nicht der Tod, sondern das Leben; der Tod ist dann nicht das, was wir fürchten, sondern begehren. Der Überdruß angesichts der Sinnlosigkeit und die Erfahrung der Todesnähe sind also zwei gegensätzliche Möglichkeiten, die jedoch darin übereinkommen, daß wir in beiden mit dem Leben als solchen konfrontiert werden, im Gegensatz zu den begrenzten Zielen. Bei Heidegger klingt diese zweite Möglichkeit höchstens am Rande an (in *Sein und Zeit* kaum, in den Vorlesungen eher; man braucht das nicht nachzulesen, weil man es sich begrifflich klarmachen kann). Schon Heideggers massive Rede vom Nichts und der Angst vor dem Nichts, als ob alles am Leben, was als nichtig erfahren würde, ungefähr dasselbe wäre, hinderte ihn daran, diese zweite Möglichkeit in ihrer Gegensätzlichkeit zur ersten zu erkennen. Dabei ist nicht abzustreiten, daß sich die beiden Erfahrungen durchaus verbinden können. So ist bekannt, daß viele, die in Depression versunken sind und am liebsten sterben würden, wenn sie sich dann durch eine schwere Krankheit, z. B. einen Infarkt, wirklich in Todesnähe sehen, um jeden Preis leben wollen. Auch schließt die Depression nicht die Todesfurcht aus, ja es ist naheliegend, daß der Depressive, obwohl er sich den Tod wünscht, ihn gleichzeitig fürchtet, weil er nicht in dieser Verfassung – im Bewußtsein, am Leben vorbeigelebt zu haben – aufhören will.

Ich will mit alledem nicht leugnen, daß es auch Menschen gibt, oder besser gesagt Menschen in bestimmten Situationen, die sich den Tod weder wünschen noch ihn fürchten, und man sollte sie nicht, wie Heidegger es tut, in die Ecke der Uneigentlichkeit schieben, in die der Lebensvergessenheit. Es kann verschiedene Gründe geben, warum man den Tod nicht fürchtet und ihn doch nicht sucht, auf der einen Seite ein bestimmtes Gefühl von Sinninsuffizienz, auf der anderen gerade das Gefühl, erfüllt gelebt zu haben. Wer das Bewußtsein hat, sinnvoll gelebt zu haben, dürfte eigentlich, wenn das bisher Ausgeführte stimmt, wenn er ein bestimmtes Alter erreicht hat, keinen Grund mehr haben, sich vor dem Tod zu fürchten. Meine Frage war hier eher hypothetisch: Was am Tod ist es, was man fürchtet, *wenn* man ihn fürchtet? Einige Anworten scheinen mir falsch oder einseitig, und meine ist gewiß auch einseitig. Z. B. habe ich, Heidegger und Nagel folgend, das Soziale ganz herausgelassen. Man könnte mir entgegenhalten, der Tod sei ein viel komplexeres Phänomen, ein Knäuel von Problemen. Das ist gewiß richtig, aber wenn wir nicht im völlig Unbestimmten bleiben wollen, müssen wir – glaube ich – irgendwo anfangen, aber mit einer Lupe, und dann ergänzen. Worauf es mir ankam, war nicht so sehr, eine bestimmte Antwort zu geben, als einen Diskurs, der schon wenig Neues zu bieten schien, wieder in Gang zu bringen.

Zumindest eine Ergänzung ist schon auf Grund meiner eigenen Gedankenführung erforderlich. Auf die Ausgangsfrage, inwiefern – um mit Nagel zu sprechen – der Tod ein Übel ist, oder – unverfänglicher formuliert – warum wir ihn fürchten, fanden wir bei Heidegger gar keine Antwort, bei Nagel eine falsche. Die Frage, so zeigte sich, kann nur lauten: Warum fürchten wir, bald zu sterben? Das war das Ergebnis bereits der Auseinandersetzung mit dem chilenischen Alten. Ich habe als eine mögliche Antwort vorgeschlagen: weil wir durch den Tod die Chance verlieren, dem Leben einen Sinn zu geben oder mehr Sinn zu geben. Ich ließ aber offen, daß diese quasi existenzphilosophische Antwort nur eine mögliche ist. Ich bezweifle, daß sie dem chilenischen Alten eingeleuchtet hätte. Er hätte – so meine ich – gesagt, daß er lediglich weiterleben wolle. Aber warum, wenn doch die Übel im Alter die Güter überwiegen?

Ich werde nur auf einem Umweg zu einer Antwort kommen, indem ich zuerst die existenzphilosophische Antwort weiter kläre. Ein Begriff, den ich an zentraler Stelle verwendete und im unklaren ließ, war der der Sinngebung. Ich kann, was ich damit meine, etwa so erläutern (alle Klärungen, so erinnere man sich, sind vorläufig und können verbessert werden): Wenn wir auf der einen Seite selbstvergessen auf irgendeinen Zweck aus sind, erfüllt dieser unser Wollen, aber das bleibt isoliert; und was kommt danach? Wir stehen dann vor der Leere des Lebens; leer, weil unser Wollen nicht mehr oder nur partiell noch greifen kann. Wenn wir hingegen das Leben selbst bejahen können, und das kann immer nur durch Tätigkeiten und Zwecke oder Haltungen, Haltungen auch zu unserem Leiden, geschehen, geben wir dem Leben Sinn. Das Leben ist für mich sinnvoll, so möchte ich das quasi definieren, wenn ich mich einerseits nicht in den begrenzten Zwecken verliere, sondern mich auf das Leben selbst beziehe, und ich mir andererseits nicht, weil es mir leer erscheint, den Tod wünsche.

Gedanken über den Tod

Diese Definition ist freilich, bewußt, völlig formal. Gibt es Rezepte? Heidegger verneint das entschieden[13], und letztlich ist das gewiß richtig, nicht nur wegen der Verschiedenheit der Lebenssituationen, sondern weil es dem Umstand widerspräche, daß die Sinngebung nur als Akt der Freiheit verstanden werden kann. Aber wenigstens die formale Charakterisierung des Existenzproblems sollte möglichst angemessen erfolgen, und ich meine, daß es, so wie Heidegger es darstellt, verengt und mit unnötigen Merkwürdigkeiten belastet ist. Die einzige Aussage, die man bei Heidegger darüber findet, wie sich das Bewußtsein der Todesnähe auf das Leben auswirkt, ist, daß es „von der Verlorenheit in die zufällig sich andrängenden Möglichkeiten" befreie.[14] Das ist sicher eine Seite, aber Heidegger schreibt so, als stehe jeder immer vor einer Menge von Möglichkeiten – das ist sein Wort für die begrenzten Zwecke – und müsse nur wählen. Wieder zeigt sich, daß Heidegger die Situation der Leere, in der jemand wenigstens meint, keine Möglichkeiten zu haben, nicht berücksichtigt. Und dann spricht er so, als gelte es, die „eigenste" Möglichkeit zu wählen. Dieser Ausdruck: „eigenste Möglichkeit", schillert in *Sein und Zeit*. Erstens steht er für den Todesbezug selbst, und hier finde ich den Ausdruck einleuchtend – es handelt sich um etwas, worin jeder ganz auf sich zurückgeworfen, „unvertretbar" ist[15] –, aber dann, im folgenden Kapitel, verwendet Heidegger den Ausdruck auch inhaltlich, als ob es darauf ankäme, einen bestimmten ganz eigenen Weg zu finden. Durch dieses Insistieren auf Eigenstes und Eigentlichkeit gibt Heidegger seinem Gedanken eine sehr eigene Wendung, durch die das Problem, vor das wir uns wirklich angesichts des Todes gestellt sehen, schon in seiner formalen Fassung vereinseitigt wird.

Tolstoi hat in seiner Erzählung „Der Tod des Iwan Iljitsch" eine allgemeinere Formulierung gewählt, die ich angemessener finde. Heidegger erwähnt diese Erzählung nebenbei in einer Anmerkung[16], aber ich meine, daß das, was Heidegger über das Sein zum Tode sagt, lediglich der Versuch ist, das, was Tolstoi in der Form einer Erzählung beschrieben hat, begrifflich zu fassen – und Tolstoi gelang das ohne die Sophistereien, die sich bei Heidegger finden und von denen ich nur einige genannt habe.[17] Die Einsicht, zu der Iwan Iljitsch am Ende seiner Krankheit und seiner Todesangst kommt, ist:

Ich habe falsch gelebt, mein Wohlbefinden war Täuschung, ich habe nicht gelebt, wie ich gesollt hätte. Ich finde diese Antwort befriedigender, schon weil sie formaler und allgemeiner ist als Heideggers Rede von Möglichkeiten und einer eigensten. Sie scheint auch genau dem zu entsprechen, was ich vorhin meinte, als ich sagte: Ich habe am Leben vorbeigelebt. Heidegger war der Bezug auf ein Sollen offensichtlich unsympathisch, und man wird in der Tat vorsichtig sein müssen, wie das Wort hier zu verstehen ist. Hat Tolstoi es auf Gott bezogen? Er sagt das aber nicht. Und moralisch wird man es auch nicht verstehen können. Ich schlage vor, es so zu verstehen: Ich habe falsch gelebt, d. h. nicht so, wie ich gesollt hätte, wenn ich, wie ich gelebt habe, angesichts des Todes bedauere. Wieder bleibt die Antwort ganz formal, formaler als die Heideggers. Wir müssen nicht Angst vor dem Tod haben, aber wenn wir sie haben, haben wir sie – meine ich – davor. Aber auch diese Aussage scheint zu stark, denn viele Menschen würden mir widersprechen und mit meinem chilenischen Alten sagen: Nicht, weil sie bedauern, wie sie gelebt hätten, hätten sie Furcht vor dem Tod, sondern einfach, weil sie weiterleben wollten. Etwas fehlt also noch.

Ich bleibe gleichwohl noch einen Moment bei Tolstoi. Für ihn war die Begegnung mit dem Tod Anlaß zur Umkehr, jedoch keiner Umkehr, wie in der christlichen Tradition, zu einer Norm. Was man erlebt, ist vielmehr wie eine Verbindung eines Ausrufezeichens mit einem Fragezeichen. Das Beängstigende ist die Unbestimmtheit des Fragezeichens. In der Erzählung erscheint schließlich ein Licht, das die Angst löst. Das wirkt erst einmal wie ein *deus ex machina* und ist gewiß nicht verallgemeinerbar.

Schlicht verallgemeinerbar ist hier wohl nichts, aber lehrreicher erscheint mir, wie Tolstoi das Bewußtsein der Todesnähe in dem zwanzig Jahre früher geschriebenen Roman *Krieg und Frieden* darstellt. Als Fürst Andrej in der Schlacht von Austerlitz tödlich verwundet wird (er stirbt dann gleichwohl nicht), sieht er, nachdem er rücklings auf die Erde gefallen war, „nichts mehr über sich als den Himmel, den hohen Himmel, der jetzt nicht klar, aber doch unermeßlich hoch war, mit ruhig über ihn hingleitenden Wolken" (III, § 16). Der Hinweis auf die Wolken scheint mir deutlich zu machen, daß nicht der christliche Himmel gemeint ist, sondern unser wirklicher, der wahrnehmbare Himmel. „Wie ist es nur zugegangen", fragt sich Andrej, „daß ich diesen hohen Himmel früher nie gesehen habe?" „Ja, alles ist nichtig, alles ist Irrtum und Lüge", sagt er, ähnlich wie Iwan Iljitsch sein früheres Leben als Irrtum und Täuschung erkennt, alles „außer diesem unendlichen Himmel". In den kurzen Momenten, in denen ihm das Bewußtsein wiederkehrt, sieht er immer wieder diesen hohen Himmel, und als zufällig Napoleon, sein früheres Idol, heranreitet und ihn anspricht, würdigt er ihn keiner Antwort. Napoleon erscheint hier als der Inbegriff der begrenzten Ziele, wie groß auch immer sie einem erscheinen mögen. „In diesem Augenblick erschien ihm Napoleon als ein so kleiner, nichtiger Mensch im Vergleich mit alledem, was jetzt zwischen seiner Seele und diesem hohen, unendlichen Himmel mit den darüber hinlaufenden Wolken vorging" (III, § 19).

Es ist ein alter Topos, daß der Mensch angesichts des Todes sich seiner Geringfügigkeit und der Geringfügigkeit seiner Sorgen bewußt werden kann. Wie anders klingt das als die Frage nach der eigensten Möglichkeit. Die Maßstäbe werden zurechtgerückt. In diesem Sinn läßt sich jetzt auch das Licht der späteren Novelle und die dortige Rede von einem Sollen verstehen. Es zeigt sich etwas Offensichtliches, was nur verdrängt worden war. Im gewöhnlichen Leben und auch gerade in der Depression neigt jeder dazu, sich als Universum zu sehen, aber es ist ein Irrtum: Ich bin *in* der Welt, diese ist das Universum, und ich nur eine Partikel. Der Tod und schon das Altern enthalten die Chance, diesen Irrtum einzusehen und sich gewissermaßen innerhalb des Theaters auf die Seite zu stellen, aus dem Zentrum heraus. Im gewöhnlichen Leben liegt die Vorstellung nahe, daß mein Bewußtsein vielmehr das Theater ist, deswegen empfindet der Depressive diese Leere, obwohl doch das Theater der Welt, wenn man nicht gerade z. B. in einem Konzentrationslager ist, voller Leben ist. Und deswegen erscheint das Aufhören des Lebens, wenn ich es nicht sehe, nicht als ein im Theater Zurück- und schließlich aus ihm Heraustreten, sondern als Aufhören des Theaters selbst, so unvorstellbar, unvorstellbar im Sinn von schrecklich. Für denjenigen hingegen, der den Tod zum Anlaß nehmen kann, sich aus dem Zentrum zurückzunehmen, das Napoleonische abzustreifen, verändern sich die Gewichte. Er läßt sich los, indem er sich in die Welt zurück und in dieser an den Rand stellt. Das bedeutet nicht, daß er entschwebt (und etwa mit Gustav Mahler sagt „Ich bin der Welt abhanden gekommen"), sondern diese Positionsänderung kann auch zu einer Quelle der Sinngebung seiner konkreten Situation werden. Es ist das, was Fürst Andrej aufgehen wird, wenn er sechs Jahre später zum zweiten Mal, und diesmal endgültig, tödlich verwundet wird. So gesehen, legt der Tod auf die Frage, vor die er stellt, selbst eine Antwort nahe, aber es ist nicht leicht, sie zu ergreifen.

Warum nicht? Ich habe vorhin von einem Irrtum gesprochen, und man kann sagen, es ist ja wirklich ein Irrtum, sich als Zentrum der Welt zu sehen, aber es ist, darin muß man Nietzsche recht geben, ein Irrtum, ohne den kein Mensch und kein Lebewesen lebensfähig wäre. Wer sich selbst nicht über alles wichtig nimmt, ist nicht lebensfähig. Es ist das, was die Stoiker mit dem Begriff der *Oikeiosis* und Rousseau mit dem des *amour de soi* im Auge hatten. Als Säugling ist jeder allemal für sich das ganze Theater, das Universum. Im Erwachen und Wachsen des Realitätssinns spaltet sich das dann: Wir lernen, daß wir das Universum uns gegenüber haben und unsere Wünsche mit ihm in Einklang bringen müssen. Aber nach wie vor sind unsere Wünsche das für uns Ausschlaggebende, wir halten an diesem Mikrokosmos fest und wir würden unsere Lebensfähigkeit verlieren, wenn wir uns nicht gegen die Grenzen stemmten, die uns die Realität vorgibt. Jeder Weg hinauf, alle Kreativität, jeder Einsatz, aber wohl auch alles Obensein, alles Glück setzt diese Selbstzentriertheit voraus und impliziert das Risiko der Verzweiflung. Die Gelassenheit, das Sichloslassen ist nicht mehr Realitätssinn, denn in dieser Haltung stemmen wir uns nicht mehr nach außen und haben das Universum nicht mehr uns gegenüber, sondern treten in dieses zurück.

Die Rede von einem Irrtum, sich als Zentrum anzusehen, ist also nicht ganz richtig. Weil es ein Irrtum ist, haben wir die Möglichkeit, uns loszulassen und zurückzustellen. Aber weil dieser Irrtum die Bedingung des individuellen Lebens ist, läßt sich das nur als Grenzmöglichkeit verstehen. Mit der Geschichte des Fürsten Andrej ist gleichzeitig die Gegenmöglichkeit, das Am-Leben-Haften meines chilenischen Alten verständlich geworden. Beide Geschichten Tolstois enthalten eine Umkehr. Geschieht diese nicht, dann ist das Weiterlebenwollen um jeden Preis selbstverständlich – nicht, weil das Leben ein Gut ist, nicht weil die Güter die Übel überwiegen, sondern weil der Wille zur Selbsterhaltung die erste, grundlegende Komponente der *Oikeiosis,* des Sichwichtignehmens ist, und das ist auch der Grund, warum das Aufhören schrecklich erscheint, wenn man im Zentrum bleibt, d. h. selbst das Theater ist. Diese Reaktion ist jetzt verständlich, aber sie wirkt unter bestimmten Bedingungen irrational, sei es, daß man sich, z. B. im Alter, in einer Situation befindet, in der es außer auf Grund dieses Triebs nicht sinnvoll erscheint, am Leben zu haften, sei es, weil man etwas als schrecklich empfindet, was man nicht als schrecklich empfinden muß, *wenn* es den anderen Weg gibt, den des Fürsten Andrej. Man kann jetzt das mysteriöse „sollte", auf das wir in der anderen Geschichte gestoßen waren, so interpretieren, daß der, der sich dem Tod nahe sieht, es bedauern würde, wenn ihm die Entzentrierung nicht gelingt, wenn es ihm also nicht gelingt, mit dem Apostel Paulus, wenn auch nicht in seinem Sinn, auszurufen: „Tod, wo ist dein Stachel?" (Kor. I, 15,55)

Man könnte die Gelassenheit vielleicht ihrerseits unter den Realitätssinn subsumieren, weil sie sich besonders dann nahelegt, wenn das Festhalten als irrational erscheint, ähnlich wie wir ein Übermaß an Emotionen zu vermeiden versuchen, wo wir dieses als realitätsunangemessen erkennen, ohne deswegen die Emotionalität als solche zu verachten. Das führt schließlich zur Frage nach der anzustrebenden Ausgewogenheit zwischen Festhalten und Kämpfen einerseits und Loslassen andererseits. Denn um Ausgewogenheit scheint es sich doch handeln zu müssen. Die schlichte Lebensverneinung, wie der Buddha sie lehrte, wirkt ebenso fragwürdig wie die sture Selbstbehauptung. Das Loslassen, die Gelassenheit, ist im übrigen eine Haltung, die wir uns nicht nur dem Tod gegenüber wünschen, sondern in allem unseren Tun und Trachten, und doch wissen wir, daß die Gelassenheit, wenn sie nicht nur als Grenzmöglichkeit verstanden wird, zur Gleichgültigkeit und Apathie führen würde. So scheint unser Leben in einer Gratwanderung zwischen diesen gegensätzlichen Haltungen zu bestehen, deren Verlauf wohl jeder für sich finden muß, wobei der Kompaß, die Anzeige des Sichverirrens, vielleicht nur in dem vorhin genannten Bedauern besteht.

Aber, so könnte man fragen, sind hier nicht einfach eine Reihe von Lebensmöglichkeiten genannt worden, ohne daß klar wurde, welche Verbindlichkeit sie haben oder welche Grundlage, sei es in unserem Wesen, sei es in sonst etwas? Warum müssen wir uns denn z. B. nicht nur auf die begrenzten Ziele, sondern auch aufs Leben selbst beziehen? Und dann: Warum müssen wir, wenn auch nicht uneingeschränkt, Gelassenheit anstreben? Und schließlich: Warum müssen wir die eben angedeutete Ausgewogenheit anstreben? Diese Fragen sind nicht sinnvoll, das „warum müssen wir?" ist nicht sinnvoll; wir müssen nichts. Die Vorstellung der tradierten Philosophie, daß wir Haltungen einnehmen *müssen*, und dies, weil sie auf etwas *beruhen*, erscheint mir nicht sinnvoll. Philosophieren geschieht nicht in dritter Person, in der wir über etwas – und auch über andere und auch über mich selbst – beschreibend und erklärend reden, sondern in erster und zweiter Person, in der wir miteinander über willentliche Einstellungen, tradierte oder auch nicht-tradierte, sprechen – Einstellungen, die wir zu haben glauben oder die wir erstrebenswert finden. Indem wir sie in ihren Implikationen klären, erweisen sich einige als konfus, und es liegt dann nahe, sich von ihnen zu trennen, aber zwingend ist das nicht; sind sie klar, so können wir uns analytisch über ihre Implikationen verständigen, Implikationen, die uns gegebenenfalls so wenig behagen, daß wir uns auch von ihnen trennen wollen könnten; aber auch das ist nicht zwingend. Schließlich zeigen sich bei der Klärung andere Haltungen, die keine unerwünschten Implikationen zu haben scheinen (über das „scheinen" kommen wir ohnehin nie hinaus), und das kann dann dazu führen – aber wieder nicht zwingend –, daß wir sie als wirkliche Optionen unseres Wollens (aber nicht unbedingt als ausschließliche) ansehen. Alle Willenseinstellungen, die faktischen und die erstrebten, haben eine mehr oder weniger weitgehende und mehr oder weniger verstandene Grundlage, eine historische z. B. oder eine biologisch-anthropologische, aber die Frage, ob es und in wie weit es das eine oder das andere oder ein drittes ist, ist nicht sehr wichtig, weil die Fragen, vor die wir uns gestellt sehen, praktische Fragen sind: Fragen, wie wir leben wollen, nicht Fragen, wie wir sind oder woher wir kommen. Wir *wollen* im Lichte dessen, was wir zu sein glauben, und je besser wir verstehen, was wir sind, desto klarer unser Wollen; aber das Wollen würde aufhören, ein Wollen zu sein, wenn sich jemand einbildete, daß, weil wir so und so sind, wir so und so wollen müssen. Wir müssen etwas wollen nur relativ zu etwas anderem, was wir wollen.

Anmerkungen

1 Cf. *Phaidon* 64a.
2 H. Friedrich, *Montaigne*, Bern 1946, 6. Kap.
3 „The Macropoulos Case; Reflections on the Tedium of Immortality", in: B. Williams, *Problems of the Self*, Cambridge 1973, S. 82–100.
4 Abgedruckt in seinen *Mortal Questions*, Cambridge 1979 (dt. *Über das Leben, die Seele und den Tod*, Königstein Ts. 1984).
5 M. Heidegger, *Sein und Zeit*, Halle a. d. Saale 1927, S. 12.
6 Loc. cit., S. 84 u. ö.
7 Loc. cit., S. 285 f.
8 Loc. cit. (cf. Anm. 4), S. 16.
9 Ibid.
10 Loc. cit., S. 23.
11 Cf. *Wie sieht erfülltes Leben aus?*, ed. H. Weigel, Stuttgart u. Berlin 1976.
12 Cf. oben S. 489 und den Aufsatz von Bernard Williams, auf den in Anm. 3 verwiesen wurde.
13 Loc. cit. (cf. Anm. 5), S. 298.
14 Loc. cit., S. 264.
15 Loc. cit., S. 239 f., 263 f.
16 Loc. cit., S. 254 Anm.
17 Der in systematischer Hinsicht entscheidende Irrtum, der Heidegger im Todeskapitel unterlaufen ist – er macht die Absicht des ganzen Buches zunichte –, besteht darin, daß er glaubte, wenn er vom Tod als Möglichkeit spricht, „Möglichkeit" im existentialen Sinn verstehen zu können. Mit Möglichkeiten im existentialen Sinn meint Heidegger Seinsweisen des Daseins. Der Tod hingegen, der „jeden Augenblick möglich ist" (d. h. eintreffen kann), läßt sich natürlich nur als Ereignis verstehen, das Er-

eignis des Aufhörens meines Lebens, und das „Vorlaufen zum Tode" ist ein Sichverhalten *zu* diesem Ereignis. Um sich gegen diesen einfachen Tatbestand zu sperren, schreckte Heidegger nicht vor den abenteuerlichsten Sätzen zurück: „Das Zu-Ende-Sein besagt existential: Sein zum Ende" (S. 250). Die Hinzufügung des Wortes „existential" soll die magische Wirkung haben, das Ende als Sein zum Ende zu verstehen, während dieser Ausdruck doch seinen Sinn verliert, wenn man nicht zwischen dem Ende und dem „Sein zu" ihm unterscheidet. Dieselbe Verdrehung wiederholt sich in dem Satz: „Das mit dem Tod gemeinte Enden bedeutet kein Zu-Ende-Sein des Daseins, sondern ein Sein zum Ende dieses Seienden" (S. 243). Man kann so eine Definition nicht verbieten, muß sich aber im klaren sein, daß sie impliziert, daß wir immer, wenn wir uns zum Tod verhalten, am Sterben sind. Daß Heidegger das, was man normalerweise als Sterben versteht, demgegenüber als „Ableben" bezeichnet, wird man wohl nur noch als geschmacklos empfinden können. – Der strukturelle Fehler, der Heidegger hier unterlaufen ist, ist derselbe, den er im § 65 begeht, wenn er behauptet, die existentiale „Zu-Kunft" sei ursprünglicher als das Künftige, und den schlichten Tatbestand übersieht, daß jemand in der Weise dieser „Zu-Kunft" auf sich – sein Leben – nur zukommen kann, wenn vorausgesetzt ist, daß es eine zukünftige Ereignisfolge gibt (cf. meine *Philosophischen Aufsätze*, Frankfurt a. M. 1992, S. 131). Die Grundthese von *Sein und Zeit*, daß das existentiale Sein ursprünglicher sei, als was Heidegger „Vorhandenheit" nennt, scheitert also in gleicher Weise bei der Todesanalyse wie bei der allgemeinen Analyse der existentialen Zeitlichkeit. (Man kann, sobald man diese Fehler durchschaut hat, nur erstaunt mit dem Kopf schütteln.) – Weil der Tod nun einmal ein Ereignis ist, spreche ich im Text dauernd von Furcht vor dem Tod, wo Heidegger von Angst spricht. Wir haben Furcht vor dem Tod, also vor etwas. Gerade wenn man, wie Heidegger es tut, die Angst in der Weise terminologisch von der Furcht unterscheidet, daß die Angst keinen intentionalen Gegenstand hat, ist es sinnwidrig, von der Angst vor dem Tod zu sprechen. Bei einer laxeren Verwendung des Wortes „Angst", wie sie dem üblichen Sprachgebrauch entspricht, ist gegen diese Redeweise natürlich nichts einzuwenden.

V.

Perspektiven in Religion und Kultur

Prospects of Civilization

Wolfhart Pannenberg

Moral und Religion

Nach antikem Sprachgebrauch bezeichnet der Begriff *religio* die Gottesverehrung, sei es im Sinne des öffentlichen *cultus deorum*, sei es auch – sekundär – in der Gottesbeziehung des einzelnen, in Gebet und Kontemplation. Seit Augustin gehört dazu auch die Gotteserkenntnis, während diese zuvor eher als Voraussetzung der Gottesverehrung galt. Jedenfalls handelt es sich bei Religion immer um die Beziehung der Menschen zum Göttlichen. Der Begriff der Moral hingegen hat es mit den Beziehungen der Menschen untereinander zu tun, nämlich mit der von den Vorfahren überkommenen guten Sitte, die im Konsens über die in der Gesellschaft maßgebenden Verhaltensnormen ihren Ausdruck findet. Zu solcher guten Sitte kann auch gehören – und gehörte in der Antike zweifellos –, daß man die Götter ehrt. Umgekehrt kann mit der Gottesverehrung eine Verpflichtung auf Normen des gemeinsamen Lebens verbunden sein, sofern solche Normen im Willen der Gottheit gründen. Es gibt also von alters her Zusammenhänge zwischen Religion und Moral. Das gilt nicht zuletzt auch für das im Christentum begründete Kulturbewußtsein. Die Beachtung der Rechte und Bedürfnisse des Mitmenschen ist schon in der Prophetie Israels und erst recht in der Botschaft Jesu als Kriterium der Gerechtigkeit vor Gott geltend gemacht worden. Aber die Nächstenliebe hat auch wiederum ihren Grund und Maßstab in der Liebe Gottes zur Welt, die in der Sendung Jesu offenbar ist. Ohne ihren Grund in Gott verliert der Gedanke der Menschenliebe sein klares christliches Profil. So bleiben Gottesliebe und Nächstenliebe in der Botschaft Jesu bei aller engen Zusammengehörigkeit unterschieden, indem die erstere der letzteren vorgeordnet wird (Mk 12,29–31).

Erst in der europäischen Moderne wurde das Moralische als der Kern der Religion schlechthin angesehen. So geschah es nach dem Vorgang Herberts von Cherbury im Deismus des frühen 18. Jahrhunderts. Dabei wurde jedoch unbeschadet der Kenntnis der moralischen Grundnormen durch Vernunft und Gewissen und in Übereinstimmung mit der christlichen Naturrechtstradition der Zusammenhang der moralischen Normen mit Gott als ihrem Ursprung und als Garanten einer über dieses gegenwärtige Leben hinausreichenden Vergeltung für die guten und bösen Taten der Menschen festgehalten. Dieser Zusammenhang galt selber als Bestandteil der dem Menschen „natürlichen" Kenntnis von den moralischen Grundnormen durch Vernunft und Gewissen.

In diesem Sinne bestand noch für Rousseau ein Zusammenhang zwischen der Geltung der durch Vernunft und Gewissen bezeugten moralischen Normen und einem aus derselben Quelle stammenden Wissen von Gott. Er hat daher auch in seinem *Contrat social* 1762 ein Minimum religiöser Überzeugung unter dem Namen einer Zivilreligion für einen unentbehrlichen Bestandteil der bürgerlichen Verfassung gehalten. Die Religion läßt jeden Bürger „seine Pflichten liebgewinnen" und stellt ihm „ein zukünftiges Leben" mit „Belohnung der Gerechten und Bestrafung der Gottlosen" vor Augen (IV,8).

Ähnlich hat Kant 1781, in der *Kritik der reinen Vernunft*, das in der Vernunft begründete Bewußtsein des moralischen Gesetzes mit dem Glauben an Gott und an ein künftiges Leben verknüpft durch den Gedanken des höchsten Gutes, das der Mensch als Vernunftwesen erstreben müsse. Die in diesem Gedanken ausgedrückte Bindung des einem jeden Menschen als Naturwesen eigenen Strebens nach Glückseligkeit an die Bedingung moralischer Würdigkeit setzt einen gemeinsamen Ursprung der Naturordnung und der moralischen Ordnung in einer höchsten, der göttlichen Vernunft voraus.

> „Gott also und ein künftiges Leben sind zwei von der Verbindlichkeit, die uns reine Vernunft auferlegt, nach Prinzipien eben derselben Vernunft nicht zu trennende Voraussetzungen."[1]

Kant ging damals so weit zu erklären, ohne die Annahme des Daseins Gottes wäre die Vernunft „genötigt", „die moralischen Gesetze als leere Hirngespinste anzusehen" (ibid.). Durch die Bezeichnung der Annahme des Daseins Gottes als „Voraussetzung" der Verbindlichkeit des moralischen Gesetzes geriet Kant jedoch in Konflikt mit der von Anfang an und in seinen späteren moralphilosophischen Schriften zunehmend betonten Autonomie der Vernunft als Quelle des moralischen Bewußtseins und auch der aus dieser folgenden Verbindlichkeit des Sittengesetzes. Wenn solche Verbindlichkeit abhängig wäre von der Annahme des Daseins Gottes, dann schiene die Geltung des Sittengesetzes von einer heteronomen Bedingung abzuhängen. Zwar hatte Kant 1781 betont, es sei dieselbe Vernunft, die unserem Handeln das moralische Gesetz vorschreibt und zur Annahme des Daseins Gottes als Bedingung seiner Verbindlichkeit nötigt. Doch wenn das moralische Gesetz nur unter der Voraussetzung des Daseins Gottes verbindlich wäre, so müßte das Dasein Gottes schon anderweitig feststehen. Dagegen hat Kant in den folgenden Jahren mit zunehmender Entschiedenheit gelehrt, die Annahme des Daseins Gottes sei nur ein Postulat, das seinerseits auf die in der autonomen Vernunft wurzelnde Unbedingtheit des Sittengesetzes begründet ist. Von einer Bedingtheit der Verbindlichkeit des moralischen Gesetzes selber durch den Glauben an das Dasein Gottes war nun keine Rede mehr. Das hatte aber wiederum zur Folge, daß das Postulat des Daseins Gottes als ein dem moralischen Bewußtsein als solchem fremder und nur seiner Verbindung mit dem Streben nach Glückseligkeit dienender Gedanke erscheinen konnte, – also als Konzession an den von Kant sonst stets bekämpften Eudämonismus. Dieser Sachverhalt führte jedoch in der Diskussion über Kants Moralphilosopie nicht etwa zum Zweifel am Prinzip der Vernunftautonomie als alleiniger Quelle des moralischen Bewußtseins, sondern zur Preisgabe der auf sie begründeten Moraltheologie, weil man ja auf der Linie der späteren Argumentation Kants meinen konnte, die Verbindlichkeit des Moralgesetzes sei auch ohne Glauben an Gott, allein aus der autonom gebietenden Vernunft, gesichert.

Es braucht in diesem Zusammenhang nicht zu interessieren, daß in der auf Kant folgenden Entwicklung des Idealismus eine Erneuerung der philosophischen Theologie aus anderen als moralphilosophischen Gründen stattfand. Wichtig ist vielmehr, daß nach dem Niedergang der philosophischen Gotteslehren des Idealismus unter dem Eindruck der junghegelschen Kritik der Glaube an die Autonomie der Vernunft als Quelle des moralischen Bewußtseins bestehen blieb. Dieser Glaube wurde durch die psychologische Moralkritik Nietzsches in Frage gestellt, aber erst durch die von Freuds Psychoanalyse ausgegangenen Wirkungen nachhaltig erschüttert. Heute ist er im allgemeinen Kulturbewußtsein der säkularisierten westlichen Gesellschaften verfallen. Das gilt auch für die philosophische Ethikdiskussion. Zwar gibt es immer noch Kantianer, die die Autonomie der Vernunft als Quelle eines verbindlichen moralischen Normbewußtseins behaupten, aber charakteristisch für die gegenwärtige Diskussionslage ist wohl eher G. E. Moore geworden, der in seinen *Principia Ethica* moralische Urteile auf rational nicht beweisbare „Intuitionen" zurückführte. Das bedeutete in der Konsequenz, wie Charles Stevenson es 1964 in seinem Buch *Ethics and Language* behauptet hat, daß die Entscheidung für ethische Normen letztlich emotional, nicht rational begründet ist. Die am Einfluß solcher Positionen erkennbare Krise der philosophischen Ethikdiskussion ist 1981 von Alasdair MacIntyre in seinem vielbeachteten Buch *After Virtue. A Study in Moral Philosophy* beschrieben worden.

Die Auflösung des Prinzips der Vernunftautonomie als vermeintlich für sich allein hinreichenden Ursprung eines allgemein gültigen und für jeden einzelnen verbindlichen moralischen Normbewußtseins bedeutet nicht die Verabschiedung der Vernunft als Quelle der Kenntnis von den Grundbedingungen menschlichen Zusammenlebens. Die Formulierung solcher Grundbedingungen kann man als den Gegenstand der Naturrechtslehren betrachten, deren Tradition im Hintergrund auch der Bemühungen Kants um eine Begründung der Ethik aus einem kategorischen Imperativ der Vernunft stand. In den Naturrechtssätzen bekundet sich ein Bewußtsein davon, daß jede Gemeinschaft von Menschen darauf angewiesen ist, daß im Zusammenleben ihrer Glieder Regeln der Gegenseitigkeit beachtet werden, deren allgemeine Form in der „goldenen Regel" ausgedrückt ist: „Was du nicht willst, daß man dir tu, das füg' auch keinem andern zu", oder in der positiven Formulierung Jesu: „Alles was ihr wollt, daß euch die Menschen tun, das tut auch ihr ihnen" (Lk 6,31; Mt 7,12). Diese in den Rechtstraditionen der Völker weit verbreitete Regel der Gegenseitigkeit liegt spezielleren Naturrechtssätzen zugrunde wie dem Imperativ *neminem laede* oder der Vorschrift *pacta sunt servanda*. Ihr ist auch die Universalisierungsforderung von Kants kategorischem Imperativ verwandt; denn die Maxime des eigenen Verhaltens als allgemeines Gesetz zu wollen schließt auch die Gegenseitigkeit ein, – allerdings nur unter der zusätzlichen Bedingung, daß Subjekt und Gegenstand der Tätigkeit beide auf den allgemeinen Begriff des Menschen überhaupt bezogen werden. Eine Maxime, die sich nur auf die Behandlung einer bestimmten Kategorie von Menschen (z. B. Kapitalisten, Schwarze oder Juden) bezieht, schließt auch als allgemeines Gesetz gedacht die Gegenseitigkeit nicht ein. Andererseits erstreckt sich die Forderung nach Universalisierbarkeit der Handlungsmaxime auch auf viele Handlungen, bei denen der Gesichtspunkt der Gegenseitigkeit keine Rolle spielt, wie schon Kants Beispiele in der Grundlegung zur Metaphysik der Sitten zeigen. Vor allem aber implizieren die Naturrechtssätze noch nicht die Motivation für den einzelnen, sich ihnen entsprechend zu verhalten, während der kategorische Imperativ als Gebot der Vernunft auch die Achtung für seine Forderung beim einzelnen Menschen begründen soll. Im Unterschied zum kategorischen Imperativ lassen die Naturrechtssätze die Frage nach der subjektiven Nötigung zu sittlichem Handeln offen. Gerade darum bleibt ihre Evidenz unberührt von der gegenwärtigen Krise des ethischen Bewußtseins, weil diese ihren Brennpunkt in der Frage nach der individuellen Verbindlichkeit moralischer Normen hat. Man kann sehr wohl einsehen, daß der Fortbestand einer Gemeinschaft an der Einhaltung gewisser Regeln durch alle, zumindest aber durch die Mehrheit ihrer Glieder hängt, dennoch aber für das eigene Verhalten eine Ausnahme beanspruchen. Das gilt auch dann, wenn, wie im Fall des Schwarzfahrers, der Handelnde selber von der Befolgung der Regel durch die andern profitiert, was allerdings auf die Dauer nur unter der Bedingung möglich ist, daß die eigene Abweichung von der Norm möglichst unbemerkt bleibt.

Für die ethische Argumentation genügt es nicht, allgemeine Handlungsnormen zu formulieren, die als Bedingungen für den Bestand der Gemeinschaft ausgewiesen werden. Vielmehr ist es erforderlich, den Begriff dessen, was für das Individuum gut ist, mit dem des allgemeinen Besten zu verbinden. Das hat in klassischer Weise die sokratisch-platonische Ethik geleistet. Dabei geht es keineswegs nur um das „Glück" des Individuums und dessen Vereinbarkeit mit der allgemeinen Regel der Vernunft. Der Begriff des Guten selber, der das wahre Glück jedes einzelnen Menschen durch Teilhabe an ihm allererst begründet, hat eine auf das je Individuelle und Besondere sich erstreckende Dimension, und das gemeinsam Gute kann gar nicht bestehen, ohne die je besondere Bestimmung der Individuen in sich zu integrieren. Umgekehrt erlangt der einzelne das für ihn oder sie wahrhaft Gute nur unter der Bedingung der Zusammenstimmung mit dem gemeinsam Guten. Das ist nirgends klarer als im christlichen Platonismus Augustins zum Ausdruck gekommen, der Gott als das höchste Gut des einzelnen, zugleich aber auch als Ursprung des gemeinsam Guten, der gerechten Ordnung des gemeinsamen Lebens erkennen lehrte.

Nach beiden Seiten hin hängen Moral und Religion zusammen. Durch Religion sind die moralischen Verhaltensregeln in der Tiefe der Gesinnung des einzelnen verankert, wird der einzelne also dazu motiviert, sich ihnen entsprechend zu verhalten. Das aber ist darum so, weil die moralische Ordnung des gemeinsamen Lebens letztlich in Gott, der die Gemeinschaft der Menschen will, begründet ist.

Gegen die Annahme eines so engen Zusammenhangs von Religion und Moral erheben sich allerdings eine Reihe von Bedenken. An erster Stelle steht ihr die selbständige, rein rationale Begründbarkeit der moralischen Normen entgegen. Sie gilt auch in der gegenwärtigen Krise der Ethik trotz aller Zweifel an der subjektiven Verbindlichkeit moralischer Normen weiterhin für die Erkenntnis der Grundbedingungen menschlicher Gemeinschaft, wie sie aus der Regel der Gegenseitigkeit folgen und in den Sätzen der Naturrechtstradition ihren Ausdruck gefunden haben, unbeschadet aller Zeitbedingtheit ihrer Formulierung. Die gegenwärtige Krise der Ethik bezieht sich ja erst in zweiter Linie auf die Inhalte dieser Regeln, vorrangig hingegen auf ihre subjektive Verbindlichkeit für das Verhalten der Individuen. Das bedeutet allerdings, daß die rationale Evidenz solcher Regeln noch nicht viel über den moralischen Zustand einer konkreten Gesellschaft aussagt. Die Frage nach der subjektiven Motivation, sich solchen Regeln entsprechend zu verhalten, bleibt also bestehen. Soweit religiöse Motivation diese Lücke füllt, geschieht das in der Überzeugung, daß der Gott des Glaubens die Gemeinschaft der Menschen in der Gegenseitigkeit eines Zusammenlebens nach Regeln der Gerechtigkeit will. Dabei ist das auf den Glauben an Gott begründete Bewußtsein der Regeln eines gemeinsamen Lebens inhaltlich nicht verschieden von der Erkenntnis der Bedingungen dafür durch die Vernunft. Nur weiß der Glaubende eben, daß Gott menschliche Gemeinschaft in Gerechtigkeit und Frieden will, so daß auch der Glaubende selber sich für die Bewahrung oder Herstellung der Bedingungen solcher Gemeinschaft einsetzt.

Die inhaltliche Identität des göttlichen Rechtswillens mit den der Vernunft erkennbaren Regeln eines gemeinsamen Lebens in gegenseitiger Verläßlichkeit macht auch verständlich, was sonst als ein weiteres Bedenken gegen die Behauptung eines engen Zusammenhangs ② von Religion und Moral geltend zu machen wäre: Das ist die Tatsache, daß viele Menschen sich moralisch untadelig verhalten, obwohl sie dem religiösen Glauben distanziert gegenüberstehen. Wenn jedoch die Motivation zu solchem Verhalten noch nicht durch die bloße Einsicht in die Bedeutung von Regeln der Gegenseitigkeit für das gedeihliche Zusammenleben der Menschen erklärt ist, so bleibt die Möglichkeit offen, daß der moralisch Handelnde trotz aller Distanzierung von den Lehren und Riten traditioneller Religion doch immer noch stärker von ihren moralischen Impulsen bestimmt ist, als es ihm selber bewußt wird. Oder die Motivation zu moralischem Handeln entspricht einfach dem Motiv des Wohlwollens gegenüber andern. Dieses Motiv bedarf keiner Begründung oder Rechtfertigung. Doch wenn sich der Handelnde dessen zu vergewissern sucht, warum er sich eigentlich von Motiven des Wohlwollens bestimmen läßt, dann führen solche Erwägungen wieder sehr schnell in den Bereich der religiösen Thematik des Lebens und der Lebensführung.

Ein drittes Bedenken, das sich heute der Behauptung eines engen ③ Zusammenhangs zwischen Moral und Religion entgegenstellt, ergibt sich aus der Tatsache zunehmender Entfremdung von der Religion in der Bevölkerung säkularisierter Staaten. Der christliche Glaube hat nicht mehr genügend Einfluß auf das Verhalten der Menschen, um bei allen oder der großen Mehrzahl von ihnen moralisches Verhalten zu motivieren.

Damit wiederholt sich, so könnte es scheinen, ein Problem, das sich schon in der frühen Neuzeit erhob, nach den Religionskriegen im Gefolge von Reformation und Gegenreformation. Damals war es die konfessionelle Zerstrittenheit, die den christlichen Glauben ungeeignet erscheinen ließ als Basis des gesellschaftlichen Konsenses und Friedens. Man suchte daher die Grundlagen des gesellschaftlichen Zusammenhalts neu zu bestimmen auf dem Boden der allen Menschen gemeinsamen Natur und Vernunft. Dazu gehörte für die Aufklärung auch die Allgemeinheit der Moral im Unterschied zur Partikularität der religiösen Bekenntnisse. Bedurfte die Moral für ihre Wirksamkeit noch der Ergänzung durch Religion, so doch nur durch die ebenfalls aus der Vernunft begründete und insofern dem Menschen „natürliche" Religion des Glaubens an einen Gott und an eine künftige Vergeltung für die Taten der Menschen. In dieser Situation verstand sich der Anspruch des Christentums auf allgemeine Wahrheit für alle Menschen nicht mehr von selbst. Es lag nahe, ihn theologisch dadurch zu rechtfertigen, daß das Christentum selber moralisch oder doch im Hinblick auf seine ethische Relevanz ausgelegt wurde. Insofern kann man die Aufklärung und die von ihr ausgehende Moderne als „das ethische Zeitalter des Christentums" bezeichnen, wie Trutz Rendtorff das im Anschluß an Ernst Troeltsch getan hat.[2] Dieses Zeitalter ist heute vorbei, weil das Bewußtsein moralischer Verbindlichkeit in der individuellen Lebensführung ebenso wie in der Theoriediskussion der Ethik in Verfall geraten ist. Ethikkommissionen und globale Forderungen nach Gerechtigkeit – als ob man sich einig wäre, worin diese besteht – und nach einem Weltethos können das nicht verdecken. Sie sind mehr Ausdruck des an dieser Stelle gefühlten Mangels, als daß sie ihn beheben könnten. Aber kann religiöse Motivation diesen Mangel ausfüllen? Das mag zwar im individuellen Fall geschehen, vielleicht auch immer noch mehr oder weniger häufig. Im Hinblick auf die Gesamtsituation der modernen Gesellschaften in der Phase fortgeschrittener Säkularisierung ist das jedoch eher unwahrscheinlich.

Moral und Religion

Nach den Religionskriegen der frühen Neuzeit stand die Partikularität des religiösen Bekenntnisses, aber mehr noch die Konfliktträchtigkeit der intoleranten Wahrheitsansprüche der christlichen Konfessionen gegeneinander dem gesellschaftlichen Frieden im Wege, so daß die moralischen Grundlagen des gemeinsamen Lebens vom Streit der Konfessionen abgelöst werden mußten. Heute, im ökumenischen Zeitalter der Christenheit, ist zwar die Intoleranz geschwunden, aber im Schwinden ist wegen der fortgeschrittenen Säkularisierung auch der Einfluß der Religion auf die moralische Lebensführung der Menschen. Hinzu kommt, daß in den Kirchen selber der ethische Konsens in Frage gestellt wird. Der Liebesgedanke Jesu wird von seiner theologischen Basis (im Gebot der Gottesliebe) abgelöst, und er wird damit entleert und mißbraucht zur Vergleichgültigung moralischer Unterscheidungen im Sinne eines *anything goes*. So schlägt die Auflösung moralischer Verbindlichkeiten im allgemeinen Bewußtsein auf die Kirche zurück und am stärksten dort, wo zuvor das Christentum auf Ethik konzentriert und reduziert worden ist.

Die Erneuerung des moralischen Bewußtseins in den Kirchen selber muß ihren Ausgangspunkt vom Glaubensbewußtsein nehmen, aus der Besinnung auf den biblischen Gott der Erwählung, der nicht nur einzelne, sondern ein Volk erwählt und darum in den zehn Geboten die Grundbedingungen der Gemeinschaft im menschlichen Zusammenleben – die auch das Naturrecht zu formulieren suchte – durch seine Autorität den Individuen verbindlich macht. Auch Jesu Auslegung der Gesetzesüberlieferung vom Gedanken der Liebe Gottes her, an der teilzunehmen die Menschen berufen sind, hat ihren Ausgangspunkt in der Partikularität jüdischen Gottesglaubens und insofern auch im kommunitaristischen Ansatz jüdischer Ethik, obwohl dieser ausgeweitet wird im Sinne des jüdischen Schöpfungsglaubens auf das Verhältnis zu allen Menschen, auch außerhalb des Gottesvolks: Gott respektieren heißt immer auch: die Mitmenschen respektieren.

Die moralische Relevanz der Religion äußert sich nicht in erster Linie durch öffentliche Erklärungen der Kirchen zu moralischen Fragen, zumal der Zerfall des moralischen Konsenses in den Kirchen leicht dazu führt, daß solche Erklärungen gerade an entscheidenden

523

Punkten undeutlich werden. Die moralische Relevanz des Glaubens sollte ihren Ausdruck vor allem im individuellen Verhalten der Christen im alltäglichen Zusammenleben der Menschen finden, besonders auch dadurch, daß Christen der Welt einen anderen Lebensstil vorleben als das, was in der heutigen Medienlandschaft für zeitgemäß gilt. Man sollte sich heute daran erinnern, daß die Anziehungskraft der christlichen Gemeinschaft in den ersten Jahrhunderten der Kirche, im Zeitalter der Verfolgungen, außer dem Bekenntnismut der Märtyrer auch darauf beruhte, daß die Gemeinschaft der Christen sich inmitten einer moralisch verkommenen Gesellschaft durch die Treue zu festen Maßstäben der Lebensführung auszeichnete.

Angesichts des schwindenden Einflusses der Religion auf das Verhalten der Menschen, sogar auch innerhalb der Kirchen, ist es heute fraglich, ob im gegenwärtigen Zeitalter eines Zerfalls moralischer Verbindlichkeit die religiöse Motivation den Mangel an rationaler Evidenz überkommener Verhaltensregeln für das Verhalten der Individuen ausgleichen kann. Und dennoch bleibt richtig, mit Iwan Karamasow zu sprechen, daß ohne den Glauben an Gott „alles erlaubt" ist. Der Versuch, das Bewußtsein moralischer Verbindlichkeit auf die bloße Autonomie der Vernunft zu gründen, ist gescheitert. Sein Scheitern sprach Max Horkheimer 1970 mit der Feststellung aus, alles, was mit Moral zusammenhängt, gehe „letzten Endes auf Theologie zurück; alle Moral, zumindest in den westlichen Ländern, gründet in der Theologie".[3] Wenn das richtig ist, dann hat der Versuch, die Moral statt dessen allein auf die Vernunft zu gründen, selber schon zum Zerfall der Moral beigetragen.

Das heißt nun allerdings nicht, daß Fragen der Moral und ihrer Begründung nur die Theologie und die positive Religion etwas angingen. Moralische Regeln der Gegenseitigkeit in den menschlichen Beziehungen sind für alle Glieder einer Gesellschaft wichtig, quer zu allen Unterschieden zwischen ihnen, auch zu Unterschieden des religiösen Bekenntnisses. Entsprechendes gilt aber auch im Außenverhältnis zu Gliedern anderer Gesellschaften. Moralisches Bewußtsein sollte daher nicht nur beinhalten, wie „man" sich in einer konkreten Gesellschaft verhält und was man dort nicht tut, sondern zumindest eine Offenheit auf das allgemein Menschliche hin haben. Die Beziehung auf das allgemein Menschliche ist für das ethische Bewußtsein der kulturellen Überlieferung in Europa sogar konstitutiv, schon von seinen Ursprüngen im griechischen Denken her. Das gilt auch für den religiösen Aspekt der Moral. Er ist in der jüdisch-christlichen Tradition primär durch die Beziehung zum Schöpfergott gegeben, der der Schöpfer aller Menschen ist, auch derer, die nicht zur eignen religiösen Gemeinschaft gehören. Wie der biblische Schöpfungsglaube in der Geschichte des Christentums die Verbindung mit dem philosophischen Monotheismus erlaubte und sogar erforderlich machte, wenn der Gott der Bibel als der eine Gott aller Menschen verkündet werden sollte, so nötigte er auch zur Aneignung der philosophischen Ethik und der Naturrechtslehren im christlichen Denken: Wie jeder Mensch als Geschöpf des einen Gottes immer schon in seiner Existenz auf diesen Gott bezogen ist, ob er nun darum weiß oder nicht, so ist er auch immer schon von ihm her in Anspruch genommen für den Willen Gottes zur Gemeinschaft der Menschen miteinander. Die religiöse Begründung der Moral bildet daher, recht verstanden, keine Alternative zur philosophischen Frage nach dem Guten auf dem Boden des allgemein Menschlichen. Andererseits ist die philosophische Frage nach dem Guten als Frage nach der Bestimmung des Menschen seit Platon immer schon mit dem Gedanken Gottes als des Einen Guten verknüpft.

Die Wahrnehmung der göttlichen Wirklichkeit in der Autorität des Guten ist nicht nur Sache der Offenbarungstheologie, sondern auch der Philosophie. Mit diesem Sachverhalt angemessen umzugehen, erfordert freilich eine philosophische Vernunft, die sich selber nicht als verschlossen gegen die Transzendenz des Göttlichen begreift, sondern als in ihrer Freiheit immer schon durch sie konstituiert. Das Dasein Gottes wird dann nicht als etwas Zusätzliches zur Autonomie dieser Vernunft erscheinen können, als Gegenstand eines Postulates dieser Vernunft zur Bewältigung eines Folgeproblems des moralischen Bewußtseins. Der in der Erfahrung sich aufdrängende Mangel an Übereinstimmung zwischen dem Ergehen der Individuen und dem Grade ihrer moralischen Würdigkeit steht gar nicht im Zentrum des Zusammenhangs von Moral und Religion. Schon bei Rousseau ist der Gesichtspunkt jenseitiger Strafen oder Belohnungen als Motivation moralischen Verhaltens in der Gegenwart ungebührlich in den Vordergrund gerückt worden. Im Mittelpunkt der Frage nach dem Verhältnis von Moral und Religion muß vielmehr die Erfahrung der Autorität des Guten selber stehen.[4] Solche Erfahrung ist eng verbunden mit der Frage nach der Bestimmung des Menschen, also danach, was seine Identität konstituiert und ausmacht, seine Identität als dieser Mensch, aber darin doch immer zugleich als Mensch überhaupt. An dieser Stelle liegen die Wurzeln des moralischen Bewußtseins und auch seines Zusammenhangs mit dem Thema der Religion.

Die Allgemeinheit dieses Zusammenhangs zwischen Religion und moralischer Bestimmung des Menschen wird leicht verdunkelt, wenn er nur von seiten der Offenbarungsreligion und ihrer Theologie geltend gemacht wird. Daher ist es wichtig, daß er immer wieder auch Thema philosophischer Ethik wird: Das höchste Gut für den Menschen ist Gott und die Gemeinschaft mit ihm. Die Harmonie zwischen moralischer Würdigkeit und Glückseligkeit ist nur eine der Folgerungen daraus, und zwar eine der entfernteren, denn die ethisch nächste Folgerung aus der Gemeinschaft mit Gott ist die Teilnahme an der Bewegung seiner Liebe zu seinen Geschöpfen, also die Moralität selber.

Anmerkungen

1 *Kritik der reinen Vernunft* A 811.
2 T. Rendtorff: *Theorie des Christentums. Historisch-theologische Studien zu seiner neuzeitlichen Verfassung,* Gütersloh 1972, S. 152. Cf. vom Vf.: *Grundlagen der Ethik. Philosophisch-theologische Perspektiven,* Göttingen 1996, S. 10 sowie 13 f.
3 M. Horkheimer: *Die Sehnsucht nach dem ganz Anderen. Ein Interview mit Kommentar von Helmut Gumnior,* Hamburg 1970, S. 61.
4 Diese Formulierung setzt voraus, daß das Gute nicht mit Kant auf eine Eigenschaft des Willens reduziert, sondern mit Platon dem Willen vorgeordnet wird als das zu Erstrebende.

Robert Spaemann

Gottesbeweise nach Nietzsche

> Ich fürchte, wir werden Gott nicht los,
> weil wir noch an die Grammatik glauben.
> Fr. Nietzsche, *Götzendämmerung*[1]

In Nietzsche kommt die *via moderna* – d. h. der Nominalismus – zur Vollendung und zum vollen Selbstbewußtsein. Was uns hinsichtlich des Gedankens eines Gottesbeweises trennt von den *quinque viae* des hl. Thomas, ist das Mißtrauen, der Zweifel an der Leistungsfähigkeit unserer Wörter und unserer Grammatik, an der Reichweite unseres Denkens. Denken, verstanden als Herrschaft, als Funktion der Selbstbehauptung, kann nicht zugleich das Sich-Zeigen dessen sein, was ist. Insofern Wissen Macht ist, gilt, was Michel Foucault so ausdrückte:

> „Wir müssen uns nicht einbilden, daß uns die Welt ein lesbares Gesicht zuwendet, welches wir nur zu entziffern haben. Die Welt ist kein Komplize unserer Erkenntnis."[2]

Sollten wir uns genötigt fühlen, einen ersten unbewegten Beweger zu denken, dann haben wir jedenfalls gelernt, diese Nötigung als eine Idiosynkrasie unseres Denkvermögens zu betrachten, das uns, wenn es außerhalb seiner pragmatischen Bestimmung gebraucht wird, zudem in Antinomien verwickelt. Der Gottesbeweis aus der Teleologie natürlicher Prozesse war selbst wohl das wirksamste Instrument zur Zerstörung seiner eigenen Voraussetzung: des teleologischen Denkens.[3] Wenn nämlich finale Prozesse dem Flug des Pfeils zu vergleichen sind, der ins Ziel fliegt, weil ein intelligentes Wesen ihn abgeschossen hat, dann muß man doch bedenken: Das *telos* ist nicht im Pfeil, sondern im Schützen. Thomas von Aquin, der dieses Bild benutzt, hat es noch *cum grano salis* verstanden. Gott als Schöpfer unterscheidet sich von irdischen Herstellern dadurch, daß er Dinge erschaffen kann, die selbst „auf etwas aus sind". Aber im Unterschied zu Aristoteles war er der Überzeugung, daß so etwas wie Aus-sein-auf doch nur gedacht werden kann, wenn es letzten Endes aus einem Bewußtsein hervorgeht. Und so nahm das Schicksal dieser Metapher seinen Lauf bis hin zu Johannes Buridan. Die Welt wird zur Maschine, die mechanisch funktioniert, also, wie die heutigen Biologen sagen, „teleonomisch". Daß so etwas wie ein *telos* nur in einem Bewußtsein sein könne, ist zum anti-aristotelischen Gemeinplatz geworden.[4] Teleonomisch strukturierte Prozesse aber bedürfen nicht mehr eines göttlichen Ingenieurs, sondern nur eines menschlichen Betrachters, für den sie so aussehen, als wären sie auf etwas aus. Wenn allerdings dieser menschliche Betrachter das Gerichtetsein seines eigenen Blicks auch nur als ein „Als ob" versteht, bricht alles Verstehen zusammen.

Der Anti-Teleologismus glaubte, mit der *causa efficiens* auszukommen. Zu diesem Zweck mußte die Regelmäßigkeit der Ursache-Folge-Beziehung, die bisher als Argument für Finalität galt, in den Begriff der Kausalursache hineindefiniert werden. Ein Ereignis B ist dann Wirkung eines Ereignisses A, wenn es auf dieses „nach einer Regel folgt", wie es bei Kant heißt. Am Ende verdrängte dann der Begriff der Regel, also des Naturgesetzes, auch den der Ursache. Die Kausalursache wird, wie zuvor das *telos*, als Anthropomorphismus entlarvt und fällt Ockhams Razor zum Opfer, – bei Nietzsche ebenso wie bei Bertrand Russell.[5] Damit spätestens aber war es natürlich auch um den Beweis der Existenz einer ersten Ursache geschehen. Denn diese ist gewiß nicht etwas, worauf etwas anderes „nach einer Regel folgt". Dabei ist zu bedenken, daß in unserem „normalen" Verständnis der Begriff einer Regelmäßigkeit in dem der Ursache nach wie vor gar nicht enthalten ist.

Die Skepsis bezüglich der Reichweite unserer Vernunft, die die *quinque viae* des hl. Thomas zu Fall brachte, hatte Thomas seinerseits schon ins Spiel gebracht gegen Anselms ontologisches Argument.[6] Aus einem bloßen Begriff kann, so war sein Einwand, niemals auf Existenz geschlossen werden, auch dann nicht, wenn Existenz zur Definition des Begriffs gehört. Ein solcher Schluß wäre nur dann möglich, wenn unserem Begriff eine wirkliche Einsicht in das Wesen Gottes zugrunde läge. Und eben dies ist nach Thomas nicht der Fall. Er spricht von der „debilitas nostri intellectus", der sich gegenüber dem „notum per se simpliciter" verhält wie das Auge des Nachtvogels zur Sonne. Er kann das Wesen Gottes nicht schauen, sondern nur von den Wirkungen auf die Ursache schließen. Kant aber hat gezeigt, daß alle von der Erfahrung ausgehenden Gottesbeweise, also vor allem der physiko-theologische, allenfalls auf einen oder mehrere Weltbaumeister schließen lassen, Baumeister, die selbst Teile des Universums sind. Wo diese Beweise darüber hinaus einen Schöpfer der endlichen Wirklichkeit selbst beweisen wollen, setzen sie sämtlich den ontologischen Beweis voraus, als den „einzig möglichen", falls es überhaupt Gottesbeweise geben könnte.[7]

Dennoch billigte Kant der spekulativen Vernunft die Fähigkeit zu, einen adäquaten Gottesbegriff als „fehlerfreies Ideal" bilden zu können, einen Begriff, „welcher die ganze menschliche Erkenntnis schließt und krönet", während es der praktischen Vernunft, also der „Moraltheologie" vorbehalten bleibt, für diesen Begriff „objektive Realität" zu postulieren.[8]

Eben hier aber setzt Nietzsches Kritik an. Wenn es ohnehin nur nützliche oder schädliche Irrtümer gibt, dann ist ein Irrtum, so schreibt er, erst dann widerlegt, wenn seine Entstehung aufgeklärt und das Interesse, das ihn hervorgebracht hat, als schädlich diskreditiert ist – und zwar als schädlich für die menschliche Rasse als ganze, nicht unbedingt schädlich für bestimmte Individuen.

> „Die Frage der bloßen Wahrheit des Christentums – sei es in Hinsicht auf die Existenz seines Gottes, oder die Geschichtlichkeit seiner Entstehungslegende [...] – ist eine ganz nebensächliche Angelegenheit, solange die Wertfrage der christlichen Moral nicht berührt ist. [...] Es gibt Schlupfwinkel für das Problem der Wahrheit, und die Gläubigsten können zuletzt sich der Logik der Ungläubigsten bedienen, um sich ein Recht zu schaffen, gewisse Dinge als unwiderlegbar zu affirmieren, nämlich als Jenseits der Mittel aller Widerlegung. (Dieser Kunstgriff heißt sich heute ‚Kantischer Kritizismus'.)"[9]

Erst die naturalistische Genealogie des „Gott-Mnems" – wie es ein evolutionärer Erkenntnistheoretiker heute nennt – läßt das Unternehmen eines Gottesbeweises, so scheint es, definitiv in sich zusammensinken. Denn gerade, *weil* die Idee Gottes als solche Sein impliziert, bricht sie bereits als Idee zusammen, wenn der Gedanke des Seins zusammenbricht und wenn David Hume recht behält mit seinem lapidaren Satz: "We never really advance a step beyond our-selves".[10] Nietzsches ganzes Werk kann als eine Paraphrase dieses Satzes gelesen werden. Die Frage nach der Wahrheit des Glaubens an Gott stellt sich nicht mehr, wenn der Gedanke der Wahrheit als solcher schon eine Selbsttäuschung ist, weil es nur nützliche und schädliche Irrtümer – das heißt Idiosynkrasien – gibt. Nietzsche hat als erster die wechselseitige Bedingtheit des Gedankens der Wahrheit und des Gottes-Gedankens klar ausgesprochen, wenn er schreibt,

> „daß auch wir Aufklärer, wir freien Geister des 19. Jahrhunderts, unser Feuer noch von dem Christenglauben nehmen, der auch der Glaube Platos war, daß Gott die Wahrheit, daß die Wahrheit göttlich ist".[11]

In diesem Sinne schreibt heute der Neopragmatist Richard Rorty:

> „Ein höheres Forschungsziel namens Wahrheit gäbe es nur dann, wenn es so etwas wie eine letzte Rechtfertigung gäbe, also keine Rechtfertigung vor einem bloß endlichen Auditorium menschlicher Hörer, sondern eine Rechtfertigung vor Gott".[12]

Die klassischen Gottesbeweise sahen zwar in Gott den Grund der Intelligibilität der Welt. Aber wenn Gott auch das πρότερον φύσει war, so war doch die Intelligibilität der Welt das γνωριμώτατον πρὸς ἡμᾶς, von dem aus wir zum γνωριμώτατον φύσει gelangen. Die beiden Wege der ontologischen und der Erkenntnisbegründung sind daher zwar gegenläufig, aber sie sind genau symmetrisch. Das ändert sich seit dem Nominalismus und dem mit ihm zusammenhängenden Voluntarismus. Wenn das So-sein der Welt nicht fundiert ist in ewigen Wesensstrukturen, die Gott in kontingentes Sein überführt, sondern wenn es nur Ausdruck des undurchdringlichen Willens Gottes ist, dann verliert in der Tat die Welt ihr „lesbares Gesicht". Bei Descartes erstmals gilt die *reductio ad absurdum* nicht mehr als Beweis für die Wahrheit des Gegenteils. Denn es könnte ja sein, daß wir im Absurden leben und daß sogar unsere klarsten Evidenzen Idiosynkrasien sind. Descartes brauchte für diese Hypothese noch die Figur der Irreführung durch einen *genius malignus*, die in der mystischen Literatur seiner Zeit geläufig war. Uns genügt heute der Naturalismus der evolutionären Erkenntnistheorie. Seit Descartes verbürgt nicht mehr die Intelligibilität des Seins das Dasein Gottes, sondern es bedarf umgekehrt der Wirklichkeit Gottes, um uns die Intelligibilität des Seins, also die Erfüllung dessen zu verbürgen, was wir meinen, wenn wir von „Wahrheit" sprechen. Gottesbeweise können unter dieser Bedingung nicht mehr Beweise sein, die, ausgehend von einem vorausgesetzten Begriff wahrer Erkenntnis, die Existenz eines absoluten und vollkommenen Wesens beweisen, wobei die Leistungsfähigkeit der Beweisgrundlagen und Beweisfiguren im vorhinein als feststehend vorausgesetzt wird. Über Gott und über das, was wir unter Wahrheit verstehen, kann vielmehr nur noch *uno actu* entschieden werden.

Hierin ist die Unzulänglichkeit der Mittel begründet, mit denen vor allem katholische Theologen und kirchliche Autoritäten metaphysischen Realismus und klassischen Wahrheitsbegriff verteidigen. Ihre Intervention will die Grundlagen der Metaphysik als *praeambula fidei* sichern, ohne das, wofür diese Grundlagen dienen sollen, bereits methodisch in Anspruch zu nehmen. Sie will sozusagen eine religiöse Verpflichtung urgieren, eine religionsneutrale und religionsunabhängige Theorie der Wahrheit zu akzeptieren. Sie statuiert eine Glaubensverpflichtung, die Glaubensunabhängigkeit von Gotteserkenntnis anzuerkennen. Sieht man hierin eine immanente Selbstinterpretation des Glaubens als „rationabile obsequium", ist dagegen nichts einzuwenden. Aber wenn es tatsächlich so ist, daß nur der Glaube an Gott einen Begriff von Erkenntnis ermöglicht, der zu einer Einsicht in die Existenz Gottes führen könnte, dann bestimmt eben dies unsere Situation. Kant definierte das Ding an sich als das Ding, wie es sich für den *intellectus archetypus* zeigt. Nietzsche versuchte zu zeigen, daß es nur unter der Voraussetzung eines *intellectus archetypus* Sinn hat, von einem Ding an sich oder einer wahren Welt zu sprechen, und der Neopragmatismus folgt ihm darin, so z. B. Rorty, wenn er den Begriff der Erkenntnis überhaupt als Illusion preisgibt und durch die grundlose Hoffnung auf eine bessere Zukunft ersetzen möchte. Dabei ist es nur konsequent, wenn Rorty sogar den Vorwurf verschwommenen und widersprüchlichen Redens nicht mehr als Vorwurf gelten läßt[13], denn bei einem Denken, das nicht mehr auf Wahrheit verpflichtet ist, sondern auf Erfolg, kann nicht einmal mehr klar gesagt werden, worin denn dieser Erfolg bestehen soll. Es kann überhaupt nicht mehr auf Klarheit ankommen. Verschwommene Gedanken können effektiver sein als klare Gedanken. Die neue Situation ist also dadurch gekennzeichnet, daß wir *uno actu* darüber entscheiden, ob wir ein Absolutes, ob wir dieses Absolute als Gott denken, ob wir so etwas wie eine nicht auf uns relative Wahrheit anerkennen und schließlich, ob wir uns für berechtigt halten, uns selbst als wahrheitsfähige Wesen, und das heißt: als Personen zu betrachten, also als Wesen, die ihrerseits einen Anspruch darauf haben, von anderen als in einem metaphysischen Sinne real anerkannt zu werden. Verschwunden ist der archimedische Punkt, von dem aus wir, von Gewißheit zu Gewißheit fortschreitend, schließlich bei der Affirmation der Existenz Gottes ankommen. Wo Gott nicht das Alpha des Weges ist, da wird er auch nicht das Omega sein können. Wer dies zuerst klar gesehen und ausgesprochen hat, war Hegel.

Ich möchte meine These über die Neuheit dieser Situation in zwei Gedankengängen verdeutlichen. Der erste stammt wiederum von Descartes.[14] Der Gottesgedanke dient Descartes bekanntlich zur Behebung seines Zweifels an der Realitätsbezogenheit unseres Denkens. Man wundert sich darüber, denn wenn unser Denken idiosynkratisch ist, wieso sollte es dann nicht auch jener Gedankengang sein, der zur Annahme der Existenz Gottes führt? Dieser Einwand übersieht, daß der Gedanke Gottes nur deshalb zur Behebung des Zweifels dient, weil wir entdecken, daß nur dieser Gedanke es war, der überhaupt erst einen solchen Zweifel möglich machte. Und zwar deshalb, weil der Gottesgedanke den Raum einer wahren Welt eröffnet, der größer ist als unser Bewußtseinsraum und der nicht als dessen Funktion gedacht werden kann. Unser Bewußtsein ist ja entweder *per definitionem* das Ganze dessen, was ist, oder es ist endliches Bewußtsein. Wenn es das Ganze dessen ist, was ist, dann macht es keinen Sinn, auch nur die Frage nach einem Außerhalb dieses Bewußtseins zu stellen. Eine solche Frage könnte gar nicht formuliert, gedacht oder verstanden werden. Ist das Bewußtsein aber endlich, dann ist es möglich, es als Idiosynkrasie eines natürlichen Wesens zu verstehen. Sein Selbstverständnis als Repräsentation der Wirklichkeit kann das Ergebnis der Täuschung durch einen *genius malignus* sein. Es kann aber auch einfach verstanden werden als Funktion der Selbstbehauptung in einer bedrohlichen Welt mit knappen Ressourcen. Nur, wenn es so wäre, könnten wir eben dies nicht wissen, ja nicht einmal denken. Die digitale Organisation unseres Denkens, das Widerspruchsprinzip, die Unterscheidung eines Innen und Außen, würde nicht die ganz andere Unterscheidung eines „sum" vom „cogito" hervorbringen.

Was Descartes diese Unterscheidung ermöglicht, ist die Anwesenheit der Gottesidee als Idee einer wahren Welt, die nicht *per definitionem* in eins fällt mit dem „Für-mich-Sein". Nur mit Bezug auf sie ist die Frage nach ihrer Erkennbarkeit sinnvoll. Indem die Gottesidee die Dimension der Wahrheit eröffnet, ermöglicht sie es Descartes, die eigene Endlichkeit und deshalb Täuschbarkeit zu denken. Der *genius malignus* ist dann der, der diese Täuschbarkeit für eine wirkliche Täuschung ausnutzen könnte. Zwar ist das *cogito sum*, wie Descartes betont, kein Syllogismus, sondern eine unmittelbare Evidenz. Es ist aber auch keine Tautologie. Denn es bedeutet, daß wir nicht in einem unendlichen *cogito me cogitare me cogitare*, oder, um mit Fichte zu sprechen, in „Bildern von Bildern von Bildern"[15] gefangen bleiben, sondern zu einer „objektiven" Selbstaffirmation gelangen können. Ich denke nicht nur, daß ich denke, daß ich denke usw., sondern die Tatsache, daß ich denke, ereignet sich als Tatsache in einer nicht durch mich definierten, also wahren Welt. Es ist an sich, und nicht nur für mich, daß ich für mich bin. Und wer immer wahr urteilen will, kann dies nicht leugnen. Mein Bewußtseinsraum ist Teil jenes absoluten Raumes, der es uns möglich macht, an der Relevanz dieses Bewußtseinsraumes zu zweifeln.

Subjekte, die als Subjekte füreinander objektiv sind, nennen wir Personen.[16] Das punktuelle *cogito* ist nicht personal. Es ist voraussetzungslos, aber es ist auch folgenlos. Es hat keine objektive Relevanz. Für eine „objektive", naturalistische Betrachtung ist es das schlechthin Nichtige, das wir durch geeignete sprachliche Transformationen ganz eliminieren können und wirklich eliminieren, wenn wir Wissenschaft treiben. Der eliminative Reduktionismus scheint mir der einzig konsequente Naturalismus zu sein. Neben ihm kann durchaus eine existentielle und geschichtliche Hermeneutik der Subjektivität existieren, eine Hermeneutik, die die Innenseite des Daseins thematisiert. Aber kein Weg führt von dieser nichtigen Innenseite zur wissenschaftlichen Rede, die uns darüber belehrt, was in Wahrheit ist. Daß Subjekte als Subjekte „in Wahrheit sind", ist eins mit der Behauptung, daß sie *als* Subjekte erkennbar und erkannt sind. Daß sie also nicht neben ihrer Innenseite auch eine Außenseite haben, sondern daß ihre Innenseite als Innenseite nicht nur für sie selbst ist. Diese Behauptung aber ist tatsächlich eine theologische Behauptung, oder sie ist sinnlos. Sagen „ich bin" heißt sagen „Gott ist" oder: „Sein selbst ist von der Weise der Innerlichkeit". (Die christliche Trinitätslehre besagt, daß das Objektivsein des Für-sich-Seins die Struktur des absoluten Seins selbst ist.)

Diese Einsicht realisieren setzt bereits Freiheit voraus. Wer gegen sich selbst als Person optiert zugunsten eines naturalistischen Monismus, kann durch kein Argument daran gehindert werden. Die Akzeptanz von Argumenten setzt schon voraus, daß man an Wahrheit in einem anderen Sinn als dem wissenschaftlicher Naturbeherrschung interessiert ist. Wer, wie z. B. Daniel Dennett, von vornherein erklärt, prinzipiell kein Argument gegen den naturalistischen Reduktionismus zu akzeptieren[17], für den ist natürlich jeder Gottesbeweis ebenso vergeblich wie jedes Plädoyer für die Anerkennung von Subjekten als Personen. Hier gilt Fichtes Wort:

> „Was für eine Philosophie man wähle, hängt [...] davon ab, was für ein Mensch man ist."[18]

Gottesbeweise nach Nietzsche können nur den Charakter von *argumenta ad hominem* haben. Aber schon Leibniz hatte geschrieben, daß es keine „absoluten Beweise" gibt und daß jeder Beweis in Wirklichkeit ein *argumentum ad hominem* ist.[19]

Ich habe das Cartesische Argument mit Hilfe der Raummetapher zu rekonstruieren versucht: Raum als Struktur des Für-einander-Seins; Gott als Konstituens eines absoluten Raumes der Wahrheit, als Bedingung des *sum* eines *cogito* und als Garant des repräsentationalen Charakters unserer Erkenntnis. Und dies wiederum als Bedingung der Wirklichkeit von Personen. Wir können uns die Unverzichtbarkeit des Gedankens der Existenz Gottes für das Selbstverständnis von Personen noch auf eine zweite Weise verdeutlichen, nämlich mit Hilfe einer Reflexion über die zeitliche Dimension der Selbstkonstitution von Personen.[20] Subjekte können für andere nur als Subjekte objektiv werden, weil sie nie reine unmittelbare Innerlichkeit, sondern sich selbst als Subjektivität immer schon objektiv geworden sind, nämlich durch Erinnerung. Ich erinnere mich meiner Zustände als der meinigen, also sozusagen von innen. Gleichwohl ist dieses Innen nicht mein jetziges Innen. Die Erinnerung an frühere Schmerzen ist nicht gleichbedeutend mit gegenwärtigen Schmerzen. Erst durch Erinnerung wird die Person ihrer Identität über das punktuelle *cogito* hinaus bewußt. Dieses *cogito* ist ja zunächst nicht nur solipsistisch, es ist auch bloß instantan. Vergangenheit impliziert es nur als *cogitatum*, also als Erinnerung. Erinnerung aber gehört nicht dem Bereich unmittelbarer Selbstgewißheit an, sondern dem Bereich dessen, worüber wir uns täuschen können. Die Einheit der Person kann deshalb nicht auf unmittelbare Selbstgewißheit gegründet werden. Wir können auch nicht wissen, ob wir uns des gegenwärtigen Bewußtseinszustandes je adäquat werden erinnern können. Der gegenwärtige Schmerz mag in Folge einer Amnesie definitiv verschwinden, die gegenwärtige Freude in späterer Depression nicht einmal mehr als erinnerte gegenwärtig sein. Zum „sum" der *res cogitans* gehört es aber, daß es nicht nur für andere, sondern auch für mich selbst ein unverrückbares Maß der Wahrheit bleibt. „Ich werde Schmerzen gehabt haben" ist genau dann wahr, wenn ich jetzt Schmerzen habe. Erst die Gottesidee aber eröffnet für Descartes den Wahrheitsraum, zu dem alles gehört, was das instantane Selbstbewußtsein transzendiert, so daß dieses sich mit seinen früheren und späteren Zuständen zur Einheit einer Person zusammenschließt. Die endliche Person konstituiert sich wesentlich zeitlich. Da für Descartes nur Gott den repräsentationalen Charakter der Erkenntnis, also auch der Erinnerung garantiert, garantiert nur er die Einheit der Person.

Aber wir müssen noch einen Schritt weitergehen. Alle Wirklichkeitsbehauptungen, alle Existenzsätze in unserer Umgangssprache sind temporaler Natur, und zwar sind sie Behauptungen über Wirklichkeit in einem emphatischen Sinne nur im Präsens. Das Vergangene und das Künftige gelten uns nicht im gleichen Sinne als wirklich wie das Gegenwärtige. – Sätze im Futurum exactum sind nur wahr, wenn ein entsprechender Satz im Präsens jetzt wahr ist oder einmal wahr gewesen ist. – Diese Implikation gilt aber auch in umgekehrter Richtung: Nur was später gewesen sein wird, ist jetzt. Das Futurum exactum impliziert das Präsens. Behaupten, etwas werde künftig nicht gewesen sein, ist gleichbedeutend mit der Behauptung, daß es auch jetzt nicht in Wahrheit ist. Die Behauptung streicht sozusagen die Gegenwart ontologisch durch, indem sie ihr eine für die Selbstkonstitution unverzichtbare Dimension entzieht. Wir können die Grammatik nicht suspendieren, ohne uns selbst durchzustreichen. Nun stellt sich aber die Frage nach dem ontologischen Status dieses Gewesenseins, wenn jede Erinnerung und jede Spur ausgelöscht sein wird. Welchen Sinn hat es zu sagen: Wenn alles bewußte Leben im Kosmos verschwunden ist, bleibt dennoch die Tatsache, daß einmal ein tiefes Glück empfunden oder ein Kind zu Tode gequält wurde? Was sollen wir unter diesem „Bleiben" denken? Aber umgekehrt: Was könnte es heißen zu sagen, einmal werde dieses beides nicht mehr gewesen sein? Die Behauptung ist sinnlos, denn das *futurum exactum* gehört zur Konstitution des Präsens, und seine Negation läuft auf eine Entwirklichung der Gegenwart hinaus. Wir können diese Entwirklichung akzeptieren und damit die Entwirklichung von Personalität als Wirklichkeit von Subjektivität. Wir *müssen* sie akzeptieren, wenn wir den Gottesgedanken aus dem Denken fernhalten wollen. Denn ein Gewesensein behaupten, das von allem Bewußtsein endlicher Personen unabhängig ist, kann nur heißen, die Existenz Gottes behaupten. Wenn wir auf die Annahme eines definitiven Aufgehobenseins aller Ereignisse der Welt in einem göttlichen Innen verzichten, müssen wir die Wirklichkeit entwirklichen. Wir müssen den absurden Gedanken akzeptieren, daß das, was jetzt ist, einmal nicht mehr gewesen sein wird. Das aber heißt, daß es überhaupt nicht in einem letzten Sinne wirklich ist – ein Gedanke, den nur der Buddhismus tatsächlich zu denken versucht. Die Konsequenz des Buddhismus ist die Verneinung des Lebens.

Nietzsche hat wie kein anderer vor ihm die Konsequenzen des Atheismus durchdacht, insofern er nicht den Weg der Lebensverneinung, sondern der Lebensbejahung gehen will. Als katastrophalste Konsequenz erschien es ihm, daß der Mensch das Woraufhin seiner Selbsttranszendenz verliert. Denn Nietzsche sah es als die größte Errungenschaft des Christentums an, daß es lehrte, den Menschen zu lieben um Gottes willen,

> „bis jetzt das vornehmste und entlegenste Gefühl, das unter Menschen erreicht worden ist".[21]

Der Übermensch und die Idee der ewigen Wiederkehr sollten der funktionale Ersatz für die Gottesidee sein. Denn Nietzsche sah genau, wer andernfalls das Gesicht der Erde in Zukunft bestimmen würde: die „letzten Menschen", die glauben, das Glück erfunden zu haben und über „Liebe", „Schöpfung", „Sehnsucht" und „Stern" spotten.[22] Sie sind nur noch mit der Manipulation ihrer eigenen Lustzustände beschäftigt und halten jeden Dissidenten für verrückt, dem es im Ernst um etwas geht, also zum Beispiel um „Wahrheit". Nietzsches heroischer Nihilismus hat sich – wie er selbst befürchtete – als ohnmächtig gegenüber dem letzten Menschen erwiesen. Die Funktion der Gottesidee beruht nämlich auf dem Glauben an eine Wahrheit, die durch keine Funktion definiert ist. Darum ist jeder funktionale Ersatz für sie unmöglich. Der banale Nihilismus des letzten Menschen wird heute z. B. von Richard Rorty propagiert. Der Mensch, der mit der Gottesidee auch der Idee der Wahrheit abgesagt hat, kennt nur noch seine eigenen subjektiven Zustände. Sein Verhältnis zur Wirklichkeit ist nicht repräsentational, sondern nur kausal. Er möchte sich als geschicktes Tier verstehen. Für ein solches Tier kann es so etwas wie Gotteserkenntnis nicht geben. Wenn aber Erfahrung der Welt als des offenen Raumes einer sich selbst zeigenden Wirklichkeit nur noch um den Preis der Affirmation der Existenz Gottes zu haben ist, dann ist das für diejenigen, die sich weiterhin als freie und wahrheitsfähige Wesen verstehen wollen, das überzeugendste Argument für die Existenz Gottes – ein *argumentum ad hominem*.

Robert Spaemann

Anmerkungen

1. Fr. Nietzsche, *Götzendämmerung*, in: *Werke: Kritische Gesamtausgabe*, ed. G. Colli u. M. Montinari, Bd. VI 3, Berlin 1969, S. 72.
2. M. Foucault, *L'ordre du discours*, Paris 1971, dt.: *Die Ordnung des Diskurses*, Frankfurt a. M. 1977, S. 36.
3. Cf. R. Spaemann, R. Löw, *Die Frage wozu?*, 3. Aufl. München 1991, S. 93 ff.
4. Cf. N. Hartmann, *Teleologisches Denken*, Berlin 1951, und W. Stegmüller, *Teleologie, Funktionsanalyse, Selbstregulation*, Berlin 1969, S. 585.
5. Cf. B. Russell, "On the Notion of Cause", in: *Proceedings of the Aristotelian Society* 13 (1912–13), S. 1–26.
6. Cf. Thomas v. Aquin, *Summa contra gentiles* I,11.
7. *Kritik der reinen Vernunft* B 653.
8. *Kritik der reinen Vernunft* B 670.
9. Fr. Nietzsche, *Nachgelassene Fragmente*, loc. cit. Bd. VIII 3, Berlin 1972, S. 211.
10. D. Hume, *A Treatise of Human Nature*, ed. L. A. Selby-Bigge, Oxford 1987, Book I, part II, sect. VI.
11. Fr. Nietzsche, *Die fröhliche Wissenschaft*, loc. cit., Bd. V 2, Berlin 1973, S. 344.
12. R. Rorty, *Hoffnung statt Erkenntnis*, Wien 1994, S. 30.
13. Loc. cit., S. 17.
14. Cf. zum folgenden R. Spaemann, „Le ‚sum' dans le ‚Cogito sum'", in: *Le Discours et sa méthode*, ed. N. Grimaldi u. J. L. Marion, Paris 1987, S. 271–284, dt. in: *Zeitschrift für philosophische Forschung* 41, Heft 3 (1987).
15. J. G. Fichte, *Die Bestimmung des Menschen*, in: *Werke*, Bd. 2, ed. I. H. Fichte, Berlin 1971, Nachdr. d. Ausg. 1845/46, S. 245.
16. Cf. R. Spaemann, *Personen*, Stuttgart 1996.
17. D. C. Dennett, *Consciousness Explained*, London 1991, dt.: *Philosophie des menschlichen Bewußtseins*, Hamburg 1994, S. 565.
18. J. G. Fichte, *Erste Einleitung in die Wissenschaftslehre*, in: *Werke*, Bd. 1, ed. I. H. Fichte, Berlin 1971, Nachdr. d. Ausg. 1845/46, S. 434.
19. G. W. Leibniz, *Opuscules et fragments inédits*, ed. L. Couturat, Paris 1903, S. 183.
20. Cf. op. cit. (cf. Anm. 16), S. 111 ff.
21. Fr. Nietzsche, *Jenseits von Gut und Böse*, loc. cit. Bd. VI 2, Berlin 1968, S. 77.
22. Fr. Nietzsche, *Also sprach Zarathustra*, loc. cit. Bd. VI 1, Berlin 1968, S. 13.

Henry E. Allison

Beauty as Mediator between Nature and Freedom
An Analysis of the Moral and Systematic Significance of Taste in Kant's *Critique of Judgment*

Introduction

As Kant makes clear in the published 'Introduction', a major concern of the *Critique of Judgment*[1] is to bridge the "immense gulf" [*die unübersehbare Kluft*] separating freedom from nature, the supersensible from appearances.[2] Such a radical separation of the two domains is not a problem for Kant's theoretical philosophy, but it is for the practical. Since the legislation of freedom enjoins ends that are to be realized in the world of sense, it is practically necessary to assume that these ends are realizable. And, according to Kant, this means that, "[I]t must be possible to think of nature as being such that the lawfulness of its form will harmonize with at least the possibility of the ends to be realized in it according to the laws of freedom".[3] At the end of the 'Introduction', Kant returns to this topic, suggesting that it is judgment, through its concept, the purposiveness of nature, that mediates between the domains of nature and freedom, thereby providing the required transition [*den Übergang*] in thought from the concept of the latter to that of the former.[4]

Elsewhere, I examined this topic in connection with teleological judgment. My aim was to show, with specific reference to the morally required end of perpetual peace, how Kant's teleological conception of history (the meeting place of natural and moral teleology), provides just such a transition, making it possible to conceive of nature (including human nature) as amenable to the realization of, or at least the gradual approximation to, this moral ideal.[5] My present concern is with the contributions of aesthetic judgment or, more precisely, since I shall not be discussing the sublime, the contributions of the judgment of taste and the experience of beauty to the bridging of this gap. In short, it is with the moral significance of taste, which I take to be equivalent to its systematic significance. Although it is not part of my present concern, it is at least worth noting that the demonstration that each part of the *Critique of Judgment* contributes in distinct, yet essential ways to this bridging project should shed some light on the thorny question of the unity of the third *Critique*.

An underlying assumption of my analysis, for which I do not intend to argue here, is that Kant's account of taste is addressed to two quite distinct concerns, which are frequently conflated in the literature: the first is the normativity of the pure judgment of taste, that is, the claim implicit in such a judgment to speak with a universal voice; the second is the question of the importance of taste, which consists in its moral (and, therefore, systematic) significance.[6] The former is the concern of the "Analytic of the Beautiful" and the "Deduction" (through § 39). Setting aside the sublime, I take the latter to be the main concern of the remainder of the *Critique of Aesthetic Judgment*. Thus, whereas I agree with the interpreters who emphasize the centrality of the connection of taste with morality for Kant's overall project in the *Critique of Aesthetic Judgment*, I reject the view that this connection is to be regarded as part of the deduction itself.[7] On the contrary, we shall see that the account of the moral significance of taste presupposes and, therefore, can hardly help to establish its normativity.

My central thesis, however, is that Kant's account of the moral significance of taste is more complex and nuanced than it is usually taken to be, and that it is best understood when viewed in connection with two relatively neglected aspects of his moral theory: the conception of indirect duty and the doctrine of radical evil (which are themselves intimately related). More specifically, I shall argue that the doctrine of an intellectual interest in natural beauty developed in § 42 and the account of the beautiful as the symbol of the morally good contained in § 59 are concerned with two distinct ways in which taste can mediate between nature and freedom and that each of these yields a distinct ground for a "duty, as it were," (or indirect duty) to develop taste. As Kant himself indicates, the first is limited to natural beauty, since it is concerned with the purposiveness of nature; but the second, I shall argue, applies to artistic as well as natural beauty, since it is linked to the *act* rather than the *object* of aesthetic appraisal.

I

The natural starting point for an analysis of the moral significance of taste in the *Critique of Judgment* is Kant's often cited but enigmatic claim at the end of § 40:

> "If we could assume that the mere universal communicability as such of our feeling must already carry with it an interest for us (something we are, however, not justified in inferring from the character of a merely reflective power of judgment), then we could explain how it is that we require from everyone as a duty, as it were [*gleichsam*], the feeling in a judgment of taste."[8]

This passage raises at least two distinct questions. One is its compatibility with Kant's doctrine (itself highly controversial) of the disinterestedness of judgments of taste.[9] The other, and by far most important one, concerns the suggestion that showing that the universal communicability of the feeling in a judgment of taste carries with it an interest would suffice to explain how we can require from others, indeed, as a duty, as it were, the feeling in a judgment of taste. In view of Kant's insistence on the demand for agreement built into the judgment of taste, it is not surprising that some interpreters have equated this mysterious "duty, as it were," with this very demand. And, as a result, they have regarded the subsequent account of interest (together with the later discussion of beauty as a symbol of the morally good) as part of an extended deduction turning on the link between beauty and morality.[10] But once a sharp distinction has been drawn between the justificatory project of the deduction and the larger concern with the significance of taste of the bulk of the *Critique of Aesthetic Judgment*, that line of interpretation is no longer available. Thus, it becomes necessary to distinguish between the aesthetic ought (the demand for agreement) and this quasi-duty to attain the feeling in a judgment of taste. Moreover, this, in turn, gives rise to the questions of the grounds for this quasi-duty and why it is described as a duty, as it were, rather than a full-fledged duty.

With regard to the first issue, it should suffice to note that the problem of connecting the universal communicability of the feeling in a judgment of taste with an interest presupposes rather than conflicts with the presumed disinterestedness of the judgment. If judgments of taste were either founded upon an interest or "of themselves" [*an sich*] gave rise to one, both of which Kant explicitly denies[11], then there would be no puzzle about how they might involve an interest. Their disinterestedness, however, still leaves open the possibility that such judgments might give rise to an interest when taken together with something else, which is precisely what Kant claims.

It is also important to keep in mind that the problem is not simply to explain how this universal communicability could "carry with it an interest", but why it *must* [*müsse*] do so. Consequently, Kant is concerned to ground a necessary connection between an interest and either the disinterested pleasure in a judgment of beauty or the universal communicability of that pleasure. Moreover, given the definition of interest as "pleasure in the existence of an object"[12], this necessary connection must be between the pleasure of taste (or its universal communicability) and a further pleasure in the existence of the objects deemed beautiful.

The disinterestedness of the judgment of taste itself also explains why such a necessary connection takes the form of an ought. Since both basing the universally communicable pleasure on an interest and deriving one directly from it are ruled out by the very nature of taste, there is no possibility of demonstrating any causal connection. Moreover, since it is hardly a matter of conceptual analysis, it cannot be an analytic necessity. Consequently, a deontic necessity would seem to be the only viable candidate. In other words, the only way in which Kant can establish such a necessary connection is by showing that one ought to take an interest in the existence of beautiful objects. And to show this may plausibly be described as establishing a "duty, as it were" to take such an interest.

The tasks, therefore, are to determine the nature of this interest and to ground the claim that one ought to develop it. Since Kant speaks of requiring as a "duty, as it were" the feeling in a judgment of taste rather than an interest in beauty, it might seem that there is a further problem of connecting this required interest with the pleasure of taste. But since taste just is the capacity to appreciate (and hence take pleasure in) beauty, it is a necessary condition of the possibility of taking an interest in objects in virtue of their beauty. Thus, the requirement to develop taste is entailed by the requirement to take an interest in beautiful objects.

Kant deals with the first of these questions explicitly and the second implicitly in § 41. As a first step, he clarifies the problem by noting that what must be done is to determine the connection between taste and something else, so that the (disinterested) liking of mere reflection can be connected with an additional pleasure in the existence of the objects of this liking. He then points out that there are only two possible candidates for this something else: it might be either something empirical, namely an inclination inherent in human nature, or something intellectual. Kant characterizes the latter as the property of the will of being able to be determined *a priori* by reason[13], which is equivalent to its capacity to be motivated by the moral law. Given these alternatives, he then argues that only the latter is capable of generating the kind of interest required.

Since the empirical interest in question concerns the universal communicability of the pleasure of taste, it initially seems to be precisely what is called for. In fact, in language reminiscent of the "duty, as it were," Kant even remarks that a regard for universal communicability is "something that everyone expects and demands from everyone else, as it were [*gleichsam*] through an original contract, which is dictated through humanity itself".[14] Nevertheless, Kant rules out this particular (empirical) interest in beauty because of its two-fold conditionality. First, it is based on an assumed inclination for society inherent in human nature. The problem, presumably, is not with the assumption that there is such an inclination, but rather with the fact that no inclination, not even one inherent in human nature, could ever support anything more than a hypothetical imperative.[15] Second, as connected with the social inclination, this interest in the universal communicability of one's feeling would be operative only in society, which means that it lacks the requisite universality. Even worse, Kant notes that the value attached to such universal communicability attains its maximum at the most advanced stage of civilization, which he later characterizes as a "glittering misery" [*glänzendes Elend*] because it involves the development of insatiable inclinations.[16]

The latter suggests a Rousseauian style critique of this empirical interest and the aestheticism to which it leads. But rather than providing such a critique, Kant dismisses this interest on the grounds that it is irrelevant to his present concern, which is only with "what may have reference *a priori*, even if only indirectly, to a judgment of taste"[17]. So far this is just what we would expect, since the aim is to establish a necessary, albeit indirect, connection with the pleasure in the judgment of taste and its universal communicability. Kant seems suddenly to change the subject, however, for he remarks that if even in this (indirect) form, such a connection with interest should be discovered, "then taste would reveal a transition of our judgmental faculty [*Beurteilungsvermögens*] from sense enjoyment to moral feeling"[18]. Moreover, he continues, "not only would we then have better guidance in using taste purposively, but it [taste or our judgmental faculty] would also be presented as a mediating link in the chain of the human *a priori* faculties, on which all legislation must depend"[19]. And, in conclusion, he remarks that precisely because an empirical interest in the beautiful is based on an inclination, "it can provide only a very ambiguous transition from the agreeable to the good"[20].

All of this makes it abundantly clear that Kant's real reason for dismissing an empirical interest in the beautiful is its unsuitability as mediator between nature and freedom, and that the considerations noted above are the reasons for this unsuitability. Consequently, it is in connection with this systematic concern, rather than the justificatory project of the deduction that we must consider the question of interest in the beautiful and, therefore, the duty, as it were, to develop taste as a precondition of taking such an interest. Nor can one argue that the demonstration that taste plays this mediating function just is the deduction, for the claim of taste to speak with a universal voice must already be presupposed, if the latter is to be accomplished.

II

The questions now are whether there is such a thing as an intellectual interest in the beautiful, that is, one that is independent of inclination and connected with our moral capacity, and, if so, whether it is better suited to the task at hand than a merely empirical interest. Kant deals with these questions in § 42 by attempting to link such an interest with a certain predisposition to morality. I shall consider the nature of this linkage in the present section and its relevance to the "duty, as it were," to develop taste in the next.

Kant's account is complicated by his rejection of the more or less orthodox enlightenment belief in an intrinsic connection between the love of beauty and moral goodness. Appealing instead to the Rousseauian thesis that "virtousi of taste" are as a rule morally corrupt, he concludes not only that a feeling for the beautiful differs in kind from moral feeling (which is not particularly controversial), but also, and more significantly, that we cannot assume an inner affinity [*eine innere Affinität*] between interest in the beautiful *per se* and moral interest, which might seem to rule out any intellectual interest in beauty. But since the Rousseauian thesis applies only to the interest in artistic beauty, Kant also maintains that this does not preclude the possibility of a connection between a moral interest and an interest in *natural* beauty. Thus, in partial agreement with the enlightenment view, he states:

"I do maintain that to take a *direct interest* in the beauty of *nature* (not merely to have the taste needed to judge it) is always the mark of a good soul; and if this interest is habitual, if it readily associates itself with the *contemplation of nature*, this indicates at least a mental attunement [*eine Gemüthsstimmung*] favorable to moral feeling."[21]

Kant also insists, however, that the interest be in beauty rather than charm and that it must be thought to pertain to nature rather than to art. Indeed, with regard to the latter point, he notes that if one were deceived into believing that something was a natural beauty and later recognized it to be artificial, then any direct interest (although not necessarily the aesthetic evaluation) would disappear. Moreover, Kant presents this conclusion not merely as his own opinion, but as the considered view of all those who have cultivated their moral feeling.[22] Accordingly, he takes his main task to be to account for this superiority of natural over artistic beauty, which cannot be a matter of purely aesthetic ranking.

It is by way of explaining this presumed superiority that Kant links the intellectual interest in natural beauty with the problem of a gap between nature and freedom. He begins by focusing on the parallel between aesthetic and moral judgments and their corresponding capacities. Both are concerned with forms (forms of objects in the one case and forms of maxims in the other); both involve a liking that is made into a law for everyone; and, finally, neither is based on an antecedent interest. They differ in that the aesthetic judgment is based on feeling and the moral on concepts and, more significantly for present purposes, in the fact that the moral, but not the aesthetic judgment of itself gives rise to an interest.

The basic moral interest is in the objective reality of our moral ideas, that is, in the realizability in nature of our moral projects, the totality of which constitutes the idea of the highest good.[23] As already indicated, it is precisely this interest that underlies the need to bridge the "immense gulf" between the realms of nature and freedom. But by way of connecting this interest with taste and an intellectual interest in natural beauty, Kant here characterizes this interest more specifically as being "that nature should at least show a trace or give a hint that it contains some basis or other [*irgend einen Grund*] for us to assume in its products a lawful harmony with that liking of ours that is independent of all interest"[24].

Kant's reasoning here seems to be roughly the following: since, as moral agents, we necessarily take a direct interest in the realization of morally required ends, and since it is nature that supplies the enabling conditions for the realization of these ends, this interest must also attach to any traces or hints that nature reveals of its harmony with these ends. Kant could not, of course, claim straightaway that natural beauties do in fact provide such traces and hints, since that would amount to a dogmatic teleological claim that goes well beyond the scope of reflective judgment. The claim, instead, is that it is reasonable to assume that morally well disposed agents will naturally take them as such and, therefore, also take a direct interest in the beautiful in nature.

This claim is based on a two-fold analogy between nature's presentation of beautiful forms (its aesthetic purposiveness) and the moral purposiveness in which we are interested. First, it is a form of purposiveness in the sense of being a mode in which nature appears to favor us. Here Kant's idea seems to be that the only way in which we can comprehend this favoring is by somehow connecting it to our moral vocation.[25] Second, like moral purposiveness, it produces a universally communicable liking that is quite distinct from one produced through the satisfaction of any of the ends of inclination. Together, they suggest (but hardly entail) that any conscientious moral agent with the capacity to appreciate such purposiveness, that is, any one with taste, will view any manifestation of it as an indication of nature's moral purposiveness and take an interest in it on that basis. Conversely, someone without a well developed moral interest will not take any additional interest in such signs, even if that person has the taste to appreciate natural beauty aesthetically. And from this Kant concludes that, "If someone is directly interested in the beauty of nature, we have cause to suppose that he has at least a predisposition [*Anlage*] to a good moral disposition [*Gesinnung*]"[26].

III

It is, however, one thing to claim that an interest in natural beauty is an indicator (of undetermined reliability) of a predisposition to morality, or even of a good moral character, and quite another to claim that one ought to develop such an interest. Accordingly, even granting that taste is itself a necessary condition of the interest, it does not follow that we have anything like a duty to develop taste. In order to establish this, it is necessary to show how taste and the intellectual interest ensuing from it can themselves help to bridge the gap between nature and freedom by bringing about a transition from sense enjoyment to moral feeling.[27] In other words, what must be shown is not merely that a person of good moral disposition will take an interest in the bridging of the gap, but that taking such an interest actually helps to bring about the desired result.

Since Kant himself does not offer an argument in support of this claim, we must attempt to do so for him on the basis of the materials he has provided, both in the *Critique of Judgment* and in his writings on moral theory. Central to this reconstruction is the idea that, precisely because it brings awareness of these traces and hints, the appreciation of natural beauty can aid in the strengthening of moral commitment by deepening the sense that "nature is on our side". Accordingly, it is by functioning in this way that taste, as the capacity to appreciate such beauty, helps to bring about the required transition from the agreeable to the morally good.

Although it seems relatively clear that some confidence that "nature is on our side" is a necessary condition of the possibility of the moral life for Kant, it does not follow from this that an aesthetic appreciation of mere traces or hints of nature's harmony with these ends is likewise a necessary condition. In fact, the Kantian emphasis on the autonomy of the will might seem to run counter to the view that one need rely upon any such extrinsic factors. Certainly, the Kantian moral agent does not stand in need of them in order to have an incentive [*Triebfeder*] to be moral. What role, then, can they play in the moral life?

The explanation which I propose is admittedly somewhat speculative, but it does closely parallel the analysis that I have offered elsewhere of Kant's puzzling claim in *The Doctrine of Virtue* that there is "an indirect duty to cultivate the compassionate natural (aesthetic [*ästhetische*]) feelings in us, and to make use of them as so many means to sympathy based on moral principles and the feeling appropriate to them"[28]. What is particularly puzzling here is that this sympathy, which is supposedly cultivated by visiting scenes of human misery, such as hospitals and debtor's prisons and the like, is characterized by Kant as "one of the impulses that nature has implanted in us to do what the representation of duty alone would not accomplish"[29]. The latter makes it appear that Kant is affirming the insufficiency of the duty-motive, which would contradict the central tenet of his moral psychology.

In brief, my claim was that the cultivation of the natural feeling of sympathy is intended to fulfill a two-fold function: on the one hand, it increases our awareness of (and sensitivity to) the true suffering of others, and, therefore, our awareness of occasions for beneficent action; on the other, it makes us more capable of being moved to action by such suffering. The first part of this claim is relatively non-problematic. In order to help others in anything more than a random way, one must be aware that they are in need of help, and the cultivation of sympathetic feelings aids in this awareness by lengthening our moral antennae, so to speak.

The second part of the claim is far from unproblematic, however, since it seems to link the sympathetic feeling directly to moral motivation. For why should the virtuous person need to be moved by sympathy, and does not such reliance upon sympathetic feeling undermine the moral worth of the action (at least according to Kant's theory)? The answer, in my view, lies in Kant's doctrine of radical evil. Contrary to some interpretations, this doctrine refers not to extreme evil, which for Kant takes the form of wickedness [*Bösartigkeit*], but, rather, to an ineliminable susceptibility to temptation that characterizes even the best of us and that provides the ultimate basis for all immoral actions.[30] Although this susceptibility applies to both narrow and wide duties, it is particularly dangerous in the case of the latter. Since such duties require the adoption of a maxim committing oneself to the pursuit of a certain end, say alleviating the suffering of others, rather than the performance of specific acts, it is all too easy to become diverted, for example, to let other, prudential considerations outweigh the claim of someone in need of help. Indeed, the temptation to do so is greatly increased by the fact that, on most occasions at least, there is no guilt or demerit in the neglect of an opportunity to offer such help.[31]

Accordingly, even the truly virtuous need to be on guard against such temptation, and it is here that the feeling of sympathy comes into play by providing a kind of "counterweight" (to use Kant's somewhat misleading term) to the claims of the self-regarding inclinations. What is crucial, however, is that this feeling functions as a weapon against the propensity to evil rather than as a directly motivating factor. Thus, it is such a weapon that it enables us to do "what the thought of duty alone could not accomplish". It is also for this reason that we have at least an indirect duty to cultivate this feeling.

The present suggestion, then, is that similar considerations apply, *mutatis mutandis*, to the development of an appreciation of the indications of nature's moral purposiveness provided by beautiful natural objects. To be sure, these indications do not fulfill the epistemological function of making us aware of occasions for moral activity which we might otherwise not notice. In this respect the analogy does not apply. Nevertheless, our awareness of these indications does also serve as a "counterweight" to the tendency to ignore occasions for dutiful action, albeit in a somewhat different way than our sympathetic feelings. Whereas the latter do so by reinforcing our sense of the genuine needs of others and, therefore, of their (non-juridical) moral claims upon us, the former does so by reinforcing the sense that nature is on our side and, therefore, that our moral efforts will not be in vain. Here the temptation to be counteracted is to succumb to the thought of the futility of moral effort, which is arguably one of the prime ways in which radically evil moral agents such as ourselves tend to evade the claims of duty, especially those that do not appear to be easily fulfillable. Accordingly, this thought must constantly be struggled against, and it is here that these traces and hints of nature's moral purposiveness enter into the moral life. They do so by helping to reinforce our all too tenuous commitment to the ends that are also duties and ultimately to the highest good.

If this is correct, it would also enable us to see why we have here merely a "duty, as it were," which I take to be equivalent to an indirect duty, rather than a genuine or direct duty. It cannot be a direct duty because the development of an appreciation of nature's traces and hints of its moral purposiveness, like the cultivation of one's sympathetic feelings, is neither itself a morally necessary end nor a necessary means to the attainment of one. One could, after all, have a good will and yet totally lack the capacity or opportunity to appreciate natural beauty. For these reasons I think that the capacity to appreciate natural beauty is best characterized as a moral facilitator. Moreover, it is precisely because of humanity's inherent propensity to evil that such a facilitator is required.[32]

Such a reading also accords with Kant's brief discussion of the proper attitude towards natural beauty in *The Doctrine of Virtue*. Although he does not there refer explicitly to an indirect duty to appreciate natural beauty, he does claim that a propensity to the wanton destruction of the beauty of natural objects is contrary to our duty to ourselves. The express reason for this is that,

> "[I]t weakens or uproots that feeling in man which though not of itself moral, is still a disposition of sensibility that greatly promotes morality or at least prepares the way for it: the disposition, namely, to love something (e. g. beautiful crystal formations, the indescribable beauty of plants) even apart from any intention to use it."[33]

To claim that the feeling for the beautiful in nature greatly promotes, or at least prepares the way for morality, without being itself moral, is to claim that it serves as a moral facilitator rather than as an absolute requirement. Nevertheless, this status is sufficient to ground both the negative duty to refrain from acts of wanton destruction of natural beauties and the positive, but merely indirect, duty to take an interest in natural beauty and to develop the taste required to appreciate it.[34]

IV

Making us sensitive to hints and traces of nature's moral purposiveness is, however, only one of the two ways in which taste helps to bridge the gap between nature and freedom. The second way, which is also suggested by the above cited passage from the *The Doctrine of Virtue*, is by weaning us from sensuous enjoyment. This produces a liking that, like moral feeling, is not based on any antecedent interest, and, in the process, prepares us for the more serious business of morality. This is, of course, the feature of Kant's position developed by Schiller, and Kant gives an indication of it already in the "General Comment" following § 29, when he remarks that, "[T]he beautiful prepares us for loving something, even nature, without interest"[35]. Although this preparatory function is quite distinct from the one discussed above, it is also clearly part of the story that Kant is telling in § 42, particularly insofar as he emphasizes the analogy between the judgment of taste and the moral judgment.

But since Kant was there concerned exclusively with the appreciation of natural beauty, whereas this new function presumably applies to artistic beauty as well, it could not there receive its full development.[36] This occurs in § 59, where Kant presents his account of the beautiful (both natural and artistic) as a symbol of the morally good. He summarizes this aspect of his position at the end of this section when he writes:

> "Taste enables us, as it were, to make the transition from sensible charm to habitual moral interest without making too violent a leap; for taste presents the imagination as admitting, even in its freedom, of determination that is purposive for the understanding, and teaches it to like even objects of sense freely, even apart from sensible charm."[37]

Since taste supposedly accomplishes this in virtue of beauty's capacity to serve as a symbol of the morally good, we must begin by considering briefly Kant's analysis of this symbolic relation. Basically, a symbol for Kant is an intuition that exhibits a conceptual content in an indirect fashion (by means of an analogy). As such, it is contrasted with a schema, which exhibits it directly. Concepts of the understanding can be directly exhibited in intuition or schematized, but ideas of reason, because of their distance from everything sensible, can only be indirectly exhibited, that is, symbolized.[38]

The discussion in the *Critique of Judgment* is a further development of this line of thought, one which not surprisingly emphasizes the role of judgment.[39] According to this account, what is directly presented [*dargestellt*] in a case of indirect exhibition or "symbolic *hypotyposis*" is not the idea to be symbolized but some other (schematizable) concept. The object, which is the sensible realization of this latter concept, then functions as the symbolic exhibition of the initial (unschematizable) idea just in case judgment's reflection on it is formally analogous to the form of reflection on the original idea.[40] As Kant indicates, this procedure involves a double function of judgment (one quasi-determinative and the other reflective). In the first, judgment applies the concept to be symbolized to the object of a sensible intuition, and in the second it applies the rule for reflecting on the former object to the thought of an entirely different object, which supposedly corresponds to the original idea.[41]

Kant illustrates this by the examples of a constitutional monarchy governed by the rule of law, which is symbolized by an animate body, and a monarchy governed by an individual will, which is symbolized by a handmill. The point is that even though there is no resemblance between these two types of institution and the two types of physical object, there is one between the nature of our reflection on each of the correlated pairs. Thus, in reflecting on an animate body one necessarily appeals to the idea of a purposive, organic connection between the parts, which is supposedly also appropriate to the thought of the *modus operandi* of a constitutional monarchy. By contrast, a hand mill suggests the thought of a blind mechanism, which supposedly captures metaphorically the functioning of a despotic government.

The key to this account is the idea of a formally analogous reflection (or reflective isomorphism), which, in the examples cited, seems to concern the manner in which the relationship between the whole and its parts is conceived. More generally, the analogy concerns the rule or organizing principle that governs reflection on the sensible and intellectual objects. When these rules of reflection are sufficiently analogous the former may serve as a symbol of the latter.[42] Consequently, to claim that the beautiful is the symbol of the morally good is just to claim that there is a sufficiently significant isomorphism between reflection on the beautiful and reflection on the morally good so that the former activity may be regarded as a sensuously directed analogue of the latter.[43]

Kant makes this clear in the paragraph immediately following the one cited above, where he presents four analogous features of the two types of reflection. These are not presented as exhaustive, but they are intended to express the major ways in which the beautiful symbolizes the morally good. 1) Both involve a direct liking (although the liking for the beautiful is based on reflection on an intuition and that for the good on a concept). 2) Both likings are independent of interest (although, again, the liking for the morally good directly gives rise to one). 3) Both involve the harmony of freedom with law (in the case of the judgment of taste it is the harmony of the imagination in its freedom with the lawfulness of the understanding and in the case of the moral judgment, the harmony of the free will with itself according to laws of reason). 4) Both involve the thought of universal validity (in the case of the beautiful this is not determinable through any universal concept, whereas in the case of the morally good it is so determinable).[44]

The same analogy that explains how the beautiful symbolizes the morally good also accounts for the preparatory function of taste. Although much more needs to be said, the main point is simply that the reflection contained in the pure judgment of taste involves the transcendence of sensuously based interest and the adoption of a universal standpoint that is the aesthetic analogue of the standpoint of the autonomous moral agent as a legislating member of a kingdom of ends. Thus the development of taste can be seen as a preparation for morality.[45]

It is, however, merely a preparation and not itself a necessary condition of a good will or virtuous character. Consequently, although Kant himself does not make the point, the requirement to develop taste must once again be seen as a matter of moral facilitation and, therefore, as taking the form of an indirect duty or "duty, as it were", rather than a genuine duty. A good will or virtuous character obviously requires the kind of distancing from sensuous interest that taste engenders, but Kant would certainly not wish to claim that this aesthetic distancing is either necessary or sufficient for moral distancing. The former would have to be rejected because it rules out the possibility of a good will for those who simply lack the physical capacities or opportunity to appreciate beauty, the latter because it would require attributing such a will to the aesthete. Nevertheless, keeping in mind the background doctrine of radical evil, it does seem reasonable to claim that, by helping to wean us from too great an attachment to sensuous satisfaction and by providing an alternative standard of evaluation that appeals to our higher cognitive powers and to the judgment of others, taste can play a significant, albeit auxiliary role in the moral life.[46]

Finally, it must be re-emphasized that this second form of moral facilitation, unlike the first, applies in principle to the appreciation of artistic as well as natural beauty.[47] Since both kinds of beauty present objects suitable for a disinterested liking, both can help to weaken the attachment to sensuous interest. In fact, although the point is often either denied or ignored, Kant's account of beauty as a symbol of morality applies to both artistic and natural beauty.[48] Indeed, it must, since the analogy concerns the *act* of reflection rather than the object reflected upon, and since the four features noted above pertain to the judgment of natural and artistic beauty.

Moreover, Kant himself suggests as much in § 52, even while insisting on the importance of connecting the fine arts, "closely or remotely, with moral ideas, which alone carry with them an independent liking"[49]. As the context makes clear, Kant's point is not that fine art has no capacity to promote morality, but, rather, that unless it is connected with moral ideas its enjoyment is in danger of degenerating into a spiritually debilitating aestheticism. Thus, rather than dismissing artistic beauty completely from the moral point of view, Kant concludes only that, "In general it is the beauties of nature that are most beneficial [*am zuträglichsten*], if we are habituated early to observe judge and admire them"[50]. Although artistic beauty is here subordinated to the natural variety for the reasons just noted, it is not completely precluded from playing a morally significant role, as it would have to be, if the only such role were to provide an appreciation of traces and hints of nature's purposiveness.

Conclusion

Perhaps the major conclusion to be drawn from these considerations is that Kant's account of taste and its relationship to morality is far more complex and nuanced than is usually thought to be the case. Not only must we distinguish sharply between the narrow legitimization task of the deduction and the overall systematic concern of the *Critique of Judgment* as a whole to demonstrate that judgment provides a mediating link, making it possible to bridge the gap between nature and freedom, but we must also distinguish between two distinct ways in which taste and the experience of beauty contribute to this larger project. First, by making us aware of traces and hints of nature's "being on our side", the experience of natural beauty both produces an intellectual interest in those who are already morally predisposed and helps to strengthen a commitment to morally necessary ends; second, because of its structural isomorphism with moral reflection, the experience of beauty (whether natural or artistic) helps to wean us from an attachment to sense and prepare us for the demands of morality. Although related, these are clearly distinct functions and should not be lumped together as ways of "symbolizing morality".[51] And, if the account offered here is correct, both of these moral functions must be understood in connection with Kant's notion of an indirect duty that is closely related to the doctrine of radical evil.[52]

But even granting all of this, it must be admitted that this account is incomplete in several essential respects. Thus, there has been no reference to Kant's important account of aesthetic ideas and no *explicit* treatment of the connection between taste and the supersensible (both within and without), which is such a central theme in the last part of the *Critique of Aesthetic Judgment*.[53] And, of course, there has been no mention of the sublime, which stands in an even closer relationship to morality than the beautiful. The sublime raises a special problem for Kant's moral teleology, however, since its function is supposedly to assure us of our superiority to a potentially hostile nature, rather than to reassure us that nature is "on our side". Accordingly, a discussion of its contribution to the resolution of the gap problem requires a separate treatment.

Notes

1. All references to Kant's writings are first to *Kant's gesammelte Schriften*, herausgegeben von der Deutschen (formerly Königlich Preußischen) Akademie der Wissenschaften (= Akademie-Ausgabe [AA]), (Berlin: Walter de Gruyter (and predecessors), 1900 ff.), with Roman numerals for the volume and Arabic numerals for the page number. Second references are, together with the German title or an abbrevation for the work cited, to the standard pagination of the first and second editions, indicated as "A" and "B" respectively. Third references in brackets give the page number in the English translation of the *Kritik der Urtheilskraft* by W. S. Pluhar (Indianapolis: Hackett Publishing Company Inc., 1987) [= Pluhar-trans.]. Although I make use of Pluhar's translation, I frequently modify it, sometimes significantly.
2. Cf. AA V 175, *Kritik der Urtheilskraft* B XIX [Pluhar-trans. p. 14].
3. AA V 176, *Kritik der Urtheilskraft* B XX [Pluhar-trans. p. 15].
4. Cf. AA V 195 f., *Kritik der Urtheilskraft* B LV [Pluhar-trans. p. 36].
5. Allison, "The Gulf between Nature and Freedom and Nature's Guarantee of Perpetual Peace", in: *Proceedings of the Eighth International Kant Congress Memphis 1995* (Milwaukee: Marquette University Press, 1996) Vol. I, pp. 37–49.
6. I discuss this conflation in more detail in "Beauty and Duty in Kant's *Critique of Judgment*", forthcoming in the *Kantian Review*. The present paper is essentially a revised and condensed version of the above; though the latter's emphasis on the question of the relationship between the deduction and the moral functions of taste is replaced by a focus on the systematic significance of these functions themselves.
7. Commentators who hold the latter view include: D. W. Crawford, *Kant's Aesthetic Theory* (Madison Wisconsin: University of Wisconsin Press,

1974); K. Rogerson, *Kant's Aesthetics, The Roles of Form and Expression* (Lanham, New York, London: University Press of America, 1986); S. Kemal, *Kant and Fine Art, An Essay on Kant and the Philosophy of Fine Art and Culture*, (Oxford: Clarendon Press, 1986); and A. Savile, *Aesthetic Reconstructions: The Seminal Writings of Lessing, Kant, and Schiller* (Oxford: Basil Blackwell, 1987), pp. 129-91.

8   AA V 296, *Kritik der Urtheilskraft* B 161 [Pluhar-trans. p. 162].
9   This disinterestedness thesis has been criticized on a number of grounds, which include a general skepticism about the possibility of disinterested likings and a specific questioning of whether the liking for the beautiful falls into that category. The basic problem is sharply expressed by J. Kulenkampff, who writes: "He who likes the state of aesthetic contemplation is as interested in the existence of some object [...] as he who likes to drink a bottle of wine" ("The Objectivity of Taste: Hume and Kant", in: *Nous* 24 (1990), p. 109). Although I cannot deal adequately with this topic here, it is easy to see that this line of objection largely misses the point of Kant's disinterestedness thesis, which turns on the claim that an antecedent interest cannot serve as part of the justifying grounds for an aesthetic evaluation. The basic intuition is that if an interest is an ingredient in the assessment (which it would be if the latter were either based on or directly gave rise to an interest), then the ensuing judgment is no longer a pure judgment of taste. As such, the disinterestedness thesis functions to support the autonomy of taste, its irreducibility either to judgments of mere agreeableness or of goodness.
10 Cf. note 7.
11 Cf. AA V 205 Anm., *Kritik der Urtheilskraft* B 7 Anm. [Pluhar-trans. p. 46 note].
12 AA V 296, *Kritik der Urtheilskraft* B 162 [Pluhar-trans. p. 163]. It should be noted that Kant here characterizes interest in terms of a pleasure [*Lust*] in the existence of something rather than, as in the initial formulation, as a liking [*Wohlgefallen*] connected with the representation of the existence (or continued existence) of an object (AA V 204; *Kritik der Urtheilskraft* B 5 [Pluhar-trans. p. 45]). Nevertheless, this does not create any major difficulties, since Kant consistently treats *Wohlgefallen* and *Lust* as equivalent in his discussions of aesthetic response.
13 Cf. AA V 296, *Kritik der Urtheilskraft* B 162 [Pluhar-trans. p. 163].
14 AA V 297, *Kritik der Urtheilskraft* B 163 [Pluhar-trans. p. 164]; cf. H. Arendt, *Lectures on Kant's Political Philosophy*, ed. R. Beiner (Chicago: University of Chicago Press, 1982), pp. 76f.

15 Paul Guyer has recently argued that Kant is here referring to and criticizing the account of Marcus Herz, *Versuch über den Geschmack* (Leipzig: Hintz, 1776; second edition Berlin: Vots, 1790). See his "Nature, Art, and Autonomy", in: *Kant and the Experience of Freedom, Essays on Aesthetics and Morality* (New York and Cambridge: Cambridge University Press, 1993), pp. 241–48. Although I find this suggestion reasonable, I do not think that it materially affects the points at issue.

16 Cf. AA V 432 f., *Kritik der Urtheilskraft* B 393 f. [Pluhar-trans. pp. 320 f.]. In addition to the conception of unsocial sociability, this Rousseauian side of Kant is perhaps best in evidence in the account of the vices of culture depicted in *Religion within the Limits of Reason Alone*: AA VI 27, *Die Religion innerhalb der Grenzen der bloßen Vernunft* B 17 f. These vices are all said to be rooted in the corruption of the predisposition to humanity, which seems to be the Kantian analogue of Rousseau's *amour propre*.

17 AA V 297, *Kritik der Urtheilskraft* B 164 [Pluhar-trans. p. 164].

18 Ibid.

19 AA V 298, *Kritik der Urtheilskraft* B 164 [Pluhar-trans. p. 164].

20 AA V 298, *Kritik der Urtheilskraft* B 165 [Pluhar-trans. p. 165].

21 AA V 298 f., *Kritik der Urtheilskraft* B 166 [Pluhar-trans. pp.165 f.].

22 Cf. AA V 297, *Kritik der Urtheilskraft* B 163 [Pluhar-trans. p. 164].

23 For a characterization of the highest good as a totalizing concept see *Religion within the Limits of Reason Alone*: AA VI 5, *Die Religion innerhalb der Grenzen der bloßen Vernunft* BA VIIIf.

24 AA V 300, *Kritik der Urtheilskraft* B 169 [Pluhar-trans. p. 167].

25 Cf. AA V 301, *Kritik der Urtheilskraft* B 170 [Pluhar-trans. p. 168].

26 AA V 300 f., *Kritik der Urtheilskraft* B 169 f. [Pluhar-trans. p. 167].

27 For a critique of Kant's argument in § 42 based on similar considerations, see Crawford, *Kant's Aesthetic Theory* (cf. note 7), pp. 148–9. In contrast to Crawford, however, I take this to indicate that the argument has not yet been formulated rather than that it simply fails. Accordingly, the argument advanced in the rest of this section may be read as a response to Crawford and other critics (including Guyer) who accept his line of criticism.

28 AA VI 457, *Metaphysik der Sitten* A 131. See Allison, *Kant's Theory of Freedom* (Cambridge: Cambridge University Press, 1990), pp. 167 f.; and *Idealism and Freedom* (Cambridge University Press, 1996), pp. 122 f..

29 AA VI 457, *Metaphysik der Sitten* A 132.

30 For my detailed discussions of this issue cf. *Kant's Theory of Freedom* (cf. note 28), pp. 146–61; and *Idealism and Freedom* (cf. note 28), pp. 169–82.
31 In the *Metaphysics of Morals* (AA VI 384, *Metaphysik der Sitten* A 10 f.) Kant characterizes the contrast between virtue and lack of virtue or moral weakness as one of logical opposition, and that between virtue and vice as real opposition. According to this view, the failure to act beneficently on a given occasion, unless it reflects a principled refusal to help others, manifests a simple lack of virtue rather than vice. For a discussion of this issue see Th. E. Hill Jr., "Imperfect Duty and Supererogation", in: *Dignity and Practical Reason in Kant's Moral Theory* (Ithaca and London: Cornell University Press, 1992), pp. 147–75.
32 The same analysis applies, *mutatis mutandis*, to that other major indirect duty in the Kantian moral scheme: the requirement to cultivate (or at least not neglect) one's own happiness. According to Kant's account of this in *The Doctrine of Virtue*, what is required is to ward off poverty, since this is a great temptation to vice (AA VI 388, *Metaphysik der Sitten* A 17 f.). Although there is no explicit reference to radical evil here, it is clear that for Kant an openness to such temptation is precisely what is meant by the propensity to evil. Kant also refers to the cultivation of one's own happiness as an indirect duty in *Groundwork* (AA IV 399, *Grundlegung der Metaphysik der Sitten* BA 11 f.) and *Critique of Practical Reason* (AA V 93, *Kritik der praktischen Vernunft* A 166 f.).
33 AA VI 443, *Metaphysik der Sitten* A 107.
34 At the end of § 42 Kant does claim that we do in fact require this direct interest, since "we consider someone's way of thinking [*Denkungsart*] to be coarse and ignoble if he has no *feeling* for the beautiful in nature" (AA V 303, *Kritik der Urtheilskraft* B 173 [Pluhar-trans. p. 169–70]).
35 AA V 267, *Kritik der Urtheilskraft* B 115 [Pluhar-trans. p. 127].
36 Kant's limitation of an intellectual interest and the associated "duty, as it were," to develop taste to natural beauty has frequently been criticized in light of his theory of genius, according to which nature, in the subject, gives the rule to art (cf. AA V 307 and 309, *Kritik der Urtheilskraft* B 181 and 185 [Pluhar-trans. pp. 175 and 177]). The point here is supposedly that the theory of genius involves the overcoming of the rigid art-nature dichotomy with which Kant seems to operate in his account of interest. For a recent statement of this view see J. Kneller, "The Interests of Disinterest", *Proceedings of the Eighth International Kant Congress Memphis 1995*, ed. H. Robinson (Milwaukee: Marquette University Press, 1996)

Vol. I, Part 2, pp. 782–84. At least part of the response to this line of criticism is indicated by G. F. Munzel in her commentary on Kneller's paper ("The Privileged Status of Interest in Nature's Beautiful Forms", loc. cit., pp. 789–90). As Munzel notes, Kant uses 'nature' in a variety of senses, and in the case of the interest in natural beauty it concerns the beautiful forms of particular objects of external nature or the physical world. By contrast, 'nature' as applicable to the genius concerns the inner nature of the individual. In addition, I would also note in this context the importance of distinguishing between what are sometimes called Kant's "reception aesthetic" and his "creation aesthetic". To appreciate the beauty of a work of art involves, for Kant, recognizing it as a product of human intention, and this is what blocks the possibility of an intellectual interest in such beauty. The theory of genius, however, is the cornerstone of Kant's "creation aesthetic", so that the idea that works of genius are somehow based on "nature" (in one sense of the term), simply does not enter into the evaluation and, therefore, cannot provide the basis for an intellectual interest in artistic beauty.

37 AA V 354, *Kritik der Urtheilskraft* B 260 [Pluhar-trans. p. 230].

38 Kant insists in all three *Critiques* that *at least* this much is necessary, if ideas are to have any regulative or even practical function. Thus, in the first *Critique*, he claims that the transcendental ideas each provide an "analogon of a schema" (AA III 440, *Kritik der reinen Vernunft* A 665/B 693), in terms of which their regulative function is to be understood. Similarly, in the second *Critique*, he presents the view, already present in the *Groundwork*, that even the moral law must be thought according to an analogy (or "Typik") as a law of nature if it is to be genuinely action guiding; cf. the *Critique of Practical Reason*: AA V 67–71, *Kritik der praktischen Vernunft* A 119–126.

39 This brief account is to be contrasted with the detailed and in many ways informative discussion of this topic by G. F. Munzel, "'The Beautiful Is the Symbol of the Morally-Good': Kant's Philosophical Basis of Proof for the Idea of the Morally-Good", in: *Journal of the History of Philosophy* 33 (1995), pp. 301–29. Although there is much of value in Munzel's paper, particularly in the discussion of Kant's use of analogy and symbol in various works, I believe that the account is vitiated by a failure to note a significant difference between the third *Critique's* account of symbolization and that found in other Kantian texts. As she quite correctly notes, the usual function of a symbol for Kant is to provide some sort of cognition by way of analogy of the purely intellectual object symbolized.

Accordingly, she takes the function of the analogy with the beautiful to be to help determine, relative to us, the meaning of the idea of the morally good [*das Sittlich-Gute*], and, on her account, it does so in virtue of the analogy in causality between the way in which the morally good and the beautiful are produced. As a direct consequence of this, she is led to conclude that only artistic beauty can symbolize the morally good because only in the case of artistic production do we find the requisite analogy with moral production (cf. esp. pp. 321–26). This result is, however, not only highly counter-intuitive but also without textual support. Since Kant was so emphatic in linking an intellectual interest in beauty specifically with natural beauty, it is only reasonable to assume that if he had intended to limit the symbolic relation to artistic beauty he would have said so. In addition, this reading fails to help explain why Kant should claim that regarding the beautiful in this way (as symbol) is both natural for everyone and regarded as a duty (a topic which she fails to discuss). In my judgment, this reading is based on a two-fold mistake: 1) a failure to recognize that Kant's concern in § 59 is not with attempting to augment our cognition of the morally good (the symbolized) but rather with underscoring the significance of its symbol (the beautiful); 2) the location of the analogy in the respective modes of causality necessary to produce the symbol and the symbolized rather than in the form of reflection on each. Thus, Munzel may be correct in arguing against Guyer (loc. cit., p. 321) that the analogy Kant intends is between the morally good and a beautiful object rather than between moral and aesthetic judgment *per se*, but she fails to note that the point of this analogy lies completely in the parallelism in the reflection on these two objects.

40 Cf. AA V 351, *Kritik der Urtheilskraft* B 254 f. [Pluhar-trans. p. 226].

41 Cf. AA V 352 f., *Kritik der Urtheilskraft* B 257 [Pluhar-trans. p. 227].

42 Although the analogy goes both ways, the symbolization relation is asymmetrical, since the symbol, as exhibition of a concept (or idea), is always something sensible (or sensibly instantiable), while that which is symbolized can be something non-sensible. This is the answer to the question posed by Ted Cohen, who asked why should a good will not be taken as a symbol of a beautiful object. Cf. "Why Beauty is a Symbol of Morality", in: *Essays in Kant's Aesthetics*, ed. T. Cohen and P. Guyer (Chicago: The University of Chicago Press, 1982), p. 232.

43 Kant does not indicate just what he means here by the morally good [*das Sittlich-Gute*] and the candidates in the literature include freedom

(Guyer, "Nature, Art, and Autonomy" (cf. note 15), p. 252); the idea of the supersensible ground at the basis of morality (Crawford, *Kant's Aesthetic Theory* (cf. note 7), p. 157); the realized object of the will determined by pure practical reason (Munzel, "The Beautiful is the Symbol of the Morally-Good" (cf. note 39), pp. 317–20). Of these, I take the latter to be closest to the truth, since Kant is presumably concerned here with the object of morality, in the sense of a realized moral good, reflection on which is analogous to reflection on a beautiful object.

44 Cf. AA V 354, *Kritik der Urtheilskraft* B 259 [Pluhar-trans. p. 229].

45 Presumably, this is the point to which Kant alludes at the end of § 22, when, after noting that the indeterminate standard of a *sensus communis* is presupposed by the judgment of taste, he mysteriously asks whether there is in fact such a common sense, which serves as constitutive principle of the possibility of experience, or whether there is "a still higher principle of reason that makes it only a regulative principle for us to bring forth, for higher purposes, a common sense in the first place?" (AA V 240, *Kritik der Urtheilskraft* B 67 f. [Pluhar-trans. p. 90]) Kant does not deal with this and related questions at this point, since that would be out of place in the "Analytic of the Beautiful". Nevertheless, it is clear that the "higher purposes" are moral and that the account of the beautiful as the symbol of the morally good is intended to support the second alternative, which involves the claim that there is at least a quasi-moral requirement to develop taste (here identified with a *sensus communis*).

46 This, again, is to be contrasted with the views of Crawford, *Kant's Aesthetic Theory* (cf. note 7), pp. 153–9. He takes the claim that the beautiful symbolizes morality to mean (in part) that it expresses the idea at the basis of all morality, and he takes this to ground a duty to be sensitive to, and cultivate an interest in, the basis of morality. In addition to (in my view) mistakenly linking this argument with the deduction of taste, Crawford neglects Kant's characterization of the requirement to develop taste and the ensuing feeling for beauty as a "duty, as it were".

47 It also applies to the sublime, though I am not discussing that here.

48 Munzel, as already noted, denies that it applies to natural beauty (cf. note 39), while Guyer denies that it applies to artistic beauty, "Nature, Art, and Autonomy" (cf. note 15), p. 268.

49 AA V 326, *Kritik der Urtheilskraft* B 214 [Pluhar-trans. p. 196].

50 Ibid.

51 This is particularly characteristic of Guyer, who neglects to distinguish

between these functions. Cf. his "Nature, Art, and Autonomy" (cf. note 15), esp. pp. 265–71.

52 It might be objected at this point that the doctrine of radical evil is only developed in *Religion within the Limits of Reason Alone* and, therefore, some two years after the *Critique of Judgment*. I have argued in *Kant's Theory of Freedom* (cf. note 28) (Chapter Eight), however, that this doctrine was implicit in Kant's moral writings from the *Groundwork* on.

53 I have emphasized 'explicit', because I believe that the account of the supersensible can be explicated in terms of the analysis of nature's traces and hints, which certainly point to what Kant terms the "supersensible substrate of nature", and the weaning, elevating function of taste, which helps to increase our awareness of our own "supersensible [moral] vocation".

Stanley Cavell

Benjamin and Wittgenstein: Signals and Affinities

If there is a variously datable split within the Western philosophical mind between traditions poorly called the Anglo-American analytical and the Continental metaphysical, it is understandable that most philosophers would not feel obliged to let this much matter to them, satisfied with their own work (or dissatisfied with it in their own ways), and attending to the other shore only when institutionally or pedagogically confronted with it, say by an international conference or by a student caught up in a foreign current. Early in the conversation Dieter Henrich and I had when we first met, in Connecticut in 1971, we recognized common ground between us in the fact that this split did matter to each of us, as if not just present opportunities for thought were denied sufficient nourishment in our current philosophical dispensations but unignorable aspirations from our own pasts were thereby perhaps rendered uninheritable. A direct response of his to this loss was to accept teaching positions on some regular basis on this shore, at Columbia and then at Harvard. I gathered that the idea of his experiment was to test both what would happen to interested American students on being introduced to this tradition by one who was native to its instruction and at the same time attentive to their American condition, and, contrariwise, to test what would happen to his own teaching and writing under the pressure of extended communication with such an audience. It was a decisively successful experience, judging from my knowledge of his effect upon students (and colleagues) at Harvard, and I do not doubt that the notable philosophical increase in the United States of interest in German Idealism is due at least as much to Dieter Henrich's visits here as to any other single cause.

My own efforts at finding communicating passages between the traditions have remained active, but, for a variety of reasons, have taken more indirect or private forms. In accepting the welcome invitation to contribute to this volume I knew that I wanted to mark the common ground of that early conversation by specifying certain of these efforts of mine. But it is the nature of the indirectness that the instances lose their interest if they are forced, and yet I did not want to repeat myself unduly – as, for instance, to recall a connection I have drawn of Wittgenstein's remark (so familiar from *Philosophical Investigations*, and rather disheartening, I believe, in the Anglo-American dispensation) that Philosophy "leaves everything as it is"[1], with Heidegger's idea of thinking as "letting-lie-before-one" in *What Is Called Thinking?*[2] The plausibility of the conjunction requires a particular preparation for each side – one which shows Wittgenstein's remark to be the invitation to a task, not the expression of an (a politically "conservative") attitude, and shows Heidegger's announcement to be open to assessment (independently of its appropriation of Parmenides) in terms of Wittgenstein's proposal of perspicuousness as a philosophical mode of presentation. These are hardly matters to be hurried.

It was the coincidence of an invitation to a conference on Walter Benjamin[3] extended to non-specialists, asking them "to evaluate Benjamin's contribution to their respective fields", that prompted me to compose an explicit if limited exercise in following the mutual receptions (or non-receptions) of one side of the philosophical mind by the other, in which one side is taken as represented in certain texts of Walter Benjamin, the other as in Wittgenstein's *Investigations*. At several points I make clear my sense that many philosophical colleagues will find the links I propose between them to be at best of questionable pertinence to philosophy, both because they may regard Benjamin's work to have at best questionable pertinence to philosophy and because the material I cite from the *Investigations*, or the way I cite it, seems to pay too little attention to its more strictly philosophical problems. But all I am counting on is that the passages or points of the texts I cite are not dismissable by philosophers without a pang of intellectual conscience, so that the impulse to dismiss them has its own chance to take on philosophical pertinence.

Dieter Henrich once remarked in a seminar of his, in response, as I recall, to a student's citing an authority in attempting to adjudicate a conflict of philosophical interpretation: "It depends on whom you believe" – meaning not whose assertions you hold to be fact, but whose procedures you find to be compelling and productive. This response seemed to me, in its timing, to suggest connections among a sequence of issues bearing on the sources of philosophical conviction, where conviction is bound up with a philosophical practice of interpreting texts: If we grant that an interpretation, a way of looking at something, inherently exists in relation to opposing possibilities; and that to invoke an authority on one side or the other is to invoke an interpretation of that authority; then we might surmise that a convincing choice among interpretations will be a function of what it is you want of a text, and hence may lead you to look for an articulation of the strange thought that a text may want something of itself. Such, at any rate, seems to me a way of putting what it is I am after in the following thoughts.

Whatever the exact perimeter of my "field", let us say, of philosophy for which the invitation I have alluded to expected me to speak, it is, and while partially and restlessly, has wanted to be, territory shared with those who, however different otherwise, acknowledge some affinity with the later Wittgenstein and with J. L. Austin, if just so far as those thinkers are recognizable as inheritors, hence no doubt betrayers, of a tradition of philosophy that definitively includes Frege, Russell, Carnap, and Quine. Judged so, an honest answer to the question of Benjamin's actual contribution to the field is that it is roughly nil. But if that were my complete or only answer, I would not have accepted the prompting to respond to the question.

Two helpful anthologies of writing about Benjamin – one edited in 1994[4] and one from eight years earlier[5] – are explicit in their wish to present Benjamin in his aspect, or should one say semblance, as a philosopher; both are explicit in wishing to counter the dominating semblance of Benjamin as a great critic, as lent to him in the English-speaking world by Hannah Arendt's portrait and collection under the title *Illuminations*[6]; as they are explicit in recognizing that Benjamin at best created, and aspired to, as Adorno put the matter, "a philosophy directed against philosophy", which they are also prepared to recognize as something that a creative canonical modern philosopher, since, I suppose, Descartes and Bacon, is rather bound to do. This gesture of a disciplinary or counter-disciplinary appropriation of Benjamin focuses two points of interest for me (I do not suppose them incompatible with those editors' intentions):

(1) Benjamin's anti- or counter-philosophy may be seen specifically as immeasurably distant from and close to Wittgenstein's anti- or counter-philosophy in *Philosophical Investigations*.

(2) There is an economy of inspiration and opacity in Benjamin's prose – sometimes it is, as Emerson puts things, a play of intuition and tuition – which suggests a reason that the idea of philosophy should not simply replace or succeed that of criticism in coming to terms with his achievement: Benjamin enacts, more or less blatantly, a contesting of the philosophical with the literary, or of what remains of each, that seems internal at once to the exceptional prestige of his work and to an effect of intimacy or concern it elicits from its readers.

A sense of affinity between Benjamin and Wittgenstein helped produce the signals in my sub-title, when with the memory in my head of Benjamin's frequently cited letter to Scholem from 1931[7] in which he expresses a phantasm of his writing as a call or signal for rescue from the top of the crumbling mast of a sinking ship, I came upon a piece of his with the title "Program for a Proletarian Children's Theater" containing these sentences: "Almost every child's gesture is command and signal" and "It is the task of the director to rescue the children's signals out of the dangerous magic realm of mere fantasy and to bring them to bear on the material".[8] One hardly knows whether Benjamin is there identifying more with the director than with the child, whose world Benjamin of course enters elsewhere as well (apart from his interest in the history of children's books).[9] And I know of no other major philosophical sensibility of this century who attaches comparable importance to the figure of the child with the exception of Wittgenstein in the *Investigations*, which opens with Augustine's portrait of himself as a child stealing language from his elders, an autobiographical image that haunts every move in Wittgenstein's drive to wrest language back from what he calls metaphysics, and what we might perhaps still call the absolute.

To the extent that opening a path for Benjamin's contribution to my field will be furthered by opening certain passages between his writing and Wittgenstein's *Investigations* – which is the object of these remarks – I have to give an idea of how I have wished to see the *Investigations* received.

My interpretation of that work is as a continuous response to the threat of skepticism, a response that does not deny the truth of skepticism – that we cannot coherently claim with certainty that the world exists and I and others in it – but recasts skepticism's significance in order to throw light upon, let's say, human finitude, above all, representing all, the human achievement of words. I also go on to relate the resulting understanding of skepticism to the problematic of knowledge worked out in Shakespearean tragedy, whether in Othello's tortured doubts about Desdemona's faithfulness, or in Macbeth's anxiety about his wife's humanity, or in Lear's presentations of his worthiness for love, or in Hamlet's desire never to have succeeded, or acceded, to existence. Reading tragedy back into philosophical skepticism I would variously, in various connections, characterize the skeptic as craving the emptiness of language, as ridding himself of the responsibilities of meaning, and as being drawn to annihilate externality or otherness, projects I occasionally summarize as seeking to escape the conditions of humanity, which I call the chronic human desire to achieve the inhuman, the monstrous, from above or from below. (I wonder what might, or should, have happened to these ideas had I read earlier than mere weeks ago Benjamin's frightening portrait of Karl Kraus[10] as a misanthrope and satirist. This is I trust for another time.) Pursuing the "I" or "We" of the *Investigations* as periodically the modern skeptical subject, I find specific, quite explicit, sketches there of this figure as characterized by fixation, strangeness, torment, sickness, self-destructiveness, perversity, disappointment, and boredom. It was in a seminar I offered three or four years ago on Heidegger and Thoreau, to a group of students with whom I could more or less assume my reading of Wittgenstein, upon my saying of *Walden*[11] that it is an exercise in replacing the melancholia of skepticism by a mourning for the world, letting it go, that a student – not of philosophy but of literary studies – blurted out that I must read Benjamin's *Trauerspiel*-book.[12]

I had years earlier read just the "Epistemo-Critical Prologue" to the book profitlessly, unprepared to divine its motivations by what I had then read of Benjamin (essentially no more than, to say the truth, the essays collected in *Illuminations*[13]), and I put the thing aside, vaguely planning to seek reliable advice and then go back. It is always an issue to determine whose advice or warning you will accept in such matters, and for some reason I allowed myself, after a while, to accept this student's unguarded appeal, with its registering of an unknown affinity. As an example of the results I want to go on here to specify something of the perspective from which I follow Benjamin's identification of saturnine melancholy as a feature of the mourning play, especially in its theological conception, as *acedia*, "dullness of the heart, or sloth", which Benjamin counts as the fourth of the deadly sins, and of which he nominates Hamlet as the greatest modern portrait. This conjunction of melancholy with, let me call it, ennui or boredom, speaks to one of the guiding forces of Wittgenstein's thoughts in the *Investigations*, the recognition that his mode of philosophizing seems to "destroy everything interesting (all that is great and important)"[14]. Wittgenstein voices this recognition explicitly just once in the *Investigations* (and once more can be taken to imply it[15]), but it is invoked each time he follows the method of language-games, that is to say, punctually through the bulk of the *Investigations*. That this destruction, as Wittgenstein notes, leaves behind as it were no scene of devastation, no place that has become "only bits of stone and rubble"[16] – everything is left as it is, your world is merely as a whole displaced, transfigured by withdrawing your words from their frozen investments, putting them back into real circulation – suggests that the imaginary destruction of what we called great and important reveals our investments to have been imaginary, with the terribly real implication that so far as philosophy was and is our life (and there is no surveying the extent) our life has been trained as a rescue from boredom, delivered to an anxious twilight of interest.

That Benjamin's *Trauerspiel*-book can thus be entered as a study of a peculiar preoccupation with Shakespeare and skepticism is of pressing interest for me. (The Baroque date seems roughly to fit, but

Benjamin's concept of the Baroque, which he ties to the Counter-Reformation, is so far as I know unsettled in its application to the English-speaking dispensation. This discrepancy may prove fateful.) Continuing for a moment the theme of melancholy, one may well be struck by the fact that Benjamin's report of the emblems of melancholy, which features the dog, the stone, and the sphere (following Panofsky and Saxl's celebrated work on Dürer), turns out to report figures that all appear in *Philosophical Investigations.*

The dog, possessed classically of a melancholic look and a downward gaze, as toward the center of gravity, appears in the *Investigations* at a moment in which Wittgenstein, in one of his images of human finitude (distinguishing that from animal limitation), remarks, "One can imagine an animal angry, frightened, unhappy, happy, startled. But hopeful? And why not?"[17] The text continues by instancing this non-despairing hopelessness, as it were, of animals as follows: "A dog believes his master is at the door. But can he also believe his master will come the day after tomorrow? – And *what* can he not do here? – How do I do it?"[18] Wittgenstein's answer here is to reflect that "the phenomena of hope are modes of [the] complicated form of life [of humans]"[19], a life form he here identifies as of those who can talk, which for him seems essentially to mean, those who can fall into philosophical perplexity.

The stone appears in an equally fateful path of the *Investigations'* territory, that of our knowledge of pain, of our basis (under the threat of skepticism) of sympathy with the suffering of others. "What gives us *so much as the idea* that living beings, things, can feel anything?"[20] Countering the theory that I transfer the idea from feelings in myself to objects outside, Wittgenstein observes:

> "I do not transfer my idea to stones, plants, etc. – Couldn't I imagine having frightful pains and turning to stone while they lasted? Well, how do I know, if I shut my eyes, whether I have not turned into a stone? And if that has happened, in what sense will *the stone* have the pains?"[21]

The further working out of metamorphosis here is briefly Kafkaesque, and the association of pain with stone has a precedent in the poem of Trakl's that Heidegger interprets in his essay entitled

"Language".[22] (Is Wittgenstein's move against a narcissistic diagnosis of our knowledge of suffering not pertinent to a political imagination?)

Of course such considerations would, at best, be responded to as curiosities by more representative members of my field, and at worst, not without proper impatience, as an avoidance or betrayal of philosophy (as if I perversely emphasize the aspect of the *Investigations* that is itself a betrayal of philosophy). And I am not even mentioning Wittgenstein's place for the fly, the beetle, the lion, and the cow. Benjamin's recurrence to animals (as well as to stone and to angels) is a principle theme of a book called *Walter Benjamin's Other History*[23], which opposes Benjamin's new conception of natural history to, importantly, Heidegger's articulation of Dasein's historicity. So I might note that I am also not mentioning in connection with Benjamin's new conception of natural history that the concept of natural history occurs significantly also in the *Investigations*, in accounting for our species' ability to attribute concepts to others that imply membership in our species, such as commanding, recounting, chatting, walking, drinking, playing[24] (and, of course, accounting for an inability to exercise this ability in particular cases).

Nor will impatience be stilled as I now list the sphere – understood as the earth, the third of the emblems of melancholy – as appearing among the countless paths along which Wittgenstein tracks the philosophical pressure on words that forces them from their orbits of meaningfulness:

> "[An] example [is] that of the application of 'above' and 'below' to the earth. [...] I see well enough that I am on top; the earth is surely beneath me! (And don't smile at this example. We are indeed all taught at school that it is stupid to talk like that. But it is much easier to bury a problem than to solve it)."[25]

Preoccupied with Benjamin, we should perhaps recall that Brecht, in his *Galileo*, found it of politically revolutionary importance to provide the right explanation for the error of supposing people at the antipodes to be "below" our part of the earth. (It is worth considering whether Brecht was in his way a bit burying the problem, I mean the intellectual resources of the Counter-Reformation Church.) Perhaps a more pertinent invocation of the sphere, or its surface – pertinent now to Benjamin's struggle with classical Idealism – is the following instance of Wittgenstein's unearthing our untiring requirement of the ideal:

> "Thought is surrounded by a halo. – It's essence, logic, presents an order, in fact the a priori order of the world. [...] We are under the illusion that [...] [this] order is a *super*-order between – so to speak – *super*-concepts."[26] "The conflict [between actual, everyday, language and our requirement of the crystalline purity of logic] becomes intolerable; the requirement now threatens to become empty [Anscombe translation modified]. – We have got on to slippery ice where there is no friction and so in a certain sense the conditions are ideal, but also, just because of that, we are unable to walk. We want to walk; so we need *friction*. Back to the rough ground!"[27]

Where other theorists of melancholy emphasize the relation of the human to earth's gravity, working out the fact of finding ourselves bound or sunk upon earth, Wittgenstein, the engineer, works out the fate of our capacity to move ourselves upon it, to go on – a different insistence upon the Benjaminian theme of our existence in materiality, our new relation to objects.

Something is right in the exasperation or amusement such considerations can cause those within the tradition of Anglo-American analytical philosophy. One who insisted on such matters as the melancholy or disappointment in the *Investigations*, in the absence of, unresponsive to, the matters it instances in its Preface – matters concerning "the concepts of meaning, of understanding, of a proposition, of logic, mathematics, states of consciousness"[28], along with attention to Wittgenstein's insistence on the procedures he calls his "methods" – would not be, I would be prepared to join in saying, talking about Wittgenstein's *Philosophical Investigations*. (Though I am not prepared to identify ahead of time every way responsiveness to such matters can look.) But then why not be content to say that? Why the exasperation? Why *does* Wittgenstein write that way? Could not the occasional animals and the odd flairings of pathos, perverseness, suffocation, lostness, be dropped or ignored and a doctrine survive? Many, most serious scholars of the *Investigations* have felt so, and behaved so.

Benjamin may provide a further fresh start here, from an odd but characteristic place, in his decisive interpretation or illumination of the animals in Kafka's stories – help specifically in grasping how it is that matters which can readily seem negligible, and which after all occupy so small a fraction of the actual sentences and paragraphs of the text of the *Investigations*, can nevertheless seem to others (who do not deny the presence of the other shore) to contain, as it were, its moral, the heart of the counsel it offers. Kafka's parables, Benjamin suggests – the old friend of Gershom Scholem's – "have [...] a similar relation to doctrine as the Aggadah [the non-legal part of the talmudic and later rabbinic literature] does to the Halakah [the law or doctrine in that literature]." And Benjamin asks:

> "But do we have the doctrine which Kafka's parables interpret and which Kafka's postures and the gestures of his animals clarify? It does not exist; all we can say is that here and there we have an allusion to it. Kafka might have said that these are relics transmitting the doctrine, although we could regard them just as well as precursors preparing the doctrine. In every case it is a question of how life and work are organized in human society."[29]

The application to the *Investigations* must be rather topsy-turvy. It is a work that quite explicitly claims not to advance *theses*[30], a claim few of its admirers, I believe, believe. The closest thing to a doctrine I discern in the *Investigations* seems to occur in three short sentences that end its opening paragraph, in which Wittgenstein announces what he calls the roots of the idea of language that he sees in the picture conveyed by the paragraph from Augustine's *Confessions* referred to earlier.[31] The idea Wittgenstein formulates as follows: "Every word has a meaning. This meaning is correlated with the word. It is the object for which the word stands."[32] The 693 ensuing sections of the *Investigations* can be said to discover relics transmitting this doctrine, or precursors preparing the doctrine, ones which show the doctrine – which seems so obvious as to be undeniable, if even noticeable – to come not merely to very little, but to come to nothing, to be empty. Yet it announces in its roots – in every one of the words Augustine employs to express his memory of receiving language – the theory of language as a means of referring to the world and as expressing our desires that every advanced philosophy since Frege and Husserl and the early Russell, up to Heidegger and Benjamin and Lacan and Derrida have in one way or another contended with. Wittgenstein's originality, to my mind, is to show that the doctrine, as reflected in its countless relics, is nothing we believe, that it is its very promise of emptiness that we crave, as if that would be not less than redemption.

Students of Wittgenstein have heard something from me over the years not unlike this skeptical news, or rather this news about skepticism, and have taken it to attribute to Wittgenstein a vision of the end of philosophy, an attribution some deplore and others embrace. It will hardly be of interest to either of these receptions of Wittgenstein to hear that the dismantling of a false redemption is work enough for an ambitious philosophy. But that is in any case not the direction of issue for me at the moment, which is to suggest that if readers of Wittgenstein should be interested in Benjamin, that is because readers of Benjamin might find they have an interest in Wittgenstein. And any specific news I have from this direction, as a beginning reader of Benjamin, can only come from testifying to specific interests that I am finding in it, its bearing on the work I do, obvious and devious.

I cite one or two sentences of Benjamin's taken from each of the two most elaborated essays in the first volume of the Harvard *Selected Writings*: from "The Concept of Criticism in German Romanticism"[33], Benjamin's doctoral dissertation and most extended, I believe, investigation of the concept of criticism; and from the essay on "Goethe's *Elective Affinities*"[34], containing stretches of Benjamin's most concentrated, I believe, work of concrete, or what used in my circles to be called practical, criticism. (Some, I know, find Benjamin's later work to surpass the earlier. But can it be true, any more than in Wittgenstein's case, that the later *obviates* the earlier?)

Start with the essay on Criticism:

> "The entire art-philosophical project of the early Romantics can [...] be summarized by saying that they sought to demonstrate in principle the criticizability of the work of art."[35]

Part of what this summarizes is the idea of criticism as a sober "continuation" or "consummation" of the work of art; together with the idea that "[e]very critical understanding of an artistic entity is, as reflection in the entity, nothing other than a higher, self-actively originated degree of this entity"[36], and the corollary idea or "principle of the uncriticizability of inferior work"[37]. That movies – the best even of Hollywood talkies – are responsive to the pressure of something like the degree of critical unfolding as, say, the texts of Shakespeare, is the explicit basis of my treatment of Hollywood comedies in *Pursuits of Happiness*.[38] It is the thing that book has often and variously had charged against it, often put as my taking these films too seriously. In part the charge is a reflection of the unexplained yet decisive fact of aesthetics in the Anglo-American dispensation of philosophy, that the questions it characteristically addresses to artistic entities neither arise from nor are answered by passages of interpretation of those entities, say as represented in Benjamin's Goethe essay, as in the following sentences from it:

> "Is Goethe [...] really closer than Kant or Mozart to the material content of marriage? One would have to deny this roundly, in the wake of all the literary scholarship on Goethe, if one were seriously determined to take Mittler's words on this subject as the writer's own. [...] After all, [Goethe] did not want, like [his character] Mittler, to establish a foundation for marriage but wished, rather, to show the forces that arise from its decay. [...] [In] truth, marriage is never justified in law (that is, as an institution) but is justified solely as an expression of continuance in love, which by nature seeks this expression sooner in death than in life."[39]

This view of the justification of marriage unnervingly resembles the view taken in my articulation of Hollywood remarriage comedies in *Pursuits of Happiness*, namely that marriage is justified not by law (secular or religious, nor in particular, to cite a more lurid connection with *Elective Affinities*, by the presence of a child), but alone by the will to remarriage. That articulation, however, denies Benjamin's rider, which proposes that continuance in love seeks its expression sooner in death than in life (perhaps Benjamin means this as a smack at a Romantic suggestion that it is easier to love eternally than diurnally). This is to say that the remarriage narratives I isolate as the best among classical Hollywood talkies (the ones best able to bear up under what I call philosophical criticism), locate the idea in a comic form, one to define which I find to require, for example, a concept of repetition grounded in Kierkegaard's and in Nietzsche's ideas of repetition and of recurrence; and a concept of the relation of appearances to things-in-themselves that challenges Kant's curtaining between them; a concept of attraction or magnetism that does not depend upon beauty; and a theory of morality that requires a working out of Emersonian perfectionism in its differences with the reigning academic forms of moral theory, deontological or Kantian, and teleological or Utilitarian. I would like to claim that this represents on my part a struggle, in Benjamin's perception, "to ascertain the place of a work or a form in terms of the history of philosophy", something Benjamin implies is his project in the *Trauerspiel*-book.[40]

I hope to get further into a discussion of this claim with Benjamin's writing more than with any other, but I anticipate trouble from the outset. For his inescapable essay of a few years later, "The Work of Art in the Age of Mechanical Reproduction"[41], in its sense of the invention of photography and of film as perhaps having "transformed the entire nature of art", does not seek confirmation for this sense of film by means of the criticism of individual films, nor does it suggest that film (some films) can be read as containing the idea which philosophical criticism is to consummate. – Of course not, if the consequence of this transformation is that we no longer possess a developing concept of art, that (in Wittgensteinian terms) nothing any longer plays this role in our form of life. – It would be worth knowing more surely (I seem to persist in counting on some reasonably positive answer) whether film, for an example, within the trauma of its role in transforming our ideas of the authorship and the audience and the work of the work of art, has mysteriously maintained, in something like the proportion of instances one would expect in any of the arts in the modern period, the definitive power of art to suffer philosophical criticism; and if film, then perhaps post-film.

Supposing for the moment that an interest in Wittgenstein's work taken from the perspective of Benjamin's would lead to contributions of Benjamin to something like my field, or to modifying the field, I ask in drawing to a close, more specifically, what the profit or amplification might be for Benjamin's projects. I cite moments from two projects which seem to me to cry out for consideration within and against a Wittgensteinian development, that is, for subjection to the exposure of mutual translation.

First from "On Language as Such and on the Language of Man": "The enslavement of language in prattle is joined by the enslavement of things in folly almost as its inevitable consequence."[42] This is an early reflection of Benjamin's insight into the language of the bourgeois for which Scholem (in the letter I alluded to earlier)[43] praises him as he rebukes him for disfiguring his metaphysics of language by claiming its relation to dialectical materialism. Benjamin responds by recognizing a necessary intellectual risk here, but what were his options in theorizing the Kierkegaardian/Heideggerean theme of "prattle"? Evidently he does not wish to endorse either Kierkegaard's Christianity nor Heidegger's own mode of explicating Dasein's thrownness and falling, which would mean in effect accepting his articulation of life in the crowded everyday. Has he an account of what language is such that it *can* corrupt itself?

Here is a great theme of Wittgenstein's *Investigations*, an essential feature of which (in which Austin's work adjoins Wittgenstein's) is the investigation of thinking's internal relation to nonsense, an investigation of course related to logical positivism's obsession with meaninglessness, and radically and specifically opposed to its mode of accounting for it. (I do not know how far one may go in taking the interest in nonsense to be definitive of what came to be called analytical philosophy, an interest that fruitfully differentiates it from its estranged sibling, called continental metaphysics.) Naturally a philosophical attention to the essential possibility of nonsense in human speech can be taken to avoid Benjamin's concern with a historically specific source of human violation, say that of late capitalism. But what is the theory (of history? of philosophy? of nature?) according to which it must be so taken? And what of the possibility that an attention to history is used to avoid the glare of philosophy?[44]

The second, related project is announced in "Theses on the Philosophy of History":

> "The themes which monastic discipline assigned to friars for meditation were designed to turn them from the world and its affairs. The thoughts we are developing here originate from similar considerations. [...] Our consideration [...] seeks to convey an idea of the high price our accustomed thinking will have to pay for a conception of history that avoids any complicity with the thinking to which these politicians [traitors to the cause of anti-Fascism] continue to adhere [or, as he goes on to say, to conform]."[45]

Here I appeal to my various efforts to show Wittgenstein's and Austin's differently cast attentions to the ordinary as underwritten in the work of Emerson and Thoreau,[46] and I note the presence of the concept of conformity, an Emersonian master-tone, in aversion to which, as aversion to which, he defines thinking. The language of conformity in his society presents itself to Emerson's ears as sounds from which he finds himself continually shrinking ("Every word they say chagrins us."[47]) and which he interprets as an expression of depression – Thoreau famously characterized the lives of the mass of people as ones of "quiet desperation"[48]; Emerson had explicitly said "secret melancholy"[49]. Thoreau's invention and demonstration of civil disobedience registers the knowledge that massive depression has, whatever else, a political basis. Specifically, it interprets the emergence of consent as a political phenomenon to signal the recognition that I must acknowledge my voice as lent to, hence as in complicity with, the injustice in my society, hence recognize that I become inexpressive, stifled, in the face of it. Pathos is one response to this knowledge, and who is capable, from time to time, of grander semblances of pathos than Benjamin (as at the close of the Goethe essay)? "Only for the sake of the hopeless ones have we been given hope."[50] Here is the point at which to assess Emerson's violent efforts at cheerfulness, at raising up the hearts of his neighbors, which so grates on intellectual ears.

I suppose that this Emersonian note is a sound of hope in democracy, a kind of cost of participation in it. Emerson's formidable essay "Experience" enacts a relentless demand for attaining, or for mourning the passing of, one's own experience – adjoining signature themes of Benjamin's – an enactment through a process of judging the world that Emerson names thinking, something he also calls patience, by which he says "we shall win at the last"[51]. I take that formula in Emerson's dialect to suggest, "ween at the last", ween meaning to think something possible, as though realization is a function of active expectation now. (As in Shakespeare's *Henry VIII*: "Ween you of better luck [...] than your Master,/Whose minister you are?"[52]) And is it sure that Emerson's affirmation is too American a proposition, asking too much of that old part of us so fascinated by the necessity and the freedom of being uncomprehended? Except of course by children.

Notes

1 Wittgenstein, *Philosophical Investigations* (Oxford: Blackwell's, 1958) § 124, in what follows: *Philosophical Investigations*.
2 Cf. M. Heidegger, *What Is Called Thinking?*, trans. J. G. Gray (New York: Harper and Row, 1968).
3 The conference, "Perspectives on Benjamin", was held at Yale's Humanities Center in September 1997.
4 Cf. *Walter Benjamin's Philosophy: Destruction and Experience*, ed. A. Benjamin and P. Osborne (London: Routledge, 1994).
5 Cf. *Benjamin: Philosophy, History, Aesthetics*, ed. G. Smith (Chicago: Chicago University Press, 1989).
6 Cf. W. Benjamin, *Illuminations*, ed. H. Arendt (New York: Schocken, 1969).
7 Cf. Benjamin's letter from April 17, 1932, in: *The Correspondence of Walter Benjamin*, ed. G. Scholem and Th. W. Adorno (Chicago: Chicago University Press, 1994).
8 W. Benjamin, "Proposal for a Proletarian Children's Theater," in: *The Weimar Republic Sourcebook*, ed. A. Kaes, M. Jay, E. Dimendberg (Berkeley: University of California Press, 1994), p. 233.
9 Cf. J. Mehlman's fascinating *Walter Benjamin for Children: An Essay on His Radio Years* (Chicago: University of Chicago Press, 1993).

10 Cf. W. Benjamin, "Karl Kraus," in: *Reflections*, ed. P. Demetz (New York: Harcourt Brace Javanovich, 1978).
11 Cf. H. D. Thoreau, *Walden, or Life in the Woods* (New York: New American Library, 1980).
12 Cf. W. Benjamin, *Ursprung des deutschen Trauerspiels*, engl.: *The Origin of German Tragic Drama*, trans. J. Osborne (London: NLB, 1985).
13 Cf. note 6.
14 *Philosophical Investigations* § 118.
15 Cf. *Philosophical Investigations* § 570. Marcelo Stamm has reminded me of a striking passage dating from 1931 in Wittgenstein's *Vermischte Bemerkungen* (trans. as *Culture and Value*) where Wittgenstein first composes the *close* of a musical theme, emphazising that he does *not know* the theme itself, and then remarks: "Es [the close] fiel mir heute ein, als ich über meine Arbeit in der Philosophie nachdachte und mir vorsagte: 'I *destroy*, I *destroy*, I *destroy* –'." (in: *Werkausgabe* Bd. 8 (Frankfurt a. M.: Suhrkamp, 1984), p. 479).
16 *Philosophical Investigations* § 118.
17 *Philosophical Investigations* Part 2, p. 174.
18 Ibid.
19 Ibid.
20 *Philosophical Investigations* § 283.
21 Ibid.
22 Cf. M. Heidegger: "Language", in: *Poetry, Language, Thought*, trans. A. Hofstadter (New York: Harper and Row, 1971), pp. 187–210.
23 Cf. B. Hanssen, *Walter Benjamin's Other History* (Berkeley: University of California Press, 1997).
24 Cf. *Philosophical Investigations* § 118.
25 *Philosophical Investigations* § 351.
26 *Philosophical Investigations* § 97.
27 *Philosophical Investigations* § 107.
28 *Philosophical Investigations* Preface, p. 9.
29 W. Benjamin, "Kafka's Stories", in: *Selected Writings*, ed. M. Bullok et M. W. Jennings, Vol. I, 1913–1926 (Cambridge, Mass.: Belknap Press, 1996), p. 122.
30 Cf. *Philosophical Investigations* § 128.
31 Cf. p. 568.
32 *Philosophical Investigations* § 1.
33 Cf. W. Benjamin, "The Concept of Criticism in German Romanticism", in: *Selected Writings* (cf. note 29).

34 Cf. W. Benjamin, "Goethe's *Elective Affinities*", in: *Selected Writings* (cf. note 29).
35 Op. cit. (cf. note 33), p. 179.
36 Loc. cit. p. 152.
37 Loc. cit. p. 159.
38 Cf. St. Cavell, *Pursuits of Happiness. The Hollywood Comedy of Remarriage* (Cambridge, Mass.: Harvard University Press, 1981).
39 Op. cit. (cf. note 34), pp. 300 f.
40 Cf. op. cit. (cf. note 12), p. 105.
41 Cf. W. Benjamin, "The Work of Art in the Age of Mechanical Reproduction", in: *Selected Writings* (cf. note 29).
42 W. Benjamin, "On Language as Such and on the Language of Man", in: *Selected Writings* (cf. note 29), p. 72.
43 Cf. note 7.
44 Winfried Menninghaus, who organized the Yale conference (cf. note 3), commented to me after my talk that Benjamin was in fact interested in nonsense, construing (if I understood) the freedom from sense in fairy tales as a rescue from the dictation of sense in myth. I am not prepared now to speak to this. Nor can I now derive the tuition from a theme from the *Trauerspiel*-book that to my ear captures the intuition in my tendency to characterize the skeptic as wishing to escape the responsibility for meaning his words; I refer to Benjamin's claim that, in the Baroque antithesis of sound and meaning, "meaning is encountered, and will continue to be encountered as the reason for mournfulness".
45 W. Benjamin, "Theses on the Philosophy of History", in: *Selected Writings* (cf. note 29), p. 258.
46 Cf. my *The Senses of Walden* (San Francisco: North Point Press, 1981) as well as my *Conditions Handsome and Unhandsome. The Constitution of Emersonian Perfectionism* (Chicago: University of Chicago Press 1990).
47 Cf. R. W. Emerson, "Self-Reliance", in: *Essays*, First Series (Columbus, Ohio: Merill, 1969) Vol. I, p. 45.
48 Cf. Thoreau, "Economy" (Chap. 1), in: *The Variorum Walden*, ed. W. Harding (New York: Twayne Publ., 1962), (§ 9) p. 5.
49 Emerson, "New England Reformers", in: *Essays*, Second Series (loc. cit.) Vol. II, p. 294.
50 W. Benjamin, "Goethe's *Elective Affinities*", in: *Selected Writings* (cf. note 29), p. 356.
51 Emerson, "Experience", in: op. cit. (cf. note 47), Vol. II, p. 93.
52 W. Shakespeare, *Henry VIII*, Act V Sc. I, 135–137.

Ernst H. Gombrich

Zeit, Zahl und Zeichen
Zur Geschichte des Gedenktages*

> Wenn die Natur des Fadens ew'ge Länge,
> Gleichgültig drehend, auf die Spindel zwingt,
> Wenn aller Wesen unharmon'sche Menge
> Verdrießlich durch einander klingt;
> Wer teilt die fließend immer gleiche Reihe
> Belebend ab, daß sie sich rhythmisch regt?
> Wer ruft das Einzelne zur allgemeinen Weihe,
> Wo es in herrlichen Akkorden schlägt?
>
> Goethe, *Faust I*

Titel, Thema und Motto dieses Beitrages entstammen einer Ansprache zur Jahrhundertfeier von Ernst Cassirers Geburt. Auf die Begründung der Verwendung einer überarbeiteten Fassung dieser Ansprache als Beitrag zu Ehren Dieter Henrichs gehe ich ausführlich in der Eingangsanmerkung ein.

Der Titel, den ich für diese Überlegungen gewählt habe – also „Zeit, Zahl und Zeichen" –, soll dazu verhelfen, möglichst direkt ins Zentrum unseres Problemkreises zu führen, d. h. die Beziehung der Theorie Cassirers zur Philosophie der Kunst. Freilich muß ich dazu erklären, wie dieser Titel zustande kam: Als ich nämlich erfuhr, daß Nelson Goodman einen seiner Beiträge englisch *Words, Worlds and Works* nannte, reizte es mich, ein deutsches Gegenstück zu seinen Alliterationen zu finden, und so kam es eben zu „Zeit, Zahl und Zeichen".

Natürlich macht ein solches Spiel mit der Sprache nicht den Anspruch, ein Kunstwerk zu sein, doch teilt es etwa mit der Dichtkunst die Eigenschaft, aus den Gegebenheiten der Sprache heraus, also aus dem geltenden Zeichensystem, geschaffen zu sein. Bei einer solchen

Schöpfung wirkt das Zeichen selbst auf das Bezeichnete, den Gedanken. Denn die Sprache spiegelt hier nicht nur das Denken wider, sie regt auch zu neuem Denken an. So will ich auch nicht leugnen, daß der alliterierende Titel, den ich der deutschen Sprache abgewann, auch meine Pläne und Absichten steuerte. Er war es eigentlich, der es mir nahelegte, statt mehr allgemein über Cassirers Verhältnis zur Kunst zu sprechen, eben diesen Anlaß selbst: d. h. die Jahrhundertfeier zum Thema zu wählen. Auch dieses Thema, so stellte sich heraus, bietet ja eine Brücke zur Kunst. Nicht umsonst heißt es bei Jacob Burckhardt, das Festwesen sei der wahre Übergang vom Leben in die Kunst, und gehört nicht die Gedenkfeier auch zum Festwesen?

Wenn der Anlaß zu feiern etwa ein hundertster Geburtstag ist, so messen wir also die abgelaufene *Zeit* durch die *Zahl* der Jahre, die verflossen sind, und *bezeichnen* die Zahl mit der Ziffer 100. Dabei dürfen wir festhalten, daß der Jahresverlauf, d. h. die Einheiten, die wir gezählt haben, zu den Naturgegebenheiten gehört und daß ihre Anzahl ebenfalls eine objektive Tatsache beschreibt, während die Bezeichnung, das Symbolsystem, das wir zu unserer Verständigung verwenden, unserer Sprache, also unserer Kultur entstammt. In der Terminologie der griechischen Denker gehört das Erste zur *Physis*, zur Natur, das Andere zur *Thesis*, zur Konvention. Ohne die Periodizität der Natur, d. h. ohne die Wahrnehmung irgendeiner Wiederholung, könnten wir den Ablauf der Zeit nicht erfassen, aber die Wahl der Perioden (ob es nun der Herzschlag ist oder der Tageslauf, die Mondphasen oder die Jahreszeiten) steht bei uns und ist nicht weniger Konvention als die Bezeichnung der Zahl. Und doch, so wesentlich diese Unterscheidung zwischen Naturereignis und menschlicher Schöpfung auch sein mag, dürfen wir sie auch nicht überspannen. Wurzelt doch auch die Konvention meist in Naturgegebenheiten, nämlich in der Natur des Menschen. Unser Zahlensystem ist hier keine Ausnahme: Nicht nur schließt es an die Gegebenheit an, daß wir zehn Finger an den Händen haben, mit denen es sich bequem zählen läßt, selbst die Periodizität, auf die sich etwa die Zahl 100 mit 10 × 10 aufbaut, ruht letztendlich auf der beschränkten Fassungskraft unseres Denkvermögens. Ein Wesen mit unbeschränkter Erfindungskraft und ebenso unbeschränktem Erinnerungsvermögen könnte wohl ein solches System entbehren. Es könnte jede Zahl entlang einer beliebigen Länge der Zahlenreihe mit einem eigenen Namen oder Zeichen bezeichnen und etwa am Ende die eine Kategorie der noch ungezählten Zahlen anfügen. Für den menschlichen Geist wäre eine solche systemlose ungegliederte Zahlenreihe ebenso nutzlos wie eine rein nominalistische Sprache, in der jedem individuellen Ding ein eigener Laut zugeordnet würde. Wir brauchen die zusammenfassenden Begriffe, die Ordnung der Dinge und Zahlen nach Klassen und Unterklassen, wir können die Welt nur erfassen, indem wir sie in ein hierarchisches System einzufangen versuchen. Alle Zahlen und Maßsysteme sind so hierarchisch aufgebaut. Hundert ist eben dadurch ein Markstein und eine ausgezeichnete Stelle in der Zahlenreihe, weil es zehn mal zehn Einheiten sind. Im Duodezimalsystem hätte natürlich 144 diese psychologische und kulturelle Bedeutung.

So kann es vielleicht nicht wunder nehmen, daß für die menschliche Psyche die Periodizitäten der Natur sozusagen mit den Periodizitäten des selbstgeschaffenen Systems verschwimmen. Wir sprechen etwa von einem „runden Geburtstag", ohne uns immer darüber im klaren zu sein, daß nicht der Geburtstag, d. h. die Zahl der verflossenen Jahre „rund" ist, sondern bloß die konventionelle Bezeichnung. Der Betrieb, der sich bereits jetzt auf das kommende „Millenium" konzentriert, beweist diesen geistigen Kurzschluß zur Genüge. Der eingelernte Stellenwert der Ziffern scheint nicht weniger wirklich zu sein als der naturgegebene Kreislauf des Jahres. Ob wir nun an den Anlaß unserer Feier denken oder an das Festwesen im allgemeinen, die Tendenz, *Physis* und *Thesis* zu verschmelzen, zeigt sich fast überall.

Die regelmäßige Erfahrung und berechtigte Erwartung der Wiederkehr, die die Natur dem Menschen einprägt (und die auch noch durch organische Prozesse verstärkt wird), hat auch dazu geführt, daß der Ablauf der Zeit selbst als ein Zyklus empfunden wird, was wohl besonders für primitive und vorgeschichtliche Kulturen gilt.[1]

In seiner *Joseph-Trilogie* hat Thomas Mann diese traumhaft wirkende Auffassung mit viel Einfühlungsvermögen beschrieben: „Was uns beschäftigt" – heißt es in der „Höllenfahrt" –, „ist nicht die bezifferbare Zeit. Es ist vielmehr ihre Aufhebung im Geheimnis der Vertauschung von Überlieferung und Prophezeiung, welche dem Worte „Einst" einen Doppelsinn von Vergangenheit und Zukunft und damit seine Ladung potentieller Gegenwart verleiht. Hier hat die Idee der Wiederverkörperung ihre Wurzel."

Bei Thomas Mann gewinnt dann diese Idee Gestalt in dem Kapitel „Vom ältesten Knechte", jenem Eliezer, hinter dem der junge Joseph „eine unendliche Perspektive von Eliezergestalten sieht".

Das Extrem dieser Auffassung ist in der Vorstellung von der ewigen Wiederkehr des Gleichen erreicht, die uns von Nietzsche her vertraut ist. Sie wurde im Altertum von den Stoikern verfochten. Von Chrysippus wird der Ausspruch berichtet:

> „Es wird wieder einen Sokrates geben und einen Plato, und jeder wird dieselben Freunde und Mitbürger haben, und diese Wiederkunft wird nicht einmal stattfinden, [...] sondern in alle Ewigkeit."

„In alle Ewigkeit", das heißt „zahllose Male". Es stellt sich die Frage, wie weit die Fähigkeit des Zählens selbst, d. h. der Begriff einer unbegrenzten Zahlenreihe, erst durch die Erfindung entsprechender Zeichen bedingt war, das heißt wohl auch, daß Zeichen und Zahlen ihrerseits die geltende Vorstellung von der Zeit mitgeprägt haben.

Es wäre gewiß vermessen, hier dogmatisch zu sein, und doch wäre es möglich, daß erst die Markierung eines Ereignisses in bleibender Form, d. h. als Zeichen, auch zu der Fähigkeit geführt hat, die Zyklen der Natur miteinander zu vergleichen und auch ihren Ablauf festzulegen. Ich denke natürlich dabei in erster Linie an die Beobachtungen der Himmelserscheinungen, die zu den frühesten Errungenschaften der Kultur gehören. Was uns diese Kulturen vererbt haben, sind ja die verschiedenen Formen des Kalenders, die immer noch unser Leben begleiten. Erst die Himmelsbeobachtungen haben dazu führen können, etwa die Anzahl der Tage zu zählen, die zwischen der Wiederkehr der Sonnenwenden ablaufen, oder auch die Mondphasen, die diesen Ablauf begleiten. Die Schwierigkeit, diese natürlichen Zyklen in Einklang zu bringen, konnte doch nicht verhindern, daß der Ablauf der Zeit nun doch sozusagen diszipliniert und auch für die Zukunft festgelegt war. Ohne diese schöpferische Leistung gäbe es auch keine Zeitrechnung und natürlich auch keine Gedenktage im Festkalender einer jeden Gemeinschaft.[2]

Zwar deckt sich der Begriff des Gedenktages nicht durchaus mit dem der festlichen Feier. Mancher religiöse und gesellschaftliche Brauch statuiert auch Gedenktage für den Einzelnen, etwa den ersten Jahrestag nach dem Tode des Vaters, der im Leben der Japaner eine entscheidende Rolle spielt, oder gar den Jahrestag eines Verbrechens, für den das österreichische Strafrecht als Verschärfung „Hartes Lager und Wasser und Brot" vorschreiben kann, aber die Regel ist doch, daß die Gemeinschaft an dem Gedenktag Anteil nimmt und mitfeiert. Und hier gehen eben die Gedenktage fast nahtlos in das Festwesen über.

Schon das Alte Testament bietet genügend Beispiele dieses Zusammenhangs. Dem Zyklus der Sieben-Tage-Woche, die wohl in der nahöstlichen Astrologie wurzelt, liegt auch die Schöpfungsgeschichte zugrunde, die ihrerseits den Sabbath (oder später Sonntag) zum Festtag bestimmt, ein Zyklus, der bereits unabhängig ist von der Periodizität der Natur. Das jüdische Osterfest, das an die Ereignisse des Auszugs aus Ägypten erinnern soll, ist wie das christliche Ostern an die Mondphasen gebunden, während das christliche Weihnachtsfest die Geburt des Erlösers mit der Wiederkehr des Lichts nach der Wintersonnenwende verbindet.

Rein psychologisch gesehen liegt bei diesen und analogen religiösen Festen die zyklische Auffassung nahe an der Oberfläche. Das vorgeschriebene Ritual und seine künstlerischen Abwandlungen sollen die Gläubigen anregen, das gefeierte Ereignis neu zu erleben, wobei der inzwischen verflossenen Zeit nicht weiter gedacht wird. Und doch gibt es auch Anzeichen dafür, daß auch unsere Vorstellung einer geradlinigen Abfolge der Jahre hier mitspielen kann: So sagt etwa Jesus im Evangelium des Lukas bei der Einsetzung des Abendmahles „Das tut zu meinem Gedächtnis", eine Aufforderung, die das Ritual des Meßopfers aus einer Gedenkfeier in eine zyklische Wiederholung verwandelt.

Bei Shakespeare allerdings verbindet sich das Ereignis selbst mit der Vorhersage ihres festlichen Gedenkens.

So heißt es in *The Life of King Henry V* (Act IV Sc. III):

"He that shall live this day, and see old age,
Will yearly on the vigil feast his neighbours,
And say, "Tomorrow is Saint Crispian":
Then will he strip his sleeve and show his scars
And say, "These wounds I had on Crispin's day."
Old men forget; yet all shall be forgot.
But he'll remember with advantages
What feats he did that day: then shall our names,
Familiar in his mouth as household words, ...
Be in their flowing cups freshly remember'd.
This story shall the good man teach his son;
And Crispin Crispian shall ne'er go by,
From this day to the ending of the world,
But we in it shall be remembered."

Die Verwurzelung des Gedenktages im Kalender ist da schon selbstverständlich. Noch vielsagender und auch unheimlicher ist die Szene in *Julius Caesar* (Act III Sc. I) direkt nach dem Mord, in der Brutus ein künftiges Festritual voraussagt, das nie Gestalt gewann:

"... Stoop, Romans, stoop,
And let us bathe our hands in Caesar's blood
Up to the elbows, and besmear our swords:
Then walk we forth, even to the market place,
And waving our red weapons over our heads,
Let's all cry *Peace! Freedom! and Liberty!*

Cassius:

Stoop then, and wash. How many ages hence
Shall this our lofty scene be acted over
In states unborn and accents yet unknown!"

Wie wir wissen, gedenken wir heute Julius Caesars nicht an einem Gedenktag, sondern eigentlich einen Monat lang, denn der Juli trägt seinen Namen.

Gewiß sollte ihn dieser Beschluß unsterblich machen. Dieselbe Sehnsucht nach Unsterblichkeit beseelt auch das Gedicht des Horaz, der stolz verkündete: „Die Reihe der Jahre und die Flucht der Zeit" könne seinen Schöpfungen nichts anhaben.

Zeit, Zahl, Zeichen

"Exegi monumentum aere perennius
regalique situ pyramidum altius
quod non imber edax, non aquilo inpotens
possit diruere aut innumerabilis
annorum series et fuga temporum.
Non omnis moriar, multaque pars mei
vitabit Libitinam: usque ego postera
crescam laude recens, dum Capitolium
scandet cum tacita virgine pontifex."

(Ich hab' ein Werck vollbracht dem Ertz nicht zu vergleichen/Dem die Pyramides an Höhe müssen weichen/Das keines Regens Macht, kein starcker Nortwind nicht/Nach Folge vieler Jahr und Flucht der Zeit zerbricht./Ich kann nicht gar vergehn, man wird mich rühmen hören/So lange man zu Rom den Jupiter wird ehren.)[3]

Auch der chinesische Dichter Li Tai Peh teilte diese Zuversicht,[4] die gegen allen Anschein dem zyklischen Zeitbild nicht zuwiderläuft. Im Denken der Menschen sind diese beiden Auffassungen nicht so unvereinbar wie sie rein logisch sein mögen.

Gerade weil der zyklische Jahresablauf immer das wesentliche Denkmodell bot, führt diese Analogie fast von selbst zu der Vorstellung einer beliebig langen Folge von Zyklen, von Wiederkehr und Erneuerungen, die in den Mythen vieler Hochkulturen ihren Niederschlag gefunden haben.

Im alten Indien findet man die kühnsten Spekulationen über die Länge dieser Zeitalter, die sich eng an das dekadische Zahlensystem anschließen. Das *mahayuga*, das selbst vier ungleiche Abschnitte hat, währt 12 000 Jahre, und dieses selbst ist nur *ein* göttliches Jahr. 360 dieser Jahre sind dann ein kosmischer Zyklus, der also 4 320 000 Jahre dauert. Tausend *mahayugas* sind ein *kalpa*, und dieses ist wie ein Tag im Leben des Brahma. Hundert dieser Jahre ist die Länge von Brahmas Leben, nach dem die Zeit zu Ende ist und eine neue Schöpfung beginnt.[5]

Auch Plato spricht im *Timäus* von dem großen Jahr, der kosmischen Epoche, die ihr Ende findet, wenn alle Planeten wieder an ihren Ausgangspunkt zurückgekehrt sind. Laut einer Stelle im *Staat* scheint es, daß sich Plato dieses große Jahr nach Analogie unseres Jahres als einen Zyklus von 360 Jahren vorgestellt hat.

Diese Vorstellung „vom großen Jahr" klingt ja auch in der berühmten *Vierten Ekloge* Vergils an, die im Mittelalter als Prophetie der Geburt des Erlösers verstanden wurde:

"ultima Cumaei venit iam carminis aetas;
magnus ab integro saeclorum nascitur ordo.
iam redit et virgo, redeunt Saturnia regna"

(Schon erfüllte sich ganz die Zeit Cumäischer Sänge/Schon von neuem beginnt der Jahrhunderte mächtige Ordnung/Kehrt uns die heilige Magd und kehrt das Reich des Saturnus.)[6]

In den erwähnten Beispielen handelt es sich wohl um esoterisches Wissen und esoterische Erwartungen, die das Leben der Allgemeinheit kaum berührt haben mögen. Dagegen scheint es in der Kultur Alt-Mexikos einen viel kurzfristigeren Zyklus gegeben zu haben, der einschneidend in das Leben der Gemeinschaft eingriff:

Dort handelt es sich um ein „Bündel" von 52 Jahren, bei dessen Zu-Ende-Gehen alle Feuer ausgelöscht werden müssen. Gemäß der grausamen Rituale dieser Kultur wurde die neue Flamme in der Brust eines Menschenopfers entzündet und von dort in alle Richtungen getragen.

Weitaus am einflußreichsten für die abendländische Kultur waren die übergreifenden Zyklen der alten Juden. Die entscheidende Stelle hier ist die Vorschrift im 3. Buch Moses, 25, die vor allem die Feldarbeit regulieren will. So wie der 7. Tag der Woche ein Ruhetag ist, so soll auch das 7. Jahr ein Ruhejahr der Felder sein, die brachliegen müssen.

Nach dem Ablauf von 7 Zyklen von 7 Jahren, d. h. nach der Vollendung von 49 Jahren, schreibt das Alte Testament ein Jubeljahr vor, das daher alle 50 Jahre stattfindet. In Luthers Übersetzung heißt es:

„Und du sollst zählen solcher Sabbatjahre sieben, daß sieben Jahre siebenmal gezählet werden, und die Zeit der sieben Sabbatjahre mache neun und vierzig Jahre. Da sollst du die Posaune lassen blasen durch all euer Land am zehnten Tage des siebenten Monats, eben am Tage der Versöhnung. Und ihr sollt das fünfzigste Jahr heiligen und sollt ein Freijahr ausrufen im Lande allen, die drinnen wohnen; denn es ist euer Halljahr. Da soll ein jeglicher bei euch wieder zu seiner Habe und zu seinem Geschlecht kommen."

Man darf wohl fragen, ob es jemals möglich war, diese Bestimmungen wörtlich einzuhalten.[7] Und doch wirkten sie auch im Christentum nach, denn der zugrunde liegende Gedanke, die zuversichtliche Hoffnung auf eine endliche Erneuerung nach langer Frist, ist ja naturgegeben durch das Absterben und Aufblühen der Pflanzenwelt. Was nicht naturgegeben ist, ist natürlich die Zahl der Jahre und Tage, auf der die Vorschrift beruht und die in diesem Falle dem Zyklus der Woche entlehnt ist.

An sich widerspricht wohl dieses Messen des Zeitablaufs dem zyklischen Gedanken, aber es wäre müßig zu fragen, wie und seit wann das Zählen der Jahre zur kulturellen Konvention wurde. Die Zahl der Lebensjahre ist es vielleicht nicht, die Anlaß zu dieser Gewohnheit gegeben hat, denn auch heute wissen viele Menschen in primitiven Kulturen nicht genau, wie alt sie sind. Anders steht es natürlich mit den Ahnenreihen bis in die graue Vergangenheit und auch mit der Hoffnung auf Nachkommenschaft bis in die fernste Zukunft, die uns aus der Bibel vertraut ist und die bereits ein lineares Zeitbild impliziert.

In den Hochkulturen sind es wohl vor allem die Lebensjahre des Herrschers und der Dynastien, die allgemein für die betreffende Gemeinschaft den Maßstab des geschichtlichen Ablaufs bilden und dadurch auch das Gefühl der jeweiligen Distanz zu der Vergangenheit befestigen. Die Herrscherlisten des alten Orients geben meist die Zahl der betreffenden Regierungsjahre an, und der hellenisierte Ägypter Manetho numerierte auch die Dynastien – ein Gebrauch, der sich bis heute erhalten hat.

Die Möglichkeit, ein einzelnes Ereignis als festen Punkt zu nehmen, von dem aus der Ablauf der Jahre gezählt wurde (also was wir die Bestimmung einer *Ära* nennen), reicht weniger weit zurück. Zwar zählten die Buddhisten die Distanz der Jahre, die sie von der Geburt oder dem Tod des Buddhas trennten, aber verschiedene lokale Traditionen kamen zu verschiedenen Resultaten. Auch die Rechnung der Zeit seit der Gründung Roms, *ab urbe condita*, schwankte lange, und dasselbe gilt für die christliche sowie für die jüdische *aera*.

Solange das Zeitbewußtsein und selbst die *aera* schwankend blieben, konnten auch Gedenktage nur proklamiert und nicht vom Kalender abgelesen werden. Das galt wohl für die Jahrhundertfeier

Roms, für die Horaz sein *Carmen Saeculare* schrieb, nicht weniger als für andere Gründungsfeiern.[8]

Erst die Konstruktion eines allgemein verbindlichen Zahlengerüsts, zu der die Anerkennung der *aera* führte, ermöglichte jene vorhersehbaren und festgelegten Feiern, die wir Gedenktage nennen.

Es kann kaum überraschen, daß die ersten solchen Feiern, von denen wir Kenntnis haben, sich an die biblische Satzung des Jubeljahres anschlossen. Dabei beruht freilich die Bezeichnung auf einem Übersetzungsfehler: Wie erinnerlich, ist im Alten Testament von einem Hornsignal zu lesen, das den Beginn der Feier proklamieren soll. Das hebräische Wort für das Widderhorn, um das es sich handelt, ist *Jobel*, was als *Jubel*, oder lateinisch *iubilatio* gedeutet wurde.

Im Jahre 1300 hat Papst Bonifaz VIII. das erste kirchliche Jubeljahr promulgiert, wobei er sich auch auf ein Gerücht bezog, demzufolge das gleiche auch hundert Jahre früher geschehen sei. Der Zustrom von Pilgern in diesem und in den folgenden Jubeljahren legte es nahe, dieses gewinnbringende Fest noch häufiger zu feiern, erst waren es alle fünfzig, dann alle dreiunddreißig Jahre, bis Pius II. dekretierte, daß alle 25 Jahre ein heiliges Jahr sei.

Es scheint, daß es der Protestantismus war, der vielleicht in Anlehnung an diesen päpstlichen Brauch die erste echte Jahrhundertfeier beging. Sie wurde im Jahre 1617 in Deutschland zum Gedenken an die Reformation des Jahres 1517 begangen, wie die aus diesem Anlaß geprägten Gedenkmünzen bezeugen. Die katholische Seite ließ nicht lange auf sich warten. Der Jesuitenorden gab seinerseits zur Feier seines hundertjährigen Bestehens ein Prachtwerk mit Emblemen heraus, mit dem Titel *Imago primi saeculi Societatis Iesu* aus dem Jahre 1640.

Was diese Beispiele bestätigen, ist die ursprüngliche Verbindung solcher Feiern mit dem Leben einer bestimmten Gemeinschaft. Es ist die eigene Geschichte, deren gedacht werden soll.

So ist bereits im 15. Jahrhundert in Florenz der zweihundertsten Wiederkehr von Dantes (wahrscheinlichem) Geburtstag gedacht worden, wobei den Florentinern besonders viel daran lag, ihren großen Dichter, den sie verbannt hatten, öffentlich zu ehren. So wurde im

Jahre 1465 beschlossen, daß Domenico Michelino ältere Gemälde im Dom durch das Portrait ersetzen sollte, das auch heute dort noch hängt.[9]

Es scheint, daß die wachsende Popularität der Jahrhundertrechnung aus dem schulmäßigen Geschichtsunterricht stammt und bereits um 1700 allgemein war.[10] So häufen sich seit dieser Epoche auch die Nachrichten von Jahrhundertfeiern.

Jedenfalls feierte die Universität von Frankfurt an der Oder im Jahre 1706 das Jubiläum ihres hundertjährigen Bestehens im Beisein des Königs von Preußen,[11] und im Jahre 1728 erschien in Goslar eine Gedenkschrift zu Ehren Albrecht Dürers „um eben die Zeit, als er vor 200 Jahren die Welt verlassen". Ein Vorreiter eines Festzuges, der kein Ende nehmen sollte.

Die erste Jahrhundertfeier zur Wiederkehr des Geburtstages eines großen Philosophen, von der ich Kenntnis habe, war zu Ehren des 100. Geburtstages von Leibniz; im Jahre 1746 hielt Johann Christian Gottsched eine lateinische Festrede an der Leipziger Universität.

Merkwürdigerweise ist das erste großaufgezogene Fest zu Ehren eines berühmten Mannes, das ausdrücklich als Jubiläum bezeichnet wurde, mit keiner runden Zahl verbunden: Ich denke an das große „Shakespeare Jubilee" des Jahres 1769 in Shakespeares Geburtsstadt Stratford upon Avon, dessen *spiritus rector* der Schauspieler David Garrick war. Viele der weniger erfreulichen Begleiterscheinungen solcher Jubiläen mit ihrem Rummel, Kitsch und ihrer Kommerzialisierung machten sich schon damals bemerkbar. Die Wahl des Datums, wie gesagt, kam dabei zufällig zustande, die Idee entwickelte sich aus einer Stiftung einer Shakespeare-Statue durch Garrick, dem dafür das Ehrenbürgerrecht von Stratford verliehen wurde. Wahrscheinlich war G. F. Händel der erste Komponist, dessen 100. Geburtstag im Jahre 1785 in England gefeiert wurde,[12] was gut zu der Tatsache paßt, daß seine Werke auch nach seinem Tode weiterhin aufgeführt wurden.

Der früheste Beleg für das Wort „centenary" in unserem Sinn findet sich im englischen Wörterbuch für das Jahr 1788, wo es sich auf die politische Gedenkfeier zur Erinnerung an die Glorious Revolution von 1688 bezieht.

Natürlich boten Festlichkeiten dieser Art dem gesteigerten Nationalbewußtsein des 19. Jahrhunderts eine willkommene Gelegenheit, das Gemeinschaftsgefühl zu stärken.[13] Als die Akademie der Künste in Berlin im Jahre 1820 eine öffentliche Säkularfeier zu Ehren Raffaels veranstaltete, wurde schon im voraus bestimmt, den Todestag Dürers nicht weniger glanzvoll zu feiern. Tatsächlich wurde aus der Dürerfeier des Jahres 1828 ein Nationalfest der deutschen Romantik. Aber auch dies wurde in den Schatten gestellt durch die große Schillerfeier des Jahres 1859 zum 100. Geburtstag des Nationaldichters, in der die patriotische Rhetorik wahre Orgien feierte.

Daß auch die regierenden Herrscherhäuser ihr angestammtes Recht auszunützen wußten, ihre Untertanen durch Familienfeste und Jubiläen fester an sich zu binden, versteht sich fast von selbst. Meine Mutter (geb. 1873) erinnerte sich noch im hohen Alter an den prunkvollen Festzug in Wien, den der Maler Makart zu Ehren der silbernen Hochzeit des Herrscherpaares im Jahre 1879 inszenierte. Auch das „Jubilee" zu Ehren der fünfzigjährigen Regierung der englischen Königin Victoria im Jahre 1887 lebte noch in der Einnerung weiter. Mit feiner Ironie hat Robert Musil seinen Roman *Der Mann ohne Eigenschaften* um die vergebliche Planung einer solchen dynastischen Feier kreisen lassen: das erhoffte siebzigste Regierungsjahr des „Friedenskaisers" Franz Joseph im Jahre 1918, dessen Festlichkeiten das dreißigste Regierungsjubiläum Kaiser Wilhelms II. im selben Jahr in den Schatten stellen sollten.

Es hätte kaum viel Sinn, wenn ich versuchte, von hier noch die Linien zu ziehen, die zu unserer heutigen Situation führen, wo schon die Kalender und Almanache des nächsten Jahres dafür sorgen, daß wir die Gelegenheit zu Gedenkfeiern nicht versäumen.[14] Verleger und Ausstellungsveranstalter, Rundfunk- und Fernsehintendanten, die Tourismusindustrie nicht zu vergessen, erweisen sich dankbar für eine solche Anregung zur Programmgestaltung. Vor einiger Zeit erhielt ich eine Einladung vom polnischen Kulturinstitut in London zu einer Ausstellung aus Anlaß des ersten polnischen Kinoplakates vor damals hundert Jahren.

Die gesellschaftlichen und wirtschaftlichen Faktoren, die zu dieser Inflation geführt haben, liegen auf der Hand. Aber gewiß gibt es auch tiefere Gründe für dieses ständige Anwachsen von Gedenktagen. In unseren schnellebigen Zeitläufen des technischen Fortschritts fällt die Vergangenheit nur allzuleicht der Vergessenheit anheim. Was seinerzeit dieser bedrohlichen Tendenz Einhalt bot – das „Denkmal" –, hat sich als wenig wirksam erwiesen. Wir gehen oder fahren an den Statuen verdienter Männer und Frauen vorbei, ohne die Inschrift zu lesen oder sie auch nur zu bemerken. Etwas besser steht es um die Gedenkstätten, den wirklichen oder legendären Schauplatz mythischer oder religiöser Ereignisse, die auch heute noch Schwärme von Pilgern anziehen. In ihrer säkularisierten Form sind sie die bewährten „Sehenswürdigkeiten" für Touristen, die gerne hören, das betreffende Haus, oder wenigstens der Raum, sei noch genauso, wie ihn der berühmte Mann verlassen habe, das heißt, etwa im Goethehaus in Weimar sei die Zeit stillgestanden. Aber nur der Gedenktag vermag einer gleichgesinnten Gemeinschaft die Sicherheit zu geben, daß Leistung und Ereignisse der Vergänglichkeit trotzen können, wie das Horaz mit Recht so zuversichtlich erhoffte. Sein Werk gehört eben der Kultur, der „allgemeinen Bildung" an, die sich bewußt ist, in der Vergangenheit zu wurzeln. So negiert der Gedenktag – im Gegensatz zur rituellen Feier – auch keineswegs den linearen Ablauf der Zeit. Er kann uns auch die Distanz bewußt machen, die uns von dem gefeierten Ereignis trennt, das uns dennoch unverlierbar sein soll.

Anmerkungen

* Auf den ersten Blick mag es abwegig wirken, daß ich hier zur Ehrung eines hochgeschätzten Kollegen einen Beitrag herangezogen habe, dessen Vorfassung auf die Jahrhundertfeier von Ernst Cassirer im Oktober 1974 zurückgeht. Und doch hege ich begründete Hoffnung, daß dieser Beitrag Dieter Henrich nicht unwillkommen sein wird: Die damalige Feier war es nämlich, die uns zusammenführte und die auch zum Anlaß wurde, daß Prof. Henrich ganz unerwarteterweise mich für den Hegelpreis der Stadt Stuttgart vorschlug. Vielleicht verdanke ich diese Auszeichnung auch dem Zufall, daß ich krankheitshalber verhindert war, nach Hamburg zu kommen, und daß Prof. Henrich es freundlicherweise übernahm, meine Rede dort zu verlesen. Wie dem auch sei, sie hat offenbar sein Interesse erregt, und ich schrieb ihm damals, daß ich an eine Veröffentlichung erst denken könnte, nachdem ich das Ganze überarbeitet und straffer gefaßt hätte. Das Resultat dieser Bemühungen liegt nun endlich hier vor. Dabei stellte sich heraus, daß ein inzwischen erschienenes einschlägiges Werk mich der Notwendigkeit enthob, viele der angeführten Tatsachen weiter durch Quellennachweise zu belegen. Es handelt sich um das unschätzbare Büchlein von Arno Borst, *Computus, Zeit und Zahl in der Geschichte Europas*, Berlin 1990, dessen 270 Fußnoten eine wahre Fundgrube zur Bibliographie des Themas bieten. So darf ich hoffen, daß diese Fassung, die freilich auch nur den Weg absteckt, der einmal zum Ziele führen mag, den Empfänger nicht zu sehr enttäuschen wird.

1 Cf. *Shapes of Philosophical History*, ed. F. E. Manuel, Stanford 1965.
2 Cf. *Festivals in World Religions*, ed. A. Brown, Essex 1985, ein Buch, das für englische Schulen bestimmt ist und Beiträge von Spezialisten enthält.
3 Übertragung von Martin Opitz.
4 Eine deutsche Paraphrase dieses Gedichts findet sich in H. Bethge, *Die Chinesische Flöte*, Leipzig 1920.
5 Ich zitiere nach M. Eliade, *Le Mythe de l'Éternel Retour*, Paris 1949, S. 169 – 171; bezüglich der mannigfaltigen Komplikationen dieser Anschauungen, cf. R. Gombrich, „Ancient Indian Cosmology", in: *Ancient Cosmologies*, ed. C. Blacker und M. Loewe, London 1975, ein Band, der auch weitere Beiträge zu unserem Thema enthält.
6 Übertragung von R. A. Schröder.
7 Für das Nachleben, cf. B. Z. Wacholder, „The Calendar of Sabbatical Cycles during the Second Temple and the Early Rabbinic Period", in: *Hebrew Union College Annual* (1973), S. 153 – 196.
8 Cf. M. Bernhart, *Handbuch zur römischen Münzkunde*, Halle 1926, S. 75 ff.
9 Cf. C. Marchisio, *Monumento pittorico a Dante in Santa Maria del Fiore*, Rom 1956.
10 Cf. J. Burkhard, *Die Entstehung der modernen Jahrhundertrechnung. Ursprung und Ausbildung einer historiographischen Technik von Flaccius bis Ranke*, Göppingen 1971, besprochen von: A. Witschi-Benz, in: *History and Theory* XIII 2 (1974).
11 Cf. H. H. Monk, *The Life of Richard Bentley, D. D.*, London 1833, S. 191.

Für dies und das Folgende bin ich meinen Kollegen am Warburg Institute, vor allem Otto Kurz, verpflichtet.
12 Dr. Burney, *An Account of the Musical Performances* [...] *in Commemoration of Händel*, s. l. 1785.
13 Cf. das Sammelwerk von E. Brix und H. Steckl, *Der Kampf um das Gedächtnis. Öffentliche Gedenktage in Mitteleuropa*, Wien 1997.
14 Der Jahreskalender des Verlags Deike in Kreuzlingen z. B. verspricht „pro Jahr ca. 1600 Geburtstage, Todestage, Denktage ...".

Hans-Georg Gadamer

Wissen zwischen gestern und morgen

Das Thema der Zeit ist vor allem durch Heideggers *Sein und Zeit* in den Vordergrund unseres philosophischen Interesses gerückt worden. Man wird sich dabei insbesondere des griechischen Hintergrunds des Problems der Zeit bewußt, wobei Augustinus das Problem auf die Formel brachte, daß man zu wissen meine, was die Zeit ist, danach gefragt aber nicht sagen könne, was sie sei.[1] Man versteht diese Schwierigkeit der Bestimmung dessen, was die Zeit *ist*, ohne weiteres, insofern die Zeit nicht eigentlich „ist", sondern *vergeht*. Die Spanne zwischen gestern und morgen scheint dem Anspruch zuwiderzulaufen, den das Wissen erhebt, denn wenn etwas Wissen auszeichnet, so ist es gerade dessen Unabhängigkeit von den Veränderlichkeiten des Geschehens. Gleichwohl ist das Problem der Zeit schon früh ein Gegenstand des philosophischen Denkens geworden, und so begegnet es im Schrifttum von Plato ebenso wie bei Aristoteles in wichtigen Zusammenhängen. Aristoteles war bemüht, von dem Begriff des „Jetzt" aus die ständig abrollende Kette der von der Zeit durchlaufenen Jetztpunkte als ihre eigentliche Struktur herauszuarbeiten. Plato hingegen betont stärker das Rätselvolle der Zeit, wenn von ihm das Herausfallen der eigentlichen Zeiterfahrung aus aller Vergänglichkeit zum Thema gemacht wird. Das griechische ἐξαίφνης übersetzt man in der Regel als das „Plötzliche", also gerade als das, das sich allem Kalkulieren und Beherrschen der Zeitlichkeit entzieht. Vollends ist die aristotelische Definition der Zeit als Kette von Jetztpunkten eine Herausforderung für unser Denken, in der ein Jetzt nur die Grenze zwischen einem Soeben und einem Alsbald darstellt: Das Jetzt ist selber gleichsam nur eine Grenzbestimmung und teilt insofern die ontologische Rätselhaftigkeit des Punktes, der ohne Ausdehnung ist.

Die Zeit ist sozusagen eine Denkfigur, der nichts entspricht, von dem man sagen möchte, daß es „Sein" hat. Deswegen habe ich die

Formel „zwischen gestern und morgen" gewählt, weil sie zwar unbestimmt und doch allgegenwärtig ist. Mit der Frage nach der Zeit ist offenkundig mehr gemeint als die logisch-begriffliche Schwierigkeit, die in dem Problem des Seins der Zeit gelegen ist, das in Wahrheit ein Vergehen ist. Gestern und morgen sind mehr als nur ein gewesener und ein kommender Jetzt-Punkt.Wie schon im Wort „morgen" anklingt, ist mit der Formel „zwischen gestern und morgen" auch kein willkürlicher Einschnitt ausgesprochen, der das „Zwischen" ausmacht; vielmehr ist eine Gliederung der Zeiterfahrung selbst zu Grunde gelegt, die alles Lebendige artikuliert: der Rhythmus von Tag und Nacht, Wachsein und Schlaf. Dieser Rhythmus hat schon früh das Denken beschäftigt. Heraklit etwa sah die unheimliche Nachbarschaft dieser täglichen Erfahrung von gestern und morgen, die als Zeit erfahren wird, mit der Todeserfahrung.[2] Sie rührt in der Rätselhaftigkeit des totenähnlichen Schlafes und der immer neuen Überraschung des Erwachens an den Tod als dem Ende aller Erfahrung.

Und doch, man kann sich gleichsam des Anspruches nicht erwehren, den das Wissen auf zeitlose Gültigkeit erhebt. Insofern auch haben nicht zufällig die Philosophie und die sie begleitende Wissenschaft in der ständigen Fühlung mit und Nachbarschaft zur Mathematik ihren ersten Weg genommen. Der griechische Ursprung von „Mathematik" – μάθημα – verweist darauf, daß ihr Gegenstand allein durch vernünftiges Denken erlernt werden kann, so daß es nicht dem vorübereilenden Fluß der Erscheinungen und Veränderungen ausgesetzt ist. In ihrer Distanz zu aller möglichen Erfahrung sind Geometrie und Zahlenkunde auf ein Jenseitiges von Raum und Zeit gerichtet. Es ist die reine Vernunft, die das eigentlich Wißbare auszeichnet, das sich nicht nur auf ein gerade Anwesendes, Jetziges und Gegenwärtiges bezieht, sondern ein Wissen von etwas Zeitlosem ist. Dieser Sinn von „Zeitlosigkeit" der Wissensinhalte steht in besonderer Weise zu dem quer, was wir in der Erfahrung der vergehenden Zeit artikulieren, wenn wir von „gestern" und von „morgen" sprechen. Was kann ein *Zwischen* zwischen diesen beiden Erfahrungen, der Erfahrung des Gestern und des Morgen, überhaupt sein? Daß zwischen beiden Erfahrungen ein Gegensatz besteht, ist unverkennbar. Beiden

Richtungen des Fragens, was das Gestern und was das Morgen ist, haftet etwas von Dunkelheit an, und doch in verschiedener Weise. Geht man von zwei Dunkelheiten aus, zwischen denen ein Augenblick der Helle auftritt, so hat für uns das Vergangene eine andere Qualität als das Kommende. Der Helle des Tages gegenüber ist das *Gestern* im Verblassen und Verdunkeln. Das Vergangene ist unabänderlich, unserer Verfügung entzogen, weswegen die Griechen Wert darauf gelegt haben zu sagen, selbst die Götter könnten Geschehenes nicht ungeschehen machen. Am Ende kann man vom Vergessen des Vergangenen sprechen: Man *kann* das vergessen, was *vergangen* ist. Umgekehrt ist das *Morgen* zwar vom Augenblick des Erwachens unserer Aufmerksamkeit an, im hellen Lichte unserer geistigen Gewärtigkeit, dasjenige, was noch „Zeit hat" und „vor uns liegt", was aber ebensosehr in die Ungewißheit des Planens, des Erwartens und des Hoffens gehüllt bleibt. So kann sich die Wissenschaft der Zukunft gegenüber nur mit der größten Vorsicht und mit zögernden Schritten bemächtigen wollen. Dennoch ist unser Leben ungeachtet der Unberechenbarkeit der Zukunft von einem Vermuten, Voraussehenwollen, Planen, Orientieren und Hoffen auf das Zukünftige hin erfüllt.

Man stellt sich unwillkürlich die Frage, ob nicht auch das Gestrige dem Wissen mehr oder minder entgeht. Die Wissenschaft hat die hinter uns liegende Vorzeit von jeher mit ganz anderen Mitteln und in ganz anderer Weise zu bestimmen versucht als die Zukunft. Von besonderer Bedeutung sind die Formen des Mythos, der Sagen und der dichterischen Wiederkehr. Die Gegenwärtigkeit des Vergangenen scheint in besonderer Weise für den Rückruf in die Gegenwart offen zu sein. Ob die Rede von einer „Wissenschaft" hier angemessen ist, ist allerdings umstritten. Die historischen Wissenschaften haben sich sogar als Bezeichnung nicht recht etablieren können, so sehr auch die griechische Kultur gerade in ihren Historikern besondere Meisterleistungen der Vergegenwärtigung und der Verständlichmachung des Vergangenen hervorgebracht hat. Das Wort *Historie*, das wir mit lateinischem Akzent aus dem Griechischen kennen, verleugnet im Grunde selber die Vergangenheit. Es ist der *Augenzeuge* – derjenige, der dabei war – der die Grenze zwischen Vergangenheit und Gegenwart leugnet. Der Raum aber, in dem die Erhellung der Vergangenheit ursprünglich statthatte, ist der öffentliche Platz, der Raum des Festes und Rituals, in dem die Vergegenwärtigung wirkliche Wiederkehr ist.

Weder Zukunft noch auch Vergangenheit sind jedoch in demselben Sinne da, in dem das Wissen, unter Durchmessung des *Gegenwärtigen*, sich vermittelt. Es ist ein großes Ereignis in der Geschichte der menschlichen Kulturen allgemein im Verhältnis zu ihrer Vergangenheit, daß neben das Gedächtnis die Schriftlichkeit getreten ist, und man fragt sich, ob nicht auch die Wissenschaft der Mathematik und der ihr innewohnende Beweisbegriff bereits einen Fortschritt an Abstraktion verrät und vorbereitet, den wir im Übergang vom Rhapsoden-Zeitalter in das Zeitalter der Schriftlichkeit und der Lesekultur vollziehen. Zu den großen Ereignissen der abendländischen Kultur im besonderen gehört ohne Zweifel, daß dieser Schritt mit der Entwicklung des Alphabets einherging, wobei ein entscheidender Schritt der Griechen der war, auch die Vokale in die Schriftzeichen aufzunehmen. Eine interessante Frage ist, wann die Lesekultur sich von der Vokalisation im Sinne des begleitenden Sprechens befreit hat und der reinen Abstraktionskraft der Zeichendeutung vertraute. Mit dem Übergang zur *Schrift* geht ein bedeutungsvoller Wandel einher: Die Übersetzung mündlicher Rede in die Schriftlichkeit ist die Umsetzung in eine neue Gattung, in der die Sprache etwas anderes leisten muß als im oralen Vortrag, der u. a. von Gesten, von der Modulation der Stimme, von der Konzentration in und auf die Rede begleitet ist. Man nimmt an, daß in der antiken Welt bis in das 12. Jahrhundert hinein die Stimme das Lesen begleitete[3]. Mit der Durchsetzung der Schriftlichkeit ist demgegenüber der Ausfall einer ganzen Dimension der Zeichengebung verbunden. Uns ist inzwischen das *nicht* von der Stimme begleitete Lesen so geläufig, daß auch das, was an der Schriftlichkeit „Stil" genannt wird, eine besondere Bedeutung entfaltet hat. Dies steht auch im Gegensatz zu der Rede, die ehedem dem vortragenden Rhapsoden überlassen und anvertraut war. Das Herauslesen des Gemeinten aus den schriftlichen Symbolen nimmt mit dem Gutenbergzeitalter eine vollends neue Entwicklung, die eine neue Lesekultur zur Folge hat. Sie trägt insbesondere dem utilitaristischen Aspekt der Informationsvermittlung

Rechung. Wir sind durch den gegenwärtigen technologischen Fortschritt, im Zeitalter des Computers und der technischen Kommunikation, im Begriff, eine abermals neue Wendung zu durchlaufen. So beobachten wir, wie mit diesem Fortschritt mehr und mehr die lyrische Poesie an Lebenskraft verliert. Daß Lyrik den stimmlichen Klang im Lesen mitverlangt und „hörbar" sein muß, macht die Selbständigkeit und damit auch die Dimension der Kunst im Gebrauch der Sprache in einem ganz anderen Grade aus, als dies den heutigen Lesegewohnheiten entspricht und dem modernen Leser abverlangt wird. Gleiche Wirkung hat auch die Ausbreitung der durch Reproduktion bestimmten Kommunikationsformen, wie sie durch die technischen Übertragungsmedien im Gebrauch der Sprache herrschend geworden sind. Es gehört zu dieser Entwicklung, daß der gewandelte Gebrauch der Sprache selber vieles ausschließt, was ehedem an Gemeinsamkeiten und Möglichkeiten der Mitteilung zwischen Menschen bestand. Die technische Vermittlung führt zu einer unaufhebbaren Verarmung der Gegenseitigkeit im Miteinander. Die Folgen werden sich auch an der Wissenschaft selber beobachten lassen, sofern die eigentliche Kunst des Erzählens, der Erzeugung von Erwartung und Spannung, der Überraschung und der unmittelbaren affektiven Berührung erlahmt und zu weiteren Abstraktionsgraden der Sprache führen wird. Eine solche Wirkung kennen wir bereits aus der Rolle, die die Information und ihre Vermittlung im öffentlichen Umgang spielt. Nicht nur der Gebrauch des Wortes selber, sondern zugleich auch die Weise des Umgangs mit der Mitteilung, die die Information enthält, wird dabei unter anderem unsere geschichtlichen Wissenschaften beeinflussen.

Wenden wir uns nun dem Wissen um die Zukunft zu. Selbstverständlich beeinflußt der Stand unseres Wissens auch die Erwartungen, die wir auf die Zukunft richten. Schon im Begriff der Information liegt in Wahrheit ein Zukunftsbezug, sofern deren Berücksichtigung dem zukünftigen Handeln entgegenkommen soll. Information ist ja eine Beschränkung, die dem Handelnden eine Entscheidung nicht suggeriert oder anrät, sondern nur eine Hilfe für die eigene Entscheidung anbieten will. (Das gerade ist es, was das Miteinander in diesen Formen der Kommunikation so verarmen läßt.) Gleichwohl bleibt alles Handeln primär auf seine Folgen hin gerichtet und damit in der Zukunftsdimension. Es ist der Entwurfscharakter, der in allem Handeln liegt, so wie umgekehrt das Bereuen oder Beklagen begangener Fehler nur von begrenzter Handlungswirkung ist. Wenn wir auch einer Wissenschaft von der Zukunft keine große Bedeutung beimessen können, so sind wir doch auf den Gebrauch der Wissenschaft überhaupt angewiesen, auch wenn die Folgen unseres Handelns in all ihrer Ungewißheit verbleiben. Wir können diese Zusammenhänge insbesondere an dem, was man Hoffnung nennt, studieren. Die Hoffnung ist eine Grundstruktur unseres Lebensbewußtseins, ohne die wir die Belastungen des Lebens wohl kaum tragen könnten. Trotzdem bleibt es eine beherzigenswerte Wahrheit, daß angesichts der Unvorhersehbarkeit der Zukunft unser Handlungsfreiraum ständig an Grenzen stößt. Freilich wird man auch nicht unterschätzen dürfen, wie sehr Wissenschaft und Technik regelnde Kräfte geworden sind, die *ihrerseits* den Handlungsfreiraum beengen. Es ist auffällig, wie der Wert der Hoffnung etwa in primitiven agrarischen Kulturen zurücktritt, weil das eigene Handeln die stärkere Triebkraft des Erfolges ist. Hoffnung ist allerdings ein Schwächezeichen des Wissens, wenn sie *eitle* Hoffnung ist. Man gibt sich leeren Hoffnungen hin, statt vorzusorgen, den Acker zur rechten Zeit zu bestellen bzw. zu tun, was die Voraussicht gebietet. Aus diesem Grund warnt Hesiod, wie auch die griechische Mythologie, vor der leeren Hoffnung, der gegenüber der Mensch vielmehr kraft seines eigenen Willens Vorsorge treffen und wachsam sein soll. An der Wiege der abendländischen Kultur steht sicherlich ein Sinn von Hoffnung, der mit einem Vorausschauen verbunden und auf ein Handeln hin ausgerichtet ist, das aus einem Planen und Sich-Orientieren hervorgeht. Man muß an dieser Stelle weiter nach dem Unterschied zwischen „Hoffnung" und „Entwurf" fragen, aber es ist zugleich offenkundig, daß die Menschen hier philosophische Fragen stellen, auf die zu antworten niemand in der Lage ist – nach der Zukunft, dem Tode, dem Sinn des Lebens, nach dem Glück. Geht man von der Grundvoraussetzung dieses Fragens aus, bezeichnet sie, um mit Kant zu sprechen, eine menschliche Naturanlage, die uns Menschen von jeher auch für die von den Religionen angebotenen Antworten empfänglich macht. Im Zusammenhang dieses Fragens steht auch das Problem eitler Hoffnung in der Weise, wie sich die christliche Tradition zu ihm gestellt hat. Mit allen Religionen ist eine Verheißung verbunden, die das Mysterium des Todes annehmbar machen und es dem Menschen ermöglichen soll, den Tod im Lebensbewußtsein zu tragen. Wir erfahren die Beschränktheit unserer Voraussicht letzten Endes auch aus der entscheidenden Beengung der menschlichen Zukunft, die der Tod darstellt. Was man in der Philosophie die Transzendenz nennt, drückt auf verschiedene Weise aus, daß aller Voraussicht und Vorsorge eine Grenze gesetzt ist. Gewiß liegt in dem Verheißungssinn über den Tod hinaus eine religiöse Urerfahrung der Menschheit. Wir müssen allerdings auch innerhalb der verschiedenen herrschenden Religionswelten mit folgenschweren Differenzen in der Wirkungsweise der industriellen Revolution rechnen. Ich denke hier im besonderen an die Bedeutung des Calvinismus für die Zivilisationsentwicklung der modernen europäischen Welt. Daß wirtschaftlicher Erfolg als ein Zeichen göttlicher Gunst gewertet wird, hat ohne Zweifel den Fortschrittsglauben und den wirtschaftlichen Wettkampf überhitzt und umgekehrt die Rolle der ritualen Lebensordnungen geschwächt, die in anderen Religionswelten weniger reduziert worden sind, selbst wenn diese sich die Errungenschaften der Technik auch angeeignet haben.

Nun aber treten wir als solche in Erscheinung, die einerseits dem Kommenden, andererseits aber dem zugewandt sind, von dem wir herkommen. Mit der Wendung in die Vergangenheit ist ohne Zweifel noch stärker die Frage nach der Möglichkeit des Wissens verbunden. Der Unwißbarkeit der Zukunft steht (in Grenzen) die Wißbarkeit der Vergangenheit gegenüber. Wie läßt sich die Rückwendung in diese unsere jeweilige Vorgeschichte anthropologisch verständlich machen? Es scheint so etwas wie ein Be- bzw. Festhaltenkönnen im Fluß des Vergehens möglich zu sein, wobei dieses Vergehen nicht ein solches der Zeit selbst, sondern vielmehr eines dessen ist, was die Zeit mit sich bringt und wieder mit sich fortreißt. Die Erinnerung geht etwa auf Prägungen (so wie ich mich erinnere, vom griechischen Denken geprägt worden zu sein). Bei den Griechen sind μνήμη, das

Gedächtnis, und ἀνάμνησις, die Wiedererinnerung, ja die eigentlichen Grundfunktionen menschlichen Denkens, das vermag, seine eigene Herkunft festzuhalten, das Erfahrene zu sammeln, zu verarbeiten und so auch zu einem vorgreifenden Wissen zu gelangen, wie es dasjenige ist, worüber etwa der erfahrene Handwerker oder der planende Ingenieur verfügt. Sicherlich liegt in der Möglichkeit der Aneignung solchen Wissens eine entscheidende Fähigkeit des Menschen.

Ich erinnere mich der Frage Heideggers an seine Schüler danach, was das Gegenteil zu *Erwarten* sei. Die Antwort aller war: *Erinnern.* Heidegger erwiderte: „Nein: *Vergessen.*" In der Tat ist uns heute in anderer Weise bewußt, daß das Fest- und Behalten ein Zeugnis für die Vormacht des Vergessens ist und welchen Lebensgehalt wiederum dieses Vergessen selbst in sich birgt. Das Vergessen kann geradezu eine Form des Verzeihens sein, eine Möglichkeit, selbst schwerstes Unrecht, das einem widerfahren ist, zu vergeben oder aber vergeben zu lernen. Folgt man bei der Frage danach, was Vergessen eigentlich ist, dem modernen technologischen Denken, müßte das eigentliche Ideal des Wissens die Speicherung, die instantane Abrufbarkeit sein. Verhielte es sich so, wäre die Zukunft der Menschheit ihrem Erstarren sehr nahe. In Wahrheit gibt es das Wunder des Vergessens, jene Gegenmöglichkeit der Verarbeitung und Überwindung dessen, was einem zu schaffen macht, weil wir es nicht einfach vergessen oder uns bzw. dem anderen nicht schlichtweg nachsehen können. All dieses wird am Ende von den wundertätigen Kräften, die im Vergessen liegen, verwunden. Daß der Mensch über eine solche Möglichkeit des Vergessens verfügt, ist von tiefgehender anthropologischer Bedeutung. Aischylos hat in seinem *Prometheus*-Drama[4] den Prometheus-Mythos unter diesem Gesichtspunkt gedeutet: Die eigentlich *prometheische* Leistung liegt in einem Vorausschauen, das den Menschen, die ihrerseits vorausschauen, ihr vorausschauendes Wissen von ihrem Ende *verhüllt.* Dem Mythos zufolge habe der Mensch anfangs in Höhlen gelebt und ein tristes, vegetierendes Dasein in der Erwartung des für ihn im voraus sichtbaren Todes geführt. Prometheus habe den Menschen dieses Wissen von ihrem Tod genommen und dadurch den Menschen die Zukunft geschenkt. Er kann sich sodann der Erfinder aller τέχναι rühmen. Das Vermögen, vorauszubauen, ist dabei in gewissen Grenzen durch die Natur vorgeprägt, im Menschen ist es allerdings in besonderer Weise entwickelt, so daß Aristoteles etwa auch von φρόνησις spricht. Den Menschen zeichnet in besonderer Weise aus, nicht allein auf das Gegenwärtige in seiner Anziehungskraft ausgerichtet zu sein, sondern dieses zugunsten fernerer Ziele auch zurücksetzen, ausblenden oder „vergessen" zu können. In diesem Sinne ist der Mensch ein Wesen mit einem Begriff von der Zeit bzw. einem Zeitsinn, was auch die Bereitschaft zu Opfern oder zur Übernahme von Bürden einschließt, wenn dies die Abwendung oder Besserung sonst fortbestehender größerer Lasten, Beschwerden oder Leiden verspricht. Betrachtet man das menschliche Verhalten von dieser Seite, ist offenkundig, daß kein Speicherungsideal leitend ist, wenn wir unser Wissen entwickeln, mehren und vertiefen. Wir übersetzen es vielmehr in prospektive, strategische Fähigkeiten, die ein kalkulierendes, antizipierendes Wählenkönnen einschließen, aus dem Präferenzordnungen hervorgehen, die sich nicht schlechthin auf das Gegenwärtige und Verfügbare beschränken.

Vor diesem Hintergrund wird nun aber auch deutlich, daß das Vergessen sehr eng im Zusammenhang mit der Frage nach dem „Wissen zwischen gestern und morgen" steht. Wir kommen so auch zu einigen Schlußfolgerungen, die im Ausgang unserer Leitfrage zu erörtern sind. Es war schon davon die Rede gewesen, daß das Wissen zwischen gestern und morgen kein solches zwischen einem Jetzt und einen anderen Jetzt ist, was ja ohnehin eine bedenkliche Redeweise wäre, weil sie davon ausgeht, daß man über das eine, erste Jetzt noch als Jetzt verfügt, wenn man das zweite Jetzt auf das erste bezieht. Von Bedeutung ist hier, daß zwischen dem „Gestern" und dem „Morgen" nicht etwa das „Jetzt", sondern vielmehr das „Heute" steht. Was ist das Heute? Ein *heutiger Tag* etwa; ein Tag, der mit seinem Licht die Dunkelheit ablöst. Gerade vor dem Hintergrund seiner Wissensauszeichnung macht der Mensch die hochbedeutsame Grunderfahrung des Rhythmus von Schlaf und Wachsein, der auch einer des Vergessens ist: Es ist die Erfahrung dieses Rhythmus, in dem das vielleicht mit wirren Traumsignalen durchsetzte Vergessen statthat, die das Erwachen zu einer großen menschlichen Möglichkeit für unser wissendes und bewußtes Dasein werden läßt. Wir kehren sozusagen zu uns zurück, nachdem wir als Schlafende gleichsam leblos dagelegen haben und am Morgen erwachen. Bereits Heraklit stellte, wie ich eingangs erwähnt habe, in tiefsinnigen Analogien das Verhältnis des todesähnlichen Schlafes und des Todesschlafes und das Erwachen wie das Anzünden einer Helle in einem selber dar.[5] Das Erwachen ist, wie sich sagen ließe, ein *Zusichkommen*. Und es eröffnet sich im jeweiligen „Heute" ein Weg in den kommenden Tag mit neuen Erwartungen und erneuertem Lebensmut. Zwischen dem Gestern und dem Morgen liegt so das Vergessen im Schlaf und das erneute Erwachen zum Wachsein.

Für unsere Frage nach dem Wissen des Menschen zwischen der Erinnerung und dem Vergessen kann aus einer erweiterten Sicht das, was zuvor über das Fest- und Behalten, über das Wieder-Holen und Abrufen anklang, nochmals bedeutsam werden. Denn das Vermögen der Erinnerung ist eben etwas anderes als die Fähigkeit des Speicherns. Es gehört zu den Absonderlichkeiten unserer objektivierenden Wissenschaft, daß man über einen langen Zeitraum hinweg immer von *Engrammen* in einer *tabula rasa* gesprochen hat, die der Mensch ursprünglich sei. Plato, bei dem die Lehre von der *Anamnesis* anhand geometrischer Beispiele entwickelt wird, bezog sich auf die griechische Mythologie. Zweifellos spielt er auf die in der orphisch-pythagoreischen Religion gelehrte mythisch-vorgeburtliche Vergangenheit des Menschen an.[6] Zugleich soll aber zur Klarheit gebracht werden, was das *Denken* ist und welcher Zusammenhang zu der Fähigkeit des Sich-Erinnerns besteht. Im *Menon* wird bekanntlich das sophistische Argument artikuliert, daß dem Menschen die Möglichkeit der Einsicht sowohl in das, was er weiß, als auch in das Ungewußte verwehrt ist.[7] Der ἀργὸς λόγος, der diese These begründen soll, zielt darauf ab, das Fragen und Suchen als unmöglich zu erweisen. Aber wir wissen, daß im Menschen immer schon Vorprägungen und Anlagen in der μνήμη liegen, sei es im „Gedächtnis" unseres Genotyps, sei es im „Gedächtnis" unserer organisch-leiblichen Funktionen, in unserem bewußten Wahrnehmen oder auch im Sprechenlernen und der Sprache überhaupt. Das „Erinnern" ist in diesem

Sinne die Aktualisierung von Möglichkeiten, die im Menschen angelegt sind. Der Gedanke einer solchen Realisierung von Möglichkeiten bzw. Anlagen wirft ein bedeutsames Licht auch auf das, was das Wissen des Menschen zwischen einem Gestern und einem Morgen im Zeichen des Vergessens und Erinnerns sowie des Vorausschauenwollens und Orientierens in die Zukunft ist. In letzterem hat zweifellos auch das, was den Menschen zu dem fragenden Menschen macht, der er ist, seine eigentliche Wurzel. Und hieraus auch versteht sich überhaupt sein Geöffnetsein für den Horizont des Fragens und den Horizont des Möglichen.

Ich habe bislang von einer Erfahrung im Erinnern gesprochen, das ein Wählen, Gewichten und Herausheben ist und das voraussetzt, etwas abblenden und von etwas absehen zu können. Was für die Erfahrung des Einzelnen zwischen gestern und morgen gilt, gilt so aber auch innerhalb der größeren Maßstäbe „des Heutigen". Auch für das Heutige unserer gesellschaftlichen Lage, das Heutige unserer Kulturwelt, Epoche etc. gilt, daß es aus Vorprägungen, die weitgehend im dunkeln liegen, in beständiger, schrittweiser „Erhellung" zum Gegenstand unseres Wissens werden kann. Mit der Formel „zwischen gestern und morgen" drückt sich offenkundig der ganze Weltort des Menschen aus, der sich seines gesellschaftlichen Daseins und seiner politischen Verantwortung vor seinen Mitmenschen und heute vielleicht mehr denn je vor der Menschheit bewußt wird. Den Raum für ein Handeln aus solcher Verantwortlichkeit muß sich der Einzelne erst erschließen – er eröffnet sich ihm zwischen einem Gestern und einem Morgen jedoch ähnlich der Art und Weise, wie sich der jeweils neue Tag dem planenden Verhalten des Menschen jeden Morgen von neuem aufschließt.

Sowohl in der Perspektive des Einzelnen als auch im überindividuellen Horizont stellt sich aber die Frage, wie unsere Vorgeschichte, die Vorprägungen etwa, von denen die Rede war und die einen Teil unserer Herkunft ausmachen, ins *Dasein* gelangen. Bedeutsam ist Platos Antwort, der er an dieser Stelle das „Plötzliche" – ἐξαίφνης – einführt[8]: Die Zeit, in der jedes Jetzt in den Abgrund des sogleich schon Vergangenseins fällt, stellte sich als Rätsel dar. Zwischen dem einen Jetzt-Punkt und dem nächsten Jetzt-Punkt kann eigentlich nur etwas Zeitloses, das nicht in der Folge der „Jetzte" steht, mithin das „Plötzliche" angenommen werden. Wir verfügen über ein reiches Vokabular, um diese Erfahrung, etwa mit der Rede von dem Einfall oder der „Eingebung", auszudrücken. (Spricht man demgegenüber von „Inspiration", liegt darin vielleicht schon der Gedanke einer anspruchsvollen Interpretation, die den Sinn von Einfall und „Eingebung" als Hinnahme von etwas Gegebenem nicht in der gleichen Weise trifft.) Ich meine, daß von diesem Gedanken her sich entwickeln läßt, was ein Fragen, Suchen und Forschen in der wissenschaftlichen Kultur des Menschen seinem Wesen nach auszeichnet. Das Plötzliche, ἐξαίφνης, bezeichnet in Wahrheit kein Zeitmoment, kein Jetzt, sondern bedeutet vielmehr *Präsenz*, die den Raum erfüllt. Analog darf man *Helle* nicht mit dem Blitz oder der Flamme als Lichtquelle gleichsetzen. Sie ist vielmehr etwas, das sich ausbreitet und einen Raum ausbildet. Eine Eingebung ist uns auf vergleichbare Weise gegenwärtig, wenn wir auch ihren Ursprung, ihre Quelle nicht einsehen können. Weist sie uns etwa den Weg zur Lösung eines uns tief bedrängenden Problems, so können wir sie oft auch dann nicht erschöpfen, wenn wir den von ihr eröffneten Weg gleichwohl mit Besonnenheit prüfen.

Es ist der *Präsenz*-Gedanke, auf den meine bisherigen Überlegungen eigentlich ausgerichtet gewesen sind. Bislang war von „Bewußtsein" nicht die Rede gewesen. Zwischen dem Bewußten und dem Unbewußten wäre, so meine ich, eine zu einfache Trennung vorgenommen, wenn man eine Trennlinie der Art zieht, wie man sie fälschlicherweise auch zwischen dem Erinnertem und dem Vergessenen ansetzt. Dem gegenüber steht, was sich zwischen gestern und morgen im Lebensprozeß des Zu-sich-Kommens ereignet, sich aber auch auf das Ganze unserer bewußten gesellschaftlichen und politischen Handlungen übertragen läßt. Das Zu-sich-Kommen, Sich-bewußt-Werden, in dem das Dunkel der Helle weicht, ereignet sich nicht in einem Jetzt, sondern in dem Raum dessen, worin *Präsenz* statthat. Die Helle der Präsenz kann immer wieder schwinden, eine Evidenz kann sich verhüllen, wie auch eine Eingebung nichts ist, was uns treu bleiben muß. Mehr noch, sie kann sich auch als Fehleingebung erweisen und uns zu einem neuen Ansatz im Suchen zwingen, bis wir finden, was uns fehlt und worum es uns geht. Im *Symposion* läßt Plato Sokrates durch Diotima darüber belehren, was Wiederholung ist: Sie ist die Voraussetzung und damit das „Leben" der Gattung, die nur durch die Reproduktion der Individuen fortexistiert.[9] In gleicher Weise versinken alle wissenden Möglichkeiten des Menschen, wenn sie nicht wiederholt werden. Keine Wiederholung ist aber bloße Wiederholung. Sie ist Leben. In jeder Wiederholung liegt etwas von unserem zukünftigen Schicksal.

Anmerkungen

1 Cf. Augustinus, *Confessiones* XI, 14 (17).
2 Cf. Heraklit, *Fragmente* B 26.
3 Augustinus zitiert die Ausnahmefigur des Bischofs Ambrosius, der über die Fähigkeit verfügte zu lesen, ohne dabei laut zu sprechen: cf. *Confessiones* VI, 3 (3) sowie J. O'Donnells aufschlußreichen Kommentar hierzu in: *Augustine, Confessions II. Commentary on Books 1–7*, Oxford 1992, S. 345.
4 Aischylos wurde die Autorschaft dieser ganz ungewöhnlichen Tragödie lange Zeit abgesprochen, weil sie sich so erheblich von den anderen von ihm überlieferten Tragödien unterschied.
5 Cf. loc. cit. (cf. Anm. 2).
6 Cf. Platon, *Menon* 80c–82a.
7 Cf. Platon, *Menon* 81a.
8 Cf. Platon, *Parmenides* 156d.
9 Cf. Platon, *Symposion* 207d–208c.

Autorenverzeichnis

Henry E. Allison is currently Professor of Philosophy at Boston University, and Adjunct Professor at the University of Oslo. Early publications include *Lessing and the Enlightenment* (1966) and *The Kant-Eberhard Controversy* (1973). Allison is known for his *Kant's Transcendental Idealism* (1983), a study on *Benedict de Spinoza* (1987), and more recently for *Kant's Theory of Freedom* (1990). A collection of his recent essays on Kant's theoretical and practical philosophy was published under the title *Idealism and Freedom* (1996). In addition to numerous articles on various aspects of Kant's thought, Allison has also written on Kierkegaard, Locke, Berkeley, and on issues in the German enlightenment and the philosophy of religion. Among the best known of his papers not dealing with Kant is "Christianity and nonsense" (1967), an analysis of Kierkegaard's *Concluding Unscientific Postscript*. Allison is presently working on a book on Kant's third *Critique*.

Wolfgang Carl ist Professor der Philosophie an der Georg-August-Universität Göttingen. Sein philosophisches Hauptinteresse gilt Problemen der Erkenntnistheorie und Philosophie des Geistes, der Sprachphilosophie und der Geschichte der Philosophie im 18. und 19. Jahrhundert. Zu seinen frühen Veröffentlichungen gehören *Das Platonische Verständnis von Philosophie* (1966) sowie *Existenz und Prädikation* (1974). Bekannt wurde Carl insbesondere durch seine Studien zu Frege und Wittgenstein einerseits und Kant andererseits, die unter den Titeln *Sinn und Bedeutung* (1982) bzw. *Der schweigende Kant* (1989) in Buchform vorliegen. Zu Carls jüngeren Publikationen gehören *Die transzendentale Deduktion der Kategorien in der ersten Auflage der Kritik der reinen Vernunft* (1992) sowie *Frege's Theory of Sense and Reference* (1994). Gegenwärtig arbeitet Carl unter anderem an einem Projekt zu den semantischen und epistemologischen Voraussetzungen des „Standpunkts der ersten Person".

Stanley Cavell is Emeritus Cabot Professor of Aesthetics and the General Theory of Value at Harvard University. A first collection of Cavell's essays, *Must We Mean What We Say?* (1969), was followed by *The World Viewed* (1971), on the ontology of film, and *The Senses of Walden* (1972), on Thoreau as a philosopher. These constitute, as it were, three beginnings to his work, variously elaborated in *The Claim of Reason* (1979), on Wittgenstein, skepticism, and tragedy, in *Pursuits of Happiness* (1981), on the Hollywood comedy of remarriage, and in *Disowning Knowledge* (1987), on six plays of Shakespeare. *Themes out of School* (1984) and *In Quest of the Ordinary* (1988), two collections spanning these interests, are to appear in German translation in the near future. Among recent publications are *Philosophical Passages* (1995), on Emerson, Wittgenstein, Austin, and Derrida, and *A Pitch of Philosophy: Autobiographical Exercises* (1997). Having retired in 1997 from some four decades of teaching at Harvard, Cavell plans to take himself by surprise.

Index of Contributors

Roderick M. Chisholm is Emeritus Andrew Mellon Professor of the Humanities at Brown University, Providence. Chisholm has published extensively and influentially in philosophy of mind, epistemology, and metaphysics. Within analytic philosophy he was mainly responsible for renewed interest in the Austrian tradition. He is best known for producing a system of epistemic principles which attribute justification based on self-presenting psychological states, and which allow increased levels of justification on the basis of coherence. His main publications include *Perceiving* (1961), *The Problem of the Criterion* (1973), *Person and Object* (1976), *Erkenntnistheorie* (1979), an investigation on reference and intentionality entitled *The First Person* (1981, translated into German as *Die erste Person* (1992)), and *The Foundations of Knowing* (1982). Further books are a *Theory of Knowledge* (1966, 1989[3]), a study coauthored with A. W. Mellon on *Brentano and Intrinsic Value* (1986), and *On Metaphysics* (1989). His latest book deals with *A Realistic Theory of Categories* (1996).

Arthur C. Danto is Johnsonian Professor Emeritus of Philosophy at Columbia University, and art critic *(The Nation)*. He is the author of an *Analytical Philosophy of Knowledge* (1968), an *Analytical Philosophy of History* (1968), and an *Analytical Philosophy of Action* (1973); the latter two appeared in German translation also. Danto has also written books on *Nietzsche as Philosopher* (1968), and Sartre (German: *Jean-Paul Sartre* (1986)). Further publications are: *The Transfiguration of the Commonplace* (1981, German: *Die Verklärung des Gewöhnlichen* (1984)), *The State of the Art* (1987), and *Connections to the World* (1989), a German translation of which is under preparation as *Wege zur Welt*. From his later books several have already been translated into German, e. g. *Beyond the Brillo Box* (1992, German: *Kunst nach dem Ende der Kunst* (1996)), and *The Philosophical Disenfranchisement of Art* (1986, German: *Die philosophische Entmündigung der Kunst* (1993)). Among his latest publications are *Embodied Meanings* (1994), and *After the End of Art* (1997) which is due to appear in German in 1998 as *Das Fortleben der Kunst.*

Donald Davidson is Willis S. and Marion Slusser Professor of Philosophy at Berkeley University. Davidson became best known for his papers on "Actions, Reasons and Causes" (1963), "Truth and Meaning" (1967), "Mental Events" (1970), "On the Very Idea of a Conceptual Scheme" (1974), "A Coherence Theory of Truth and Knowledge" (1983), and "The Structure and Content of Truth" (1990). His *Essays on Actions and Events* (1980) brings together some of his central writings on action, and *Inquiries into Truth and Interpretation* (1984) contains some of his most important work on language. Both volumes have been translated into German: *Handlung und Ereignis* (1985) and *Wahrheit und Interpretation* (1986). "The Structure and Content of Truth" (1990) presents a unified picture of language and action. Some of Davidson's more recent essays on the philosophy of mind are collected and translated into German in *Der Mythos des Subjektiven* (1993). Davidson's present work is concerned with the source and nature of the concept of objectivity, and with extending his inquiries on the concept of truth.

Autorenverzeichnis

Michael Dummett is Emeritus Wykeham Professor of Logic at Oxford University. His philosophical work has lain chiefly in the areas of philosophy of mathematics, philosophy of logic, philosophy of language, and the relation between the latter and metaphysics. His first book was *Frege: Philosophy of Language* (1973). Since then Dummett has published three other books on Frege, among others *The Interpretation of Frege's Philosophy* (1981), the most recent being *Frege: Philosophy of Mathematics* (1991). His work furthermore includes *Elements of Intuitionism* (1977), two books of essays, *Truth and Other Enigmas* (1978, German: *Wahrheit* (1982)), and *Ursprünge der analytischen Philosophie* (1988), with a revised English version: *Origins of Analytical Philosophy* (1993). His Williams James Lectures of 1976 appeared as *The Logical Basis of Metaphysics* (1991), followed by *The Seas of Language* (1993). Dummett is preparing his Gifford Lectures (under the title *Thought and Reality*) for publication, and hopes to demonstrate that the intuitionistic continuum gives a better model of physical magnitudes than the classical continuum.

Helmut Fahrenbach ist Professor der Philosophie an der Eberhard-Karls-Universität Tübingen. Von historisch-systematischen Interpretationen (zu Kant, Kierkegaard, Marx, Nietzsche-Wittgenstein, Jaspers, Bloch, Sartre, Plessner u. a.) ausgehend suchen Fahrenbachs Arbeiten die systematischen Zusammenhänge zwischen „Philosophischer Anthropologie, Ethik und kritischer Gesellschaftstheorie", „Marxismus und Existentialismus" und „Philosophie und Politik im 20. Jahrhundert" aufzuklären. Zu seinen frühen Publikationen gehören *Kierkegaards existenzdialektische Ethik* (1968), *Existenzphilosophie und Ethik* (1970), *Zur Problemlage der Philosophie* (1975) und *Brecht zur Einführung* (1986). Beiträge aus der jüngeren Zeit sind „Philosophie und Politik nach der Erfahrung des Nationalsozialismus" (1993), „Philosophie, Marxismus und sozialistische Theorie" (1993) und „Philosophie kommunikativer Vernunft – in weltbürgerlicher Absicht und sozialistischer Perspektive" (1995).

Dagfinn Føllesdal is C. I. Lewis Professor of Philosophy at Stanford University, and also Professor at the University of Oslo. He wrote his dissertation with Quine on *Referential Opacity and Modal Logic* (1961), and works mainly in the philosophy of language, philosophy of logic, and on Husserl's phenomenology. His first philosophical publication was *Husserl und Frege* (1958), an investigation of the origins and development of Phenomenology. It has been followed by more than a hundred articles, many of them in German and variously anthologized, and some books, one of which has been translated into German as *Rationale Argumentation* (1986, written together with L. Walløe and J. Elster), on argumentation theory and issues in the philosophy of science. From 1970 to 1982 Føllesdal was an editor of *The Journal of Symbolic Logic*. He is also the co-editor of *Phenomenology and the Formal Sciences* (1991). Among his recent publications are "Gödel and Husserl" (1995) and „Die öffentliche Natur der Sprache" (1997).

Index of Contributors

Harry Frankfurt is Professor of Philosophy at Princeton University. His early work on 17th century rationalism includes *Demons, Dreamers, and Madmen. The Defense of Reason in Descartes' Meditations* (1970). Frankfurt's more recent work has been on the philosophy of action and moral philosophy. Among his most widely cited papers are "Alternate Possibilities and Moral Responsibility" (1969), "Freedom of the Will and the Concept of a Person" (1971), "The Importance of What We Care About" (1982), which gave the title to a first collection of his philosophical essays published in 1988, "On Bullshit" (1986), and "The Faintest Passion" (1992), his Presidential Address to the American Philosophical Association (Eastern Division). A second collection of essays entitled *Necessity, Volition and Love* is due to appear by the end of 1998. Frankfurt is currently engaged in trying to develop a general account of the distinction between being active and being passive, as well as in extending his inquiries into the concept of caring.

Hans-Georg Gadamer ist emeritierter Professor der Philosophie der Ruprecht-Karls-Universität Heidelberg. Sein Œuvre umfaßt Arbeiten zur antiken Philosophie, Ästhetik, Geschichtsphilosophie, zur philosophischen Hermeneutik und zur Anthropologie, die in einer zehnbändigen Werkausgabe wiederveröffentlicht sind. Zu Gadamers Buchpublikationen gehören u. a. sein Hauptwerk *Wahrheit und Methode* (1960, engl.: *Truth and Method* (1975)), *Parmenides* (1970), *Hegels Dialektik* (1971, engl.: *Hegel's Dialectic* (1976)), *Vernunft im Zeitalter der Wissenschaft* (1976, engl.: *Reason in the Age of Science* (1981)), *Die Aktualität des Schönen* (1977, engl.: *The Relevance of the Beautiful and Other Essays* (1986)) und *Die Idee des Guten zwischen Plato und Aristoteles* (1978, engl.: *The Idea of the Good in Platonic-Aristotelian Philosophy* (1986)). Weitere Werke und Beitragssammlungen Gadamers in englischer Übersetzung sind *Philosophical Hermeneutics* (1977), *Dialogue and Dialectic* (1980) sowie, jüngeren Datums, *Plato's Dialectical Ethics* (1991) und *Literature and Philosophy in Dialogue* (1994).

Ernst H. Gombrich ist Professor emeritus der Universität London, war von 1959 bis 1976 Direktor des Warburg-Instituts und bekleidete den Lehrstuhl für „Geschichte des Nachlebens der Antike". Gombrichs Hauptarbeitsgebiet umfaßt neben der Geschichte vor allem die Methode und Theorie der bildenden Künste, auch im Zusammenhang mit Problemen der modernen Wahrnehmungstheorie. Zu Gombrichs wichtigsten Publikationen zählen *The Story of Art* (1950, 1995[16], dt.: *Die Geschichte der Kunst* (1996[16])), *Art and Illusion* (1960, dt.: *Kunst und Illusion* (1967)), *The Sense of Order* (1979, dt.: *Ornament und Kunst* (1982)), *Aby Warburg. An Intellectual Biography* (1970, dt. 1981), vier Bände *Studies in the Art of the Renaissance* (1966, 1972, 1976, 1986, dt.: *(Zur) Kunst der Renaissance* (1985–1988)) sowie weitere Arbeiten zur Theorie und Geschichte der Kunst, unter anderem *The Image and the Eye* (1982, dt.: *Bild und Auge* (1984)) und *Reflections on the History of Art* (1987, dt.: *Kunst und Kritik* (1993)). Zu Gombrichs jüngeren, auf Deutsch erschienenen Büchern gehören *Gastspiele* (1992) und *Das forschende Auge* (1994).

Autorenverzeichnis

Paul Guyer is the Florence R. C. Murray Professor in the Humanities at the University of Pennsylvania. He has written widely on the history of modern philosophy and on aesthetics, but is best known for his work on Kant. He is the author of two books on Kant's aesthetics, *Kant and the Claim of Taste* (1979; second, expanded edition 1997) and *Kant and the Experience of Freedom* (1993), a book on Kant's theoretical philosophy, *Kant and the Claims of Knowledge* (1987), and, in recent years, of numerous articles on Kant's practical philosophy. He is the editor of the *Cambridge Companion to Kant* (1993) and *Kant's Groundwork of the Metaphysics of Morals* (1998). P. Guyer is the General Co-Editor of the *Cambridge Edition of the Works of Immanuel Kant*, and, with A. W. Wood, has edited and translated the *Critique of Pure Reason* for that series (1998). Kant's practical philosophy and the systematic relations of Kant's theoretical and practical philosophy with his teleology continue to be foremost among his research interests. He is also currently translating the *Critique of Judgment* for the Cambridge edition of Kant.

Colin McGinn is Professor of Philosophy at Rutgers University. He has worked and published mainly in the philosophy of mind and language, on Wittgenstein, and in ethics. He first became known for *The Subjective View* (1982), an investigation on secondary qualities and indexical thoughts, followed by *Wittgenstein on Meaning* (1984) which combines an interpretation and evaluation of Wittgenstein's philosophy of language. Thereafter appeared *Mental Content* (1989), and *The Problem of Consciousness* (1991) which brings together essays towards the problem's resolution. His book on *Problems in Philosophy* (1993) was also translated into German as *Die Grenzen vernünftigen Fragens* (1996). Recent publications are an introduction to the philosophy of mind entitled *The Character of Mind* (1997), *Ethics, Evil, and Fiction* (1997), and *Minds and Bodies* (1997). Colin McGinn is at present working on a book on philosophical logic and engaged in further inquiries on the mind-body problem.

Jürgen Mittelstraß ist Professor der Philosophie und Wissenschaftstheorie an der Universität Konstanz und Direktor des dortigen Zentrums Philosophie und Wissenschaftstheorie. Seine wichtigsten Arbeitsgebiete sind Wissenschaftstheorie und Wissenschaftsgeschichte, ferner Erkenntnistheorie und Sprachphilosophie. Zum Werk von Mittelstraß gehören neben der Herausgabe der *Enzyklopädie Philosophie und Wissenschaftstheorie* (I–IV, 1980–1996) die Monographien *Neuzeit und Aufklärung* (1970), *Die Möglichkeit von Wissenschaft* (1974), *Wissenschaft als Lebensform* (1982), *Die Wahrheit des Irrtums* (1989) und, aus dem selben Jahr, *Der Flug der Eule*. Zu seinen jüngeren Publikationen zählen *Leonardo-Welt* (1992) und *Die unzeitgemäße Universität* (1994). Mittelstraß ist zudem Koautor der Denkschrift *Geisteswissenschaften heute* (1991) und hat zusammen mit M. Carrier das Buch *Geist, Gehirn, Verhalten* (1989) geschrieben, das in ergänzter Form auch in englischer Sprache unter dem Titel *Mind, Brain, Behavior* (1991) vorliegt.

Index of Contributors

Wolfhart Pannenberg lehrte Systematische Theologie und ist Professor emeritus der Ludwig-Maximilians-Universität München. Er wurde bekannt durch den von ihm herausgegebenen Band *Offenbarung als Geschichte* (1961). Seine Hauptwerke sind: *Grundzüge der Christologie* (1964, 1990[7], engl.: *Jesus – God and Man* (1970)), *Wissenschaftstheorie und Theologie* (1973), *Anthropologie in theologischer Perspektive* (1983) sowie vor allem seine dreibändige *Systematische Theologie* (1988, 1991, 1993); diese Werke liegen unter anderem auch in englischer Übersetzung vor. Ferner erschienen von ihm *Gottesgedanke und menschliche Freiheit* (1972), *Was ist der Mensch?* (1962, 1995[8]), *Das Glaubensbekenntnis* (1972, 1995[6]) und *Gottesgedanke und Metaphysik* (1988). Zu seinen jüngeren Veröffentlichungen gehören *Toward a Theology of Nature* (1993), *Theologie und Philosophie* (1996), *Grundlagen der Ethik* (1996) und *Problemgeschichte der neueren evangelischen Theologie in Deutschland. Von Schleiermacher bis zu Barth und Tillich* (1997).

Charles Parsons is Edgar Pierce Professor of Philosophy at Harvard University. He has worked chiefly on mathematical logic, philosophy of logic and mathematics, and certain historical figures such as Kant, Frege, and Gödel. Some of his philosophical essays are collected in *Mathematics in Philosophy* (1983). More recent articles include "The Structuralist View of Mathematical Objects" (1990), "The Transcendental Aesthetic" (1992), "Platonism and Mathematical Intuition in Kurt Gödel's Thought" (1995), "What Can We Do 'In Principle'?" (1997), and "Husserl and the Linguistic Turn" (forthcoming). Parsons is editor, with S. Feferman and others, of volume III, *Unpublished Essays and Lectures* (1995) of Gödel's *Collected Works*. In addition to participating in the editing of Gödel's correspondence, he is engaged in a larger project in the philosophy of mathematics, in which intuition is a central theme.

John Perry is the Henry Walgrave Stuart Professor of Philosophy at Stanford University, and the Director of Stanford's Center for the Study of Language and Information. Perry has worked extensively in the philosophy of mind and the philosophy of language. His early work focused on identity and personal identity, and included *A Dialogue on Personal Identity and Immortality* (1978). He coauthored *Situations and Attitudes* (1983) with J. Barwise (German: *Situationen und Einstellungen* (1984)), and wrote a number of papers, some on information, with D. Israel, e. g. *What is Information?* (1991) and *Fodor and Psychological Explanations* (1991). More recent publications include a volume of selected essays, *The Problem of the Essential Indexical* (1993), including "Frege on Demonstratives", which has been translated into German as „Frege über indexikalische Ausdrücke" (1995). Perry is presently working on an integrated account of information and action.

Autorenverzeichnis

Hilary Putnam is Cogan University Professor at Harvard University. He has worked extensively on the philosophy of science (including philosophy of mathematics), as well as the philosophy of mind and philosophy of language. Many of his books have been translated into German. His work includes *Language, Mind and Knowledge* (1975), three volumes of *Philosophical Papers* (vols. 1 and 2 (1975), vol. 3 (1981)), *Reason, Truth and History* (1981, German: *Vernunft, Wahrheit und Geschichte* (1990)), and *Representation and Reality* (1988, German: *Repräsentation und Realität* (1991)). A selection of Putnam's papers has appeared in German as *Von einem realistischen Standpunkt* (1993). Among his most recent books are *Realism with a Human Face* (1992), *Renewing Philosophy* (1992, German: *Für eine Erneuerung der Philosophie* (1997)), *Words and Life* (1994), and *Pragmatism* (1994, German: *Pragmatismus* (1995)). Hilary Putnam's most recent work is concerned with interpreting and applying the insights of American Pragmatism and the insights of the later philosophy of Wittgenstein, which Putnam sees as having a certain relation to Pragmatism.

Wolfgang Schluchter ist Professor der Soziologie an der Ruprecht-Karls-Universität Heidelberg und Leiter des Max-Weber-Kollegs für kultur- und sozialwissenschaftliche Studien an der Universität Erfurt. Schluchter hat insbesondere umfangreiche Forschungen zu Max Weber unternommen. Er ist Herausgeber von und Beiträger in einer fünfbändigen Reihe, die sich mit Webers Studien zur Religionssoziologie befaßt (1981–87). Zu Schluchters Buchpublikationen gehören *Die Einheit von Wissenschaft und Geschichte* (1981), *Max Webers Kultur- und Werttheorie* (1988) sowie *Religions- und Herrschaftssoziologie* (1988). *Die Entwicklung des okzidentalen Rationalismus* (1979) liegt auch auf Englisch als *The Rise of Western Rationalism* (1985) vor. Schluchter ist zudem Koautor von *Max Weber's Vision of History* (1984). Zu seinen neueren Veröffentlichungen gehören *Rationalism, Religion, and Domination* (1989), *Unversöhnte Moderne* (1996, engl.: *Paradoxes of Modernity* (1996)) und *Neubeginn durch Anpassung?* (1996).

Hans Sluga ist Professor der Philosophie an der Universität Kalifornien in Berkeley. Sein philosophisches Hauptinteresse gilt Frege, Grundproblemen der Epistemologie, unter anderem aber auch historischen Aspekten der analytischen Philosophie und der Beziehung von Philosophie und Politik. In diesen letzten Bereich fallen Abhandlungen wie *The Break: Habermas, Heidegger and the Nazis* (1992), *Truth and Power* (1993) sowie *Heidegger's Crisis* (1993), eine Untersuchung des Verhältnisses von Philosophie und Politik im Nationalsozialismus. Slugas philosophisches Profil ist darüber hinaus durch seine Arbeiten zu Frege bestimmt. Er ist Autor von *Gottlob Frege* (1990) sowie der Herausgeber einer umfangreichen, vierbändigen Sammlung von Beiträgen zu allen Aspekten der Fregeschen Philosophie unter dem Titel *The Philosophy of Frege* (1993). Sluga ist auch Mitherausgeber des *Cambridge Companion to Wittgenstein* (1996). Er arbeitet gegenwärtig an dem Abschluß einer Studie zur politischen Philosophie.

Index of Contributors

Ernest Sosa is Romeo Elton Professor of Natural Theology, Professor of Philosophy at Brown University, Providence, and is also on the faculty at Rutgers University. He is the editor of a number of volumes among others on the philosophy of R. Chisholm (1979), on *Knowledge and Justification* (1991), and on *Causation* (1993). He is particularly known for papers collected in *Knowledge in Perspective* (1991), for more recent publications in epistemology, and for work in metaphysics and philosophy of mind. Several of his papers have been widely anthologized; among them are "The Raft and the Pyramid" (1980); "Putnam's Pragmatic Realism" (1993) and "Philosophical Skepticism and Epistemic Circularity" (1994). Sosa is now engaged in developing his favored *via media* in epistemology between internalism and externalism, and between foundationalism and coherentism, propounded as *virtue perspectivism*. He is also investigating how this *via media* is related to recent varieties of contextualism and naturalism in epistemology.

Robert Spaemann ist emeritierter Professor der Philosophie der Ludwig-Maximilians-Universität München. Seine Arbeiten befassen sich mit der Ideengeschichte der Neuzeit und der Naturphilosophie, aber auch mit Problemen der Ethik, Anthropologie und Religionsphilosophie. Zu Spaemanns frühen Veröffentlichungen zählen Studien zu L. G. H. de Bonald: *Der Ursprung der Soziologie aus dem Geist der Restauration* (1998^2) und *Zur Kritik der politischen Utopie* (1977). Zu den späteren wichtigen Veröffentlichungen gehören Studien zu Fénelon: *Reflexion und Spontaneität* (1990^2) und zu *Rousseau* (1980). In englischer Übersetzung erschienen die *Moralischen Grundbegriffe* (1996^5) als *Basic Moral Concepts* (1987) sowie *Glück und Wohlwollen* (1989) als *Happiness and Benevolence* (1998). Zu Spaemanns jüngeren Arbeiten gehören eine Untersuchung der Geschichte und Wiederentdeckung des teleologischen Denkens unter dem Titel *Die Frage wozu?* (1991^3), die Überarbeitung seiner *Philosophischen Essays* (1994^2) und eine Studie zum Unterschied zwischen „etwas" und „jemand" unter dem Titel *Personen* (1996).

Michael Theunissen ist Professor der Metaphysik und Ontologie an der Freien Universität Berlin. Seine Bücher über Sozialontologie – *Der Andere* (1965, engl.: *The Other: Studies in the Social Ontology of Husserl, Heidegger, Sartre, and Buber* (1984)) – und Hegel – *Hegels Lehre vom absoluten Geist als theologisch-politischer Traktat* (1970) sowie *Sein und Schein. Die kritische Funktion der Hegelschen Logik* (1978) – und Abhandlungen zu Kierkegaard, bes. "Kierkegaard's Negativistic Method" (1981), repräsentieren Theunissens philosophische Arbeit bis in die 80er Jahre. Aus seiner späteren philosophischen Arbeit gingen unter anderem eine *Negative Theologie der Zeit* (1991), *Der Begriff Verzweiflung* (1993) und *Vorentwürfe von Moderne. Antike Melancholie und die Acedia des Mittelalters* (1996) hervor. Ins Englische übersetzt wurden auch Beiträge zur Rechtsphilosophie Hegels ("The Repressed Intersubjectivity in Hegel's Philosophy of Right" (1991)) und zu Zeittheorie und Metaphysik ("Metaphysic's Forgetfulness of Time" (1992)). Theunissen bereitet ein umfangreiches Werk mit philosophischen Interpretationen zu Pindar und zur archaischen Lyrik vor.

Autorenverzeichnis

Hann Trier ist emeritierter Professor der Berliner Hochschule der Künste, an der er über dreiundzwanzig Jahre hinweg eine Malklasse leitete. Er gilt als einer der Protagonisten des abstrakten Expressionismus. Sein umfangreiches Œuvre umfaßt neben dem graphischen Werk z. T. großformatige Leinwandbilder (der Œuvrekatalog Triers verzeichnet über 850 Arbeiten) sowie unter anderem die Deckengemälde im Schloß Charlottenburg in Berlin (1974), das auf Initiative Dieter Henrichs hin entstandene Deckenbild in der Bibliothek des philosophischen Seminars der Universität Heidelberg (1978) sowie der freischwebende Baldachin in der Kölner Rathaushalle (1980). Später entstanden unter anderem ein Deckenbild in Rom (1984), eine Supraporta in Bonn (1986) sowie Wandbilder in Museen in Köln (1986) und Wuppertal (1990). Von Hann Trier liegen auch eigene theoretische Texte vor, so etwa „Wie ich ein Bild male" (1959), „Einige Betrachtungen über die Beziehungen zwischen Kunst und Natur" (1965) und *Ut poesis pictura?* (1985). (Cf. S. 625 „Bildlegenden")

Ernst Tugendhat ist emeritierter Professor der Philosophie der Freien Universität Berlin. Seine frühe philosophische Arbeit galt der kritischen Auseinandersetzung mit Heidegger sowie Untersuchungsgängen im Rahmen der Sprachphilosophie. Zu seinen Haupttiteln in diesem Zusammenhang zählen *Selbstbewußtsein und Selbstbestimmung* (1979) und seine *Vorlesungen zur Einführung in die sprachanalytische Philosophie* (1976), die auch in englischer Übersetzung unter dem Titel *Traditional and Analytical Philosophy* (1982) vorliegen. Insbesondere durch sie wurde Tugendhat auch im englischsprachigen Raum bekannt. In der zweiten Hälfte der 70er Jahre setzte eine wachsende Beschäftigung mit Themen der praktischen Philosophie ein. Hieraus gingen unter anderem die *Vorlesungen über Ethik* (1993) hervor. Eine Sammlung *Philosophische Aufsätze*, die das Spektrum der philosophischen Themen Tugendhats weiter beleuchtet, erschien 1992. Tugendhats jüngste Buchveröffentlichung trägt den Titel *Dialog in Leticia* (1997) und schließt kritisch an seine Ethik-Vorlesungen von 1993 an.

Gianni Vattimo is Professor of Philosophy at the University of Torino. He has worked extensively on ancient aesthetics, Nietzsche, Heidegger, and contemporary hermeneutics. Early publications include *Essere, storia e linguaggio in Heidegger* (1963, 1986[2]), and a book on Nietzsche entitled *Il soggetto e la maschera* (1974). Most of Vattimo's later books have been published in translations also, e. g. *Al di là del soggetto* (1981, German: *Jenseits vom Subjekt* (1986)), *Le avventure della differenza* (1980, Engl.: *The Adventure of Difference* (1993)), *La fine della modernità* (1985, Engl.: *The End of Modernity* (1992), German: *Das Ende der Moderne* (1992)). Most recent publications include *Oltre l'interpretazione* (1994), a study on hermeneutics (Engl.: *Beyond Interpretation* (1996), German: *Jenseits der Interpretation* (1997)), and *Credere di credere* (1996, German: *Glauben – Philosophieren* (1997)). Vattimo is currently preparing a book on the relationship between post-metaphysical philosophy and the Christian tradition under the title *After Christianity*.

Index of Contributors

Vincenzo Vitiello ist Professor der Theoretischen Philosophie an der Universität Salerno. Seine Hauptarbeitsgebiete liegen in der Philosophie des 19. und 20. Jahrhunderts, insbesondere der Hermeneutik und der Philosophie der Religion. Vitiello ist durch frühe Studien zu *Heidegger: Il Nulla e la fondazione della storicità* (1976), zur Beziehung von Hegel und Heidegger, *Dialettica ed ermeneutica* (1979) und seine *Utopia del nichilismo* (1983) bekannt geworden. Die wichtigsten späteren Publikationen sind eine *Topologia del moderno* (1992), *Elogio dello spazio* (1994), eine topologische Theorie der Hermeneutik, deren erster Teil in *Beiträgen zur Hermeneutik aus Italien* (1993) auch in deutscher Übersetzung vorliegt, des weiteren *La voce riflessa* (1994), *Cristianesimo senza redenzione* (1995) und zuletzt *Non dividere il sì dal no* (1996). Vitiellos jüngste Arbeit ist eine Weiterentwicklung der topologischen Theorie der Hermeneutik unter dem Titel *La favola di Cadmo. La storia tra scienza e mito da Blumenberg a Vico* (1998).

Bernard Williams is Monroe Deutsch Professor of Philosophy at the University of California at Berkeley, and a Fellow of All Souls College, Oxford. He has worked principally in ethics, but also in the history of philosophy, the philosophy of mind, and political philosophy. Bernard Williams is well known for his criticism of utilitarianism in *Utilitarianism: For and Against* (together with J. J.C. Smart (1973, German: *Kritik des Utilitarismus* (1979)) and his account of ethical thought in *Ethics and the Limits of Philosophy* (1985). Most of Williams's other books have been translated into German: *Problems of the Self* (1973, German: *Probleme des Selbst* (1978)), *Morality* (1976, German: *Der Begriff der Moral* (1978)), *Descartes, The Project of Pure Enquiry* (1978, German: *Descartes* (1981)), and *Moral Luck* (1981, German: *Moralischer Zufall* (1984)). More recent publications are *Shame and Necessity* (1993), an important account of ethical ideas of ancient Greece, and their relation to modern experience, and a collection of essays, *Making Sense of Humanity and Other Philosophical Papers* (1995). Bernard Williams is currently working on a study of the relations between truth and truthfulness.

Richard Wollheim is Professor of Philosophy at the University of California at Berkeley, and Emeritus Grote Professor of the Philosophy of Mind and Logic at the University of London. Wollheim's work has been mainly concerned with a wide range of problems of the philosophy of mind, including aesthetics and the philosophy of psychoanalysis. His early work includes books on *F. H. Bradley* (1959) and *Freud* (1971), the latter translated into German as *Sigmund Freud* (1972). From this early period is also *Art and Its Objects* (1968), a book Wollheim became particularly known for, published in German as *Objekte der Kunst* (1982). A first collection of Wollheim's essays and lectures appeared under the title *On Art and the Mind* (1974), his William James Lectures where published as *The Thread of Life* (1984), and his Andrew W. Mellon Lectures in the Fine Arts as *Painting as an Art* (1987). Among his more recent publications is a second collection of essays and lectures entitled *The Mind and its Depths* (1993). Wollheim is now preparing his Cassirer Lectures, delivered at Yale in 1991, for a book entitled *On the Emotions*.

Autorenverzeichnis

Der Herausgeber: Marcelo Stamm ist wissenschaftlicher Assistent am Institut für Philosophie der Ludwig-Maximilians-Universität München und studierte Philosophie, Wissenschaftstheorie/Logik, Theoretische Linguistik und Literaturwissenschaften in München und Oxford. Neben der klassischen deutschen Philosophie als einem Hauptarbeitsgebiet gilt sein besonderes Interesse Wittgenstein und der zeitgenössischen Debatte in der Philosophie des Geistes. Im Kontext von Forschungsprojekten Dieter Henrichs zur Formationsgeschichte des Deutschen Idealismus entstand eine Reihe von Beiträgen insbesondere zu Problemen der Prinzipienphilosophie zwischen Kant und Fichte sowie eine Konstellationsstudie zum Programm einer Philosophie aus einem Grundsatz unter dem Titel *Systemkrise. Die Elementarphilosophie in der Debatte 1789–1794* (1999). Marcelo Stamm arbeitet zur Zeit vor allem an epistemologischen und semantischen Problemen einer Theorie der Subjektivität im Anschluß an Wittgensteins Spätphilosophie.

Bildlegenden

Umschlag: Hann Triers Vorlage für den Umschlag ist eine Tusch-Pinselzeichnung auf weißem Papier im Format 62,5 × 48,5 cm. Das Blatt stammt aus dem Jahr 1961 und ist links unten „hT 61" signiert.

S. 13: Triers Gouache ist eine Malerei aus dem Jahr 1996 auf weißem Papier mit gerissenem Rand im Format 61,5 × 61,5 cm. Sie trägt am unteren Rand eine Widmung für Dieter Henrich *(septuagenario octogenarius)* sowie die Signatur „hTrier".

Im synthetischen Gestus

Hann Trier begann seine systematische künstlerische Tätigkeit 1946, im Alter von 31 Jahren, und lebte in der ersten Hälfte der 50er Jahre für einige Zeit in der Neuen Welt. Von dieser Zeit an entwickelte er das beidhändige Malen in simultanen Bewegungen zum Stilprinzip: „Malen heißt in zusammenhängendem Ablauf auf überschaubarer Fläche tanzen. Im Fließen, im Staccato, im Anhalten, in der Wiederkehr der Pinselschläge tanzt der Rhythmus. Ich springe in ihn hinein, indem ich mit den Pinseln so tanze, daß Tanz sichtbar wird."

Bei aller *Choreographie* und „bei aller Methodik des Prozessualen, die sie zustande bringt", sollen Triers Bilder jedoch „die Phantasie nicht binden, die Deutung offenlassen und durch ihre Mehrschichtigkeit der Wirklichkeit des Denkens auf ihre Weise antworten, einer Wirklichkeit, die der Malerei besser dient, je weniger sie sich in den Dienst nehmen läßt."

So sind Hann Triers Bilder in besonderer Weise geeignet, einen Band mit Beiträgen *in synthetischer Absicht* zu umfassen und zu eröffnen. Sie können dies nicht nur kraft ihres Offenseins. Daß es sich hier wie dort um einen abgeschlossenen Prozeß handeln könnte, dagegen – so Trier im Raisonnieren über das Programm zu den vorliegenden Beiträgen – „spricht die 'Absicht', die ja erst ins Werk zu setzen wäre".

Trier selbst setzt einen *synthetischen Gestus* ins Werk. Dieser findet seinen Ausdruck in einer *Bewegung*, die sich in seinen Bildern als ein *Pas de deux* der beiden malenden Hände manifestiert. Die Hände folgen dem Gestus des „tastenden und atmenden Fortschreitens von der Mitte her". Dieses Prinzip des Trier'schen Malens sucht und fordert ein Pendant im Betrachter: Der kann und muß „von seiner eigenen Mitte her eins zum anderen fügen und so nachdenklich in die Lage dessen kommen, der den Malprozeß umstülpt, die Zeit wieder rinnen läßt und so zum potentiellen Maler dieser Bilder wird. Immer wieder können die Bilder – obwohl auf Dauer gemeint – auf diese Weise neu und anders entstehen."

Wie das Malen ist insofern auch das Betrachten „das Setzen von Klängen", wobei ein „Klang" selbst ein „Farbton [ist], der sichtbar zwischen seinen warmen und kalten Qualitäten vibriert und darin seinen Ort sucht". Triers Gouache steht in ihrer Palette und ihrem Aufbau in der Tradition sakraler Decken- und Wandmalerei. Das Bild mutet, wie das für viele Arbeiten Triers gilt, wie eine auf die Leinwand bzw. aufs Papier heruntergeholte Deckenmalerei an. Als Deckenbild installiert würde sie aufgrund der in ihr gesetzten Verläufe mehrerer Achsen „von der Mitte her" die illusionistische Überhöhung des Raumes bewirken. In der Tuschmalerei für den Umschlag wiederum schlägt sich *eine* Schrittfolge nieder, die eine exzentrische Bahn beschreibt, aus deren Spuren der Part der beiden Hände und „Tendenzen", die der linken und rechten Hand eigen sind, sichtbar werden.

Im Ziel, eine Konstellation der Farben bzw. Bewegungen hervorzubringen, liegt eine synthetische Absicht eigener Art. Indem Triers Bilder verlangen, auf sie zu- und in sie einzugehen, setzen sie voraus, daß man in sie eintreten *kann*: Eine solche Forderung ginge ins Leere, wären Triers Bilder nicht *offen* in dem weiteren Sinne, unverdeckt zugänglich zu sein. Mehr noch, sie blieben unwirklich ohne eine besondere Weise des *„Entgegenkommens"*, die Hann Trier von jedem Betrachter seiner Kunst fordert und die ihm, so Trier, von Dieter Henrich zuteil wurde, dem die beiden diesen Band begleitenden Bilder gewidmet sind: „Denn so abstrakt, daß sie sich einfach erledigen ließe, gewissermaßen von Amts wegen, zuständigkeitshalber und unter Aktenzeichen abzuheften, ist die Kunst wohl selten oder nie. Meine jedenfalls braucht einen, dem die reine Anschauung dessen, was schon da ist, nicht genügt – einen, der ihr so zugetan ist, daß er sie hervorbringen möchte."

Die Zitate von Hann Trier sind „Wie ich ein Bild male (1959)", wiederabgedruckt in: *Hann Trier. Dokumentation der Galerie Hennemann*, ed. Manfred de la Motte, Bonn 1980 (S. 159–64), sowie seiner „Heidelberger Rede", in: *Heidelberger Jahrbücher* XXV, 1981 (S. 26 f.), entnommen.

Klett-Cotta
© J. G. Cotta'sche Buchhandlung Nachfolger GmbH, gegr. 1659,
Stuttgart 1998
Alle Rechte vorbehalten
Fotomechanische Wiedergabe nur mit Genehmigung des Verlages
Printed in Germany
Schutzumschlag: Philippa Walz, Stuttgart
mit einer Tusch-Pinselzeichnung von Hann Trier
Gesetzt aus der 10 Punkt Bodoni Old Face
von Fotosatz Janß, Pfungstadt
Auf säure- und holzfreiem Werkdruckpapier gedruckt
von Gutmann, Talheim
In Fadenheftung gebunden
von Lachenmaier, Reutlingen
Einbandstoff: Regent-Leinen

Die Deutsche Bibliothek – CIP-Einheitsaufnahme
Philosophie in synthetischer Absicht = Synthesis in mind / hrsg.
von Marcelo Stamm. – Stuttgart: Klett-Cotta, 1998
ISBN 3-608-91861-2